Applied Numerical Analysis Using MATLAB®

Laurene V. Fausett
University of South Carolina Aiken

Prentice Hall
Upper Saddle River, NJ 07458

Library of Congress Cataloging-in-Publication Data

Fausett, Laurene V.
    Applied numerical analysis using MATLAB/Laurene V. Fausett
    p. cm.
  Includes bibliographic references and index.
  ISBN 0-13-319849-9
  1. Numerical analysis—Data processing. 2. MATLAB. I. Title.
  QA297.F38 1999
  519.4'0285—dc21

Publisher: *Tom Robbins*
Editor-in-Chief: *Marcia Horton*
Production editors: *Carole Suraci and Scott Disanno*
Managing editor: *Eileen Clark*
Art director: *Jayne Conte*
Cover design: *Bruce Kenselaar*
Manufacturing manager: *Trudy Pisciotti*
Assistant vice president of production and manufacturing: *David W. Riccardi*

Printed in the United States of America

10 9 8 7 6 5 4 3 2 1

ISBN 0-13-319849-9

PRENTICE-HALL INTERNATIONAL (UK) LIMITED, *London*
PRENTICE-HALL OF AUSTRALIA PTY. LIMITED, *Sydney*
PRENTICE-HALL CANADA INC., *Toronto*
PRENTICE-HALL HISPANOAMERICANA, S.A., *Mexico*
PRENTICE-HALL OF INDIA PRIVATE LIMITED, *New Delhi*
PRENTICE-HALL OF JAPAN, INC., *Tokyo*
SIMON & SCHUSTER ASIA PTE. LTD., *Singapore*
EDITORA PRENTICE-HALL DO BRASIL, LTDA., *Rio de Janeiro*

Books extend our world through time and space.
In that spirit, I dedicate this work to all of my teachers
and all of my students.

Contents

3   SOLVING SYSTEMS OF LINEAR EQUATIONS: DIRECT METHODS   77

4   SOLVING SYSTEMS OF LINEAR EQUATIONS: ITERATIVE METHODS   109

5   NONLINEAR FUNCTIONS OF SEVERAL VARIABLES   135

Preface

The purpose of this text is to present the fundamental numerical techniques used in engineering, applied mathematics, computer science, and the physical and life sciences in a manner that is both interesting and understandable to undergraduate and beginning graduate students in those fields. The organization of the chapters, and of the material within each chapter, the use of MATLAB functions and scripts to illustrate the methods, and the exercises provided are all designed with student learning as the primary objective.

The first chapter sets the stage for the material in the rest of the text; it gives a brief introduction to the long history of numerical techniques, and a "preview of coming attractions" for some of the recurring themes of the remainder of the text. It also presents enough description of MATLAB to allow students to use the MATLAB functions presented for each of the numerical methods discussed in the other chapters. The MATLAB function may be used directly for computer solutions, as a structured algorithm for hand computations, or as a guide for coding in other programming languages.

Each of the subsequent chapters begins with a one page overview of the subject matter, together with an indication as to how the topics presented in the chapter are related to those in previous and subsequent chapters. Introductory examples are presented to suggest a few of the types of problems for which the topics of the chapter may be used. Following the presentation of its methods, each chapter concludes with a summary of the most important formulas, a selection of suggestions for further reading, and an extensive set of exercises. The first group of problems provides fairly routine practice of the techniques; the second group presents applications adapted from a variety of fields; and the final group of problems encourages students to extend their understanding of either the theoretical or the computational aspects of the methods.

The presentation of each numerical technique is based on the successful teaching methodology of providing examples and geometric motivation for a method, and a concise statement of the steps to carry out the computation, before giving a mathematical development of the process or a discussion of the more theoretical issues that are relevant to the use and understanding of the topic. Each topic is illustrated by examples that range in complexity from very simple to moderate. Geometrical or graphical illustrations are included whenever they are appropriate. A simple MATLAB function is presented for each method, which also serves as a clear step-by-step description of the process; discussion of theoretical considerations is placed at the conclusion of the section. The last section of each chapter gives a brief discussion of MATLAB built-in functions for solving the kinds of problems covered in the chapter.

The chapters are arranged according to the following general areas:

Chapters 2–5 deal with solving linear and nonlinear equations.
Chapters 6 and 7 treat topics from numerical linear algebra.
Chapters 8–10 cover numerical methods for data interpolation and approximation.
Chapters 11 presents numerical differentiation and integration.
Chapters 12–15 introduce numerical techniques for solving differential equations.

For much of the material, a calculus sequence that includes an introduction to differential equations and linear algebra provides adequate background. For more in-depth coverage of the topics from linear algebra (especially the QR method for eigenvalues), a linear algebra course would be an appropriate prerequisite. The coverage of Fourier approximation and FFT (Chapter 10), and partial differential equations (Chapter 15) also assumes that the students have somewhat more mathematical maturity than the other chapters, since the material is intrinsically more challenging. The subject matter included is suitable for a two-semester sequence of courses, or for any of several different one-term courses, depending on the desired emphasis, student background, level of theoretical development included, and selection of topics.

There are so many people who have contributed to the development of this text that I cannot name them all. First of all, I thank my colleagues at Florida Institute of Technology, the Naval Postgraduate School, and the University of South Carolina Aiken for their support, encouragement, and suggestions. I also appreciate the comments made by the reviewers of the text, which helped greatly in the fine-tuning of the final presentation. All of my students have contributed to the text, in a variety of ways, but I especially thank Wael Elwasif for his work on many of the MATLAB programs. The editorial and production staff at Prentice Hall have my heartfelt gratitude for their efforts in insuring that the text is as accurate and as well designed as possible. And, saving the most important for last, I thank my husband and colleague, Don Fausett, for his patience and support.

Laurene V. Fausett

1

Foundations

From the earliest times, the search for solutions of real-world problems has been an important aspect of mathematical study. In many interesting applications, an exact solution may be unattainable, or it may not give the answer in a convenient form. Useful answers may involve finding good approximate results with a reasonable amount of computational effort.

Many numerical methods have a very long history. There is evidence that the Babylonians (more than 3700 years ago) knew how to find numerical solutions of quadratic equations and approximations to the square root of an integer. They also used linear interpolation to solve problems involving compound interest.

An example of the method of solving systems of linear equations that we know as Gaussian elimination appears in a Chinese manuscript (the *Nine Chapters*) from the Han Dynasty (approximately 2000 years ago); matrix notation was used. The famous German mathematician Carl Friedrich Gauss (1777–1855) indicated that the method was well known.

Chinese mathematics during the Sung dynasty (960–1279) generalized the method of successive approximations from the *Nine Chapters* to find numerical solutions of higher degree equations. Matrix solution techniques for linear systems were also extended to equations of higher degree (an approach similar to work in the West in the 19th century).

Greek mathematics included methods of calculating areas based on approximating the desired quantity by a large number of regions of known area. (A similar process was used for volumes.) A letter from Archimedes to Eratosthenes (c. 250 B.C.) describes one of these methods; the letter was discovered in 1906.

The continuation of the Greek mathematical traditions by Middle Eastern scholars tended to stress computational and practical aspects. Omar Khayyam, who lived 900 years ago, wrote a treatise on algebra that includes a systematic investigation of cubic equations. (He is perhaps better known as the author of the *Rubaiyat of Omar Khayyam.*) Jemshid Al-Kashi (who died about 1436), another Persian mathematician, solved cubic equations by iterative and trigonometric methods and also knew the method for solving general algebraic equations, which is now usually called Horner's method. W. G. Horner published the method in 1819, presumably without being aware of its previous history.

Leonardo Fibonacci (c. 1200) showed that certain cubic equations cannot be solved in terms of square roots, but that very accurate approximate solutions can be generated.

The first tables of logarithms were published by the Scotsman John Napier in 1614; they were revised by Henry Briggs (based on Napier's suggestions) in 1624 and provided a great tool for improving computation.

The connection between mathematics and astronomy has been extremely close throughout history. Leaders of the Copernican revolution ventured into a number of areas of mathematics. For example, Johannes Kepler published the *New solid geometry of wine barrels* in 1615, in which he used geometric approximations to calculate the volume of a solid of revolution.

A widely known method for approximating the roots of an equation called Newton's method (or the Newton–Raphson method) is a generalization of an iterative approach to finding the roots of polynomials published in the early 1700s. According to recent research, Thomas Simpson (well known for Simpson's rule for the numerical approximation of definite integrals) extended Newton's method to more general functions and published the results in 1740.

Taylor's formula is the theoretical basis for many numerical techniques. Taylor polynomials were introduced in an article by Brook Taylor published in 1715; the remainder term first appeared in a book by Joseph Louis Lagrange in 1797.

One of the most popular approaches to finding numerical approximations to ordinary differential equations, the Runge–Kutta method, was developed 100 years ago by the German applied mathematicians Carl Runge (1856–1927) and M. W. Kutta (1867–1944). Runge is also known for his work on the Zeeman effect and Kutta for his contributions to the theory of airfoil lift in aerodynamics.

Our modern-day calculators follow the basic design introduced in Blaise Pascal's adding machine (1642) and Gottfried Wilhelm Leibniz's multiplication machine (1671). The origin of computers, on the other hand, is usually traced to Charles Babbage's analytical engine (developed in the 1830s).

New methods continue to be developed in numerical analysis. The iterative methods for solving linear systems that are included as built-in functions in MATLAB are the result of research in the 1970s and 1980s.

Many of the issues that confront a scientist or engineer who uses numerical methods are the same today as throughout the history of the subject, although the relative importance of the competing considerations may change, depending on the computational resources available. Two primary considerations are the computational effort required and the accuracy of the resulting solution. Numerical methods for solving a problem may be classified as either direct or iterative. A direct method, such as Gaussian elimination, produces an answer to a problem in a fixed number of computational steps. An iterative method produces a sequence of approximate answers (designed to converge ever closer to the true solution, under the proper conditions).

For a direct method that would give an exact result if the computations were carried out in exact arithmetic, such as Gaussian elimination, the effect of numerical round-off may be significant. Also, since the linear systems that occur in modern applications may be extremely large, efficiency of computation is a critical aspect of choosing a solution technique for these types of problems. Other direct methods, such as techniques for numerical integration, are developed by replacing the given function by an approximating function (such as a Taylor polynomial) for which the integral can be found. The accuracy of the method depends in part on the number of terms that are retained before the Taylor series is truncated.

For iterative techniques, it is imperative that questions of convergence be understood. Do the successive approximate answers actually approach the true answer? If so, how quickly? How should the decision be made to terminate the process?

In the next section, we present three problems that illustrate basic types of numerical methods and significant issues, such as convergence and computational effort, which form the recurring themes of subsequent chapters. We conclude this chapter with an introduction to the capabilities of MATLAB, the programming environment used throughout the text.

In the remainder of the text, numerical methods are grouped according to the types of problems for which they are intended. Techniques for solving nonlinear equations of a single variable and systems of linear or nonlinear equations are presented in Chapters 2–5. Some basic methods from numerical linear algebra are given in Chapters 6 and 7. Functional approximation, including interpolation, least squares approximation, and Fourier methods, are discussed in Chapters 8–10. Numerical approximation of differentiation and integration, the basic operations of calculus, are the subject of Chapter 11. Numerical solutions of ordinary and partial differential equations are considered in Chapters 12–15.

1.1 APPLIED PROBLEMS

To illustrate the types of problems for which a numerical solution may be desired, we consider three examples. The simple problems presented in these examples can be solved exactly by techniques that are well known in algebra or calculus. However, there are closely related problems for which no exact solution can be found.

1.1.1 Nonlinear Functions

Although the zeros of a quadratic function such as $y = x^2 - 3$ can be found exactly by the quadratic formula, no such exact methods exist for most nonlinear functions. The formula for finding the zeros of a cubic function is much more complicated, and Niels Henrik Abel (1802–1829) proved that no formula exists for fifth-order polynomials. (A translation of Abel's paper appears in Smith [1959].)

There are many methods for finding approximate zeros of nonlinear functions. The simplest, the bisection method, is a systematic searching technique; the secant, false-position, and Newton's methods use a straight-line approximation to the function whose zero is sought. More powerful methods use a quadratic approximation to the function or a combination of these techniques. Each approach produces a succession of approximations. One consideration in choosing such a technique is whether, and how rapidly, these approximations approach the desired solution. The computational effort required for each iteration may also be important.

Finding the zeros of $y = x^2 - 3$ is equivalent to the problem of finding the square root of 3. A simple iterative method for finding square roots is illustrated in Section 1.2. The graph of $y = x^2 - 3$ is shown in Fig. 1.1.

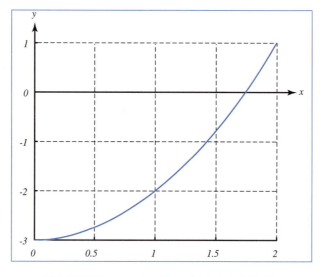

FIGURE 1.1 $y = x^2 - 3$ on the interval $[0, 2]$.

1.1.2 Linear Systems

If a linear system of equations has a unique solution, then a (nonzero) linear combination of two of the equations produces another linear equation that also passes through the same solution point. The well-known Gaussian elimination method systematically transforms the original system into an equivalent system (with the same solution) for which the solution point can be more easily identified. The process is illustrated in Section 1.2 for two equations in two unknowns. The graphs of the following two linear equations are illustrated in Fig. 1.2:

L_1: $\qquad\qquad\qquad\qquad 4x_1 + x_2 = 6,$

M_1: $\qquad\qquad\qquad\qquad -x_1 + 5x_2 = 9.$

Linear systems can be written more compactly in matrix-vector form. Thus, the foregoing system is written as $\mathbf{A}\,\mathbf{x} = \mathbf{b}$, where

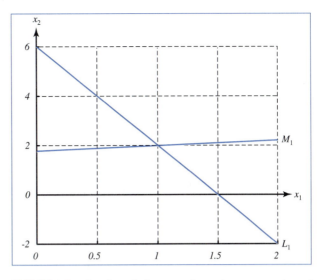

FIGURE 1.2 Graphs of the equations $4x_1 + x_2 = 6$ and $-x_1 + 5x_2 = 9$ on $[0, 2]$.

$$\mathbf{A} = \begin{bmatrix} 4 & 1 \\ -1 & 5 \end{bmatrix}, \quad \mathbf{x} = \begin{bmatrix} x_1 \\ x_2 \end{bmatrix}, \quad \mathbf{b} = \begin{bmatrix} 6 \\ 9 \end{bmatrix}.$$

If the computations in Gaussian elimination could be carried out exactly, then the main issue would be computational efficiency, since the systems for which numerical techniques are required are frequently very large. However, not all numbers are represented in exact form in computer calculations; the extent of the difficulties this causes depends on certain characteristics of the coefficient matrix of the linear system.

In many important applications, the coefficient matrix has a particular structure that allows specialized solution techniques, which reduce computation and memory requirements.

1.1.3 Numerical Integration

The fundamental theorem of calculus states that the definite integral of a function may be found from the antiderivative of the function. However, for many functions, it is much easier to show that they have a definite integral than it is to find an expression for the antiderivative in terms of elementary functions. Several numerical techniques for finding definite integrals are based on approximating the function to be integrated by a simpler function whose antiderivative can be found exactly.

The area represented by $\int_1^3 \frac{1}{x^3}\,dx$ is illustrated in Fig. 1.3. A simple numerical method for approximating this area is introduced in Section 1.2. Several methods for numerical integration are presented in Chapter 11. The accuracy of the approximate integral depends on the form of the approximating function and the number of function evaluations.

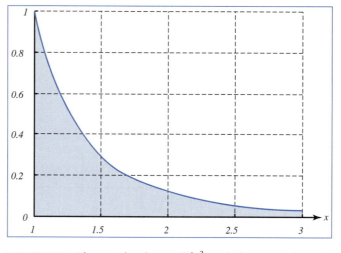

FIGURE 1.3 The graph of $y = 1/x^3$ and the area given by $\int_1^3 \dfrac{1}{x_3}\, dx.$

1.2 NUMERICAL TECHNIQUES

There are many numerical methods for solving problems such as those introduced in the previous section. We now consider one method for each problem presented, to illustrate some of the basic issues and themes that recur throughout numerical analysis.

1.2.1 Fixed-Point Iteration

To find the square root of a positive number c, it is convenient to rewrite the equation $x^2 = c$ as the implicit equation

$$x = \frac{1}{2}\left(x + \frac{c}{x}\right);$$

this form provides the basis for an iterative solution technique by using the right-hand side of the equation to generate an updated estimate for the desired value of x.

A solution of an implicit equation of the form $x = g(x)$ is called a *fixed point*. In more detail, starting with an initial guess x_0, we evaluate

$$x_1 = \frac{1}{2}\left(x_0 + \frac{c}{x_0}\right); \qquad x_2 = \frac{1}{2}\left(x_1 + \frac{c}{x_1}\right); \ldots$$

and, at the kth stage,

$$x_k = \frac{1}{2}\left(x_{k-1} + \frac{c}{x_{k-1}}\right).$$

Geometrically, this corresponds to finding the intersection of the line $y = x$ and the curve $y = \dfrac{1}{2}\left(x + \dfrac{c}{x}\right) = g(x)$. The method is known as fixed-point iteration, since we are seeking a value of x for which $x_k = x_{k+1} = g(x_k)$.

Example 1.1 Fixed-Point Iterations to Find $\sqrt{3}$

The process of generating x_1 from $x_0 = 1$ is illustrated in Fig. 1.4.

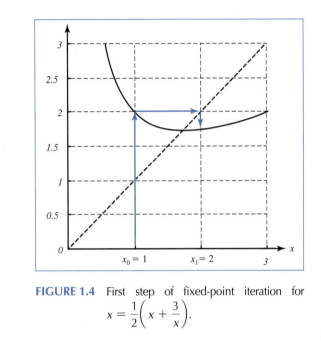

FIGURE 1.4 First step of fixed-point iteration for
$$x = \frac{1}{2}\left(x + \frac{3}{x}\right).$$

The first two iterations in the procedure for finding a root of $x^2 = 3$ give

$$x_1 = \frac{1}{2}\left(1 + \frac{3}{1}\right) = 2; \qquad x_2 = \frac{1}{2}\left(2 + \frac{3}{2}\right) = \frac{7}{4}.$$

1.2.2 Gaussian Elimination

Basic Gaussian elimination systematically transforms a system of linear equations into an equivalent system for which the solution is easier to find.

Example 1.2 Solving a Linear System

To illustrate this process, consider the following simple system:

L_1: $\qquad\qquad\qquad\qquad 4x + y = 6,$

M_1: $\qquad\qquad\qquad\qquad -x + 5y = 9.$

Using basic Gaussian elimination, we multiply the first equation by 0.25 and add the result to the second equation to give the new (equivalent) system

L_1: $4x + \quad y = \quad 6,$

M_2: $+\ 5.25y = 10.5.$

Solving the second equation gives $y = 2$; substituting that value for y into the first equation yields $x = 1$.

The original two equations are shown as lines L_1 and M_1 in Fig. 1.5. The modified second equation is shown as M_2. The solution for y is found from M_2; substituting into the first equation gives $x = 1$, as indicated by the boldface dashed vertical line.

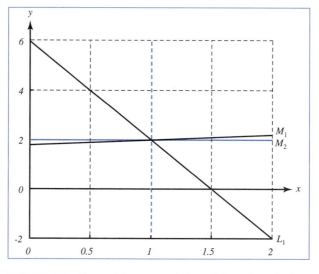

FIGURE 1.5 Geometric representation of Gaussian elimination for two equations.

1.2.3 Trapezoid Rule

The trapezoid rule approximates the definite integral

$$\int_a^b f(x)\, dx$$

by the integral of the straight line that passes through the points $(a, f(a))$ and $(b, f(b))$. The length of the interval of interest is $h = b - a$. By the trapezoid rule,

$$\int_a^b f(x)\,dx \approx \frac{h}{2}[f(a) + f(b)].$$

The accuracy of this straight-line approximation depends on the length of the interval over which the approximation is imposed, i.e., on the value of h. The accuracy is also influenced by the characteristics of the function f—in particular, by how well it is approximated by a straight line.

Example 1.3 Approximating an Integral

The trapezoid rule approximation to the definite integral

$$I = \int_1^3 \frac{1}{x^3}\, dx$$

gives

$$I \approx \frac{h}{2}[f(a) + f(b)] = 1 + 1/27 = 28/27.$$

As shown in Fig. 1.6, there is a large discrepancy between the area under the curve and the area under the straight-line approximation. We consider the error in using this method, and ways to reduce the error, in Section 1.3.

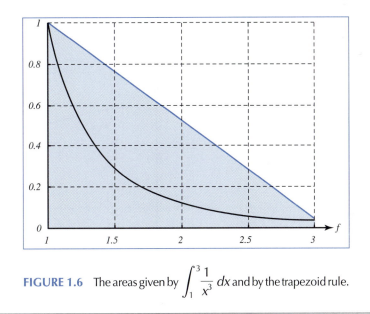

FIGURE 1.6 The areas given by $\displaystyle\int_1^3 \frac{1}{x^3}\, dx$ and by the trapezoid rule.

1.3 ANALYSIS

We now introduce some of the recurring themes in the analysis of numerical methods; these ideas are revisited in various settings in the remainder of the text. First we consider the two primary issues for iterative methods: "does the process converge?" and "when do we stop?" We then discuss some issues related to the question of how good the result of a numerical method is, and how the result can be improved.

1.3.1 Key Issues for Iterative Methods

For iterative techniques, it is imperative to know whether the method converges, i.e., whether the sequence of approximate results approaches the true solution. If the method does converge, we must decide when to terminate the process. For an important class of methods, the convergence depends on the eigenvalues of the iteration matrix; a useful theorem for bounds on the eigenvalues is given below.

Convergence of Iterative Methods

For some iterative techniques, the convergence or divergence of the method can be illustrated geometrically. The sequence of points generated by the fixed-point formula $x_k = g(x_{k-1})$ is shown in the next examples.

Example 1.4 Convergent Fixed-Point Iteration

Figure 1.7 shows the first two steps of the convergent fixed-point iteration for $x = \cos(x)$, starting with $x_0 = 0.5$.

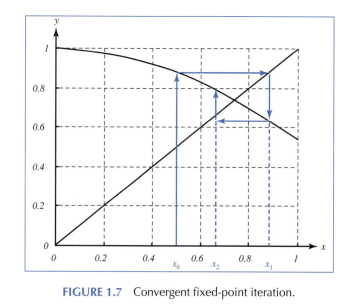

FIGURE 1.7   Convergent fixed-point iteration.

Example 1.5 Divergent Fixed-Point Iteration

Figure 1.8 shows the first two steps of the divergent fixed-point iteration for $x = g(x) = 1 - x^3$ with $x_0 = 0.5$.

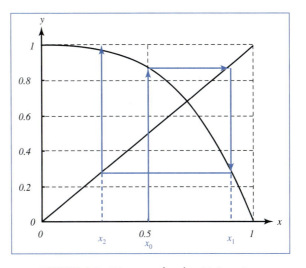

FIGURE 1.8 Divergent fixed-point iteration.

It is very useful to be able to analyze algebraically whether a fixed-point formula will converge, and if so, to estimate how rapidly. The following theorem states conditions which guarantee that

    i) the equation $x = g(x)$ has a fixed point in the interval $I = [a, b]$, and

    ii) the iterative procedure $x_k = g(x_{k-1})$ will converge to that fixed point.

Fixed-Point Convergence Theorem

If

1. $g(x)$ maps $[a, b]$ into $[a, b]$,
2. $g'(x)$ is continuous on $[a, b]$, and
3. there is a number $N < 1$ such that $|g'(x)| \leq N$ for all x in $[a, b]$,

then

1. $x = g(x)$ has exactly one solution (call it x^*) in the interval $[a, b]$, and
2. the fixed-point iteration $x_k = g(x_{k-1})$ converges to x^*, for any starting estimate in $[a, b]$.

Furthermore, the value of N gives an estimate of the error at any stage of the iteration, in that the error $e_k = x_k - x^*$ satisfies the inequalities

$$|e_{k+1}| \leq N|e_k| \qquad \text{and } |e_{k+1}| \leq N^{k+1}|e_0|.$$

It is easy to construct examples of functions $g(x)$ that do not map a given interval $I = [a, b]$ into I and for which the curves $y = x$ and $y = g(x)$ do not cross (at least for x in I). If g is continuous and does map I into I, then the curves will cross (at lease once) in the interval. The guarantee of convergence of the iterative process hinges on the magnitude of $g'(x)$ being less than 1, at least near the fixed point.

To illustrate what this theorem says, consider the fixed-point iteration $x = \cos(x)$ illustrated in Example 1.4. For $0 \leq x \leq 1$, $\cos(x)$ is also between 0 and 1, so $g(x)$ does map $[0, 1]$ into $[0, 1]$. Furthermore, $g'(x) = -\sin(x)$ ranges between 0 and $-\sin(1)$, so $|g'(x)| \leq 0.85$ for all x in $[0, 1]$, and the theorem guarantees convergence of the iterations.

On the other hand, for $x = g(x) = 1 - x^3$ (Example 1.5), $g'(x) = -3x^2$, which is not bounded by a number less than 1 on $[0, 1]$. Although there is a fixed point in the interval (and $g(x)$ does map $[0, 1]$ into $[0, 1]$), the conditions of the theorem are not satisfied, and in fact, the iterations do not converge. The difficulty is that in any neighborhood of the fixed point, $|g'(x)| > 1$.

Estimating Eigenvalues

The convergence of iterative methods based on repeated multiplication by a matrix (call it $\mathbf{M}$) often depends on the eigenvalues of $\mathbf{M}$. A number λ is an *eigenvalue* of $\mathbf{M}$ (with a corresponding nonzero eigenvector $\mathbf{v}$) if and only if $\mathbf{Mv} = \lambda\mathbf{v}$. Eigenvalues are extremely useful in many applications; methods for calculating them form the subject of Chapter 7. However, in some situations it is sufficient to be able to estimate the eigenvalues (especially if we can show that all of the eigenvalues are positive, for example). The following theorem gives bounds on the location of the eigenvalues of $\mathbf{M}$; as in standard matrix notation, the element in the ith row, jth column of $\mathbf{M}$ is denoted m_{ij}.

Gerschgorin Circle Theorem

If, for $i = 1, \ldots, n$, C_i is the circle in the complex plane with center at $(m_{ii}, 0)$ and radius $r_i = \sum_{j \in I} |m_{ij}|$, where I indicates the index set $\{1, 2, \ldots, i-1, i+1, \ldots, n\}$, then all of the eigenvalues of $\mathbf{M}$ lie within the union of the disks bounded by these circles.

Furthermore, if there are k disks, the union of which is disjoint from the other disks, then exactly k eigenvalues lie within that union.

Example 1.6 Bounds on Eigenvalues

To illustrate the Gerschgorin circle theorem, consider the problem of finding bounds on the eigenvalues of the matrix

$$\mathbf{M} = \begin{bmatrix} 2 & -1/2 & 0 \\ -1/2 & 3 & 1/2 \\ 0 & 1/2 & 6 \end{bmatrix}.$$

We find that
C_1 has center $(2, 0)$ and radius $|-1/2| + |0| = 1/2$;
C_2 has center $(3, 0)$ and radius $|-1/2| + |1/2| = 1$;
C_3 has center $(6, 0)$ and radius $|0| + |1/2| = 1/2$.

The union of the interiors of circles C_1 and C_2 is disjoint from the disk bounded by circle C_3, so we know that there are exactly two eigenvalues in the union of the regions enclosed by circles C_1 and C_2. Furthermore, there is one eigenvalue in the region bounded by circle C_3. These regions are illustrated in Fig. 1.9.

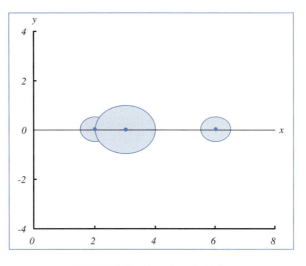

FIGURE 1.9 Gerschgorin disks.

Termination Conditions

A variety of conditions can be used for deciding when to stop an iterative procedure; however, there is no perfect test for a "stopping condition." The conditions may be characterized as being of three general types: the problem is "solved," the iteration has "converged," or the iteration process has continued "long enough." For the example of finding the zero of $f(x) = x^2 - 3$, with the true zero denoted $x*$, possible convergence tests include the following:

The problem is "solved":

$$|f(x_k)| \le f_{\text{tol}} \qquad \text{(function value reduced to specified tolerance)}.$$

The iteration has "converged":

$$|x_{k+1} - x_k| \le \text{tol} \quad \text{(absolute change is within specified tolerance)};$$
if tol $= 10^{-n}$, then x_{k+1} should approximate $x*$ to n decimal places.

$$|x_{k+1} - x_k| \le \text{tol } x_{k+1} \text{ (relative change is within specified tolerance)};$$
if tol $= 10^{-n}$, then x_{k+1} should approximate $x*$ to n significant digits.

The iterations have gone on "long enough":

$$k \ge \text{max\_it} \qquad \text{(iteration counter exceeds a specified limit)}.$$

It may also be desirable to check whether "the solution is looking bad":

$$|f(x_k)| \ge f_{\text{big}} \qquad \text{(function value exceeds a specified limit)};$$
$$|x_k| \ge x_{\text{big}} \qquad \text{(value of iterated variable exceeds a specified limit)}.$$

It is important to realize that none of these tests guarantees the desired result, namely, that $|x_k - x*| < \text{tol}$. In addition, an iterative process could pass the successive iterates test at the same time that the iterates were diverging to ∞. As an example, consider a process in which $x_k = 1 + \dfrac{1}{2} + \dfrac{1}{3} + \cdots + \dfrac{1}{k}$. The difference between successive iterates, $|x_{k+1} - x_k| = \dfrac{1}{k+1} \to 0$ as $k \to \infty$, but $x_{k+1} \to \infty$ as $k \to \infty$.

The relative-change test is appropriate for problems in which the desired roots may be of greatly differing magnitudes. It is not suitable, however, if $x = 0$ is a desired root and the method is converging rapidly, since that would produce a relatively large change in the iterates.

1.3.2 How Good is the Result?

There are several reasons that the results of a numerical solution to a problem from the "real world" may not be the exact answer. Simplifying assumptions made in modeling the original problem are one source of inaccuracies. Errors arising from data collection are another.

In this section we illustrate several basic types of errors that are more directly linked to the numerical solution of the stated problem. We first define some standard terminology for describing errors that occur in numerical methods. We then summarize the fundamentals of computer arithmetic and illustrate two types of error that arise because computers do not represent most numbers in an exact form; i.e., they do not do exact arithmetic. The third example in this section illustrates one common form of error introduced in replacing a continuous process by a discrete approximation.

Measuring Error

If x is our approximate result, and the exact (but usually unknown) result is denoted x^*, then the error in using the approximate result is

$$\text{Error}(x) = x^* - x.$$

However, especially for problems in which the magnitude of the true value may be very large, or very small, the relative error may be more important than the actual error:

$$\text{Rel Error}(x) = \frac{x - x^*}{x^*}.$$

In computing the relative error, the approximate value is often used in the denominator in place of the unknown true value x^*.

For errors that come from using a finite step size, h, in approximating a continuous process by a discrete one, it is often useful to describe how the error depends on h, as h approaches zero. We say a function $f(h)$ is "Big Oh" of h if $|f(h)| \le c|h|$ for some constant c, when h is near 0. This is written $f(h) = O(h)$. Similarly, $f(h) = O(h^2)$ means that $|f(h)| \le c|h^2|$ for some constant c, when h is near 0. If a method has an error term that is $O(h^k)$, the method is often called a kth-order method. For example, if we use a Taylor polynomial to approximate the function f at $x = a + h$, we have

$$f(x) = f(a + h) = f(a) + hf'(a) + \frac{h^2}{2!}f''(a) + \frac{h^3}{3!}f'''(\eta);$$

for some η such that $a \le \eta \le a + h$.

Assuming that f is sufficiently smooth, we let **M** be the maximum of $f'''(x)$ for $a \le x \le a + h$. Then this approximation is $\mathbb{O}(h^3)$, since the error, $\frac{h^3}{3!} f'''(\eta)$, satisfies

$$\left| \frac{h^3}{3!} f'''(\eta) \right| \le c|h^3|$$

where $c = \frac{1}{3!} M$.

Errors from Inexact Arithmetic

Computers represent real numbers in a form, called *floating point,* that is similar to scientific notation. For example, a number N is stored as

$$N = \pm .d_1 d_2 d_3 \ldots d_p B^e,$$

where B is the base and the d_is are the digits. For a computer, the base is usually 2, 8, or 16; in scientific notation, the base is 10. Each digit is an integer between 0 and $B - 1$. There are a fixed number of digits, p, and the integer exponent, e, is restricted to a range of values; i.e., $e \in [e_{min}, e_{max}]$. If, as is generally the case, it is required that $d_1 \ne 0$, the system is called a *normalized floating-point system.* Note that for a binary system, this means that $d_1 = 1$, so there is, in fact, no need to store its value.

The precision with which numbers can be stored, and computations carried out, depends on the number of digits and the range of exponents used to represent a real number. In single precision, a real variable is stored in four words, or 32 bits. A bit is a binary digit (0 or 1); a byte is 4 bits (so a byte can have $2^4 = 16$ possible values); a word is 2 bytes (8 bits). Of the 32 bits, 23 are used for the digits, 8 for the exponent, and 1 for the sign. The 8 bits for the exponent can take on 256 possible values, from $0 = 00000000_2$ to $255 = 11111111_2$. In double precision, each floating-point number occupies eight words (64 bits, 11 for the exponent, 52 for the digits, and 1 for the sign).

The range of exponents that are available determines the smallest and largest numbers (in magnitude) that can be represented. For single precision, the binary numbers in the interval $[00000000_2, 11111111_2]$ are mapped to the interval $[-128, 127]$, so the smallest number is approximately 0.14693×10^{-38} and the largest number is approximately 0.9414×10^{127}. Numbers smaller that 10^{-38} cause *underflow* (which is often set to be zero). Numbers larger than 10^{127} (or 10^{1023} for double precision) cause *overflow* (which usually halts the program).

The numbers that can be represented exactly in a system which uses a fixed range of exponents are not distributed evenly. In general, the total number of values, V, that can be represented (assuming that $d_1 \ne 0$) is given by

$$V = 2 \ (B - 1) \ (B^{p-1}) \ \text{(total number of exponents)} + 1.$$

The factor of 2 corresponds to the sign bit; the factor of $(B - 1)$ gives the number of possible values for the first digit. Each of the digits $d_2 \ldots d_p$ can take on B different values. The bit required to store zero accounts for the one additional value not counted in the product.

For a base-10 system, with two digits and exponents of 0 or 1, we have $V = 2 (9)(10)(2) + 1 = 361$. The maximum value is $.99 \times 10 = 9.9$, and the minimum value is -9.9. The positive numbers that can be represented with the exponent 1 are of the form $1.0, 1.1, 1.2, \ldots, 2.0, 2.1, 2.3, \ldots, 9.9$; the positive numbers represented with the exponent 0 are $0.10, 0.11, 0.12, \ldots, 0.20, 0.21, 0.23, \ldots, 0.99$. Thus, there are 91 values in the interval $[0, 0.99]$, but only 10 values in the interval $[1.0, 1.9]$.

In a binary floating-point system, the decimals correspond to sums of negative powers of 2. For example,

$$0.10_2 = (1)\frac{1}{2} + (0)\frac{1}{4} = \frac{1}{2} \quad \text{and} \quad 0.11_2 = (1)\frac{1}{2} + (1)\frac{1}{4} = \frac{3}{4}.$$

These are the only positive numbers that can be represented in a binary normalized floating-point system with two digits and an exponent of 0, since the normalization requires that the first digit in the expansion be 1. The positive numbers that can be represented with two digits and exponents of $-1, 0$, and 1 are illustrated in Fig. 1.10. Notice that they are not evenly distributed on the interval $[0, 2]$.

FIGURE 1.10   Positive numbers that can be represented in a binary system with two digits and exponents of -1, 0, or 1.

Round-Off Error

There are two approaches to shortening a number that has more digits than can be represented by the available floating-point system. The simplest is to *chop* the number by discarding any digits beyond what the system can accommodate. The second method is to *round* the number; the result depends on the value of the first digit to be discarded. If the system allows for n digits, rounding produces the same result as chopping if the $(n+1)$st digit is $0, 1, 2, 3$, or 4. If the $(n+1)$st digit is $6, 7, 8$, or 9, the nth digit is increased by 1. If the $(n+1)$st digit is 5, it is common to round so that the nth digit is even, rounding up about half of the time.

The errors that occur from rounding are less likely to accumulate during repeated calculations, since the true value is larger than the rounded value about half of the time and smaller about half of the time. Furthermore, the largest absolute error that can occur is twice as large for chopping as for rounding. On the other hand, chopping requires no decisions as to whether to change the last retained digit. The inaccuracies that result from either rounding or chopping are known as round-off errors.

We now consider some examples of the difficulties that can occur due to inexact computations.

Example 1.7 Effect of Order of Operations

As example of the effect of round-off, consider the following addition problem:

$$0.99 + 0.0044 + 0.0042.$$

With exact arithmetic, the result is 0.9986, regardless of the order in which the additions are performed. However, if we have three-digit arithmetic, and the operations are nested from left to right, we find that

$$(0.99 + 0.0044) + 0.0042 = 0.994 + 0.0042 = 0.998.$$

On the other hand, if we change the nesting so that the small numbers are added together first, we have

$$0.99 + (0.0044 + 0.0042) = 0.99 + 0.0086 = 0.999.$$

The number x is said to approximate x^* to t significant digits if t is the largest nonnegative integer for which

$$\left| \frac{x - x^*}{x} \right| < 5 \cdot 10^{-t}.$$

Using this definition, we see that 0.998 approximates the true solution, $x^* = 0.9986$, to three significant digits, since

$$\left| \frac{0.998 - 0.9986}{0.998} \right| = 6.012 \cdot 10^{-4} < 5 \cdot 10^{-3}.$$

On the other hand, 0.999 approximates the true solution, $x^* = 0.9986$, to four significant digits, since

$$\left| \frac{0.999 - 0.9986}{0.999} \right| = 4.004 \cdot 10^{-4} < 5 \cdot 10^{-4}.$$

For cases with greater difference in the sizes of the numbers, and with more terms, the loss of significance can be extreme.

Cancellation Error

A second example of the effect of inexact calculations occurs when a computation involves the subtraction of two nearly equal numbers. It is advisable to rewrite the formula to avoid the difficulty if possible. Consider the problem of using the quadratic formula to solve the quadratic equation

$$x^2 - bx + 1 = 0.$$

The effect of rounding the discriminant $r = \sqrt{b^2 - 4}$ is illustrated in this example; note that for large b ($b \gg 4$), r is quite close to b.

The quadratic formula gives $x_1 = \dfrac{b + r}{2}$ and $x_2 = \dfrac{b - r}{2}$. If b is positive, x_2 will involve the difference of two numbers that are very close to each other, a dangerous situation. This difficulty can be avoided by rationalizing the numerator in the quadratic formula:

$$x_2 = \frac{(b - r)}{2} \frac{(b + r)}{(b + r)} = \frac{(b^2 - r^2)}{2(b + r)} = \frac{4}{2(b + r)} = \frac{2}{(b + r)}.$$

If the same process is applied to the formula for x_1 (with which the standard quadratic formula does not have a problem), the rationalized numerator formula results in division by a quantity that is close to zero, which is a much worse situation.

Example 1.8 Cancellation Errors

To illustrate the effect of rounding, consider the problem of solving the quadratic equation $x^2 - 97x + 1 = 0$. The exact roots (shown to nine digits) and the approximations computed with rounding to five digits are summarized in Table 1.1. For the standard quadratic formula, rounding has a much larger effect on x_2 than on x_1, as expected. Using the rationalized quadratic formula for x_2 gives the correct result to the number of digits used in the rounded computation. On the other hand, if the rationalized formula is used for x_1, for which it is not appropriate, the results for the rounded computations approximate the true solution only to two digits.

Table 1.1   Effect of Rounding for Roots of Quadratic Equation

	x_1	x_2
exact	96.9896896	0.0103103743
standard quadratic formula rounded	96.990	0.01050
rationalized quadratic formula rounded	95.238	0.01031

Errors from Mathematical Approximation

Truncation Error

To introduce the analysis of the error which is produced by approximating a function by a simpler function, consider again the trapezoid rule for numerical integration, which we write now as

$$\int_a^{a+h} f(x)dx \approx \frac{h}{2}[f(a) + f(a + h)].$$

Define the function

$$F(t) = \int_a^t f(x)\,dx.$$

We can represent F by its Taylor polynomial with remainder, as follows

$$F(a + h) = F(a) + hF'(a) + \frac{h^2}{2!}F''(a) + \frac{h^3}{3!}F'''(c_1)$$

for some c_1 such that $a \le c_1 \le a + h$. Since $F' = f, F'' = f', F''' = f'', \ldots$, and $F(a) = 0$, we have

$$\int_a^{a+h} f(x)\,dx = F(a + h) = hf(a) + \frac{h^2}{2!}f'(a) + \frac{h^3}{3!}f''(c_1). \qquad (1.1)$$

On the other hand, the Taylor polynomial with remainder for f is

$$f(a + h) = f(a) + hf'(a) + \frac{h^2}{2!}f''(c_2),$$

for some c_2 such that $a \leq c_2 \leq a + h$, which gives (after a little algebra)

$$\frac{h}{2}[f(a + h) + f(a)] = hf(a) + \frac{h^2}{2}f'(a) + \frac{h^3}{4}f''(c_2). \qquad (1.2)$$

The error in the trapezoid rule is the difference of eqs. (1.1) and (1.2), or

$$\int_a^{a+h} f(x)dx - \frac{h}{2}[f(a + h) + f(a)] = \frac{h^3}{6}f''(c_1) - \frac{h^3}{4}f''(c_2).$$

We now show that if f is sufficiently smooth, i.e., f'' is continuous and bounded on $[a, a + h]$, we can combine these two remainder terms. If

$$m \leq f''(x) \leq M, \text{ for all } x \text{ on } [a, a + h],$$

then

$$\frac{h^3}{6}m \leq \frac{h^3}{6}f''(c_1) \leq \frac{h^3}{6}M,$$

and

$$\frac{h^3}{4}m \leq \frac{h^3}{4}f''(c_2) \leq \frac{h^3}{4}M,$$

so

$$\frac{-h^3}{12}m \leq \frac{h^3}{6}f''(c_1) - \frac{h^3}{4}f''(c_2) \leq \frac{-h^3}{12}M.$$

By the Intermediate Value Theorem (applied to f''), there is some point η in the interval $[a, a + h]$ such that

$$f''(\eta) = \frac{-12}{h^3}\left[\frac{h^3}{6}f''(c_1) - \frac{h^3}{4}f''(c_2)\right].$$

Thus we have

$$\int_a^{a+h} f(x)\,dx - \frac{h}{2}[f(a + h) + f(a)] = \frac{-h^3}{12}f''(\eta)$$

for some η in the interval $[a, a + h]$. This is the local truncation error, which comes from truncating the Taylor-series expansions, for one step of the trapezoid rule.

To improve the results, it is useful to subdivide the interval into n equal subintervals $[a, x_1], [x_1, x_2], \ldots, [x_{n-1}, b]$ and apply the method in each region. The length of each subinterval is $h = (b-a)/n$. This gives the more general (composite) trapezoid rule:

$$\int_a^b f(x)dx \approx \frac{h}{2}[f(a) + 2f(x_1) + \cdots + 2f(x_{n-1}) + f(b)].$$

The global error is the result of adding the local error in each of the regions. If f is sufficiently smooth, the global error can represented as $\dfrac{-(b-a)h^2}{12} f''(\eta)$ for some $a \le \eta \le b$.

Thus, the global error for the trapezoid rule is proportional to h^2, and the method is $O(h^2)$. This means that if the step size is cut in half, the bound on the global truncation error is reduced by a factor of one-fourth. In fact, the trapezoid rule is one of several numerical methods for which the error can be improved even more rapidly by combining two approximations in a manner known as acceleration (or extrapolation), which we introduce following the next example.

Example 1.9 Composite Trapezoid Rule

Consider the problem of using the trapezoid rule to approximate the integral

$$I = \int_1^3 \frac{1}{x^3} dx.$$

If we take $h = 2$, we find that $I \approx \dfrac{h}{2}[f(a) + f(b)] \approx 1.0370$. (See Example 1.3.)

As illustrated in Fig. 1.6, the area under this straight-line approximation is quite a bit larger than the true area. To improve the result, we subdivide the interval of integration, as shown in Fig. 1.11, so that $h = 1$. We find that

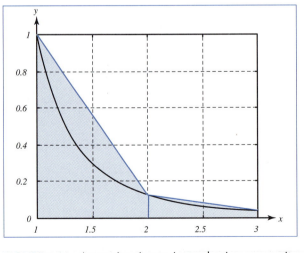

FIGURE 1.11   Approximation to integral using composite trapezoid rule.

$$I \approx \frac{h}{2}\left[f(1) + 2f(2) + f(3)\right] = \frac{1}{2}\left[1 + 2\left(\frac{1}{8}\right) + \frac{1}{27}\right] \approx 0.6435. \text{ For comparison,}$$

the exact value of the integral is $\dfrac{-1}{2}\left[1 - \dfrac{1}{3^2}\right] = \dfrac{4}{9} \approx 0.4444.$

1.3.3 Getting Better Results

Two of the important issues in judging a numerical method are the accuracy of the results and the amount of computational effort required to achieve them. For many methods, the accuracy of the results can be improved by reducing the step size; e.g., taking more subdivisions of the interval of integration for the trapezoid method. However, the increased computational effort may be an unacceptably high price to pay for the improvement. Carried to an extreme, this approach also leads to round-off errors. We begin this section with a method, acceleration, which can be used to improve the results of certain basic approximation formulas (one of which is the trapezoid rule); it is considered further in Chapter 11. We also illustrate the effect on the results when an algorithm (such as Gaussian elimination) is applied carefully or in an unwise manner. Finally, we introduce some of the ideas of computational efficiency.

Acceleration

A technique known as acceleration provides a method of improving the accuracy of an approximation formula $A(h)$ whose error can be expressed as

$$A - A(h) = a_2 h^2 + a_4 h^4 + \ldots,$$

where A is the true (unknown) value of the quantity being approximated by $A(h)$ and the coefficients of the error terms do not depend on the step size h. To apply acceleration, we form approximations to A using steps h and $h/2$. Let A_1 be the approximation using (the larger) step $h_1 = h$, and let A_2 be the approximation using step $h_2 = h/2$. These are combined to give an $O(h^4)$ approximation to A by means of two applications of an $O(h^2)$ formula:

$$A = \frac{1}{3}[4A_2 - A_1].$$

Example 1.10 Improving an Integral by Acceleration

Employing the results of Example 1.9, we can find an improved approximation to the integral by combining these results using $h = 2$ and $h = 1$:

$$I \approx \frac{1}{3}[4(0.6435) - 1.0370] = 0.51233.$$

The acceleration process can be continued, as we see by considering

$$A = B(h) + b_4 h^4 + b_6 h^6 + b_8 h^8 + \ldots,$$

where $B(h)$ is simply the extrapolated approximation to A, using step sizes h and $h/2$. If we can also find an approximation to A using step sizes $\frac{h}{2}$ and $\frac{h}{4}$, this would correspond to $B\frac{h}{2}$. Utilizing the notation introduced previously, we let B_1 be the extrapolated approximation using h and $h/2$ and B_2 be the result for $h/2$ and $h/4$. Then the second level of extrapolation gives

$$C = \frac{1}{15}[16B_2 - B_1],$$

which has error $O(h^6)$.

Since the error for the trapezoid rule can be expressed as a power series in even powers of the step size h (although we do not show this), acceleration is often used to improve the accuracy of results. This use of acceleration is generally known as *Richardson extrapolation.*

Apply the Algorithm Carefully

Consider again the system introduced in the previous sections, but assume now that there is some error in the values on the right-hand side of the equation (either as a result of round-off in previous computations, or from inaccuracies in data measurement, or whatever):

$$L_1: \qquad\qquad 4x + y = 6 \pm 0.4, \qquad\qquad (1.3)$$

$$M_1: \qquad\qquad -x + 5y = 9 \pm 0.4. \qquad\qquad (1.4)$$

The region represented by these pairs of lines, bordering the true solution, is indicated in Fig. 1.12.

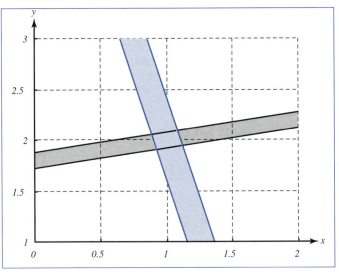

FIGURE 1.12 Graphical representation of a linear system with uncertainties.

After Gaussian elimination, the system becomes

L_1: $\qquad\qquad\qquad\qquad\qquad 4x + y = \quad 6 \pm 0.4,$ (1.3)

M_2: $\qquad\qquad\qquad\qquad\qquad 5.25y = 10.5 \pm 0.5.$ (1.5)

Solving eq. (1.5) for y gives $y = 2 \pm 0.0952\ldots$, and back substitution gives $x = 1 \pm 0.1238.\ldots$

The estimated solution is bounded within the region shown in Fig. 1.13; this is very close to the region containing the actual solution (shown in Fig. 1.12).

On the other hand, if the equations are listed in the opposite order, and the computations of Gaussian elimination are carried out without modification, the final result is much less accurate. This is illustrated in Fig. 1.14. The system is now

M_1: $\qquad\qquad\qquad\qquad\qquad -x + 5y = 9 \pm 0.4,$ (1.4)

L_1: $\qquad\qquad\qquad\qquad\qquad 4x + y = 6 \pm 0.4.$ (1.3)

After Gaussian elimination, the system becomes

M_1: $\qquad\qquad\qquad\qquad\qquad -x + 5y = \quad 9 \pm 0.4,$ (1.4)

L_2: $\qquad\qquad\qquad\qquad\qquad 21y = 42 \pm 2.$ (1.6)

Solving eq. (1.6) for y gives $y = 2 \pm 0.0952\ldots$, as before, but now back substitution results in $x = 1 \pm 0.876\ldots.$

Efficient Computations

Problems of interest for numerical methods often require many applications of certain computations that individually are not too time consuming. As computing capabilities have developed, the time required for basic operations, such as addition,

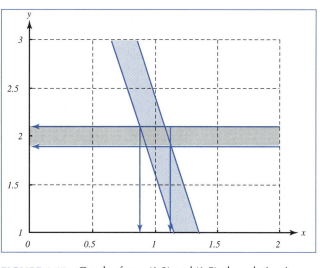

FIGURE 1.13 Graph of eqs. (1.3) and (1.5); the solution is bounded by the solid horizontal and vertical lines.

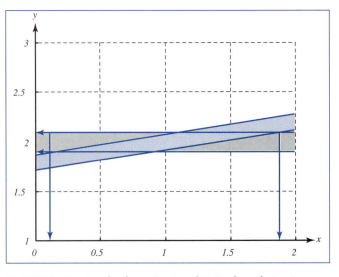

FIGURE 1.14 Graph of eqs. (1.4) and (1.6); the solution is bounded by the solid horizontal and vertical lines.

subtraction, multiplication, and division, has been reduced dramatically. Not too many years ago, multiplication and division required significantly more computational effort than addition and subtraction; it was common then to analyze algorithms based on counting only multiplications and divisions. The differential between multiplication and addition is much less now, and effort is usually evaluated in terms of floating-point operations (flops). In this section, we consider the computational effort (flops) for polynomial evaluation.

The straightforward evaluation of each term in the polynomial

$$P(x) = a_n x^n + a_{n-1} x^{n-1} + \cdots + a_1 x + a_0$$

requires n multiplications for the highest (nth degree) term and one less for each lower term. The total number of multiplications for the polynomial is

$$\sum_{k=1}^{n} k = \frac{n(n+1)}{2}.$$

There are n additions, giving the final count for the individual-term evaluation as

$$\text{flops} = \frac{n(n+3)}{2}.$$

Of course, no one would evaluate each term independently if he or she were doing it by hand. Each power of x would utilize the value of the previous power; i.e., $x^k = x \cdot x^{k-1}$. This approach requires $n - 1$ multiplications by x, n multiplications by the coefficients, and n additions. The corresponding count of operations is flops $= 3n - 1$.

A more efficient algorithm, Horner's method for evaluating polynomials, is based on expressing $P(x)$ as $(x - c)Q(x) + P(c)$, where

$$P(x) = a_n x^n + a_{n-1} x^{n-1} + \cdots + a_1 x + a_0,$$
$$Q(x) = b_n x^{n-1} + b_{n-1} x^{n-2} + \cdots + b_2 x + b_1, \text{ and } b_0 = P(c).$$

Horner's Algorithm

> Define $b_n = a_n$.
> For $\quad k = n - 1, \ldots, 0$, compute
> $\qquad b_k = a_k + b_{k+1} c$.
> End $\quad (b_0 = P(c))$.

Each of the n stages requires one multiplication and one addition, giving flops $= 2n$. In some applications, the value of the derivative of P is also required. Since $P'(x) = (x - c)Q'(x) + Q(x)$, we have $P'(c) = Q(c)$, which can be found by applying Horner's algorithm to $Q(x)$.

1.4 USING MATLAB

As the long history of numerical techniques indicates, numerical analysis does not require any particular computer resources. On the other hand, the scale and complexity of the problems that can be solved in a practical manner are strongly influenced (indeed, greatly expanded) by the availability of high-speed computers and efficient software implementation of numerical algorithms. Understanding the basic numerical methods and the issues involved in designing and analyzing them is a first step in the use of these techniques for real-world problems. Implementing the appropriate method, or using existing software, or a combination of the two approaches is necessary to achieve the final goal.

The student edition of MATLAB has been chosen as the programming environment for the presentation of the numerical techniques in this text for two main reasons. First, MATLAB provides outstanding graphing and programming capabilities, together with the ability to solve many types of problems symbolically as well. And second, MATLAB's underlying matrix structure makes the software especially useful for focusing on the aspects of various numerical techniques that can be described conveniently in vector form. This is a particularly valuable feature because vectorization is one important approach to parallel computing. MATLAB programs are presented for each of the techniques discussed in subsequent chapters. These programs can also be used as the basis for programming in other languages if that is desired. A brief summary of the most basic features of MATLAB is presented here; more details are given in the MATLAB User's Guide (Student Edition, version 5).

MATLAB originated in the late 1970s as a "matrix laboratory" for use in courses in matrix theory, linear algebra, and numerical analysis. Although today's MATLAB has vastly expanded capabilities, the basic data element is still an array, which does not require the declaration of either dimensions or variable types (integer, real, or complex). MATLAB is an interactive system; commands may be entered in the Command Window or by creating scripts or functions. Scripts and functions are known as m-files and are discussed later. First we summarize a few of the most basic MATLAB features that are useful for working in both the Command Window and m-file settings.

1.4.1 Command Window Computation

Simple computation may be carried out in the Command Window by entering an instruction at the prompt, much as you would on a calculator. For instance, in the code

```
EDU> 3*4 + 5
ans =      17
```

the result is displayed as ans (which is short for "answer").

The symbols for the basic arithmetic operations are as follows:

addition	$a + b$	subtraction	$a - b$
multiplication	$a * b$	division	$a \, / \, b$
exponentiation	$a \wedge b$		

Expressions are evaluated from left to right, with exponentiation having the highest precedence, followed by multiplication and division (with equal precedence) and then addition and subtraction (also with equal precedence).

If we wish to use the result of a computation later, we can give it a name; e.g., in the following code we define the variable s as the sum:

```
EDU> s = 3 + 4 + 5
s = 12
```

MATLAB Variables

Variable names in MATLAB may consist of up to 31 characters, starting with a letter and followed by any combination of letters, digits, and underscores. Variable names are case sensitive. Punctuation marks and spaces may not be included in a variable name.

MATLAB treats all variables as matrices, although scalar quantities are not entered or displayed in array notation. A row vector is a 1-by-n matrix; a column vector is an n-by-1 matrix. For example, a row vector may be defined as $x = [1 \quad 2 \quad 3]$. The elements, enclosed between the left bracket and the right bracket, are separated by either commas or spaces. The individual elements are $x(1) = 1$, $x(2) = 2$, and $x(3) = 3$. A column vector may be given as

```
y = [ 4
      5
      6]
```

or as

```
y = [4;    5;    6], or as y = [4    5    6]'
```

Thus, we see that a new row may be indicated either by a new line or by a semicolon. The individual elements are $y(1) = 4$, $y(2) = 5$, and $y(3) = 6$.

An example of a 3-by-4 matrix is

```
Z = [  1        2        3        4
       5        6        7        8
       9       10       11       12]
```

The element in the ith row, jth column is $Z(i,j)$, which is also denoted as z_{ij} in standard matrix notation. For this example, $Z(2,4) = 8$. (*Note:* Elements in MATLAB arrays are indexed starting from 1.)

In many situations, we need an array with a particular structure. For example, an array (row vector) of the integers from 1 to 10 is created by the command

```
x = 1:10
```

A more general form gives numbers from a to b with the specified step between the elements:

```
x = a : step : b
```

An example is

```
EDU> x = 1 : 0.5 : 3
x =
        1.5000    2.0000    2.5000    3.0000
```

In other cases, we wish to have a specified number of values, evenly distributed between the first and last element. If the desired spacing is linear, the MATLAB function linspace can be used. The command

```
x = linspace(1, n)
```

gives 100 points, evenly spaced from 1 to n, inclusive.

The user can also specify the number of points (including the first and last values) with the command

```
x = linspace(a, b, n_pts)
```

An example,

```
EDU> x = linspace(1,4,10)
x =
Columns 1 through 7
1.0000     1.3333     1.6667     2.0000     2.3333     2.6667   3.0000
Columns 8 through 10
3.6667     4.0000
```

MATLAB displays the results without enclosing the array in square brackets.

MATLAB has a number of special matrices that are very useful in applications. The following are examples of matrices that are used in examples in the remainder of this text.

The identity matrix:

```
EDU> eye(3)
ans =
     1     0     0
     0     1     0
     0     0     1
```

A square matrix of all 1's:

```
EDU> ones(3)
ans =
     1     1     1
     1     1     1
     1     1     1
```

A row vector of all 1's:

```
EDU> ones(1,4)
ans =
     1     1     1     1
```

An array of all 0's:

```
EDU> zeros(2,3)
ans =
     0     0     0
     0     0     0
```

As with the function ones, a square matrix is generated if only one argument is given. Matrices can be combined by concatenation, as in the code

```
x = [ 1      2       3]
y = [ 5     10      15 ]
z = [x      y ] = [ 1  2  3  5  10  15]
```

and the code

```
w =    [ x
         y ]

  =    [ 1      2       3
         5     10      15 ]
```

Vector and Matrix Computation

Addition and subtraction of vectors or matrices of the same dimensions are defined in the usual way. For example, if **x** and **y** are the preceding row vectors (1-by-3 matrices), then standard matrix addition is the component-by-component sum:

```
x + y = [1 + 5    2 + 10    3 + 15] = [7    12    18]
```

However, a special notation is required when component-by-component multiplication, division, or exponentiation is needed for vectors or matrices; such operations are indicated by a period immediately before the corresponding operation symbol. Thus, the component-by-component product of the vectors **x** and **y** is indicated as

```
x. * y = [(1)(5)    (2)(10)    (3)(15)] = [5    20    45]
```

In this example, **x** * **y** is not defined, since **x** and **y** are not conformable for matrix multiplication.

In MATLAB, the matrix transpose operation is denoted by the prime symbol, ';
e.g., for **x** as previously defined,

```
x' = [ 1
       2
       3 ]
```

In this example **x**′ * **y** and **x** * **y**′ are both defined:

```
x' * y = [   5      10      15
            10      20      30
            15      30      45]
```

and $\mathbf{x} * \mathbf{y}' = 70$. (For a matrix $\mathbf{M}$ with complex elements, $\mathbf{M}'$ gives the complex-conjugate transpose of $\mathbf{M}$; the transpose without conjugation is given by preceding the prime with a period, i.e., $\mathbf{M.}'$)

Any matrix $\mathbf{M}$ can be converted to a column vector $\mathbf{x}$ by setting $\mathbf{x}(:) = \mathbf{M}$.

MATLAB offers many common mathematical functions. Input to the trigonometric functions is in radians. The function $\log(x)$ indicates the natural logarithm; the base-10 logarithm is indicated by $\log10(x)$.

Plotting

To graph a function in MATLAB, we create a vector (call it $\mathbf{x}$) of the values of the independent variable that are to be graphed and a corresponding vector $\mathbf{y}$ of the values of the dependent variable. The graph is then generated by issuing the MATLAB command

```
plot (x, y)
```

The following set of commands generates the graph for Fig. 1.1:

```
x = 0 : 0.01 : 2;    y = x.^2-3;
plot(x,y);    hold on
xx = [ 0  2 ];    yy = [ 0  0 ];
plot(xx, yy);  grid on
hold off
```

The function is graphed first and the x-axis is plotted second, but the `hold on` command causes them to be drawn on the same set of axes. The first two lines compute the vectors $\mathbf{x}$ and $\mathbf{y}$, and plot the function (using straight lines between the indicated points); plotting $\mathbf{xx}$ versus $\mathbf{yy}$ gives a straight line along the x-axis. The grid lines on the graph are created using the `grid on` command. Note that a plot can be made smaller by shrinking the size of the graph window.

This example also illustrates the fact that several commands can be placed on one line if they are separated by commas or semicolons.

Output

A MATLAB command that is not terminated with a semicolon will display the result, together with the variable name (if there is one) or `ans`. A command followed by a semicolon will not display the result of the calculation. The function

```
disp(variable)
```

can be used to display the value of a variable without the variable name.

MATLAB has several number display formats; a few of the most useful are summarized here. For fixed-point numbers, `format short` displays 5 digits; `format long` displays 16 digits. For floating-point representation, `format short e` gives 5 digits plus the exponent; `format long e` gives 16 digits plus the exponent. Two combination formats, `format short g` and `format long g`, use fixed-point display (5 digits and 16 digits, respectively), unless a number is so small that floating point is necessary to show its value meaningfully. For results that are ratios of small integers, `format rat` is convenient.

The internal representation of a number is not changed when the display format is altered.

The user input and Command Window output can be saved in a text file (named `file_name`) by using the command `diary file_name`. The workspace can be saved and reloaded using commands in the File menu or using the `save` and `load` commands.

1.4.2 MATLAB Programs

There are two types of programs (known as m-files) in MATLAB: scripts and functions. To generate an m-file, choose New / m-file from the File menu, and enter the desired commands. Text following a percent sign (%) is treated as a comment. Save the file as `file_name.m`. The differences between scripts and functions are summarized next.

Scripts

Scripts provide a set of MATLAB commands, comments, definitions of parameter values, plotting commands, etc. A script that has been created and saved is executed by typing the file name at the MATLAB prompt in the Command Window. As an example, the following script calculates the trapezoid rule approximation to the integral of $1/x^3$ on the interval $[1, 3]$, as in Example 1.3:

```
% S_Ex_1_3
a = 1; b = 3;
x = [ a   b ]
y = x.^(-3)
I = (b - a)*(y(1) + y(2))/2
```

The first line is a comment, giving the name of the script. This script will display the vectors **x** and **y** and the approximate value of the integral *I*.

Scripts do not accept input arguments, but they do allow user input (via the `input` function). The previous script becomes slightly more general by replacing the values of *a* and *b* by a prompt for user input:

```
% S_Ex_1_3a
a = input('enter left-hand endpoint, a = ')
b = input ('enter right-hand endpoint, b = ')
x = [ a   b ]
y = x.^(-3)
I =(b - a)*(y(1) + y(2))/2
```

We can also define the function to be integrated as a string and evaluate the string using the MATLAB function `eval`, as illustrated in this variation on the previous script:

```
% S_Ex_1_3b
a = 1; b = 3;
f = 'x^(-3)';
x = a;    ya = eval(f);
x = b;    yb = eval(f);
I = (b - a)*(ya + yb)/2
```

For further discussion of scripts, see the MATLAB User's Guide (pp. 29–33). We now turn our attention to the creation and use of MATLAB functions.

Functions

A MATLAB function communicates with the MATLAB workspace through the variables passed into the function, the output variables it creates, and the use of global variables. A function is distinguished from a script by the fact that the first line of a function is of the form

```
function y = function_name(input arguments)
```

where y is the output variable computed by the function. If more than one output variable is specified, the form is

```
function [y, z] = function_name(input arguments)
```

The name of the function and the name of the file in which it is stored are the same, except that the name of the file ends in ".m."

To illustrate the use of a (user-created) MATLAB function, consider the following code for finding the approximate integral of $f(x) = 1/x^3$, using the basic trapezoid rule:

```
function t = trap_ex(a, b)
t = (b-a)*(a^(-3) + b^(-3))/2;
```

The function, which is created as an m-file and saved as `trap_ex.m`, can then be executed from the Command Window by entering the appropriate function call at the prompt. The response from MATLAB appears on the next line. The code is as follows:

```
EDU> t = trap_ex(1, 3)
t =        1.037
```

This function is still much more specific than we would like. A more useful function for the basic trapezoid rule allows us to give the name of the function to be integrated as an input argument. We illustrate this with the following two functions, the first of which, `my_func`, defines the function to be integrated, the second of which, `basic_trap`, implements the basic trapezoid rule:

```
function y = my_func(x)
y = x.^(-3);

function q = basic_trap(f, a, b)
ya = feval(f,a);
yb = feval(f,b);
q = (b-a)*(ya + yb)/2;
```

To use the function `basic_trap`, we must specify the name of the function to be integrated, enclosed in single quotes:

```
EDU>q = basic_trap('my_func', 1, 3)
q =
      1.037
```

We could streamline the computations even further by defining the interval of integration as a vector and finding a vector of function values.

In the chapters that follow, MATLAB functions are given for each of the numerical methods presented. A brief discussion of MATLAB's built-in functions for solving numerical problems is also included at the end of each chapter.

A function may itself contain one or more functions (defined at the end of the main function); such "subfunctions" can be called only from within the main function.

Editing

The first time MATLAB executes a function or a script, it compiles the commands; this means that if changes are made to the function, care must be taken to recompile it, either by saving the modified function with a new name or by using the `clear` command to clear the current compiled function from the working memory before the modified function is used. Executing a script by typing its name in the Command Window (followed by a carriage return) will run the most recently saved version, but changes to any functions the script calls will not be incorporated unless the previously compiled version of the function has been cleared. (The "Save and Execute" command from the File menu on Macintosh computers is recommended only for the first time a script is executed in a particular session, since this command does not recompile the script if changes have been made.)

Fixed-Point Iteration (p. 6): For finding a solution $x_k = g(x_{k-1})$ of $x = g(x)$. To find a numerical approximation to $\sqrt{c}$ by fixed-point iteration, use

$$x = g(x) = \frac{1}{2}\left(x + \frac{c}{x}\right),$$

so that the iteration formula is

$$x_k = \frac{1}{2}\left(x_{k-1} + \frac{c}{x_{k-1}}\right).$$

The Trapezoid Rule (p. 8): Approximates the definite integral

$$\int_a^b f(x)\, dx \approx \frac{b-a}{2}[f(a) + f(b)].$$

A computationally efficient method of evaluating the polynomial

$$P(x) = a_n x^n + a_{n-1} x^{n-1} + \cdots + a_1 x + a_0$$

at $x = c$ is given by Horner's algorithm:

Begin by setting $b_n = a_n$.
For $k = n - 1,\ldots,0,$
$\qquad b_k = a_k + b_{k+1}c.$
The result is: $b_0 = P(c).$

The quantities $b_n, \ldots, b_1$ are the coefficients of $Q(x)$, with $P(x) = (x - c)\, Q(x) + P(c)$. $P'(c)$ can be found by evaluating $Q(c)$ using Horner's method.

Gerschgorin Circle Theorem (p. 12): All eigenvalues of the matrix **A** lie within the union of the disks bounded by the n circles, $C_1, \ldots, C_n$, where circle C_i has center at a_{ii} and radius

$$r_i = -|a_{ij}| + \sum_{j=1}^{n} |a_{ij}|.$$

Acceleration (p. 9): The order of convergence for some approximation formulas, including the trapezoid rule for numerical integration, can be improved by combining the approximate values obtained with step size h and step size $h/2$. If we denote these approximations as $T(h)$ and $T(h/2)$, respectively, a better estimate of the desired result is given by

$$T \approx \frac{1}{3}[4T(h/2) - T(h)].$$

The trapezoid rule is a formula of order $O(h^2)$, but the extrapolated value is an approximation of order $O(h^4)$.

Much of the historical discussion in the introduction to this chapter is based on material in the following excellent books:

Struik, D. J., *A Concise History of Mathematics* (4th ed.), Dover, New York, 1987.

Eves, H., *Great Moments in Mathematics* (v. 1, before 1650; v. 2, after 1650), The Mathematical Association of America, Washington, DC, 1983.

Smith, D. E., *A Source Book in Mathematics*, Dover, New York, 1959.

For historical notes related to calculus or differential equations, the following books are especially recommended:

Boyer, C. B., *The History of the Calculus and Its Conceptual Development*, Dover, New York, 1949.

Simmons, G. F., *Calculus with Analytic Geometry*, McGraw-Hill, New York, 1985.

Simmons, G. F., *Differential Equations with Applications and Historical Notes*, McGraw-Hill, New York, 1972.

The following are a sampling of interesting articles on the history of computational aspects of mathematics:

Reynolds, B. E., "The Algorists vs. the Abacists: An Ancient Controversy on the Use of Calculators," *The College Mathematics Journal*, v. 24, no. 3, May 1993, pp. 218–223.

Weinstock, R., "Isaac Newton: Credit Where Credit Won't Do," *The College Mathematics Journal*, v. 25, no. 3, May 1994, pp. 179–192.

Kollerstrom, N., "Thomas Simpson and 'Newton's Method of Approximation': An Enduring Myth," *British Journal for the History of Science*, v. 25 (1992), pp. 347–354.

Among the references for more theoretical and advanced treatments of numerical methods are:

Atkinson, K. E., *An Introduction to Numerical Analysis* (2d ed.), John Wiley, New York, 1989.

Dahlquist, G., and A. Bjorck, *Numerical Methods*, (Translated by Ned Anderson), Prentice-Hall, Englewood Cliffs, NJ, 1974.

Isaacson, E., and H. B. Keller, *Analysis of Numerical Methods*, Dover, New York, 1994 (original, John Wiley & Sons, 1966).

Ralston, A., and P. Rabinowitz, *A First Course in Numerical Analysis* (2d ed.), McGraw-Hill, New York, 1978.

For further discussion of stopping conditions for iterative methods, see:

Maron, M. J., *Numerical Analysis: A Practical Approach*, Macmillan, New York, 1982.

Rice, J. R., *Numerical Methods, Software, and Analysis*, McGraw-Hill, New York, 1983.

The following are references for the use of MATLAB:

Student Edition of MATLAB, The Language of Technical Computing, Version 5 User's Guide, Prentice Hall, Upper Saddle River, NJ, 1997.

Van Loan, C. F., *Introduction to Scientific Computing: A Matrix-Vector Approach Using MATLAB*, Prentice Hall, Upper Saddle River, NJ, 1997.

PRACTICE THE TECHNIQUES

For problems P1.1– P1.5, investigate the use of Gaussian elimination to solve systems of two equations in two unknowns.

   a.   Solve the system as given.

   b.   Graph the given equations, and graph the transformed second equation after the elimination step.

   c.   Repeat Parts a and b for the system consisting of the same two equations, but given in reverse order.

P1.1 $4x + y = 6,$
         $-x + 2y = 3.$

P1.2 $4x + y = 9,$
         $x + 2y = 4.$

P1.3 $3x + y = 4,$
         $6x + 7y = 13.$

P1.4 $5x + y = 17,$
         $-10x + 17y = 4.$

P1.5 $3x + y = 6,$
         $x + 5y = 16.$

For problems P1.6–P1.10, investigate the convergence of the given fixed-point iteration formula.

   a.   Show the first three iterations graphically.

   b.   Compute the first three iterates algebraically.

   c.   Determine whether the conditions of the fixed-point convergence theorem are satisfied.

P1.6 $x = g(x) = 0.5x^3 + 0.3.$

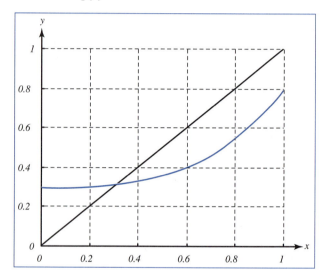

P1.7 $x = g(x) = \sin(2x).$

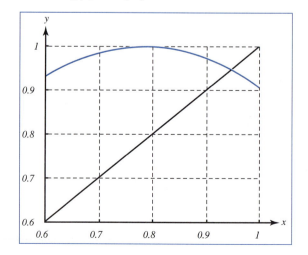

P1.8 $x = g(x) = -0.5x^3 + 0.8$.

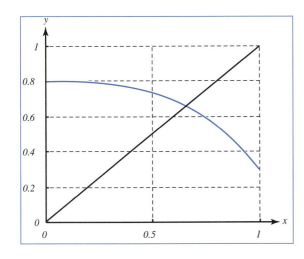

P1.9 $x = g(x) = 1 - x^2$.

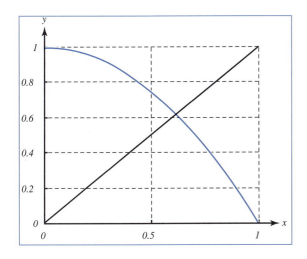

P1.10 $x = g(x) = \dfrac{1}{2} + \dfrac{1}{2}\sin(3x)$.

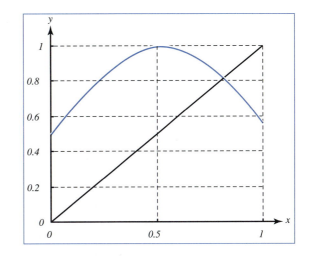

Problems P1.11–P1.15 illustrate the use of the Gerschgorin theorem to find bounds on the eigenvalues of a matrix. Find the Gerschgorin circles for each row of the given matrix. Graph the regions, and give bounds on the eigenvalues.

P1.11 $\mathbf{A} = \begin{bmatrix} 1 & 1/8 & 1/4 \\ 1/2 & 2 & 0 \\ 0 & 0 & 3 \end{bmatrix}$.

P1.12 $\mathbf{A} = \begin{bmatrix} 1 & 3/4 & 0 \\ 1/2 & 2 & -1/8 \\ 0 & 1/8 & 3 \end{bmatrix}$.

P1.13 $\mathbf{A} = \begin{bmatrix} 1 & 1/4 & 0 \\ 1/4 & 2 & 1/4 \\ 0 & 1/4 & 3 \end{bmatrix}$.

P1.14 $\mathbf{A} = \begin{bmatrix} 1 & 1/3 & 1/3 \\ 1/4 & 2 & 1/4 \\ 1/2 & 1/4 & 3 \end{bmatrix}$.

P1.15 $\mathbf{A} = \begin{bmatrix} 1 & -1/2 & 0 \\ 1/2 & 2 & 1/8 \\ 0 & 1/8 & 3 \end{bmatrix}$.

Problems P1.16–P1.17 illustrate the effect of round-off error in adding numbers of differing magnitudes.

a. *Add from left to right, rounding to three digits at each step.*
b. *Add from right to left, rounding to three digits at each step.*
c. *Compare the relative error for the results from Parts a and b.*

P1.16 $100 + 0.49 + 0.49$.

P1.17 $10.0 + 0.333 + 0.333 + 0.333$.

Problems P1.18–P1.20 illustrate the effect of round-off in the quadratic formula.

a. *Use the standard quadratic formula with rounding.*
b. *Use the rationalized-numerator quadratic formula with rounding.*
c. *Compare the results from Parts a and b with the results found without rounding.*

P1.18 $x^2 - 973x + 1 = 0$. (Round to three digits.)

P1.19 $x^2 - 57x + 1 = 0$. (Round to four digits.)

P1.20 $x^2 - 23x + 1 = 0$. (Round to four digits.)

Problems P1.21–P1.25 illustrate the use of the trapezoid rule for numerical integration.

a. *Approximate the given integral, using the basic trapezoid rule with $h = b - a$.*
b. *Approximate the integral, using the composite trapezoid rule with $h = \dfrac{b - a}{2}$.*
c. *Improve the approximation by acceleration, using results from Parts a and b.*

P1.21 Find $\displaystyle\int_0^2 \frac{1}{1 + x^2}\, dx$.

P1.22 Find $\displaystyle\int_0^{\pi/2} \sin(x)\, dx$.

P1.23 Find $\displaystyle\int_0^2 2^x\, dx$.

P1.24 Find $\displaystyle\int_0^2 e^{-x^2}\, dx$.

P1.25 Find $\displaystyle\int_0^{\pi/2} \frac{3}{1 + \sin(x)}\, dx$.

Problems P1.26–P1.30 illustrate the effect of the order of the equations in Gaussian elimination (with error).

a. *Solve the equations in the order given; determine bounds on x and y. Graph the given equations and the transformed second equation*
b. *Solve the equations in reverse order; determine bounds on x and y. Graph the given equations, and the transformed second equation*
c. *Compare the relative error in the values of x and y found in Parts a and b.*

P1.26 $4x + y = 6 \pm 0.1$,
$-x + 2y = 3 \pm 0.1$.

P1.27 $4x + y = 9 \pm 0.1$,
$x + 2y = 4 \pm 0.1$.

P1.28 $3x + y = 4 \pm 0.1$,
$6x + 7y = 13 \pm 0.1$.

P1.29 $5x + y = 17 \pm 0.2$,
$-10x + 17y = 4 \pm 0.2$.

P1.30 $3x + y = 6 \pm 0.2$,
$x + 5y = 16 \pm 0.2$.

EXTEND YOUR UNDERSTANDING

U1.1 For each of the Problems P1.6–P1.10 for which the conditions of the theorem are not satisfied on $[0, 1]$, investigate the following questions.

a. Is there a starting value of x for which the iterations do not converge? (Show this on the graph.)
b. Is there a subinterval on which the conditions are satisfied?

U1.2 Use the Gerschgorin circle theorem to show that, for any matrix

$$\mathbf{A} = \begin{bmatrix} 1 + 2r & -r & 0 \\ -r & 1 + 2r & -r \\ 0 & -r & 1 + 2r \end{bmatrix},$$

any eigenvalue m satisfies $|m| \geq 1$, regardless of the value of r. This result is used in Chapter 15. Extend the pattern to larger dimension matrices (e.g., tridiagonal, with $1 + 2r$ on the diagonal and $-r$ on the subdiagonal and superdiagonal).

U1.3 Show that Horner's method is equivalent to synthetic division.

U1.4 Show that Horner's method for evaluating polynomials can be viewed as rearranging the polynomial such that

$$P(x) = a_n x^n + a_{n-1} x^{n-1} + \ldots + a_1 x + a_0$$
$$= (\ldots((a_n x + a_{n-1})x + a_{n-1})x + \ldots + a_1)x + a_0.$$

If only the value of $P(c)$ is required, it is not necessary to save the intermediate quantities (the b_i in the statement of the algorithm in the text).

Write an algorithm for Horner's method using a single temporary variable.

U1.5 Consider a very limited binary normalized floating-point system in which there are four bits to store the positive numbers. What exponents can be represented if two bits are used? What numbers can be represented if two bits are used for digits and two for exponents? What numbers can be represented if three bits are used for digits and one for the exponents?

U1.6 Find the positive numbers that can be represented with only one digit and exponents of 0 or 1 in a base-10 normalized floating-point system.

2

Solving Equations of One Variable

As discussed in Chapter 1, the problem of finding the zeros of a nonlinear function (or roots of a nonlinear equation) has a long history. Although quadratic equations of one variable can be solved analytically, numerical estimation of the zeros may be desired. For many other types of equations, it is either difficult or impossible to find an exact solution. In this chapter, we investigate several techniques for finding roots or zeros of nonlinear equations of a single variable.

The first technique presented, bisection, is a systematic approach to subdividing an interval on which we know the function has a zero. In addition to being simple and intuitive, this method can be used to obtain an adequate initial estimate of the zero that will be refined by more powerful methods. The second group of solution techniques—the *regula falsi*, secant, and Newton methods—are based on approximating the function whose zero is desired by a straight-line approximation, either a secant line through two points on the function or a tangent line to the function. We then investigate a technique, known as Muller's method, that is based on a quadratic approximation to the function. The presentation of each technique includes several simple examples and a MATLAB function implementing the method.

Applications of zero-finding techniques occur throughout science and engineering. We begin with two examples, which we also use to illustrate the techniques throughout the chapter. Further examples from fields such as statics occur in the exercises.

In Chapters 3 and 4, we consider some methods for solving systems of linear equations; Chapter 5 presents techniques for dealing with systems of nonlinear equations.

Example 2-A Floating Sphere

According to Archimedes, if a solid that is lighter than a fluid is placed in the fluid, the solid will be immersed to such a depth that the weight of the solid is equal to the weight of the displaced fluid. For example, a spherical ball of unit radius will float in water at a depth x (the distance from the bottom of the ball to the water line) determined by ρ, the specific gravity of the ball ($\rho < 1$).

The volume of the submerged segment of the sphere is

$$V = \pi x(3r^2 + x^2)/6,$$

where r and x are related by the Pythagorean theorem, $r^2 + (1 - x)^2 = 1$. (See Fig. 2.1.)

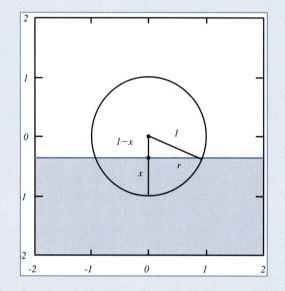

FIGURE 2.1 Floating Sphere.

To find the depth at which the ball floats, we must solve the equation stating that the volume of the submerged segment is ρ times the volume of the entire sphere, i.e.,

$$\pi x(3r^2 + x^2)/6 = \rho(4\pi/3),$$

which simplifies to

$$x^3 - 3x^2 + 4\rho = 0.$$

In general, the zero that is of physical interest is between 0 and 2 (since the ball is of unit radius and x is measured up from the bottom of the ball).

Representative values of specific gravity include $\rho \approx 0.25$ for cork and $0.33 < \rho < 0.99$ for air-dried timber, depending on the type of wood. We investigate several methods of solving the preceding equation in this chapter.

Example 2-B Planetary Orbits

The position of a moon that revolves around a planet in an elliptical orbit can be described by Kepler's equation, which gives the central angle θ as a function of time. The relationship between time t and the central angle is given by

$$2\pi t = P(\theta - e \sin \theta),$$

where P is the period of revolution of the moon about the planet, e is the eccentricity of the moon's orbit, and the moon is at $(a, 0)$ at $t = 0$. The planet is located at a focus of the ellipse, $(a\,e, 0)$. To find the central angle for any given time t, we must find the root of the equation

$$2\pi t - P\theta + Pe \sin \theta = 0.$$

If the period of revolution is 100 days, and the eccentricity is 0.5, then, for any specified time t, the central angle can be found from the relation

$$2\pi t - 100\theta + 50 \sin \theta = 0.$$

Kepler's law says that the orbit sweeps out equal areas in equal times. The position of the planet at 10-day intervals and the areas swept out between $t = 0$ and $t = 10$ and between $t = 60$ and $t = 70$ are illustrated in Fig. 2.2.

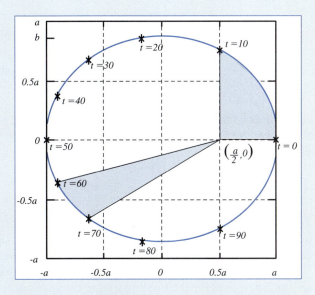

FIGURE 2.2 Position of the moon at 10-day intervals and areas swept out from days 0 to 10 and days 60 to 70.

The equation of the ellipse is $x(\theta) = a \cos(\theta)$, $y(\theta) = b \sin(\theta)$, where the coefficients a and b and the eccentricity e are related by the equation

$$b^2 = a^2 (1 - e^2).$$

Bisection is a systematic search technique for finding a zero of a continuous function. The method is based on finding an interval in which a zero is known to occur, dividing the interval into two equal subintervals, and determining which subinterval contains a zero.

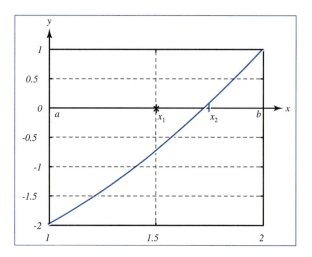

FIGURE 2.3   The graph of $y = x^2 - 3$ and the first two approximations to its zero on $[1, 2]$ using the bisection method.

Suppose that an interval $[a, b]$ has been located which is known to contain a zero, since the function changes signs between a and b. (See Fig. 2.3.) The midpoint of the interval is

$$m = \frac{a + b}{2},$$

and a zero must lie in either $[a, m]$ or $[m, b]$. The appropriate subinterval is determined by testing the function to see whether it changes sign on $[a, m]$. If so, the search continues on that interval; otherwise it continues on $[m, b]$.

We illustrate this process first for the very simple example of finding the square root of 3 and then for the floating sphere discussed in Example 2-A.

Example 2.1 Finding the Square Root of 3 Using Bisection

To find a numerical approximation to $\sqrt{3}$, we approximate the zero of

$$y = f(x) = x^2 - 3.$$

Since $f(1) = -2$ and $f(2) = 1$, we take as our starting bounds on the zero $a = 1$ and $b = 2$; the corresponding function values are $y(a) = -2$ and $y(b) = 1$. Our first approximation to the zero is the midpoint of this interval, namely, $x_1 = (1+2)/2 = 1.5$. We then find the value of the function, $y_1 = f(x_1) = (1.5)^2 - 3 = -0.75$. Since $y(a)$ and y_1 have the same sign, but y_1 and $y(b)$ have opposite signs, we know that there is a zero in the interval $[x_1, b]$. By setting $a = 1.5$, the improved left-hand endpoint of the interval, we can repeat the process; we now have $y(a) = -0.75$. The right-hand end of the interval remains unchanged, so $b = 2$ and $y(b) = 1$. It is convenient to keep track of the calculations in a tabular form; Table 2.1 shows the results of five iterations through this process.

Table 2.1 Calculation of $\sqrt{3}$ using bisection.

Step	a	b	x_i	$y(a)$	$y(b)$	y_i
1	1.0000	2.0000	1.5000	−2.0000	1.0000	−0.7500
2	1.5000	2.0000	1.7500	−0.7500	1.0000	0.0625
3	1.5000	1.7500	1.6250	−0.7500	0.0625	−0.3594
4	1.6250	1.7500	1.6875	−0.3594	0.0625	−0.1523
5	1.6875	1.7500	1.7188	−0.1523	0.0625	−0.0459

We have an estimate of the zero at each stage of the iteration, and we know that after k iterations, the error is at most

$$\frac{b_1 - a_1}{2^k},$$

where $[a_1, b_1]$ is the original interval within which the zero was bracketed. In many cases, we would not choose to retain the entire sequence of values of the endpoints of the interval bracketing the zero, but the values could be stored in vectors **a** and **b** if desired.

As indicated by the values of the function at the approximate zeros, it is possible to be quite close to the true zero at some stage of the iteration and then move away from the zero before returning to a good approximation later (with a smaller error bracket for the zero). In the foregoing calculations, we had a better approximation at step 2 than we had at step 3 or step 4.

Example 2.2 Approximating the Floating Depth for a Cork Ball by Bisection

To find the floating depth for a cork ball of radius 1 whose density is one-fourth that of water, we must find the zero (between 0 and 1) of

$$y = x^3 - 3x^2 + 1.$$

The function is shown in Fig. 2.4 for the region of interest.

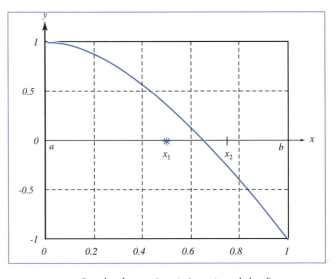

FIGURE 2.4 Graph of $y = x^3 - 3x^2 + 1$ and the first two approximations to its zero in [0, 1].

A summary of the calculations for the first 10 iterations is given in Table 2.2.

Table 2.2 Calculation of floating depth using bisection method.

i	x_i	y_i
1	0.5	0.375
2	0.75	−0.26562
3	0.625	0.072266
4	0.6875	−0.093018
5	0.65625	−0.0093689
6	0.64062	0.031712
7	0.64844	0.011236
8	0.65234	0.00094932
9	0.6543	−0.0042058
10	0.65332	−0.0016273

The MATLAB function shown next finds a zero of a function in the interval $[a, b]$; $f(a)$ and $f(b)$ must have opposite signs. The process stops if either:

1. The change in the successive iterates is less than "tol" or
2. The maximum number of iterations, "max," has been reached.

Although the change in the estimated zero at the kth iteration can be calculated directly from the length of the initial interval for the bisection method, both tests are included for user flexibility.

2.1.1 MATLAB Function for Bisection

```
function [x, y] = Bisect(fun, a, b, tol, max)
%               Input and output variables
%     fun       string containing name of function
%     [a, b]    interval containing zero
%     tol       allowable tolerance in computed zero
%     max       maximum number of iterations
%     x         vector of approximations to zero
%     y         vector of function values, fun(x)

a(1) = a;       b(1) = b;
ya(1) = feval(fun, a(1));      yb(1) = feval(fun, b(1));
if ya(1) * yb(1) > 0.0
    error('Function has same sign at end points')
end
for i = 1 : max
    x(i) = (a(i) + b(i))/2;  y(i) = feval(fun, x(i));
    if ((x(i)-a(i)) < tol)
        disp('Bisection method has converged'); break;
    end
    if y(i) == 0.0
        disp('exact zero found'); break;
    elseif y(i)*ya(i) < 0
        a(i+1) = a(i); ya(i+1) = ya(i);
        b(i+1) = x(i); yb(i+1) = y(i);
    else
        a(i+1) = x(i); ya(i+1) = y(i);
        b(i+1) = b(i); yb(i+1) = yb(i);
    end;
    iter = i ;
end
if (iter >= max)
    disp('zero not found to desired tolerance');
end
n = length(x); k = 1:n; out = [k'  a(1:n)'  b(1:n)'  x'  y'];
disp('        step           a          b          x          y')
disp(out)
```

2.1.2 Discussion

The bisection method is based on a well-known property of continuous functions, the intermediate-value theorem. Applied specifically to the cases we are interested in, the theorem states that if $f(a) > 0$ and $f(b) < 0$, or if $f(a) < 0$ and $f(b) > 0$, then there is a number c between a and b such that $f(c) = 0$.

It is helpful to know how good our answers are for any numerical technique. In general, bisection is slow, but sure. At the first stage, the length of the interval is $b - a$. The furthest that our estimated zero (the midpoint of the interval) can be from the true solution is $(b - a)/2$. At each stage the length of the interval is halved, so the maximum possible error is reduced by a factor of one-half. The error at stage k is at most $(b - a)/2^k$.

One definition of *linear convergence* is that the inequality

$$|x^* - x_k| \leq r^k |x^* - x_1|$$

holds for some constant $r < 1$, where x^* is the true zero, r is the convergence rate, x_k is the approximate zero at the kth stage, and $x_1 = (a + b)/2$ is the first approximate zero. Thus, bisection is linearly convergent with rate $1/2$.

Bisection works well with problems that cause difficulties for other methods. It is also useful as a preprocessing algorithm for the methods we discuss in the remainder of the chapter.

2.2   *Regula Falsi* and Secant Methods

Bisection makes no use of information about the shape of the function $y = f(x)$ whose zero is desired. The first way to incorporate such information is to consider a straight-line approximation to the function. Since we know how to find the zero of a linear function, it is not much more work to find our approximation to the zero of $f(x)$ not as the midpoint of the interval, but as the point where the straight-line approximation to f crosses the x-axis. In this section, we consider two closely related methods based on straight-line approximations using two initial values of the independent variable that bracket the desired zero (as with the bisection method).

The *regula falsi* and secant methods start with two points, $(a, y(a))$ and $(b, y(b))$, satisfying the condition that $y(a) \cdot y(b) < 0$. The next approximation to the zero is the value of x where the straight line through the initial points crosses the x-axis; this approximate zero is

$$x = b - \frac{b - a}{y(b) - y(a)} y(b).$$

The *regula falsi* and secant methods may differ in the choice of the points to be used to define the next iteration.

2.2.1 Regula Falsi

The *regula falsi* method, or the rule of false position, proceeds as in bisection to find the subinterval $[a, x]$ or $[x, b]$ that contains the zero by testing for a change of sign of the function, i.e., testing whether $y(a) \cdot y < 0$ or $y \cdot y(b) < 0$. If there is a zero in the interval $[a, x]$, we leave the value of a unchanged and set $b = x$. On the other hand, if there is no zero in $[a, x]$, the zero must be in the interval $[x, b]$; so we set $a = x$ and leave b unchanged.

The stopping condition may test the size of y, the amount by which the approximate solution x has changed on the last iteration, or whether the process has continued too long. Typically, a combination of these conditions is used.

Example 2.3 Finding the Cube Root of 2 Using *Regula Falsi*

To find a numerical approximation to $\sqrt[3]{2}$, we seek the zero of $y = f(x) = x^3 - 2$, illustrated, with the first approximation, in Fig. 2.5. Since $f(1) = -1$ and $f(2) = 6$, we

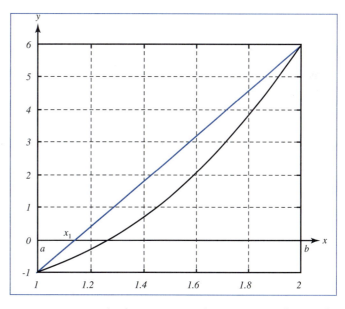

FIGURE 2.5 Graph of $y = x^3 - 2$ and approximation line on the interval [1, 2].

take as our starting bounds on the zero $a = 1$ and $b = 2$; the corresponding function values are $y(a) = -1$ and $y(b) = 6$. Our first approximation to the zero is

$$x = b - \frac{b - a}{y(b) - y(a)}(y(b)) = 2 - \frac{2 - 1}{6 + 1} \quad (6)$$

$$= 2 - 6/7 = 8/7 \approx 1.1429.$$

We then find the value of the function: $y = f(x) = (8/7)^3 - 2 \approx -0.5073$. Since $y(a)$ and y are both negative, but y and $y(b)$ have opposite signs, we know that there is a zero in the interval $[8/7, 2]$. By setting $a = 8/7$, we can repeat the process. Now $y(a) \approx -0.5073$; the right-hand end of the interval remains unchanged, so $b = 2$ and $y(b) = 6$. The computations are summarized in Table 2.3.

Table 2.3 Calculation of $\sqrt[3]{2}$ using *regula falsi*.

Step	a	b	x	y
1	1	2	1.1429	−0.50729
2	1.1429	2	1.2097	−0.22986
3	1.2097	2	1.2388	−0.098736
4	1.2388	2	1.2512	−0.041433
5	1.2512	2	1.2563	−0.017216
6	1.2563	2	1.2584	−0.0071239
7	1.2584	2	1.2593	−0.0029429
8	1.2593	2	1.2597	−0.0012148
9	1.2597	2	1.2598	−0.00050134
10	1.2598	2	1.2599	−0.00020687

The next MATLAB function finds a zero of a function in the interval $[a, b]$ using the *regula falsi* method. As with the bisection method, $f(a)$ and $f(b)$ must have opposite signs. The process stops if either:

1. The change in successive iterates is less than "tol" or
2. The maximum number of iterations, "max", has been reached.

MATLAB Function for *Regula Falsi*

```
function [x, y] = Falsi(fun, a, b, tol, max)
%    fun          string containing name of function
%    [a, b]       interval containing zero
%    tol          allowable change in successive iterates
%    max          maximum number of iterations
%    x            vector of approximations to zero
%    y            vector of function values fun(x)
```

```
a(1) = a;    b(1) = b;
ya(1) = feval(fun, a(1)); yb(1) = feval(fun, b(1));
if ya(1) * yb(1) > 0.0
    error('Function has same sign at end points')
end
for i = 1 : max
    x(i) = b(i) - yb(i) * (b(i) - a(i))/(yb(i) - ya(i));
    y(i) = feval(fun, x(i));
    if y(i) == 0.0
        disp('exact zero found'); break;
    elseif y(i) * ya(i) < 0
        a(i+1) = a(i); ya(i+1) = ya(i);
        b(i+1) = x(i); yb(i+1) = y(i);
    else
        a(i+1) = x(i); ya(i+1) = y(i);
        b(i+1) = b(i); yb(i+1) = yb(i);
    end;
    if ((i>1) & (abs(x(i)-x(i-1)) < tol))
        disp('Falsi method has converged'); break;
    end
    iter = i ;
end
if (iter >= max)
    disp('zero not found to desired tolerance');
end
n = length(x);  k = 1:n;  out = [k'  a(1:n)'  b(1:n)'  x'  y'];
disp('            step        a           b           x            y')
disp(out)
```

Example 2.4 Finding the Central Angle at Day 10 of an Elliptical Orbit, Using *Regula Falsi*

To find the central angle θ at $t = 10$ days (see Example 2-B), we must find the zero of the equation

$$y = 10\pi - 50\theta + 25 \sin \theta,$$

illustrated in Fig. 2.6.

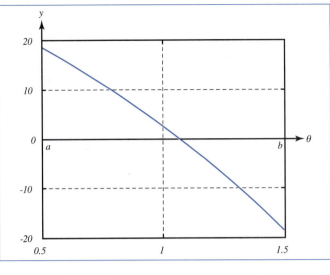

FIGURE 2.6 $y = 10\pi - 50\theta + 25\sin\theta$.

The calculations are summarized in Table 2.4. The *regula falsi* method has converged, with tol $= 0.0001$.

Table 2.4   Calculation of central angle at day 10, using *regula falsi*.

Step	a	b	θ	y(θ)
1	0.5	1.5	0.99669	2.5733
2	0.99669	1.5	1.0577	0.31063
3	1.0577	1.5	1.065	0.036638
4	1.065	1.5	1.0658	0.0043094
5	1.0658	1.5	1.0659	0.0005067
6	1.0659	1.5	1.0659	5.9575e-05

Discussion

The standard method of comparing how fast various iterative zero-finding methods converge is to investigate the behavior of $\dfrac{|x_k - x^*|}{|x_{k-1} - x^*|^p}$ for large values of k; as in the discussion of the bisection method, we denote the true zero x^*.

Rate of Convergence

If

$$\lim_{k \to \infty} \frac{|x_k - x^*|}{|x_{k-1} - x^*|^p} = \lambda \text{ for some } \lambda > 0,$$

we say that the sequence x_k converges to x^* with order $p > 0$; the number λ is called the *asymptotic error constant*. In general, higher values of p give faster convergence.

If a sequence converges with $p = 1$, we say it is linearly convergent;

If a sequence converges with $p = 2$, we say it converges quadratically.

It is not too hard to see that if a function is concave up on the interval $[a_k, b_k]$, the point $(b_k, y(b_k))$ will not change during the *regula falsi* iterations $(k+1, \dots)$; similarly, if the function is concave down, the point $(a_k, y(a_k))$ does not change. At some stage, one or the other of these conditions will be met, and from that stage onward, the convergence is linear. The *regula falsi* method can be modified to improve the convergence order to 1.4 or 1.6. (See Ralston and Rabinowitz, 1978, for further discussion.)

Although it is appealing to know that the zero is bracketed at each step of the process, some effort is required to find the appropriate subinterval at each stage. Also, an iterative process in which the form of the function being iterated can change at each stage (as is the case for a process wherein a choice must be made as to which subinterval to pursue) is more difficult to analyze.

We conclude our discussion of the *regula falsi* method by considering the challenging problem of finding the zero of a function that is quite flat near the desired zero.

Example 2.5 A Challenging Problem

Find the positive real zero of $y = x^5 - 0.5$. The function and the first three straight-line approximations are illustrated in Fig. 2.7. The calculations are summarized in Table 2.5. The *regula falsi* method converges in nine iterations with tol $= 0.0001$.

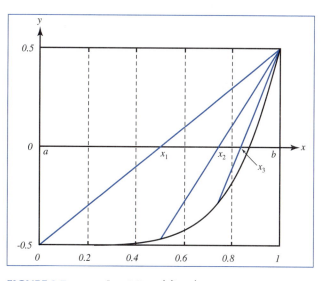

FIGURE 2.7 $y = x^5 - 0.5$ and first three approximations using *regula falsi*.

Table 2.5 Calculation of $\sqrt[5]{0.5}$ using *regula falsi*.

Step	a	b	x	y
1	0	1	0.5	−0.46875
2	0.5	1	0.74194	−0.27518
3	0.74194	1	0.83355	−0.09761
4	0.83355	1	0.86801	−0.0072543
6	0.86801	1	0.8699	−0.0018732
7	0.8699	1	0.87038	−0.00048132
8	0.87038	1	0.87051	−0.00012352
9	0.87051	1	0.87054	−3.1687e−05

2.2.2 Secant Method

The secant method, closely related to the *regula falsi* method, results from a slight modification of the latter. Instead of choosing the subinterval that must contain the zero, we form the next approximation from the two most recently generated points:

$$x_2 = x_1 - \frac{x_1 - x_0}{y_1 - y_0} y_1.$$

At the kth stage, the new approximation to the zero is

$$x_{k+1} = x_k - \frac{x_k - x_{k-1}}{y_k - y_{k-1}} y_k.$$

This process does not require any testing to determine the action to take at the next step. It also converges more rapidly than the *regula falsi* method, in general, even though the zero is not required to lie within the interval at each stage.

Example 2.6 Finding the Square Root of 3 by the Secant Method

To find a numerical approximation to $\sqrt{3}$, we seek the zero of $y = f(x) = x^2 - 3$. Since $f(1) = -2$ and $f(2) = 1$, we take as our starting bounds on the zero $x_0 = 1$ and $x_1 = 2$; the corresponding function values are $y_0 = -2$ and $y_1 = 1$. Our first approximation to the zero is

$$x_2 = x_1 - \frac{x_1 - x_0}{y_1 - y_0} y_1 = 2 - \frac{2 - 1}{1 - (-2)} (1) = 5/3 \approx 1.667.$$

The secant method does not require that the points used to compute the next approximation bracket the zero (or even that $x_0 < x_1$). It is convenient to keep track of the calculations in a tabular form; the results of four iterations through the process are shown in Table 2.6. The secant method has converged with a tolerance of 10^{-4}. Note that the first two steps in the table list the initial values for x and y and therefore do not actually represent iterations.

Table 2.6 Calculation of $\sqrt{3}$ using secant method.

Step	x	y
1	1	−2
2	2	1
3	1.6667	−0.22222
4	1.7273	−0.016529
5	1.7321	0.00031888
6	1.7321	−4.4042e-07

Example 2.7 Finding the Central Angle at Day 20 of an Elliptical Orbit

The calculations to find the central angle θ at $t = 20$ days (see Example 2-B) using the secant method are summarized in Table 2.7.

Table 2.7 Finding a zero of $y = 20\pi - 50\theta + 25 \sin \theta$ using the secant method.

k	θ_k	y_k
1	1	33.869
2	2	−14.436
3	1.7012	2.5622
4	1.7462	0.13835
5	1.7488	−0.0015105
6	1.7487	8.6907e-07

The next MATLAB function utilizes the secant method to find a zero of the given function, using the starting estimates $x_0 = a$ and $x_1 = b$. In contrast to the bisection and *regula falsi* methods, $f(a)$ and $f(b)$ need not have opposite signs, and there is no guarantee that there is a zero in the interval between two successive approximations, either initially or at any stage of the iteration. The process stops if either:

1. The change in the successive iterates is less than "tol" or
2. The maximum number of iterations, "max", has been reached.

MATLAB Function for the Secant Method

```
function [x, y] = Secant(fun, a, b, tol, max)
% Find a zero using secant method.
%       fun        string containing name of function
%       a, b       first two estimates of the zero
%       tol        tolerance for change in computed zero
```

```
%       max           maximum number of iterations
%       x             vector of approximations to zero
%       y             vector of function values fun(x)
x(1) = a;                    x(2) = b;
y(1) = feval(fun, x(1));     y(2) = feval(fun, x(2));
for i = 2 : max
        x(i+1) = x(i) - y(i) * (x(i) - x(i-1))/(y(i) - y(i-1));
        y(i+1) = feval(fun, x(i+1));
        if (abs(x(i+1)-x(i)) < tol)
                disp('method has converged'); break;
        end
        if y(i) == 0.0
                disp('exact zero found'); break;
        end
        iter = i;
end
if (iter >= max)
        disp('zero not found to desired tolerance');
end
n = length(x);      k = 1:n;      out = [k'  x'  y'];
disp('          step          x              y'), disp(out)
```

Discussion

The calculation of the update formula for the secant method is the same as that for the *regula falsi* method; only the choice of which two of the x values are used for the next iteration differs. Because the secant method does not bracket the zero at each iteration (as do the bisection and *regula falsi* methods), the secant method is not guaranteed to converge. However, when it does, the convergence is usually more rapid than for either bisection or *regula falsi*. Typically, as the iterations progress, the secants become increasingly more accurate approximations to $f(x)$.

The rate of convergence is $p = \dfrac{1 + \sqrt{5}}{2} \approx 1.62$, so convergence is faster than linear, but less than quadratic. The asymptotic error constant is

$$\lambda = \left| \frac{f''(x^*)}{2f'(x^*)} \right|^{\beta}, \text{ with } \beta = \frac{\sqrt{5} - 1}{2}.$$

Convergence Theorem for the Secant Method

If

1. $f(x), f'(x)$, and $f''(x)$ are continuous on $I = [x^* - e, x^* + e]$,
2. $f'(x^*) \neq 0$, and
3. the initial estimates x_0 and x_1 (in I) are sufficiently close to x^*,

then the secant method will converge.

The requirements for "sufficiently close" can be made more precise by defining $M = \dfrac{\max |f''|}{2 \min |f'|}$, where max and min are for all x in the interval $I = [x^* - e,$ $x^* + e]$. Then if $\max \{ M|x^* - x_0|, M|x^* - x_1| \} < 1$, the secant method will converge. It may converge for starting values that do not satisfy this inequality, but in general, the larger the value of M (if it can be computed), the closer the starting values should be to the zero. (See Atkinson, 1989, pp. 65–73, for a development of these results.)

Example 2.8 A Challenging Problem Revisited

Consider again the problem of finding the positive real zero of $y = x^5 - 0.5$. (See Fig. 2.8.) As shown in Table 2.8, the third approximation is outside the original interval that contains the root. Nevertheless, after seven iterations, the method has achieved essentially the same result as *regula falsi*.

On the other hand, if we give the starting values as $a = 1$ and $b = 0$, we again find $x_1 = 0.5$, but the calculation of x_2 is based on a straight line with almost zero slope (the line determined by the points $(0, -0.5)$ and $(0.5, -0.46875)$). There are extreme oscillations before the method converges to the correct value. Although it may

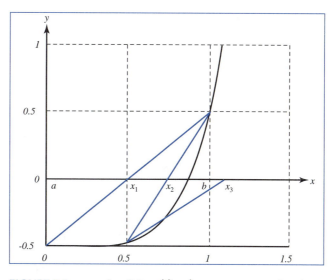

FIGURE 2.8 $y = x^5 - 0.5$ and first three secant approximations.

Table 2.8 Calculation of $\sqrt[5]{0.5}$ using the secant method.

Step	x	y
1	0.5	−0.46875
2	0.74194	−0.27518
3	1.0859	1.0098
4	0.81559	−0.13911
5	0.84832	−0.060656
6	0.87362	0.008891
7	0.87039	−0.00046064

seem contrived to give the starting estimates in this "nonnatural" order, completely analogous behavior occurs for $y = x^5 + 0.5$ when the starting estimates are $a = -1$ and $b = 0$.

2.3   NEWTON'S METHOD

Like the *regula falsi* and secant methods, Newton's method uses a straight-line approximation to the function whose zero we wish to find, but in this case the line is the tangent to the curve. The next approximation to the zero is the value of x where the tangent crosses the x-axis. This requires additional information about the function (i.e., its derivative). The secant method discussed in the previous section can be viewed as Newton's method with the derivative approximated by a difference quotient.

Given an initial estimate of the zero, x_0; the value of the function at x_0, $y_0 = f(x_0)$; and the value of the derivative at x_0, $y_0' = f'(x_0)$, the x-intercept of the tangent line, which is the new approximation to the zero, is

$$x_1 = x_0 - \frac{y_0}{y_0'}.$$

The process continues until the change in the approximations is sufficiently small or some other stopping condition is satisfied. At the kth stage, we have

$$x_{k+1} = x_k - \frac{y_k}{y_k'}.$$

Example 2.9 Finding the Square Root of 3/4 Using Newton's Method

To find a numerical approximation to $\sqrt{3/4}$, we approximate the zero of $y = f(x) = 4x^2 - 3$ (see Fig. 2.9) using the fact that $y' = f'(x) = 8x$. Since $f(0) = -3$ and $f(1) = 1$, we take as our starting estimate of the zero $x_0 = 0.5$; the corresponding function value is $y_0 = -2$, and the derivative value is $y_0' = 4$. Our first approximation to the zero is

$$x_1 = x_0 - \frac{y_0}{y_0'} = 0.5 - \frac{-2}{4} = 1.$$

Continuing for one more step yields

$$x_2 = x_1 - \frac{y_1}{y_1'} = 1.0 - \frac{1}{8} = 7/8 = 0.875.$$

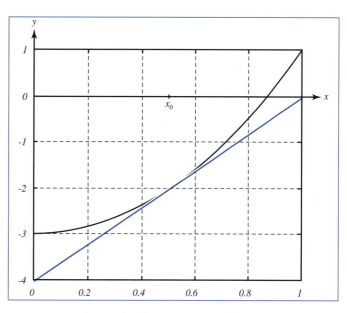

FIGURE 2.9   The graph of $y = 4x^2 - 3$ and the tangent-line approximation at $x = 0.5$.

Example 2.10 Finding the Floating Depth for a Wooden Ball

To find the depth at which a ball of radius 1 whose density is one-third that of water floats, we must find the zero (between 0 and 1) of $y = x^3 - 3x^2 + 4/3$. (See Fig. 2.10.) The calculations are summarized in Table 2.9.

Table 2.9   Floating depth of a wooden ball, using Newton's method.

Step	x	y
1	0.5	0.70833
2	0.81481	−0.11746
3	0.77427	−0.00097989
4	0.77393	−8.0255e-08
5	0.77393	−4.4409e-16

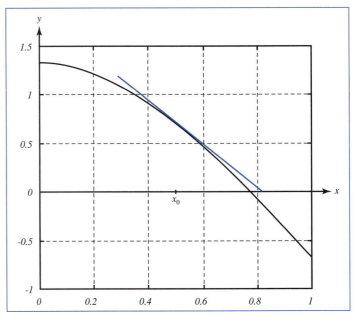

FIGURE 2.10 Floating depth of wooden ball.

The next MATLAB function finds a zero of a function near the initial estimate x_1 using Newton's method. The process stops if either:

1. the change in successive iterates is less than "tol" or
2. the maximum number of iterations, "max", has been reached.

2.3.1 MATLAB Function for Newton's Method

```
function [x, y] = Newton(fun, fun_pr, x1, tol, max)
% Find zero near x1 using Newton's method.
% Input :
%      fun          string containing name of function
%      fun_pr       name of derivative of function
%      x1           starting estimate
%      tol          allowable tolerance in computed zero
%      max          maximum number of iterations
% Output :
%      x            (row) vector of approximations to zero
%      y            (row) vector fun(x)
```

```
x(1) = x1;
y(1) = feval(fun, x(1));
y_pr(1) = feval(fun_pr, x(1));
for i = 2 : max
        x(i) = x(i-1) - y(i-1)/y_pr(i-1);
        y(i) = feval(fun, x(i));
        if abs(x(i) - x(i-1)) > tol
                disp('Newton method has converged'); break;
        end
        y_pr(i) = feval(fun_pr, x(i));
        iter = i;
end
if (iter >= max)
        disp('zero not found to desired tolerance');
end
n = length(x);    k = 1:n;  out = [k'  x'  y'];
disp('          step         x            y')
disp(out)
```

2.3.2 Discussion

We can obtain more information about the approximation to the zero x^* if we consider the Taylor series expansion for $f(x)$ near x_k, i.e.,

$$f(x) = f(x_k) + (x - x_k)f'(x_k) + 0.5(x - x_k)^2 f''(\eta),$$

where η is some (unknown) point between x and x_k. If $x = x^*$ and $f(x^*) = 0$, then

$$0 = f(x_k) + (x^* - x_k) f'(x_k) + 0.5(x^* - x_k)^2 f''(\eta),$$

and

$$x^* = x_k - \frac{f(x_k)}{f'(x_k)} - 0.5(x^* - x_k)^2 \frac{f''(\eta)}{f'(x_k)}.$$

If we now set

$$x_{k+1} = x_k - \frac{f(x_k)}{f'(x_k)}$$

and substitute this into the previous equation, we can solve for the error at the $(k + 1)$st approximation:

$$x^* - x_{k+1} = -0.5(x^* - x_k)^2 \frac{f''(\eta)}{f'(x_k)}.$$

Convergence Theorem for Newton's Method

If

1. $f(x), f'(x),$ and $f''(x)$ are continuous for all x in a neighborhood of x^*,
2. $f'(x^*) \neq 0$, and
3. x_0 is chosen sufficiently close to x^*,

then the iterates

$$x_{k+1} = x_k - \frac{f(x_k)}{f'x_k}$$

will converge to x^*.
Furthermore,

$$\lim_{k \to \infty} \frac{x_k - x^*}{(x_{k-1} - x^*)^2} = \frac{f''(x^*)}{2f'(x^*)}.$$

This result can be used to obtain some information about how close the initial estimate x_0 must be to the actual zero. Let I be an interval around x^* such that $f'(x) \neq 0$ on I, and let

$$M = \frac{\max|f''(x)|}{2\min|f'(x)|},$$

where the max and min are taken over all x in I; then convergence is guaranteed if the initial estimate is chosen close enough to the true zero so that $|x^* - x_0| < 1/M$. (See Atkinson, 1989, p. 60, for further discussion.)

Newton's method is quadratically convergent (the order of convergence is $p = 2$), with asymptotic error constant $\left|\dfrac{f''(x^*)}{2f'(x^*)}\right|$.

Newton's method has a high order of convergence and a fairly simple statement; hence, it is often the first method people use. However, the method can encounter difficulties, as illustrated in the next example.

Furthermore, the derivative must not be zero at any approximation to the zero, or Newton's method will fail. The stopping condition should be a combination of a specified maximum number of iterations and minimum tolerance on the change in the computed zero. Because of the potential for divergence, it is also wise to test for large changes in the value of the computed zero, which might signal difficulties.

Example 2.11 Oscillations in Newton's Method

Newton's method can give oscillatory results for some functions and some initial estimates. For example, consider the cubic equation

$$y = x^3 - 3x^2 + x + 3.$$

The derivative is $y' = 3x^2 - 6x + 1$. If we don't consider the graph, we might guess $x_0 = 1$ as the initial point. The calculations for the first three iterations are summarized in Table 2.10. The tangent approximations for the first two iterations are illustrated in Fig. 2.11. It is easy to see that the process will oscillate between these two values.

Table 2.10 Oscillations resulting from the use of Newton's method.

Step	x_{i-1}	x_i	y_{i-1}	y_i
1	1	2	2	1
2	2	1	1	2
3	1	2	2	1

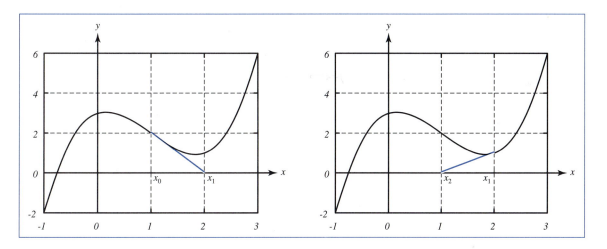

FIGURE 2.11 Oscillatory behavior of Newton's method.

2.4 MULLER'S METHOD

A logical extension of the methods based on linear approximations to the function whose zero we are seeking is to approximate the function by a quadratic function. This method is known as Muller's method. It has the advantage of being able to generate approximations to complex zeros even if the initial estimates are real. The idea is quite simple, although the formulas are more complicated than in the previous methods. Using three points on the function, we can find the equation of the quadratic that passes through those points and then find the zeros of that quadratic. It is also possible to start with two points that bracket the zero and use the midpoint of the interval between the points as the third point. Of course, once the formulas for the new approximation are derived, it is not necessary to actually find the equation of the quadratic at each step.

The parabola passing through the points (x_1, y_1), (x_2, y_2), and (x_3, y_3) can be written as $y = y_3 + c_2(x - x_3) + d_1(x - x_3)(x - x_2)$; we find the coefficients from

$$c_1 = \frac{y_2 - y_1}{x_2 - x_1}, \quad c_2 = \frac{y_3 - y_2}{x_3 - x_2} \quad \text{and} \quad d_1 = \frac{c_2 - c_1}{x_3 - x_1}.$$

This somewhat strange form is closely related to Newton's form of an interpolating polynomial, which is discussed in Chapter 8. It has the advantage of allowing some computations to carry forward from one iteration to the next. Letting $s = c_2 + d_1(x_3 - x_2)$ and solving for the zero that is closest to x_3 gives the next approximation to the desired zero:

$$x_4 = x_3 - \frac{2y_3}{s + \text{sign}(s)\sqrt{s^2 - 4y_3 d_1}}.$$

In general, Muller's method is less sensitive to starting values than Newton's method is.

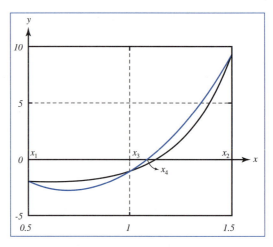

FIGURE 2.12 $y = x^6 - 2$ (black line) and parabola (blue line) for Muller's method.

Example 2.12 Finding the Sixth Root of 2 Using Muller's Method

To approximate the real zero of $y = f(x) = x^6 - 2$ (see Fig. 2.12), take as starting estimates $x_1 = 0.5$, $x_2 = 1.5$, and $x_3 = 1.0$; the corresponding function values are $y_1 = -1.9844$, $y_2 = 9.3906$, and $y_3 = -1$. Then, to find the next approximation to the zero, compute

$$c_1 = \frac{y_2 - y_1}{x_2 - x_1} = 11.375, \quad c_2 = \frac{y_3 - y_2}{x_3 - x_2} = 20.781,$$

$$d_1 = \frac{c_2 - c_1}{x_3 - x_1} = 18.812,$$

$$s = c_2 + d_1(x_3 - x_2) = 20.781 + 18.812(-0.5) = 11.375,$$

$$x_4 = x_3 - \frac{2y_3}{s + \text{sign}(s)\sqrt{s^2 - 4y_3 d_1}}$$

$$= 1 - \frac{2(-1)}{11.375 + \sqrt{11.375^2 - 4(-1)18.812}} = 1.0779.$$

The results are summarized in Table 2.11. The first two values of x are user-supplied starting estimates, and the third value of x is the midpoint of the interval defined by x_1 and x_2; values calculated by Muller's method start with x_4.

Table 2.11 Calculation of $\sqrt[6]{2}$ using Muller's method.

i	x	y
1	0.5	−1.9844
2	1.5	9.3906
3	1	−1
4	1.0779	−0.43172
5	1.117	−0.057635
6	1.1225	0.00076162
7	1.1225	−4.7432e-07

The change in the value of x_k is less than the stopping tolerance of 10^{-5}.

The following MATLAB function for Muller's method requires two user-supplied starting estimates for the zero. (Typically, these are chosen so that they define an interval that brackets the zero.) The midpoint of the interval is taken to be the third starting point. The function returns vectors x and y that give the approximate zero and corresponding function value at each step of the process (including the starting values).

2.4.1 MATLAB Function for Muller's Method

An array of output, including the step numbers, can be generated by including the following as part of the script to call the function `Muller`, which follows.

```
[x, y] = Muller('flat10', a, b, tol, max);
n = length(x);
disp('          i          x          y');
out = [1:n; x; y]'
```

The function whose zero is desired, named `flat10` in this segment of MATLAB code, is used in the next example.

```
function [x, y] = Muller(fun, x1, x2, tol, max)
% Find zero using Muller's method
% Input :
%    fun       string containing name of function
%    x1, x2    first two starting estimates,
%              3rd estimate is (x1 + x2)/2
%    tol       allowable change in successive iterates
%    max       maximum number of iterations
% Output :
%    x         (row) vector of approximations to zero
%    y         (row) vector fun(x)
x(1) = x1;       x(2) = x2;       x(3) = (x(2) + x(1))/2;
y(1) = feval(fun, x1);     y(2) = feval(fun, x2);
y(3) = feval(fun, x(3));
c(1) = (y(2) - y(1))/(x(2) - x(1));

for i = 3 : max
     c(i-1) = (y(i) - y(i-1))/(x(i) - x(i-1));
     d(i-2) = (c(i-1) - c(i-2))/(x(i) - x(i-2));
     s = c(i-1) + (x(i) - x(i-1))*d(i-2);
     x(i+1) = x(i) - ...
              2*y(i)/(s + sign(s)*sqrt(s^2 - 4*y(i)*d(i-2)));
     y(i+1) = feval(fun, x(i+1));
     if abs(x(i + 1) - x(i)) < tol
          disp('Muller method has converged'); break;
     end
     iter = i;
end
if iter >= max
     disp('zero not found to desired tolerance');
end
```

Example 2.13 Another Challenging Problem

Consider the problem of finding a zero of $y = x^{10} - 0.5$. As shown in Table 2.12, Muller's method performs well on this fairly challenging problem. The method converges to the zero $x_r = 0.9330$, with the specified tolerance of 0.0001, in six iterations. The function and the first parabolic approximation are shown in Fig. 2.13.

Table 2.12   Calculation of $\sqrt[10]{0.5}$ using Muller's method.

Step	x	y
1	0	−0.5
2	1	0.5
3	0.5	−0.49902
4	0.80875	−0.38029
5	0.9081	−0.11862
6	0.94325	0.057542
7	0.93269	−0.0018478
8	0.93303	−6.3021e-06
9	0.93303	−3.1235e-10

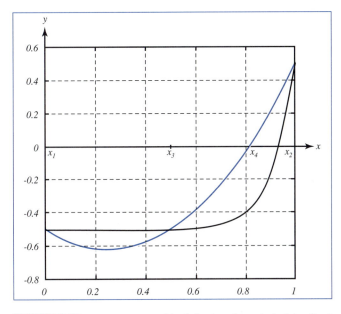

FIGURE 2.13 $y = x^{10} - 0.5$ (black line) and parabola (blue line) for Muller's method.

2.4.2 Discussion

The parabola passing through the points $(x_1, y_1), (x_2, y_2)$, and (x_3, y_3) can be written as

$$y = y_3 + c_2(x - x_3) + d_1(x - x_3)(x - x_2),$$ (2.1)

where the coefficients are found by first calculating

$$c_1 = \frac{y_2 - y_1}{x_2 - x_1}.$$

Then the coefficients are found to be

$$c_2 = \frac{y_3 - y_2}{x_3 - x_2}$$

and

$$d_1 = \frac{c_2 - c_1}{x_3 - x_1}.$$

We write the equation for the zeros of eq. (2.1) in terms of powers of $(x - x_3)$:

$$0 = y_3 + c_2(x - x_3) + d_1(x - x_3)(x - x_2),$$

$$0 = y_3 + c_2(x - x_3) + d_1(x - x_3)(x - x_3 + x_3 - x_2),$$

$$0 = y_3 + c_2(x - x_3) + d_1(x - x_3)(x - x_3) + d_1(x - x_3)(x_3 - x_2).$$

Letting $s = c_2 + d_1(x_3 - x_2)$, we wish to find the zero of

$$0 = y_3 + s(x - x_3) + d_1(x - x_3)^2$$

that is closest to x_3; so we divide by $(x - x_3)^2$, set $z = (x - x_3)^{-1}$, and find the smallest zero of

$$0 = y_3 z^2 + sz + d_1.$$

Using the quadratic formula (and choosing the zero with the largest magnitude, so that $z^{-1} = x - x_3$ will be as small as possible) gives

$$z = \frac{-s - \text{sign}(s)\sqrt{s^2 - 4y_3 d_1}}{2y_3},$$

which, after some algebra, yields

$$x = x_3 - \frac{2y_3}{s + \text{sign}(s)\sqrt{s^2 - 4y_3 d_1}}.$$

In contrast to Newton's method, Muller's method requires only function values; the derivative need not be calculated. Another advantage of Muller's method is that it may be used to find complex as well as real zeros. The method fails if $f(x_1) = f(x_2) = f(x_3)$, which can occur if x is a zero of multiplicity greater than 2.

The rate of convergence of Muller's method is slightly less than quadratic, since $p \approx 1.84$; the asymptotic error constant is $\left|\frac{f'''(x^*)}{6f'(x^*)}\right|^\beta$, where p is the positive root of $g(x) = x^3 - x^2 - x - 1$ and $\beta = \frac{p - 7}{2}$. (See Atkinson, 1989, p. 74, for a development of these results.)

2.5   FIXED-POINT ITERATION

A fixed point is a solution of the equation $x = g(x)$. A specific example of fixed-point iteration for finding the square root of a positive number was introduced in Chapter 1. A zero-finding problem, to solve $f(x) = 0$, can be converted into a fixed-point problem, to solve $x = g(x)$, in a variety of ways. However, not all such formulations will converge. A convergence theorem for fixed-point iteration is given in Chapter 1. As a practical guide, this kind of iteration is seldom used, unless $|g'(x)| \leq 1/2$ in the vicinity of the fixed point. If $-1 < g'(x) \leq 1/2$ and $x*$ is the true fixed point, then $|x_k - x*| \leq |x_k - x_{k-1}|$, so the change in successive iterates gives a bound on the error. (See Jensen and Rowland, 1975, for further discussion.)

We illustrate the use of fixed-point iteration for finding the zero of a cubic polynomial in the next example.

Example 2.14 Fixed-Point Iteration to Find a Zero of a Cubic Function

Consider the problem of solving $f(x) = 5x^3 - 10x + 3 = 0$. By writing this equation as $10x = 5x^3 + 3$, we can reformulate the problem as finding a fixed point of the equation $x = g(x) = 0.5x^3 + 0.3$. Since $g'(x) = 1.5x^2$, we restrict our interest to the interval $I = [0, 0.5]$, so that $|g'(x)| \leq 0.375$ on I. In addition, the function $g(x)$ maps I into I ($0.3 \leq g(x) \leq 0.3625$ for $0 \leq x \leq 0.5$), so there is a fixed point on I.

The iteration formula for this example is

$$x_{k+1} = 0.5(x_k)^3 + 0.3.$$

Taking $x_0 = 0.1$ as a starting estimate and rounding the result at each step to five digits, we find that

$$x_1 = 0.5(0.1)^3 + 0.3 = 0.3005,$$

$$x_2 = 0.5(0.3005)^3 + 0.3 = 0.31357,$$

$$x_3 = 0.5(0.31357)^3 + 0.3 = 0.31542.$$

If, on the other hand, we add x to both sides of the equation $f(x) = 0$ and write the fixed-point problem as $x = h(x) = 5x^3 - 9x + 3$, we find that $h'(x) = 15x^2 - 9$. Since $h'(x)$ is not small near the desired value of x, (e.g., $h'(0.3) = 15(0.09) - 9 = -7.65$), this formulation will not be convergent.

2.6   MATLAB'S METHODS

MATLAB has two built-in functions for solving problems of the type discussed in this chapter. For finding the zeros of a polynomial, the function `roots(p)` is appropriate. The polynomial is given as the (row) vector **p** of the coefficients, in descending order of the power of the variable. The roots are returned as a column vector. The function `poly(r)` constructs the polynomial with the roots given in column vector **r**. Truncation errors may lead to near-zero components; the command `real` can be used to remove any spurious imaginary components.

For example, to find the roots of $p(x) = x^3 - 7x^2 + 14x - 7$, the coefficient vector is $p = [1 \quad -7 \quad 14 \quad -7]$, and the MATLAB command

```
EDU> r = roots(p)
```

produces the result

```
r =
        3.8019
        2.445
        0.75302
```

If the polynomial is $p(x) = c_n x^n + c_{n-1} x^{n-1} + \ldots + c_1 x + c_0$, then the coefficient vector is $\mathbf{p} = [c_n \, c_{n-1} \ldots c_1 \, c_0]$. The MATLAB function `roots` is based on results from matrix theory.

To find a zero of a function of one variable, the appropriate MATLAB function is `fzero('function name', x0)`, where x_0 is the initial estimate of the root. For example, for the function `flat10` from Example 2.13, i. e.,

```
function y = flat10(x)
    y = x.^10 - 0.5;
```

and an initial estimate of $x = 0.5$, we find

```
z = fzero('flat10', 0.5)
z =        0.93303
```

As is generally the case for built-in MATLAB functions, there are several options for calling `fzero(f, x0)` to find a zero of f, which is a string containing the name of a real-valued function of a single real variable. If the starting estimate x_0 is a scalar (as in this case), `fzero` searches out from x_0 to find (if possible) an interval where f changes sign. If x_0 is a vector of length 2, `fzero` assumes that the sign of $f(x_0(1))$ differs from the sign of $f(x_0(2))$; an error occurs if this is not true. Additional input arguments may be used to specify a relative tolerance for the convergence test, information at each iteration, or additional arguments to be passed to the function f. (For further information, see the comments at the beginning of the function `fzero` (using the `help fzero` or `open fzero` commands).)

Bisection (p. 44): To find a root in $[a, b]$, where $f(a)\, f(b) < 0$:
Find $m = (a + b)/2$;
determine whether the root is in $[a, m]$ or in $[m, b]$ by testing
whether $f(a)\, f(m) < 0$;
continue the process on an appropriate subinterval.

Regula falsi and Secant Methods (p. 48): Given two estimates of the desired root, x_a and x_b, and the corresponding function values, y_a and y_b, form

$$x_c = x_b - \frac{x_b - x_a}{y_b - y_a}\, y_b$$

and proceed as follows:

Regula Falsi (p. 49): If $y_a \cdot y_c < 0$, set $x_b = x_c$ and continue. Otherwise, set $x_a = x_c$ and continue.

Secant Method (p. 54): Set $x_a = x_b, x_b = x_c$ and continue.

Newton's Method (p. 58): Given the current estimate of the root, x_k, the value of the function at x_k, i.e., $y_k = f(x_k)$, and the value of the derivative at x_k, i.e., $y'_k = f'(x_k)$, it follows that

$$x_{k+1} = x_k - \frac{y_k}{y'_k}.$$

Muller's Method (p. 63): Given three points (x_1, y_1), (x_2, y_2), and (x_3, y_3), compute

$$c_1 = \frac{y_2 - y_1}{x_2 - x_1}, \quad c_2 = \frac{y_3 - y_2}{x_3 - x_2}, \quad d_1 = \frac{c_2 - c_1}{x_3 - x_1}, \quad \text{and } s = c_2 + d_1(x_3 - x_2).$$

The next approximate root is then

$$x = x_3 - \frac{2y_3}{s + \text{sign}(s)\sqrt{s^2 - 4y_3 d_1}}.$$

SUGGESTIONS FOR FURTHER READING

For additional information on root-finding techniques, the following references are recommended:

Atkinson, K. E., *An Introduction to Numerical Analysis* (2d ed.), John Wiley & Sons, New York, 1989.

Press, W. H., B. P. Flannery, S. A. Teukolsky, and W. T. Vetterling, *Numerical Recipes: The Art of Scientific Computing*, Cambridge University Press, Cambridge, U.K., 1986.

Ralston, A., and P. Rabinowitz, *A First Course in Numerical Analysis,* McGraw-Hill, New York, 1978.

Rice, J. R., *Numerical Methods, Software, and Analysis,* McGraw-Hill, New York, 1983.

For a particularly nice discussion on special methods for treating polynomials and why they are worthwhile, see

Hamming, R. W., *Numerical Methods for Scientists and Engineers* (2d ed.), McGraw-Hill, New York, 1973.

The algorithm implemented in `fzero` was originated by T. Dekker. Descriptions, with computer code and some improvements, are given in the following sources:

Brent, R., *Algorithms for Minimization without Derivatives,* Prentice-Hall, Englewood Cliffs, NJ, 1973.

Forsythe, G. E., M. A. Malcolm, and C. B. Moler, *Computer Methods for Mathematical Computations,* Prentice-Hall, Englewood Cliffs, NJ, 1976.

Examples of applications of root-finding techniques occur throughout science and engineering. Following are a few sources:

Edwards, C. H., Jr., and D. E. Penney, *Calculus and Analytic Geometry* (5th ed.), Prentice Hall, Englewood Cliffs, NJ, 1998.

Greenberg, M. D., *Foundations of Applied Mathematics,* Prentice Hall, Englewood Cliffs, NJ, 1978.

Hibbeler, R. C., *Engineering Mechanics: Statics* (7th ed.), Prentice Hall, Englewood Cliffs, NJ, 1995.

Hibbeler, R. C., *Engineering Mechanics: Dynamics* (7th ed.), Prentice Hall, Englewood Cliffs, NJ, 1995.

For further discussion and other references to the interesting question of comparing power and exponential functions, see

Swenson, C. and A. Yandl, "An Alternative Definition of the Number *e*," *The College Mathematics Journal,* v. 24, no. 5, Nov. 1993, pp. 458–461.

PRACTICE THE TECHNIQUES

For Problems P2.1–P2.10, find the positive real zero of the functions that follow; find consecutive integers a *and* b *that bracket the root to use as starting values for the bisection,* regula falsi, *or secant method. Use* $\dfrac{a + b}{2}$ *as the starting value for Newton's method and as the third starting value for Muller's method.*

    a.   *Find the zero using bisection.*
    b.   *Find the zero using* regula falsi.
    c.   *Find the zero using the secant method.*
    d.   *Find the zero using Newton's method.*
    e.   *Find the zero using Muller's method.*

P2.1 $f(x) = x^2 - 2.$

P2.2 $f(x) = x^2 - 5.$

P2.3 $f(x) = x^2 - 7.$

P2.4 $f(x) = x^3 - 3.$

P2.5 $f(x) = x^3 - 4.$

P2.6 $f(x) = x^3 - 6.$

P2.7 $f(x) = x^4 - 0.06.$

P2.8 $f(x) = x^4 - 0.25.$

P2.9 $f(x) = x^4 - 0.45.$

P2.10 $f(x) = x^4 - 0.65.$

For Problems P2.11–P2.20, find all real zeros of the functions that follow; choose starting values as described for Problems P2.1–P2.10.

    a.   Find the zeros using bisection.
    b.   Find the zeros using regula falsi.
    c.   Find the zeros using the secant method.
    d.   Find the zeros using Newton's method.
    e.   Find the zeros using Muller's method.

P2.11 $f(x) = x^3 + 3x^2 - 1$.

P2.12 $f(x) = x^3 - 4x + 1$.

P2.13 $f(x) = x^3 - 9x + 2$.

P2.14 $f(x) = x^3 - 2x^2 - 5$.

P2.15 $f(x) = x^3 - x^2 - 4x - 3$.

P2.16 $f(x) = x^3 - 6x^2 + 11x - 5$.

P2.17 $f(x) = x^3 - x^2 - 24x - 32$.

P2.18 $f(x) = x^3 - 7x^2 + 14x - 7$.

P2.19 $f(x) = 6x^3 - 23x^2 + 20x$.

P2.20 $f(x) = 3x^3 - x^2 - 18x + 6$.

P2.21 Find a zero of $f(x) = 2x^2 - 5x + 1$ by finding a fixed point of $x = g(x) = 0.4x^2 + 0.2$.

P2.22 Find a zero of $f(x) = x - x^3$ by finding a fixed point of $x = g(x) = x^3$.

P2.23 Find a zero of $f(x) = x - x^3$ by finding a fixed point of $x = g(x) = \sqrt[3]{x}$.

P2.24 Find a zero of $f(x) = 9x^3 - 10x + 1$ by finding a fixed point of $x = g(x) = 0.9x^3 + 0.1$.

P2.25 Find a fixed point of $x = g(x) = \frac{1}{2} + \frac{1}{4}\sin(3x)$.

P2.26 Find zeros of the following functions using fixed-point iteration, or explain why iteration fails.
    a. $5x^3 + 10x - 8 = 0$.   b. $x^2 + 3x - 1 = 0$.

P2.27 For each of the following equations, use Newton's method with the specified starting value to find a root; discuss the source of the difficulty if Newton's method fails.
    a. $f(x) = -5x^4 + 11x^2 - 2$ $x_0 = 1$
    b. $f(x) = x^3 - 4x + 1$ $x_0 = 0$
    c. $f(x) = 5x^4 - 11x^2 + 2$ $x_0 = 1/2; x_0 = 0$
    d. $f(x) = x^5 - 0.5$ $x_0 = 1$

P2.28 Find the zeros of the following Legendre polynomials:
    a. $P_2(x) = (3x^2 - 1)/2$.
    b. $P_3(x) = (5x^3 - 3x)/2$.
    c. $P_4(x) = (35x^4 - 30x^2 + 3)/8$.
    d. $P_5(x) = (63x^5 - 70x^3 + 15x)/8$.

P2.29 Find the first three positive zeros of $y = x\cos x + \sin x$.

P2.30 Find the intersection(s) of $y = e^x$ and $y = x^3$; i.e., find the zeros of $f(x) = e^x - x^3$.

P2.31 Find the intersection(s) of $y = e^x$ and $y = x^2$.

P2.32 Find the intersection(s) of $y = 2^x$ and $y = x^2$.

P2.33 Find the point(s) of intersection of x^c and c^x for different values of c.
    a. $c = 3$ b. $c = 2.7$
(It is interesting to note that for $c = e$, $x^c \leq c^x$ for all x.)

P2.34 Find the intersection(s) of $y = -a + e^x$ and $y = b + \log(x)$.
    a. $a = 5, b = 1$.
    b. $a = 3, b = 2$.
    c. $a = 1, b = 5$.

P2.35 Find the zeros of $y = f(x) = \log(x + 0.1) + 1.5$.

EXPLORE SOME APPLICATIONS

The following problems suggest the variety of settings in which roots of nonlinear functions of a single variable may be required.

A2.1 To determine the displacement d of a spring of stiffness 400 N/m and unstretched length 6 m when a force of 200 N is applied, as illustrated in the following figure, two expressions are found for the tension T in each half of the spring:

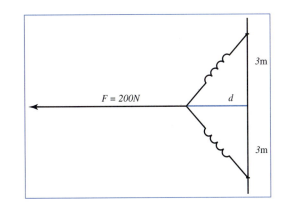

First, T is half the horizontal component of the applied force; i.e., $T = 100\sqrt{9 + d^2}/d$. Second, T is the product of the spring constant and the amount by which the spring is stretched; i.e., $T = 400(\sqrt{9 + d^2} - 3)$. Find d by finding a root of the equation

$$4(\sqrt{9 + d^2} - 3) - \sqrt{9 + d^2}/d = 0.$$

(See Hibbeler, *Statics*, 1995 for a discussion of similar problems.)

A2.2   A boat can travel with a speed of $v_b = 20$ in still water. (See accompanying figure.) Determine the bearing angle θ of the boat in a river flowing at $v_w = -5$. (The bearing angle is measured from the longitudinal axis along which the river flows.) Let v be the velocity of the boat along the desired path, which is at $60°$ from the transverse axis (across the river). Equating the longitudinal and transverse components of the velocities gives

$$v\cos(60°) = 20\sin\theta,$$

$$v\sin(60°) = -5 + 20\cos\theta.$$

Eliminating v gives the equation for θ:

$$1.732\sin\theta - \cos\theta + 0.25 = 0.$$

(See Hibbeler, *Dynamics*, 1995, p. 88.)

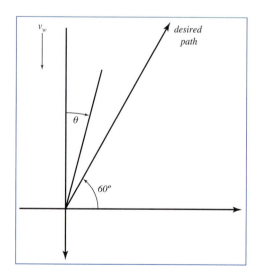

A2.3   The van der Waals equation of state, a simple extension of the ideal-gas law discovered in 1873 by the Dutch physicist Johanes Diderik van der Waals, is

$$\left(P + \frac{n^2 a}{V^2}\right)(V - nb) = nRT,$$

where the constants a and b, characteristic of the substance of the gas, are determined experimentally. For P in atmospheres, V in liters, n in moles, and T in kelvins, R is approximately 0.0820 liter atm deg^{-1} mole^{-1}. The volume of 1 mole of a perfect gas at standard conditions (1 atm, 273 K) is 22.415 liters. Find the volume occupied by 1 mole of the following gases, with given values of a and b:

Gas	a	b
O_2	1.36	0.0318
N_2O	3.78	0.0441
SO_2	6.71	0.0564

(See Pauling, *General Chemistry*, 1988, p. 337.)

A2.4   A simple model of oxygen diffusion around a capillary leads to an equation of the form

$$C(r) = \frac{Rr^2}{4K} + B_1\log(r) + B_2,$$

where R, K, B_1, and B_2 depend on the geometry, reaction rates, and other specifics of the problem. As an example, without considering realistic values of these constants, find the value of r such that

$$C(r) = 2r^2 + 3\log(r) + 1 = 2;$$

this corresponds to finding a zero of the function $y(r) = 2r^2 + 3\log(r) - 1$. (See Simon, 1986, pp. 185–189, for a discussion of the derivation of this equation.)

A2.5   The flow rate in a pipe system connecting two reservoirs (at different surface elevations) depends on the characteristics of the pump, the roughness of the pipe, the length and diameter of the pipe, and the specific gravity of the fluid. For an 800-ft section of 6″ pipe connecting two reservoirs (with a 5-ft differential in elevation) containing oil of specific gravity 0.8, with a 6-hp pump, the equation for the flow rate Q is

$$12Q^3 + 5Q - 40 = 0;$$

approximate the real root of the equation in the interval $0 \le Q \le 2$.

(For a derivation of this equation, see Ayyub and McCuen, 1996, pp. 53–59.)

A2.6   The Peng–Robinson equation of state

$$P = \frac{RT}{V - b} - \frac{a}{V(V + b) + b(V - b)}$$

is a two-parameter extension of the ideal-gas law. Find the volume of 1 mole of a gas at $P = 10^4$ kPa and $T =$

340 K; take as the parameter values $a = 364$ m⁶kPa/(kg mole)², $b = 0.03$ m³/kg mole, and $R = 1.618$. Use $V = 0.055$ m³/kg mole as an initial estimate (from the ideal-gas law). (See Hanna and Sandall, 1995, pp. 161ff, for discussion.)

A2.7 The Beattie–Bridgeman equation of state

$$P = \frac{RT}{V} + \frac{a}{V^2} + \frac{b}{V^3} + \frac{c}{V^4}$$

is a three-parameter extension of the ideal-gas law. Using $a = -1.06$, $b = 0.057$, and $c = -0.0001$, find the volume of 1 mole of a gas at $P = 25$ atm and $T = 293$ K. The constant $R = 0.082$ liter-atm/K-g mole.(See Ayyub and McCuen, 1996, p. 91.)

A 2.8 For given values of s (the length of the cable) and x (the distance between the support positions of the ends), the problem of finding the deflection of the hanging cable shown in the following diagram requires (as an intermediate step) the solution (for F) of the equation

$$s = F \sinh (x / F).$$

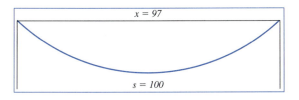

Find F for $s = 100$ and $x = 97$ (from Hibbeler, *Statics*, 1996).

A2.9 The position of a ball, thrown up with a given initial velocity v_0, and initial position x_0, subject to air resistance proportional to its velocity, is given by

$$x(t) = \rho^{-1} (v_0 + v_r)(1 - e^{-\rho t}) - v_r t + x_0,$$

where ρ is the drag coefficient, g is the gravitational constant, and $v_r = g/\rho = mg/k$ is the terminal velocity. Find when the ball hits the ground, if $x_0 = 0$, $v_0 = 20$ m/s, $\rho = 0.35$, $g = 9.8$ m/s². See a differential equations text (e.g., Edwards and Penney, Boyce and DiPrima, etc.) for further discussion.

A2.10 Some techniques for solving the differential equation describing the deflection of a uniform beam with both ends fixed, subject to a load that is proportional to the distance from one end of the beam, require the positive roots of the function $f(x) = \cosh x \cos x - 1$. In order to keep the function values within a reasonable range, it is better to consider the equivalent problem of finding the zeros of $g(x) = \cos x - 1/\cosh x$. Find the first five roots. (For more discussion of the deflection of a beam, see Edwards and Penney, *Differential Equations with Boundary Value Problems*, 1996, p. 624.)

A2.11 For a cantilever beam (one end fixed, the other free) the required parameters are the positive roots of $f(x) = \cosh x \cos x + 1$; in order to keep the function values within a reasonable range, consider zeros of $g(x) = \cos x + 1/\cosh x$. Find the first five roots.

EXTEND YOUR UNDERSTANDING

U2.1 Muller's method can also be given in the following form:
Given three initial approximations to the root: (x_0, y_0), (x_1, y_1) and (x_2, y_2), find a and b:

$$b = \frac{(x_0 - x_2)^2(y_1 - y_2) - (x_1 - x_2)^2(y_0 - y_2)}{(x_0 - x_2)(x_1 - x_2)(x_0 - x_1)}$$

$$a = \frac{(x_1 - x_2)(y_0 - y_2) - (x_0 - x_2)(y_1 - y_2)}{(x_0 - x_2)(x_1 - x_2)(x_0 - x_1)}$$

The next approximation is

$$x = x_2 + \frac{-2c}{b + \text{sign}(b)\sqrt{b^2 - 4ac}}.$$

Compare the computational effort for performing one step of this algorithm to the effort required for the algorithm given in the text.

U2.2 Use Newton's method, or the secant method, to find a root of

$$f(x) = -0.01 + \frac{1}{1 + x^2}.$$

Compare the use of a convergence test of the form $|f(x_k)| < f_{\text{tol}}$ with a test of the form

$$|x_{k+1} - x_k| < \text{tol}.$$

U2.3 Show that for the bisection method

$$\frac{|x_k - x^*|}{|x_{k-1} - x^*|} \leq \frac{1}{2}$$

is equivalent to $|x^* - x_k| \leq \dfrac{1}{2^k} |x^* - x_1|$, so that bisection is linearly convergent according to the general definition.

U2.4 Show that even without the initial estimates bracketing the zero, the secant method converges for Example 2.7; take $a = 2, b = 3$.

3

Solving Systems of Linear Equations: Direct Methods

We now extend our investigation of numerical methods for solving equations to the consideration of linear systems. In this chapter, we present the method known as Gaussian elimination.

We begin with two examples that are used to illustrate basic Gaussian elimination and two important variations. Gaussian elimination is based on the fact that if two equations have a point in common, then that point also satisfies any linear combination of the two equations. If we can find linear combinations of suitably simple form, we will be able to find the solution of the original system more easily. The form that we desire is one in which certain of the variables have been eliminated from some of the equations.

Variations of Gaussian elimination are also presented for row pivoting and tridiagonal systems. These methods are direct techniques that require a single pass through the appropriate algorithm. The specific form of the resulting (equivalent) system of equations is illustrated in the examples that follow and in MATLAB functions. We restrict our inquiry to systems in which we have the same number of equations as unknowns.

Systems of linear equations occur in a wide variety of settings, including the analysis of electrical circuits, the determination of forces on a truss, balancing the reactants in a chemical reaction, economics, traffic flow, queuing theory, and calculating the equilibrium heat distribution in a plate.

In Chapters 4 and 5, we consider iterative techniques for linear and nonlinear systems. In Chapters 6 and 7, we investigate several topics from numerical linear algebra, including two important types of matrix factorization that can be useful in solving linear systems as well as in other applications. The first of these factorizations is closely related to the Gaussian elimination techniques presented here.

Example 3-A Circuit Analysis Application

Consider the problem of finding the currents in different parts of an electrical circuit, with resistors as shown in Fig. 3.1.

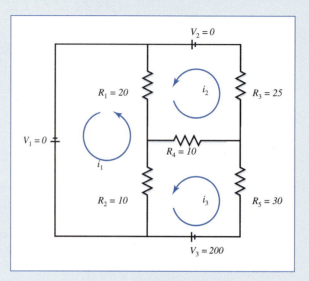

FIGURE 3.1 Simple electrical circuit.

The analysis tools come from elementary physics:

1. The sum of the voltage drops around a closed loop is zero;
2. The voltage drop across a resistor is the product of the current and the resistance.

We define each unknown current to be positive if it flows in the counterclockwise direction; if a computed current is negative, the flow is clockwise.

The analysis of the voltages around the three loops gives three equations, which we solve later in the chapter:

Flow around left loop

$$20(i_1 - i_2) + 10(i_1 - i_3) = 0.$$

Flow around upper right loop

$$25i_2 + 10(i_2 - i_3) + 20(i_2 - i_1) = 0.$$

Flow around lower right loop

$$30i_3 + 10(i_3 - i_2) + 10(i_3 - i_1) = 200.$$

Example 3-B Forces on a Truss

A lightweight structure constructed of triangular elements may be capable of supporting large weights. To analyze the forces on such a structure, known as a *truss,* a system of linear equations describing the equilibrium of the horizontal and vertical forces on each node (or joint) of the truss must be solved. A single triangular element is shown in Fig. 3.2.

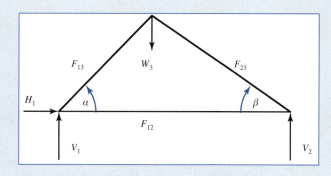

FIGURE 3.2 Element of a simple truss.

We assume that the forces in each of the members of the truss (F_{12}, F_{13}, and F_{23}) are acting to pull the structure together. V_1 and V_2 are unknown vertical forces supporting the structure (at nodes 1 and 2, respectively), H_1 is an unknown horizontal bracing force at node 1, and W_3 is a known force (at node 3) representing the weight of the structure. We define forces to be positive if they act to the right, or in an upward direction. If a computed quantity is negative, it indicates that the force acts in the opposite direction. The system of equations represents the conditions for vertical and horizontal equilibrium at the three nodes:

Node 1

$$V_1 \qquad\qquad + F_{13} \sin \alpha \qquad\qquad = 0,$$

$$H_1 \quad + F_{12} + F_{13} \cos \alpha \qquad\qquad = 0.$$

Node 2

$$V_2 \qquad\qquad\qquad + F_{23} \sin \beta = 0,$$

$$- F_{12} \qquad\qquad - F_{23} \cos \beta = 0.$$

Node 3

$$- F_{13} \sin \alpha - F_{23} \sin \beta = W_3,$$

$$- F_{13} \cos \alpha + F_{23} \cos \beta = 0.$$

3.1   GAUSSIAN ELIMINATION

The process of Gaussian elimination was introduced in Chapter 1 for a system of two equations. Example 3.1 illustates the steps for a system of three equations in three unknowns.

Example 3.1 Three-by-Three System

The three-by-three system

$$x + 2y + 3z = 1,$$
$$2x + 6y + 10z = 0,$$
$$3x + 14y + 28z = -8,$$

can be solved by Gaussian elimination as described in the following steps:

Step 1

Use the first equation to eliminate x in the second and third equations.

Multiply the first equation by -2 and add it to the second equation to get a new second equation with the x variable eliminated.

Also, multiply the first equation by -3 and add it to the third equation to get a new third equation with the x variable eliminated. The resulting system is

$$x + 2y + 3z = 1,$$
$$2y + 4z = -2,$$
$$8y + 19z = -11.$$

Step 2

Use the second equation to eliminate the y term in the third equation.

Multiply the second equation by -4 and add it to the third equation to get a new third equation with the y variable eliminated. The system now looks like this:

$$x + 2y + 3z = 1,$$
$$2y + 4z = -2,$$
$$3z = -3.$$

This completes the "forward elimination" phase; we have an upper triangular system. We now use "back substitution" to find the values of the unknowns:

$$3z = -3 \qquad \Rightarrow z = -1,$$
$$2y + 4(-1) = -2 \qquad \Rightarrow y = 1,$$
$$x + 2(1) + 3(-1) = 1 \Rightarrow x = 2.$$

3.1.1 Using Matrix Notation

We see in the preceding example that all of the computations are based on the coefficients and elements of the right-hand side of the system of equations. This system is written in matrix-vector form as $\mathbf{Ax} = \mathbf{b}$ (see Chapter 1) with

$$\mathbf{A} = \begin{bmatrix} 1 & 2 & 3 \\ 2 & 6 & 10 \\ 3 & 14 & 28 \end{bmatrix}, \qquad \mathbf{b} = \begin{bmatrix} 1 \\ 0 \\ -8 \end{bmatrix}.$$

Since the same operations are performed on the matrix $\mathbf{A}$ and the vector $\mathbf{b}$, they are often combined in the augmented matrix:

$$\begin{bmatrix} 1 & 2 & 3 & | & 1 \\ 2 & 6 & 10 & | & 0 \\ 3 & 14 & 28 & | & -8 \end{bmatrix}.$$

There are a variety of ways to transform a linear system of equations into an equivalent system having the same solution. However, the basic Gaussian elimination procedure follows a specific sequence of steps and only uses operations of the following form:

Add a multiple m of row R_i onto row R_j to form a new row R_j, or

$$R_j \leftarrow mR_i + R_j.$$

At the kth stage of the basic Gaussian elimination procedure, the appropriate multiples of the kth equation are used to eliminate the kth variable from equations $k+1, \ldots, n$; in terms of the coefficient matrix $\mathbf{A}$, the appropriate multiple of the kth row is used to reduce each of the entries in the kth column below the kth row to zero. The kth row is called the *pivot row*, the kth column is the *pivot column*, and the element a_{kk} is the *pivot element*. Since finding the appropriate multiplier for each row requires dividing by the pivot element for that stage, the process fails if the pivot element is zero. Possible remedies for this situation are discussed later in the chapter; they allow interchanging the order of the rows of the augmented matrix.

The Gaussian elimination process is illustrated in the next example using the equations for the electrical circuit in Example 3–A.

Example 3.2 Circuit Analysis

The equations describing the electrical circuit in Example 3–A simplify to

$$+30i_1 - 20i_2 - 10i_3 = 0,$$
$$-20i_1 + 55i_2 - 10i_3 = 0,$$
$$-10i_1 - 10i_2 + 50i_3 = 200.$$

In matrix form, the system is $\mathbf{A}\mathbf{x} = \mathbf{b}$, with

$$\mathbf{A} = \begin{bmatrix} 30 & -20 & -10 \\ -20 & 55 & -10 \\ -10 & -10 & 50 \end{bmatrix}, \qquad \mathbf{b} = \begin{bmatrix} 0 \\ 0 \\ 200 \end{bmatrix}.$$

Step 1

The pivot is $a_{11} = 30$.

Multiply the first row by $m_{21} = 20/30 = 2/3$ and add the result to the second row to get

$$a_{21} = 0, \qquad a_{22} = 55 + (2/3)(-20) = 125/3, \qquad a_{23} = -10 + (2/3)(-10) = -50/3.$$

Transform the right-hand side in the same way:

$$b_2 = 0 + (2/3)(0) = 0.$$

Multiply the first row by $m_{31} = 10/30 = 1/3$ and add the result to the third row to get

$$a_{31} = 0, \quad a_{32} = -10 + (1/3)(-20) = -50/3, \quad a_{33} = 50 + (1/3)(-10) = 140/3.$$

Transform the right-hand side in the same way:

$$b_3 = 200 + (1/3)(0) = 200.$$

After the first stage of Gaussian elimination,

$$\mathbf{A} = \begin{bmatrix} 30 & -20 & -10 \\ 0 & 125/3 & -50/3 \\ 0 & -50/3 & 140/3 \end{bmatrix}, \qquad \mathbf{b} = \begin{bmatrix} 0 \\ 0 \\ 200 \end{bmatrix}.$$

Step 2

The pivot is $a_{22} = 125/3$.

Multiply the second row by $m_{32} = 2/5$ and add the result to the third row to get

$$a_{31} = 0, \qquad a_{32} = 0, \qquad a_{33} = 140/3 + (2/5)(-50/3) = 40.$$

Transform the right-hand side in the same way:

$$b_3 = 200 + (2/5)(0) = 200.$$

After the second stage of Gaussian elimination,

$$\mathbf{A} = \begin{bmatrix} 30 & -20 & -10 \\ 0 & 125/3 & -50/3 \\ 0 & 0 & 40 \end{bmatrix}, \qquad \mathbf{b} = \begin{bmatrix} 0 \\ 0 \\ 200 \end{bmatrix}.$$

By back substitution (starting with the last equation and proceeding up one equation at each stage),

$$x_3 = b_3/a_{33} = 200/40 = 5,$$

$$x_2 = \frac{b_2 - a_{23}x_3}{a_{22}} = [0 + (-50/3)(5)]/[125/3] = 2,$$

$$x_1 = \frac{b_1 - a_{12}x_2 - a_{13}x_3}{a_{11}} = [0 - (-20)(2) - (-10)(5)]/30 = 3.$$

In order to implement the basic Gaussian elimination process in a computer program, it is helpful to describe the steps illustrated in Example 3.2 in somewhat more general terms. A general four-by-four system of equations can be represented in matrix form as $\mathbf{Ax} = \mathbf{b}$, where

$$\mathbf{A} = \begin{bmatrix} a_{11} & a_{12} & a_{13} & a_{14} \\ a_{21} & a_{22} & a_{23} & a_{24} \\ a_{31} & a_{32} & a_{33} & a_{34} \\ a_{41} & a_{42} & a_{43} & a_{44} \end{bmatrix} \quad \text{and} \quad \mathbf{b} = \begin{bmatrix} b_1 \\ b_2 \\ b_3 \\ b_4 \end{bmatrix}.$$

Step 1

The pivot is a_{11}.

Multiply the first row by $m_{21} = -a_{21}/a_{11}$ and add the result to the second row to get

$$a_{21} \Leftarrow 0; \qquad\qquad a_{22} \Leftarrow a_{22} + m_{21}a_{12};$$

$$a_{23} \Leftarrow a_{23} + m_{21}a_{13}; \qquad a_{24} \Leftarrow a_{24} + m_{21}a_{14}.$$

Transform the right-hand side:

$$b_2 \Leftarrow b_2 + m_{21}b_1.$$

Multiply the first row by $m_{31} = -a_{31}/a_{11}$ and add the result to the third row to get

$$a_{31} \Leftarrow 0; \qquad\qquad a_{32} \Leftarrow a_{32} + m_{31}a_{12};$$

$$a_{33} \Leftarrow a_{33} + m_{31}a_{13}; \qquad a_{34} \Leftarrow a_{34} + m_{31}a_{14}.$$

Transform the right-hand side:

$$b_3 \Leftarrow b_3 + m_{31}b_1.$$

Multiply the first row by $m_{41} = -a_{41}/a_{11}$ and add the result to the fourth row to get

$$a_{41} \Leftarrow 0; \qquad\qquad a_{42} \Leftarrow a_{42} + m_{41}a_{12};$$

$$a_{43} \Leftarrow a_{43} + m_{41}a_{13}; \qquad a_{44} \Leftarrow a_{44} + m_{41}a_{14}.$$

Transform the right-hand side:

$$b_4 \Leftarrow b_4 + m_{41}b_1.$$

Step 2

The pivot is a_{22}.

Multiply the second row by $m_{32} = -a_{32}/a_{22}$ and add the result to the third row to get

$$a_{31} = 0; \qquad a_{32} \Leftarrow 0; \qquad a_{33} \Leftarrow a_{33} + m_{32}a_{23}; \qquad a_{34} \Leftarrow a_{34} + m_{32}a_{24}.$$

Transform the right-hand side:

$$b_3 \Leftarrow b_3 + m_{32}b_2.$$

Multiply the second row by $m_{42} = -a_{42}/a_{22}$ and add the result to the fourth row to get

$$a_{41} = 0; \qquad a_{42} \Leftarrow 0; \qquad a_{43} \Leftarrow a_{43} + m_{42}a_{23}; \qquad a_{44} \Leftarrow a_{44} + m_{42}a_{24}.$$

Transform the right-hand side:

$$b_4 \Leftarrow b_4 + m_{42}b_2.$$

Step 3

The pivot is a_{33}.

Multiply the third row by $m_{43} = -a_{43}/a_{33}$ and add the result to the fourth row to get

$$a_{41} = 0; \qquad a_{42} = 0; \qquad a_{43} \Leftarrow 0; \qquad a_{44} \Leftarrow a_{44} + m_{43}a_{34}.$$

Transform the right-hand side:

$$b_4 \Leftarrow b_4 + m_{43}b_3.$$

Back Substitution

$$x_4 = b_4/a_{44},$$
$$x_3 = (b_3 - a_{34}x_4)/a_{33},$$
$$x_2 = (b_2 - a_{23}x_3 - a_{24}x_4)/a_{22},$$
$$x_1 = (b_1 - a_{12}x_2 - a_{13}x_3 - a_{14}x_4)/a_{11}.$$

We now consider a MATLAB function to solve an n-by-n system of linear equations using Gaussian elimination. The function allows us to solve k systems of the form $\mathbf{Ax} = \mathbf{b}_1, \ldots, \mathbf{Ax} = \mathbf{b}_k$, at the same time.

3.1.2 MATLAB Function for Basic Gaussian Elimination

```
function x = Gauss(A, b)
%  Solve Ax = b using Gaussian elimination without pivoting
%  Inputs :
%      A is the n-by-n coefficient matrix
%      b is the n-by-k right-hand-side matrix
%  Outputs :
%      x is the n-by-k solution matrix
[ n, k1] = size(A);    [n1, k] = size(b);    x = zeros(n, k);
for i = 1 : n-1
        m = -A(i+1:n,i)/A(i,i);
        A(i+1:n,:) = A(i+1:n,:) + m*A(i,:);
        b(i+1:n,:) = b(i+1:n,:) + m*b(i,:);
```

```
    end;
x(n,:) = b(n,:) ./ A(n,n);
for i = n-1 : -1 : 1
      x(i,:) = (b(i,:) - A(i,i+1:n)*x(i+1:n,:)) ./ A(i,i);
end
```

Example 3.3 Analysis of Forces on a Simple Truss

To illustrate the use of the preceding Gaussian elimination function, we investigate the effect of two different values of W_3 on the forces in the single-triangle truss shown in Fig. 3.2. Since varying W_3 affects only the right-hand side of the system, matrix $\mathbf{A}$ is unchanged as long as the geometry of the structure is not modified. We take $\alpha = \pi/6$ and $\beta = \pi/3$.

To find the forces for $W_3 = 100$ units and $W_3 = 75$ units, we solve the linear system $\mathbf{Ax} = \mathbf{b}_1$ and $\mathbf{Ax} = \mathbf{b}_2$ for

$$
\mathbf{b}_1 = \begin{bmatrix} 0 \\ 0 \\ 0 \\ 0 \\ 100 \\ 0 \end{bmatrix} \quad \text{and} \quad \mathbf{b}_2 = \begin{bmatrix} 0 \\ 0 \\ 0 \\ 0 \\ 75 \\ 0 \end{bmatrix}.
$$

Using the MATLAB function, we find that the force matrix is

$$
\mathbf{x} = \begin{bmatrix} 25.0000 & 18.7500 \\ -0.0000 & -0.0000 \\ 75.0000 & 56.2500 \\ 43.3013 & 32.4760 \\ -50.0000 & -37.5000 \\ -86.6025 & -64.9519 \end{bmatrix}.
$$

The first column gives the forces for a vertical force of 100 units at node 3; the second column gives the results for the second scenario: The smaller vertical force gives correspondingly smaller forces in each node.

3.1.3 Discussion

There are two key aspects to understanding why Gaussian elimination works. The first is to see why a linear combination of two equations passes through the point of intersection of the two equations. The second is to consider why (or when) the sequence of steps for Gaussian elimination produces a system that can be solved by back substitution. Analyzing these two questions suggests when Gaussian elimination works well, when it works poorly or fails, and when it can be improved.

If two equations have a point in common, then that point is also a solution of any equation formed as a linear combination of the equations. This result can be shown by simple algebra. Consider two linear equations,

S_1: $$a_0 + a_1 x_1 + a_2 x_2 + \ldots + a_n x_n = 0$$

and

T_1: $$b_0 + b_1 x_1 + b_2 x_2 + \ldots + b_n x_n = 0,$$

and assume that the point $\mathbf{r} = (r_1, r_2, \ldots, r_n)$ satisfies both equations. Then $\mathbf{r}$ also satisfies the linear combination $C = m_1 S_1 + m_2 T_1$, or

$$m_1 a_0 + m_1 a_1 x_1 + m_1 a_2 x_2 + \ldots + m_1 a_n x_n$$
$$+ m_2 b_0 + m_2 b_1 x_1 + m_2 b_2 x_2 + \ldots + m_2 b_n x_n = 0.$$

Substituting $(r_1, r_2, \ldots, r_n)$ in the equation C and using the fact that $\mathbf{r}$ satisfies S_1 and T_1 gives the desired result.

Now consider the specific sequence of transformations on the linear system given in the basic Gaussian elimination algorithm presented earlier. The description assumes that it is possible to find the necessary multiplier to reduce each column to zero as indicated. Two situations can arise if a zero pivot element is encountered, depending on whether or not there are any nonzero elements in the pivot column below the pivot row.

If a zero pivot occurs (in an n-by-n linear system), and the entire pivot column below the pivot row is also zero, then the system of equations does not have a unique solution. The equations are either inconsistent or redundant.

On the other hand, if a zero element is encountered in a pivot position, but there is a nonzero element in the pivot column below the pivot element, the Gaussian elimination process can be modified to allow for interchanging the row whose pivot element is zero with a row below it. This process is called *(partial) pivoting* and is the subject of the next section.

Several considerations are operative in determining how well a particular numerical method works. Among the most important are questions dealing with the quality of the solution, the sensitivity of the method to errors (including inexact arithmetic), and the computational effort required.

Computational effort is usually measured in terms of the number of multiplications and divisions ($m + d$) or in terms of the number of floating-point operations (flops). On early computers, multiplication and division were much more time intensive than addition and subtraction, which led researchers to analyze algorithms in terms of multiplication and division. It is also typical for the number of additions and subtractions to be directly related to the number of multiplications and divisions. Today, because the difference in effort for different operations has been reduced, analysis in terms of flops has become more common. Since the linear systems that arise in practice are often very large, it is important to see how the computational effort required for Gaussian elimination is related to the size of the coefficient matrix $\mathbf{A}$ (assumed to be n-by-n).

At the first stage of Gaussian elimination, one division is required to find the multiplier for the second row ($m_{12} = -a_{12}/a_{11}$). Then, n multiplications (and n additions) are required to form the new second row. Note that we must also multiply the right-hand side, but we do not have to multiply the first element in the row, since we know that the new first element in the second row will be zero. This process must be performed for each of the rows below the first row. Thus, the first stage requires $(n+1)(n-1)$ multiplications and divisions, as well as $n(n-1)$ additions.

At the kth stage of elimination, there is one division to form the multiplier m_{ki} and $(n-k)$ multiplications to generate the new ith row (for $i = k+1, \ldots, n$). There are also $n-k$ additions required for each new row.

The total number of multiplications and divisions is

$$\sum_{k=1}^{n-1} (n - k + 1)(n - k) = \sum_{k=1}^{n-1} n^2 - 2nk + k^2 + n - k$$

$$= \sum_{k=1}^{n-1} (n^2 + n) - \sum_{k=1}^{n-1} (2n + 1)k + \sum_{k=1}^{n-1} k^2$$

which simplifies to

$$= \frac{n^3}{3} - \frac{n}{3}.$$

If there is a unique solution, if computations are exact, and if the pivot element is not zero at any stage, Gaussian elimination gives the solution. However, since computer computations are not exact, we may be faced with errors in the calculations that result from round-off. We illustrate here two types of difficulties that can occur. The first can be avoided by a suitable reordering of the rows of the augmented matrix, which is the subject of the next section. The second example is indicative of a more serious problem.

Gaussian elimination works well for systems with coefficient matrices with special properties. For example, if $\mathbf{A}$ is *strictly diagonally dominant* (i.e., for each i, $|a_{ii}| > \sum_{j \neq i} |a_{ij}|$), Gaussian elimination will work well [Golub and Van Loan, 1996, p. 120].

Some Difficulties Are Solvable with Pivoting

Consider the following system of two equations in two unknowns, and suppose that we have arithmetic with rounding to two digits at each stage of the Gaussian elimination process:

$$0.001x_1 + x_2 = 3,$$
$$x_1 + 2x_2 = 5.$$

Proceeding according to the basic Gaussian elimination procedure, we multiply the first equation by -1000 and add it to the second equation to give (if arithmetic were exact)

$$-998x_2 = -2995.$$

After rounding, this equation becomes $-1000x_2 = -3000$, which gives $x_2 = 3$. Substitution of this value into the first equation then yields $x_1 = 0$. Clearly, this is not a good approximation to a solution of the second equation. In the next section, we discuss an enhancement to Gaussian elimination to avoid such a dilemma.

An Ill-Conditioned Matrix Causes More Serious Difficulties

Consider the linear system

$$x_1 + \frac{1}{2} x_2 = \frac{3}{2},$$

$$\frac{1}{2} x_1 + \frac{1}{3} x_2 = \frac{5}{6}.$$

Using exact arithmetic gives the exact solution $x_1 = x_2 = 1$. However, if the right-hand side is modified slightly, to

$$x_1 + \frac{1}{2} x_2 = \frac{3}{2},$$

$$\frac{1}{2} x_1 + \frac{1}{3} x_2 = 1,$$

the exact solution becomes $x_1 = 0$ and $x_2 = 3$.

This extreme sensitivity to small changes in the right-hand side is evidence of the fact that the coefficient matrix is "ill conditioned." The difficulties arising from ill conditioning cannot be solved by simple refinements in the Gaussian elimination procedure. If the *condition number* of a matrix is defined as the ratio of the largest eigenvalue to the smallest eigenvalue, a matrix with a large condition number is ill conditioned. Eigenvalues are discussed in Chapter 7. The condition number of a matrix can also be found by using the built-in MATLAB function cond. The coefficient matrix in this example is a two-by-two Hilbert matrix, and the MATLAB code is as follows:

```
EDU>   H = [ 1        1/2
             1/2      1/3]
EDU>   cond(H)
ans =      19.281
```

3.2 GAUSSIAN ELIMINATION WITH ROW PIVOTING

Basic Gaussian elimination, as presented in the previous section, fails if the pivot element at any stage of the elimination process is zero, because division by zero is not possible. In addition, difficulties that are not as easy to detect arise if the pivot element is significantly smaller than the coefficients it is being used to eliminate. In this section, we investigate an enhancement to Gaussian elimination that prevents or alleviates some of these shortcomings of the basic procedure.

In order to reduce the inaccuracies that occur in solutions computed with Gaussian elimination and avoid (if possible) the failure of the method resulting from a zero coefficient in the pivot position at some stage of the process, we may need to interchange selected rows of the augmented matrix. We illustrate this process, known as row pivoting, in Example 3.4.

Example 3.4 Difficult System

Consider again the following simple system of two equations in two unknowns, to be solved by Gaussian elimination with rounding to two significant digits at each stage of the process:

$$0.001x_1 + x_2 = 3,$$
$$x_1 + 2x_2 = 5.$$

With basic Gaussian elimination (with rounding), we found that $x_2 = 3$ and $x_1 = 0$. This is not a good approximation to a solution of the second equation.

If, instead of solving the system with the equations in the order given, we recognize that the very small coefficient of x_1 in the first equation is dangerous (because we would be dividing by something that is close to zero), we can interchange the order of the equations as follows

$$x_1 + 2x_2 = 5,$$
$$0.001x_1 + x_2 = 3.$$

Now we multiply the first equation by -0.001 and add it to the second equation to give (if arithmetic were exact)

$$0.998x_2 = 2.995.$$

After rounding, this equation becomes $x_2 = 3$. Substitution of this value into the first equation yields $x_1 = -1$, a much better approximation to a solution of the system.

The small pivot element shown in the previous example could occur at any stage of elimination. Gaussian elimination with row pivoting checks all entries in the pivot column (from the current diagonal element to the bottom of the column) and chooses the largest element as the pivot. The current row and the selected pivot row are interchanged. The following example illustrates a more limited use of pivoting, with row interchanges performed only if a zero pivot is encountered.

Example 3.5 A Three-By-Three System in which Pivoting Is Required

Consider the system of equations

$$2x + 6y + 10z = 0,$$
$$x + 3y + 3z = 2,$$
$$3x + 14y + 28z = -8.$$

The augmented matrix is

$$\left[\begin{array}{ccc|c} 2 & 6 & 10 & 0 \\ 1 & 3 & 3 & 2 \\ 3 & 14 & 28 & -8 \end{array}\right].$$

The first stage of elimination gives

$$\left[\begin{array}{ccc|c} 2 & 6 & 10 & 0 \\ 0 & 0 & -2 & 2 \\ 0 & 5 & 13 & -8 \end{array}\right].$$

We are unable to continue, unless we interchange the second and third rows:

$$\left[\begin{array}{ccc|c} 2 & 6 & 10 & 0 \\ 0 & 5 & 13 & -8 \\ 0 & 0 & -2 & 2 \end{array}\right].$$

In this simple example, after the row pivoting, no further elimination is required. By back substitution,

$$x_3 = -1;$$

$$x_2 = \frac{1}{5}[-13(-1) - 8] = 1;$$

$$x_1 = \frac{1}{2}[-6(1) - 10(-1) + 0] = 2.$$

3.2.1 MATLAB Function for Gaussian Elimination with Row Pivoting

```
function x = Gauss_pivot(A, b)
%  function x = Gauss_pivot(A, b)
%  Solution of the system of linear equations Ax = b
%  using Gaussian elimination with row pivoting
%  Inputs :
%      A is the n-by-n coefficient matrix
%      b is the n-by-1 right-hand-side vector
%  Outputs :
%      x is the n-by-1 solution vector
[ n, n1] = size(A);
for i = 1:n-1
    [ pivot, k] = max(abs(A(i:n,i)));
            % k is position of pivot, relative to row i
            % do not check rows above current row
```

```
if k > 1
    temp1 = A(i,:);        temp2 = b(i,:);
    A(i,:) = A(i+k-1,:);  b(i,:) = b(i+k-1,:);
    A(i+k-1,:) = temp1;   b(i+k-1,:) = temp2;
end
for h = i+1 : n
    m = A(h,i)/A(i,i);
    A(h,:) = A( h,:) - m* A(i,:);
    b(h,:) = b( h,:) - m* b(i,:);
end;
end;
%    back substitution
x(n,:) = b(n,:)./ A(n,n);
for i = n-1 :-1 : 1
    x(i,:) = (b(i,:)-A(i,i+1:n)*x(i+1:n,:))./A(i,i);
end
```

Note that although the preceding function actually performs the row interchanges, more sophisticated programs keep track of the indices of the pivots selected at each stage without carrying out the row interchanges.

Example 3.6 Forces in a Simple Truss

Consider the triangular truss shown in Fig. 3.3.

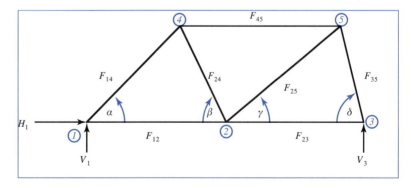

FIGURE 3.3   Triangular truss.

Assuming that the weight of the structure (100 kg) is localized at node 2 (bottom center of the figure), the following linear system describes the truss:

$$
\begin{array}{llll}
V_1 & + F_{14} \sin \alpha & & = 0, \\
H_1 & + F_{12} + F_{14} \cos \alpha & & = 0, \\
& + F_{24} \sin \beta + F_{25} \sin \gamma & & = 100, \\
-F_{12} & + F_{23} - F_{24} \cos \beta + F_{25} \cos \gamma & & = 0, \\
V_3 & & + F_{35} \sin \delta & = 0, \\
-F_{23} & & - F_{35} \cos \delta & = 0, \\
-F_{14} \sin \alpha & - F_{24} \sin \beta & & = 0, \\
-F_{14} \cos \alpha & + F_{24} \cos \beta & + F_{45} = & 0, \\
& - F_{25} \sin \gamma - F_{35} \sin \delta & & = 0, \\
& - F_{25} \cos \gamma + F_{35} \cos \delta - F_{45} = & & 0.
\end{array}
$$

The equations, in the order written, cannot be solved without pivoting. Taking $\alpha = \beta = \gamma = \delta = \pi/4$, we find that $V_1 = 50, H_1 = 0, V_3 = 50, F_{12} = 50, F_{14} = -70.7, F_{23} = 50, F_{24} = 70.7, F_{25} = 70.7, F_{35} = -70.7$, and $F_{45} = -100$.

3.2.2 Discussion

For situations in which row pivoting is desirable because some pivot elements are significantly smaller than others, some form of row scaling should also be used, since, of course, the difficulties illustrated in Example 3.4 could be masked by multiplying the first equation by 1000 to give

$$
\begin{array}{rl}
x_1 + 1000x_2 = & 3000, \\
x_1 + 2x_2 = & 5.
\end{array}
$$

Now no row interchange occurs, because the elements in the first column are equal. However, the computational difficulties described in Example 3.4 are still present. Those difficulties were more apparent with the first equation in its original form.

Scaling strategies vary and are difficult to include in general-purpose computer codes. One possible approach is to scale each row by the appropriate power of 10 (including, of course, the corresponding right-hand side if it has been retained in a separate vector) so that the magnitude of the largest element in each row of the coefficient matrix is between 0.1 and 1. Dividing by a power of 2 is actually better, since it avoids any round-off error. An even easier method to incorporate into the foregoing functions for Gaussian elimination is to divide each row of **A** by the largest element in the row, making the corresponding scaling on **b** also. However, this may introduce additional round-off error. The MATLAB function max can be used to find the largest element in a vector. (It was used to find the pivot element in the function gauss_pivot.) Scaling is sometime suggested on the columns of the coefficient matrix also; this corresponds to changing the units in which the corresponding unknown is measured. Scaling does not generally mitigate problems caused by ill conditioning.

The computational effort for Gaussian elimination is proportional to n^3, so, for large systems of equations, more efficient methods may be desirable. Improved methods have been developed in recent years that reduce the exponent to values less than 2.5. (See Hager, 1988, or Strang, 1988.) When the system has the appropriate structure, iterative techniques, which we examine in Chapter 4, may be appropriate. In the next section, we consider Gaussian elimination for the special case of a tridiagonal matrix.

3.3 GAUSSIAN ELIMINATION FOR TRIDIAGONAL SYSTEMS

In many applications, the linear system to be solved has a banded structure. For a tridiagonal system, the only nonzero entries in the coefficient matrix are the diagonal, the subdiagonal, and the superdiagonal. To take advantage of this special structure, we apply a modified form of Gaussian elimination in which, following each elimination step, the pivot row is scaled so that the diagonal element is 1. We begin by illustrating the process for a four-by-four system.

Example 3.7 Solving a Tridiagonal System by Gaussian Elimination with Row Scaling

Consider the following system of equations:

$$
\begin{aligned}
2x_1 \quad -x_2 \qquad\qquad\quad &= 1, \\
-x_1 + 2x_2 \quad -x_3 \qquad\quad &= 0, \\
-x_2 + 2x_3 \quad -x_4 &= 0, \\
-x_3 + 2x_4 &= 1.
\end{aligned}
$$

First, scale the first equation by dividing through by a_{11}, so that the new first equation has 1 on the diagonal:

$$
\begin{aligned}
x_1 \quad -\frac{1}{2}x_2 \qquad\qquad\quad &= \frac{1}{2}, \\
-x_1 + \quad 2x_2 \quad -x_3 \qquad\quad &= 0, \\
-x_2 + 2x_3 \quad -x_4 &= 0, \\
-x_3 + 2x_4 &= 1.
\end{aligned}
$$

This modifies two other elements also: the element on the upper diagonal and the one on the right-hand side.

Second, use the first equation to eliminate the x_1 term in the second equation (because of the tridiagonal structure, that is the only equation below the first in which x_1 appears):

$$
\begin{aligned}
x_1 - \frac{1}{2}x_2 \qquad\qquad\quad &= \frac{1}{2}, \\
+ \frac{3}{2}x_2 \quad -x_3 \qquad\quad &= \frac{1}{2}, \\
-x_2 + 2x_3 \quad -x_4 &= 0, \\
-x_3 + 2x_4 &= 1.
\end{aligned}
$$

Complete this step by scaling the second equation:

$$x_1 - \frac{1}{2}x_2 \qquad\qquad = \frac{1}{2},$$

$$+\, x_2 - \frac{2}{3}x_3 \qquad\quad = \frac{1}{3},$$

$$-\,x_2 + 2x_3 + -x_4 = 0,$$

$$-\,x_3 + 2x_4 = 1.$$

Next, use the second equation to eliminate the x_2 term in the third equation:

$$x_1 - \frac{1}{2}x_2 \qquad\qquad = \frac{1}{2},$$

$$+\, x_2 - \frac{2}{3}x_3 \qquad\quad = \frac{1}{3},$$

$$\frac{4}{3}x_3 \quad -x_4 = \frac{1}{3},$$

$$-\,x_3 + 2x_4 = 1.$$

Now scale the third equation:

$$x_1 - \frac{1}{2}x_2 \qquad\qquad = \frac{1}{2},$$

$$+\, x_2 - \frac{2}{3}x_3 \qquad\quad = \frac{1}{3},$$

$$+\, x_3 - \frac{3}{4}x_4 = \frac{1}{4},$$

$$-\,x_3 + 2x_4 = 1.$$

Finally, use the third equation to eliminate x_3 in the last equation:

$$x_1 - \frac{1}{2}x_2 \qquad\qquad = \frac{1}{2},$$

$$+\, x_2 - \frac{2}{3}x_3 \qquad\quad = \frac{1}{3},$$

$$+\, x_3 - \frac{3}{4}x_4 = \frac{1}{4},$$

$$+\, \frac{5}{4}x_4 = \frac{5}{4}.$$

And scale the last equation:

$$x_1 - \frac{1}{2}x_2 \qquad\qquad = \frac{1}{2},$$

$$+ x_2 - \frac{2}{3}x_3 \qquad\quad = \frac{1}{3},$$

$$+ x_3 - \frac{3}{4}x_4 = \frac{1}{4},$$

$$+ x_4 = 1.$$

Now solve by back substitution to obtain

$$x_4 = 1; \qquad\qquad\qquad x_3 = 1/4 - (-3/4)(1) = 1;$$

$$x_2 = 1/3 - (-2/3)(1) = 1; \qquad x_1 = 1/2 - (-1/2)(1) = 1.$$

Because of the special form of the matrix $\mathbf{A}$, we can reduce the storage requirements from n^2 to $3n$ by storing only the vector $\mathbf{d}$ containing the **d**iagonal elements, the vector $\mathbf{a}$ containing the elements **a**bove the diagonal, and the vector $\mathbf{b}$ containing the elements **b**elow the diagonal. Note that elements b_1 and a_n are zero. The right-hand side is stored as the vector $\mathbf{r}$. In this notation, the general tridiagonal system of equations can be written as

$$d_1x_1 + a_1x_2 \qquad\qquad\qquad\qquad = r_1,$$

$$b_2x_1 + d_2x_2 + a_2x_3 \qquad\qquad\qquad = r_2,$$

$$\cdots\cdots$$

$$+ b_{n-1}x_{n-2} + d_{n-1}x_{n-1} + a_{n-1}x_n = r_{n-1},$$

$$+ \quad b_nx_{n-1} + \quad d_nx_n = r_n.$$

An efficient algorithm for the solution of a tridiagonal system is based on Gaussian elimination with the coefficients of the diagonal elements scaled to 1 at each stage. This algorithm takes advantage of the zero elements that are already present in the coefficient matrix and avoids unnecessary arithmetic operations. Thus, we need to store only the new vectors $\mathbf{a}$ and $\mathbf{r}$. This procedure is known in the engineering literature as the *Thomas method*.

Step 1

For the first equation, form the new elements a_1 and r_1:

$$a_1 = \frac{a_1}{d_1}, \qquad r_1 = \frac{r_1}{d_1}.$$

Step 2

For each of the equations, from $i = 2, \ldots, n - 1$,

$$a_i = \frac{a_i}{d_i - b_ia_{i-1}}, \qquad r_i = \frac{r_i - b_ir_{i-1}}{d_i - b_ia_{i-1}}.$$

Step 3

For the last equation:

$$r_n = \frac{r_n - b_n r_{n-1}}{d_n - b_n a_{n-1}}.$$

Step 4

Solve by back substitution:

$$x_n = r_n,$$

$$x_i = r_i - a_i x_{i+1}, \quad i = n-1, n-2, n-3, \ldots, 2, 1.$$

Example 3.8 Solving a Tridiagonal System Using the Thomas Method

We use the tridiagonal system from Example 3.7 to illustrate the steps of the Thomas method:

$$\begin{array}{rcl}
2x_1 - x_2 & = 1, \\
-x_1 + 2x_2 - x_3 & = 0, \\
-x_2 + 2x_3 - x_4 & = 0, \\
-x_3 + 2x_4 & = 1.
\end{array}$$

$$d = (2, 2, 2, 2); a = (-1, -1, -1, 0); b = (0, -1, -1, -1); r = (1, 0, 0, 1).$$

First, form the new elements a_1 and r_1:

$$a_1 = \frac{a_1}{d_1} = -\frac{1}{2}, \qquad r_1 = \frac{r_1}{d_1} = \frac{1}{2}.$$

For the second equation,

$$a_2 = \frac{a_2}{d_2 - b_2 a_1} = \frac{-1}{2 - (-1)(-1/2)} = -\frac{2}{3},$$

$$r_2 = \frac{r_2 - b_2 r_1}{d_2 - b_2 a_1} = \frac{0 - (-1)(1/2)}{2 - (-1)(-1/2)} = \frac{1}{3}.$$

For the third equation,

$$a_3 = \frac{a_3}{d_3 - b_3 a_2} = \frac{-1}{2 - (-1)(-2/3)} = -\frac{3}{4},$$

$$r_3 = \frac{r_3 - b_3 r_2}{d_3 - b_3 a_2} = \frac{0 - (-1)(1/3)}{2 - (-1)(-2/3)} = \frac{1}{4}.$$

For the last equation,

$$r_4 = \frac{r_4 - b_4 r_3}{d_4 - b_4 a_3} = \frac{1 - (-1)(1/4)}{2 - (-1)(-3/4)} = 1.$$

Finally, solve by back substitution to obtain

$$x_4 = r_4 = 1,$$

$$x_3 = r_3 - a_3 x_4 = 1/4 - (-3/4)(1) = 1,$$

$$x_2 = r_2 - a_2 x_3 = 1/3 - (-2/3)(1) = 1,$$

$$x_1 = r_1 - a_1 x_2 = 1/2 - (-1/2)(1) = 1.$$

3.3.1 MATLAB Function for Solving a Tridiagonal System

```
function x = Thomas(a, d, b, r)
%   solve A x = b, where A is a tridiagonal matrix
%   Input
%      a     upper diagonal of matrix A, a(n) = 0.
%      d     diagonal of matrix A
%      b     lower diagonal of matrix A, b(1) = 0
%      r     right-hand side of equation
n = length(d)
a(1) = a(1)/d(1)
r(1) = r(1)/d(1)
for i = 2 : n-1
    denom = d(i) - b(i)*a(i-1);
    if (denom ==0), error('zero in denominator'), end
    a(i) = a(i)/denom;
    r(i) = (r(i) - b(i)*r(i-1))/denom;
end
r(n) = (r(n) - b(n)*r(n-1))/(d(n) - b(n)*a(n-1));
x(n) = r(n);
for i = n-1: -1 : 1
    x(i) = r(i) - a(i)*x(i+1);
end
```

3.3.2 Discussion

In addition to the greatly reduced storage requirements achieved by taking advantage of the special structure of a tridiagonal matrix, the computational effort is much less for the Thomas method than for the general form of Gaussian elimination. The required multiplications and divisions for the Thomas method are as follows:

For the first equation, 2 divisions are needed.

For each of the next $n - 2$ equations, 2 multiplications and 2 divisions are needed.

For the last equation, 2 multiplications and 1 division are required.

The total for elimination is $5 + 4(n - 2)$.

For the back substitution, $n - 1$ multiplications are needed.

The Thomas algorithm requires that $d_1 \neq 0$ and that $d_i - b_i a_{i-1} \neq 0$ for each i. For many applications, the structure of the tridiagonal matrix guarantees that these quantities will not be zero. In other cases, if we do encounter a zero value (but the system is, in fact, nonsingular) we can solve for the appropriate variable directly, reduce the size of the system, and solve the new reduced system, as illustrated in the next example.

In general, the Thomas method works well when the system is diagonally dominant.

Example 3.9 Using the Thomas Method for a System That Would Require Pivoting for Gaussian Elimination

To illustrate the possibility of continuing the solution process with the Thomas method when a division by zero is encountered, consider the following system:

$$
\begin{aligned}
2x_1 \;-x_2 && = \;1, \\
-x_1 + 2x_2 \;-x_3 && = \;0, \\
-x_2 + \frac{2}{3}x_3 \;-x_4 && = -\frac{4}{3}, \\
-x_3 + 2x_4 \;-x_5 && = \;0, \\
-x_4 + 2x_5 \;-x_6 &= \;0, \\
-x_5 + 2x_6 &= \;1.
\end{aligned}
$$

The solution begins in the normal manner by scaling the first equation and using the result to eliminate the x_1 term in the second equation. Continuing by scaling the second equation and using the result to eliminate the x_2 term in the third equation, we obtain

$$
\begin{aligned}
x_1 - \frac{1}{2}x_2 && = \frac{1}{2}, \\
+ x_2 - \frac{2}{3}x_3 && = \frac{1}{3}, \\
-x_4 && = -1, \\
-x_3 + 2x_4 \;-x_5 && = \;0, \\
-x_4 + 2x_5 \;-x_6 &= \;0, \\
-x_5 + 2x_6 &= \;1.
\end{aligned}
$$

However, we are unable to scale the third equation so as to have 1 on the diagonal, since the coefficient of x_3 is now 0. But because the third row does have a nonzero coefficient (for variable x_4), we can solve for that variable and proceed. Thus, the third equation is solved for x_4, giving $x_4 = 1$. The fourth equation is skipped for now, and the computed value of x_4 is substituted into the fifth equation. The elimination proceeds, using the fifth equation to eliminate x_5 from the final equation:

$$x_1 - \frac{1}{2}x_2 \qquad\qquad\qquad\qquad = \frac{1}{2},$$

$$+\, x_2 - \frac{2}{3}x_3 \qquad\qquad\qquad = \frac{1}{3},$$

$$-x_4 \qquad\qquad\quad = -1 \ \text{(solve)},$$

$$-x_3 + 2x_4 \quad -x_5 \qquad = \ \ 0 \ \text{(skip for now)},$$

$$+\, 2x_5 \quad -x_6 = \ \ 1 \ \text{(using } x_4 = 1\text{)},$$

$$-x_5 + 2x_6 = \ \ 1.$$

Finally, we scale the fifth equation, use it to eliminate x_5 in the last equation, and scale the last equation:

$$x_1 - \frac{1}{2}x_2 \qquad\qquad\qquad\qquad = \frac{1}{2},$$

$$+\, x_2 - \frac{2}{3}x_3 \qquad\qquad\qquad = \frac{1}{3},$$

$$-x_4 \qquad\qquad\quad = -1,$$

$$-x_3 + 2x_4 \quad -x_5 \qquad = \ \ 0,$$

$$x_5 - \frac{1}{2}x_6 = \frac{1}{2},$$

$$x_6 = \ \ 1.$$

Solving by back substitution yields

$$x_6 \qquad\qquad\qquad = 1,$$

$$x_5 = \frac{1}{2} + \frac{1}{2}x_6 = 1,$$

$$x_4 \qquad\qquad\qquad = 1 \ \text{(computed previously)},$$

$$x_3 = 2x_4 - x_5 \quad = 1 \ \text{(skipped previously)},$$

$$x_2 = \frac{1}{3} + \frac{2}{3}x_3 = 1,$$

$$x_1 = \frac{1}{2} + \frac{1}{2}x_2 = 1.$$

3.4   MATLAB's METHODS

We conclude the chapter with a brief discussion of solving linear systems by means of MATLAB's built-in capabilities. The methods implemented in high-quality professionally developed software, such as MATLAB, are efficient and easy to use. They often combine the best features from several of the basic techniques presented in this chapter. In other cases, the methods use more sophisticated procedures that are beyond the scope of the text.

There are two division symbols in MATLAB, the forward slash (/) and the backslash (\ ). It is useful to think of each as indicating multiplication by the inverse of the quantity under the slash. In this way of interpreting the symbols, $a/b = a(b^{-1})$ and $c\backslash d = c^{-1}(d)$. Since scalar multiplication is commutative, we can write the fraction $\frac{1}{2}$ as either $1/2$ or $2\backslash 1$. However, matrix multiplication is not commutative, and "backslash" division gives us a convenient way of solving the linear system $\mathbf{Ax} = \mathbf{b}$. The solution of $\mathbf{Ax} = \mathbf{b}$ is $\mathbf{x} = \mathbf{A}\backslash\mathbf{b}$, which is suggestive of $\mathbf{x} = \mathbf{A}^{-1}\,\mathbf{b}$, where it is important that the implied multiplication by the inverse of $\mathbf{A}$ is from the left. The backslash division operator is also called the matrix left-division operator.

If $\mathbf{A}$ is an n-by-n matrix and $\mathbf{b}$ is a column vector with n components (or a matrix with several such columns), then $\mathbf{x} = \mathbf{A}\backslash\mathbf{b}$ is the solution of the equation $\mathbf{Ax} = \mathbf{b}$, computed by Gaussian elimination (not computed by multiplying by the inverse of $\mathbf{A}$). A warning message is printed if $\mathbf{A}$ is badly scaled or nearly singular. The left-division operator can also be used when $\mathbf{A}$ is n-by-m ($n \neq m$) to obtain a solution of the over- or under-determined system. A system is *underdetermined* if there are more unknowns than equations and *overdetermined* if there are fewer unknowns than equations. In each case, it is the number of linearly independent equations that is important. The concept of linear independence is discussed in standard texts on linear algebra.

Information about MATLAB's operations can be found using the command

```
help matlab:ops
```

The matrix left-division operator is implemented in the function `mldivide`, which provides a brief description of its approach in the comments at the beginning of the function.

It is also possible to solve the linear system $\mathbf{Ax} = \mathbf{b}$ by using MATLAB's function for finding a matrix inverse (discussed in Chapter 5); however, multiplication by a matrix inverse is usually not the best way to solve a linear system.

SUMMARY

Basic Gaussian Elimination (p. 84): To solve $\mathbf{Ax} = \mathbf{b}$, transform matrix $\mathbf{A}$ into an upper triangular matrix by systematically applying the following row transformations to the augmented matrix consisting of $\mathbf{A}$ together with $\mathbf{b}$, i.e., $[\mathbf{A} : \mathbf{b}]$.

Add a multiple m of row R_i onto row R_j to form a new row R_j:

$$R_j \leftarrow mR_i + R_j.$$

Solve the resulting linear system by back substitution:

$$x_n = b_n/a_{nn},$$
$$x_{n-1} = (b_{n-1} - a_{n-1,n}x_n)/a_{n-1,n-1}.$$
$$x_2 = (b_2 - a_{23}x_3 - \ldots - a_{2n}x_n)/a_{22}.$$
$$x_1 = (b_1 - a_{12}x_2 - \ldots - a_{1,n-1}x_{n-1} - a_{1,n}x_n)/a_{11}.$$

Gaussian Elimination with Row Pivoting (p. 90): To solve $\mathbf{Ax} = \mathbf{b}$, transform matrix $\mathbf{A}$ into an upper triangular matrix at each stage perform row interchanges on the augmented matrix so that the pivot element is as large as possible. Then perform the same row transformations as for basic Gaussian elimination.

Thomas Method (Modified Gaussian Elimination for Tridiagonal Systems) (p. 95): Let

$$
\begin{aligned}
d_1x_1 + a_1x_2 &= r_1, \\
b_2x_1 + d_2x_2 + a_2x_3 &= r_2, \\
b_3x_2 + d_3x_3 + a_3x_4 &= r_3, \\
b_nx_{n-1} + d_nx_n &= r_n.
\end{aligned}
$$

Step 1

For the first equation, form the new elements a_1 and r_1,

$$a_1 = \frac{a_1}{d_1}, \qquad r_1 = \frac{r_1}{d_1}.$$

Step 2

For each of the equations, from $i = 2, \ldots, n - 1$,

$$a_i = \frac{a_i}{d_i - b_ia_{i-1}}, \qquad r_i = \frac{r_i - b_ir_{i-1}}{d_i - b_ia_{i-1}}.$$

Step 3

For the last equation,

$$r_n = \frac{r_n - b_nr_{n-1}}{d_n - b_na_{n-1}}.$$

Step 4

Solve by back substitution, yielding

$$x_n = r_n,$$
$$x_i = r_i - a_ix_{i+1}, \quad i = n - 1, n - 2, n - 3, \ldots, 2, 1.$$

SUGGESTIONS FOR FURTHER READING

The topics introduced in this chapter are part of the field of numerical linear algebra. We consider other topics from this area in Chapters 6 and 7. For more in-depth treatments of these techniques, the following are a few suggested sources:

Hager, W. W., *Applied Numerical Linear Algebra,* Prentice Hall, Englewood Cliffs, NJ, 1988. This book includes a discussion of the relative merits of row and column pivoting.

Strang, G., *Linear Algebra and Its Applications,* 3d ed., Harcourt Brace Jovanovich, San Diego, 1988.

For a discussion of the issues of scaling, operations counts, etc., see any of the following texts:

Atkinson, K. E., *An Introduction to Numerical Analysis,* 2d ed., John Wiley, New York, 1989.

Golub, G. H., and C. F. Van Loan, *Matrix Computations,* 3d ed., Johns Hopkins University Press, Baltimore, 1996.

Jensen, J. A., and J. H. Rowland, *Methods of Computation,* Scott, Foresman and Company, Glenview, IL, 1975.

Press, W. H., B. P. Flannery, S. A. Teukolsky, and W. T. Vetterling, *Numerical Recipes: The Art of Scientific Computing,* Cambridge University Press, Cambridge, U.K., 1986.

PRACTICE THE TECHNIQUES

For problems P3.1–P3.5, solve the linear system $\mathbf{Ax} = \mathbf{b}$ using basic Gaussian elimination.

P3.1 $\mathbf{A} = \begin{bmatrix} 3 & -1 & 2 \\ 1 & 2 & 3 \\ 2 & -2 & -1 \end{bmatrix}$, $\mathbf{b} = \begin{bmatrix} 1 \\ 1 \\ 1 \end{bmatrix}$.

P3.2 $\mathbf{A} = \begin{bmatrix} 2 & 5 & 3 \\ 8 & 9 & 7 \\ 4 & 6 & 1 \end{bmatrix}$, $\mathbf{b} = \begin{bmatrix} 2 \\ 14 \\ 3 \end{bmatrix}$.

P3.3 $\mathbf{A} = \begin{bmatrix} 10 & -2 & 1 \\ -2 & 10 & -2 \\ -2 & -5 & 10 \end{bmatrix}$, $\mathbf{b} = \begin{bmatrix} 9 \\ 12 \\ 18 \end{bmatrix}$.

P3.4 $\mathbf{A} = \begin{bmatrix} -1 & 5 & 2 \\ 2 & 3 & 1 \\ 3 & 2 & 1 \end{bmatrix}$, $\mathbf{b} = \begin{bmatrix} -2 \\ 7 \\ 3 \end{bmatrix}$.

P3.5 $\mathbf{A} = \begin{bmatrix} 8 & 1 & -1 \\ -1 & 7 & -2 \\ 2 & 1 & 9 \end{bmatrix}$, $\mathbf{b} = \begin{bmatrix} 8 \\ 4 \\ 12 \end{bmatrix}$.

For problems P3.6–P3.10, solve the linear system $\mathbf{Ax} = \mathbf{b}$

a. *using basic Gaussian elimination.*
b. *using the* MATLAB *function* Gauss *given in the text.*

P3.6 $\mathbf{A} = \begin{bmatrix} 2 & 0 & -2 \\ 3 & -4 & -4 \\ -2 & 2 & -1 \end{bmatrix}$

   i) $\mathbf{b} = [-10 \quad -8 \quad 3]'$
   ii) $\mathbf{b} = [6 \quad 2 \quad 15]'$

P3.7 $\mathbf{A} = \begin{bmatrix} 3 & -5 & -5 \\ 5 & -5 & -2 \\ 2 & 3 & 4 \end{bmatrix}$

   i) $\mathbf{b} = [-37 \quad -17 \quad 32]'$
   ii) $\mathbf{b} = [-14 \quad -32 \quad -7]'$

P3.8 $\mathbf{A} = \begin{bmatrix} 4 & 12 & 8 & 4 \\ 1 & 7 & 18 & 9 \\ 2 & 9 & 20 & 20 \\ 3 & 11 & 15 & 14 \end{bmatrix}$, $\mathbf{b} = \begin{bmatrix} -4 \\ -5 \\ -25 \\ -18 \end{bmatrix}$.

P3.9 $\mathbf{A} = \begin{bmatrix} 1 & 1 & 0 & 3 \\ 2 & 1 & -1 & 1 \\ 3 & -1 & -1 & 2 \\ -1 & 2 & 3 & -1 \end{bmatrix}$, $\mathbf{b} = \begin{bmatrix} 4 \\ 1 \\ -3 \\ 4 \end{bmatrix}$.

P3.10 $\mathbf{A} = \begin{bmatrix} 1 & 1 & 1 & 1 \\ 2 & 4 & 4 & 4 \\ 3 & 11 & 14 & 14 \\ 5 & 17 & 38 & 42 \end{bmatrix}$, $\mathbf{b} = \begin{bmatrix} 0 \\ -2 \\ -8 \\ -20 \end{bmatrix}$.

For problems P3.11–P3.14, solve the linear system $\mathbf{Ax} = \mathbf{b}$ using Gaussian elimination with row pivoting.

P3.11 $\mathbf{A} = \begin{bmatrix} 6 & 2 & 2 \\ 6 & 2 & 1 \\ 1 & 2 & -1 \end{bmatrix}$, $\mathbf{b} = \begin{bmatrix} 0 \\ 5 \\ 0 \end{bmatrix}$.

P3.12 $\mathbf{A} = \begin{bmatrix} 1 & 2 & 3 \\ 2 & 4 & 10 \\ 3 & 14 & 28 \end{bmatrix}$, $\mathbf{b} = \begin{bmatrix} 1 \\ -2 \\ -8 \end{bmatrix}$.

P3.13 $\mathbf{A} = \begin{bmatrix} 2 & 6 & 10 \\ 1 & 3 & 3 \\ 3 & 14 & 28 \end{bmatrix}$, $\mathbf{b} = \begin{bmatrix} 0 \\ 2 \\ -8 \end{bmatrix}$.

P3.14 $\mathbf{A} = \begin{bmatrix} -1 & 1 & 0 & 0 \\ 1 & -1 & 1 & 0 \\ 0 & 1 & -1 & 1 \\ 0 & 0 & 1 & -1 \end{bmatrix}$, $\mathbf{b} = \begin{bmatrix} 1 \\ 1 \\ -1 \\ -1 \end{bmatrix}$.

P3.15
$$\mathbf{A} = \begin{bmatrix} 2 & -1 & 0 & 0 & 0 & 0 \\ -1 & 2 & -1 & 0 & 0 & 0 \\ 0 & -1 & 2/3 & -1 & 0 & 0 \\ 0 & 0 & -1 & 2 & -1 & 0 \\ 0 & 0 & 0 & -1 & 2 & -1 \\ 0 & 0 & 0 & 0 & -1 & 2 \end{bmatrix}, \quad \mathbf{b} = \begin{bmatrix} 1 \\ 0 \\ -4/3 \\ 0 \\ 0 \\ 1 \end{bmatrix}.$$

For problems P3.16–P3.20, solve the linear system $\mathbf{Ax} = \mathbf{b}$ using Gaussian elimination with rounding. Compare the results using basic Gaussian elimination with those from Gaussian eliminated with row pivoting.

P3.16 $0.001x_1 + 2x_2 = 4$ (round to 2 digits)
$x_1 + 2x_2 = 5$

P3.17 $0.01x_1 + 10x_2 = 30$ (round to 2 digits)
$x_1 + x_2 = 2$

P3.18 $0.001x_1 + 2x_2 = 6$ (round to 2 digits)
$x_1 + 3x_2 = 8$

P3.19 $0.001x_1 + x_2 + x_3 = 5$ (round to 3 digits)
$x_1 + x_2 \phantom{{}+ x_3} = 3$
$x_1 \phantom{{}+ x_2} + x_3 = 4$

P3.20 $6x_1 - 2.2x_2 + 3x_3 = 20$ (round to 2 digits)
$-3x_1 + x_2 - 1.1x_3 = -8.1$
$-1x_1 - 3x_2 + 0.9x_3 = 6$

For problems P3.21–3.25, solve the linear system $\mathbf{Ax} = \mathbf{b}$; round to two digits.

    a. Use basic Gaussian elimination.
    b. Use Gaussian elimination with row pivoting.
    c. Use Gaussian elimination with scaling and pivoting; scale each row so that the largest element is 1 before choosing the pivot element.

P3.21 $x_1 + 2000x_2 = 4000$
$\phantom{x_1 + {}}x_1 + 2x_2 = 5$

P3.22 $x_1 + 1000x_2 = 3000$
$x_1 + x_2 = 2$

P3.23 $x_1 + 2000x_2 = 6000$
$x_1 + 3x_2 = 8$

P3.24 $x_1 + 1000x_2 + 1000x_3 = 5000$
$x_1 + x_2 \phantom{{}+ 1000x_3} = 3$
$x_1 \phantom{{}+ 1000x_2} + x_3 = 4$

P3.25 $600x_1 - 220x_2 + 300x_3 = 2000$
$-300x_1 + 100x_2 - 110x_3 = -810$
$-1x_1 - 3x_2 + 0.9x_3 = 6$

For problems P3.26–3.35, solve the linear system $\mathbf{Ax} = \mathbf{r}$

    a. using Gaussian elimination.
    b. using the Thomas method for tridiagonal systems.

P3.26 $\mathbf{A} = \begin{bmatrix} 1 & 2 & 0 \\ 1 & 3 & 3 \\ 0 & 3 & 10 \end{bmatrix}$, $\mathbf{r} = [10 \quad 17 \quad 22]'$.

P3.27 $\mathbf{A} = \begin{bmatrix} 1 & 2 & 0 \\ 1 & 3 & 4 \\ 0 & 3 & 13 \end{bmatrix}$, $\mathbf{r} = [3 \quad 8 \quad 16]'$.

P3.28 $\mathbf{A} = \begin{bmatrix} -2 & 1 & 0 & 0 \\ 1 & -2 & 1 & 0 \\ 0 & 1 & -2 & 1 \\ 0 & 0 & 1 & -2 \end{bmatrix}$, $\mathbf{r} = \begin{bmatrix} -1 \\ 0 \\ 0 \\ 0 \end{bmatrix}$.

P3.29 $\mathbf{A} = \begin{bmatrix} 2 & 1 & 0 & 0 \\ -1 & 2 & 1 & 0 \\ 0 & 1 & 2 & -1 \\ 0 & 0 & -1 & 2 \end{bmatrix}$, $\mathbf{r} = \begin{bmatrix} 0 \\ 0 \\ 0 \\ 11 \end{bmatrix}$.

P3.30 $\mathbf{A} = \begin{bmatrix} 5 & 1 & 0 & 0 \\ 1 & 5 & 1 & 0 \\ 0 & 1 & 5 & 1 \\ 0 & 0 & 1 & 5 \end{bmatrix}$, $\mathbf{r} = \begin{bmatrix} 33 \\ 26 \\ 30 \\ 15 \end{bmatrix}$.

P3.31 $\mathbf{A} = \begin{bmatrix} -3 & -4 & 0 & 0 & 0 & 0 \\ -3 & 4 & 5 & 0 & 0 & 0 \\ 0 & 1 & -1 & -3 & 0 & 0 \\ 0 & 0 & 0 & 4 & -5 & 0 \\ 0 & 0 & 0 & 3 & 1 & -5 \\ 0 & 0 & 0 & 0 & -1 & 2 \end{bmatrix}$

$\mathbf{r} = \begin{bmatrix} 14 & -36 & -6 & 14 & -9 & 6 \end{bmatrix}'$

P3.32 $\mathbf{A} = \begin{bmatrix} 1 & 3 & 0 & 0 & 0 & 0 & 0 \\ 5 & -4 & -1 & 0 & 0 & 0 & 0 \\ 0 & 5 & -2 & -1 & 0 & 0 & 0 \\ 0 & 0 & 2 & 3 & 1 & 0 & 0 \\ 0 & 0 & 0 & 5 & -3 & -1 & 0 \\ 0 & 0 & 0 & 0 & 1 & -1 & 0 \\ 0 & 0 & 0 & 0 & 0 & -2 & 4 \end{bmatrix}$

$\mathbf{r} = \begin{bmatrix} 14 & 1 & 28 & 0 & -25 & 0 & 2 \end{bmatrix}'$

P3.33

$\mathbf{A} = \begin{bmatrix} -1 & 1 & 0 & 0 & 0 & 0 & 0 & 0 \\ -1 & 4 & 1 & 0 & 0 & 0 & 0 & 0 \\ 0 & 4 & 1 & 3 & 0 & 0 & 0 & 0 \\ 0 & 0 & 0 & -1 & -2 & 0 & 0 & 0 \\ 0 & 0 & 0 & -2 & -2 & -2 & 0 & 0 \\ 0 & 0 & 0 & 0 & -4 & -2 & -2 & 0 \\ 0 & 0 & 0 & 0 & 0 & 2 & 4 & 0 \\ 0 & 0 & 0 & 0 & 0 & 0 & 0 & 2 \end{bmatrix}$

$\mathbf{r} = \begin{bmatrix} 7 & 13 & -3 & -2 & -4 & -28 & 26 & 10 \end{bmatrix}'$

P3.34

$\mathbf{A} = \begin{bmatrix} -1 & 1 & 0 & 0 & 0 & 0 & 0 & 0 & 0 \\ 2 & 3 & 1 & 0 & 0 & 0 & 0 & 0 & 0 \\ 0 & 3 & -3 & -1 & 0 & 0 & 0 & 0 & 0 \\ 0 & 0 & -4 & 3 & 4 & 0 & 0 & 0 & 0 \\ 0 & 0 & 0 & 3 & 3 & 5 & 0 & 0 & 0 \\ 0 & 0 & 0 & 0 & -1 & -5 & 0 & 0 & 0 \\ 0 & 0 & 0 & 0 & 0 & -5 & 1 & -4 & 0 \\ 0 & 0 & 0 & 0 & 0 & 0 & -2 & 2 & -4 \\ 0 & 0 & 0 & 0 & 0 & 0 & 0 & -4 & 2 \end{bmatrix}$

$\mathbf{r} = \begin{bmatrix} -1 & 19 & 20 & -1 & -19 & 14 & 0 & -4 & -2 \end{bmatrix}'$

P3.35

$\mathbf{A} = \begin{bmatrix} 3 & -4 & 0 & 0 & 0 & 0 & 0 & 0 & 0 & 0 \\ 3 & 3 & 5 & 0 & 0 & 0 & 0 & 0 & 0 & 0 \\ 0 & -1 & 1 & 2 & 0 & 0 & 0 & 0 & 0 & 0 \\ 0 & 0 & -2 & -4 & 5 & 0 & 0 & 0 & 0 & 0 \\ 0 & 0 & 0 & 1 & 0 & -2 & 0 & 0 & 0 & 0 \\ 0 & 0 & 0 & 0 & 5 & -3 & -2 & 0 & 0 & 0 \\ 0 & 0 & 0 & 0 & 0 & 1 & 0 & -5 & 0 & 0 \\ 0 & 0 & 0 & 0 & 0 & 0 & -3 & 0 & -1 & 0 \\ 0 & 0 & 0 & 0 & 0 & 0 & 0 & -3 & 0 & 1 \\ 0 & 0 & 0 & 0 & 0 & 0 & 0 & 0 & -4 & 1 \end{bmatrix}$

$\mathbf{r} = \begin{bmatrix} -13 & -11 & -6 & 25 & 6 & 29 & 1 & 0 & 3 & -12 \end{bmatrix}'$

For Problems P3.36–P3.40, solve the linear system $\mathbf{Ax} = \mathbf{b}$ using the MATLAB function in the text, MATLAB's built-in methods, or your own computer program.

P3.36 $\mathbf{A} = \begin{bmatrix} -5 & 0 & -4 & 1 & 4 & 5 \\ 3 & 5 & -2 & -4 & 3 & -2 \\ -1 & -3 & 3 & 4 & 3 & 1 \\ 0 & 1 & 1 & 1 & -1 & -4 \\ -4 & -1 & -4 & -3 & 2 & 0 \\ -3 & -3 & -4 & 5 & 3 & 1 \end{bmatrix}$

a. $\mathbf{b} = \begin{bmatrix} 14 & -26 & 0 & -16 & 0 & -17 \end{bmatrix}'$
b. $\mathbf{b} = \begin{bmatrix} 19 & -3 & -15 & -4 & 15 & 10 \end{bmatrix}'$
c. $\mathbf{b} = \begin{bmatrix} -16 & 29 & -4 & 2 & -13 & -31 \end{bmatrix}'$
d. $\mathbf{b} = \begin{bmatrix} -44 & 3 & -23 & 3 & -10 & -40 \end{bmatrix}'$

P3.37

$\mathbf{A} = \begin{bmatrix} -4 & -2 & -1 & 4 & 5 & -2 & -1 & 5 \\ -4 & 1 & 3 & -4 & -4 & -4 & -2 & -3 \\ 2 & 1 & -2 & 3 & -4 & -1 & -3 & 0 \\ 1 & 2 & -2 & 5 & 2 & -5 & 1 & 3 \\ 0 & -4 & 4 & -2 & -1 & -3 & 1 & 4 \\ 4 & -1 & 5 & 0 & 3 & 3 & 0 & 3 \\ 4 & 3 & 2 & 2 & -1 & -3 & -1 & 1 \\ 0 & -5 & 4 & 1 & 2 & 3 & 3 & 1 \end{bmatrix}$

a. $\mathbf{b} = \begin{bmatrix} 10 & -30 & 0 & -16 & 23 & 61 & 9 & 40 \end{bmatrix}'$
b. $\mathbf{b} = \begin{bmatrix} 46 & -13 & -14 & 18 & 16 & 20 & 0 & 7 \end{bmatrix}'$
c. $\mathbf{b} = \begin{bmatrix} 48 & -10 & -27 & 24 & 16 & -13 & -22 & 16 \end{bmatrix}'$
d. $\mathbf{b} = \begin{bmatrix} -19 & -7 & 7 & 23 & -12 & -11 & 21 & -38 \end{bmatrix}'$

P3.38

$$A = \begin{bmatrix} 0 & -3 & -3 & -2 & 3 & 3 & 1 & 2 \\ 3 & 1 & 0 & -4 & 4 & -4 & 2 & -1 \\ -3 & 2 & 3 & -5 & 3 & 5 & -2 & 0 \\ -1 & 0 & -1 & 0 & 4 & -1 & -4 & -5 \\ 5 & -1 & -2 & -1 & 4 & 0 & 2 & 3 \\ -4 & -3 & -2 & -3 & 0 & -2 & -1 & 0 \\ -3 & -3 & -4 & 1 & -3 & 2 & 4 & 0 \\ -4 & 0 & -3 & 0 & 2 & 3 & 3 & -3 \end{bmatrix}$$

a. $\mathbf{b} = [-18 \quad -13 \quad -77 \quad 25 \quad -8 \quad 4 \quad 13 \quad -15]'$
b. $\mathbf{b} = [3 \quad 14 \quad -53 \quad 3 \quad 14 \quad -7 \quad 36 \quad 25]'$
c. $\mathbf{b} = [14 \quad -30 \quad 36 \quad -7 \quad -18 \quad 26 \quad 3 \quad -7]'$
d. $\mathbf{b} = [-28 \quad -3 \quad -36 \quad -49 \quad 5 \quad -24 \quad -6 \quad -37]'$

P3.39

$$A = \begin{bmatrix} 1 & -4 & 4 & 1 & 2 & 1 & 3 & -1 & -2 & 4 \\ 2 & 2 & -3 & -4 & 5 & 5 & -4 & -2 & 0 & -2 \\ 2 & 3 & 1 & 0 & -2 & 1 & -1 & 1 & -3 & 1 \\ 1 & -4 & -4 & -3 & -2 & -3 & -1 & 1 & 0 & 4 \\ 1 & 3 & -2 & 0 & -5 & -3 & 3 & -2 & 3 & -1 \\ -1 & -1 & -2 & 0 & -1 & -4 & 0 & -3 & -2 & -3 \\ 4 & -5 & 2 & 0 & 1 & -3 & -4 & 1 & -5 & -2 \\ 5 & -2 & 3 & 1 & 3 & 1 & 2 & 1 & -3 & -5 \\ 0 & -4 & 3 & -4 & -1 & -1 & -2 & -1 & -2 & -5 \\ -4 & 5 & 3 & 5 & -2 & -2 & 1 & -1 & 0 & 4 \end{bmatrix}$$

a. $\mathbf{b} = [14 \quad 42 \quad -3 \quad -22 \quad -28 \quad 21 \quad 38 \quad 34 \quad 31 \quad -16]'$
b. $\mathbf{b} = [-12 \quad -47 \quad 15 \quad 28 \quad 17 \quad 28 \quad 37 \quad -2 \quad -5 \quad 15]'$
c. $\mathbf{b} = [-16 \quad 6 \quad 14 \quad 20 \quad -16 \quad -10 \quad -10 \quad -44 \quad -46 \quad 26]'$
d. $\mathbf{b} = [-9 \quad 46 \quad 16 \quad -21 \quad -20 \quad 6 \quad 27 \quad 21 \quad 36 \quad -25]'$

P3.40

$$A = \begin{bmatrix} 2 & -2 & -3 & 1 & 3 & 5 & 3 & 3 & -1 & -5 \\ 1 & 2 & 3 & 2 & -2 & -3 & 0 & 5 & -4 & 3 \\ 0 & 2 & 1 & -4 & 0 & -4 & 4 & -1 & 2 & 0 \\ -2 & -2 & 0 & -3 & -4 & 2 & -4 & 4 & -4 & 2 \\ 2 & -3 & -2 & -4 & -2 & 2 & -1 & 0 & 4 & -2 \\ 4 & -5 & -1 & -1 & 3 & -4 & 2 & 4 & 4 & -5 \\ 1 & 0 & 0 & 5 & 1 & 4 & 1 & -3 & 3 & -3 \\ 0 & -4 & 1 & -1 & 3 & -4 & -4 & 1 & -4 & -2 \\ 5 & 0 & 4 & -3 & -5 & -2 & 1 & -3 & 4 & 4 \\ -2 & -3 & 1 & -5 & 1 & -3 & 4 & 5 & 2 & 4 \end{bmatrix}$$

a. $\mathbf{b} = [16 \quad -37 \quad 36 \quad -43 \quad 33 \quad 66 \quad -7 \quad 18 \quad 11 \quad 5]'$
b. $\mathbf{b} = [0 \quad 29 \quad -29 \quad 25 \quad -3 \quad 12 \quad -11 \quad 17 \quad -3 \quad 7]'$
c. $\mathbf{b} = [34 \quad -54 \quad -1 \quad -2 \quad 47 \quad -3 \quad 35 \quad -39 \quad 11 \quad -27]'$
d. $\mathbf{b} = [-15 \quad 16 \quad -8 \quad -35 \quad -54 \quad -40 \quad 29 \quad -6 \quad -22 \quad -38]'$

EXPLORE SOME APPLICATIONS

A3.1 Linear systems occur in many other problems involving numerical methods. The following system is a small example of the type of system encountered as part of a quadratic spline interpolation problem (see Example 8.15):

$$\begin{aligned} a_1 - a_2 \quad\quad + b_1 \quad\quad &= 4, \\ + a_2 - a_3 \quad + b_1 + b_2 &= 12, \\ + a_3 - a_4 \quad + b_2 &= -4, \\ a_1 + a_2 \quad\quad - b_1 \quad\quad &= 0, \\ + a_2 + a_3 \quad + b_1 - b_2 &= 0, \\ + a_3 + a_4 \quad + b_2 &= 0. \end{aligned}$$

Solve for the unknowns $a_1, a_2, a_3, b_1, b_2,$ and b_3.

A3.2 This is a small example of the type of system encountered as part of the cubic spline interpolation technique (discussed in Section 8.4.3). Solve for the unknowns $a_1, a_2, \ldots, a_7$.

$$\begin{aligned} \tfrac{2}{3}a_1 + \tfrac{1}{6}a_2 \quad\quad\quad\quad\quad\quad\quad &= 1.2 \\ \tfrac{1}{6}a_1 + \tfrac{2}{3}a_2 + \tfrac{1}{6}a_3 \quad\quad\quad\quad &= 1.97 \\ + \tfrac{1}{6}a_2 + \tfrac{2}{3}a_3 + \tfrac{1}{6}a_4 \quad\quad &= 2 \\ + \tfrac{1}{6}a_3 + \tfrac{2}{3}a_4 + \tfrac{1}{6}a_5 \quad &= 0 \\ + \tfrac{1}{6}a_4 + \tfrac{2}{3}a_5 + \tfrac{1}{6}a_6 &= -2 \\ + \tfrac{1}{6}a_5 + \tfrac{2}{3}a_6 + \tfrac{1}{6}a_7 &= -1.97 \\ + \tfrac{1}{6}a_6 + \tfrac{2}{3}a_7 &= -1.2 \end{aligned}$$

A3.3 Tridiagonal systems also occur in solutions of ordinary differential equations with boundary conditions when the equations are solved by means of finite differences. For this example, solve the system $Ax = b$

$$A = \begin{bmatrix} -1.99 & 1.00 & 0 & 0 & 0 & 0 & 0 & 0 & 0 \\ 1.00 & -1.99 & 1.00 & 0 & 0 & 0 & 0 & 0 & 0 \\ 0 & 1.00 & -1.99 & 1.00 & 0 & 0 & 0 & 0 & 0 \\ 0 & 0 & 1.00 & -1.99 & 1.00 & 0 & 0 & 0 & 0 \\ 0 & 0 & 0 & 1.00 & -1.99 & 1.00 & 0 & 0 & 0 \\ 0 & 0 & 0 & 0 & 1.00 & -1.99 & 1.00 & 0 & 0 \\ 0 & 0 & 0 & 0 & 0 & 1.00 & -1.99 & 1.00 & 0 \\ 0 & 0 & 0 & 0 & 0 & 0 & 1.00 & -1.99 & 1.00 \\ 0 & 0 & 0 & 0 & 0 & 0 & 0 & 1.00 & -1.99 \end{bmatrix}$$

$b = [-0.99 \ \ 0.002 \ \ 0.0031 \ \ 0.0042 \ \ 0.0055 \ \ 0.0068 \ \ 0.0084 \ \ 0.0103 \ \ -0.6874]'$

A3.4 Consider the single triangle truss shown in Fig. 3.2, but take $\alpha = \beta = \pi/4$, so that $\cos \alpha = \sin \alpha = \cos \beta = \sin \beta = \sqrt{2}/2$. Take $W_3 = 100$.

$$
\begin{aligned}
V_1 \qquad\qquad + \sqrt{2}/2\, F_{13} \qquad\qquad &= 0 \\
H_1 \qquad + F_{12} + \sqrt{2}/2\, F_{13} \qquad\qquad &= 0 \\
V_2 \qquad\qquad\qquad + \sqrt{2}/2\, F_{23} &= 0 \\
- F_{12} \qquad - \sqrt{2}/2\, F_{23} &= 0 \\
- \sqrt{2}/2\, F_{13} - \sqrt{2}/2\, F_{23} &= 100 \\
- \sqrt{2}/2\, F_{13} + \sqrt{2}/2\, F_{23} &= 0
\end{aligned}
$$

A3.5 A 10-stage equilibrium process such as liquid extraction or gas absorption can be modeled by a tridiagonal system of linear equations; solve using $rr = 0.9$ (this depends on the ratio of flow rates (left to right and right to left) and the ratio of weight fractions of the two components that are flowing). Assume that the flow in is 0.05 and that the flow out is 0.5.

Equations for A3.7

$$
\begin{aligned}
V_1 \qquad\qquad\qquad + F_{14} \sin \alpha \qquad\qquad\qquad\qquad\qquad\qquad &= 0 \\
H_1 \qquad + F_{12} + F_{14} \cos \alpha \qquad\qquad\qquad\qquad\qquad\qquad &= 0 \\
+ F_{24} \sin \beta \ + F_{25} \sin \gamma \qquad\qquad\qquad &= 100 \\
- F_{12} \qquad + F_{23} - F_{24} \cos \beta \ + F_{25} \cos \gamma \qquad\qquad\qquad &= 0 \\
V_3 \qquad\qquad\qquad\qquad\qquad + F_{35} \sin \delta \qquad &= 0 \\
- F_{23} \qquad\qquad\qquad - F_{35} \cos \delta \qquad &= 0 \\
- F_{14} \sin \alpha \qquad - F_{24} \sin \beta \qquad\qquad\qquad &= 0 \\
- F_{14} \cos \alpha \qquad + F_{24} \cos \beta \qquad\qquad + F_{45} &= 0 \\
- F_{25} \sin \gamma \ - F_{35} \sin \delta \qquad &= 0 \\
- F_{25} \cos \gamma \ + F_{35} \cos \delta \ - F_{45} &= 0
\end{aligned}
$$

$-(1 + rr)x_1 + rr\, x_2 \qquad = -(\text{flow into compartment 1})$

$x_{i-1} - (1 + rr)x_i + rrx_{i+1} = 0 \qquad i = 2, \ldots, n-1$

$x_{n-1} - (1 + rr)x_n \qquad = -(\text{flow out of compartment } n)$

(See Hanna and Sandall, p. 58 for a discussion of similar problems.)

A3.6 The equilibrium positions of a system of blocks coupled by springs is described by a linear system of equations. Suppose that there are four blocks arranged as shown below. The unstretched length of the ith spring is L_i, and its spring constant is k_i. The distance between the two walls is L. The equation stating that the ith block is in equilibrium states that the forces on the block (from the springs on either side of it) are equal. For example, for B_2, this gives $K_2(X_1 + L_2 - X_2) = K_3(X_2 + L_3 - X_3)$.

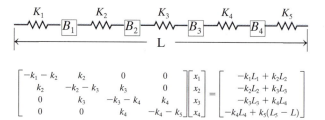

$$\begin{bmatrix} -k_1 - k_2 & k_2 & 0 & 0 \\ k_2 & -k_2 - k_3 & k_3 & 0 \\ 0 & k_3 & -k_3 - k_4 & k_4 \\ 0 & 0 & k_4 & -k_4 - k_5 \end{bmatrix} \begin{bmatrix} x_1 \\ x_2 \\ x_3 \\ x_4 \end{bmatrix} = \begin{bmatrix} -k_1 L_1 + k_2 L_2 \\ -k_2 L_2 + k_3 L_3 \\ -k_3 L_3 + k_4 L_4 \\ -k_4 L_4 + k_5(L_5 - L) \end{bmatrix}$$

Solve the system for $L_1 = 2; L_2 = 2; L_3 = 2; L_4 = 2; L_5 = 2; L_w = 8$. $k_1 = 1; k_2 = 1; k_3 = 1; k_4 = 1; k_5 = 5$. See Garcia, 1994, p. 103 for discussion of a similar problem.

A3.7 Consider the simple truss shown in Fig. 3.3, but take the angles to be $\alpha = \pi/6, \beta = \pi/3, \gamma = \pi/6, \delta = \pi/3$. Solve the linear system, and compare the forces to those found in Example 3.6. See equations below.

A3.8 Consider the same truss as in A 3.7, but assume that half of the load is applied at node 4 and half at node 5, instead of the entire load being localized at node 2.

A3.9 Find the currents in the electrical circuit shown in Fig. 3.1 if the resistances are $R_1 = 12$, $R_2 = 4$, $R_3 = 5$, $R_4 = 2$, $R_5 = 10$, and the voltages are $V_1 = 100$, $V_2 = 0$, $V_3 = 0$.

A3.10 Find the currents in the electrical circuit shown in Fig. 3.1 if the resistances are $R_1 = 15$, $R_2 = 5$, $R_3 = 20$, $R_4 = 0$, $R_5 = 10$, and the voltages are $V_1 = 0$, $V_2 = 200$, $V_3 = 100$.

A3.11 Find the currents in the electrical circuit shown in Fig. 3.1 if the resistances are $R_1 = 10$, $R_2 = 5$, $R_3 = 0$, $R_4 = 10$, $R_5 = 5$, and the voltages are $V_1 = -200$, $V_2 = 0$, $V_3 = 35$.

EXTEND YOUR UNDERSTANDING

U3.1 In Gauss–Jordan elimination, elements above the diagonal are eliminated in the same manner as are elements below the diagonal, thus avoiding the back-substitution phase of the solution process. In a modified Gauss–Jordan technique, the elimination of elements below the diagonal is done in a first phase (as with basic Gaussian elimination), but the second phase eliminates elements above the diagonal (rather than using back substitution). Compare the number of operations (flops) required for the ordinary Gauss–Jordan and the modified Gauss–Jordan techniques to the number of flops required for basic Gaussian elimination.

U3.2 Consider the problem of solving the system $\mathbf{Ax} = \mathbf{b}$, where

$$\mathbf{A} = \begin{bmatrix} 1 & 1/2 & 1/3 \\ 1/2 & 1/3 & 1/4 \\ 1/3 & 1/4 & 1/5 \end{bmatrix}$$

and $\mathbf{b}$ is four different, but similar, right-hand sides:

$$\mathbf{b} = \begin{bmatrix} 3.0000 & 2.9000 & 3.1000 & 3.0000 \\ 1.9000 & 2.0000 & 1.8000 & 2.0000 \\ 1.4330 & 1.5000 & 1.4000 & 1.4000 \end{bmatrix}$$

Compare the solutions to $\mathbf{x} = [1 \quad 2 \quad 3]'$, the solution to

$$\mathbf{Ax} = [3.0000 \quad 1.9167 \quad 1.4333].$$

U3.3 Compare the computational effort required to solve various linear systems by means of the Gaussian elimination function in the text with that needed with MATLAB's matrix left-division operator. The number of floating-point operators can be obtained by the MATLAB command `flops`.

U3.4 Solve the following tridiagonal system, performing steps of the Thomas algorithm by hand (note that the process can be separated into two parts when division by zero would occur in the basic process):

$$
\begin{array}{rcl}
1x_1 + 1x_2 & = & 2 \\
2x_1 + 3x_2 + 1x_3 & = & 5 \\
+ 2x_2 + 3x_3 + 2x_4 & = & 3 \\
+ 1x_3 + 2x_4 + 1x_5 & = & 2 \\
+ 1x_4 + 1x_5 + 1x_6 & = & 3 \\
+ 2x_5 + 1x_6 + 2x_7 & = & 4 \\
+ 2x_6 + 5x_7 + 2x_8 & = & 6 \\
+ 1x_7 + 1x_8 & = & 3
\end{array}
$$

4

Solving Systems of Linear Equations: Iterative Methods

Systems of linear equations for which numerical solutions are needed are often very large, making the computational effort of general, direct methods, such as Gaussian elimination, prohibitively expensive. For systems that have coefficient matrices with the appropriate structure—especially large, sparse systems (i.e., systems with many coefficients whose value is zero)—iterative techniques may be preferable.

We begin this chapter with an example of a linear system that occurs in the solution of Poisson's equation by a finite-difference method. (See Chapter 15.) For applications such as this, in which the elements of the coefficient matrix can be generated as needed from a simple formula, it is beneficial to use a method that does not require storing (and modifying) the entire coefficient matrix, as was the case with Gaussian elimination.

We then consider the three most common classical iterative techniques for linear systems: the Jacobi, Gauss–Seidel, and successive overrelaxation (SOR) methods. The performance of each technique is illustrated for several small systems and for the linear system in the example from Poisson's equation. Some theoretical results are presented to give guidance in determining when the method may be useful. A MATLAB function is provided for each technique.

Several iterative methods developed relatively recently are implemented in MATLAB's built-in functions; these are discussed briefly in the last section of the chapter.

The convergence of each of the iterative techniques examined in this chapter depends on results from linear algebra. The eigenvalues of the iteration matrix play a crucial role in determining whether these methods will converge; numerical methods for finding eigenvalues are discussed in Chapter 7, but MATLAB's built-in function `eig` provides an efficient way of checking the conditions of the theorems given in this chapter.

Example 4-A A Linear System That Comes from Solving a Partial Differential Equation Numerically

The two-dimensional potential equation can be solved numerically by defining a mesh of points in the region of interest and approximating the derivatives by finite differences. For example, to solve the potential equation

$$u_{xx} + u_{yy} = 0, \qquad 0 \le x \le 1, \qquad 0 \le y \le 1,$$

with boundary conditions

$$u(0, y) = y^2, \qquad u(1, y) = 1, \qquad 0 < y < 1,$$
$$u(x, 0) = x^2, \qquad u(x, 1) = 1, \qquad 0 < x < 1,$$

and a mesh of $\Delta x = \Delta y = 0.2$, we obtain the following linear system:

$$
\begin{bmatrix}
4 & -1 & & & -1 & & & & & & & & & & & \\
-1 & 4 & -1 & & & -1 & & & & & & & & & & \\
& -1 & 4 & -1 & & & -1 & & & & & & & & & \\
& & -1 & 4 & & & & -1 & & & & & & & & \\
-1 & & & & 4 & -1 & & & -1 & & & & & & & \\
& -1 & & & -1 & 4 & -1 & & & -1 & & & & & & \\
& & -1 & & & -1 & 4 & -1 & & & -1 & & & & & \\
& & & -1 & & & -1 & 4 & & & & -1 & & & & \\
& & & & -1 & & & & 4 & -1 & & & -1 & & & \\
& & & & & -1 & & & -1 & 4 & -1 & & & -1 & & \\
& & & & & & -1 & & & -1 & 4 & -1 & & & -1 & \\
& & & & & & & -1 & & & -1 & 4 & & & & -1 \\
& & & & & & & & -1 & & & & 4 & -1 & & \\
& & & & & & & & & -1 & & & -1 & 4 & -1 & \\
& & & & & & & & & & -1 & & & -1 & 4 & -1 \\
& & & & & & & & & & & -1 & & & -1 & 4
\end{bmatrix}
\cdot
\begin{bmatrix}
u_1 \\ u_2 \\ u_3 \\ u_4 \\ u_5 \\ u_6 \\ u_7 \\ u_8 \\ u_9 \\ u_{10} \\ u_{11} \\ u_{12} \\ u_{13} \\ u_{14} \\ u_{15} \\ u_{16}
\end{bmatrix}
=
\begin{bmatrix}
0.08 \\ 0.16 \\ 0.36 \\ 1.64 \\ 0.16 \\ 0.0 \\ 0.0 \\ 1.0 \\ 0.36 \\ 0 \\ 0 \\ 1.0 \\ 1.64 \\ 1.0 \\ 1.0 \\ 2.0
\end{bmatrix}
$$

This system is well suited for an iterative solution scheme, such as any of the methods we consider in this chapter (since it is diagonally dominant and quite sparse). We solve the system in Examples 4.3, 4.6, and 4.8.

In practice, the linear system would often be very large, and the coefficient matrix would not actually be generated. The finite-difference method used to form the linear system and the solution of the system by means of the iterative techniques introduced in the following sections, but without the explicit generation of the coefficient matrix, are discussed in Chapter 15.

Classical iterative methods for solving linear systems are based on converting the system $\mathbf{Ax} = \mathbf{b}$ into the equivalent system $\mathbf{x} = \mathbf{Cx} + \mathbf{d}$ and generating a sequence of approximations $\mathbf{x}^{(1)}, \mathbf{x}^{(2)}, \ldots$, where

$$\mathbf{x}^{(k)} = \mathbf{Cx}^{(k-1)} + \mathbf{d}.$$

This methodology is similar to the fixed-point iteration method introduced in Chapter 1 for nonlinear functions of a single variable.

In this chapter, we consider three common iterative techniques for solving linear systems: the Jacobi, Gauss–Seidel, and SOR methods. The basic idea is to solve the ith equation in the system for the ith variable, in order to convert the given system (using a four-by-four system for illustration)

$$a_{11}x_1 + a_{12}x_2 + a_{13}x_3 + a_{14}x_4 = b_1,$$
$$a_{21}x_1 + a_{22}x_2 + a_{23}x_3 + a_{24}x_4 = b_2,$$
$$a_{31}x_1 + a_{32}x_2 + a_{33}x_3 + a_{34}x_4 = b_3,$$
$$a_{41}x_1 + a_{42}x_2 + a_{43}x_3 + a_{44}x_4 = b_4,$$

into the system

$$x_1 = \qquad\qquad -\frac{a_{12}}{a_{11}}x_2 - \frac{a_{13}}{a_{11}}x_3 - \frac{a_{14}}{a_{11}}x_4 + \frac{b_1}{a_{11}},$$

$$x_2 = -\frac{a_{21}}{a_{22}}x_1 \qquad\qquad -\frac{a_{23}}{a_{22}}x_3 - \frac{a_{24}}{a_{22}}x_4 + \frac{b_2}{a_{22}},$$

$$x_3 = -\frac{a_{31}}{a_{33}}x_1 - \frac{a_{32}}{a_{33}}x_2 \qquad\qquad -\frac{a_{34}}{a_{33}}x_4 + \frac{b_3}{a_{33}},$$

$$x_4 = -\frac{a_{41}}{a_{44}}x_1 - \frac{a_{42}}{a_{44}}x_2 - \frac{a_{43}}{a_{44}}x_3 \qquad\qquad + \frac{b_4}{a_{44}}.$$

The Jacobi and Gauss–Seidel methods differ in the manner in which they update the values of the variables on the right-hand side of the equations. The SOR update is a convex combination of the previous solution vector and the Gauss–Seidel update.

Stopping conditions must be specified for any iterative process. Two possibilities are to stop the iterations when the norm of the change in the solution vector $\mathbf{x}$ from one iteration to the next is sufficiently small or to stop the iterations when the norm of the residual vector, $|\mathbf{Ax} - \mathbf{b}|$, is below a specified tolerance.

4.1   JACOBI METHOD

The Jacobi method is based on the transformation of the linear system $\mathbf{Ax} = \mathbf{b}$ into the system $\mathbf{x} = \mathbf{Cx} + \mathbf{d}$, in which the matrix $\mathbf{C}$ has zeros on the diagonal. The vector $\mathbf{x}$ is updated using the previous estimate for all components of $\mathbf{x}$ to evaluate the right-hand side of the equation.

Example 4.1 Illustrating the Jacobi Method Graphically

To visualize the Jacobi iterations, consider the two-by-two system

$$2x + y = 6,$$
$$x + 2y = 6.$$

For the Jacobi method, the equations are written as

$$x = -\frac{1}{2}y + 3,$$

$$y = -\frac{1}{2}x + 3.$$

Starting with $x^{(1)} = 1/2$ and $y^{(1)} = 1/2$, the first equation produces the next estimate for x (using $y^{(1)}$), and the second equation gives the next value of y (using $x^{(1)}$):

$$x^{(2)} = -\frac{1}{2}y^{(1)} + 3 = -\frac{1}{4} + 3 = \frac{11}{4},$$

$$y^{(2)} = -\frac{1}{2}x^{(1)} + 3 = -\frac{1}{4} + 3 = \frac{11}{4}.$$

Notice that new values of the variables are not used until a new iteration step is begun. This is called *simultaneous updating*. The first iteration is illustrated in Fig. 4.1.

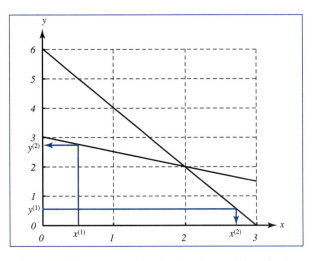

FIGURE 4.1 The first iteration for the Jacobi method.

Example 4.2 Solving a Three-by-Three System Using Jacobi Iteration

Consider the three-by-three system of equations

$$2x_1 - x_2 + x_3 = -1,$$
$$x_1 + 2x_2 - x_3 = 6,$$
$$x_1 - x_2 + 2x_3 = -3,$$

which are converted to

$$x_1 = +0.5x_2 - 0.5x_3 -0.5,$$
$$x_2 = -0.5x_1 + 0.5x_3 + 3.0,$$
$$x_3 = -0.5x_1 + 0.5x_2 + -1.5.$$

In matrix notation, the original system, $\mathbf{Ax} = \mathbf{b}$, i.e.,

$$\begin{bmatrix} 2 & -1 & 1 \\ 1 & 2 & -1 \\ 1 & -1 & 2 \end{bmatrix} \begin{bmatrix} x_1 \\ x_2 \\ x_3 \end{bmatrix} = \begin{bmatrix} -1 \\ 6 \\ -3 \end{bmatrix},$$

has been transformed to

$$\begin{bmatrix} x_1^{(k)} \\ x_2^{(k)} \\ x_3^{(k)} \end{bmatrix} = \begin{bmatrix} 0.0 & 0.5 & -0.5 \\ -0.5 & 0.0 & 0.5 \\ -0.5 & 0.5 & 0.0 \end{bmatrix} \begin{bmatrix} x_1^{(k-1)} \\ x_2^{(k-1)} \\ x_3^{(k-1)} \end{bmatrix} + \begin{bmatrix} -0.5 \\ 3.0 \\ -1.5 \end{bmatrix},$$

where the iteration counter is indicated by a superscript.

Starting with $x^{(0)} = (0, 0, 0)$ we find

$$\begin{bmatrix} x_1^{(1)} \\ x_2^{(1)} \\ x_3^{(1)} \end{bmatrix} = \begin{bmatrix} 0.0 & 0.5 & -0.5 \\ -0.5 & 0.0 & 0.5 \\ -0.5 & 0.5 & 0.0 \end{bmatrix} \begin{bmatrix} 0 \\ 0 \\ 0 \end{bmatrix} + \begin{bmatrix} -0.5 \\ 3.0 \\ -1.5 \end{bmatrix} = \begin{bmatrix} -0.5 \\ 3.0 \\ -1.5 \end{bmatrix}.$$

For the second iteration, we have

$$\begin{bmatrix} x_1^{(2)} \\ x_2^{(2)} \\ x_3^{(2)} \end{bmatrix} = \begin{bmatrix} 0.0 & 0.5 & -0.5 \\ -0.5 & 0.0 & 0.5 \\ -0.5 & 0.5 & 0.0 \end{bmatrix} \begin{bmatrix} -0.5 \\ 3.0 \\ -1.5 \end{bmatrix} + \begin{bmatrix} -0.5 \\ 3.0 \\ -1.5 \end{bmatrix} = \begin{bmatrix} 1.75 \\ 2.50 \\ 0.25 \end{bmatrix}.$$

The Jacobi method converges in 13 iterations to the vector

$$\mathbf{x} = [\, 1.0002 \quad 2.0001 \quad -0.9997 \,]'.$$

The stopping condition used is that the Euclidean norm of the difference of the solution vectors between two successive iterations be less than 0.001. The true solution is $\mathbf{x}^* = [\, 1 \quad 2 \quad -1 \,]'$.

4.1.1 Matlab Function for Jacobi Method

```
function x = Jacobi_f(A, b, x0, tol, max)
%    Solution of the system of linear equations
%       Ax = b
%    using iterative Jacobi algorithm
%    Inputs :
%       A         coefficient matrix (n-by-n)
%       b         right-hand side (n-by-1)
%       x0        initial solution (n-by-1)
%       tol       stop if norm of change in x < tol.
%       max       maximum number of iterations
%    Outputs :
%       x         solution vector (n-by-1)
[n  m] = size(A);
xold = x0;
C = -A;
for i = 1:n
   C(i,i) = 0;
end
for i = 1:n
   C(i,:) = C(i,:)/A(i,i);
end
for i = 1:n
   d(i,1) = b(i)/A(i,i);
end
i = 1;
disp('    i          x1        x2         x3          . . . .');
while (i <= max)
   xnew = C * xold + d;
   if norm(xnew-xold) <=tol
      x = xnew;
      disp('Jacobi method converged');
      return;
   else
      xold = xnew;
   end
```

```
   disp([i      xnew']);
   i = i + 1;
end
disp('Jacobi method did not converge');
disp('results after maximum number of iterations');
x = xnew;
```

This function displays the iteration number and the current approximate solution at each step. The final approximate solution is returned, along with a message stating whether the convergence criterion was met.

Example 4.3 A Linear System That Comes from a PDE

Consider the linear system presented in Example 4-A. The variables represent function values at the grid points in a rectangular array as follows:

	0.04	**0.16**	**0.36**	**0.64**	
0.04	u_1	u_2	u_3	u_4	**1**
0.16	u_5	u_6	u_7	u_8	**1**
0.36	u_9	u_{10}	u_{11}	u_{12}	**1**
0.64	u_{13}	u_{14}	u_{15}	u_{16}	**1**
	1	**1**	**1**	**1**	

The values of the solution, as specified by the boundary conditions, are shown in boldface in this diagram and in each of the following ones.

The computed results for the first iteration are as follows:

	0.04	**0.16**	**0.36**	**0.64**	
0.04	0.0200	0.0400	0.0900	0.4100	**1.00**
0.16	0.0400	0.0000	0.0000	0.2500	**1.00**
0.36	0.0900	0.0000	0.0000	0.2500	**1.00**
0.64	0.4100	0.2500	0.2500	0.5000	**1.00**
	1.00	**1.00**	**1.00**	**1.00**	

The computed results for the second iteration are as follows:

	0.04	**0.16**	**0.36**	**0.64**	
0.04	0.0400	0.0675	0.2025	0.4950	**1.00**
0.16	0.0675	0.0200	0.0850	0.4150	**1.00**
0.36	0.2025	0.0850	0.1250	0.4375	**1.00**
0.64	0.4950	0.4150	0.4375	0.6250	**1.00**
	1.00	**1.00**	**1.00**	**1.00**	

The Jacobi method requires 51 iterations to reach the stopping condition (that the Euclidean norm of the difference between two successive solution vectors be less than 10^{-5}). The computed solution is as follows:

	0.04	0.16	0.36	0.64	
0.04	0.1921	0.3442	0.5261	0.7467	**1.00**
0.16	0.3442	0.4988	0.6533	0.8206	**1.00**
0.36	0.5261	0.6533	0.7679	0.8824	**1.00**
0.64	0.7467	0.8206	0.8824	0.9412	**1.00**
	1.00	**1.00**	**1.00**	**1.00**	

4.1.2 Discussion

The Jacobi method is often derived by converting the original system, $\mathbf{Ax} = \mathbf{b}$, into a decomposed form $(\mathbf{L} + \mathbf{D} + \mathbf{U})\,\mathbf{x} = \mathbf{b}$, where $\mathbf{D}$ is a diagonal matrix, $\mathbf{L}$ is a lower triangular matrix, and $\mathbf{U}$ is an upper triangular matrix. The decomposed form is expressed as $\mathbf{x} = \mathbf{Cx} + \mathbf{d}$ in the following way:

$$\mathbf{Dx} = (-\mathbf{L} - \mathbf{U})\mathbf{x} + \mathbf{b},$$

$$\mathbf{x} = \mathbf{D}^{-1}(-\mathbf{L} - \mathbf{U})\mathbf{x} + \mathbf{D}^{-1}\mathbf{b},$$

$$\mathbf{x} = \mathbf{Cx} + \mathbf{d}.$$

This formulation assumes that the diagonal of $\mathbf{A}$ contains no element that is zero. If $\mathbf{A}$ is nonsingular, but has a zero element on the diagonal, rows and columns may be permuted to obtain a form with nonsingular $\mathbf{D}$. It is desirable to have the diagonal elements large relative to the off-diagonal elements.

The primary considerations in determining when the Jacobi method (or some other iterative method) works well are convergence and computational effort.

To illustrate the sensitivity of the Jacobi method to the form of the coefficient matrix $\mathbf{A}$ (or equivalently, to the form of the iteration matrix $\mathbf{C}$), consider the simple system from the beginning of this section, but with the order of the equations reversed, so that the system is no longer diagonally dominant:

$$x + 2y = 6,$$

$$2x + y = 6.$$

In the Jacobi iterative form, we have (see Fig. 4.2)

L_1: $\qquad\qquad\qquad\qquad x = -2y + 6,$

L_2: $\qquad\qquad\qquad\qquad y = -2x + 6.$

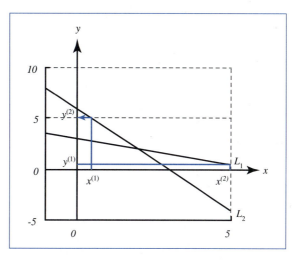

FIGURE 4.2 Divergent Jacobi iterations.

Starting with $x^{(1)} = 1/2$ and $y^{(1)} = 1/2$, we obtain

$$x^{(2)} = -2\, y^{(1)} + 6 = 5,$$

$$y^{(2)} = -2\, x^{(1)} + 6 = 5.$$

Further iterations show that the solution diverges, with x and y alternating between large positive and large negative values.

There are several useful theoretical results concerning the relationships between the characteristics of the matrix $\mathbf{A}$ (or the iteration matrix $\mathbf{C}$) and the convergence of Jacobi iteration for the system $\mathbf{Ax} = \mathbf{b}$. Two such results are summarized next.

A *sufficient* condition for Jacobi iteration to converge to the solution of the system $\mathbf{Ax} = \mathbf{b}$ is that the original matrix $\mathbf{A}$ be strictly diagonally dominant. This means that, for each row, the magnitude of the diagonal element is greater than the sum of the magnitudes of the other elements in the row.

A *necessary and sufficient* condition for the convergence of the Jacobi method is that the magnitude of the largest eigenvalue of the iteration matrix $\mathbf{C}$ be less than 1. Eigenvalues and eigenvectors are discussed further in Chapter 7. Using the MATLAB function to compute eigenvalues of the iteration matrix $\mathbf{C}$ for the previous system, we find values of

$$3.4641 \quad \text{and} \quad -3.4641.$$

Clearly, Jacobi iteration is not suitable for this problem. The eigenvalues of the iteration matrix for the original ordering of the equations are

$$0.28868 \quad \text{and} \quad -0.28868.$$

Of course, we would not normally use an iterative method on such a small system, but the point is that the method will not converge for this simple example. (For further discussion of these results, see Atkinson, 1989, pp. 546–7.)

Each iteration of the Jacobi method requires one matrix–vector multiplication, or $(n-1)^2$ scalar multiplications. Thus, if the method converges in a reasonable number of iterations, the computational effort could be significantly less than the $\mathbb{O}(n^3)$ multiplications required for Gaussian elimination.

The Jacobi method is particularly convenient for parallel computation, because each component of the solution can be updated independently of the other components.

4.2 GAUSS–SEIDEL METHOD

The Gauss–Seidel method of solving linear systems is a simple iterative technique obtained by transforming the linear system $\mathbf{Ax} = \mathbf{b}$ into the system $\mathbf{x} = \mathbf{Cx} + \mathbf{d}$, in which the matrix $\mathbf{C}$ has zeros on the diagonal. However, in contrast to the Jacobi method, each component of the vector $\mathbf{x}$ on the right-hand side of the transformed equation is updated immediately as each iteration progresses. This procedure is called *sequential updating*.

Example 4.4 Graphical Illustration of the Gauss–Seidel Method

To visualize the Gauss–Seidel iterations, consider the two-by-two system introduced in Example 4.1; the equations are written as

$$x = -\frac{1}{2}y + 3,$$

$$y = -\frac{1}{2}x + 3.$$

The first iteration is illustrated in Fig. 4.3 for the starting values of $x^{(1)} = 1/2$ and $y^{(1)} = 1/2$. The first equation then produces the next estimate for x (using $y^{(1)}$), and the second equation is used to find the next value of y (using the newly computed value $x^{(2)}$). The result is

$$x^{(2)} = -\frac{1}{2}y^{(1)} + 3 = -\frac{1}{4} + 3 = \frac{11}{4},$$

$$y^{(2)} = -\frac{1}{2}x^{(2)} + 3 = -\frac{11}{8} + 3 = \frac{13}{8}.$$

Table 4.1 shows the first four steps of the iteration.

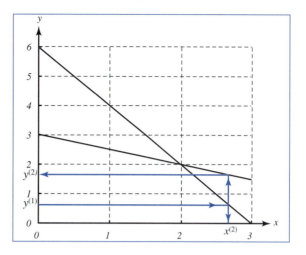

FIGURE 4.3 First step of Gauss–Seidel iteration.

Table 4.1 Four Steps of Gauss–Seidel Iteration

i	x	y
1	2.75	1.625
2	2.1875	1.9062
3	2.0469	1.9766
4	2.0117	1.9941

Example 4.5 Solving a Three-by-Three System Using Gauss–Seidel Iteration

Consider the three-by-three system of equations (as in Example 4.2)

$$2x_1 - x_2 + x_3 = -1,$$
$$x_1 + 2x_2 - x_3 = 6,$$
$$x_1 - x_2 + 2x_3 = -3,$$

which are converted to the iterative system

$$x_1^{(new)} = \phantom{-0.5x_1^{(new)}} + 0.5x_2^{(old)} - 0.5x_3^{(old)} -0.5,$$
$$x_2^{(new)} = -0.5x_1^{(new)} \phantom{+ 0.5x_2^{(old)}} + 0.5x_3^{(old)} + 3.0,$$
$$x_3^{(new)} = -0.5x_1^{(new)} + 0.5x_2^{(new)} \phantom{+ 0.5x_3^{(old)}} -1.5.$$

Note that the most recent estimate for each of the unknowns is used in evaluating the right-hand side of each equation.

Starting with $x^{(0)} = (0, 0, 0)$, we find

$$x_1 = \qquad\qquad (0.5)(0) \quad + (-0.5)(0) \quad - 0.5 = -0.5,$$

$$x_2 = (-0.5)(-0.5) \qquad\qquad + (0.5)(0) \quad + \quad 3 = 3.25,$$

$$x_3 = (-0.5)(-0.5) + (0.5)(3.25) \qquad\qquad - 1.5 = 0.375.$$

For the second iteration,

$$x_1 = \qquad\qquad (0.5)(3.25) \quad + (-0.5)(0.375) - 0.5 = 0.9375,$$

$$x_2 = (-0.5)(0.9375) \qquad\qquad + (0.5)(0.375) \quad + \quad 3 = 2.7188,$$

$$x_3 = (-0.5)(0.9375) + (0.5)(2.7188) \qquad\qquad - 1.5 = -0.6094.$$

The Gauss–Seidel method converges in 10 iterations to the vector

$$\mathbf{x} = [1.0001 \quad 1.9999 \quad -1.0001]'.$$

The stopping condition is that the Euclidean norm of the difference of the solutions between two successive iterations be less than 0.001.

As a transition to the general MATLAB function for the Gauss–Seidel method presented next, we illustrate the process for a general four-by-four system:

$$a_{11}x_1 + a_{12}x_2 + a_{13}x_3 + a_{14}x_4 = b_1,$$

$$a_{21}x_1 + a_{22}x_2 + a_{23}x_3 + a_{24}x_4 = b_2,$$

$$a_{31}x_1 + a_{32}x_2 + a_{33}x_3 + a_{34}x_4 = b_3,$$

$$a_{41}x_1 + a_{42}x_2 + a_{43}x_3 + a_{44}x_4 = b_4.$$

The iterative form of the equations is

$$x_1^{(new)} = \qquad\qquad -\frac{a_{12}}{a_{11}}x_2^{(old)} - \frac{a_{13}}{a_{11}}x_3^{(old)} - \frac{a_{14}}{a_{11}}x_4^{(old)} + \frac{b_1}{a_{11}},$$

$$x_2^{(new)} = -\frac{a_{21}}{a_{22}}x_1^{(new)} \qquad\qquad - \frac{a_{23}}{a_{22}}x_3^{(old)} - \frac{a_{24}}{a_{22}}x_4^{(old)} + \frac{b_2}{a_{22}},$$

$$x_3^{(new)} = -\frac{a_{31}}{a_{33}}x_1^{(new)} - \frac{a_{32}}{a_{33}}x_2^{(new)} \qquad\qquad - \frac{a_{34}}{a_{33}}x_4^{(old)} + \frac{b_3}{a_{33}},$$

$$x_4^{(new)} = -\frac{a_{41}}{a_{44}}x_2^{(new)} - \frac{a_{42}}{a_{44}}x_2^{(new)} - \frac{a_{43}}{a_{44}}x_3^{(new)} \qquad\qquad + \frac{b_4}{a_{44}}.$$

4.2.1 MATLAB Function for Gauss–Seidel Method

Note that the matrix $\mathbf{C}$ in the MATLAB function that follows does not represent the matrix used in the theoretical investigation of convergence.

```
function x = Seidel_f(A, b, x0, tol, max)
%   Solution of the system of linear equations Ax = b
%       using Gauss-Seidel iterative algorithm
%   Inputs :
%       A           coefficient matrix (n-by-n)
%       b           right-hand side (n-by-1)
%       x0          initial solution (n-by-1)
%       tol         stop if norm of change in x < tol.
%       max         maximum number of iterations
%   Outputs :
%       x           solution vector (n-by-1)
[ n, m ] = size(A);   x = x0;   C = -A;
for i = 1:n
   C(i,i) = 0;
end
for i = 1:n
   C(i,1:n) = C(i,1:n)/A(i,i);
end
for i = 1:n
   r(i,1) = b(i)/A(i,i);
end
i = 1;
disp('    i            x1          x2          x3      ....')
while (i <= max)
   xold = x;                % save solution from previous step
   for j = 1: n
      x(j) = C( j, : ) * x + r(j);
   end
   if norm(xold -x) <= tol
      disp('Gauss-Seidel method converged');
      return;
   end
   disp([ i       x' ])
   i = i + 1;
end
disp('Gauss-Seidel method did not converge');
```

Example 4.6 A Linear System That Comes from a PDE

For the linear system presented in Example 4-A, describing the numerical solution of the potential equation using finite differences (see Chapter 15), the Gauss–Seidel iterative method achieves the same solution as the Jacobi method (Example 4.3), but in 29 iterations rather than 51. The stopping condition is that the Euclidean norm of the difference between two successive iterates be $\leq 10^{-5}$.

4.2.2 Discussion

The Gauss–Seidel method is usually derived by converting the original system, $\mathbf{Ax} = \mathbf{b}$, into a decomposed form $(\mathbf{L} + \mathbf{D} + \mathbf{U})\,\mathbf{x} = \mathbf{b}$, where $\mathbf{D}$ is a diagonal matrix, $\mathbf{L}$ is a lower triangular matrix, and $\mathbf{U}$ is an upper triangular matrix. The decomposed form is expressed as $\mathbf{x} = \mathbf{Tx} + \mathbf{c}$ in the following way:

$$(\mathbf{D} + \mathbf{L})\mathbf{x} = -\mathbf{Ux} + \mathbf{b},$$

$$\mathbf{x} = (\mathbf{D} + \mathbf{L})^{-1}\,(-\mathbf{U})\mathbf{x} + (\mathbf{D} + \mathbf{L})^{-1}\mathbf{b},$$

$$\mathbf{x} = \mathbf{T}\,\mathbf{x} + \mathbf{c}.$$

Like the Jacobi method, the Gauss–Seidel method is sensitive to the form of the coefficient matrix $\mathbf{A}$ (or equivalently, to the form of the iteration matrix $\mathbf{T}$); reversing the order of the equations in Example 4.4 shows a divergence similar to that for the Jacobi method.

There are several useful theoretical results concerning the relationships between the characteristics of the matrix $\mathbf{A}$ (or the iteration matrix $\mathbf{T}$) and the convergence of Gauss–Seidel iteration for the system $\mathbf{Ax} = \mathbf{b}$. The matrix form of the Gauss–Seidel method is used primarily for analyzing the convergence of the method; however, general theoretical results that guarantee convergence (which depend on the eigenvalues of the matrix $\mathbf{T}$) are not necessarily the most convenient for important applications.

The numerical solution of partial differential equations (see Chapter 15) leads to linear systems in which the matrix $\mathbf{A}$ is real and symmetric, with positive diagonal elements. For such matrices, the Gauss–Seidel method will converge (for any $x^{(0)}$) if and only if all of the eigenvalues of $\mathbf{A}$ are real and positive. (See Atkinson, 1989, pp. 499, 551; a proof is given in Isaacson and Keller, 1966, pp. 70–71.) For an example that does not satisfy the symmetry requirement, theoretical analysis is more difficult to carry out.

If $\mathbf{A}$ is positive definite, Gauss–Seidel iteration converges for any initial vector. (For a proof of this result, see Ralston and Rabinowitz, 1978, p. 445.) We discuss some tests for positive definite matrices in the next section.

If the iteration matrix $\mathbf{C}$ for the Jacobi method is nonnegative (a situation that often occurs in the numerical solution of partial differential equations), then the Jacobi and Gauss–Seidel methods either both converge or both diverge; when they both converge, Gauss–Seidel iteration converges more rapidly (except in the trivial case when the largest eigenvalue of the iteration matrix for both methods is zero; see Ralston and Rabinowitz, 1978, p. 446.)

The Gauss–Seidel method typically converges more rapidly than the Jacobi method, although it is more difficult to use for parallel computation.

It is possible to modify the Gauss–Seidel method by introducing an additional parameter, ω (omega), that may accelerate the convergence of the iterations. The idea is to take a combination of the previous value of x and the current update (from the Gauss–Seidel method). The parameter ω controls the proportion of the update that comes from the previous solution and the proportion that comes from the current calculation. For $0 < \omega < 1$, the method is called successive underrelaxation; for $1 < \omega < 2$, the method is called successive over relaxation (SOR).

Consider the three-by-three system

$$a_{11}x_1 + a_{12}x_2 + a_{13}x_3 = b_1,$$
$$a_{21}x_1 + a_{22}x_2 + a_{23}x_3 = b_2,$$
$$a_{31}x_1 + a_{32}x_2 + a_{33}x_3 = b_3.$$

The SOR equations are

$$x_1^{(new)} = (1 - \omega)x_1^{(old)} + \frac{\omega}{a_{11}}(b_1 - a_{12}x_2^{(old)} - a_{13}x_3^{(old)}),$$

$$x_2^{(new)} = (1 - \omega)x_2^{(old)} + \frac{\omega}{a_{22}}(b_2 - a_{21}x_1^{(new)} - a_{23}x_3^{(old)}),$$

$$x_3^{(new)} = (1 - \omega)x_3^{(old)} + \frac{\omega}{a_{33}}(b_3 - a_{31}x_1^{(new)} - a_{32}x_2^{(new)}).$$

The right-hand side of each equation is a linear combination of the previous estimate for all components of x and the estimate used in the Gauss–Seidel method. For $\omega = 1$, SOR reduces to the Gauss–Seidel method.

Example 4.7 Solving a Three-by-Three System Using SOR

Consider the three–by-three system $\mathbf{Ax} = \mathbf{b}$, where

$$\mathbf{A} = \begin{bmatrix} 4 & -2 & 0 \\ -2 & 6 & -5 \\ 0 & -5 & 11 \end{bmatrix}, \qquad \mathbf{b} = [8 \quad -29 \quad 43]'.$$

The system is converted to

$$x_1 = (1 - \omega)x_1^{(old)} + \omega\left(\qquad + \frac{1}{2}x_2^{(old)} + \qquad + 2 \right),$$

$$x_2 = (1 - \omega)x_2^{(old)} + \omega\left(\frac{1}{3}x_1^{(new)} \qquad + \frac{5}{6}x_3^{(old)} - \frac{29}{6} \right),$$

$$x_3 = (1 - \omega)x_3^{(old)} + \omega\left(\qquad + \frac{5}{11}x_2^{(new)} \qquad + \frac{43}{11} \right).$$

We illustrate the first iteration, using $\omega = 1.2$.

Starting with $x^{(0)} = (0, 0, 0)$, we find

$$x_1 = -0.8(0) + 1.2 \qquad\qquad + (1/2)(0) \qquad\qquad\qquad + 2 \qquad = 2.4,$$

$$x_2 = -0.8(0) + 1.2(1/3)(2.4) + \qquad\qquad\qquad + (5/6)(0) - 29/6 \quad = -4.84,$$

$$x_3 = -0.8(0) + 1.2 \qquad\qquad + (5/11)(-4.84) \qquad\qquad + 43/11 = 2.05.$$

Results from the MATLAB function presented in Section 4.3.1 are shown in Table 4.2.

Table 4.2 Results for SOR Iterations

i	x_1	x_2	x_3
1	2.4	−4.84	2.0509
2	−0.984	−3.1747	2.5491
3	0.69199	−2.3392	2.9052
4	0.85809	−2.0838	2.9733
5	0.97813	−2.0187	2.9951
6	0.99314	−2.0039	2.9989
7	0.99905	−2.0007	2.9998

The stopping condition is that the Euclidean norm of the difference of the solutions betweeen two successive iterations be less than tol = 0.001.

Example 4.8 A Linear System of PDEs

We investigate the convergence of the boundary value problem discussed in Examples 4.3 and 4.6, with $x^{(0)} = [0\ 0 \ldots 0]'$ and tolerance = 0.00001 for several values of ω. Of course, for $\omega = 1$, the SOR method is the same as Gauss–Seidel iteration. The required number of iterations for selected values of ω are shown in Table 4.3.

Table 4.3 Required Number of Iterations for Different Values of the Relaxation Parameter

ω	0.8	0.9	1.0	1.2	1.25	1.3	1.4
No. of iterations	44	36	29	18	15	13	16

4.3.1 MATLAB Function for SOR

```
function x = SOR_f(A, b, x0, w, tol, max)
%   Solution of the system of linear equations
%      Ax = b
%   using SOR iterative algorithm
%   Inputs :
%      A          coefficient matrix (n-by-n)
```

```
%       b           right-hand side (n-by-1)
%       x0          initial solution (n-by-1)
%       tol         stop if norm of change in x < tol.
%       max         maximum number of iterations
%   Outputs :
%       x           solution vector (n-by-1)
[ n, m ] = size(A);   x = x0;   C = -A;
for i = 1:n
    C(i,i) = 0;
end
for i = 1:n
    C(i,1:n) = C(i,1:n)/A(i,i);
end
for i = 1:n
    r(i,1) = b(i)/A(i,i);
end
i = 1;
disp('    i         x1          x2          x3      . . .')
while (i <= max)
    xold = x;               % save solution from previous step
    for j = 1: n
        x(j) = (1-w)*xold(j) + w*(C(j, :) * x + r(j)) ;
    end
    if norm(xold -x) <= tol
        disp('SOR method converged');
        return;
    end
    disp([ i        x' ])
    i = i + 1;
end
disp('SOR method did not converge');
```

4.3.2 Discussion

The SOR method can be derived by multiplying the decomposed system obtained from the Gauss–Seidel method by the relaxation parameter ω, i.e.,

$$\omega(\mathbf{D} + \mathbf{L})\mathbf{x} = -\omega\mathbf{U}\mathbf{x} + \omega\mathbf{b},$$

and adding $(1 - \omega)\mathbf{D}\mathbf{x}$ to each side of the equation. This gives

$$(\mathbf{D} - \omega\mathbf{L})\mathbf{x} = ((1 - \omega)\mathbf{D} - \omega\mathbf{U})\mathbf{x} + \omega\mathbf{b},$$

which can be solved for $\mathbf{x}$ (for purposes of analysis) to obtain

$$\mathbf{x} = (\mathbf{D} - \omega\mathbf{L})^{-1}((1 - \omega)\mathbf{D} + \omega\mathbf{U})\mathbf{x} + \omega(\mathbf{D} - \omega\mathbf{L})^{-1}\mathbf{b}.$$

The SOR iteration matrix is $\mathbf{C} = (\mathbf{D} - \omega\mathbf{L})^{-1}((1 - \omega)\mathbf{D} + \omega\mathbf{U})$. It can be shown that det $\mathbf{C} = (1 - \omega)^n$. Since the determinant of a matrix is equal to the product of its eigenvalues, at least one eigenvalue of $\mathbf{C}$ must be greater than or equal to 1 in absolute value if either $\omega \leq 0$ or $\omega \geq 2$. Therefore, the iteration parameter ω should always be chosen such that $0 < \omega < 2$.

Given an approximate solution $\mathbf{x}^{(k)}$ to the linear system $\mathbf{A}\mathbf{x} = \mathbf{b}$, the residual vector $\mathbf{r}$ is defined to be $\mathbf{r} = \mathbf{b} - \mathbf{A}\mathbf{x}^{(k)}$. The SOR method is designed to reduce the residual vector more rapidly than the Gauss–Seidel method does. (See Golub and Ortega, 1992, p. 299.)

4.3.3 Some Useful Theoretical Results

It is always important to consider whether an iterative process will converge to a solution. The Ostrowski theorem gives some information on the convergence of the SOR method for an important class of matrices, namely, positive definite matrices.

Ostrowski Theorem

If $\mathbf{A}$ is a positive definite matrix and $0 < \omega < 2$, then the SOR method will converge for any initial vector $\mathbf{x}$. (See Golub and Ortega, 1992, p. 298.)

The matrix $\mathbf{A}$ is *positive definite* if $\mathbf{x}'\mathbf{A}\mathbf{x} > 0$ for any vector $\mathbf{x}$ that is not the zero vector. Unfortunately, this definition does not provide a convenient way to check whether a particular matrix is positive definite. Since symmetric matrices occur in many applications for which SOR is important, we summarize a few useful results for testing whether a symmetric matrix is positive definite.

Necessary and Sufficient Tests for a Positive Definite Matrix

For a real, symmetric matrix $\mathbf{A}$, each of the following tests is a necessary and sufficient condition for $\mathbf{A}$ to be positive definite:

$\mathbf{x}^T\mathbf{A}\mathbf{x} > 0$ for all $\mathbf{x} \neq \mathbf{0}$.

All eigenvalues of $\mathbf{A}$ are positive.

All upper left submatrices of $\mathbf{A}$ have positive determinants.

All pivots of $\mathbf{A}$ (without row interchanges) are positive.

(See Strang, 1988, p. 331.)

Another Test for a Positive Definite Matrix

A symmetric matrix is positive definite if it is diagonally dominant and each diagonal element is positive. (Golub and Van Loan, 1996, p. 141.)

Test to Exclude Matrix from Being Positive Definite

If **A** is symmetric and positive definite, then

1. **A** is nonsingular.
2. $a_{ii} > 0$ for $i = 1, \ldots, n$.
3. $a_{ii}a_{jj} > (a_{ij})^2$ for $i \neq j$.

(Faires and Burden, 1998, p. 276.)

Tridiagonal coefficient matrices occur in connection with finite-difference methods for solving boundary value problems (cf. Chapter 14), some finite-difference methods for solving partial differential equations (cf. Chapter 15), and cubic spline interpolation (cf. Chapter 8). A useful result pertaining to such matrices is the following.

Optimal ω for Tridiagonal, Positive Definite Matrix

If **A** is positive definite and tridiagonal, then the optimal ω is

$$\omega = \frac{2}{1 + \sqrt{1 - \rho^2}}$$

where ρ is the eigenvalue of largest magnitude of the iteration matrix for the Jacobi method.

4.4   MATLAB's METHODS

MATLAB provides functions for iteratively solving the linear system $\mathbf{Ax} = \mathbf{b}$ using the preconditioned conjugate gradients method, the biconjugate gradients method, the conjugate gradients squared method, the generalized minimum residual method, and the quasi-minimal residual method. These methods make fewer assumptions about the structure of the matrix **A** than do the methods presented in this chapter. For each of the conjugate gradients methods, the basic call to the appropriate function requires only the matrix **A** and the right-hand side **b** as input. The user can supply the stopping tolerance, the maximum number of iterations, a preconditioning matrix, or the initial estimate of the solution if any of these is desired. The default initial estimate is the zero vector. Convergence is achieved when the iterated solution has a relative residual `norm(b - Ax)/norm(b)` less than or equal to a specified tolerance. (The default tolerance is 10^{-6}.) The default maximum number of iterations is the minimum of n and 20. The details of these methods are beyond the scope of this text, but the characteristics of each function are summarized briefly here, with suggestions for further reading. (For more information, see the on-line help for each function.)

For the preconditioned conjugate gradients method, the matrix **A** must be symmetric and positive definite. The basic call for this function is x = pcg(A, b). For the system given in Example 4.7, pcg converged at iteration 3 to a solution with relative residual 1.4e-16; **x** = [1, −2, 3]′. For a user-specified stopping tolerance, the call is x = pcg(A, b, tol). For a user-specified tolerance and maximum number of iterations, the syntax is x = pcg(A, b, tol, maxit). The function pcg can also be used with a user-supplied symmetric positive definite (left) preconditioner **M**; the syntax is x = pcg(A, b, tol, maxit, M). If a preconditioner is given, the function solves the system $M^{-1} A x = M^{-1} b$ for **x**. To supply an initial estimate x_0 of the solution vector, the function is called as x = pcg(A, b, tol, maxit, M, x0). (For a discussion of conjugate gradient methods and preconditioning, see Golub and Ortega, 1992, pp. 300–303.)

There are forms of the biconjugate gradients method corresponding to each of the options for the conjugate gradients method just summarized. The basic call is x = bicg(A, b). (For a discussion of the biconjugate gradients method, see Golub and Van Loan, 1996, pp. 550–551.) There are also stabilized forms of each of the options for the biconjugate gradients method. The function is bicgstab. (For a discussion of stabilized biconjugate gradient methods, see Freund, Golub, and Nachtigal, 1992, pp. 81–82.) The conjugate gradients squared method is implemented in the function cgs. (See Freund et al., 1992, pp. 81–83.)

The generalized minimum residual method, GMRES, is implemented in the function gmres. The user may instruct the method to restart after the number of iterations specified by the parameter restart by calling the function as x = gmres(A, b, restart); the default value of restart is *n*, in which case the method does not actually restart at all. (See Freund et al., 1992, pp. 66–68.) There are forms of the quasi-minimal residual method, QMR, corresponding to each of the options for the methods summarized. The basic call is x = qmr(A,b). (See Freund et al., 1992, pp. 76–79.)

SUMMARY

In this chapter, we solve the linear system **Ax** = **b** iteratively by converting it into an equivalent system **x** = **Cx** + **d** to generate a sequence of approximations $\mathbf{x}^{(1)}, \mathbf{x}^{(2)}, \ldots$, according to the formula $\mathbf{x}^{(k)} = \mathbf{C}\mathbf{x}^{(k-1)} + \mathbf{d}$. The *i*th equation is solved explicitly for the *i*th component of **x**.

Jacobi Method (p. 111): The equations (illustrated for $N = 4$) are

$$x_1^{(k)} = \qquad\qquad -\frac{a_{12}}{a_{11}} x_2^{(k-1)} - \frac{a_{13}}{a_{11}} x_3^{(k-1)} - \frac{a_{14}}{a_{11}} x_4^{(k-1)} + \frac{b_1}{a_{11}},$$

$$x_2^{(k)} = -\frac{a_{21}}{a_{22}} x_1^{(k-1)} \qquad\qquad -\frac{a_{23}}{a_{22}} x_3^{(k-1)} - \frac{a_{24}}{a_{22}} x_4^{(k-1)} + \frac{b_2}{a_{22}},$$

$$x_3^{(k)} = -\frac{a_{31}}{a_{33}} x_1^{(k-1)} - \frac{a_{32}}{a_{33}} x_2^{(k-1)} \qquad\qquad -\frac{a_{34}}{a_{33}} x_4^{(k-1)} + \frac{b_3}{a_{33}},$$

$$x_4^{(k)} = -\frac{a_{41}}{a_{44}} x_1^{(k-1)} - \frac{a_{42}}{a_{44}} x_2^{(k-1)} - \frac{a_{43}}{a_{44}} x_3^{(k-1)} \qquad\qquad + \frac{b_4}{a_{44}}.$$

Gauss–Seidel Method (p. 118): The equations (shown for $n = 4$) are

$$x_1^{(k)} = \quad\quad -\frac{a_{12}}{a_{11}}x_2^{(k-1)} - \frac{a_{13}}{a_{11}}x_3^{(k-1)} - \frac{a_{14}}{a_{11}}x_4^{(k-1)} + \frac{b_1}{a_{11}},$$

$$x_2^{(k)} = -\frac{a_{21}}{a_{22}}x_1^{(k)} \quad\quad -\frac{a_{23}}{a_{22}}x_3^{(k-1)} - \frac{a_{24}}{a_{22}}x_4^{(k-1)} + \frac{b_2}{a_{22}},$$

$$x_3^{(k)} = -\frac{a_{31}}{a_{33}}x_1^{(k)} - \frac{a_{32}}{a_{33}}x_2^{(k)} \quad\quad -\frac{a_{34}}{a_{33}}x_4^{(k-1)} + \frac{b_3}{a_{33}},$$

$$x_4^{(k)} = -\frac{a_{41}}{a_{44}}x_1^{(k)} - \frac{a_{42}}{a_{44}}x_2^{(k)} - \frac{a_{43}}{a_{44}}x_3^{(k)} \quad\quad + \frac{b_4}{a_{44}}.$$

SOR method (p. 123): For the relaxation parameter ω satisfying $1 < \omega < 2$, we have the equations (for $n = 4$)

$$x_1^{(k)} = (1 - \omega)x_1^{(k-1)} + \frac{\omega}{a_{11}}(b_1 \quad\quad - a_{12}x_2^{(k-1)} - a_{13}x_3^{(k-1)} - a_{14}x_4^{(k-1)}),$$

$$x_2^{(k)} = (1 - \omega)x_2^{(k-1)} + \frac{\omega}{a_{22}}(b_2 - a_{21}x_1^{(k)} \quad\quad - a_{23}x_3^{(k-1)} - a_{24}x_4^{(k-1)}),$$

$$x_3^{(k)} = (1 - \omega)x_3^{(k-1)} + \frac{\omega}{a_{33}}(b_3 - a_{31}x_1^{(k)} - a_{32}x_2^{(k-1)} \quad\quad - a_{34}x_4^{(k)} \quad),$$

$$x_4^{(k)} = (1 - \omega)x_4^{(k-1)} + \frac{\omega}{a_{44}}(b_4 - a_{41}x_1^{(k)} - a_{42}x_2^{(k)} \quad - a_{43}x_3^{(k)} \quad\quad).$$

SUGGESTIONS FOR FURTHER READING

For further discussions of matrix computation, see the following texts:

> Golub, G. H., and C. F. Van Loan, *Matrix Computations* (3d ed.), Johns Hopkins University Press, Baltimore, 1996.

> Coleman, T. F., and C. Van Loan, *Handbook for Matrix Computations,* SIAM, Philadelphia, 1988.

For a discussion of the conjugate gradients methods implemented in MATLAB's built-in functions and a discussion of the relationship between iterative and direct methods, see the following sources:

> Freund, R. W., G. H. Golub, and N. M. Nachtigal, "Iterative Solution of Linear Systems," *Acta Numerica I,* 1992, pp. 57–100.

> Forsythe, G. E., M. A. Malcolm, and C. B. Moler, *Computer Methods for Mathematical Computations,* Prentice-Hall, Englewood Cliffs, NJ, 1977.

The following are excellent references for applied linear algebra:

> Strang, G., *Linear Algebra and Its Applications,* (3d ed.), Harcourt Brace Jovanovich, San Diego, CA, 1988.

Hager, W. W., *Applied Numerical Linear Algebra,* Prentice-Hall, Englewood Cliffs, NJ, 1988.

Datta, B. N., *Numerical Linear Algebra and Applications,* Brooks Cole, Pacific Grove, CA, 1995.

For more advanced discussion of iterative methods for linear systems, see the following texts:

Greenbaum, A., *Iterative Methods for Solving Linear Systems,* SIAM, Philadelphia, 1997.

Barrett, R., J. Donato, J. Dongarra, V. Eijkhout, R. Pozo, C. Romine, and H. van der Vorst, *Templates for the Solution of Linear Systems: Building Blocks for Iterative Methods,* SIAM, Philadelphia, 1993.

PRACTICE THE TECHNIQUES

For problems P4.1–P4.5, approximate the solution of the system $\mathbf{Ax} = \mathbf{b}$, *iteratively (if possible); let* $x^{(0)} = [0, 0, 0]'$.

   a. Use Jacobi iteration, and perform three iterations by hand.

   b. Use Gauss–Seidel iteration, and perform three iterations by hand.

   c. Use Jacobi iteration, and perform 10 iterations with a MATLAB function.

   d. Use Gauss–Seidel iteration and perform 10 iterations with a MATLAB function.

P4.1 $\mathbf{A} = \begin{bmatrix} 10 & -2 & 1 \\ -2 & 10 & -2 \\ -2 & -5 & 10 \end{bmatrix}$, $\mathbf{b} = \begin{bmatrix} 9 \\ 12 \\ 18 \end{bmatrix}$.

P4.2 $\mathbf{A} = \begin{bmatrix} 4 & 1 & 0 \\ 1 & 3 & -1 \\ 1 & 0 & 2 \end{bmatrix}$, $\mathbf{b} = \begin{bmatrix} 3 \\ -4 \\ 5 \end{bmatrix}$.

P4.3 $\mathbf{A} = \begin{bmatrix} 5 & -1 & 0 \\ -1 & 5 & -1 \\ 0 & -1 & 5 \end{bmatrix}$, $\mathbf{b} = \begin{bmatrix} 9 \\ 4 \\ -6 \end{bmatrix}$.

P4.4 $\mathbf{A} = \begin{bmatrix} 8 & 1 & -1 \\ -1 & 7 & -2 \\ 2 & 1 & 9 \end{bmatrix}$, $\mathbf{b} = \begin{bmatrix} 8 \\ 4 \\ 12 \end{bmatrix}$.

P4.5 $\mathbf{A} = \begin{bmatrix} 4 & 1 & 0 \\ 1 & 3 & -1 \\ 0 & -1 & 4 \end{bmatrix}$, $\mathbf{b} = \begin{bmatrix} 3 \\ 4 \\ 5 \end{bmatrix}$.

For Problems P4.6–P4.18, approximate the solution of the system $\mathbf{Ax} = \mathbf{b}$ *iteratively; unless otherwise indicated, let* $\mathbf{x}^{(0)} = [0, 0, 0]'$.

   a. Use Jacobi iteration, and perform 10 iterations with a MATLAB function.

   b. Use Gauss–Seidel iteration, and perform 10 iterations with a MATLAB function.

   c. Use SOR with $\omega = 1.25$, $\omega = 1.5$, $\omega = 1.75$, and $\omega = 1.9$.

P4.6 $\mathbf{A} = \begin{bmatrix} -2 & 1 & 0 & 0 \\ 1 & -2 & 1 & 0 \\ 0 & 1 & -2 & 1 \\ 0 & 0 & 1 & -2 \end{bmatrix}$, $\mathbf{b} = \begin{bmatrix} -1 \\ 0 \\ 0 \\ 0 \end{bmatrix}$.

P4.7 $\mathbf{A} = \begin{bmatrix} 5 & 1 & 0 & 0 \\ 1 & 5 & 1 & 0 \\ 0 & 1 & 5 & 1 \\ 0 & 0 & 1 & 5 \end{bmatrix}$, $\mathbf{b} = \begin{bmatrix} 33 \\ 26 \\ 30 \\ 15 \end{bmatrix}$.

P4.8 $\mathbf{A} = \begin{bmatrix} 1 & 2 & 0 & 0 \\ 2 & 6 & 8 & 0 \\ 0 & 8 & 35 & 18 \\ 0 & 0 & 18 & 112 \end{bmatrix}$,

$\mathbf{b} = [2 \quad 6 \quad -10 \quad -112]'$;
(the optimal value is $\omega = 1.9387$.)

P4.9 $\mathbf{A} = \begin{bmatrix} 4 & 8 & 0 & 0 \\ 8 & 18 & 2 & 0 \\ 0 & 2 & 5 & 1.5 \\ 0 & 0 & 1.5 & 1.75 \end{bmatrix}$,

$\mathbf{b} = [8 \quad 18 \quad 0.50 \quad -1.75]'$;
(the optimal value is $\omega = 1.634$.)

P4.10 $\mathbf{A} = \begin{bmatrix} 4 & -8 & 0 & 0 \\ -8 & 18 & -2 & 0 \\ 0 & -2 & 5 & -1.5 \\ 0 & 0 & -1.5 & 1.75 \end{bmatrix}$,

$\mathbf{b} = [-12 \quad 22 \quad 5 \quad 2]'$;
(the optimal value is $\omega = 1.634$.)

P4.11 $\mathbf{A} = \begin{bmatrix} 1 & -2 & 0 & 0 \\ -2 & 5 & -1 & 0 \\ 0 & -1 & 2 & -0.5 \\ 0 & 0 & -0.5 & 1.25 \end{bmatrix}$,

$\mathbf{b} = [-3 \quad 5 \quad 2 \quad 3.5]'$;
(the optimal value is $\omega = 1.5431$.)

P4.12 $\mathbf{A} = \begin{bmatrix} 1 & -2 & 0 & 0 & 0 \\ -2 & 5 & 1 & 0 & 0 \\ 0 & 1 & 2 & -2 & 0 \\ 0 & 0 & -2 & 5 & 1 \\ 0 & 0 & 0 & 1 & 2 \end{bmatrix}$,

$\mathbf{b} = [5 \quad -9 \quad 0 \quad 3 \quad 0]'$;
(the optimal value is $\omega = 1.7684$.)

P4.13 $\mathbf{A} = \begin{bmatrix} 1 & -2 & 0 & 0 & 0 \\ -2 & 6 & 4 & 0 & 0 \\ 0 & 4 & 9 & -0.5 & 0 \\ 0 & 0 & -0.5 & 1.25 & 0.5 \\ 0 & 0 & 0 & 0.5 & 3.25 \end{bmatrix}$,

$\mathbf{b} = [5 \quad -2 \quad 18 \quad 0.5 \quad -2.25]'$;
(the optimal value is $\omega = 1.7064$.)

P4.14 $\mathbf{A} = \begin{bmatrix} 1 & -2 & 0 & 0 & 0 & 0 \\ -2 & 6 & 4 & 0 & 0 & 0 \\ 0 & 4 & 9 & -0.5 & 0 & 0 \\ 0 & 0 & -0.5 & 3.25 & 1.5 & 0 \\ 0 & 0 & 0 & 1.5 & 1.75 & -3 \\ 0 & 0 & 0 & 0 & -3 & 13 \end{bmatrix}$,

$\mathbf{b} = [-3 \quad 22 \quad 35.5 \quad -7.75 \quad 4 \quad -33]'$;
(the optimal value is $\omega = 1.7113$.)

P4.15 $\mathbf{A} = \begin{bmatrix} 7.63 & 0.3 & 0.15 & 0.5 & 0.34 & 0.84 \\ 0.38 & 6.4 & 0.7 & 0.9 & 0.29 & 0.57 \\ 0.83 & 0.19 & 8.33 & 0.82 & 0.34 & 0.37 \\ 0.5 & 0.68 & 0.86 & 10.21 & 0.53 & 0.7 \\ 0.71 & 0.3 & 0.85 & 0.82 & 5.95 & 0.55 \\ 0.43 & 0.54 & 0.59 & 0.66 & 0.31 & 9.25 \end{bmatrix}$,

$\mathbf{b} = [-9.44 \quad 25.27 \quad -48.01 \quad 19.76 \quad -23.63 \quad 62.59]'$;

P4.16 $\mathbf{A} = \begin{bmatrix} 85.57 & 0.46 & 0.92 & 0.41 & 0.14 & 0.02 \\ 0.23 & 52.53 & 0.74 & 0.89 & 0.2 & 0.75 \\ 0.61 & 0.82 & 20.44 & 0.06 & 0.2 & 0.45 \\ 0.49 & 0.44 & 0.41 & 67.57 & 0.6 & 0.93 \\ 0.89 & 0.62 & 0.94 & 0.81 & 84.08 & 0.47 \\ 0.76 & 0.79 & 0.92 & 0.01 & 0.2 & 2.38 \end{bmatrix}$,

$\mathbf{b} = [85.61 \quad -267.18 \quad 54.91 \quad -140.66 \quad 331.55 \quad -18.69]'$

P4.17 $\mathbf{A} = \begin{bmatrix} 14.38 & 0.59 & 0.44 & 0.12 & 0.8 & 0.84 & 0.39 & 0.16 \\ 0.09 & 81.93 & 0.35 & 0.45 & 0.91 & 0.17 & 0.59 & 0.87 \\ 0.04 & 0.37 & 43.17 & 0.72 & 0.23 & 0.17 & 0.12 & 0.24 \\ 0.61 & 0.63 & 0.68 & 89.93 & 0.24 & 0.99 & 0.04 & 0.65 \\ 0.61 & 0.72 & 0.7 & 0.27 & 73.54 & 0.44 & 0.46 & 0.97 \\ 0.02 & 0.69 & 0.73 & 0.25 & 0.08 & 69.07 & 0.87 & 0.66 \\ 0.02 & 0.08 & 0.48 & 0.87 & 0.64 & 0.31 & 35.55 & 0.87 \\ 0.19 & 0.45 & 0.55 & 0.23 & 0.19 & 0.37 & 0.26 & 16.61 \end{bmatrix}$,

$\mathbf{b} = [23.49 \quad 87.25 \quad 170.88 \quad -530.36 \quad 227.13 \quad 141.59 \quad -136.83 \quad 117.43]$

P4.18 $\mathbf{A} = \begin{bmatrix} 10 & 0 & 1 & 0 & 0 & 0 & 0 & 0 \\ 0 & 10 & 0 & 0 & 0 & 0 & -1 & 0 \\ 0 & 0 & 10 & 0 & 0 & -2 & 0 & 0 \\ 2 & 0 & 0 & 10 & 0 & 0 & 0 & 0 \\ 0 & 0 & 1 & 0 & 10 & 0 & 0 & 0 \\ 0 & 0 & 0 & -3 & 0 & 10 & 0 & 0 \\ 0 & 3 & 0 & 0 & 0 & 0 & 10 & 0 \\ 0 & 0 & 0 & 0 & 1 & 0 & 0 & 10 \end{bmatrix}$,

$\mathbf{b} = [13 \quad 13 \quad 18 \quad 42 \quad 53 \quad 48 \quad 76 \quad 85]'$

EXPLORE SOME APPLICATIONS

A4.1 A script for the single-triangle truss is given in the following m-file. (note that the order of the last two equations has been reversed to improve diagonal dominance):

$$a = \pi/6;$$

$$b = \pi/6$$

$$T = \begin{bmatrix} 1 & 0 & 0 & 0 & \sin(a) & 0 \\ 0 & 1 & 0 & 1 & \cos(a) & 0 \\ 0 & 0 & 1 & 0 & 0 & \sin(b) \\ 0 & 0 & 0 & -1 & 0 & -\cos(b) \\ 0 & 0 & 0 & 0 & -\cos(a) & \cos(b) \\ 0 & 0 & 0 & 0 & -\sin(a) & -\sin(b) \end{bmatrix}$$

$$b = [0 \ 0 \ 0 \ 0 \ 0 \ 10]'$$

$$x0 = \text{zeros } (6,1)$$

$$\text{max\_iter} = 25$$

$$\text{tol} = 0.0001$$

$$x = \text{jacobi } (T, b, x0, \text{tol, max\_iter, tol})$$

A4.2 Iterative methods may be useful for systems that have a few small non-zero elements outside of a fairly pronounced banded structure (such elements prevent the application of the Thomas method and cause extensive fill in the lower triangular portion of the coefficient matrix if Gaussian elimination is used). For example, solve $\mathbf{Ax} = \mathbf{b}$:

$$\mathbf{A} =$$

$$\begin{bmatrix} -2.9 & 0.9 & 0 & 0 & 0 & 0.01 & 0 & 0 & 0 & 0 \\ 1.0 & -2.9 & 0.9 & 0 & 0 & 0 & 0 & 0 & 0.01 & 0 \\ 0 & 1.0 & -2.9 & 0.9 & 0 & 0 & 0 & 0 & 0 & 0 \\ 0 & 0 & 1.0 & -2.9 & 0.9 & 0 & 0 & 0 & 0 & 0 \\ 0.01 & 0 & 0 & 1.0 & -2.9 & 0.9 & 0 & 0 & 0 & 0 \\ 0 & 0 & 0 & 0 & 1.00 & -2.9 & 0.9 & 0 & 0 & 0 \\ 0 & 0 & 0 & 0 & 0 & 1.0 & -2.9 & 0.9 & 0 & 0 \\ 0 & 0 & 0.01 & 0 & 0 & 0 & 1.0 & -2.9 & 0.9 & 0 \\ 0.01 & 0 & 0 & 0 & 0 & 0 & 0 & 1.0 & -2.9 & 0.9 \\ 0 & 0 & 0 & 0 & 0 & 0 & 0 & 0 & 1.0 & -2.9 \end{bmatrix}$$

b =
[−0.1395 −0.080 −0.153 −0.173 −0.1842 −0.255 −0.296 −0.3826 −0.3492 −1.05]

A4.3 Modify the right hand side of Example 4.3 as follows (this reflects adding a strong heat source in the PDE as discussed in Chapter 15)

b = [0.08 0.16 0.36 1.64 0.16 0.0 25 1.0 0.36 0.0 0.0 1.0 1.64 1.0 1.0 2.0]'

A4.4 Modify the right hand side of Example 4.3 as follows (this reflects different boundary conditions)

b = [0.208 0.4 0.6 1.8 0.264 0.0 0.0 1.0 0.216 0.0 0.0 1.0 1.512 1.0 1.0 2.0]'

A4.5 The following linear system corresponds to the finite difference solution to a PDE, with unequal spacing in the x and y directions.

$$\mathbf{A} = \begin{bmatrix} -68 & 9 & 25 & 0 & 0 & 0 & 0 & 0 \\ 9 & -68 & 0 & 25 & 0 & 0 & 0 & 0 \\ 25 & 0 & -68 & 9 & 25 & 0 & 0 & 0 \\ 0 & 25 & 9 & -68 & 0 & 25 & 0 & 0 \\ 0 & 0 & 25 & 0 & -68 & 9 & 25 & 0 \\ 0 & 0 & 0 & 25 & 9 & -68 & 0 & 25 \\ 0 & 0 & 0 & 0 & 25 & 0 & -68 & 9 \\ 0 & 0 & 0 & 0 & 0 & 25 & 9 & -68 \end{bmatrix}$$

b = [−25.6667 −8.6933 −8.0 −1.44 −9.0 −3.24 −34.0 −30.76]'

EXPAND YOUR UNDERSTANDING

U4.1 For each of the linear systems in problems P3.1–P3.5, determine whether **A** is strictly diagonally dominant. Also, if possible, solve the system of equations using the iterative methods presented in this chapter.

For problems U4.2–U4.6, write the linear system $\mathbf{Ax} = \mathbf{b}$ in the explicit iterative form for the Jacobi method, i.e., $\mathbf{x} = \mathbf{Tx} + \mathbf{c}$, where $\mathbf{A} = \mathbf{D} - \mathbf{L} - \mathbf{U}$ and $\mathbf{T} = \mathbf{D}^{-1}(\mathbf{L} + \mathbf{U})$; find the eigenvalues of $\mathbf{T}$ using the MATLAB function *"eig". For those problems to which the theorems apply, find the optimal SOR parameter.*

U4.2 $\mathbf{A} = \begin{bmatrix} 10 & -2 & 1 \\ -2 & 10 & -2 \\ -2 & -5 & 10 \end{bmatrix}$, $\mathbf{b} = \begin{bmatrix} 9 \\ 12 \\ 18 \end{bmatrix}$.

U4.3 $\mathbf{A} = \begin{bmatrix} 5 & -1 & 0 \\ -1 & 5 & -1 \\ 0 & -1 & 5 \end{bmatrix}$, $\mathbf{b} = \begin{bmatrix} 9 \\ 4 \\ -6 \end{bmatrix}$.

U4.4 $\mathbf{A} = \begin{bmatrix} 4 & 1 & 0 \\ 1 & 3 & -1 \\ 0 & -1 & 4 \end{bmatrix}$, $\mathbf{b} = \begin{bmatrix} 3 \\ 4 \\ 5 \end{bmatrix}$.

U4.5 $\mathbf{A} = \begin{bmatrix} -2 & 1 & 0 & 0 \\ 1 & -2 & 1 & 0 \\ 0 & 1 & -2 & 1 \\ 0 & 0 & 1 & -2 \end{bmatrix}$, $\mathbf{b} = \begin{bmatrix} -1 \\ 0 \\ 0 \\ 0 \end{bmatrix}$.

U4.6 $\mathbf{A} = \begin{bmatrix} 5 & 1 & 0 & 0 \\ 1 & 5 & 1 & 0 \\ 0 & 1 & 5 & 1 \\ 0 & 0 & 1 & 5 \end{bmatrix}$, $\mathbf{b} = \begin{bmatrix} 33 \\ 26 \\ 30 \\ 15 \end{bmatrix}$.

U4.7 Suppose Jacobi's method is used for the linear system $\mathbf{Ax} = \mathbf{b}$, with

$$\mathbf{A} = \begin{bmatrix} 4 & 12 & 8 & 4 \\ 1 & 7 & 18 & 9 \\ 2 & 9 & 20 & 20 \\ 3 & 11 & 15 & 14 \end{bmatrix}, \quad \mathbf{b} = \begin{bmatrix} -4 \\ -5 \\ -25 \\ -18 \end{bmatrix}.$$

Perform two iterations and discuss the expected results.

U4.8 Other decompositions of the matrix $\mathbf{A}$ may be appropriate for solving the system $\mathbf{Ax} = \mathbf{b}$ iteratively when $\mathbf{A}$ has a special structure. In particular, if $\mathbf{A} = \mathbf{B} + \mathbf{C}$, where $\mathbf{B}$ is tridiagonal and the elements of $\mathbf{C}$ are small, consider the iterative scheme

$$\mathbf{Ax} = \mathbf{b},$$

$$(\mathbf{B} + \mathbf{C})\mathbf{x} = \mathbf{b},$$

$$\mathbf{Bx} = -\mathbf{Cx} + \mathbf{b}.$$

The method will converge if the elements of $\mathbf{C}$ are sufficiently small so that $\|\mathbf{B}^{-1}\mathbf{C}\| < 1$. The usefulness of this method depends on the fact that the tridiagonal system $\mathbf{Bx}$ is relatively easy to solve at each stage. (See Hager, 1988, p. 334.)

U4.9 MATLAB's function "diag" can be used to construct the iteration matrix for the Jacobi, Gauss–Seidel, and SOR methods. Modify the following MATLAB functions that use "diag", and compare the number of flops required with those for the loop methods:

```
xold = x0;
C = diag(diag(A)) - A;
                % diag(A) is vector [a11, ... ann]'
                % diag(diag(A)) is n x n diag matrix
C = diag(1 ./ diag(A)) * C;
                % multiply ith row of C by 1/aii
d = diag(1 ./ diag(A)) * b;
```

U4.10 Add a test on the relative residual, as defined in Section 4.4, to the functions for Jacobi, Gauss–Seidel, and SOR iteration, and compare the computational effort required to achieve convergence for these methods and the built-in MATLAB methods; use some of the sample problems and exercises as test cases.

Nonlinear Functions of Several Variables

Several of the methods introduced in Chapter 2 for finding a zero of a nonlinear function of a single variable can be extended to nonlinear functions of several variables. However, the problem is much more difficult in several variables. For two nonlinear functions of two variables, $z = f(x, y)$ and $z = g(x, y)$, finding a zero of the system requires finding the intersection of the curves $f(x, y) = 0$ and $g(x, y) = 0$. It is very important to use any information available about the specific problem to identify the region where these curves may intersect, i.e., the possible location of a zero.

We begin this chapter by considering the extension of Newton's method to systems of nonlinear equations. Starting with an initial estimate of the solution, each nonlinear function is approximated by its tangent plane (at the current approximate solution); the common root of the resulting linear equations provides the next approximation to the desired zero. Forming the linear system requires either computation of the Jacobian matrix (the matrix of partial derivatives) for the nonlinear system or approximation of the Jacobian numerically.

Fixed-point iteration, introduced for functions of a single variable in Chapter 1, provides an approach to solving a system of nonlinear equations that does not require the computation of partial derivatives. However, the transformation of the original problem into fixed-point form is more straightforward for some problems than for others.

We also consider the problem of finding the minimum of a scalar function of several variables. In addition to many other applications of minimization, root-finding problems may be solved by constructing a function whose minimum corresponds to the desired root. A basic gradient-descent minimization function is presented in Section 5.3. A more powerful approach, implemented in MATLAB's built-in function `fmins`, is based on a "simplex search," a logical extension of bisection.

Nonlinear systems of equations occur in many settings, including the solution of nonlinear partial differential equations by means of finite differences.

Example 5-A Nonlinear System from Geometry

The problem of finding the points of intersection of two curves in the xy-plane may require solving a nonlinear system of equations. For example, suppose we would like to know where the ellipse of eccentricity 0.5 (which described the orbit in an example in Chapter 2) would intersect a circle with the same area and the same center. (See Fig. 5.1.) The area of an ellipse is πab; for this example, with an eccentricity of 0.5, we take $a = 1$ and $b = \sqrt{3}/2$, so the equation of the ellipse is

$$x^2 + 4y^2/3 = 1.$$

Since the area of a circle is πr^2, the equation of a circle with the same area as the ellipse is

$$x^2 + y^2 = r^2 = \sqrt{3}/2.$$

The points of intersection are solutions of the nonlinear system

$$3x^2 + 4y^2 - \quad 3 \quad = 0,$$
$$x^2 + \quad y^2 - \sqrt{3}/2 = 0.$$

We solve this system in Example 5.3.

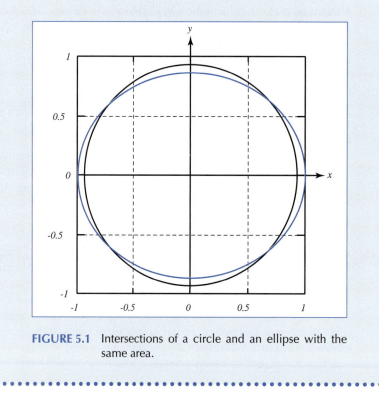

FIGURE 5.1 Intersections of a circle and an ellipse with the same area.

Example 5-B Position of a Two-Link Robot Arm

The position of a two-link robot arm can be described in terms of the angle that the first link makes with the horizontal axis and the angle that the second link makes with the first link. In this example, we assume that the lengths of the two links are d_1 and d_2; the first link makes an angle α with the horizontal axis, and the second link makes an angle β with the direction defined by the first link. Our problem is to find the angles α and β that allow the end of the second link to be at a specified point, with coordinates (p_1, p_2). The arrangement is illustrated in Fig. 5.2. The equations for these requirements are as follows:

Location of the end of the first link (x_1, y_1)

$$x_1 = d_1 \cos(\alpha),$$

$$y_1 = d_1 \sin(\alpha);$$

Location of the end of the second link (x_2, y_2)

$$x_2 = x_1 + d_2 \cos(\alpha + \beta),$$

$$y_2 = y_1 + d_2 \sin(\alpha + \beta).$$

Thus, we need to solve

$$p_1 = d_1 \cos(\alpha) + d_2 \cos(\alpha + \beta),$$

$$p_2 = d_1 \sin(\alpha) + d_2 \sin(\alpha + \beta),$$

for the unknown angles α and β.

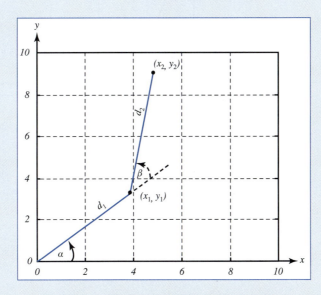

FIGURE 5.2 Two-link robot arm, initial position.

We solve a problem of this type in Example 5.4.

Newton's method for finding the root of a nonlinear function, discussed in Chapter 2, can be extended to solving a system of nonlinear equations. In the following examples, we show iterations as superscripts (in parentheses), since we often use vector notation, denoting components of the unknown vector by subscripts. In cases where we do not wish to retain all iterates, we denote the current estimate as x_old, and the next estimate as x_new.

Example 5.1 Intersection of a Circle and a Parabola

We first consider a system of two equations describing the intersection of the unit circle (centered at the origin) and a given parabola (with vertex at the origin). The curves are illustrated in Fig. 5.3. We are looking for the common zeros of the functions

$$f(x, y) = x^2 + y^2 - 1 \quad \text{and} \quad g(x, y) = x^2 - y.$$

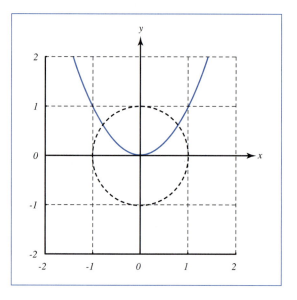

FIGURE 5.3   Intersections of a circle and a parabola.

We start with an initial estimate of a common solution, $(x^{(0)}, y^{(0)})$. The plane that is tangent to the function $z = f(x, y)$ at $(x^{(0)}, y^{(0)}, f(x^{(0)}, y^{(0)}))$ has the equation:

$$z - f(x^{(0)}, y^{(0)}) = f_x(x^{(0)}, y^{(0)})(x - x^{(0)}) + f_y(x^{(0)}, y^{(0)})(y - y^{(0)}),$$

where $f_x(x^{(0)}, y^{(0)})$ is the partial derivative of $f(x, y)$ with respect to x, evaluated at $(x^{(0)}, y^{(0)})$, and $f_y(x^{(0)}, y^{(0)})$ is the partial derivative of $f(x, y)$ with respect to y, evaluated at $(x^{(0)}, y^{(0)})$.

Similarly, the equation of the plane tangent to $z = g(x, y)$ at $(x^{(0)}, y^{(0)}, g(x^{(0)}, y^{(0)}))$ is

$$z - g(x^{(0)}, y^{(0)}) = g_x(x^{(0)}, y^{(0)})(x - x^{(0)}) + g_y(x^{(0)} y^{(0)})(y - y^{(0)}).$$

To find the next approximation to the desired solution, we find the intersection of these two tangent planes with the xy-plane (i.e., with $z = 0$). We define $r = x - x^{(0)}$ and $s = y - y^{(0)}$ and solve the linear system

$$f_x(x^{(0)}, y^{(0)})r + f_y(x^{(0)}, y^{(0)})s = -f(x^{(0)}, y^{(0)}),$$
$$g_x(x^{(0)}, y^{(0)})r + g_y(x^{(0)}, y^{(0)})s = -g(x^{(0)}, y^{(0)}).$$

Note that r and s give the location of the intersection point in terms of its displacement from the point $(x^{(0)}, y^{(0)})$; i.e., $(x, y) = (r + x^{(0)}, s + y^{(0)})$. For this example, $f_x = 2x$, $f_y = 2y$, $g_x = 2x$, and $g_y = -1$.

Choosing the initial estimate as $(x^{(0)}, y^{(0)}) = (1/2, 1/2)$, we have

$$f_x = 1, f_y = 1, g_x = 1, g_y = -1, f(1/2, 1/2) = -1/2, \text{ and } g(1/2, 1/2) = -1/4.$$

The resulting linear system to be solved is

$$r + s = 1/2,$$
$$r - s = 1/4.$$

Its solution is $r = 3/8$, $s = 1/8$.

The second approximate solution, $(x^{(1)}, y^{(1)})$ is the intersection point in terms of its (x, y) coordinates:

$$x^{(1)} = x^{(0)} + r = 1/2 + 3/8 = 7/8,$$
$$y^{(1)} = y^{(0)} + s = 1/2 + 1/8 = 5/8.$$

The process is repeated, using the new approximate solution to evaluate the partial derivatives $f_x, f_y, g_x,$ and g_y, and the functions, f and g. A summary of the results for the first two iterations is given in Table 5.1. The last column gives the Euclidean norm of the change in the solution vector at each step. The true solution is $(x, y) = (0.78615, 0.61803)$. (See Fig. 5.4.)

Table 5.1 Approximate solutions to intersection of a circle and a parabola.

Step	x	y	$|\Delta|$
0	0.5	0.5	
1	0.875	0.625	0.39528
2	0.79067	0.61806	0.084611

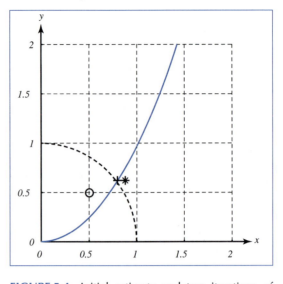

FIGURE 5.4 Initial estimate and two iterations of Newton's method.

5.1.1 Matrix-Vector Notation

The general nonlinear system

$$f_1(x_1, x_2, x_3, \ldots, x_n) = 0,$$
$$f_2(x_1, x_2, x_3, \ldots, x_n) = 0,$$
$$f_3(x_1, x_2, x_3, \ldots, x_n) = 0,$$
$$\vdots$$
$$f_n(x_1, x_2, x_3, \ldots, x_n) = 0,$$

can be written in a more compact vector form as $F(\mathbf{x}) = \mathbf{0}$, where

$$\mathbf{x} = \left[x_1, x_2, x_3, \ldots, x_n \right],$$

$$F(\mathbf{x}) = \begin{bmatrix} f_1(\mathbf{x}) \\ f_2(\mathbf{x}) \\ \cdot \\ \cdot \\ \cdot \\ f_n(\mathbf{x}) \end{bmatrix},$$

and

$$\mathbf{0} = \begin{bmatrix} 0 \\ 0 \\ \cdot \\ \cdot \\ \cdot \\ 0 \end{bmatrix}.$$

Newton's method uses the Jacobian (matrix of partial derivatives) of the system:

$$J(x_1, \ldots, x_n) = \begin{bmatrix} \partial f_1/\partial x_1 & \cdots & \partial f_1/\partial x_n \\ \cdot & \cdots & \cdot \\ \cdot & \cdots & \cdot \\ \cdot & \cdots & \cdot \\ \partial f_n/\partial x_1 & \cdots & \partial f_n/\partial x_n \end{bmatrix}.$$

At each stage of the iterative process, an updated approximate solution vector **x_new** is found from the current approximate solution **x_old** according to the equation

$$\mathbf{x\_new} = \mathbf{x\_old} - J^{-1}(\mathbf{x\_old})F(\mathbf{x\_old}).$$

In the case of a single equation and a single variable, this reduces to the Newton iteration introduced in Section 2.3:

$$\text{x\_new} = \text{x\_old} - \frac{f(\text{x\_old})}{f'(\text{x\_old})}.$$

However, evaluating the inverse of the Jacobian matrix is an expensive computation, so in practice, the equivalent system of linear equations

$$J(\mathbf{x\_old})\mathbf{y} = -F(\mathbf{x\_old}), \text{ where } \mathbf{y} = \mathbf{x\_new} - \mathbf{x\_old},$$

is solved for the vector **y**, which is used to update **x_old**. That is,

$$\mathbf{x\_new} = \mathbf{x\_old} + \mathbf{y}.$$

When $n = 2$, the corresponding system of equations is

$$f_x(\text{x\_old}, \text{y\_old})r + f_y(\text{x\_old}, \text{y\_old})s = -f(\text{x\_old}, \text{y\_old}),$$
$$g_x(\text{x\_old}, \text{y\_old})r + g_y(\text{x\_old}, \text{y\_old})s = -g(\text{x\_old}, \text{y\_old}),$$

where the updated approximate solution is given by

$$\text{x\_new} = \text{x\_old} + r,$$
$$\text{y\_new} = \text{y\_old} + s.$$

In vector-matrix notation, these equations can be written as

$$\begin{bmatrix} f_x(\text{x\_old}, \text{y\_old}) & f_y(\text{x\_old}, \text{y\_old}) \\ g_x(\text{x\_old}, \text{y\_old}) & g_y(\text{x\_old}, \text{y\_old}) \end{bmatrix} \begin{bmatrix} r \\ s \end{bmatrix} = \begin{bmatrix} -f(\text{x\_old}, \text{y\_old}) \\ -g(\text{x\_old}, \text{y\_old}) \end{bmatrix}$$

and

$$\begin{bmatrix} \text{x\_new} \\ \text{y\_new} \end{bmatrix} = \begin{bmatrix} \text{x\_old} \\ \text{y\_old} \end{bmatrix} + \begin{bmatrix} r \\ s \end{bmatrix}.$$

The MATLAB function for Newton's method, presented next, uses this vector-matrix formulation. The notation is illustrated for three equations in the example that follows.

5.1.2 MATLAB Function for Newton's Method for Nonlinear Systems

```
function x = Newton_sys(F, JF, x0, tol, max_it)
% Solve the nonlinear system F(x) = 0 using Newton's method
% vectors x and x0 are row vectors (for display purposes)
% function F returns a column vector, [f1(x), ..fn(x)]'
% stop if norm of change in solution vector is less than tol
% solve JF(x) y = - F(x) using Matlab's "backslash operator"
% y = - feval(JF, xold) \ feval(F, xold);
% the next approximate solution is    x_new = xold + y';
 x_old = x0;
 disp([0 x_old ]);
 iter = 1;
 while (iter <= max_it)
     y = - feval(JF, x_old) \ feval(F, x_old);
     x_new = x_old + y';
     dif = norm(x_new - x_old);
     disp([iter   x_new    dif]);
     if dif <= tol
         x = x_new;
         disp('Newton method has converged')
         return;
     else
         x_old = x_new;
     end
     iter = iter + 1;
 end
 disp('Newton method did not converge')
 x = x_new;
```

Example 5.2 Newton's Method for a System of Three Equations

To illustrate the use of Newton's method, we seek a common solution of the following three equations, which represent the unit sphere centered at the origin, a cylinder with radius 1/2 and axis along the x_2–axis, and a paraboloid of revolution around the x_3-axis:

$$f_1(x_1, x_2, x_3) = x_1^2 + x_2^2 + x_3^2 - 1 \quad = 0,$$
$$f_2(x_1, x_2, x_3) = x_1^2 \quad\quad + x_3^2 - 1/4 = 0,$$
$$f_3(x_1, x_2, x_3) = x_1^2 + x_2^2 - 4x_3 \quad\quad = 0.$$

In vector form,

$$F(\mathbf{x}) = \begin{bmatrix} x_1^2 + x_2^2 + x_3^2 - 1 \\ x_1^2 \quad\quad + x_3^2 - 1/4 \\ x_1^2 + x_2^2 - 4x_3 \end{bmatrix}.$$

The Jacobian is

$$J(\mathbf{x}) = \begin{bmatrix} 2x_1 & 2x_2 & 2x_3 \\ 2x_1 & 0 & 2x_3 \\ 2x_1 & 2x_2 & -4 \end{bmatrix}.$$

Using an initial estimate of $x^{(0)} = [1\ 1\ 1]$, a tolerance of 0.00001 to test for the stopping condition, and the MATLAB function `Newton_sys`, we obtain the results summarized in Table 5.2. Here we represent the change in the components of the approximate solution vector at each stage of iteration as $\Delta x = x\_new - x\_old$. With this notation, the stopping conditions can be written as $\|\Delta x\| < 0.00001$. Newton's method has converged in seven iterations.

Table 5.2 Newton iterations for a system of three equations.

Step	$x(1)$	$x(2)$	$x(3)$	$\|\Delta x\|$
0	1	1	1	
1	0.79167	0.875	0.33333	0.70956
2	0.44345	0.86607	0.42857	0.36111
3	0.28027	0.86603	0.44538	0.16405
4	0.2296	0.86603	0.44705	0.0507
5	0.22371	0.86603	0.4472	0.0058853
6	0.22361	0.86603	0.44721	0.00010352
7	0.22361	0.86603	0.44721	2.4665e-06

Example 5.3 Intersection of a Circle and an Ellipse

Consider now the problem of finding the points of intersection of two curves. The first equation represents an ellipse of eccentricity 0.5. The second equation represents a circle with the same area as the ellipse. Both curves are centered at the origin. The equations are, respectively,

$$3x^2 + 4y^2 - 3 = 0,$$
$$x^2 + y^2 - \sqrt{3}/2 = 0.$$

The Jacobian of this system is the matrix

$$J(x, y) = \begin{bmatrix} 6x & 8y \\ 2x & 2y \end{bmatrix}.$$

The MATLAB functions to evaluate the system and its Jacobian are given here for illustration; the unknowns are denoted $x(1)$ and $x(2)$ rather than x and y:

```
function f = orbit_cross(x)
    f = [ ( 3*x(1)^2 + 4*x(2)^2 - 3  )
        (   x(1)^2 +   x(2)^2 - sqrt(3)/2 )  ]  ;
```

```
function df = orbit_cross_j(x)
    df = [ 6*x(1)        8*x(2)
           2*x(1)        2*x(2) ]  ;
```

Table 5.3 gives a summary of the computations using the MATLAB function Newton_sys, with a starting estimate of $\mathbf{x}^{(0)} = [0.5 \quad 0.5]'$. The curves are illustrated in Fig. 5.1.

Table 5.3 Intersection of circle and ellipse using Newton's method.

Step	x(1)	x(2)	$\|\Delta x\|$
0	0.5	0.5	
1	0.7141	0.65192	0.26253
2	0.68201	0.63422	0.036654
3	0.68125	0.63397	0.00079461
4	0.68125	0.63397	4.2138e-07

Example 5.4 Positioning a Robot Arm

Consider a two-link robot arm, as introduced in Example 5-B. Let the length of the first link be 5 and the length of the second link be 6. We wish to find the angles so that the arm will move to the point $(10, 4)$, starting from initial angles of $\alpha = 0.7$ and $\beta = 0.7$.

The system of equations in this case is

$$5\cos(\alpha) + 6\cos(\alpha + \beta) - 10 = 0,$$

$$5\sin(\alpha) + 6\sin(\alpha + \beta) - 4 = 0.$$

Table 5.4 Iterations to find position of robot arm using Newton's method.

Step	α	β	$\|\Delta\|$
0	0.7	0.7	
1	−0.59855	1.8339	1.724
2	−0.10782	0.89987	1.0551
3	0.086882	0.53893	0.4101
4	0.14791	0.426	0.12837
5	0.15585	0.41139	0.016621
6	0.15598	0.41114	0.00029053

Table 5.4 gives the results of six iterations. The initial position and final position of the arm are illustrated in Fig. 5.5.

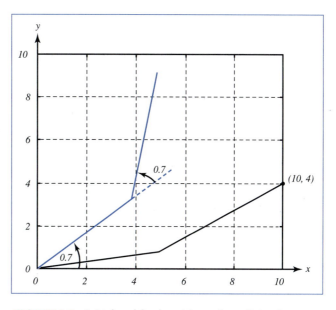

FIGURE 5.5 Initial and final positions of two-link robot arm.

5.2 FIXED-POINT ITERATION FOR NONLINEAR SYSTEMS

It is sometimes convenient to solve a system of nonlinear equations by an iterative process that does not require the computation of partial derivatives. An example of the use of fixed-point iteration for finding a zero of a nonlinear function of a single variable appears in Chapter 1. The extension of this idea to systems is straightforward.

Example 5.5 Fixed-Point Iteration for a System of Two Nonlinear Functions

To introduce the use of fixed-point iteration for nonlinear systems, consider the problem of finding a zero of the system

$$f_1(x_1, x_2) = x_1^3 + 10x_1 - x_2 - 5 = 0,$$
$$f_2(x_1, x_2) = x_1 + x_2^3 - 10x_2 + 1 = 0,$$

by converting these equations to the form $x_1 = g_1(x_1, x_2)$, $x_2 = g_2(x_1, x_2)$, in the following manner:

$$x_1 = -0.1x_1^3 + 0.1x_2 + 0.5,$$
$$x_2 = 0.1x_1 + 0.1x_2^3 + 0.1.$$

The graphs of the equations $f_1 = 0$ and $f_2 = 0$ are shown in Fig. 5.6. The results are summarized in Table 5.6.

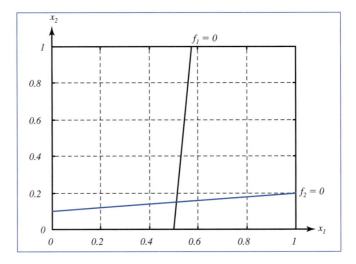

FIGURE 5.6 System of two nonlinear equations.

Table 5.6 Approximate solutions at each stage of iteration.

Iteration	x_1	x_2	$\|\Delta x\|$
0	0.6	0.6	
1	0.5384	0.1816	0.42291
2	0.50255	0.15444	0.044975
3	0.50275	0.15062	0.0038204
4	0.50235	0.15062	0.00039661
5	0.50238	0.15058	4.9381e-05

5.2.1 MATLAB Function for Fixed-Point Iteration for Nonlinear Systems

```
function x = Fixed_pt_sys(G, x0, tol, max_it)
%  Solve the nonlinear system x = G(x)
%  using fixed-point iteration
%  vector x and x0 are row vectors (for display purposes)
%  function G returns a column vector of values,
%       [g1(x), ..., gn(x)]'
%  stop if norm of change in solution is less than tol
% y = feval (G, x_old); the next solution is x_new = y';
disp([0     x0]);              % display initial estimate
```

```
x_old = x0;
iter = 1;
while (iter <= max_it)
    y = feval(G, x_old);
    x_new =  y';
    dif = norm(x_new - x_old);
    disp([iter x_new dif]);
    if dif <= tol
        x = x_new
        disp('Fixed-point iteration converged')
        return;
    else
        x_old = x_new;
    end
    iter = iter + 1;
end
disp('Fixed-point iteration did not converge')
x = x_new;
```

The function in Example 5.5 is expressed in MATLAB as follows:

```
function G = ex5_5(x)
G = [ (-0.1*x(1)^3 + 0.1*x(2) + 0.5)
      (0.1*x(1) + 0.1*x(2)^3 + 0.1)];
```

Example 5.6 Fixed-Point Iteration for a System of Three Nonlinear Equations

As another illustration of the use of fixed-point iteration, we seek a common solution of the following three equations:

$$
\begin{aligned}
f_1(x_1, x_2, x_3) &= \quad x_1^2 + 50x_1 + \quad x_2^2 + \quad x_3^2 - 200 = 0, \\
f_2(x_1, x_2, x_3) &= \quad x_1^2 \qquad\quad + 20x_2 + \quad x_3^2 - \quad 50 = 0, \\
f_3(x_1, x_2, x_3) &= -x_1^2 \qquad\qquad - \quad x_2^2 + 40x_3 + \quad 75 = 0.
\end{aligned}
$$

These equations can be written compactly in vector form as $\mathbf{f}(\mathbf{x}) = \mathbf{0}$, where $\mathbf{x}, \mathbf{f}$ and $\mathbf{0}$ are vectors in R_3. There are many possibilities for converting this system to a fixed-point iteration form $\mathbf{x} = \mathbf{g}(\mathbf{x})$, but convergence depends on the magnitude of the partial derivatives of $\mathbf{g}$ being sufficiently small, so we choose to rewrite the system as

$$50x_1 = -x_1^2 - x_2^2 - x_3^2 + 200,$$

$$20x_2 = -x_1^2 \qquad - x_3^2 + 50,$$

$$40x_3 = \quad x_1^2 + x_2^2 \qquad - 75.$$

The desired iterative form is obtained by dividing each equation by the coefficient of the variable on the left-hand side:

$$x_1 = g_1(x_1, x_2, x_3) = -0.02x_1^2 - 0.02x_2^2 - 0.02x_3^2 + 4,$$

$$x_2 = g_2(x_1, x_2, x_3) = -0.05x_1^2 \qquad - 0.05x_3^2 + 2.5,$$

$$x_3 = g_3(x_1, x_2, x_3) = \quad 0.025x_1^2 + 0.025x_2^2 \qquad - 1.875.$$

Using the preceding MATLAB function and a starting estimate of $(2, 2, 2)$, we find that the fixed-point iteration converges in 10 iterations to the solution $(3.6328, 1.7321, -1.4701)$; the stopping condition is that the norm of the change in the solution vector be less than 10^{-4}. The results are summarized in Table 5.7.

Table 5.7 Approximate solution at each stage of iteration.

Iteration	x_1	x_2	x_3	$\|\Delta x\|$
0	2	2	2	
1	3.76	2.1	−1.675	4.0759
2	3.5729	1.6528	−1.4113	0.5518
3	3.6502	1.7621	−1.4876	0.15403
4	3.6272	1.7232	−1.4643	0.050903
5	3.6346	1.735	−1.4719	0.015899
6	3.6323	1.7312	−1.4695	0.0050696
7	3.633	1.7324	−1.4702	0.0016031
8	3.6328	1.732	−1.47	0.00050866
9	3.6328	1.7321	−1.4701	0.00016117
10	3.6328	1.7321	−1.4701	5.1098e-05

5.2.2 Discussion

The conditions that guarantee a fixed point for the vector function $g(x)$ are similar to those presented in Chapter 1 for a fixed point of a function of 1 variable. We consider the extension of the interval $a \le x \le b$ in R^1 into R^n by assuming that $g(x)$ is defined on an n-dimensional rectangle D, the set of all points $(x_1, x_2, \ldots, x_n)$ such that $a_i \le x_i \le b_i$ for some constants $a_1, \ldots, a_n$ and $b_1, \ldots, b_n$. We assume further that all components of the Jacobian matrix $G(x)$ are continuous on D.

Fixed-Point Convergence Theorem for R^n

If $g(x)$ maps D into D, then g has a fixed point in D. In other words, if $g(x)$ is in D whenever x is in D, then there is some point p in D such that $p = g(p)$.

If

$$\|\mathbf{G}(\mathbf{p})\|_\infty < 1,$$

then the sequence of approximations to the fixed point, defined by

$$\mathbf{x}^{(k+1)} = \mathbf{g}(\mathbf{x}^{(k)}),$$

converges, as long as the initial point $\mathbf{x}^{(0)}$ is sufficiently close to the fixed point $\mathbf{p}$. The matrix norm $\|\mathbf{G}(\mathbf{p})\|_\infty$ is the maximum of the row sums of $\mathbf{G}$. (For a proof of this theorem, see Atkinson, 1989.)

As a corollary to the fixed-point convergence theorem, we have the following result:

If there is a constant $K < 1$ such that for every $\mathbf{x}$ in $\mathbf{D}$,

$$\left| \frac{\partial g_i(\mathbf{x})}{\partial x_j} \right| \leq \frac{K}{n} \qquad \text{for each } i = 1, \ldots, n, \text{ and each } j = 1, \ldots, n,$$

then, for any initial point $\mathbf{x}^{(0)}$ in D, the sequence of approximations to the fixed point defined by

$$\mathbf{x}^{(k+1)} = \mathbf{g}(\mathbf{x}^{(k)})$$

converges.

A bound on the error at the mth step is given by

$$\|\mathbf{x}^{(m)} - \mathbf{p}\|_\infty \leq \frac{K^m}{1 - K} \|\mathbf{x}^{(1)} - \mathbf{x}^{(0)}\|_\infty.$$

Proofs of these results, a special case of the contraction mapping theorem, can be found in more advanced numerical analysis texts, e.g., Ortega (1972) and Atkinson (1989).

To apply the fixed-point convergence theorem to Example 5.5, i.e.,

$$x_1 = -0.1x_1^3 + 0.1x_2 + 0.5 = g_1(x_1, x_2),$$

$$x_2 = 0.1x_1 + 0.1x_2^3 + 0.1 = g_2(x_1, x_2),$$

we first check to make sure that $\mathbf{g}(\mathbf{x})$ maps the rectangle $0 \leq x_1 \leq 1, 0 \leq x_2 \leq 1$ into itself; that is, for $0 \leq x_1, x_2 \leq 1$, we have $0 \leq g_1, g_2 \leq 1$. In fact $0.4 \leq g_1 \leq 0.6$ and $0.1 \leq g_2 \leq 0.3$. We also investigate the partial derivatives

$$\frac{\partial g_1(\mathbf{x})}{\partial x_1} = -0.3x_1^2, \quad \frac{\partial g_1(\mathbf{x})}{\partial x_2} = 0.1, \quad \frac{\partial g_2(\mathbf{x})}{\partial x_1} = 0.1, \quad \text{and} \quad \frac{\partial g_2(\mathbf{x})}{\partial x_2} = 0.3x_2^2,$$

which are all less than 0.5 (for $0 \leq x_1, x_2 \leq 1$), as is required for the corollary.

5.3   MINIMUM OF A NONLINEAR FUNCTION OF SEVERAL VARIABLES

In this section, we turn our attention to the problem of finding a minimum of a scalar function of several variables. Minimization problems are important in many applications. Also, the problem of finding the common zeros of several nonlinear functions can be converted into a minimization problem, as illustrated in Example 5.7. An interesting geometric problem is presented in Example 5.8.

The gradient of a function of several variables is a vector in the direction of most rapid increase, and the negative of the gradient gives the direction of most rapid decrease. A simple gradient search technique starts with an initial estimate of the location of a minimum and determines the direction in which the function is decreasing most rapidly. A new approximate solution is found by moving a specified distance in the direction of the negative gradient. If the function value is lower at the new point, it is accepted as the new solution; if not, a smaller step in the direction of the negative gradient is taken. The step size is reduced until the new point is an improvement (i.e., the function value is smaller at the new point than at the previous point) or until the step size is less than a given tolerance, in which case convergence has been achieved.

Example 5.7 Finding a Zero of a Nonlinear System by Minimization

To use minimization techniques to find a zero of a system of nonlinear functions, we define a new function that is the sum of the squares of the functions whose common zero is desired. For example, if we want a zero of the functions

$$f(x, y) = x^2 + y^2 - 1 \quad \text{and} \quad g(x, y) = x^2 - y,$$

we define

$$h(x, y) = (x^2 + y^2 - 1)^2 + (x^2 - y)^2.$$

The minimum value of $h(x, y)$ is 0, which occurs when $f(x, y) = 0$ and $g(x, y) = 0$. The derivatives for the gradient are

$$h_x(x, y) = 2(x^2 + y^2 - 1)2x + 2(x^2 - y)2x,$$
$$h_y(x, y) = 2(x^2 + y^2 - 1)2y + 2(x^2 - y)(-1).$$

A summary of the results using the MATLAB function ffmin are given in Table 5.8. Example 5.1 solved the same problem by Newton's method.

Table 5.8   Approximate zeros at each step of iteration.

Step	x	y	Change
0	0.5	0.5	
1	0.875	0.625	−0.26831
2	0.74512	0.61133	−0.035987
3	0.79251	0.61902	−0.0079939
4	0.78446	0.6178	−0.00019414
5	0.78657	0.6181	−1.3631e-05

5.3.1 MATLAB Function for Minimization by Gradient Descent

```
function xmin = ffmin(my_func, my_func_g, x0, tol, max_it)
% find the minimum of a scalar function of several variables
% the function is defined in "my_func"
% the negative gradient is given in "my_func_g"
iter = 1;
x_old = x0;
disp([ 0      x0])
while (iter <= max_it)
    dx = feval(my_func_g, x_old);
    x_new = x_old + dx;
    z0 = feval(my_func, x_old);
    z1 = feval(my_func, x_new);
    ch = z1 - z0;
    while ( ch >= 0 )
        dx = dx/2;
        if ( norm(dx) < 0.00001 )
            break;
        else
        x_new = x_old + dx/2;
        z1 = feval(my_func, x_new);
        ch = z1 - z0;
        end
    end
    if (abs(ch) < tol)            % iterations have converged
        disp(' iterations converged')
        break;
    end
    disp([ iter     x_new     ch] )
    x_old = x_new;
    iter = iter + 1;
end
xmin = x_new;
```

For Example 5.7, the function to be minimized and its (negative) gradient function are given by the following code:

```
function h = ex_min(x)
h =  ( x(1)^2 + x(2)^2 - 1 )^2 + ( x(1)^2 -x(2) )^2;
function dh = ex_min_g(x)
% direction of greatest decrease
dh = [ -(4*(x(1)^2 + x(2)^2 - 1)*x(1) + 4*(x(1)^2 + x(2))*x(1))
        -(4*(x(1)^2 + x(2)^2 + 1)*x(2) - 2*(x(1)^2 - x(2)))]';
```

We now consider an example in which finding the minimum of a function is the primary objective.

Example 5.8 Optimal Location of a Point in the Plane

Given three points in the plane, we wish to find the location of the point $P = (x, y)$ so that the sum of the squares of the distances from P to the three given points, (x_1, y_1), (x_2, y_2), and (x_3, y_3), is as small as possible. In other words, we need to find the minimum of

$$f(x, y) = (x - x_1)^2 + (y - y_1)^2 + (x - x_2)^2 + (y - y_2)^2 + (x - x_3)^2 + (y - y_3)^2.$$

The necessary derivatives are

$$f_x(x, y) = 2(x - x_1) + 2(x - x_2) + 2(x - x_3) = 6x - 2x_1 - 2x_2 - 2x_3,$$
$$f_y(x, y) = 2(y - y_1) + 2(y - y_2) + 2(y - y_3) = 6y - 2y_1 - 2y_2 - 2y_3.$$

The initial estimate of $(0.2, 0.2)$ and the results of the first two updates are shown in Fig. 5.7, together with the three given points, $(0, 0)$, $(1, 0)$, and $(1/2, 1)$.

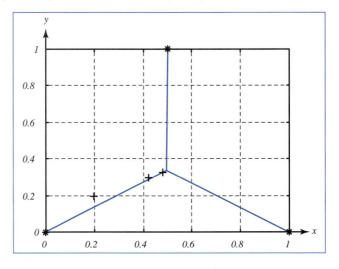

FIGURE 5.7 First three iterations to find optimal location of P.

MATLAB's built-in function to find the minimum of a function of several variables uses a Nelder–Mead type of simplex search. We sketch the method first and then summarize the options for using MATLAB's implementation.

In two dimensions, a *simplex* is a geometrical figure consisting of three points (vertices), together with all line segments connecting them—in other words, a triangle. In three dimensions, a simplex is a tetrahedron, i.e., four points and the polygonal faces connecting them. In R^n, a simplex consists of $n+1$ points and the hyperplane segments connecting them. For simplicity, we limit our description of the simplex method to two dimensions. The method starts with an initial simplex (triangle) and identifies the vertex (call it "bad") where the function to be minimized is largest. Each iteration of the simplex method transforms the simplex by a combination of reflections, expansions, and contractions. A reflection takes the vertex "bad" and projects it through the center of the opposite face of the simplex. If the new point is better (i.e., if the function evaluated at "new" is smaller), the method continues expanding the simplex by moving "new" further along the same ray, until the improvement stops. Other possible moves include contraction along the ray from the vertex "bad" to the center of the opposite face and contraction of all vertices (except the best) towards the best. (For a more detailed description, see Press et al., 1986.)

MATLAB provides an implementation of the simplex search method in the function `fmins`. The basic function call is

```
x = fmins('F', x0)
```

where 'F' is a string containing the name of the function to be minimized, $F(x)$ is a scalar-valued function of a vector variable, and x0 is the initial estimate of location of the (local) minimum.

As is typically the case with built-in MATLAB functions, the user can supply values for option parameters that control the printout of intermediate steps, the termination tolerance for x, the termination tolerance for $F(x)$, and the maximum number of evaluations of $F(x)$. The default values for these specify no intermediate printout, tolerance on x and on $F(x)$ of 0.0001, and a maximum of 200*length(x) function evaluations. (See the comments at the beginning of the function listing (or enter `help fmins`) for more information on the syntax for specifying other values and for other options.)

SUMMARY

The general nonlinear system

$$f_1(\mathbf{x}_1, \mathbf{x}_2, \mathbf{x}_3, \ldots, \mathbf{x}_n) = 0,$$
$$f_2(\mathbf{x}_1, \mathbf{x}_2, \mathbf{x}_3, \ldots, \mathbf{x}_n) = 0,$$
$$f_3(\mathbf{x}_1, \mathbf{x}_2, \mathbf{x}_3, \ldots, \mathbf{x}_n) = 0,$$
$$\cdots$$
$$f_n(\mathbf{x}_1, \mathbf{x}_2, \mathbf{x}_3, \ldots, \mathbf{x}_n) = 0,$$

is written in vector form as $\mathbf{F}(\mathbf{x}) = \mathbf{0}$.

Newton's Method (p. 138): The update for Newton's method is given by

$$\mathbf{x\_new} = \mathbf{x} - \mathbf{J}^{-1}(\mathbf{x})\mathbf{F}(\mathbf{x}).$$

To avoid computing the inverse of the Jacobian, the equivalent system of linear equations

$$\mathbf{J}(\mathbf{x})\mathbf{y} = -\mathbf{F}(\mathbf{x}), \quad \text{where } \mathbf{y} = \mathbf{x\_new} - \mathbf{x},$$

is solved for the vector $\mathbf{y}$, which is used to update $\mathbf{x}$. That is,

$$\mathbf{x\_new} = \mathbf{x} + \mathbf{y}.$$

Fixed-Point Iteration (p. 145): The system $\mathbf{F}(\mathbf{x}) = \mathbf{0}$ may be converted to fixed-point form $\mathbf{x} = \mathbf{g}(\mathbf{x})$ in many different ways.

The fixed-point iteration $\mathbf{x}^{(k+1)} = \mathbf{g}(\mathbf{x}^{(k)})$ will converge if there is a region $\mathbf{D}$, such that $\mathbf{g}(\mathbf{D})$ is in $\mathbf{D}$, and the Jacobian of $\mathbf{g}$ satisfies $\|\mathbf{G}(\mathbf{p})\|_\infty < 1$.

Minimization of a Scalar Function of Several Variables (p. 149): The problem of solving the nonlinear system $\mathbf{F}(\mathbf{x}) = \mathbf{0}$ may be converted to a minimization problem by defining

$$\mathbf{h}(\mathbf{x}) = (\mathbf{F}_1(\mathbf{x}))^2 + (\mathbf{F}_2(\mathbf{x}))^2 + \cdots + (\mathbf{F}_n(\mathbf{x}))^2$$

The minimum value of $\mathbf{h}(\mathbf{x})$ is 0, which occurs when each of the component functions of $\mathbf{F}(\mathbf{x})$ is zero.

Minimization problems occur in many areas of application.

A simple gradient search for the minimum of $\mathbf{h}(\mathbf{x})$ begins with an initial estimate $\mathbf{x}^{(0)}$; at each iteration the approximate solution is moved a small distance in the direction of the negative gradient of $\mathbf{h}$. Care must be taken in determining the distance the solution should be moved.

MATLAB implements a more reliable search technique which does not require the gradient of the function.

SUGGESTIONS FOR FURTHER READING

The following texts examine numerical methods applied to nonlinear functions of several variables:

Acton, F. S., *Numerical Methods That (Usually) Work*, Harper and Row, New York, 1970.

Ortega, J. M., *Numerical Analysis: A Second Course*, Academic Press, New York, 1972.

Press, W. H., B. P. Flannery, S. A. Teukolsky, and W. T. Vetterling, *Numerical Recipes: The Art of Scientific Computing*, Cambridge University Press, Cambridge, U.K., 1986.

Reinboldt, W. C., *Methods for Solving Systems of Nonlinear Equations*, SIAM, Philadelphia, 1974.

For a discussion of the simplex search method, see (in addition to Press et al., 1986)

Nelder, J. A., and Mead, R., *Computer Journal*, vol. 7, 1965, p. 308.

A reference for the MATLAB implementation in `fmins` is

J. E. Dennis, Jr., and D. J. Woods, *New Computing Environments*: *Microcomputers in Large-Scale Computing*, edited by A. Wouk, SIAM, Philadelphia, 1987, pp. 116–122.

The following are among the well-respected texts that provide a more in-depth treatment of multivariable analysis:

Dillon, W. R., and M. Goldstein, *Multivariate analysis*: *Methods and applications*, John Wiley and Sons, New York, 1984.

Hair, J. F., R. E. Anderson, R. L. Tatham, and W. Black, *Multivariate Data Analysis* (5th ed.), Prentice Hall, Englewood Cliffs, NJ, 1998.

Johnson, R. A., and D. W. Wichern, *Applied Multivariate Statistical Analysis* (4th ed.), Prentice Hall, Englewood Cliffs, NJ, 1998.

Kachigan, S. K., *Multivariate Statistical Analysis*: *A Conceptual Introduction* (2d ed.), Radius Press, New York, 1991.

Mardia, K. V., *Multivariate Analysis*, Academic Press, London, 1980.

Morrison, D. F., *Multivariate Statistical Methods* (3d ed.), McGraw-Hill, New York, 1990.

PRACTICE THE TECHNIQUES

For Problems P5.1–P5.10, solve the nonlinear system

   a. *using Newton's method.*

   b. *by finding the minimimum of the function $f^2 + g^2$ or $f^2 + g^2 + h^2$.*

P5.1 $f(x,y) = x^2 - \sqrt{3}xy + 2y^2 - 10 = 0,$
$g(x,y) = 4x^2 + 3\sqrt{3}xy + y^2 - 22 = 0.$

P5.2 $f(x,y) = x^2 - \sqrt{3}xy + 2y^2 - 10 = 0,$
$g(x,y) = x^2 - \sqrt{3}xy + 2 = 0.$

P5.3 $f(x,y) = 4x^2 + 3\sqrt{3}xy + y^2 - 22 = 0,$
$g(x,y) = x^2 - \sqrt{3}xy + 2 = 0.$

P5.4 $f(x,y) = -x^2 + xy - y + 7x - 11 = 0,$
$g(x,y) = x^2 + y^2 - 9 = 0.$

P5.5 $f(x,y) = x^2 + 4y^2 - 16 = 0,$
$g(x,y) = xy^2 - 4 = 0.$

P5.6 $f(x,y) = x^3y - y - 2x^3 + 16 = 0,$
$g(x,y) = x - y^2 + 1 = 0.$

P5.7 $f(x,y,z) = x\,y\,z - 1 = 0,$
$g(x,y,z) = x^2 + y^2 + z^2 - 4 = 0,$
$h(x,y,z) = x^2 + 2y^2 - 3 = 0.$

P5.8 $f(x,y,z) = x^2 + 4y^2 + 9z^2 - 36 = 0,$
$g(x,y,z) = x^2 + 9y^2 \qquad - 47 = 0,$
$h(x,y,z) = x^2\,z - 11 \qquad\qquad = 0.$

P5.9 $f(x,y,z) = x^2 + 2y^2 + 4z^2 - 7 = 0,$
$g(x,y,z) = 2x^2 + y^3 + 6z - 10 = 0,$
$h(x,y,z) = xyz + 1 = 0.$

P5.10 $f(x,y,z) = x^2 + y^2 + z^2 - 14 = 0,$
$g(x,y,z) = x^2 + 2y^2 \qquad - 9 = 0,$
$h(x,y,z) = x - 3y^2 + z^2 \qquad = 0.$

For Problems P5.11–P5.15, solve the nonlinear system

   a. *using Newton's method*

   b. *by finding the minimimum of the function $f^2 + g^2$ or $f^2 + g^2 + h^2$.*

   c. *using fixed-point iteration.*

P5.11 $f(x,y,z) = x^3 - 10x + y - z + 3 = 0,$
$g(x,y,z) = y^3 + 10y - 2x - 2z - 5 = 0,$
$h(x,y,z) = x + y - 10z + 2\sin(z) + 5 = 0.$

P5.12 $f(x,y,z) = x^2 + 20x + y^2 + z^2 - 20 = 0,$
$g(x,y,z) = x^2 + 20y + z^2 - 20 = 0,$
$h(x,y,z) = x^2 + y^2 - 40z = 0.$

P5.13 $f(x,y,z) = x^2 + y^2 + z^2 + 10x - 4 = 0,$
$g(x,y,z) = x^2 - y^2 + z^2 + 10y - 5 = 0,$
$h(x,y,z) = x^2 + y^2 - z^2 + 10z - 6 = 0.$

P5.14 $f(x,y,z) = 10x - x^2 - y - z^2 - 4 = 0,$
$g(x,y,z) = 10y - x^2 - y^2 - z - 5 = 0,$
$h(x,y,z) = 10z - x - y^2 - z^2 - 6 = 0.$

P5.15 $f(x,y,z) = 10x - x^3 + y^2 - z - 5 = 0,$
$g(x,y,z) = 10y + 0.5x^2 - y^2 - z - 3 = 0,$
$h(x,y,z) = 10z - x - y^2 - z^3 - 6 = 0.$

EXPLORE SOME APPLICATIONS

A5.1 Find the minimum of the following function using MATLAB's function `fmins`:

$$f(x,y) = -y + x^{-1} + \frac{y^2 - y + 1}{(y - y^2)(1 - x)}.$$

Find the minimum by setting the partial derivatives f_x and f_y equal to zero and solving the resulting nonlinear system using Newton's method. Investigate the effect of different starting estimates; $x = y = 0.5$ is one suitable choice.

A5.2 The equations for the optimal two-stage finite-difference scheme for a parabolic PDE are

$$12rq = 6r - 1,$$

$$60r^2 - 180r^2\,q - 30rq = 1.$$

Compare your result with the exact solution, which is $r = \dfrac{\sqrt{5}}{10}$ and $q = \dfrac{3 - \sqrt{5}}{6}$. (See Ames, 1992, p. 65.)

A5.3 Solve the following nonlinear system using Newton's method (this gives the coefficients and evaluation points for Gauss–Legendre quadrature with $n = 2$, which are discussed in Chapter 11):

$$2 = a_1 + a_2, \qquad 0 = a_1 x_1 + a_2 x_2,$$

$$\frac{2}{3} = a_1 x_1^2 + a_2 x_2^2, \qquad 0 = a_1 x_1^3 + a_2 x_2^3.$$

A5.4 Find the roots of the steady-state of the Lorenz equations

$$y - x = 0,$$
$$5x - y - xz = 0,$$
$$xy - 16z = 0.$$

(See Garcia, 1994, p. 109, for a discussion of a similar problem.)

A5.5 The steady state of the concentration of two chemical species in an oscillatory chemical system described by the Brusselator model is given by the nonlinear system

$$0 = A + x^2y - (B + 1)x,$$

$$0 = Bx - x^2y.$$

Find the solution for the following values of the parameters A and B:

    a. $B = 1, A = 1.$

    b. $B = 3, A = 1.$

    c. $B = 2, A = 1.$

(See Garcia, 1994, p. 111, for a discussion of a similar problem.)

A5.6 Find the angles of a two-link robot arm that enable it to reach the point $(3, 4)$; the lengths of the two links are $d_1 = 5$ and $d_2 = 6$. Use the starting values for the angles of $\alpha = 1, \beta = 1$.

A5.7 Find the location of two points (x_1, x_2) and (x_3, x_4) so that the sum of the squares of the distances required to link the four given points by the paths shown in the figure is minimal.

$$p_1 = (0, 0), \; p_2 = (1.8, 0),$$

$$p_3 = (1.5, 1), \; p_4 = (0.3, 1.6).$$

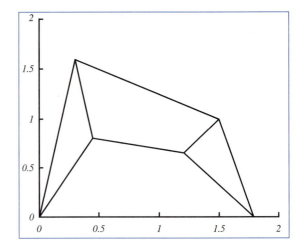

A5.8 Find the location of two points (x_1, x_2) and (x_3, x_4) so that the sum of the *distances* required to link the four given points by the paths shown in the figure is minimal.

```
p1 = [0   0]; p2 = [1.8   0 ];
p3 = [1.5   1]; p4 = [0.3   1.6];
```

EXTEND YOUR UNDERSTANDING

U5.1–U5.10 For each of Problems P5.1–P5.10, compare the computational effort required to solve the problem using Newton's method with that required using MATLAB's function `fmins`. (Use the MATLAB `flops` command.)

U5.11–U5.15 For each of Problems P5.11–P5.15, determine whether the conditions of the fixed-point convergence theorem or the corollary are satisfied.

U5.16 Compare the sum of the distances found in A5.8 for the optimal placement of the two points with the sum of the distances if only one interior point is used.

U5.17 Repeat A5.7 and A5.8 using the four given points $(0, 0)$, $(1, 0)$, $(1, 1)$ and $(0, 1)$. Compare your results with those found using only one interior point.

6

LU Factorization

In Chapters 3 and 4 we used vector-matrix notation and operations to solve systems of linear equations. In this chapter and the next, we investigate numerical methods for carrying out several important tasks from linear algebra. In this chapter, we consider the factorization of a matrix into the product of a lower triangular matrix $\mathbf{L}$ and an upper triangular matrix $\mathbf{U}$. For a three-by-three matrix $\mathbf{A}$, the problem is to find $\mathbf{L}$ and $\mathbf{U}$ so that $\mathbf{LU} = \mathbf{A}$, i.e.,

$$\begin{bmatrix} \ell_{11} & 0 & 0 \\ \ell_{21} & \ell_{22} & 0 \\ \ell_{31} & \ell_{32} & \ell_{33} \end{bmatrix} \cdot \begin{bmatrix} u_{11} & u_{12} & u_{13} \\ 0 & u_{22} & u_{23} \\ 0 & 0 & u_{33} \end{bmatrix} = \begin{bmatrix} a_{11} & a_{12} & a_{13} \\ a_{21} & a_{22} & a_{23} \\ a_{31} & a_{32} & a_{33} \end{bmatrix}.$$

There are two common methods of finding an LU factorization: Gaussian elimination and direct computation. The first creates an upper triangular matrix during the elimination process; the corresponding lower triangular matrix, with 1's on the diagonal, can be constructed from the multipliers used during the elimination. In the special case of a tridiagonal matrix, an LU factorization can be found very efficiently from the vectors containing the elements on the main diagonal, the elements above the main diagonal, and the elements below the main diagonal.

The second method, direct decomposition, is somewhat more general, in that it allows for the fact that the LU factorization of a given matrix is not unique; the three most common forms correspond to three different assumptions about the diagonal elements of $\mathbf{L}$ and $\mathbf{U}$. The Doolittle form, with 1's on the diagonal of $\mathbf{L}$, gives the same factors produced by Gaussian elimination. The Crout form places 1's on the diagonal of $\mathbf{U}$. The Cholesky form requires that the corresponding diagonal elements of $\mathbf{L}$ and $\mathbf{U}$ be equal, i.e., $u_{ii} = \ell_{ii}$; it is especially useful for symmetric positive definite matrices, since in that case it preserves the symmetry and produces a factorization with $\mathbf{L} = \mathbf{U}'$. For a positive symmetric matrix, a slight modification of the Cholesky form gives a factorization as $\mathbf{LDL}'$.

An LU factorization of $\mathbf{A}$ can be used to solve linear systems of equations efficiently, especially when the system $\mathbf{Ax} = \mathbf{b}$ must be solved repeatedly using a given matrix $\mathbf{A}$ with different values of $\mathbf{b}$ that are not known in advance. LU factorization can also be used to find the inverse and the determinant of $\mathbf{A}$.

Example 6-A Circuit Analysis Application

Consider the problem of finding the currents in different parts of an electrical circuit, as shown originally in Figure 3.1. Suppose now that we want to investigate the effect of changing the size of the voltage drop and even its position, placing it perhaps in one of the other two subloops of the circuit. (See Fig. 6.1.) This corresponds to changing the right-hand side of the system of equations developed in Chapter 3.

    The equations for the three loops can be written in a more general form as follows:

Flow around left loop

$$20(i_1 - i_2) + 10(i_1 - i_3) = V_1.$$

Flow around upper right loop

$$25i_2 + 10(i_2 - i_3) + 20(i_2 - i_1) = V_2.$$

Flow around lower right loop

$$30i_3 + 10(i_3 - i_2) + 10(i_3 - i_1) = V_3.$$

In Figure 3.1 we had $V_1 = 0$, $V_2 = 0$, and $V_3 = 200$.

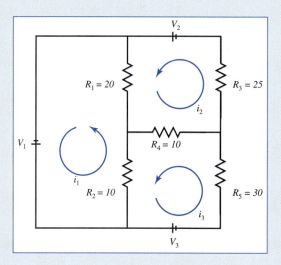

FIGURE 6.1 Simple electrical circuit.

    We can solve the new circuit equations efficiently by finding the LU factorization of the coefficient matrix (which does not change as long as we do not modify the sizes or positions of the resistors).

6.1 LU FACTORIZATION FROM GAUSSIAN ELIMINATION

The process of Gaussian elimination forms the basis for finding a very useful representation of a matrix $\mathbf{A}$ known as an LU factorization. A lower triangular matrix $\mathbf{L}$, with 1's on the diagonal, can be constructed from the multipliers used in Gaussian elimination. (See Chapter 3.) The elimination process transforms the original matrix $\mathbf{A}$ into an upper triangular matrix $\mathbf{U}$. The lower triangular matrix $\mathbf{L}$ is formed by placing the negatives of the multipliers (as used in the multiply-and-add procedure) in the appropriate positions as shown in the following examples. In the following illustrative example, we create new matrices $\mathbf{L}$ and $\mathbf{U}$ so that we can verify the result; for efficient use of computer memory, $\mathbf{L}$ and $\mathbf{U}$ can be stored in the locations originally occupied by matrix $\mathbf{A}$.

Example 6.1 Three-by-Three System

We first illustrate LU factorization for the coefficient matrix from Example 3.1; the $\mathbf{L}$ and $\mathbf{U}$ matrices are initialized as $\mathbf{L} = \mathbf{I}$ and $\mathbf{U} = \mathbf{A}$. The matrices are

$$\mathbf{A} = \begin{bmatrix} 1 & 2 & 3 \\ 2 & 6 & 10 \\ 3 & 14 & 28 \end{bmatrix}, \quad \mathbf{L} = \begin{bmatrix} 1 & 0 & 0 \\ 0 & 1 & 0 \\ 0 & 0 & 1 \end{bmatrix}, \quad \mathbf{U} = \begin{bmatrix} 1 & 2 & 3 \\ 2 & 6 & 10 \\ 3 & 14 & 28 \end{bmatrix}.$$

Step 1: The first row of $\mathbf{U}$ remains unchanged.
Multiply the first row by -2, and add the result to the second row.
Store the negative of the multiplier in the first column, second row, of $\mathbf{L}$.
Also, multiply the first row by -3, and add the result to the third row.
Store the negative of the multiplier in the first column, third row, of $\mathbf{L}$.
The resulting matrices are

$$\mathbf{L} = \begin{bmatrix} 1 & 0 & 0 \\ 2 & 1 & 0 \\ 3 & 0 & 1 \end{bmatrix}, \quad \mathbf{U} = \begin{bmatrix} 1 & 2 & 3 \\ 0 & 2 & 4 \\ 0 & 8 & 19 \end{bmatrix}.$$

Step 2: The first and second rows of $\mathbf{U}$ remain unchanged.
Multiply the second row by -4, and add the result to the third row.
Store the negative of the multiplier in the second column, third row, of $\mathbf{L}$.
The matrices that result are

$$\mathbf{L} = \begin{bmatrix} 1 & 0 & 0 \\ 2 & 1 & 0 \\ 3 & 4 & 1 \end{bmatrix}, \quad \mathbf{U} = \begin{bmatrix} 1 & 2 & 3 \\ 0 & 2 & 4 \\ 0 & 0 & 4 \end{bmatrix}.$$

Multiply $\mathbf{L}$ by $\mathbf{U}$, and verify the result:

$$\mathbf{LU} = \begin{bmatrix} 1 & 0 & 0 \\ 2 & 1 & 0 \\ 3 & 4 & 1 \end{bmatrix} \cdot \begin{bmatrix} 1 & 2 & 3 \\ 0 & 2 & 4 \\ 0 & 0 & 3 \end{bmatrix} = \begin{bmatrix} 1 & 2 & 3 \\ 2 & 6 & 10 \\ 3 & 14 & 28 \end{bmatrix} = \mathbf{A}.$$

Example 6.2 Four-by-Four System

We now consider the LU factorization of a four-by-four matrix

$$\mathbf{A} = \begin{bmatrix} 4 & 12 & 8 & 4 \\ 1 & 7 & 18 & 9 \\ 2 & 9 & 20 & 20 \\ 3 & 11 & 15 & 14 \end{bmatrix}.$$

Step 1: Row 1 is unchanged, and rows 2–4 are modified to give

$$\ell_{21} = \frac{a_{21}}{a_{11}} = \frac{1}{4},$$

$$\ell_{31} = \frac{a_{31}}{a_{11}} = \frac{1}{2}, \qquad \mathbf{U} = \begin{bmatrix} 4 & 12 & 8 & 4 \\ 0 & 4 & 16 & 8 \\ 0 & 3 & 16 & 18 \\ 0 & 2 & 9 & 11 \end{bmatrix}.$$

$$\ell_{31} = \frac{a_{41}}{a_{11}} = \frac{3}{4},$$

Step 2: Rows 1 and 2 are unchanged; rows 3 and 4 are transformed, yielding

$$\ell_{32} = \frac{a_{32}}{a_{22}} = \frac{3}{4},$$

$$\mathbf{U} = \begin{bmatrix} 4 & 12 & 8 & 4 \\ 0 & 4 & 16 & 8 \\ 0 & 0 & 4 & 12 \\ 0 & 0 & 1 & 7 \end{bmatrix}.$$

$$\ell_{42} = \frac{a_{42}}{a_{22}} = \frac{1}{2},$$

Step 3: The fourth row is modified to complete the forward elimination stage:

$$\ell_{43} = \frac{a_{43}}{a_{33}} = \frac{1}{4}, \qquad \mathbf{U} = \begin{bmatrix} 4 & 12 & 8 & 4 \\ 0 & 4 & 16 & 8 \\ 0 & 0 & 4 & 12 \\ 0 & 0 & 0 & 4 \end{bmatrix}.$$

Multiply **L** by **U** to verify the result:

$$\begin{bmatrix} 1 & 0 & 0 & 0 \\ 1/4 & 1 & 0 & 0 \\ 1/2 & 3/4 & 1 & 0 \\ 3/4 & 1/2 & 1/4 & 1 \end{bmatrix} \cdot \begin{bmatrix} 4 & 12 & 8 & 4 \\ 0 & 4 & 16 & 8 \\ 0 & 0 & 4 & 12 \\ 0 & 0 & 0 & 4 \end{bmatrix} = \begin{bmatrix} 4 & 12 & 8 & 4 \\ 1 & 7 & 18 & 9 \\ 2 & 9 & 20 & 20 \\ 3 & 11 & 15 & 14 \end{bmatrix}.$$

$$\mathbf{L} \qquad \cdot \qquad \mathbf{U} \qquad = \qquad \mathbf{A}$$

6.1.1 MATLAB Function for LU Factorization Using Gaussian Elimination

```
function [L, U] = LU_factor(A)
%       LU factorization of matrix A
%         using Gaussian elimination without pivoting
%       Input : A   --> n-by-n matrix
%       Output  L (lower triangular) and
%               U (upper triangular)
[ n,  m ] = size(A);
L = eye(n);                             % initialize matrices
U = A;
for j = 1 : n
    for i = j+1 : n
        L( i, j ) = U( i, j ) / U( j, j );
        U( i, : ) = U( i, : ) - L( i, j )*U( j, : );
    end
end
%  display L and U
L
U
%  verify results
B = L*U
A
```

We have chosen to use separate matrices for **L** and **U** in this MATLAB function, so that we can show the verification of the factorization at the end of the program. If this is not desired, both **L** and **U** can be stored in the same matrix that originally held matrix **A**. The 1's on the diagonal of **L** are not explicitly stored in that case. We are assuming that **A** is square, i.e., that the number of rows in **A** equals the number of columns. A test that $n = m$ could be added easily to this function to check for this feature, giving an error message if **A** is not square. Similarly, a test could be added to check that the pivot element is nonzero at each stage ($U(j, j) \neq 0$). We discuss the case of LU factorization with pivoting in Section 6.3.

Example 6.3 LU Factorization for Circuit Analysis Example

Consider the LU factorization of the coefficient matrix of the circuit analysis example from Chapter 3. The matrix is

$$\mathbf{A} = \begin{bmatrix} 30 & -20 & -10 \\ -20 & 55 & -10 \\ -10 & -10 & 50 \end{bmatrix}.$$

The matrices after the first stage of Gaussian elimination are

$$
\mathbf{L} = \begin{bmatrix} 1 & 0 & 0 \\ -2/3 & 1 & 0 \\ -1/3 & 0 & 1 \end{bmatrix}, \quad \mathbf{U} = \begin{bmatrix} 30 & -20 & -10 \\ 0 & 125/3 & -50/3 \\ 0 & -50/3 & 140/3 \end{bmatrix}.
$$

The matrices after the second stage of Gaussian elimination are

$$
\mathbf{L} = \begin{bmatrix} 1 & 0 & 0 \\ -2/3 & 1 & 0 \\ -1/3 & -2/5 & 1 \end{bmatrix}, \quad \mathbf{U} = \begin{bmatrix} 30 & -20 & -10 \\ 0 & 125/3 & -50/3 \\ 0 & 0 & 40 \end{bmatrix}.
$$

6.1.2 Discussion

The operations of Gaussian elimination can be expressed as actions performed on matrix $\mathbf{A}$ by certain elementary matrices. First consider the effect of multiplying a matrix by several simple matrices. (We use three-by-three matrices for purposes of illustration.)

Multiply the first row of $\mathbf{A}$ by c, and add the result to the second row to form the new second row:

$$
\begin{bmatrix} 1 & 0 & 0 \\ c & 1 & 0 \\ 0 & 0 & 1 \end{bmatrix} \cdot \begin{bmatrix} a_{11} & a_{12} & a_{13} \\ a_{21} & a_{22} & a_{23} \\ a_{31} & a_{32} & a_{33} \end{bmatrix} = \begin{bmatrix} a_{11} & a_{12} & a_{13} \\ d_{21} & d_{22} & d_{23} \\ a_{31} & a_{32} & a_{33} \end{bmatrix}.
$$

Here, $d_{21} = ca_{11} + a_{21}$, $d_{22} = ca_{12} + a_{22}$, and $d_{32} = ca_{13} + a_{32}$. For convenience, we write this as $\mathbf{CA} = \mathbf{D}$.

We also need the inverse of the matrix $\mathbf{C}$; i.e., we want $\mathbf{C}^{-1}\mathbf{C} = \mathbf{I}$. By direct calculation, it is evident that

$$
\begin{bmatrix} 1 & 0 & 0 \\ -c & 1 & 0 \\ 0 & 0 & 1 \end{bmatrix} \cdot \begin{bmatrix} 1 & 0 & 0 \\ c & 1 & 0 \\ 0 & 0 & 1 \end{bmatrix} = \begin{bmatrix} 1 & 0 & 0 \\ 0 & 1 & 0 \\ 0 & 0 & 1 \end{bmatrix},
$$

or

$$
\mathbf{C}^{-1} \quad \cdot \quad \mathbf{C} \quad = \quad \mathbf{I}.
$$

We can combine several such operations in a single matrix. For instance, the operations that perform the first stage of Gaussian elimination can be written as

$$
\begin{bmatrix} 1 & 0 & 0 \\ m_{21} & 1 & 0 \\ m_{31} & 0 & 1 \end{bmatrix} \cdot \begin{bmatrix} a_{11} & a_{12} & a_{13} \\ a_{21} & a_{22} & a_{23} \\ a_{31} & a_{32} & a_{33} \end{bmatrix} = \begin{bmatrix} a_{11} & a_{12} & a_{13} \\ 0 & a'_{22} & a'_{23} \\ 0 & a'_{32} & a'_{33} \end{bmatrix},
$$

where the elements $a'_{22}, a'_{23}, a'_{32}$, and a'_{33} have been modified by the actions needed to reduce the first column of $\mathbf{A}$ to zero (below the diagonal element).

To show that we can obtain the LU factorization of $\mathbf{A}$ as previously illustrated, we define the matrices

$$\mathbf{M}_1 = \begin{bmatrix} 1 & 0 & 0 \\ m_{21} & 1 & 0 \\ m_{31} & 0 & 1 \end{bmatrix} \quad \text{and} \quad \mathbf{M}_1^{-1} = \begin{bmatrix} 1 & 0 & 0 \\ -m_{21} & 1 & 0 \\ -m_{31} & 0 & 1 \end{bmatrix},$$

where the values of m_{21} and m_{31} are determined as before. In a similar manner, we define

$$\mathbf{M}_2 = \begin{bmatrix} 1 & 0 & 0 \\ 0 & 1 & 0 \\ 0 & m_{32} & 1 \end{bmatrix} \quad \text{and} \quad \mathbf{M}_2^{-1} = \begin{bmatrix} 1 & 0 & 0 \\ 0 & 1 & 0 \\ 0 & -m_{32} & 1 \end{bmatrix},$$

where m_{32} is found in the manner required to reduce to zero the second column of the transformed matrix $\mathbf{A}$, below the diagonal. Thus, $\mathbf{U} = \mathbf{M}_2 \cdot (\mathbf{M}_1 \cdot \mathbf{A})$.

The following identities provide the justification for the LU factorization of $\mathbf{A}$ (using the steps of Gaussian elimination without pivoting):

$$\mathbf{M}_1^{-1} \cdot (\mathbf{M}_1 \cdot \mathbf{A}) = \mathbf{A},$$

$$(\mathbf{M}_1^{-1} \cdot \mathbf{M}_2^{-1}) \cdot \{\mathbf{M}_2 \cdot (\mathbf{M}_1 \cdot \mathbf{A})\} = \mathbf{A}$$

Now consider the elements of $\mathbf{M}_1^{-1} \cdot \mathbf{M}_2^{-1} = \mathbf{L}$, or

$$\begin{bmatrix} 1 & 0 & 0 \\ -m_{21} & 1 & 0 \\ -m_{31} & 0 & 1 \end{bmatrix} \cdot \begin{bmatrix} 1 & 0 & 0 \\ 0 & 1 & 0 \\ 0 & -m_{32} & 1 \end{bmatrix} = \begin{bmatrix} 1 & 0 & 0 \\ -m_{21} & 1 & 0 \\ -m_{31} & -m_{32} & 1 \end{bmatrix}.$$

Thus, the lower triangular matrix with 1's on the diagonal and the negatives of the Gaussian elimination multipliers in the appropriate lower triangular positions, together with the upper triangular matrix formed during the elimination process, provides an LU factorization of matrix $\mathbf{A}$.

6.2 LU FACTORIZATION OF TRIDIAGONAL MATRICES

As we found with Gaussian elimination, the LU factorization of a tridiagonal matrix $\mathbf{T}$ can be accomplished using much less computation (and less computer memory for the storage of the matrices) than for a full matrix $\mathbf{A}$ of the same size.

6.2.1 MATLAB Function for LU Factorization of a Tridiagonal Matrix

In the MATLAB code that follows, the multipliers that are stored in vector **bb** and that form the lower diagonal of the matrix **L** could be written directly into the original vector **L**, and the modified main diagonal of the upper triangular matrix, **dd**, could be written over the original diagonal **d**. We have chosen to use somewhat more vectors than necessary to try to make the process as clear as possible and to allow verification of the result if necessary.

```
function [dd, bb] = LU_tridiag(a, d, b)
%  LU factorization of a tridiagonal matrix T
%  Input
%    a     vector of elements above main diagonal, a(n) = 0
%    d     diagonal of matrix T
%    b     vector of elements below main diagonal, b(1) = 0
% The factorization of T consists of
%       Lower bidiagonal matrix,
%         1's on main diagonal; lower diagonal is bb
%       Upper bidiagonal matrix,
%          main diagonal is dd; upper diagonal is a
n = length(d)
bb(1) = 0;
dd(1) = d(1);
for i = 2 : n
    bb(i) = b(i)/dd(i-1);
    dd(i) = d(i) - bb(i)*a(i-1);
end
```

Note that this factorization follows the basic Gaussian elimination process and does not scale the diagonal elements to 1, as in the Thomas method. It is not, in general, possible to obtain an LU factorization with all of the diagonal elements of both **L** and **U** set equal to 1.

Example 6.4 LU Factorization of Tridiagonal System

Consider again the four-by-four tridiagonal matrix from Example 3.7,

$$\mathbf{M} = \begin{bmatrix} 2 & -1 & 0 & 0 \\ -1 & 2 & -1 & 0 \\ 0 & -1 & 2 & -1 \\ 0 & 0 & -1 & 2 \end{bmatrix},$$

which can be represented by the vectors

$$\mathbf{d} = [\, 2, 2, 2, 2 \,], \quad \mathbf{a} = [\, -1, -1, -1, 0 \,], \quad \mathbf{b} = [\, 0, -1, -1, -1 \,].$$

For this example, $n = 4$. Following the steps in the MATLAB function, we have $dd_1 = d_1 = 2$. For $i = 2$,

$$bb_2 = b_2/dd_1 = -1/2,$$
$$dd_2 = d_2 - bb_2 a_1 = 2 - (-1/2)(-1) = 3/2.$$

For $i = 3$,

$$bb_3 = b_3/dd_2 = -1/(3/2) = -2/3,$$

$$dd_3 = d_3 - bb_3 a_2 = 2 - (-2/3)(-1) = 4/3.$$

For $i = 4$,

$$bb_4 = b_4/dd_3 = -1/(4/3) = -3/4,$$

$$dd_4 = d_4 - bb_4 a_3 = 2 - (-3/4)(-1) = 5/4.$$

In general, the factorization is

$$\mathbf{L} = \begin{bmatrix} 1 & 0 & 0 & 0 \\ bb_2 & 1 & 0 & 0 \\ 0 & bb_3 & 1 & 0 \\ 0 & 0 & bb_4 & 1 \end{bmatrix}, \quad \mathbf{U} = \begin{bmatrix} dd_1 & a_1 & 0 & 0 \\ 0 & dd_2 & a_2 & 0 \\ 0 & 0 & dd_3 & a_3 \\ 0 & 0 & 0 & dd_4 \end{bmatrix},$$

which, for this example, is

$$\mathbf{L} = \begin{bmatrix} 1 & 0 & 0 & 0 \\ -1/2 & 1 & 0 & 0 \\ 0 & -2/3 & 1 & 0 \\ 0 & 0 & -3/4 & 1 \end{bmatrix}, \quad \mathbf{U} = \begin{bmatrix} 2 & -1 & 0 & 0 \\ 0 & 3/2 & -1 & 0 \\ 0 & 0 & 4/3 & -1 \\ 0 & 0 & 0 & 5/4 \end{bmatrix}.$$

6.3   LU FACTORIZATION WITH PIVOTING

For problems in which row pivoting must be performed on the coefficient matrix $\mathbf{A}$ during Gaussian elimination, we can obtain an LU factorization of the permuted matrix $\mathbf{PA}$, where $\mathbf{P}$ is the permutation matrix that represents the row interchanges which occurred during the pivoting. If we store the elements of $\mathbf{L}$ below the diagonal in the positions of $\mathbf{A}$ that have been reduced to zero by the elimination process, the elements of $\mathbf{L}$ will appear in the correct positions, even when pivoting is used. However, a record of the row interchanges that are performed must be kept so that one can determine which permutation of $\mathbf{A}$ will be produced by the product $\mathbf{LU}$, in order to permute the right-hand side of a system of equations if the permuted $\mathbf{LU}$ factorization is used to solve the system. If we store $\mathbf{L}$ as a separate matrix, then, whenever pivoting occurs, the elements of $\mathbf{L}$ that have been already been computed must be permuted along with matrix $\mathbf{A}$. However, the diagonal elements of $\mathbf{L}$ are not permuted. We first illustrate the process for a three-by-three matrix and then give a MATLAB function and an algebraic justification for using the method.

Example 6.5 Effect of Pivoting on LU Factorization

Consider the matrix

$$\mathbf{A} = \begin{bmatrix} 2 & 6 & 10 \\ 1 & 3 & 3 \\ 3 & 14 & 28 \end{bmatrix}$$

from Example 3.5. The first stage of elimination gives

$$
\overset{\mathbf{L}}{\begin{bmatrix} 1 & 0 & 0 \\ 1/2 & 1 & 0 \\ 3/2 & 0 & 1 \end{bmatrix}}, \quad \overset{\mathbf{U}}{\begin{bmatrix} 2 & 6 & 10 \\ 0 & 0 & -2 \\ 0 & 5 & 13 \end{bmatrix}}.
$$

We are unable to continue unless we interchange row 2 and row 3:

$$
\begin{bmatrix} 1 & 0 & 0 \\ 3/2 & 1 & 0 \\ 1/2 & 0 & 1 \end{bmatrix} \quad \begin{bmatrix} 2 & 6 & 10 \\ 0 & 5 & 13 \\ 0 & 0 & -2 \end{bmatrix},
$$

Note that the elements in the first column of **L** are also permuted.

For this small example, no further elimination is required. The product **LU** gives a permutation of the original matrix **A**:

$$
\overset{\mathbf{L}}{\begin{bmatrix} 1 & 0 & 0 \\ 3/2 & 1 & 0 \\ 1/2 & 0 & 1 \end{bmatrix}} \cdot \overset{\mathbf{U}}{\begin{bmatrix} 2 & 6 & 10 \\ 0 & 5 & 13 \\ 0 & 0 & -2 \end{bmatrix}} = \overset{\mathbf{P} \cdot \mathbf{A}}{\begin{bmatrix} 2 & 6 & 10 \\ 3 & 14 & 28 \\ 1 & 3 & 3 \end{bmatrix}}.
$$

6.3.1 MATLAB Function for LU Factorization with Row Pivoting

```
function [L, U, P] = LU_pivot(A)
[n, n1] = size(A);
L = eye(n);   P = eye(n);   U = A;   % initialize matrices
for j = 1 : n
    [pivot    m] = max(abs( U(j:n, j) ));
    m = m + j - 1;                % index of pivot
    if m ~= j                     % interchange rows m and j
        % interchange rows m and j in U
            temp1 = U( j, : );
            U(j, :) = U(m, :);
            U( m, :) = temp1;
        % interchange rows m and j in P
            temp2 = P(j, :);
            P(j, :) = P(m, :); P(m, :) = temp2;
```

```
    if j >= 2                           % interchange rows m and j
                                        % in columns 1:j-1 of L
            temp3 = L( j, 1 : j-1 );
            L( j, 1 : j-1 ) = L( m, 1 : j-1 );
            L( m, 1 : j-1 ) = temp3;
        end
    end
    for i = j+1 : n
        L( i, j ) = U( i, j ) / U( j, j );
        U( i, : ) = U( i, : ) - L( i, j )*U( j, : );
    end
end
L, U% display L and U
T1 = L*U% verify results
T2 = P*A
```

This MATLAB function uses the built-in function max to find the desired pivot element at each stage. At the jth stage, the search is conducted in the jth column from the diagonal element U_{jj} to the bottom of the column (element U_{nj}). To find the element of the largest magnitude, the search is conducted after applying the absolute-value function to the elements of the vector being searched. Calling the function as [big k] = max(x) gives the largest element as big and k as the index pointing to that element; i.e., $x(k) =$ big. Since the index is counted from the beginning of the vector, and the vector being searched starts with the jth element of the pivot column, we add $(j-1)$ to the index returned by the function max to express the pivot position.

6.3.2 Discussion

When row pivoting is used in Gaussian elimination, the matrices **L** and **U** that are obtained give a factorization of a *permutation* of **A**, corresponding to the row interchanges performed during pivoting. Row interchanges on matrix **A** correspond to multiplying **A** on the left by a permutation matrix—that is, a matrix with elements that are either 0 or 1 and with the further property that there is exactly one 1 in each row and in each column. In other words, the matrix **P** is a permutation of the identity matrix. Column interchanges are accomplished by multiplying **A** on the right by a permutation matrix. The inverse of a permutation matrix is the matrix itself.

For example, to interchange the second and third rows of **A**, we perform the following multiplication:

$$
\begin{bmatrix} 1 & 0 & 0 \\ 0 & 0 & 1 \\ 0 & 1 & 0 \end{bmatrix} \cdot \begin{bmatrix} a_{11} & a_{12} & a_{13} \\ a_{21} & a_{22} & a_{23} \\ a_{31} & a_{32} & a_{33} \end{bmatrix} = \begin{bmatrix} a_{11} & a_{12} & a_{13} \\ a_{31} & a_{32} & a_{33} \\ a_{21} & a_{22} & a_{23} \end{bmatrix}.
$$

Now, consider a simple three-by-three example. The operations that perform the first stage of Gaussian elimination can be written as

$$
\begin{bmatrix} 1 & 0 & 0 \\ m_{21} & 1 & 0 \\ m_{31} & 0 & 1 \end{bmatrix} \cdot \begin{bmatrix} a_{11} & a_{12} & a_{13} \\ a_{21} & a_{22} & a_{23} \\ a_{31} & a_{32} & a_{33} \end{bmatrix} = \begin{bmatrix} a_{11} & a_{12} & a_{13} \\ 0 & a'_{22} & a'_{23} \\ 0 & a'_{32} & a'_{33} \end{bmatrix},
$$

where the new elements $a'_{22}, a'_{23}, a'_{32},$ and a'_{33} are the result of the actions needed to reduce the first column of $\mathbf{A}$ to zero, below the diagonal.

To show that we can obtain the LU factorization of $\mathbf{A}$ as illustrated, we define the following matrices:

$$
\mathbf{M}_1 = \begin{bmatrix} 1 & 0 & 0 \\ m_{21} & 1 & 0 \\ m_{31} & 0 & 1 \end{bmatrix}, \qquad M_1^{-1} = \begin{bmatrix} 1 & 0 & 0 \\ -m_{21} & 1 & 0 \\ -m_{31} & 0 & 1 \end{bmatrix},
$$

where the values of m_{21} and m_{31} are those required to produce zeros in the desired positions.

For the second stage of Gaussian elimination, we work with the transformed matrix, which is actually $\mathbf{M}_1\mathbf{A}$. If we interchange the second and third rows of $\mathbf{M}_1\mathbf{A}$, we will find $\mathbf{M}_2$ on the basis of the permuted matrix $\mathbf{PM}_1\mathbf{A}$. Accordingly, we define

$$
\mathbf{M}_2 = \begin{bmatrix} 1 & 0 & 0 \\ 0 & 1 & 0 \\ 0 & m_{32} & 1 \end{bmatrix} \quad \text{and} \quad \mathbf{M}_2^{-1} = \begin{bmatrix} 1 & 0 & 0 \\ 0 & 1 & 0 \\ 0 & -m_{32} & 1 \end{bmatrix},
$$

where m_{32} is found to reduce the second column of $\mathbf{PM}_1\mathbf{A}$ to zero, below the diagonal.

As in Section 6.1.2, we first consider the identity

$$
\mathbf{M}_1^{-1} \cdot (\mathbf{M}_1 \cdot \mathbf{A}) = \mathbf{A}.
$$

The product $\mathbf{M}_1 \cdot \mathbf{A}$ has the form

$$
\begin{bmatrix} x & x & x \\ 0 & x & x \\ 0 & x & x \end{bmatrix},
$$

and $\mathbf{M}_1^{-1}$ has the form

$$
\begin{bmatrix} \# & 0 & 0 \\ \# & \# & 0 \\ \# & 0 & \# \end{bmatrix}.
$$

Before $\mathbf{M}_2$ is constructed, the second and third rows of the matrix $\mathbf{M}_1 \cdot \mathbf{A}$ are interchanged; we express this interchange as multiplication by the permutation matrix $\mathbf{P}$. Making use of the fact that $\mathbf{P}$ is its own inverse, we have the identity

$$
\mathbf{M}_1^{-1} \cdot \mathbf{P} \cdot \mathbf{P} \cdot (\mathbf{M}_1 \cdot \mathbf{A}) = \mathbf{A}.
$$

Now, $\mathbf{M}_2$ is found to reduce the (3,2) element in the matrix $\mathbf{P} \cdot (\mathbf{M}_1 \cdot \mathbf{A})$ to zero; we thus have the identity

$$
\mathbf{M}_1^{-1} \cdot \mathbf{P} \cdot \mathbf{M}_2^{-1} \cdot \{\mathbf{M}_2 \cdot \mathbf{P} \cdot \mathbf{M}_1 \cdot \mathbf{A}\} = \mathbf{A}.
$$

Hence, $\mathbf{M}_2 \cdot \mathbf{P} \cdot \mathbf{M}_1 \cdot \mathbf{A}$ is the upper triangular matrix formed by the Gaussian elimination. However, $\mathbf{M}_1^{-1} \cdot \mathbf{P} \cdot \mathbf{M}_2^{-1}$ is not lower triangular. In order to construct the lower triangular matrix with the negatives of the multipliers in the right places, we need $\mathbf{P} \cdot \mathbf{M}_1^{-1} \cdot \mathbf{P} \cdot \mathbf{M}_2^{-1}$. This gives

$$\mathbf{P} \cdot \mathbf{M}_1^{-1} \cdot \mathbf{P} \cdot \mathbf{M}_2^{-1} \cdot \{\mathbf{M}_2 \cdot \mathbf{P} \cdot \mathbf{M}_1 \cdot \mathbf{A}\} = \mathbf{PA},$$

or $\mathbf{LU} = \mathbf{PA}$ when row interchanges are performed during elimination. The permutation matrix $\mathbf{P}$ performs the bookkeeping associated with the row interchanges.

Finally, consider the actual elements of $\mathbf{B} = \mathbf{P} \cdot \mathbf{M}_1^{-1} \cdot \mathbf{P}$:

$$\begin{bmatrix} 1 & 0 & 0 \\ 0 & 0 & 1 \\ 0 & 1 & 0 \end{bmatrix} \cdot \begin{bmatrix} 1 & 0 & 0 \\ -m_{21} & 1 & 0 \\ -m_{31} & 0 & 1 \end{bmatrix} \cdot \begin{bmatrix} 1 & 0 & 0 \\ 0 & 0 & 1 \\ 0 & 1 & 0 \end{bmatrix} =$$

$$\begin{bmatrix} 1 & 0 & 0 \\ -m_{31} & 0 & 1 \\ -m_{21} & 1 & 0 \end{bmatrix} \cdot \begin{bmatrix} 1 & 0 & 0 \\ 0 & 0 & 1 \\ 0 & 1 & 0 \end{bmatrix} = \begin{bmatrix} 1 & 0 & 0 \\ -m_{31} & 1 & 0 \\ -m_{21} & 0 & 1 \end{bmatrix}.$$

We now verify that $\mathbf{P} \cdot \mathbf{M}_1^{-1} \cdot \mathbf{P} \cdot \mathbf{M}_2^{-1} = \mathbf{B} \cdot \mathbf{M}_2^{-1} = \mathbf{L}$:

$$\begin{bmatrix} 1 & 0 & 0 \\ -m_{31} & 1 & 0 \\ -m_{21} & 0 & 1 \end{bmatrix} \cdot \begin{bmatrix} 1 & 0 & 0 \\ 0 & 1 & 0 \\ 0 & -m_{32} & 1 \end{bmatrix} = \begin{bmatrix} 1 & 0 & 0 \\ -m_{31} & 1 & 0 \\ -m_{21} & -m_{32} & 1 \end{bmatrix}.$$

Thus, the positions of the elements of $\mathbf{L}$ reflect the interchanges that occurred during elimination; the matrix formed from the product of $\mathbf{L}$ and $\mathbf{U}$ is a permuted form of the original matrix $\mathbf{A}$.

6.4 DIRECT LU FACTORIZATION

An alternative approach to Gaussian elimination for finding the LU factorization of matrix $\mathbf{A}$ is based on equating the elements of the product $\mathbf{LU}$ with the corresponding elements of $\mathbf{A}$, in a systematic manner. The three most common forms of LU factorization correspond to three different choices for the form of the diagonal elements in $\mathbf{L}$ and $\mathbf{U}$. For Doolittle's method, the diagonal elements of $\mathbf{L}$ are 1; for Crout's method, the diagonal elements of $\mathbf{U}$ are 1, and for Cholesky's method, the diagonal elements of $\mathbf{L}$ and $\mathbf{U}$ are equal.

6.4.1 Doolittle LU Factorization

The Doolittle form of LU factorization assumes that the diagonal elements of matrix $\mathbf{L}$ are 1's. Thus, for a three-by-three matrix $\mathbf{A}$, the problem is to find matrices $\mathbf{L}$ and $\mathbf{U}$ so that $\mathbf{LU} = \mathbf{A}$:

$$\begin{bmatrix} 1 & 0 & 0 \\ \ell_{21} & 1 & 0 \\ \ell_{31} & \ell_{32} & 1 \end{bmatrix} \cdot \begin{bmatrix} u_{11} & u_{12} & u_{13} \\ 0 & u_{22} & u_{23} \\ 0 & 0 & u_{33} \end{bmatrix} = \begin{bmatrix} a_{11} & a_{12} & a_{13} \\ a_{21} & a_{22} & a_{23} \\ a_{31} & a_{32} & a_{33} \end{bmatrix}.$$

We begin by finding $u_{11} = a_{11}$ and then solving for the remaining elements in the first row of $\mathbf{U}$ and the first column of $\mathbf{L}$. At the second stage, we find u_{22} and then the remainder of the second row of $\mathbf{U}$ and the second column of $\mathbf{L}$. Continuing in this manner, we determine all of the elements of $\mathbf{U}$ and $\mathbf{L}$. This process is implemented in the following MATLAB function and illustrated in Example 6.6. Crout factorization follows a similar procedure, but assumes that there are 1's on the diagonal of $\mathbf{U}$ rather than $\mathbf{L}$.

MATLAB Function for Doolittle LU Factorization

```
function [L, U] = Doolittle(A)
[n, m] = size(A);              % The dimension of A
U = zeros(n, n);               % Initialize U
L = eye(n);                    % Initialize L
for k = 1 : n                  % compute stage k
    U(k, k) = A(k, k) - L( k, 1:k-1 )*U(1:k-1, k );
    for j = k+1 : n
        U(k, j) = A(k, j)-L(k, 1:k-1)*U(1:k-1, j);
        L(j, k) = (A(j,k)-L(j,1:k-1)*U(1:k-1,k))/U(k,k);
    end
end
```

Note that although MATLAB correctly interprets the empty product L(1,1:0)*U(1:0,1) in the function `Doolittle`, matrix indexing starts with 1, not 0, in MATLAB.

Example 6.6 Doolittle LU Factorization

To find the LU factorization for $\mathbf{A} = \begin{bmatrix} 1 & 4 & 5 \\ 4 & 20 & 32 \\ 5 & 32 & 64 \end{bmatrix}$ by Doolittle's computation, we write the desired product as

$$\begin{bmatrix} 1 & 0 & 0 \\ \ell_{21} & 1 & 0 \\ \ell_{31} & \ell_{32} & 1 \end{bmatrix} \cdot \begin{bmatrix} u_{11} & u_{12} & u_{13} \\ 0 & u_{22} & u_{23} \\ 0 & 0 & u_{33} \end{bmatrix} = \begin{bmatrix} 1 & 4 & 5 \\ 4 & 20 & 32 \\ 5 & 32 & 64 \end{bmatrix}.$$

We begin by solving for the first row of $\mathbf{U}$ and the first column of $\mathbf{L}$:

$$(1)u_{11} = a_{11} = 1, \qquad (1)u_{12} = a_{12} = 4, \qquad (1)u_{13} = a_{13} = 5;$$

$$\ell_{21}u_{11} = a_{21} = 4, \qquad \ell_{31}u_{11} = a_{31} = 5.$$

Next, using these values, we find the second row of $\mathbf{U}$ and the second column of $\mathbf{L}$:

$$
\begin{bmatrix} 1 & 0 & 0 \\ 4 & 1 & 0 \\ 5 & \ell_{32} & 1 \end{bmatrix} \cdot \begin{bmatrix} 1 & 4 & 5 \\ 0 & u_{22} & u_{23} \\ 0 & 0 & u_{33} \end{bmatrix} = \begin{bmatrix} 1 & 4 & 5 \\ 4 & 20 & 32 \\ 5 & 32 & 64 \end{bmatrix},
$$

$$(4)(4) + u_{22} = 20 \quad \Rightarrow u_{22} = 20 - 16 = 4;$$

$$(4)(5) + u_{23} = 32 \quad \Rightarrow u_{23} = 32 - 20 = 12;$$

$$(5)(4) + \ell_{32} u_{22} = 32 \quad \Rightarrow \ell_{32} = (32 - 20)/4 = 3.$$

Finally, the only remaining unknown in matrix $\mathbf{U}$ is determined:

$$
\begin{bmatrix} 1 & 0 & 0 \\ 4 & 1 & 0 \\ 5 & 3 & 1 \end{bmatrix} \cdot \begin{bmatrix} 1 & 4 & 5 \\ 0 & 4 & 12 \\ 0 & 0 & u_{33} \end{bmatrix} = \begin{bmatrix} 1 & 4 & 5 \\ 4 & 20 & 32 \\ 5 & 32 & 64 \end{bmatrix},
$$

$$(5)(5) + (3)(12) + u_{33} = 64 \Rightarrow u_{33} = 64 - 25 - 36 = 3.$$

The factorization is

$$
\mathbf{L} = \begin{bmatrix} 1 & 0 & 0 \\ 4 & 1 & 0 \\ 5 & 3 & 1 \end{bmatrix}, \quad \mathbf{U} = \begin{bmatrix} 1 & 4 & 5 \\ 0 & 4 & 12 \\ 0 & 0 & 3 \end{bmatrix}.
$$

6.4.2 Cholesky LU Factorization

If the matrix $\mathbf{A}$ is symmetric positive definite, there is a very convenient form of LU factorization, called Cholesky factorization, for which the upper triangular matrix $\mathbf{U}$ is the transpose of the lower triangular matrix $\mathbf{L}$; i.e., $\mathbf{A} = \mathbf{L}\mathbf{L}'$. Furthermore, only $n(n + 1)/2$ storage locations are required, rather than the usual n^2. In its more general form, for a three-by-three matrix $\mathbf{A}$, the problem is to find matrices $\mathbf{L}$ and $\mathbf{U}$ so that $\mathbf{L}\mathbf{U} = \mathbf{A}$; that is, we seek

$$
\begin{bmatrix} x_{11} & 0 & 0 \\ \ell_{21} & x_{22} & 0 \\ \ell_{31} & \ell_{32} & x_{33} \end{bmatrix} \cdot \begin{bmatrix} x_{11} & u_{12} & u_{13} \\ 0 & x_{22} & u_{23} \\ 0 & 0 & x_{33} \end{bmatrix} = \begin{bmatrix} a_{11} & a_{12} & a_{13} \\ a_{21} & a_{22} & a_{23} \\ a_{31} & a_{32} & a_{33} \end{bmatrix},
$$

where the corresponding diagonal elements of $\mathbf{L}$ and $\mathbf{U}$ are required to be equal ($u_{ii} = \ell_{ii} = x_{ii}$).

The following MATLAB function for Cholesky LU factorization assumes that $\mathbf{A}$ is symmetric. A check for the symmetry of $\mathbf{A}$ could easily be added, by testing to see whether $\mathbf{A} = \mathbf{A}'$. The function does not exploit the storage savings that can be accomplished by writing $\mathbf{L}$ and $\mathbf{U}$ over the original matrix $\mathbf{A}$; instead, $\mathbf{A}$ is saved to allow verification of the factorization.

MATLAB Function for Cholesky LU Factorization

```
function [L, U] = Cholesky(A)
%    A is assumed to be symmetric
%    L is computed, and U = L'
[ n, m ] = size(A);  % The dimension of A
L = zeros(n, n);      % Initialize L
for k = 1:n
    L(k,k) = sqrt( A(k, k) - L(k,1:k-1)*L(k,1:k-1)' );
    for i = k+1:n
        L(i,k) = (A(i,k) - L(i,1:k-1) * L(k,1:k-1)')/L(k,k);
    end
end
U = L'
```

If the matrix $\mathbf{A}$ is symmetric and positive definite, the Cholesky factorization can be carried out without pivoting or scaling. If $\mathbf{A}$ is not positive definite, the procedure may encounter the square root of a negative number at some stage of the computation. (See Atkinson, 1989.)

Example 6.7 Cholesky LU Factorization

The Cholesky form of LU factorization for $\mathbf{A} = \begin{bmatrix} 1 & 4 & 5 \\ 4 & 20 & 32 \\ 5 & 32 & 64 \end{bmatrix}$ requires the diagonal of the $\mathbf{L}$ and $\mathbf{U}$ matrices to be equal, so we write the desired product as

$$\begin{bmatrix} x_{11} & 0 & 0 \\ \ell_{21} & x_{22} & 0 \\ \ell_{31} & \ell_{32} & x_{33} \end{bmatrix} \cdot \begin{bmatrix} x_{11} & u_{12} & u_{13} \\ 0 & x_{22} & u_{23} \\ 0 & 0 & x_{33} \end{bmatrix} = \begin{bmatrix} 1 & 4 & 5 \\ 4 & 20 & 32 \\ 5 & 32 & 64 \end{bmatrix}$$

and proceed to solve for the unknowns in a systematic manner. The first stage of calculations gives

$$x_{11} x_{11} = a_{11} = 1 \Rightarrow x_{11} = 1;$$

$$x_{11} u_{12} = a_{12} = 4 \Rightarrow u_{12} = 4/1 = 4;$$

$$x_{11} u_{13} = a_{13} = 5 \Rightarrow u_{13} = 5/1 = 5;$$

$$\ell_{21} x_{11} = a_{21} = 4 \Rightarrow \ell_{21} = 4/1 = 4;$$

$$\ell_{31} x_{11} = a_{31} = 5 \Rightarrow \ell_{31} = 5/1 = 5.$$

Note that if $\mathbf{A}$ is symmetric, $a_{1j} = a_{j1}$, and it is automatic that $\ell_{j1} = u_{1j}$.

Next, from the values computed in the first stage, the product is

$$\begin{bmatrix} 1 & 0 & 0 \\ 4 & x_{22} & 0 \\ 5 & \ell_{32} & x_{33} \end{bmatrix} \cdot \begin{bmatrix} 1 & 4 & 5 \\ 0 & x_{22} & u_{23} \\ 0 & 0 & x_{33} \end{bmatrix} = \begin{bmatrix} 1 & 4 & 5 \\ 4 & 20 & 32 \\ 5 & 32 & 64 \end{bmatrix};$$

we thus compute

$$(4)(4) + (x_{22})(x_{22}) = 20 \Rightarrow x_{22} = (20 - 16)^{1/2} = 2;$$

$$(4)(5) + (x_{22})u_{23} = 32 \Rightarrow u_{23} = (32 - 20)/2 = 6;$$

$$(5)(4) + \ell_{32}(x_{22}) = 32 \Rightarrow \ell_{32} = (32 - 20)/2 = 6.$$

Finally, we find the last unknown:

$$\begin{bmatrix} 1 & 0 & 0 \\ 4 & 2 & 0 \\ 5 & 6 & x_{33} \end{bmatrix} \cdot \begin{bmatrix} 1 & 4 & 5 \\ 0 & 2 & 6 \\ 0 & 0 & x_{33} \end{bmatrix} = \begin{bmatrix} 1 & 4 & 5 \\ 4 & 20 & 32 \\ 5 & 32 & 64 \end{bmatrix},$$

$$(5)(5) + (6)(6) + (x_{33})(x_{33}) = 64 \Rightarrow x_{33} = (64 - 25 - 36)^{1/2} = \sqrt{3}.$$

The LU factorization, with $\mathbf{L}$ and $\mathbf{U}$ as follows, satisfies $\mathbf{L} = \mathbf{U}'$:

$$\mathbf{L} = \begin{bmatrix} 1 & 0 & 0 \\ 4 & 2 & 0 \\ 5 & 6 & \sqrt{3} \end{bmatrix}, \qquad \mathbf{U} = \begin{bmatrix} 1 & 4 & 5 \\ 0 & 2 & 6 \\ 0 & 0 & \sqrt{3} \end{bmatrix}.$$

6.5 APPLICATIONS OF LU FACTORIZATION

6.5.1 Solving Systems of Linear Equations

One advantage of saving the multipliers so that the $\mathbf{L}$ matrix can be formed is evident from the situation in which the same system of equations must be solved again later, with a different right-hand side. If the coefficient matrix $\mathbf{A}$ of a linear system of equations is written as the product of a lower triangular matrix $\mathbf{L}$ and an upper triangular matrix $\mathbf{U}$, the linear system can be solved easily in two steps.

The original matrix-vector equation, $\mathbf{Ax} = \mathbf{b}$, is written in terms of the LU factorization of $\mathbf{A}$ as $\mathbf{LUx} = \mathbf{b}$. We introduce the unknown vector $\mathbf{y}$, defined as $\mathbf{Ux} = \mathbf{y}$. We first solve the system $\mathbf{Ly} = \mathbf{b}$ for $\mathbf{y}$ by "forward substitution"; i.e., we solve for y_1 first, y_2 next, etc. We then solve the system $\mathbf{Ux} = \mathbf{y}$ for $\mathbf{x}$ by "backward substitution," finding x_n first, then x_{n-1} next, etc.

Example 6.8 Solving Electrical Circuit for Several Voltages

Consider again the electric circuit of Figure 6.1 with resistances as shown, but with $V_1 = 0$, $V_2 = 80$, and $V_3 = 0$. The system to be solved is $\mathbf{Ax} = \mathbf{b}$, where

$$\mathbf{A} = \begin{bmatrix} 30 & -20 & -10 \\ -20 & 55 & -10 \\ -10 & -10 & 50 \end{bmatrix} \quad \text{and} \quad \mathbf{b} = \begin{bmatrix} 0 \\ 80 \\ 0 \end{bmatrix}.$$

As found in Example 6.3, $\mathbf{A} = \mathbf{LU}$, for

$$\mathbf{L} = \begin{bmatrix} 1 & 0 & 0 \\ -2/3 & 1 & 0 \\ -1/3 & -2/5 & 1 \end{bmatrix} \quad \text{and} \quad \mathbf{U} = \begin{bmatrix} 30 & -20 & -10 \\ 0 & 125/3 & -50/3 \\ 0 & 0 & 40 \end{bmatrix}.$$

We first solve $\mathbf{Ly} = \mathbf{b}$, i.e.,

$$\begin{bmatrix} 1 & 0 & 0 \\ -2/3 & 1 & 0 \\ -1/3 & -2/5 & 1 \end{bmatrix} \begin{bmatrix} y_1 \\ y_2 \\ y_3 \end{bmatrix} = \begin{bmatrix} 0 \\ 80 \\ 0 \end{bmatrix},$$

and find, by forward substitution, that

$$y_1 = 0, \quad y_2 = 80, \quad \text{and} \quad y_3 = (2/5)(80) = 32.$$

Next, we solve $\mathbf{Ux} = \mathbf{y}$, or

$$\begin{bmatrix} 30 & -20 & -10 \\ 0 & 125/3 & -50/3 \\ 0 & 0 & 40 \end{bmatrix} \begin{bmatrix} x_1 \\ x_2 \\ x_3 \end{bmatrix} = \begin{bmatrix} 0 \\ 80 \\ 32 \end{bmatrix},$$

and find, by backward substitution, that

$$x_3 = 32/40 = 4/5,$$

$$x_2 = (80 + 40/3)(3/125) = 56/25,$$

and

$$x_1 = (1/30)[-20(56/25) - 10(4/5)] = 44/25.$$

The resulting electrical currents in each of the three loops are

$$i_1 = 1.76, \quad i_2 = 2.24, \quad \text{and} \quad i_3 = 0.80.$$

MATLAB Function to Solve the Linear System LU $x = b$

```
function x = LU_Solve(L, U, b)
% Function to solve the equation L U x = b
      L    --> Lower triangular matrix (with 1's on diagonal)
      U    --> Upper triangular matrix
      b    --> Right-hand side vector
[n m] = size(L);   z = zeros(n,1);   x = zeros(n,1);
% Solve L z = b using forward substitution
z(1) = b(1);
for i = 2:n
    z(i) = b(i) - L(i, 1:i-1) * z(1:i-1);
end
```

```
% Solve U x = z using back substitution
x(n) = z(n) / U(n, n);
for i = n-1 : -1 : 1
    x(i) = (z(i) - U(i,i+1:n) * x(i+1:n)) / U(i, i);
end
```

Note that if pivoting had been used in decomposing $\mathbf{A}$, then the system to be solved no longer would be $\mathbf{Ax} = \mathbf{b}$, but rather would be $\mathbf{PAx} = \mathbf{Pb}$, where $\mathbf{PA} = \mathbf{LU}$. In such a case, the original right-hand side must be transformed to $\mathbf{c} = \mathbf{Pb}$. The right-hand side $\mathbf{b}$ (or $\mathbf{c}$ if pivoting has been used) may be entered as either a row or a column vector in the MATLAB function. The initialization of the vectors $\mathbf{z}$ and $\mathbf{x}$ forces them to be column vectors, as required for the matrix-vector multiplications to be defined.

As described for Gaussian elimination in Chapter 3, this routine can be generalized easily to the case of multiple right-hand sides. For each column of the right-hand-side matrix $\mathbf{b}$, there will be a corresponding column in the solution matrices $\mathbf{z}$ and $\mathbf{x}$. A MATLAB function for multiple right-hand sides is presented in Section 6.5.4, where it is used to find the inverse of a matrix.

6.5.2 Solving a Tridiagonal System Using LU Factorization

A tridiagonal system whose coefficient matrix has been factored as described in Section 6.2 can also be solved by a MATLAB function.

MATLAB Function for Solving a Tridiagonal System Using LU Factorization

```
function x = LU_tridiag_solve(a, d, b, r)
%   Function to solve the equation A x = r
%   LU factorization of A is expressed as
%   Lower bidiagonal matrix:
%       diagonal is 1s, lower diagonal is b; b(1) = 0.
%   Upper bidiagonal matrix: diagonal is d, upper diagonal is a
%   Right-hand-side vector is r
%   Solve L z = r using forward substitution
n = length(d);
z(1) = r(1);
for i = 2:n
    z(i) = r(i) - b(i) * z(i-1);
end
% Solve U x = z using back substitution
x(n) = z(n) / d(n);
for i = n-1 : -1 : 1
    x(i) = (z(i) - a(i) * x(i+1)) / d(i);
end
```

Example 6.9 Solving a Tridiagonal System Using LU Factorization

To solve the system $\mathbf{Ax} = \mathbf{r}$, where

$$\mathbf{A} = \begin{bmatrix} 1 & 4 & 0 & 0 & 0 \\ 4 & 15 & 1 & 0 & 0 \\ 0 & -2 & 3 & 2 & 0 \\ 0 & 0 & 3 & 7 & 5 \\ 0 & 0 & 0 & 4 & 21 \end{bmatrix}$$

and $\mathbf{r} = [-7 \quad -23 \quad 5 \quad 6 \quad 89]'$, we can take advantage of the tridiagonal structure of $\mathbf{A}$ to represent it more efficiently in terms of the vectors $\mathbf{a}$, $\mathbf{d}$, and $\mathbf{b}$:

$$\mathbf{a} = [4 \quad 1 \quad 2 \quad 5 \quad 0],$$

$$\mathbf{d} = [1 \quad 15 \quad 3 \quad 7 \quad 21],$$

$$\mathbf{b} = [0 \quad 4 \quad -2 \quad 3 \quad 4].$$

Using the MATLAB function from Section 6.2, we find that the $\mathbf{L}$ matrix is specified by the vector of elements on the subdiagonal:

$$\mathbf{bb} = [0 \quad 4 \quad 2 \quad 3 \quad 4].$$

The matrix $\mathbf{U}$ has the same superdiagonal vector $\mathbf{a}$ as the original matrix, but the elements on the diagonal of $\mathbf{U}$ are given by the vector

$$\mathbf{dd} = [1 \quad -1 \quad 1 \quad 1 \quad 1]$$

Solving the system using the MATLAB function

$$\mathbf{x} = \text{LU\_tridiag\_solve}(a, dd, bb, r)$$

gives

$$\mathbf{x} = [1 \quad -2 \quad 3 \quad -4 \quad 5].$$

6.5.3 Determinant of a Matrix

The determinant of a matrix is useful in a variety of situations, including solving eigenvalue problems and making a change of variable in a multiple integral. Cramer's rule for solving systems of linear equations is based on the ratio of two determinants, but it is not an efficient numerical method for solving large systems.

The determinant of **A** can be found as follows:

If $\mathbf{A} = \mathbf{LU}$, then $\det(\mathbf{A}) = \prod_{i=1}^{n} \ell_{ii} \prod_{i=1}^{n} u_{ii}$.

If pivoting is used, so that $\mathbf{A} = \mathbf{P}^{-1}\mathbf{LU}$, we have

$$\det(\mathbf{A}) = (-1)^k \prod_{i=1}^{n} \ell_{ii} \prod_{i=1}^{n} u_{ii},$$

where k is the number of row interchanges that occurred during the LU factorization.

Example 6.10 Finding the Determinant of a Matrix

To find the determinant of the three-by-three matrix

$$\mathbf{A} = \begin{bmatrix} 1 & -1 & 2 \\ -2 & 1 & 1 \\ -1 & 2 & 1 \end{bmatrix},$$

we begin by finding its LU factorization, where

$$\mathbf{L} = \begin{bmatrix} 1 & 0 & 0 \\ -2 & 1 & 0 \\ -1 & -1 & 1 \end{bmatrix} \quad \text{and} \quad \mathbf{U} = \begin{bmatrix} 1 & -1 & 2 \\ 0 & -1 & 5 \\ 0 & 0 & 8 \end{bmatrix}.$$

Since pivoting was not required, we obtain

$$\det(\mathbf{A}) = u_{11}u_{22}u_{33} = (1)(-1)(8) = -8.$$

6.5.4 Inverse of a Matrix

The inverse of an n-by-n matrix **A** can be found by solving the system of equations

$$\mathbf{A}\mathbf{x}_i = \mathbf{e}_i \quad (i = 1, \ldots, n)$$

for the vectors $\mathbf{e}_i = [0 \quad 0 \quad \ldots \quad 1 \quad \ldots \quad 0 \quad 0]'$, where the 1 appears in the ith position. The matrix **X** whose columns are the solution vectors $\mathbf{x}_1, \ldots, \mathbf{x}_n$ is $\mathbf{A}^{-1}$. The process is illustrated in Example 6.11.

Example 6.11 Finding a Matrix Inverse Using LU Factorization

Find the inverse of the three-by-three matrix $\mathbf{A} = \mathbf{LU}$, where

$$\mathbf{A} = \begin{bmatrix} 1 & -1 & 2 \\ -2 & 1 & 1 \\ -1 & 2 & 1 \end{bmatrix}, \quad \mathbf{L} = \begin{bmatrix} 1 & 0 & 0 \\ -2 & 1 & 0 \\ -1 & -1 & 1 \end{bmatrix}, \quad \mathbf{U} = \begin{bmatrix} 1 & -1 & 2 \\ 0 & -1 & 5 \\ 0 & 0 & 8 \end{bmatrix}.$$

First we solve $\mathbf{LY} = \mathbf{I}$ for $\mathbf{Y}$, i.e.,

$$\begin{bmatrix} 1 & 0 & 0 \\ -2 & 1 & 0 \\ -1 & -1 & 1 \end{bmatrix} \cdot \begin{bmatrix} y_{11} & y_{12} & y_{13} \\ y_{21} & y_{22} & y_{23} \\ y_{31} & y_{32} & y_{33} \end{bmatrix} = \begin{bmatrix} 1 & 0 & 0 \\ 0 & 1 & 0 \\ 0 & 0 & 1 \end{bmatrix}.$$

The first column of $\mathbf{Y}$ is the solution vector for the system

$$\begin{bmatrix} 1 & 0 & 0 \\ -2 & 1 & 0 \\ -1 & -1 & 1 \end{bmatrix} \cdot \begin{bmatrix} y_{11} \\ y_{21} \\ y_{31} \end{bmatrix} = \begin{bmatrix} 1 \\ 0 \\ 0 \end{bmatrix}.$$

The second and third columns of $\mathbf{Y}$ are found in a similar manner, using the second and third columns of $\mathbf{I}$. Each column of $\mathbf{Y}$ is found by forward substitution, using the corresponding column of $\mathbf{I}$. The solution that is obtained is

$$\mathbf{Y} = \begin{bmatrix} 1 & 0 & 0 \\ 2 & 1 & 0 \\ 3 & 1 & 1 \end{bmatrix}.$$

Finally, we solve $\mathbf{U\,X} - \mathbf{Y}$ for $\mathbf{X}$; then $\mathbf{A}^{-1} = \mathbf{X}$. We have

$$\begin{bmatrix} 1 & -1 & 2 \\ 0 & -1 & 5 \\ 0 & 0 & 8 \end{bmatrix} \cdot \begin{bmatrix} x_{11} & x_{12} & x_{13} \\ x_{21} & x_{22} & x_{23} \\ x_{31} & x_{32} & x_{33} \end{bmatrix} = \begin{bmatrix} 1 & 0 & 0 \\ 2 & 1 & 0 \\ 3 & 1 & 1 \end{bmatrix}.$$

The solution is easily found for each column of $\mathbf{X}$, using back substitution and the corresponding column of $\mathbf{Y}$. The solution is

$$\mathbf{X} = \mathbf{A}^{-1} = \begin{bmatrix} 1/8 & -5/8 & 3/8 \\ -1/8 & -3/8 & 5/8 \\ 3/8 & 1/8 & 1/8 \end{bmatrix}.$$

Using the LU factorization of $\mathbf{A}$ and the general LU-solve function given next, we can construct $\mathbf{X}$. It is not necessary to write a separate MATLAB function for the matrix inverse using LU factorization. The function LU_Solve_Gen (L, U, B) will produce $\mathbf{A}^{-1}$ when $\mathbf{B}$ is the identity matrix.

```
function x = LU_Solve_Gen(L, U, B)
% Function to solve the equation L U x = B
%    L  --> Lower triangular matrix (1's on diagonal)
%    U  --> Upper triangular matrix
%    B  --> Right-hand-side matrix
[n    n2] = size(L);    [m1    m] = size(B);
% Solve L z = B using forward substitution
```

```
for j = 1:m
    z(1, j) = b(1, j);
    for i = 2 : n
        z(i,j) = B(i,j) - L(i, 1:i-1) * z(1:i-1, j);
    end
end
% Solve U x = z using back substitution
for j = 1:m
    x(n, j) = z(n, j) / U(n, n);
    for i = n-1 : -1 : 1
        x(i,j) = (z(i,j)-U(i,i+1:n)*x(i+1:n,j))/ U(i,i);
    end
end
```

6.6 MATLAB's METHODS

MATLAB has four built-in functions that perform the numerical linear algebra operations discussed in this chapter. To find the LU decomposition of a square matrix $\mathbf{A}$, the function `lu` can be used. The function call `[L, U] = lu(A)` returns an upper triangular matrix in $\mathbf{U}$ and a product of lower triangular and permutation matrices in $\mathbf{L}$ such that $\mathbf{A} = \mathbf{LU}$. Calling the function with three output arguments, i.e., `[L, U, P] = lu(A)`, returns the upper triangular, lower triangular, and permutation matrices such that $\mathbf{PA} = \mathbf{LU}$. Additional options for the function `lu` allow the user to control the pivoting in sparse matrices. More information is provided in the comments at the beginning of the function. Calling `lu(A)` with one output argument (or with no output argument specifically defined) returns the output from LINPACK's ZGEFA routine.

For Cholesky factorization, the built-in MATLAB function is `chol`. This function uses only the diagonal and upper triangular part of $\mathbf{A}$. The lower triangular part is assumed to be the (complex conjugate) transpose of the upper part. If $\mathbf{A}$ is positive definite, then `R = chol(A)` produces an upper triangular $\mathbf{R}$ so that $\mathbf{R}'\mathbf{R} = \mathbf{A}$. If $\mathbf{A}$ is not positive definite, an error message is printed. For more information on using `chol`, see the comment statements at the beginning of the function.

To find the determinant of a matrix, use the function `det`. To find the inverse of a matrix, use the function `inv`.

SUMMARY

In LU factorization, we factor $\mathbf{A} = \mathbf{LU}$, where $\mathbf{U}$ is the upper triangular matrix obtained by Gaussian elimination (without pivoting) and

$$\mathbf{L} = \begin{bmatrix} 1 & 0 & 0 & 0 \\ -m_{21} & 1 & 0 & 0 \\ -m_{31} & -m_{32} & 1 & 0 \\ -m_{41} & -m_{42} & -m_{43} & 1 \end{bmatrix}$$

is the lower triangular matrix formed from the multipliers used in the elimination (illustrated for $n = 4$).

LU Factorization of Tridiagonal System (Illustrated for $n = 4$):

$$\begin{aligned} d_1 x_1 + a_1 x_2 &= r_1, \\ b_2 x_1 + d_2 x_2 + a_2 x_3 &= r_2, \\ b_3 x_2 + d_3 x_3 + a_3 x_4 &= r_3, \\ b_4 x_3 + d_4 x_4 &= r_4. \end{aligned}$$

Compute

$$\begin{aligned} dd_1 &= d_1, \\ bb_2 &= b_2/d_1, & dd_2 &= d_2 - bb_2 a_1, \\ bb_3 &= b_3/dd_2, & dd_3 &= d_3 - bb_3 a_2, \\ bb_4 &= b_4/dd_3, & dd_4 &= d_4 - bb_4 a_3. \end{aligned}$$

The factorization is

$$\mathbf{L} = \begin{bmatrix} 1 & 0 & 0 & 0 \\ bb_2 & 1 & 0 & 0 \\ 0 & bb_3 & 1 & 0 \\ 0 & 0 & bb_4 & 1 \end{bmatrix}, \quad \mathbf{U} = \begin{bmatrix} dd_1 & a_1 & 0 & 0 \\ 0 & dd_2 & a_2 & 0 \\ 0 & 0 & dd_3 & a_3 \\ 0 & 0 & 0 & dd_4 \end{bmatrix}.$$

Direct LU Factorization: Doolittle form puts 1's on the diagonal of $\mathbf{L}$:

$$\begin{bmatrix} 1 & 0 & 0 \\ \ell_{21} & 1 & 0 \\ \ell_{31} & \ell_{32} & 1 \end{bmatrix} \cdot \begin{bmatrix} u_{11} & u_{12} & u_{13} \\ 0 & u_{22} & u_{23} \\ 0 & 0 & u_{33} \end{bmatrix} = \begin{bmatrix} a_{11} & a_{12} & a_{13} \\ a_{21} & a_{22} & a_{23} \\ a_{31} & a_{32} & a_{33} \end{bmatrix}.$$

Crout form puts 1's on the diagonal of $\mathbf{U}$:

$$\begin{bmatrix} \ell_{11} & 0 & 0 \\ \ell_{21} & \ell_{22} & 0 \\ \ell_{31} & \ell_{32} & \ell_{33} \end{bmatrix} \cdot \begin{bmatrix} 1 & u_{12} & u_{13} \\ 0 & 1 & u_{23} \\ 0 & 0 & 1 \end{bmatrix} = \begin{bmatrix} a_{11} & a_{12} & a_{13} \\ a_{21} & a_{22} & a_{23} \\ a_{31} & a_{32} & a_{33} \end{bmatrix}.$$

Cholesky form makes the diagonals of $\mathbf{L}$ and $\mathbf{U}$ equal:

$$\begin{bmatrix} x_{11} & 0 & 0 \\ \ell_{21} & x_{22} & 0 \\ \ell_{31} & \ell_{32} & x_{33} \end{bmatrix} \cdot \begin{bmatrix} x_{11} & u_{12} & u_{13} \\ 0 & x_{22} & u_{23} \\ 0 & 0 & x_{33} \end{bmatrix} = \begin{bmatrix} a_{11} & a_{12} & a_{13} \\ a_{21} & a_{22} & a_{23} \\ a_{31} & a_{32} & a_{33} \end{bmatrix}.$$

The following are a few of the many excellent undergraduate texts on linear algebra:

Kolman, B., *Introductory Linear Algebra with Applications* (6th ed.), Prentice Hall, Upper Saddle River, NJ, 1997.

Leon, S. J., *Linear Algebra with Applications* (5th ed.), Prentice Hall, Upper Saddle River, NJ, 1998.

Strang, G., *Linear Algebra and Its Applications* (3d ed.), Harcourt Brace Jovanovich, San Diego, 1988.

The following two references are at a somewhat more advanced level:

Golub, G. H., and C. F. Van Loan, *Matrix Computations* (3d ed.), Johns Hopkins University Press, Baltimore, 1996.

Fox, L., *An Introduction to Numerical Linear Algebra*, Oxford University Press, New York, 1965. This classic work also contains many bibliographic entries.

PRACTICE THE TECHNIQUES

For Problems P6.1–P6.15,

a. *find the LU factorization of the matrix, using Gaussian elimination.*
b. *find the inverse.*
c. *find the determinant.*
d. *solve $\mathbf{Ax} = \mathbf{b}$ with $\mathbf{b} = [1 \quad 1 \quad \ldots \quad 1]'$; then solve $\mathbf{Ay} = \mathbf{x}$.*

P6.1

$$\mathbf{A} = \begin{bmatrix} 1 & 2 & 3 \\ 2 & 8 & 11 \\ 3 & 22 & 35 \end{bmatrix}.$$

P6.2

$$\mathbf{A} = \begin{bmatrix} 3 & 6 & 12 \\ -1 & 0 & 2 \\ 3 & 2 & 1 \end{bmatrix}.$$

P6.3

$$\mathbf{A} = \begin{bmatrix} 2 & 1 & -2 \\ 4 & -1 & 2 \\ 2 & -1 & 1 \end{bmatrix}.$$

P6.4

$$\mathbf{A} = \begin{bmatrix} 3/2 & -1 & 1/2 \\ -1/2 & 1/2 & -1/4 \\ 1/2 & -1/2 & 1/2 \end{bmatrix}.$$

P6.5

$$\mathbf{A} = \begin{bmatrix} 1 & 1/2 & 1/3 \\ 1/2 & 1/3 & 1/4 \\ 1/3 & 1/4 & 1/5 \end{bmatrix}.$$

P6.6

$$\mathbf{A} = \begin{bmatrix} 1/5 & 0 & 0 & 0 \\ -26 & 13 & -4 & 2 \\ 12 & -6 & 2 & -1 \\ -3/2 & 3/4 & -1/4 & 1/4 \end{bmatrix}.$$

P6.7

$$\mathbf{A} = \begin{bmatrix} 1 & 1 & 0 & 3 \\ 2 & 1 & -1 & 1 \\ 3 & -1 & -1 & 2 \\ -1 & 2 & 3 & -1 \end{bmatrix}.$$

P6.8

$$\mathbf{A} = \begin{bmatrix} 1 & -2 & 6 & -12 \\ 0 & 1 & -3 & 6 \\ 0 & -5 & 16 & -32 \\ 0 & 15 & -48 & 97 \end{bmatrix}.$$

P6.9

$$\mathbf{A} = \begin{bmatrix} 3 & 7 & 4 & 0 \\ 0 & 3 & 13 & 3 \\ 0 & 0 & 1 & 4 \\ 1 & 2 & 0 & 0 \end{bmatrix}.$$

P6.10

$$\mathbf{A} = \begin{bmatrix} 1 & 2 & 3 & -1 \\ 1 & 1 & -1 & 2 \\ 0 & -1 & -1 & 3 \\ 3 & 1 & 2 & -1 \end{bmatrix}.$$

P6.11

$$\mathbf{A} = \begin{bmatrix} 1 & 2 & 3 & 1 & 0 & 0 \\ 2 & 6 & 10 & 2 & 1 & 0 \\ 3 & 14 & 28 & 3 & 4 & 1 \\ 1 & 2 & 3 & 4 & 6 & 12 \\ 0 & 2 & 4 & -1 & 1 & 2 \\ 0 & 0 & 3 & 3 & 2 & 2 \end{bmatrix}.$$

P6.12

$$\mathbf{A} = \begin{bmatrix} 2 & 1 & -2 & 1 & 0 & 0 \\ 4 & -1 & 2 & 2 & 1 & 0 \\ 2 & -1 & 1 & 1 & 2/3 & 1 \\ 2 & 1 & -2 & 5/2 & -1 & 1/2 \\ 0 & -3 & 6 & -1/2 & 10/3 & -7/6 \\ 0 & 0 & -1 & 1/2 & -7/3 & 29/12 \end{bmatrix}.$$

P6.13

$$\mathbf{A} = \begin{bmatrix} 1 & 2 & 1 & 1 & 0 & 0 \\ 2 & 6 & 4 & 2 & 1 & 0 \\ 3 & 14 & 12 & 3 & 4 & 1 \\ 1 & 2 & 1 & 2 & 6 & 12 \\ 0 & 2 & 2 & -1 & -3 & -6 \\ 2 & 4 & 3 & 3 & 2 & 2 \end{bmatrix}.$$

P6.14

$$\mathbf{A} = \begin{bmatrix} 1 & 2 & 1 & 1 & 0 & 0 & 1 & 0 & -1 & 0 \\ 2 & 6 & 4 & 2 & 1 & 0 & 2 & 2 & 0 & 1 \\ 3 & 14 & 12 & 3 & 4 & 1 & 4 & 9 & 6 & 5 \\ 1 & 2 & 1 & 2 & 2 & 3 & 1 & 1 & 1 & 3 \\ 0 & 2 & 2 & -1 & 1 & 3 & 2 & 0 & 1 & -1 \\ 2 & 4 & 3 & 3 & -2 & -7 & -1 & 4 & 0 & 2 \\ 1 & 2 & 0 & 1 & 0 & 1 & 1 & 0 & -1 & 0 \\ 0 & 2 & 4 & 0 & -1 & -4 & 3 & 9 & 0 & 7 \\ 1 & 0 & -3 & 2 & 1 & 2 & -1 & -3 & -1 & 0 \\ 0 & 2 & 2 & 1 & 3 & 4 & 0 & 4 & 5 & 7 \end{bmatrix}.$$

P6.15

$$\mathbf{A} = \begin{bmatrix} 1 & 1 & 1 & 1 & 0 & 0 & 1 & 0 & -1 & 0 \\ 1 & 3 & 2 & 1 & 1 & 0 & 1 & 1 & 0 & 1 \\ 1 & 3 & 3 & 1 & 1 & 1 & 2 & 2 & 1 & 2 \\ 1 & 1 & 1 & 3 & 1 & 1 & 1 & 1 & 1 & 1 \\ 0 & 2 & 1 & -2 & 2 & 0 & 1 & -1 & 0 & 1 \\ 1 & 1 & 2 & 3 & -1 & 2 & 1 & 3 & 2 & 1 \\ 1 & 1 & 0 & 1 & 0 & 0 & 2 & 0 & -2 & 0 \\ 0 & 2 & 2 & 0 & -1 & 0 & 2 & 6 & 0 & 3 \\ 1 & -1 & -1 & 3 & 0 & 1 & 0 & -1 & 2 & -1 \\ 0 & 2 & 1 & 2 & 2 & 2 & 0 & 4 & 4 & 4 \end{bmatrix}.$$

For Problems P6.16–P6.25, find an LU factorization of the given matrix
  a. *using the method for tridiagonal matrices.*
  b. *using Gaussian elimination.*

P6.16

$$\mathbf{A} = \begin{bmatrix} 5 & 0 & 0 \\ 5 & 3 & 1 \\ 0 & 9 & 7 \end{bmatrix}.$$

P6.17

$$\mathbf{A} = \begin{bmatrix} 4 & 2 & 0 \\ 16 & 12 & 1 \\ 0 & 8 & 5 \end{bmatrix}.$$

P6.18

$$\mathbf{A} = \begin{bmatrix} 2 & 4 & 0 \\ 2 & 8 & 2 \\ 0 & 4 & 4 \end{bmatrix}.$$

P6.19

$$\mathbf{A} = \begin{bmatrix} 5 & 1 & 0 \\ 15 & 6 & 3 \\ 0 & 9 & 11 \end{bmatrix}.$$

P6.20

$$\mathbf{A} = \begin{bmatrix} 3 & 5 & 0 \\ 12 & 24 & 3 \\ 0 & 8 & 7 \end{bmatrix}.$$

P6.21

$$\mathbf{A} = \begin{bmatrix} 1 & 3 & 0 & 0 \\ 2 & 7 & 2 & 0 \\ 0 & 2 & 5 & 5 \\ 0 & 0 & 1 & 6 \end{bmatrix}.$$

P6.22

$$\mathbf{A} = \begin{bmatrix} 3 & 1 & 0 & 0 \\ 12 & 5 & 2 & 0 \\ 0 & 2 & 8 & 5 \\ 0 & 0 & 16 & 23 \end{bmatrix}.$$

P6.23

$$\mathbf{A} = \begin{bmatrix} 1 & 4 & 0 & 0 \\ 1 & 6 & 2 & 0 \\ 0 & 6 & 10 & 3 \\ 0 & 0 & 12 & 13 \end{bmatrix}.$$

P6.24

$$\mathbf{A} = \begin{bmatrix} 2 & 1 & 0 & 0 \\ 6 & 5 & 1 & 0 \\ 0 & 2 & 3 & 5 \\ 0 & 0 & 8 & 22 \end{bmatrix}.$$

P6.25

$$\mathbf{A} = \begin{bmatrix} 5 & 0 & 0 & 0 \\ 10 & 1 & 2 & 0 \\ 0 & 3 & 7 & 4 \\ 0 & 0 & 1 & 8 \end{bmatrix}.$$

P6.26

$$\mathbf{A} = \begin{bmatrix} 1 & 2 & 0 & 0 & 0 & 0 \\ 2 & 6 & 2 & 0 & 0 & 0 \\ 0 & 8 & 9 & 0 & 0 & 0 \\ 0 & 0 & 0 & 1 & 6 & 0 \\ 0 & 0 & 0 & -1 & -4 & 6 \\ 0 & 0 & 0 & 0 & -4 & -11 \end{bmatrix}.$$

P6.27

$$\mathbf{A} = \begin{bmatrix} 1 & -5 & 0 & 0 & 0 & 0 \\ 2 & -8 & -4 & 0 & 0 & 0 \\ 0 & 6 & -9 & -3 & 0 & 0 \\ 0 & 0 & 12 & -8 & -2 & 0 \\ 0 & 0 & 0 & 20 & -5 & -1 \\ 0 & 0 & 0 & 0 & 30 & 0 \end{bmatrix}.$$

P6.28

$$\mathbf{A} = \begin{bmatrix} 4 & 4 & 0 & 0 & 0 & 0 \\ 16 & 20 & 0 & 0 & 0 & 0 \\ 0 & 4 & 3 & 1 & 0 & 0 \\ 0 & 0 & 9 & 5 & 4 & 0 \\ 0 & 0 & 0 & 10 & 21 & 2 \\ 0 & 0 & 0 & 0 & 3 & 7 \end{bmatrix}.$$

P6.29

$$\mathbf{A} = \begin{bmatrix} 5 & 2 & 0 & 0 & 0 & 0 \\ 15 & 10 & 0 & 0 & 0 & 0 \\ 0 & 8 & 2 & 2 & 0 & 0 \\ 0 & 0 & 2 & 5 & 4 & 0 \\ 0 & 0 & 0 & 9 & 16 & 4 \\ 0 & 0 & 0 & 0 & 16 & 17 \end{bmatrix}.$$

P6.30

$$\mathbf{A} = \begin{bmatrix} 1 & 1 & 0 & 0 & 0 & 0 & 0 & 0 & 0 & 0 \\ 1 & 3 & 1 & 0 & 0 & 0 & 0 & 0 & 0 & 0 \\ 0 & 4 & 3 & 1 & 0 & 0 & 0 & 0 & 0 & 0 \\ 0 & 0 & 3 & 5 & 1 & 0 & 0 & 0 & 0 & 0 \\ 0 & 0 & 0 & -2 & 1 & 1 & 0 & 0 & 0 & 0 \\ 0 & 0 & 0 & 0 & -4 & -1 & 0 & 0 & 0 & 0 \\ 0 & 0 & 0 & 0 & 0 & -3 & 2 & 1 & 0 & 0 \\ 0 & 0 & 0 & 0 & 0 & 0 & 2 & 3 & 0 & 0 \\ 0 & 0 & 0 & 2 & 1 & 0 & 0 & 4 & 2 & 0 \\ 0 & 0 & 0 & 2 & 1 & 0 & 0 & 0 & 6 & 1 \end{bmatrix}.$$

For Problems P6.31–P6.35, find an LU factorization of a permutation of **A**, *using Gaussian elimination with row pivoting.*

P6.31

$$\mathbf{A} = \begin{bmatrix} 6 & 2 & 2 \\ 6 & 2 & 1 \\ 1 & 2 & -1 \end{bmatrix}.$$

P6.32

$$\mathbf{A} = \begin{bmatrix} 1 & 2 & 3 \\ 2 & 4 & 10 \\ 3 & 14 & 28 \end{bmatrix}.$$

P6.33

$$\mathbf{A} = \begin{bmatrix} -1 & 1 & 0 & 0 \\ 1 & -1 & 1 & 0 \\ 0 & 1 & -1 & 1 \\ 0 & 0 & 1 & -1 \end{bmatrix}.$$

P6.34

$$\mathbf{A} = \begin{bmatrix} 2 & -1 & 0 & 0 & 0 & 0 \\ -1 & 2 & -1 & 0 & 0 & 0 \\ 0 & -1 & 2/3 & -1 & 0 & 0 \\ 0 & 0 & -1 & 2 & -1 & 0 \\ 0 & 0 & 0 & -1 & 2 & -1 \\ 0 & 0 & 0 & 0 & -1 & 2 \end{bmatrix}.$$

P6.35

$$\mathbf{A} = \begin{bmatrix} 1 & -2 & 0 & 0 & 0 & 0 \\ -2 & 6 & 4 & 0 & 0 & 0 \\ 0 & 4 & 8 & -1/2 & 0 & 0 \\ 0 & 0 & -1/2 & 13/4 & 3/2 & 0 \\ 0 & 0 & 0 & 3/2 & 7/4 & -3 \\ 0 & 0 & 0 & 0 & -3 & 13 \end{bmatrix}.$$

For Problems P6.36–P6.40, find the LU factorization of the given matrix

    a.   *in Doolittle form.*
    b.   *in Cholesky form.*
    c.   *Use the LU factorization from Part a or b to solve the linear system* $\mathbf{Ax} = \mathbf{b}$ *for the given* $\mathbf{b}$.

P6.36

$$\mathbf{A} = \begin{bmatrix} 1 & 2 & 3 \\ 2 & 20 & 26 \\ 3 & 26 & 70 \end{bmatrix}.$$

i. $\mathbf{b} = [14 \quad 120 \quad 265]'$.

ii. $\mathbf{b} = [7 \quad 38 \quad 123]'$.

iii. $\mathbf{b} = [10 \quad 48 \quad 173]'$.

P6.37

$$\mathbf{A} = \begin{bmatrix} 9 & 18 & 36 \\ 18 & 40 & 84 \\ 36 & 84 & 181 \end{bmatrix}.$$

i. $\mathbf{b} = [63 \quad 146 \quad 313]'$.
ii. $\mathbf{b} = [0 \quad -8 \quad -25]'$.
iii. $\mathbf{b} = [-18 \quad -32 \quad -59]'$.

P6.38

$$\mathbf{A} = \begin{bmatrix} 9 & 18 & 36 \\ 18 & 52 & 116 \\ 36 & 116 & 265.25 \end{bmatrix}.$$

i. $\mathbf{b} = [63.00 \quad 186.00 \quad 417.25]'$.
ii. $\mathbf{b} = [-9.00 \quad -46.00 \quad -113.25]'$.
iii. $\mathbf{b} = [81 \quad 306 \quad 721]'$.

P6.39

$$\mathbf{A} = \begin{bmatrix} 2 & -1 & 0 & 0 & 0 & 0 \\ -1 & 2 & -1 & 0 & 0 & 0 \\ 0 & -1 & 2/3 & -1 & 0 & 0 \\ 0 & 0 & -1 & 2 & -1 & 0 \\ 0 & 0 & 0 & -1 & 2 & -1 \\ 0 & 0 & 0 & 0 & -1 & 2 \end{bmatrix}.$$

i. $\mathbf{b} = [3 \quad -3 \quad 2 \quad -2 \quad -3 \quad -1]'$.
ii. $\mathbf{b} = [0 \quad 0 \quad 1 \quad -2 \quad -3 \quad -1]'$.
iii. $\mathbf{b} = [3 \quad -5 \quad 13/3 \quad -9 \quad 11 \quad -9]'$.

P6.40

$$\mathbf{A} = \begin{bmatrix} 1 & 1 & 1 & 1 & 0 & 0 & 1 & 0 & -1 & 0 \\ 1 & 5 & 3 & 1 & 2 & 0 & 1 & 2 & 1 & 2 \\ 1 & 3 & 3 & 1 & 1 & 1 & 2 & 2 & 1 & 2 \\ 1 & 1 & 1 & 5 & 2 & 2 & 1 & 2 & 3 & 2 \\ 0 & 2 & 1 & 2 & 6 & 3 & 2 & 0 & 5 & 4 \\ 0 & 0 & 1 & 2 & 3 & 4 & 2 & 1 & 5 & 3 \\ 1 & 1 & 2 & 1 & 2 & 2 & 7 & 2 & -1 & 4 \\ 0 & 2 & 2 & 2 & 0 & 1 & 2 & 9 & 2 & 5 \\ -1 & 1 & 1 & 3 & 5 & 5 & -1 & 2 & 14 & 4 \\ 0 & 2 & 2 & 2 & 4 & 3 & 4 & 5 & 4 & 7 \end{bmatrix}.$$

i. $\mathbf{b} = [0 \quad 8 \quad 3 \quad -14 \quad -39 \quad -32 \quad -1 \quad 45 \quad -56 \quad -1]'$.
ii. $\mathbf{b} = [-15 \ -43 \ -43 \ -27 \ -12 \ -14 \ -59 \ -79 \ 2 \ -63]'$.
iii. $\mathbf{b} = [-6 \ -10 \ -8 \ -12 \ -7 \ 0 \ -29 \ -19 \ 24 \ -21]'$.

EXPLORE SOME APPLICATIONS

LU factorization is especially useful for solving linear systems that must be solved for several different right-hand sides which are not known in advance. One place that this occurs is in using the inverse power method, discussed in the next chapter.

For each of the following matrices, find the LU decomposition, and use it to solve the sequence of linear systems. Start with $\mathbf{b} = [1 \ 1 \ 1]'$, *and solve* $\mathbf{Ax} = \mathbf{b}$. *Then find* $\mathbf{y}$ *such that* $\mathbf{Ay} = \mathbf{x}$.

A6.1

$$\mathbf{A} = \begin{bmatrix} 1 & 0 & 0 \\ 2 & -1 & 2 \\ 4 & -4 & 5 \end{bmatrix}.$$

A6.2

$$\mathbf{A} = \begin{bmatrix} 5 & -2 & 1 \\ 3 & 0 & 1 \\ 0 & 0 & 2 \end{bmatrix}.$$

A6.3

$$\mathbf{A} = \begin{bmatrix} 2 & 2 & -1 \\ -5 & 9 & -3 \\ -4 & 4 & 1 \end{bmatrix}.$$

A6.4

$$\mathbf{A} = \begin{bmatrix} -19 & 20 & -6 \\ -12 & 13 & -3 \\ 30 & -30 & 12 \end{bmatrix}.$$

Problems A6.5–A6.7 make use of a matrix formulation of quadratic equations. The quadratic form $ax^2 + bxy + cy^2 = F(x,y)$ *can be written in matrix form as* $[\mathbf{Av}]\mathbf{v} = F(x,y)$, *with* $v = [x, y]'$ *and* $\mathbf{A} = \begin{bmatrix} a & b/2 \\ b/2 & c \end{bmatrix}$. *The form of the graph of the quadratic equation*

$$ax^2 + bxy + cy^2 = d, (d \neq 0)$$

is given by the sign of the determinant of the matrix $\mathbf{A}$:

If $det(\mathbf{A}) < 0$, *the graph is a hyperbola;*
if $det(\mathbf{A}) > 0$, *the graph is an ellipse or a circle (or is degenerate);*
if $det(\mathbf{A}) = 0$, *the graph is a pair of straight lines (or is degenerate).*

(For further discussion of these ideas, see Grossman and Derrick, 1988, p. 490.)

Write the following equations in matrix form, and determine whether the equation is a hyperbola, an ellipse, a circle, or a pair of straight lines.

A6.5 $x^2 - \sqrt{3}xy + 2y^2 = 10.$

A6.6 $4x^2 + 3\sqrt{3}xy + y^2 = 22.$

A6.7 $x^2 - \sqrt{3}xy = -2.$

EXTEND YOUR UNDERSTANDING

U6.1 Compare the computational effort required to find the LU factorization for a tridiagonal system by means of the standard Gaussian elimination with the effort needed if one uses the special form of the algorithm. Consider the operation count for each method, and then find the flops for the MATLAB functions. (Take Problems P6.16, P6.21, P6.26, and P6.30 as examples.)

U6.2 Compare the computational efforts required to find the Doolittle and Cholesky LU factorizations for a symmetric matrix. Consider the operation count for each method, and then find the flops for the MATLAB functions. (Take Problems P6.36, P6.39, and P6.40 as examples.)

U6.3 Construct an example of a symmetric matrix for which the Cholesky factorization fails.

Eigenvalues, Eigenvectors, and QR Factorization

The factorization of a matrix $\mathbf{A}$ into the product of lower triangular and upper triangular matrices $\mathbf{L}$ and $\mathbf{U}$, discussed in Chapter 6, provides a method for finding several quantities associated with $\mathbf{A}$, including the determinant of $\mathbf{A}$, the inverse of $\mathbf{A}$, and the solution of the linear system $\mathbf{Ax} = \mathbf{b}$. In this chapter, we conclude our investigation into topics from numerical linear algebra by considering techniques for finding the eigenvalues and eigenvectors of a matrix. We already have encountered eigenvalues in Chapter 4, where they appear in the analysis of the convergence characteristics of iterative methods for solving linear systems. The estimation of eigenvalues based on the Gerschgorin theorem was presented in Chapter 1.

We first consider a method, known as the power method, for finding a specific eigenvalue and its associated eigenvector for a given matrix $\mathbf{A}$. The basic power method finds the dominant eigenvalue, i.e., the eigenvalue of largest magnitude. Variations of the power method can be used to find the eigenvalue of smallest magnitude or the eigenvalue closest to a specified value.

We next consider the factorization of $\mathbf{A}$ into the product of an orthogonal matrix $\mathbf{Q}$ and a right (upper) triangular matrix $\mathbf{R}$. *QR factorization* can be used for a number of types of problems, including solving a linear system and finding an orthonormal basis for the space spanned by a collection of vectors. We restrict our application of QR factorization to its use in finding the eigenvalues of $\mathbf{A}$.

Eigenvalues and eigenvectors are important in many areas of science and engineering, including solving differential equations and finding physical characteristics of a structure, such as the principal stress, moments of inertia, etc.

Example 7-A Inertia

The principal inertias and principal axes of a three-dimensional object can be found from the eigenvalues and eigenvectors, respectively, of its inertial matrix. For example, consider a body consisting of unit point masses at $(1, 0, 0)$, $(1, 2, 0)$, and $(0, 0, 1)$. (See Fig. 7.1.) Its inertial matrix is

$$\mathbf{G} = \begin{bmatrix} 5 & -2 & 0 \\ -2 & 3 & 0 \\ 0 & 0 & 6 \end{bmatrix}.$$

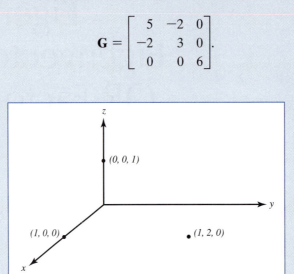

FIGURE 7.1 A body consisting of three unit point masses.

In general, the inertial matrix is

$$\mathbf{G} = \begin{bmatrix} I_{xx} & -I_{xy} & -I_{xz} \\ -I_{yx} & I_{yy} & -I_{yz} \\ -I_{zx} & -I_{zy} & I_{zz} \end{bmatrix},$$

where the moments of inertia of the body around the x-, y-, and z-axes are, respectively

$$I_{xx} = \int (y^2 + z^2)\, dm, \qquad I_{yy} = \int (x^2 + z^2)\, dm, \qquad I_{zz} = \int (x^2 + y^2)\, dm,$$

and the corresponding products of inertia are

$$I_{xy} = I_{yx} = \int xy\, dm, \qquad I_{xz} = I_{zx} = \int xz\, dm, \qquad I_{yz} = I_{zy} = \int yz\, dm.$$

(See Greenberg, 1998, p. 581, or Thomson, 1986, p. 103 for further discussion.)

Example 7-B Buckling and Breaking of a Beam

The bending moment of a simply supported beam (see Fig. 7.2) is described by the differential equation

$$-x'' = \lambda x, \quad 0 \le x \le 1,$$

with boundary conditions

$$x(0) = x(1) = 0,$$

where λ is the applied load. When λ reaches a critical value, the beam buckles (and may break soon after the load exceeds that value). This smallest eigenvalue of the differential equation can be approximated by the smallest eigenvalue of the linear system obtained by the finite-difference techniques we consider in Chapter 14. Thus, for large n, we are interested in the smallest eigenvalue of the n-by-n matrix

$$\mathbf{A} = (n+1)^2 \begin{bmatrix} 2 & -1 & & & & \\ -1 & 2 & -1 & & & \\ & -1 & 2 & -1 & & \\ & & \cdot & \vdots & \cdot & \\ & & & -1 & 2 & -1 \\ & & & & -1 & 2 \end{bmatrix}.$$

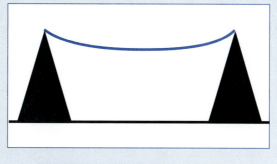

FIGURE 7.2 Simply supported beam.

The eigenvalues of the boundary value problem can be shown to be

$$\mu_j = (j\pi)^2$$

Using the MATLAB functions for finding eigenvalues discussed in this chapter, one can experiment to investigate how large n should be to achieve a reasonably accurate estimate of the smallest eigenvalue of the differential equation, namely $\mu_1 = \pi^2$, by using the eigenvalue of the discrete system. One might also compare the next smallest eigenvalue of the discrete system with the corresponding eigenvalue for the continuous problem, i.e., $\mu_2 = 4\pi^2$. (See Hager, 1988, for further discussion.)

A (real or complex) number λ is an eigenvalue of a matrix $\mathbf{A}$, and a nonzero vector $\mathbf{x}$ is a corresponding eigenvector of $\mathbf{A}$, if and only if $\mathbf{Ax} = \lambda\mathbf{x}$. A fundamental property is that λ is an eigenvalue of $\mathbf{A}$ if and only if it is a zero of the characteristic polynomial $f(\lambda) = \det(\mathbf{A} - \lambda\mathbf{I})$.

If $\mathbf{A}$ is an n-by-n matrix, the characteristic polynomial $f(\lambda)$ is an nth degree polynomial. Therefore, the fundamental theorem of algebra applies to the eigenvalues of $\mathbf{A}$, as well as to the zeros of the characteristic polynomial, and guarantees that $\mathbf{A}$ has n (complex) eigenvalues.

Except for very small matrices, direct calculation of the characteristic equation is not practical. If the determinant of $\mathbf{A} - \lambda\mathbf{I}$ can be calculated, the roots of the characteristic equation can be found by methods from Chapter 2. There are, however, other methods of finding the characteristic equation without direct evaluation of the determinant. (See Ralston and Rabinowitz, 1978, pp. 485–486.)

We first consider the power method, an iterative technique for finding the dominant eigenvalue (the eigenvalue of largest magnitude) of a matrix. If an eigenvalue of $\mathbf{A}$ is known, another eigenvalue can be found by applying the power method to a matrix formed by subtracting the known value from the diagonal elements of $\mathbf{A}$. Using results from linear algebra relating the eigenvalues of a matrix to those of its inverse leads to the inverse power method, which finds the eigenvalue of smallest magnitude. The inverse power method can be generalized to find the eigenvalue closest to a given value. Information from the Gerschgorin theorem presented in Chapter 1 could be used to provide an estimate of the locations of the eigenvalues if that is desired.

We next study the factorization of a matrix into an orthogonal matrix $\mathbf{Q}$ (which has the property that its inverse is equal to its transpose) and an upper (or right) triangular matrix $\mathbf{R}$. QR factorization can be used to find all of the eigenvalues of a matrix. In addition, QR factorization may be preferable to other approaches for solving the linear system $\mathbf{Ax} = \mathbf{b}$ when $\mathbf{A}$ is ill conditioned. (See Wilkinson, 1965, or Hager, 1988.)

The ratio of the largest to the smallest eigenvalue of a matrix is a useful measure of the "condition" of a matrix; a matrix with a large condition number is called ill conditioned. The Hilbert matrix, introduced in Chapter 1, is a famous example of an ill-conditioned matrix.

7.1 POWER METHOD

The power method is an iterative procedure for determining the dominant eigenvalue of a matrix $\mathbf{A}$. The basic idea behind the power method is that the defining relationship which is satisfied if $\mathbf{x}$ is an eigenvector of $\mathbf{A}$, namely,

$$\lambda\mathbf{x} = \mathbf{Ax},$$

can be converted into a sequence of approximations to λ and $\mathbf{x}$. We start with an initial guess $\mathbf{z}$ for the true eigenvector $\mathbf{x}$ and compute

$$\mathbf{w} = \mathbf{Az}.$$

If $\mathbf{z}$ is an eigenvector, then for any component of $\mathbf{z}$ and $\mathbf{w}$, we would have $\lambda z_k = w_k$. If $\mathbf{z}$ is not an eigenvector, we would like to use $\mathbf{w}$ as the next approximation and iterate until the process converges (if it does). However, because an eigenvector is determined only up to a scale factor, we normalize $\mathbf{w}$ before using it as the next approximation $\mathbf{z}$; the normalization is chosen so that the largest component of $\mathbf{z}$ is 1 at each stage of the iteration.

The method will converge if the initial estimate of the eigenvector has a (nonzero) component in the direction of the eigenvector corresponding to the dominant eigenvalue. For that reason, a starting vector with all components equal to 1 is used in the computations of the power method.

Briefly, the power method approach is based on the following observations. We iterate according to the equation $\mathbf{w} = \mathbf{Az}$. From the basic definition of an eigenvalue, we also have the approximate relationship $\lambda \mathbf{z} \approx \mathbf{Az}$. Therefore, $\mathbf{w} \approx \lambda \mathbf{z}$.

Denoting the dominant component of $\mathbf{w}$ as w_k, we have

$$w_k \approx \lambda z_k \Rightarrow \lambda \approx \frac{w_k}{z_k}.$$

Since we scale the vector $\mathbf{z}$ at each stage so that $z_k = 1$, we have the approximation

$$\lambda \approx w_k.$$

Carrying out the iterations has the effect of multiplying the original estimate by successively higher powers of $\mathbf{A}$—hence the name of the method. The first two iterations, shown here, illustrate the basic pattern:

$$\mathbf{w}^{(1)} = \mathbf{Az}^{(1)};$$

$$\mathbf{z}^{(2)} = \frac{1}{w^{(1)}_k} \mathbf{w}^{(1)} = \frac{1}{w^{(1)}_k} \mathbf{Az}^{(1)};$$

$$\mathbf{w}^{(2)} = \mathbf{Az}^{(2)} = \mathbf{A} \frac{1}{w^{(1)}_k} \mathbf{Az}^{(1)} = \frac{1}{w^{(1)}_k} \mathbf{A}^2 \mathbf{z}^{(1)};$$

$$\mathbf{z}^{(3)} = \frac{1}{w^{(2)}_k} \mathbf{w}^{(2)} = \frac{1}{w^{(2)}_k} \frac{1}{w^{(1)}_k} \mathbf{A}^2 \mathbf{z}^{(1)}.$$

7.1.1 Basic Power Method

The basic power method is illustrated in the following example.

Example 7.1 Using the Basic Power Method

To find the eigenvalue λ of largest magnitude, and a corresponding eigenvector, of

$$\mathbf{A} = \begin{bmatrix} 21 & 7 & -1 \\ 5 & 7 & 7 \\ 4 & -4 & 20 \end{bmatrix},$$

we start with the initial vector $\mathbf{z} = [1, 1, 1]'$.

Step 1: $\mathbf{w} = \mathbf{Az} = [27, 19, 20]'$.

Since the first component of **w** has the largest magnitude, the first estimate of λ is $w_1 = 27$. We use that component to scale the approximate eigenvector:

$$\mathbf{z} = \mathbf{w}/w_1 = [1, 19/27, 20/27]' = [1.0000, 0.7037, 0.7407]'.$$

Step 2: $\mathbf{w} = \mathbf{Az} = [25.1852, 15.1111, 16.0000]'.$

Since the first component of **w** has the largest magnitude, the estimate of λ is $w_1 = 25.1852$, and

$$\mathbf{z} = \mathbf{w}/w_1 = [1.0000, 0.6000, 0.6353]'.$$

Step 3: $\mathbf{w} = \mathbf{Az} = [24.5647, 13.6471, 14.3059]'.$

The estimate of λ is $w_1 = 24.5647$, and

$$\mathbf{z} = \mathbf{w}/w_1 = [1.0000, 0.5556, 0.5824]'.$$

Step 4: $\mathbf{w} = \mathbf{Az} = [24.3065, 12.9655, 13.4253]'.$

The estimate of λ is $w_1 = 24.3065$, and

$$\mathbf{z} = \mathbf{w}/w_1 = [1.0000, 0.5334, 0.5523]'.$$

The final estimate of the dominant eigenvalue is $\lambda \approx w_1$, and the final estimate of the corresponding eigenvector is **z**.

Checking the accuracy of our estimate, $\lambda = 24.3065$ and

$$\mathbf{z} = (1.0000, 0.5334, 0.5523)',$$

we compute $\mathbf{Az} - \lambda\mathbf{z} = [-0.1249, -0.3653, -0.5123]'.$

The maximum norm of this vector gives us a bound on the accuracy of the estimate after four steps, namely, $\|\mathbf{Az} - \lambda\mathbf{z}\|_\infty = 0.5123$.

Using MATLAB's built-in function `eig` to compute the eigenvalues of **A** gives

$$\text{eig}(\mathbf{A}) = [\, 24.0000, 8.0000, 16.0000 \,]'.$$

From this, we see that the largest eigenvalue is 24. The successive approximations of the power method converge toward that value.

The following MATLAB function implements the basic power method; the display format is designed for matrices that are no larger than five by five.

MATLAB Function for the Basic Power Method

```
function [z, m] = Power_m(A, max_it, tol)
[ n, nn ] = size(A);   z = ones(n, 1);
it = 0;                error = 100;
disp('  it    m      z(1)     z(2)     z(3)     z(4)     z(5)')
while (it < max_it & error > tol)
    w = A*z;           ww = abs(w);
    [k, kk] = max(ww); % kk is index of max element of ww
```

```
    m = w(kk);              % estimate of eigenvalue
    z = w/w(kk);            % estimate of eigenvector
    out = [ it+1    m    z' ];          disp(out)
    error = norm(A * z - m * z);
    it = it + 1;
  end
  error
```

Example 7.2 Using MATLAB Function for the Power Method

The maximal component of the estimated eigenvector may change during the first few iterations, as is illustrated in this example.

Let

$$\mathbf{A} = \begin{bmatrix} -44 & 9 & -6 \\ -280 & 57 & -40 \\ -75 & 15 & -13 \end{bmatrix}.$$

Table 7.1 shows 15 iterations.

Table 7.1	Iterations of the power method.			
Step	m	z(1)	z(2)	z(3)
1	−263.0000	0.1559	1.0000	0.2776
2	2.2471	0.2115	1.0000	−0.1337
3	3.1252	0.1586	1.0000	0.2799
4	1.3855	0.2458	1.0000	−0.3873
5	3.6667	0.1387	1.0000	0.4362
6	−1.0699	−0.2635	−0.6804	1.0000
7	−5.0131	0.1060	1.0000	0.6874
8	−1.8843	−0.1129	0.0894	1.0000
9	−3.2827	0.0689	1.0000	0.9714
10	−2.7992	−0.0493	0.4147	1.0000
11	−3.0823	0.0320	0.8303	1.0000
12	−2.9466	−0.0217	0.5556	1.0000
13	−3.0362	0.0143	0.7398	1.0000
14	−2.9761	−0.0096	0.6175	1.0000
15	−3.0160	0.0064	0.6993	1.0000

Given additional iterations, the dominant eigenvalue is found to be −3; the corresponding eigenvector is [0   2/3   1]′.

In the previous example, we estimated the dominant eigenvalue at each step of the process; this procedure is used for checking convergence for a residual stopping condition of the form $\|\mathbf{Az} - \lambda\mathbf{z}\| < \text{tolerance}$. A combination of this condition and a specified upper limit on the total number of iterations is used in the MATLAB function for the basic power method.

Accelerated Power Method

In some cases, it is possible to accelerate the convergence of the power method by using an estimate of λ that does not rely on a single component of the current vectors $\mathbf{w}$ and $\mathbf{z}$. The improved estimate of λ is called the *Rayleigh quotient* and is given by:

$$\lambda = (\mathbf{z}'\mathbf{w})/(\mathbf{z}'\mathbf{z}).$$

When $\mathbf{A}$ is symmetric, the power method with the Rayleigh quotient converges more rapidly than the standard power method. The accelerated power method can be implemented by replacing the definition of λ in the MATLAB function for the basic power method.

Example 7.3 Dominant Eigenvalue for Symmetric Matrix

To illustrate the acceleration in convergence of the dominant eigenvalue of a symmetric matrix that generally results when using the Rayleigh quotient, consider the following four-by-four matrix:

$$\mathbf{A} = \begin{bmatrix} 4 & 2/3 & -4/3 & 4/3 \\ 2/3 & 4 & 0 & 0 \\ -4/3 & 0 & 6 & 2 \\ 4/3 & 0 & 2 & 6 \end{bmatrix}.$$

The estimate of the dominant eigenvalue from the basic power method λ_b, the estimate from the Rayleigh quotient λ_r, and the eigenvector $\mathbf{z}$ are shown in Table 7.2. After 10 iterations, the error from the basic method is 0.1328; that from the Rayleigh quotient approximation is 0.1036.

Table 7.2 Iterations of basic and accelerated power methods.

Step	λ_b	λ_r	$z(1)$	$z(2)$	$z(3)$	$z(4)$
1	9.3333	6.3333	0.5000	0.5000	0.7143	1.0000
2	8.0952	7.2792	0.3353	0.2882	0.6941	1.0000
3	7.8353	7.6621	0.2477	0.1757	0.7297	1.0000
4	7.7898	7.8286	0.1885	0.1114	0.7764	1.0000
5	7.8042	7.9083	0.1443	0.0732	0.8210	1.0000
6	7.8344	7.9495	0.1104	0.0497	0.8595	1.0000
7	7.8661	7.9718	0.0842	0.0346	0.8911	1.0000
8	7.8945	7.9842	0.0640	0.0246	0.9164	1.0000
9	7.9181	7.9911	0.0485	0.0178	0.9362	1.0000
10	7.9371	7.9950	0.0366	0.0131	0.9516	1.0000

We may need to find eigenvalues besides (or instead of) the eigenvalue of largest magnitude. Some simple properties of eigenvalues can help us do this. In particular, we can make use of the fact that if a matrix $\mathbf{A}$ has eigenvalues $\lambda_1, \lambda_2, \ldots, \lambda_n$, with corresponding eigenvectors $\mathbf{v}_1, \mathbf{v}_2, \ldots, \mathbf{v}_n$, then the eigenvalues of $\mathbf{A} - b\mathbf{I}$ are $\mu_1 = \lambda_1 - b, \mu_2 = \lambda_2 - b, \ldots, \mu_n = \lambda_n - b$; the eigenvectors are unchanged by the shift.

7.1.2 Shifted Power Method

If we already know an eigenvalue λ of a matrix $\mathbf{A}$, we can find another eigenvalue of $\mathbf{A}$ by applying the power method to the matrix $\mathbf{B} = \mathbf{A} - \lambda\mathbf{I}$. We denote the dominant eigenvalue of the shifted matrix $\mathbf{B}$ as μ.

Example 7.4 Dominant Eigenvalue of Shifted Matrix

Consider the inertial matrix introduced in Example 7-A. One eigenvalue of

$$\mathbf{G} = \begin{bmatrix} 5 & -2 & 0 \\ -2 & 3 & 0 \\ 0 & 0 & 6 \end{bmatrix}$$

is 6; to find another eigenvalue, we apply the power method to the shifted matrix

$$\mathbf{B} = \mathbf{G} - 6\mathbf{I} = \begin{bmatrix} -1 & -2 & 0 \\ -2 & -3 & 0 \\ 0 & 0 & 0 \end{bmatrix}.$$

We start with $\mathbf{z} = [1, 1, 1]'$ and use the Rayleigh quotient approximation.

Step 1: $\mathbf{w} = \mathbf{Bz} = [-3, -5, 0]'$,

$$\mu = \frac{\mathbf{z'w}}{\mathbf{z'z}} = -\frac{8}{3}, \qquad \mathbf{z} = \frac{\mathbf{w}}{w_2} = [3/5, 1, 0]'.$$

Step 2: $\mathbf{w} = \mathbf{Bz} = [-13/5, -21/5, 0]'$,

$$\mu = \frac{\mathbf{z'w}}{\mathbf{z'z}} = -\frac{72}{17}, \qquad \mathbf{z} = \frac{\mathbf{w}}{w_2} = [13/21, 1, 0]'.$$

The results of the first four iterations using a MATLAB function for the power method with Rayleigh quotient to estimate the eigenvalue are summarized in Table 7.3. Using the basic power method requires one more iteration to achieve the stopping condition, $\|\mathbf{Az} - \mu\mathbf{z}\| < 0.0001$.

Table 7.3 Iterations of the shifted power method.

Step	μ	$z(1)$	$z(2)$	$z(3)$
1	−2.6667	0.6000	1.0000	0
2	−4.2353	0.6190	1.0000	0
3	−4.2361	0.6180	1.0000	0
4	−4.2361	0.6180	1.0000	0

7.1.3 Inverse Power Method

The inverse power method provides an estimate of the eigenvalue of $\mathbf{A}$ that is of smallest magnitude. It is based on the fact that eigenvalues of $\mathbf{B} = \mathbf{A}^{-1}$ are the reciprocals of the eigenvalues of $\mathbf{A}$. Therefore, we apply the power method to $\mathbf{B} = \mathbf{A}^{-1}$ to find its dominant eigenvalue μ. The reciprocal of μ will give the smallest magnitude eigenvalue μ of $\mathbf{A}$. However, it is not desirable to actually compute $\mathbf{A}^{-1}$; instead, at the stage where the power method would compute $\mathbf{A}^{-1}\mathbf{z} = \mathbf{w}$ to find the next approximation to the eigenvector $\mathbf{w}$, we solve the system $\mathbf{A}\mathbf{w} = \mathbf{z}$ for $\mathbf{w}$. This is an example of a situation in which the LU factorization is useful, since we must solve a linear system with the same coefficient matrix, but different right-hand sides, at each stage.

The inverse power method can also be generalized to find the eigenvalue that is closest to a given number. This procedure is discussed further in the next section.

Example 7.5 Using the Inverse Power Method

To find the smallest eigenvalue of

$$\mathbf{A} = \begin{bmatrix} 21 & 7 & -1 \\ 5 & 7 & 7 \\ 4 & -4 & 20 \end{bmatrix} = \begin{bmatrix} 1 & 0 & 0 \\ 0.24 & 1 & 0 \\ 0.19 & -1 & 1 \end{bmatrix} \begin{bmatrix} 21 & 7 & -1 \\ 0 & 5.33 & 7.24 \\ 0 & -0 & 27.43 \end{bmatrix},$$

we apply the inverse power method with initial vector $\mathbf{z} = [1, 1, 1]'$.

Step 1: Solve $\mathbf{A}\mathbf{w} = \mathbf{z} \Rightarrow \mathbf{w} = [0.0286, 0.0651, 0.0573]'$.

Since the largest component of $\mathbf{w}$ is w_2, the estimate of the largest eigenvalue of $\mathbf{A}^{-1}$ is $\mu = \dfrac{w_2}{z_2} = 0.0651$.

The estimate of the smallest eigenvalue of $\mathbf{A}$ is $\lambda = 1/\mu = \dfrac{z_2}{w_2} = 15.3610$, and

$$\mathbf{z} = \frac{\mathbf{w}}{w_2} = [0.4400, 1.0001, 0.8801]'.$$

Step 2: Solve $\mathbf{A}\mathbf{w} = \mathbf{z} \Rightarrow \mathbf{w} = [-0.0042, 0.0842, 0.0617]'$.
Since the largest component of $\mathbf{w}$ is w_2, we have

$$\mu = \frac{w_2}{z_2} = 0.0842, \qquad \lambda = 1/\mu = \frac{z_2}{w_2} = 11.8777,$$

$$\mathbf{z} = \frac{\mathbf{w}}{w_2} = [-0.0495, 0.9997, 0.7324]'.$$

Step 3: Solve $\mathbf{A}\mathbf{w} = \mathbf{z} \Rightarrow \mathbf{w} = [-0.0336, 0.1029, 0.0639]'$.

The estimate of λ is $\dfrac{z_2}{w_2} = 9.7153$.

Using MATLAB to compute the eigenvalues of $\mathbf{A}$ gives

$$\text{eig}(\mathbf{A}) = [24.00, 8.00, 16.00]'.$$

```
function [z, m] = InvPower( A, max_it, tol )
[n, nn] = size(A);   z = ones(n,1);   it = 0;   error = 100;
[L, U] = LU_factor(A);
while (it < max_it & error > tol)
     w = LU_solve(L, U, z);   ww = abs(w);   [k, kk] = max(ww);
     m = (z'*z)/(z'*w);        z = w/w(kk);
     out = [ it+1    m    z' ];  disp(out)
     error = norm(A * z - m * z);
     it = it + 1;
end
```

Example 7.6 Using the MATLAB Function `InvPower`

Consider the matrix

$$\mathbf{A} = \begin{bmatrix} 66 & -21 & 9 \\ 228 & -73 & 33 \\ 84 & -28 & 16 \end{bmatrix},$$

and take as the initial estimate of the eigenvector $z = [1 \quad 1 \quad 1]'$. Compute the LU factorization of $\mathbf{A}$:

$$\mathbf{L} = \begin{bmatrix} 1.0000 & 0 & 0 \\ 3.4545 & 1.0000 & 0 \\ .2727 & 2.8000 & 1.0000 \end{bmatrix}, \quad \mathbf{U} = \begin{bmatrix} 66.0000 & -21.0000 & 9.0000 \\ 0 & -0.4545 & 1.9091 \\ 0 & 0 & -0.8000 \end{bmatrix}.$$

The results of the first 10 iterations are given in Table 7.4.

Table 7.4 Iterations of the inverse power method.

Step	m	$z(1)$	$z(2)$	$z(3)$
1	−0.0657	0.2792	1.0000	0.2821
2	1.2111	0.2878	1.0000	0.2605
3	1.5947	0.2920	1.0000	0.2430
4	1.7672	0.2946	1.0000	0.2301
5	1.8585	0.2963	1.0000	0.2209
6	1.9111	0.2975	1.0000	0.2143
7	1.9430	0.2983	1.0000	0.2098
8	1.9630	0.2989	1.0000	0.2067
9	1.9758	0.2992	1.0000	0.2045
10	1.9840	0.2995	1.0000	0.2030

The eigenvalue of smallest magnitude is $m = 2.0$; the corresponding eigenvector is $\mathbf{z} = [0.3000 \ 1.0000 \ 0.2000]$.

Example 7.7 Buckling Beams

The buckling and subsequent breaking of a simply supported beam is approximated by the smallest eigenvalue of the n-by-n matrix

$$
\mathbf{A} = (n+1)^2
\begin{bmatrix}
2 & -1 & & & & \\
-1 & 2 & -1 & & & \\
& -1 & 2 & -1 & & \\
& & \cdot & \vdots & \cdot & \\
& & & -1 & 2 & -1 \\
& & & & -1 & 2
\end{bmatrix}.
$$

A better approximation is obtained for larger values of n.

For $n = 6$, with five iterations of the inverse power method and a tolerance equal to 10^{-5}, we find that $m = 0.1981$, and therefore, the first buckling mode is approximately $(6+1)^2(0.198) = 9.7069$.

For $n = 10$, performing five iterations of the inverse power method with a tolerance equal to 10^{-5}, we find that $m = 0.0810$, and the estimate of the first buckling mode is $(10+1)^2(0.081) = 9.8027$.

7.1.4 General Inverse Power Method

The ideas of the shifted power method and the simple inverse power method can be combined to enable us to find the eigenvalue of a matrix $\mathbf{A}$ that is closest to a given number b. This method is based on the fact that if the eigenvalues of a matrix $\mathbf{C}$ are $\lambda_1, \ldots, \lambda_n$, then the eigenvalues of $\mathbf{D} = \mathbf{C} - b\mathbf{I}$ are $\lambda_1 - b, \ldots, \lambda_n - b$. Furthermore, the eigenvalues of $\mathbf{D}^{-1}$ are $\dfrac{1}{\lambda_1 - b}, \ldots, \dfrac{1}{\lambda_n - b} = \mu_1, \ldots, \mu_n$. So μ_1, the dominant eigenvalue of $\mathbf{D}^{-1}$, corresponds to the eigenvalue of $\mathbf{C}$ that is closest to b, according to the relation $\mu_1 = \dfrac{1}{\lambda_1 - b}$.

Example 7.8 Finding the Eigenvalue Closest to a Given Number

Let

$$
\mathbf{A} =
\begin{bmatrix}
21 & 7 & -1 \\
5 & 7 & 7 \\
4 & -4 & 20
\end{bmatrix}, \quad \text{and} \quad
\mathbf{B} =
\begin{bmatrix}
6 & 7 & -1 \\
5 & -8 & 7 \\
4 & -4 & 5
\end{bmatrix}.
$$

Find the eigenvalue of $\mathbf{A}$ that is closest to $b = 15$ by applying the inverse power method to $\mathbf{B} = \mathbf{A} - 15\mathbf{I}$.

Start with $\mathbf{z} = [1, 1, 1]'$

Step 1: Solve $\mathbf{Bw} = \mathbf{z} \Rightarrow \mathbf{w} = [0.0317, 0.1587, 0.3016]'$;

estimate of largest eigenvalue of $\mathbf{B}^{-1}$: $\mu = \dfrac{w_3}{z_3} = 0.3016$;

estimate of smallest eigenvalue of $\mathbf{B}$: $1/\mu = \dfrac{z_3}{w_3} = 3.3158$;

$$\mathbf{z} = \frac{\mathbf{w}}{w_3} = [0.1053, 0.5263, 1.000]'.$$

Step 2: Solve $\mathbf{Bw} = \mathbf{z} \Rightarrow \mathbf{w} = [0.3718, 0.4570, 0.8630]'$;

estimate of largest eigenvalue of $\mathbf{B}^{-1}$: $\mu = \dfrac{w_3}{z_3} = 0.8630$;

estimate of smallest eigenvalue of $\mathbf{B}$: $1/\mu = \dfrac{z_3}{w_3} = 1.1588$;

$$\mathbf{z} = \frac{\mathbf{w}}{w_3} = [-0.4308, 0.5295, 1.000]'.$$

Step 3: Solve $\mathbf{Bw} = \mathbf{z} \Rightarrow \mathbf{w} = [-0.4723, 0.4808, 0.9624]'$;

estimate of smallest eigenvalue of $\mathbf{B}$: $1/\mu = \dfrac{z_3}{w_3} = 1.0390$;

The estimate of the desired eigenvalue of $\mathbf{A}$ is $b + 1/\mu$, where μ is the estimated largest eigenvalue of $\mathbf{B}^{-1}$ and $1/\mu$ is the estimated smallest eigenvalue of $\mathbf{B}$. Thus, the estimated eigenvalue of $\mathbf{A}$ that is closest to 15 is approximately 16.

The *trace* of a square matrix $\mathbf{A}$, $\text{tr}(\mathbf{A})$, is defined as the sum of the diagonal elements of $\mathbf{A}$. The trace is also equal to the sum of the eigenvalues of $\mathbf{A}$. (Cf. Golub and Van Loan, 1996, p. 310.) This fact can be used to help determine values of the shift parameter b to use for finding other eigenvalues. It is especially useful when all diagonal element are nonnegative. In such a case, after the dominant eigenvalue λ_1 has been found, one might try a value of b given by $b = \dfrac{\text{tr}(\mathbf{A}) - \lambda_1}{n - 1}$.

7.1.5 Discussion

The proof of the convergence of the basic power method assumes that the dominant eigenvalue is real and not a repeated eigenvalue, so that the eigenvalues can be ordered as $|\lambda_1| > |\lambda_2| \geq |\lambda_3| \geq \ldots \geq |\lambda_n|$. Often, however, the method is applicable even if these assumptions are not met. (See Ralston and Rabinowitz, 1978.)

The proof is based on the fact that if the matrix $\mathbf{A}$ is diagonalizable (i.e., if $\mathbf{A}$ has n linearly independent eigenvectors $\mathbf{v}^{(1)}, \ldots, \mathbf{v}^{(n)}$), then any vector $\mathbf{z}$ can be written as a unique linear combination of the eigenvectors:

$$\mathbf{z} = \sum_{i=1}^{n} c_i \mathbf{v}^{(i)} \Rightarrow \mathbf{A}^j \mathbf{z} = \sum_{i=1}^{n} c_i \mathbf{A}^j \mathbf{v}^{(i)}.$$

Since λ_i is the eigenvalue corresponding to eigenvector $\mathbf{v}^{(i)}$, it follows that

$$\mathbf{A}\mathbf{v}^{(i)} = \lambda_i\mathbf{v}^{(i)} \quad \text{and} \quad \mathbf{A}^j\mathbf{v}^{(i)} = \lambda_i^j\mathbf{v}^{(i)}.$$

Therefore,

$$\mathbf{A}^j\mathbf{z} = \sum_{i=1}^{n} c_i\lambda_i^j\mathbf{v}^{(i)} = \lambda_1^j\left[c_1\mathbf{v}^{(1)} + \sum_{i=2}^{n} c_i\frac{\lambda_i^j}{\lambda_1^j}\mathbf{v}^{(i)}\right].$$

If $\mathbf{A}$ has a single dominant eigenvalue (i.e., if $|\lambda_1| > |\lambda_2| \geq |\lambda_3| \ldots \geq |\lambda_n|$), then $\dfrac{\lambda_i^j}{\lambda_1^j} \to 0$ as $j \to \infty$.

Without some control over the iterative process that this suggests, we cannot distinguish the unknown quantities λ_1^j, c_1, and $\mathbf{v}^{(1)}$ on the right-hand side of the equation for $\mathbf{A}^j\mathbf{z}$. It is also quite likely that all components of the limiting vector will grow without bound. However, by an appropriate scaling of the vectors produced during iteration, we can assure that this limit is finite and nonzero.

The convergence of the estimate at the jth iteration depends on $|\lambda_2/\lambda_1|^j$, so the method will converge more rapidly when the dominant eigenvalue is much larger than the next most dominant eigenvalue.

Convergence may be improved for symmetric matrices by using the Rayleigh quotient to estimate the eigenvalue. In this case, the estimate at the jth iteration depends on $|\lambda_2/\lambda_1|^{2j}$ (because the eigenvectors can be taken to be orthonormal).

7.2 QR FACTORIZATION

We begin this section by considering two transformations that can be used to obtain the QR factorization of a real matrix. We require a transformation that will reduce certain elements of a given vector to zero. This can be accomplished using either Householder reflections or Givens rotations.

We next investigate the construction of the QR factorization, $\mathbf{A} = \mathbf{QR}$, where $\mathbf{R}$ is upper (also known as right) triangular, $\mathbf{Q}$ is orthogonal (so that $\mathbf{Q}^{-1} = \mathbf{Q}'$), and both are real. The general QR factorization is based on the use of Householder transformations.

In Section 7.3, we consider a standard method of finding all eigenvalues of a real matrix $\mathbf{A}$. This approach is based on a sequence of transformations of $\mathbf{A}$ (using QR factorizations) that preserve the eigenvalues while generating a matrix for which the eigenvalues are much easier to obtain.

7.2.1 Householder and Givens Transformations

The QR factorization of a matrix requires that we reduce to zero certain elements of a vector (a column or portion of a column of the matrix whose factorization is sought). The transformations are often described in terms of multiplication by a matrix with the appropriate special properties, although in practice the equivalent operations are usually carried out more efficiently without explicitly forming the matrix or performing the matrix multiplication.

Householder Matrix

The Householder transformation (or reflection) is often described in terms of multiplication by a matrix known as a *Householder matrix*. A Householder matrix is a matrix of the form $\mathbf{H} = \mathbf{I} - 2\mathbf{w}\mathbf{w}'$, where $\mathbf{w}$ is a unit (column) vector, i.e., $\|\mathbf{w}\|_2 = 1$. The formation of the Householder matrix to reduce to zero a vector $\mathbf{x}$ (an n-tuple), from position k through position n, is summarized in the following algorithm.

Algorithm for Householder Matrix: Given an n-dimensional vector $\mathbf{x}$ and an index k such that $1 \le k \le n$, find a vector $\mathbf{w}$ so that the matrix $\mathbf{H} = \mathbf{I} - 2\mathbf{w}\mathbf{w}'$ reduces positions $k+1, \ldots, n$ of vector $\mathbf{x}$ to zero—i.e., so that $\mathbf{H}\mathbf{x}$ has the form $[z_1, \ldots, z_k, 0, 0, \ldots, 0]'$.

Step 1: Set $w_i = 0$ for $i = 1, \ldots, k-1$.

Step 2: Find $g = \sqrt{x_k^2 + \cdots + x_n^2}$.

Find $s = \sqrt{2g(g + |x_k|)}$.

Step 3: Set $w_k = (x_k + \text{sign}(x_k)\, g)/s$.

Set $w_i = \dfrac{x_i}{s}$ for $i = k+1, \ldots, n$.

The following MATLAB function for the construction of a Householder matrix is presented for instructional purposes. In practice, the Householder matrix is seldom explicitly formed. (Cf. Golub and Van Loan, 1996, p. 211.) An example of how to avoid constructing a Householder matrix is described following the analysis of the Householder transformation.

MATLAB Function for Householder Transformation

```
function H = Householder(x, k)
[n, nn] = size(x)
w = zeros(n, 1)
g = norm(x(k : n))
p = sign(x(k));
s = sqrt(2*g*(g+p*x(k)))
w(k) = (x(k) + p*g)/s
w(k+1 : n) = x(k+1 : n)/s
H = eye(n) - 2*w*w'
```

The next example illustrates the use of Householder matrices as part of the process of transforming a matrix $\mathbf{A}$ into a similar upper triangular matrix. In this setting, Householder matrices are determined for each column of $\mathbf{A}$, except the last, in order to reduce the elements below the diagonal of the matrix to zero.

Example 7.9 Householder Transformation of Three-By-Three Matrix

We start by applying the Householder algorithm to reduce the subdiagonal elements of the first column of the matrix

$$\mathbf{A} = \begin{bmatrix} 21 & 7 & -1 \\ 5 & 7 & 7 \\ 4 & -4 & 20 \end{bmatrix}$$

to zero. The vector we wish to transform is the first column of $\mathbf{A}$, so $k = 1$. We have

$$\mathbf{x} = \mathbf{A}(:, 1) = [21, 5, 4]'.$$

We find $g = \sqrt{x_1^2 + x_2^2 + x_3^2} = 21.9545$ and $s = \sqrt{2g(g + |x_k|)} = 43.4291$. Also, $w(1) = (21 + g)/s; w(2) = 5/s; w(3) = 4/s$, so that

$$\mathbf{w} = [0.9891, 0.1151, 0.0921]',$$

$$\mathbf{H} = \begin{bmatrix} 1 & 0 & 0 \\ 0 & 1 & 0 \\ 0 & 0 & 1 \end{bmatrix} - 2\mathbf{w}\mathbf{w}^T = \begin{bmatrix} -0.9565 & -0.2277 & -0.1822 \\ -0.2277 & 0.9735 & -0.0212 \\ -0.1822 & -0.0212 & 0.9830 \end{bmatrix},$$

and

$$\mathbf{B} = \mathbf{H}\mathbf{A} = \begin{bmatrix} -21.9545 & -7.5611 & -4.2816 \\ 0.0000 & 5.3051 & 6.6180 \\ 0.0000 & -5.3560 & 19.6944 \end{bmatrix}.$$

Example 7.10 Using the MATLAB Function Householder

As an example of the use of the MATLAB function Householder, we reduce the subdiagonal elements of the second column of the preceding matrix $\mathbf{B}$ to zero. The following output has been edited slightly to conserve space:

$$H = \text{Householder}(\mathbf{B}(:, 2), 2),$$

$$g = 7.5386,$$

$$s = 13.9156,$$

$$\mathbf{w} = [0, 0.9230, -0.3849]',$$

$$\mathbf{H} = \begin{bmatrix} 1.0000 & 0.0000 & 0.0000 \\ 0.0000 & -0.7037 & 0.7105 \\ 0.0000 & 0.7105 & 0.7037 \end{bmatrix}, \quad \mathbf{HB} = \begin{bmatrix} -21.9545 & -7.5611 & -4.2816 \\ 0.0000 & -7.5386 & 9.3351 \\ 0.0000 & -0.0000 & 18.5613 \end{bmatrix}.$$

Analysis of the Householder Transformation

To understand how the Householder transformation works, we must do a little analysis. The basic ideas are as follows.

Any matrix formed according to the equation $\mathbf{H} = \mathbf{I} - 2\mathbf{ww}'$ is symmetric. If $\mathbf{w}$ is a unit vector ($\|\mathbf{w}\|_2 = 1$), then $\mathbf{H}$ is orthogonal, since

$$\mathbf{H}'\mathbf{H} = (\mathbf{I} - 2\mathbf{ww}')\,(\mathbf{I} - 2\mathbf{ww}') = \mathbf{I} - 4\mathbf{ww}' + 4\mathbf{ww}'\mathbf{ww}' = \mathbf{I}.$$

Because it is both symmetric and orthogonal, $\mathbf{H}$ is its own inverse!

Any vector $\mathbf{v} \neq 0$ that is not a unit vector can be scaled to produce a unit vector $\mathbf{w}$ in the same direction by defining $\mathbf{w} = \dfrac{\mathbf{v}}{\|\mathbf{v}\|_2}$.

Now we outline how we can determine the vector $\mathbf{v}$ that will provide a Householder matrix of the form $\mathbf{H} = \mathbf{I} - \dfrac{2}{\mathbf{v}'\mathbf{v}}\,\mathbf{vv}'$ such that multiplication of an n-dimensional vector $\mathbf{x}$ by $\mathbf{H}$ will reduce all the components of $\mathbf{x}$ to zero, except for the kth component.

Let $\mathbf{e}_k$ denote the n-dimensional vector with a 1 as its kth component and 0's for all other components. Then we want to determine $\mathbf{v}$ such that $\mathbf{Hx} = \alpha\mathbf{e}_k$, for some scalar α. Some matrix algebra tells us that $\mathbf{v}$ must be a linear combination of $\mathbf{x}$ and $\mathbf{e}_k$. We set $\mathbf{v} = \mathbf{x} + \alpha\mathbf{e}_k$ and find (after more algebra) that $\mathbf{v} = \mathbf{x} \pm \|\mathbf{x}\|_2\mathbf{e}_k$ and $\mathbf{Hx} \pm \|\mathbf{x}\|_2\mathbf{e}_k = 0$, as desired.

It is good practice to choose the sign of $\alpha = \pm\|\mathbf{x}\|_2$ to agree with the sign of x_k, in order to avoid cancellation in the kth component of v. It is for this reason that we compute $w_k = (x_k + \text{sign}(x_k)g)/s$ in step 3 of the algorithm for the Householder transformation.

To apply the Householder transformation to the first column of a matrix $\mathbf{A}$, we compute the vector $\mathbf{v}$ with $k = 1$, using the first column of $\mathbf{A}$ as the vector $\mathbf{x}$. For columns other than the first, we have $k > 1$, and we want to reduce to zero only elements after the kth component of column k. Therefore, we set the components of $\mathbf{v}$ before the kth component equal to zero; i.e., $v_i = 0$ for $i = 1, \ldots, k-1$. We use only components k through n to compute the norm of the $\mathbf{x}$ term, denoted as g in step 2. We ignore the first $k - 1$ components and treat the remaining components as an $(n - k + 1)$-dimensional vector. The norm of $\mathbf{v}$ is denoted as s in step 2. The vector $\mathbf{w}$ is obtained by dividing the component of $\mathbf{v}$ by the norm of $\mathbf{v}$. That is the reason for division by s in step 3.

Householder Transformations in Practice

In applications, Householder matrices are not explicitly constructed. To see how their construction can be avoided, we observe that

$$\mathbf{HA} = (\mathbf{I} - 2\mathbf{ww}')\mathbf{A} = \mathbf{A} - 2\mathbf{ww}'\mathbf{A} = \mathbf{A} - \mathbf{wu}',$$

where $\mathbf{u} = 2\mathbf{A}'\mathbf{w}$. Computation of $\mathbf{u}$ requires the multiplication of a matrix and a vector, that of $\mathbf{wu}'$ requires the outer product of two vectors, and that of $\mathbf{A} - \mathbf{wu}'$ requires the subtraction of one matrix from another. Altogether, these steps require $4n^2$ flops if $\mathbf{A}$ is an n-by-n matrix and $\mathbf{w}$ is n by 1.

On the other hand, explicit formation of the matrix $\mathbf{H} = \mathbf{I} - 2\mathbf{w}\mathbf{w}'$ requires the outer product of a vector with itself and multiplication of the matrices $\mathbf{H}$ and $\mathbf{A}$, for a total of $2n^3$ flops. This is an order of magnitude more computational effort than it takes to compute $\mathbf{A} - \mathbf{w}\mathbf{u}'$. For that reason, Householder matrices are virtually never explicitly formed in practice.

Example 7.11 Householder Transformation of a Three-by-Three Matrix Revisited

Consider once more the matrix

$$\mathbf{A} = \begin{bmatrix} 21 & 7 & -1 \\ 5 & 7 & 7 \\ 4 & -4 & 20 \end{bmatrix}$$

from Example 7.9. Again, we begin by introducing zeros below the diagonal in the first column, by taking $\mathbf{x} = [21,5,4]'$, $g = \text{norm}(\mathbf{x}) = 21.954$, $\mathbf{v} = \mathbf{x} + g[1,0,0]' = [42.954,5,4]'$, $s = \text{norm}(\mathbf{v}) = 43.429$, and $\mathbf{w} = \mathbf{v}/s = [0.98907, 0.11513, 0.092104]'$. This gives

$$\mathbf{u} = 2\mathbf{A}'\mathbf{w} = [43.429, 14.722, 3.3178]',$$

$$\mathbf{w}\mathbf{u} = \begin{bmatrix} 42.954 & 14.561 & 3.2816 \\ 5 & 1.6949 & 0.38198 \\ 4 & 1.356 & 0.30559 \end{bmatrix},$$

and

$$\mathbf{B} = \mathbf{A} - \mathbf{w}\mathbf{u}' = \begin{bmatrix} -21.954 & -7.5611 & -4.2816 \\ 0 & 5.3051 & 6.618 \\ 0 & -5.3560 & 19.694 \end{bmatrix}.$$

For the second column, to introduce zeros below the diagonal, we find $\mathbf{w}$ from $\mathbf{x} = [0, 5.3051, -5.3560]'$. That is, the first component is zero, and the second and third elements come from the second column of $\mathbf{B}$; this gives $\mathbf{w} = [0, 0.92296, -0.38489]'$ and $\mathbf{u} = 2\mathbf{B}'\mathbf{w} = [0, 13.916, -2.9436]'$. Then

$$\mathbf{w}\mathbf{u}' = \begin{bmatrix} 0 & 0 & 0 \\ 0 & 12.844 & -2.7169 \\ 0 & -5.356 & 1.133 \end{bmatrix}$$

and

$$\mathbf{R} = \mathbf{B} - \mathbf{w}\mathbf{u}' = \begin{bmatrix} -21.954 & -7.5611 & -4.2816 \\ 0 & -7.5386 & 9.3349 \\ 0 & 0 & 18.561 \end{bmatrix}.$$

As we shall see in Example 7.12, this upper triangular matrix is the desired matrix $\mathbf{R}$ for the QR factorization of the matrix $\mathbf{A}$.

Givens Rotations

A Givens rotation is a matrix of the form

$$\mathbf{G} = \begin{bmatrix} 1 & 0 & 0 & 0 & 0 \\ 0 & c & 0 & -s & 0 \\ 0 & 0 & 1 & 0 & 0 \\ 0 & s & 0 & c & 0 \\ 0 & 0 & 0 & 0 & 1 \end{bmatrix} \begin{matrix} \\ \leftarrow \text{row } i \\ \\ \leftarrow \text{row } j \\ \\ \end{matrix}$$

where $c^2 + s^2 = 1$.

In general, the c's occur in row i and row j; a Givens rotation matrix is orthogonal, since $\mathbf{G}'\mathbf{G} = \mathbf{I}$. If c and s are interpreted as $\cos(\theta)$ and $\sin(\theta)$, then multiplication by the two-by-two Givens matrix

$$\mathbf{G} = \begin{bmatrix} c & -s \\ s & c \end{bmatrix}$$

corresponds to rotation by the angle θ in R^2.

By selecting the appropriate values for c and s, a Givens rotation can be used to reduce a specific matrix element to zero. In particular, if

$$c = \frac{x_1}{\sqrt{x_1^2 + x_2^2}} \quad \text{and} \quad s = \frac{-x_2}{\sqrt{x_1^2 + x_2^2}},$$

then $c^2 + s^2 = 1$ and

$$\begin{bmatrix} c & -s \\ s & c \end{bmatrix} \begin{bmatrix} x_1 \\ x_2 \end{bmatrix} = \begin{bmatrix} \sqrt{x_1^2 + x_2^2} \\ 0 \end{bmatrix}.$$

Thus, a sequence of Givens rotations could be applied to reduce to zero all elements below the diagonal in a matrix to transform it to upper triangular form.

The product $\mathbf{B} = \mathbf{GA}$ transforms rows i and j of matrix $\mathbf{A}$, so that

$$\mathbf{B}(i,:) = c\mathbf{A}(i,:) - s\mathbf{A}(j,:),$$
$$\mathbf{B}(j,:) = s\mathbf{A}(i,:) + c\mathbf{A}(j,:),$$

and

$$\mathbf{B}(k,:) = \mathbf{A}(k,:), \text{for } k \neq i, j.$$

Similarly, $\mathbf{D} = \mathbf{CG}'$ modifies only the ith and jth columns of $\mathbf{C}$. Hence, the actions of the multiplication on the left or the right by $\mathbf{G}$ or $\mathbf{G}'$ can be accomplished without explicitly forming $\mathbf{G}$ or $\mathbf{G}'$ and without performing the matrix multiplication.

Givens rotations require approximately twice as many multiplications as Householder reflections. However, in the case of matrices with only a few elements that must be reduced to zero, Givens rotations are the method of choice. More efficient implementations of the Givens scheme are also available. (See Hager, 1988 for further discussion.)

7.2.2 Basic QR Factorization

A real matrix $\mathbf{A}$ can be factored into the form

$$\mathbf{A} = \mathbf{QR},$$

where $\mathbf{Q}$ is orthogonal, $\mathbf{R}$ is upper triangular, and both are real. The following algorithm summarizes the process.

> **Algorithm for QR Factorization (Using Householder Matrices):**
> Given a real n-by-n matrix $\mathbf{A}$ with columns denoted $\mathbf{A}(:, 1), \ldots, \mathbf{A}(:, n)$:
> Define $\mathbf{R}^{(0)} = \mathbf{A}$.
> For $k = 1, \ldots, n-1$,
>> Find $\mathbf{H}^{(k)}$ in order to reduce positions $k+1, \ldots, n$, in the kth column of $\mathbf{R}^{(k-1)}$ to zero;
>> Define $\mathbf{R}^{(k)} = \mathbf{H}^{(k)} \mathbf{R}^{(k-1)}$.
> end.
> Define $\mathbf{Q} = \mathbf{I}$.
> For $k = n-1, \ldots, 1$,
>> $\mathbf{Q} = \mathbf{H}^{(k)} \mathbf{Q}$
> end.
> Define $\mathbf{R} = \mathbf{R}^{(n-1)}$.

Notice that the computation of $\mathbf{Q}$ in this algorithm is a backward accumulation of the product of the $\mathbf{H}$ matrices. Taking the products in this order permits a reduction in the number of required flops by exploiting the structure of $\mathbf{H}^{(k)}$. At each step, the leading $(k-1)$-by-$(k-1)$ block of $\mathbf{H}^{(k)}$ is a $(k-1)$-by-$(k-1)$ identity matrix. This advantage is exploited in "industrial-strength" mathematical software, such as MATLAB, to provide efficient QR factorization routines.

Example 7.12 QR Factorization

In Examples 7.9 and 7.10, we computed the Householder matrices required to form the QR factorization of the matrix

$$\mathbf{A} = \begin{bmatrix} 21 & 7 & -1 \\ 5 & 7 & 7 \\ 4 & -4 & 20 \end{bmatrix}.$$

First we found

$$\mathbf{H}^{(1)} = \begin{bmatrix} -0.9565 & -0.2277 & -0.1822 \\ -0.2277 & 0.9735 & -0.0212 \\ -0.1822 & -0.0212 & 0.9830 \end{bmatrix},$$

which we used to reduce the first column of $\mathbf{A}$ to zero. Then we set $\mathbf{R}^{(1)} = \mathbf{H}^{(1)}\mathbf{A}$. Next we found

$$\mathbf{H}^{(2)} = \begin{bmatrix} 1.0000 & 0.0000 & 0.0000 \\ 0.0000 & -0.7037 & 0.7105 \\ 0.0000 & 0.7105 & 0.7037 \end{bmatrix},$$

which we used to reduce the third element in the second column of $\mathbf{R}^{(1)}$ to zero. The required upper triangular matrix is

$$\mathbf{R}^{(2)} = \mathbf{H}^{(2)}\mathbf{R}^{(1)} = \begin{bmatrix} -21.9545 & -7.5611 & -4.2816 \\ 0.0000 & -7.5386 & 9.3351 \\ 0.0000 & 0.0000 & 18.5613 \end{bmatrix},$$

and the orthogonal matrix $\mathbf{Q}$ is given by

$$\mathbf{Q} = \mathbf{H}^{(1)}\mathbf{H}^{(2)} = \begin{bmatrix} -0.9565 & 0.0308 & -0.2900 \\ -0.2277 & -0.7001 & 0.6768 \\ -0.1822 & 0.7133 & 0.6767 \end{bmatrix}.$$

To check the accuracy of our computations, we find

$$\mathbf{QR} = \begin{bmatrix} 21 & 7 & -1 \\ 5 & 7 & 7 \\ 4 & -4 & 20 \end{bmatrix} = \mathbf{A},$$

and it follows that $\mathbf{Q}'\mathbf{Q} = \mathbf{I}$.

The MATLAB function that follows illustrates the use of Householder transformations, without explicitly forming the Householder matrices, to obtain the QR factorization of a matrix $\mathbf{A}$. It does not take advantage of the zeros in the vector $\mathbf{x}$ at each iteration to reduce the number of computations required. It is used in the next section to find the QR factorizations needed in the general QR-eigenvalue method.

MATLAB Function to Find QR Factorization by Householder Transformations

```
function [Q, R] = QR_factor(A)
[n, nn] = size(A); R = A; Q = eye(n);
for k = 1:n-1
    x = zeros(n,1);   x(k:n, 1) = R(k:n, k)
    g = norm(x);      v = x;      v(k) = x(k) + g
    s = norm(v);      w = v/s;    u = 2*R'*w;
    R = R-w*u' ;      Q = Q - 2*Q*w*w' ;
end
```

7.3   FINDING EIGENVALUES USING QR FACTORIZATION

To find the eigenvalues of a real matrix $\mathbf{A}$ using QR factorization, we generate a sequence of matrices $\mathbf{A}^{(m)}$ that are orthogonally similar to $\mathbf{A}$ (and thus have the same eigenvalues as $\mathbf{A}$). A similarity transformation is a transformation of the form $\mathbf{H}^{-1}\mathbf{AH}$, where $\mathbf{H}$ is any nonsingular matrix. The sequence $\mathbf{A}^{(m)}$ converges to a matrix from which the eigenvalues can be found easily. If the eigenvalues of $\mathbf{A}$ satisfy

$|\lambda_1| > |\lambda_2| > \ldots > |\lambda_n|$, the iterates converge to an upper triangular matrix with the eigenvalues on the diagonal. If $\mathbf{A}$ is symmetric, the iterates will converge to a block diagonal matrix in which all blocks have order 1 or 2. (For further discussion and original references, see Atkinson, 1989, pp. 625–626.)

We first consider the basic QR-eigenvalue algorithm and a MATLAB function to implement it. However, since the QR-eigenvalue method involves a sequence of factorizations, we conclude the chapter with a more efficient QR factorization method for finding eigenvalues. This approach is based on a preliminary transformation of $\mathbf{A}$ into Hessenberg form—i.e., upper triangular, except for the first subdiagonal. The QR factorization of a matrix that is in Hessenberg form is computationally more efficient, since there is only one element that must be transformed to zero in each column. The QR factorization in this case is usually based on Givens rotations. The similarity transformations guarantee that the eigenvalues of the original and final matrices are the same.

7.3.1 Basic QR Eigenvalue Method

The following is the basic procedure for finding eigenvalues using QR factorization. The matrices formed at each iteration are indicated by superscripts.

> **Algorithm for Finding Eigenvalues Using QR Factorization:**
> Given a real n-by-n matrix $\mathbf{A}$:
> Define $\mathbf{A}^{(1)} = \mathbf{A}$.
> For $k = 1: \text{k\_max}$,
>   Factor $\mathbf{A}^{(k)} = \mathbf{Q}^{(k)}\mathbf{R}^{(k)}$ (so that $\mathbf{Q}^{(k)T}\mathbf{A}^{(k)} = \mathbf{R}^{(k)}$).
>   Define $\mathbf{A}^{(k+1)} = \mathbf{R}^{(k)}\mathbf{Q}^{(k)}$ (so that $\mathbf{A}^{(k+1)} = \mathbf{Q}(k)^{\text{T}}\mathbf{A}^{(k)}\mathbf{Q}^{(k)}$).
> end.

MATLAB Function for Finding Eigenvalues by QR Factorization

```
function e = QR_eig(A, max)
%    find eigenvalues using QR
for i = 1:max
    [Q, R] = QR_factor(A)
    A = R*Q
end
e = diag(A)
```

Example 7.13 Finding Eigenvalues Using QR Factorization

Consider again the matrix introduced in Example 7.3:

$$\mathbf{A} = \begin{bmatrix} 4 & 2/3 & -4/3 & 4/3 \\ 2/3 & 4 & 0 & 0 \\ -4/3 & 0 & 6 & 2 \\ 4/3 & 0 & 2 & 6 \end{bmatrix}$$

Starting with $A^{(1)} = A$, the first five iterations (using `QR_eig`) $\mathbf{A}^{(2)} = \mathbf{A}$ give.

$$\mathbf{A}^{(2)} = \begin{bmatrix} 5.6000 & 0.2769 & -0.3819 & -1.1034 \\ 0.2769 & 3.9148 & 0.1175 & 0.3395 \\ -0.3819 & 0.1175 & 7.4099 & -1.7047 \\ -1.1034 & 0.3395 & -1.7047 & 3.0753 \end{bmatrix}$$

$$\mathbf{A}^{(3)} = \begin{bmatrix} 5.9512 & 0.0541 & -0.0401 & 0.4338 \\ 0.0541 & 3.9703 & 0.0220 & -0.2377 \\ -0.0401 & 0.0220 & 7.9498 & 0.5429 \\ 0.4338 & -0.2377 & 0.5429 & 2.1286 \end{bmatrix}$$

$$\mathbf{A}^{(4)} = \begin{bmatrix} 5.9945 & 0.0092 & -0.0035 & -0.1476 \\ 0.0092 & 3.9922 & 0.0029 & 0.1241 \\ -0.0035 & 0.0029 & 7.9967 & -0.1399 \\ -0.1476 & 0.1241 & -0.1399 & 2.0165 \end{bmatrix}$$

$$\mathbf{A}^{(5)} = \begin{bmatrix} 5.9994 & 0.0015 & -0.0003 & 0.0494 \\ 0.0015 & 3.9980 & 0.0004 & -0.0624 \\ -0.0003 & 0.0004 & 7.9998 & 0.0351 \\ 0.0494 & -0.0624 & 0.0351 & 2.0028 \end{bmatrix}$$

$$\mathbf{A}^{(6)} = \begin{bmatrix} 5.9999 & 0.0003 & -0.0000 & -0.0165 \\ 0.0003 & 3.9995 & 0.0000 & 0.0312 \\ -0.0000 & 0.0000 & 8.0000 & -0.0088 \\ -0.0165 & 0.0312 & -0.0088 & 2.0006 \end{bmatrix}$$

We see that the off-diagonal elements are going to zero very slowly, although the eigenvalues found by taking the diagonal elements after 5 iterations are not a bad approximation to the exact values. The results after 5 and 10 iterations are summarized in Table 7.5.

Table 7.5 Eigenvalues found by basic QR eigenvalue method.

Iterations	Eigenvalues			
5	5.9999	3.9995	8.0000	2.0006
10	6.0000	4.0000	8.0000	2.0000

7.3.2 Improved QR Eigenvalue Method

As mentioned in the previous section, in employing QR factorizations to find the eigenvalues of matrix $\mathbf{A}$, it is preferable to first use a similarity transformation to convert $\mathbf{A}$ to Hessenberg form. As described earlier, the required computations can be performed more efficiently without explicitly forming the Householder matrices.

MATLAB Function for Similarity Transformation to Hessenberg Form

```
function A = Hessenberg(A)
[n  nn] = size(A);
for k = 1:n-2
    H = Householder(A(:, k ), k+1);
    A = H*A*H;
end
```

We illustrate the use of this function to transform a matrix $\mathbf{A}$ into Hessenberg form in the next example. Note that we set the very small, but nonzero, entries that appear in the lower triangular region of the transformed matrix due to round-off errors to zero in order to make the Hessenberg form more evident.

Example 7.14 Similarity Transformation to Hessenberg Form

Consider the matrix

$$\mathbf{A} = \begin{bmatrix} 2 & 0 & 0 & 0 \\ -4 & 4 & 0 & 0 \\ 12 & -6 & 6 & 0 \\ 48 & 24 & -8 & 8 \end{bmatrix}.$$

Step 1: Find $\mathbf{H}$ to reduce $\mathbf{A}(3:4, 1)$ to zero:

$$\mathbf{H} = \begin{bmatrix} 1.0000 & 0 & 0 & 0 \\ 0 & -0.0806 & 0.2417 & -0.9670 \\ 0 & 0.2417 & 0.9459 & 0.2163 \\ 0 & -0.9670 & 0.2163 & 0.1347 \end{bmatrix}$$

Transform **A** by setting **A** = **HAH**:

$$
\mathbf{A} = \begin{bmatrix} 2.0000 & 0 & 0 & 0 \\ 49.6387 & 11.7143 & 0.9771 & 25.1014 \\ -0.0000 & -0.7588 & 4.2228 & 0.6189 \\ 0.0000 & -0.8326 & -0.0257 & 2.0629 \end{bmatrix}
$$

Step 2: Find **H** to reduce **A**(4:4, 2) to zero:

$$
\mathbf{H} = \begin{bmatrix} 1.0000 & 0 & 0 & 0 \\ 0 & 1.0000 & 0 & 0 \\ 0 & 0 & -0.6736 & -0.7391 \\ 0 & 0 & -0.7391 & 0.6736 \end{bmatrix}
$$

Transform **A** by setting **A** = **HAH**:

$$
\mathbf{A} = \begin{bmatrix} 2.0000 & 0 & 0 & 0 \\ 49.6387 & 11.7143 & -19.2099 & 16.1869 \\ -0.0000 & 1.1265 & 3.3383 & 0.7804 \\ 0.0000 & 0.0000 & 1.4250 & 2.9474 \end{bmatrix}
$$

The last transformed matrix is in upper Hessenberg form, with the same eigenvalues as the original matrix **A**: eig(**A**) = [4, 6, 8, 2].

The following MATLAB function includes conversion to Hessenberg form and QR factorization based on Givens rotations. As with the use of Householder reflections, it is computationally more efficient to write out the specific actions performed by the Givens rotation, rather than using the more concise and elegant description in terms of multiplication by the entire Givens matrix.

MATLAB Function for Improved QR Eigenvalue Method

```
function e = QR_eig_g(A, max)
%  Improved algorithm for finding eigenvalues using QR
[n  nn] = size(A);
% convert to Hessenberg form
for k = 1:n-2
    H = Householder(A(:, k ), k+1); A = H*A*H;
end
```

```
for i = 1:max
    [Q, R] = QR_factor_g(A);  A = R*Q
end
e = diag(A)
```

MATLAB Function for Improved QR Factorization

```
function [Q, R] = QR_factor_g(A)
[n, nn] = size(A);
Q = eye(n);  R = A;
for k = 1:n-1
    x1 = R(k,k);  x2 = R(k+1,k);  rr = sqrt(x1^2 + x2^2);
    c = x1/rr; s = -x2/rr;
    R_new = R; Q_new = Q;
    R_new(k,:) = c*R(k,:) - s*R(k+1,:);
    R_new(k+1,:) = s*R(k,:) +c*R(k+1,:);
    Q_new(:,k) = c*Q(:,k) - s*Q(:,k+1);
    Q_new(:,k+1) = s*Q(:,k) +c*Q(:,k+1);
    R = R_new; Q = Q_new;
end
```

Example 7.15 Finding Eigenvalues Using QR Factorization

Consider again the matrix introduced in Example 7.3 and revisited in Example 7.13:

$$\mathbf{A} = \begin{bmatrix} 4 & 2/3 & -4/3 & 4/3 \\ 2/3 & 4 & 0 & 0 \\ -4/3 & 0 & 6 & 2 \\ 4/3 & 0 & 2 & 6 \end{bmatrix}.$$

After conversion to Hessenberg form (which is tridiagonal for this example, since the original $\mathbf{A}$ is symmetric), we have our starting matrix:

$$\mathbf{A}^{(1)} = \begin{bmatrix} 4.0000 & -2.0000 & 0.0000 & 0.0000 \\ -2.0000 & 4.0000 & -0.0000 & -0.0000 \\ 0.0000 & -0.0000 & 4.9172 & -1.6815 \\ 0.0000 & 0.0000 & -1.6815 & 7.0828 \end{bmatrix}$$

Using `QR_eig_g`, the first five iterations give

$$\mathbf{A}^{(2)} = \begin{bmatrix} 5.6000 & -1.2000 & 0.0000 & 0.0000 \\ -1.2000 & 2.4000 & -0.0000 & -0.0000 \\ 0.0000 & -0.0000 & 6.1736 & -1.9925 \\ 0.0000 & 0.0000 & -1.9925 & 5.8264 \end{bmatrix}$$

$$\mathbf{A}^{(3)} = \begin{bmatrix} 5.9512 & -0.4390 & -0.0000 & 0.0000 \\ -0.4390 & 2.0488 & -0.0000 & -0.0000 \\ 0.0000 & -0.0000 & 7.3056 & -1.5151 \\ 0.0000 & 0.0000 & -1.5151 & 4.6944 \end{bmatrix}$$

$$\mathbf{A}^{(4)} = \begin{bmatrix} 5.9945 & -0.1479 & -0.0000 & 0.0000 \\ -0.1479 & 2.0055 & -0.0000 & -0.0000 \\ 0.0000 & -0.0000 & 7.8004 & -0.8709 \\ 0.0000 & 0.0000 & -0.8709 & 4.1996 \end{bmatrix}$$

$$\mathbf{A}^{(5)} = \begin{bmatrix} 5.9994 & -0.0494 & -0.0000 & 0.0000 \\ -0.0494 & 2.0006 & -0.0000 & -0.0000 \\ 0.0000 & -0.0000 & 7.9482 & -0.4524 \\ 0.0000 & 0.0000 & -0.4524 & 4.0518 \end{bmatrix}$$

$$\mathbf{A}^{(6)} = \begin{bmatrix} 5.9999 & -0.0165 & -0.0000 & 0.0000 \\ -0.0165 & 2.0001 & -0.0000 & -0.0000 \\ -0.0000 & -0.0000 & 7.9869 & -0.2284 \\ 0.0000 & 0.0000 & -0.2284 & 4.0131 \end{bmatrix}$$

Table 7.6 shows the results of using this method for 5 and 10 iterations.

Table 7.6 Results for 5 and 10 iterations of better QR_eigenvalue method.

Iterations	Eigenvalues			
5	5.9999	2.0001	7.9869	4.0131
10	6.0000	2.0000	8.0000	4.0000

The computational effort for the two approaches, as used in this problem, is summarized in Table 7.7.

Table 7.7 Flops required for 5, 10, and 15 iterations.

	5	10	15
Basic	4081	8161	12,241
Better	2222	3783	5343

7.4 MATLAB's METHODS

MATLAB has built-in functions for finding eigenvalues and eigenvectors and for performing QR factorization. The function `eig` has been used repeatedly in the previous chapters to find eigenvalues of a matrix. When called with a single output variable, such as, $\mathbf{e} = \texttt{eig}(\mathbf{A})$, the function returns a vector containing the eigenvalues of $\mathbf{A}$, where $\mathbf{A}$ is a square matrix. When called with two output variables, as in $[\mathbf{Z}, \mathbf{m}] = \texttt{eig}(\mathbf{A})$, the function produces a full matrix $\mathbf{Z}$ whose columns are the eigenvectors corresponding to the eigenvalues that appear on the diagonal of the matrix $\mathbf{m}$. The eigenvalues and eigenvectors satisfy $\mathbf{AZ} = \mathbf{Zm}$. The eigenvectors are scaled to be of unit Euclidean length.

The function eig can also be called with two input matrices, i.e. $[\mathbf{V}, \mathbf{D}] = \texttt{eig}(\mathbf{A}, \mathbf{B})$; in this case, the function produces the generalized eigenvalues and corresponding eigenvectors such that $\mathbf{AV} = \mathbf{BVD}$.

MATLAB's built-in function for QR (orthogonal-triangular) decomposition has the form $[\mathbf{Q}, \mathbf{R}] = \texttt{qr}(\mathbf{A})$. It produces an upper triangular matrix $\mathbf{R}$ of the same dimension as $\mathbf{A}$ and a unitary matrix $\mathbf{Q}$ such that $\mathbf{A} = \mathbf{QR}$. If a third output matrix is specified, in the call $[\mathbf{Q}, \mathbf{R}, \mathbf{E}] = \texttt{qr}(\mathbf{A})$, the function produces a permutation matrix $\mathbf{E}$, an upper triangular matrix $\mathbf{R}$, and a unitary matrix $\mathbf{Q}$ such that $\mathbf{AE} = \mathbf{QR}$. The column permutation $\mathbf{E}$ is chosen so that abs(diag($\mathbf{R}$)) is decreasing.

For sparse matrices, the qr function can compute a "Q-less QR decomposition"; i.e., $\mathbf{R} = \texttt{qr}(\mathbf{A})$ returns only $\mathbf{R}$. Note that $\mathbf{R} = \texttt{chol}(\mathbf{A}'\mathbf{A})$. The least squares approximate solution to $\mathbf{Ax} = \mathbf{b}$ can be found with the Q-less QR decomposition and one step of iterative refinement, as indicated in the comments at the beginning of the function `qr`:

$$\% \quad \mathbf{x} = \mathbf{R} \backslash (\mathbf{R}' \backslash (\mathbf{A}' * \mathbf{b}))$$

$$\% \quad \mathbf{r} = \mathbf{b} - \mathbf{A} * \mathbf{x}$$

$$\% \quad \mathbf{e} = \mathbf{R} \backslash (\mathbf{R}' \backslash (\mathbf{A}' * \mathbf{r}))$$

$$\% \quad \mathbf{x} = \mathbf{x} + \mathbf{e};$$

(See any standard text on linear algebra for a discussion of least squares approximate solutions.)

The basic power method for finding the dominant eigenvalue of matrix $\mathbf{A}$ is

$$\mathbf{z}^{(1)} = [1 \quad 1 \quad 1 \quad \ldots \quad 1]',$$

$$\mathbf{w}^{(1)} = \mathbf{A}\mathbf{z}^{(1)}; \mathbf{z}^{(2)} = \frac{1}{w^{(1)}k} \mathbf{w}^{(1)},$$

where $w^{(1)}k$ is the component of $\mathbf{w}$ that is of largest magnitude and is the first estimate of the dominant eigenvalue and $\mathbf{z}^{(2)}$ is the corresponding (estimate of the) eigenvector.

Continuing, we have

$$\mathbf{w}^{(2)} = \mathbf{A}\mathbf{z}^{(2)}, \quad \mathbf{z}^{(3)} = \frac{1}{w^{(2)}k} \mathbf{w}^{(2)},$$

and so on until the estimates have converged. The Rayleigh quotient gives an improved estimate of the eigenvalue, especially for symmetric matrices:

$$\lambda = (\mathbf{z}'\mathbf{w})/(\mathbf{z}'\mathbf{z}).$$

The inverse power method finds the eigenvalue of $\mathbf{A}$ that is of smallest magnitude. We apply the power method to $\mathbf{B} = \mathbf{A}^{-1}$ to find its dominant eigenvalue, μ. Then the reciprocal of μ gives the smallest magnitude eigenvalue λ of $\mathbf{A}$.

To avoid computing $\mathbf{A}^{-1}$, instead of finding $\mathbf{A}^{-1}\mathbf{z} = \mathbf{w}$, we solve the system $\mathbf{A}\mathbf{w} = \mathbf{z}$ for $\mathbf{w}$. The inverse power method applied to a shifted matrix, $\mathbf{A} - b\,\mathbf{I}$, finds the eigenvalue closest to b.

QR factorization of a matrix $\mathbf{A}$ can be accomplished using Householder matrices, as described in the following algorithm:

Define $R^{(0)} = A$.
For $k = 1, \ldots, n$ ab; 1
        Find $H^{(k)}$ to reduce positions $k + 1, \ldots, n$ in the kth column of $R(k - 1)$
        to zero;
        Define $R^{(k)} = H^{(k)} R^{(k-1)}$.
end.
Define $Q = I$.
For $k = n - 1, \ldots, 1,$
        $Q = H^{(k)} Q$
end.
Define $R = R^{(n-1)}$.

For a matrix in Hessenberg form, it is more efficient to perform the factorization using Givens rotations. The preprocessing to Hessenberg form and the use of Givens rotations for QR factorization are discussed in Section 7.3.2.

QR method for eigenvalues:

Define $\mathbf{A}(1) = \mathbf{A}$.
For $k = 1 : k\_\text{max}$,
    Factor $\mathbf{A}(k) = \mathbf{Q}(k)\,\mathbf{R}(k)$
    Define $\mathbf{A}(k+1) = \mathbf{R}(k)\,\mathbf{Q}(k)$
end.

SUGGESTIONS FOR FURTHER READING

The following are a few of the many excellent undergraduate texts on linear algebra:

Kolman, B., *Introductory Linear Algebra with Applications,* 6th ed., Prentice Hall, Upper Saddle River, NJ, 1997.

Leon, S. J., *Linear Algebra with Applications,* 5th ed., Prentice Hall, Upper Saddle River, NJ, 1998.

Strang, G., *Linear Algebra and Its Applications,* 3rd ed., Harcourt Brace Jovanovich, San Diego, CA, 1988.

Some references at a somewhat more advanced level include:

Golub, G. H. and C. F. Van Loan, *Matrix Computations,* 3d ed., Johns Hopkins University Press, Baltimore, 1996.

Fox, L., *An Introduction to Numerical Linear Algebra,* Oxford University Press, New York, 1965. This classic work also contains many bibliographic entries.

For further discussion of application of eigenvalues, see:

Thomson, W. T., *Introduction to Space Dynamics,* Dover, New York, 1986. (Originally published by John Wiley & Sons, 1961.)

Greenberg, M. D., *Foundations of Applied Mathematics,* Prentice Hall, Englewood Cliffs, NJ, 1977.

PRACTICE THE TECHNIQUES

In Problems P7.1–P7.20, use the power method to find the specified eigenvalue, and a corresponding eigenvector, of the given matrix.

    a. Use the basic power method to find the dominant eigenvalue.

    b. Use the inverse power method to find the eigenvalue of smallest magnitude.

P7.1 $A = \begin{bmatrix} 1 & 0 & 0 \\ 2 & -1 & 2 \\ 4 & -4 & 5 \end{bmatrix}$.

P7.2 $A = \begin{bmatrix} -2 & 2 & -1 \\ -2 & 2 & 0 \\ 2 & -2 & 3 \end{bmatrix}$.

P7.3 $A = \begin{bmatrix} 5 & -2 & 1 \\ 3 & 0 & 1 \\ 0 & 0 & 2 \end{bmatrix}$.

P7.4 $A = \begin{bmatrix} 2 & 2 & -1 \\ -5 & 9 & -3 \\ -4 & 4 & 1 \end{bmatrix}$.

P7.5 $A = \begin{bmatrix} -19 & 20 & -6 \\ -12 & 13 & -3 \\ 30 & -30 & 12 \end{bmatrix}$.

P7.6 $A = \begin{bmatrix} 25 & -26 & 8 \\ 15 & -16 & 4 \\ -39 & 39 & -15 \end{bmatrix}$.

P7.7 $A = \begin{bmatrix} -36 & 10 & -5 \\ -172 & 47 & -22 \\ -16 & 4 & 1 \end{bmatrix}$.

P7.8 $A = \begin{bmatrix} 2 & 0 & 0 \\ -180 & 47 & -15 \\ -600 & 150 & -48 \end{bmatrix}$.

P7.9 $A = \begin{bmatrix} 104 & -34 & 8 \\ 357 & -117 & 28 \\ 204 & -68 & 18 \end{bmatrix}$.

P7.10 $A = \begin{bmatrix} 66 & -21 & 9 \\ 228 & -73 & 33 \\ 84 & -28 & 16 \end{bmatrix}$.

P7.11 $A = \begin{bmatrix} 4 & 0 & 0 & 0 \\ -4 & 8 & -4 & 2 \\ -7 & 7 & -3 & 3 \\ -2 & 2 & -2 & 4 \end{bmatrix}$.

P7.12 $A = \begin{bmatrix} 11 & -6 & 4 & -2 \\ 4 & 1 & 0 & 0 \\ -9 & 9 & -6 & 5 \\ -6 & 6 & -6 & 7 \end{bmatrix}$.

P7.13 $A = \begin{bmatrix} 20 & -15 & 10 & -5 \\ 26 & -21 & 16 & -8 \\ 11 & -11 & 11 & -5 \\ 4 & -4 & 4 & -1 \end{bmatrix}$.

P7.14 $A = \begin{bmatrix} -6 & 6 & -4 & 2 \\ -8 & 8 & -4 & 2 \\ 0 & 0 & 2 & 0 \\ 0 & 0 & 0 & 2 \end{bmatrix}$.

P7.15 $A = \begin{bmatrix} -3 & 2 & -8 & 0 \\ -21 & 10 & -20 & 0 \\ 0 & 0 & 5 & 0 \\ 0 & 0 & 8 & 0 \end{bmatrix}$.

P7.16 $A = \begin{bmatrix} 11 & -8 & 6 & -4 & 2 \\ 16 & -13 & 12 & -8 & 4 \\ 4 & -4 & 5 & 0 & 0 \\ -9 & 9 & -9 & 12 & -5 \\ -6 & 6 & -6 & 6 & -1 \end{bmatrix}$.

P7.17 $A = \begin{bmatrix} 2 & 0 & 0 & 0 & 0 \\ 3 & -1 & 3 & -2 & 1 \\ 2 & -2 & 4 & 0 & 0 \\ -5 & 5 & -5 & 8 & -3 \\ -4 & 4 & -4 & 4 & 0 \end{bmatrix}$.

P7.18 $A = \begin{bmatrix} -7 & 8 & -6 & 4 & -2 \\ -13 & 14 & -9 & 6 & -3 \\ -2 & 2 & 1 & 0 & 0 \\ 5 & -5 & 5 & -3 & 3 \\ 4 & -4 & 4 & -4 & 5 \end{bmatrix}$.

P7.19 $\mathbf{A} = \begin{bmatrix} -8 & 8 & -6 & 4 & -2 \\ -7 & 7 & -3 & 2 & -1 \\ 8 & -8 & 10 & -6 & 3 \\ 8 & -8 & 8 & -5 & 4 \\ 4 & -4 & 4 & -4 & 5 \end{bmatrix}$.

P7.20 $\mathbf{A} = \begin{bmatrix} -1 & 4 & -3 & 2 & -1 \\ -11 & 14 & -9 & 6 & -3 \\ -6 & 6 & -2 & 2 & -1 \\ 6 & -6 & 6 & -4 & 4 \\ 6 & -6 & 6 & -6 & 7 \end{bmatrix}$.

For the symmetric matrices in Problems P7.21–P7.40, find the dominant eigenvalue
  a. *using the power method and*
  b. *using the accelerated power method (Rayleigh quotient).*

P7.21 $\mathbf{A} = \begin{bmatrix} 6 & -1 & -2 \\ -1 & 8 & 1 \\ -2 & 1 & 2 \end{bmatrix}$.

P7.22 $\mathbf{A} = \begin{bmatrix} 1 & 0 & 1 \\ 0 & 9 & -2 \\ 1 & -2 & 11 \end{bmatrix}$

P7.23 $\mathbf{A} = \begin{bmatrix} 11 & -2 & -4 \\ -2 & 15 & 2 \\ -4 & 2 & 3 \end{bmatrix}$.

P7.24 $\mathbf{A} = \begin{bmatrix} 10 & 3 & 6 \\ 3 & 4 & -3 \\ 6 & -3 & 22 \end{bmatrix}$.

P7.25 $\mathbf{A} = \begin{bmatrix} 8 & -6 & -9 \\ -6 & 44 & 0 \\ -9 & 0 & 14 \end{bmatrix}$.

P7.26 $\mathbf{A} = \begin{bmatrix} -9 & 0 & 1 \\ 0 & -1 & -2 \\ 1 & -2 & 1 \end{bmatrix}$.

P7.27 $\mathbf{A} = \begin{bmatrix} 1 & -2 & -4 \\ -2 & 5 & 2 \\ -4 & 2 & -7 \end{bmatrix}$.

P7.28 $\mathbf{A} = \begin{bmatrix} 5 & -3 & -9 & -7 \\ -3 & 33 & 3 & 10 \\ -9 & 3 & 9 & -3 \\ -7 & 10 & -3 & 37 \end{bmatrix}$.

P7.29 $\mathbf{A} = \begin{bmatrix} 50 & 3 & 2 & -11 \\ 3 & 8 & 10 & 5 \\ 2 & 10 & 18 & -4 \\ -11 & 5 & -4 & 42 \end{bmatrix}$.

P7.30 $\mathbf{A} = \begin{bmatrix} 51 & 5 & 11 & 1 \\ 5 & 5 & 3 & -8 \\ 11 & 3 & 37 & 1 \\ 1 & -8 & 1 & 21 \end{bmatrix}$.

P7.31 $\mathbf{A} = \begin{bmatrix} 11 & -6 & -8 & 6 \\ -6 & 47 & -4 & 0 \\ -8 & -4 & 19 & 4 \\ 6 & 0 & 4 & 15 \end{bmatrix}$.

P7.32 $\mathbf{A} = \begin{bmatrix} 4 & 2/3 & -4/3 & 4/3 \\ 2/3 & 4 & 0 & 0 \\ -4/3 & 0 & 12 & 8 \\ 4/3 & 0 & 8 & 12 \end{bmatrix}$.

P7.33 $\mathbf{A} = \begin{bmatrix} 81/2 & 21/2 & -21 & 21 \\ 21/2 & 41/2 & -5 & 5 \\ -21 & -5 & 37 & -1 \\ 21 & 5 & -1 & 37 \end{bmatrix}$.

P7.34 $\mathbf{A} = \begin{bmatrix} 32 & -2 & -5 & -8 & 1 \\ -2 & 20 & 8 & 6 & 0 \\ -5 & 8 & 6 & 0 & -3 \\ -8 & 6 & 0 & 32 & -2 \\ 1 & 0 & -3 & -2 & 24 \end{bmatrix}$.

P7.35 $\mathbf{A} = \begin{bmatrix} 6 & 2 & -1 & -3 & -5 \\ 2 & 18 & -2 & 5 & 4 \\ -1 & -2 & 20 & -5 & -4 \\ -3 & 5 & -5 & 28 & 1 \\ -5 & 4 & -4 & 1 & 12 \end{bmatrix}$.

P7.36 $\mathbf{A} = \begin{bmatrix} 35 & 5 & 9 & -1 & 4 & -3 \\ 5 & 5 & 3 & -8 & 2 & 0 \\ 9 & 3 & 33 & -1 & 4 & -3 \\ -1 & -8 & -1 & 21 & 0 & 1 \\ 4 & 2 & 4 & 0 & 29 & -2 \\ -3 & 0 & -3 & 1 & -2 & 31 \end{bmatrix}$.

P7.37 $\mathbf{A} = \begin{bmatrix} 52 & 6 & 15 & 1 & 5 & 3 & 5 \\ 6 & 16 & 0 & -13 & 4 & -9 & -2 \\ 15 & 0 & 58 & -3 & 8 & 1 & 6 \\ 1 & -13 & -3 & 30 & 1 & -7 & -3 \\ 5 & 4 & 8 & 1 & 42 & 3 & 5 \\ 3 & -9 & 1 & -7 & 3 & 28 & -1 \\ 5 & -2 & 6 & -3 & 5 & -1 & 44 \end{bmatrix}.$

P7.38

$\mathbf{A} = \begin{bmatrix} 46 & 0 & 5 & 14 & 10 & 2 & 5 & 4 \\ 0 & 46 & -5 & -14 & -10 & -2 & -5 & -4 \\ 5 & -5 & 56 & 9 & 14 & -1 & 7 & 3 \\ 14 & -14 & 9 & 18 & 2 & -11 & 1 & -7 \\ 10 & -10 & 14 & 2 & 64 & -4 & 9 & 2 \\ 2 & -2 & -1 & -11 & -4 & 44 & -3 & -5 \\ 5 & -5 & 7 & 1 & 9 & -3 & 58 & 1 \\ 4 & -4 & 3 & -7 & 2 & -5 & 1 & 42 \end{bmatrix}.$

P7.39

$\mathbf{A} = \begin{bmatrix} 84 & -8 & -3 & 25 & -3 & -10 & -23 & -12 & -5 \\ -8 & 132 & -18 & -7 & -12 & 22 & 14 & 18 & 2 \\ -3 & -18 & 110 & 13 & 7 & -18 & -17 & -16 & -3 \\ 25 & -7 & 13 & 62 & 13 & 2 & 29 & 8 & 7 \\ -3 & -12 & 7 & 13 & 100 & -14 & -20 & -14 & -4 \\ -10 & 22 & -18 & 2 & -14 & 126 & 8 & 22 & 0 \\ -23 & 14 & -17 & 29 & -20 & 8 & 60 & 0 & -11 \\ -12 & 18 & -16 & 8 & -14 & 22 & 0 & 122 & -2 \\ -5 & 2 & -3 & 7 & -4 & 0 & -11 & -2 & 94 \end{bmatrix}.$

P7.40

$\mathbf{A} = \begin{bmatrix} 84 & 1 & 1 & -9 & 23 & 7 & 1 & -7 & 1 & -3 \\ 1 & 46 & 15 & -5 & -11 & -17 & 7 & 1 & 3 & 1 \\ 1 & 15 & 50 & 5 & 11 & 17 & -7 & -1 & -3 & -1 \\ -9 & -5 & 5 & 68 & -17 & -12 & 3 & 4 & 1 & 2 \\ 23 & -11 & 11 & -17 & 100 & -3 & 9 & -13 & 5 & -5 \\ 7 & -17 & 17 & -12 & -3 & 44 & 11 & -2 & 5 & 0 \\ 1 & 7 & -7 & 3 & 9 & 11 & 58 & -1 & -3 & -1 \\ -7 & 1 & -1 & 4 & -13 & -2 & -1 & 72 & -1 & 3 \\ 1 & 3 & -3 & 1 & 5 & 5 & -3 & -1 & 64 & -1 \\ -3 & 1 & -1 & 2 & -5 & 0 & -1 & 3 & -1 & 70 \end{bmatrix}.$

For the matrices given in Problems P7.1–P7.40,

a. Find the QR factorization.
b. Find the eigenvalues, using the MATLAB function QR_eigen.
c Use a Householder similarity transformation to transform the given matrix to Hessenberg form.
d. Find the eigenvalues of the transformed matrix from Part c.

EXPLORE SOME APPLICATIONS

A7.1 Show that the quadratic equation in three variables,

$$ax^2 + by^2 + cz^2 + 2dxy + 2exz + 2fyz = g,$$

can be written as $[\mathbf{A}\ \mathbf{v}]\mathbf{v} = g$, with

$$\mathbf{A} = \begin{bmatrix} a & d & e \\ d & b & f \\ e & f & c \end{bmatrix}.$$

The surfaces described by the equation can be classified according to the signs of the eigenvalues of $\mathbf{A}$, as indicated in the following table (degenerate cases may occur; cf. Fraleigh and Beauregard, 1987, p. 381):

Eigenvalues		Surface
$+\ +\ +$ or	$-\ -\ -$	Ellipsoid
$+\ +\ -$ or	$+\ -\ -$	Elliptic cone or hyperboloid (1 or 2 sheets)
$+\ +\ 0$ or	$-\ -\ 0$	Elliptic paraboloid or elliptic cylinder
$+\ -\ 0$		Hyperbolic paraboloid or hyperbolic cylinder
$+\ 0\ 0$ or	$-\ 0\ 0$	Parabolic cylinder or two parallel planes

In Problems A7.2–A7.12, write the equation as a quadratic form as in A7.1, find the eigenvalues of $\mathbf{A}$, and classify the surface.

A7.2 $6x^2 + 8y^2 + 2z^2 - 2xy - 4xz + 2yz = 12$.

A7.3 $x^2 + 9y^2 + 11z^2 + 2xz - 4yz = 24$.

A7.4 $11x^2 + 15y^2 + 3z^2 - 4xy - 8xz + 4yz = 21$.

A7.5 $10x^2 + 4y^2 + 22z^2 + 6xy + 12xz - 6yz = 48$.

A7.6 $8x^2 + 44y^2 + 14z^2 - 12xy - 18xz = 36$.

A7.7 $x^2 + 9y^2 + 11z^2 + 2xz - 4yz = 24$.

A7.8 $11x^2 + 15y^2 + 3z^2 - 4xy - 8xz + 4yz = 21$.

A7.9 $7x^2 + 10y^2 + 19z^2 - 28xy - 8xz - 20yz = 18$.

A7.10 $-4x^2 + 3y^2 + z^2 - 4xy + 12xz - 16yz = -36$.

A7.11 $-16x^2 - 7y^2 - 13z^2 + 4xy + 20xz - 16yz = -28$.

A7.12 $16x^2 - y^2 + 11z^2 - 20xy - 28xz + 8yz = 82$.

For Problems A7.13–A7.16, find the eigenvalues and eigenvectors of $\mathbf{A}$, the matrix of the quadratic form

$$\begin{bmatrix} x & y \end{bmatrix} \mathbf{A} \begin{bmatrix} x & y \end{bmatrix}' = g.$$

(See Problems A6.4–A6.6.) If $\mathbf{Q}$ is the matrix whose columns are the eigenvectors of $\mathbf{A}$ (with each eigenvector of unit length), then the change of variables

$$\begin{bmatrix} x \\ y \end{bmatrix} = \mathbf{Q} \begin{bmatrix} t \\ u \end{bmatrix}$$

performs the necessary rotation so that, in the new coordinate system (t, u), the cross-product terms do not appear. Use the eigenvalues of $\mathbf{A}$ to find the quadratic equation in terms of the rotated axes that eliminate the mixed terms. (Ignore any linear terms, they can be eliminated by a translation of axes after the rotation.)

A7.13 $x^2 - \sqrt{3}xy + 2y^2 = 10$.

A7.14 $4x^2 + 3\sqrt{3}xy + y^2 = 22$.

A7.15 $x^2 - \sqrt{3}xy = -2$.

A7.16 $-x^2 + xy - y + 7x = 11$.

In Problems A7.17–A7.22, find the principal inertias and principal axes of the three-dimensional object consisting of point masses $m_1, \ldots, m_k$ located at $(x_1, y_1, z_1), \ldots, (x_k, y_k, z_k)$, respectively. The inertial matrix is as given in Example 7-A, but for point masses, the moment of inertias of the body around the x, y, and z-axes are, respectively,

$$I_{xx} = \sum_{i=1}^{k} (y_i^2 + z_i^2) m_i,$$

$$I_{yy} = \sum_{i=1}^{k} (x_i^2 + z_i^2) m_i,$$

$$I_{zz} = \sum_{i=1}^{k} (x_i^2 + y_i^2) m_i,$$

and the products of inertia are, similarly,

$$I_{xy} = I_{yx} = \sum_{i=1}^{k} (x_i y_i) m_i,$$

$$I_{xz} = I_{zx} = \sum_{i=1}^{k} (x_i z_i) m_i,$$

$$I_{yz} = I_{zy} = \sum_{i=1}^{k} (y_i z_i) m_i.$$

A7.17 Unit point masses ($m = 1$) at $(1, 0, 0)$, $(1, 1, 0)$, $(1, 1, 1)$.

A7.18 Unit point masses at $(1, 0, 0)$, $(0, 1, 0)$, $(1, 1, 0)$, $(1, 0, 1)$, $(1, 1, 1)$.

A7.19 Unit point masses at $(0, 1, 0)$, $(0, 0, 1)$, $(1, 1, 0)$, $(1, 0, 1)$, $(1, 1, 1)$.

A7.20 Unit point masses at $(1, 0, 0)$, $(0, 2, 0)$, $(0, 0, 1)$, $(1, 1, 0)$, $(1, 0, 1)$, $(0, 1, 1)$, $(1, 1, 2)$.

A7.21 Unit point masses at $(1, 0, 0)$, $(0, 1, 0)$, $(0, 0, 1)$, $(1, 1, 0)$, $(1, 0, 1)$, $(0, 1, 1)$; point mass with $m = 2$ at $(1, 1, 1)$.

A7.22 Unit point masses at $(1, 0, 0)$, $(0, 1, 0)$, $(1, 1, 0)$, $(1, 0, 1)$; point masses with $m = 2$ at $(0, 0, 1)$, $(0, 1, 1)$, $(1, 1, 1)$.

Problems A7.23–A7.26 explore the eigenvalues of matrices whose shapes resemble letters of the alphabet. (See Leon, et al., 1996.)

A7.23 Find the eigenvalues and eigenvectors of the following matrices:

$$\mathbf{L3} = \begin{bmatrix} 1 & 0 & 0 \\ 1 & 0 & 0 \\ 1 & 1 & 1 \end{bmatrix},$$

$$\mathbf{L4} = \begin{bmatrix} 1 & 0 & 0 & 0 \\ 1 & 0 & 0 & 0 \\ 1 & 0 & 0 & 0 \\ 1 & 1 & 1 & 1 \end{bmatrix},$$

$$\mathbf{L5} = \begin{bmatrix} 1 & 0 & 0 & 0 & 0 \\ 1 & 0 & 0 & 0 & 0 \\ 1 & 0 & 0 & 0 & 0 \\ 1 & 0 & 0 & 0 & 0 \\ 1 & 1 & 1 & 1 & 1 \end{bmatrix}.$$

Generate some larger $\mathbf{L}$ matrices, and discuss any patterns you find in the eigenvalues and eigenvectors.

A7.24 Find the eigenvalues and eigenvectors of the following matrices:

$$\mathbf{H3} = \begin{bmatrix} 1 & 0 & 1 \\ 1 & 1 & 1 \\ 1 & 0 & 1 \end{bmatrix},$$

$$\mathbf{H5} = \begin{bmatrix} 1 & 0 & 0 & 0 & 1 \\ 1 & 0 & 0 & 0 & 1 \\ 1 & 1 & 1 & 1 & 1 \\ 1 & 0 & 0 & 0 & 1 \\ 1 & 0 & 0 & 0 & 1 \end{bmatrix},$$

$$\mathbf{H7} = \begin{bmatrix} 1 & 0 & 0 & 0 & 0 & 0 & 1 \\ 1 & 0 & 0 & 0 & 0 & 0 & 1 \\ 1 & 0 & 0 & 0 & 0 & 0 & 1 \\ 1 & 1 & 1 & 1 & 1 & 1 & 1 \\ 1 & 0 & 0 & 0 & 0 & 0 & 1 \\ 1 & 0 & 0 & 0 & 0 & 0 & 1 \\ 1 & 0 & 0 & 0 & 0 & 0 & 1 \end{bmatrix}.$$

Generate some larger **H** matrices, and discuss any patterns you find in the eigenvalues and eigenvectors.

A7.25 Find the eigenvalues and eigenvectors of the following matrices:

$$\mathbf{T3} = \begin{bmatrix} 1 & 1 & 1 \\ 0 & 1 & 0 \\ 0 & 1 & 0 \end{bmatrix},$$

$$\mathbf{T5} = \begin{bmatrix} 1 & 1 & 1 & 1 & 1 \\ 0 & 0 & 1 & 0 & 0 \\ 0 & 0 & 1 & 0 & 0 \\ 0 & 0 & 1 & 0 & 0 \\ 0 & 0 & 1 & 0 & 0 \end{bmatrix},$$

$$\mathbf{T7} = \begin{bmatrix} 1 & 1 & 1 & 1 & 1 & 1 & 1 \\ 0 & 0 & 0 & 1 & 0 & 0 & 0 \\ 0 & 0 & 0 & 1 & 0 & 0 & 0 \\ 0 & 0 & 0 & 1 & 0 & 0 & 0 \\ 0 & 0 & 0 & 1 & 0 & 0 & 0 \\ 0 & 0 & 0 & 1 & 0 & 0 & 0 \\ 0 & 0 & 0 & 1 & 0 & 0 & 0 \end{bmatrix}.$$

Generate some larger **T** matrices, and discuss any patterns you find in the eigenvalues and eigenvectors.

A7.26 Find the eigenvalues and eigenvectors of the following matrices:

$$\mathbf{N3} = \begin{bmatrix} 1 & 0 & 1 \\ 1 & 1 & 1 \\ 1 & 0 & 1 \end{bmatrix},$$

$$\mathbf{N4} = \begin{bmatrix} 1 & 0 & 0 & 1 \\ 1 & 1 & 0 & 1 \\ 1 & 0 & 1 & 1 \\ 1 & 0 & 0 & 1 \end{bmatrix},$$

$$\mathbf{N5} = \begin{bmatrix} 1 & 0 & 0 & 0 & 1 \\ 1 & 1 & 0 & 0 & 1 \\ 1 & 0 & 1 & 0 & 1 \\ 1 & 0 & 0 & 1 & 1 \\ 1 & 0 & 0 & 0 & 1 \end{bmatrix},$$

$$\mathbf{N6} = \begin{bmatrix} 1 & 0 & 0 & 0 & 0 & 1 \\ 1 & 1 & 0 & 0 & 0 & 1 \\ 1 & 0 & 1 & 0 & 0 & 1 \\ 1 & 0 & 0 & 1 & 0 & 1 \\ 1 & 0 & 0 & 0 & 1 & 1 \\ 1 & 0 & 0 & 0 & 0 & 1 \end{bmatrix}.$$

Generate some larger **N** matrices, and discuss any patterns you find in the eigenvalues and eigenvectors.

Problems A7.27–A7.50 introduce the application of eigenvalues and eigenvectors to the solution of linear systems of first-order ordinary differential equations (ODEs). (These problems are related to problems in Chapter 13.)

If the real matrix **A** *has distinct, real eigenvalues* μ_1 *and* μ_2 *with eigenvectors* $\mathbf{v}_1$ $\mathbf{v}_2$, *respectively, the general solution of the linear system of ODEs,* $\mathbf{x}' = \mathbf{A}\mathbf{x}$, *is*

$$\mathbf{x} = c_1 e^{\mu_1 t} \mathbf{v}_1 + c_2 e^{\mu_2 t} \mathbf{v}_2.$$

If the matrix **A** *has a complex eigenvalue* $\mu = a + bi$, *with eigenvector* **v**, *the general solution of* $\mathbf{x}' = \mathbf{A}\mathbf{x}$ *is*

$$\mathbf{x} = c_1 e^{at}[\cos(bt)\,\mathrm{Re}(\mathbf{v}) - \sin(bt)\,\mathrm{Im}(\mathbf{v})] \\ + c_2[\cos(bt)\,\mathrm{Im}(\mathbf{v}) + \sin(bt)\,\mathrm{Re}(\mathbf{v})].$$

Note that the complex conjugate of μ *is also an eigenvalue, and its eigenvector is the complex conjugate of* **v**. *(See Leon, 1998, for a discussion of these basic ideas; the extension to n-by-n systems follows in a similar manner, as long as A has n linearly independent eigenvectors. For a discussion of the more general case, see, e.g., Zill, 1986.)*

In problems A7.27–A7.50, find the general solution of $\mathbf{x}' = \mathbf{A}\mathbf{x}$.

A7.27 $\mathbf{A} = \begin{bmatrix} 3 & -3 & 2 & -1 \\ 12 & -12 & 10 & -5 \\ 15 & -15 & 14 & -7 \\ 6 & -6 & 6 & -3 \end{bmatrix}$.

A7.28 $\mathbf{A} = \begin{bmatrix} -26 & 21 & -14 & 7 \\ -34 & 29 & -20 & 10 \\ -13 & 13 & -11 & 7 \\ -8 & 8 & -8 & 7 \end{bmatrix}$.

A7.29 $\mathbf{A} = \begin{bmatrix} 1 & -3 & 2 & -1 \\ 4 & -6 & 2 & -1 \\ -5 & 5 & -8 & 5 \\ -10 & 10 & -10 & 7 \end{bmatrix}$.

A7.30 $\mathbf{A} = \begin{bmatrix} -6 & 6 & -4 & 2 \\ -16 & 16 & -12 & 6 \\ -17 & 17 & -15 & 9 \\ -10 & 10 & -10 & 8 \end{bmatrix}$.

A7.31 $\mathbf{A} = \begin{bmatrix} 3 & -3 & 2 & -1 \\ 10 & -10 & 8 & -4 \\ 10 & -10 & 9 & -4 \\ 2 & -2 & 2 & 0 \end{bmatrix}$.

A7.32 $\mathbf{A} = \begin{bmatrix} 29 & -24 & 16 & -8 \\ 52 & -46 & 34 & -17 \\ 35 & -34 & 30 & -16 \\ 14 & -14 & 14 & -9 \end{bmatrix}$.

A7.33 $\mathbf{A} = \begin{bmatrix} 3 & -6 & 4 & -2 \\ 30 & -32 & 24 & -12 \\ 38 & -37 & 31 & -17 \\ 14 & -14 & 14 & -10 \end{bmatrix}$.

A7.34 $\mathbf{A} = \begin{bmatrix} 16 & -15 & 10 & -5 \\ 42 & -40 & 30 & -15 \\ 35 & -34 & 29 & -14 \\ 8 & -8 & 8 & -3 \end{bmatrix}$.

A7.35 $\mathbf{A} = \begin{bmatrix} 9 & -9 & 6 & -3 \\ 24 & -23 & 16 & -8 \\ 14 & -13 & 9 & -3 \\ -4 & 4 & -4 & 5 \end{bmatrix}$.

A7.36 $\mathbf{A} = \begin{bmatrix} -9 & 9 & -6 & 3 \\ -10 & 11 & -6 & 3 \\ 3 & -2 & 4 & -2 \\ 4 & -4 & 4 & -2 \end{bmatrix}$.

A7.37 $\mathbf{A} = \begin{bmatrix} 20 & -18 & 12 & -6 \\ 34 & -31 & 20 & -10 \\ 14 & -13 & 8 & -5 \\ 2 & -2 & 2 & -3 \end{bmatrix}$.

A7.38 $\mathbf{A} = \begin{bmatrix} -19 & 18 & -12 & 6 \\ -26 & 26 & -16 & 8 \\ -2 & 3 & 1 & -1 \\ 6 & -6 & 6 & -4 \end{bmatrix}$.

A7.39 $\mathbf{A} = \begin{bmatrix} 14 & -9 & 6 & -3 \\ 3 & 3 & -4 & 2 \\ -23 & 24 & -21 & 12 \\ -15 & 15 & -14 & 10 \end{bmatrix}$.

A7.40 $\mathbf{A} = \begin{bmatrix} 11 & -12 & 8 & -4 \\ 25 & -25 & 16 & -8 \\ 7 & -6 & 2 & 0 \\ -9 & 9 & -8 & 6 \end{bmatrix}$.

A7.41 $\mathbf{A} = \begin{bmatrix} 2 & 3 & 2 & 1 \\ 1 & 1 & 2 & -1 \\ 10 & -9 & 12 & -7 \\ 9 & -9 & 10 & -7 \end{bmatrix}$.

A7.42 $\mathbf{A} = \begin{bmatrix} -13 & 12 & -8 & 4 \\ -24 & 21 & -14 & 7 \\ -14 & 12 & -9 & 6 \\ -6 & 6 & -6 & 6 \end{bmatrix}$.

A7.43 $\mathbf{A} = \begin{bmatrix} -16 & 18 & -12 & 6 \\ -39 & 38 & -24 & 12 \\ -19 & 16 & -8 & 4 \\ 4 & -4 & 4 & -2 \end{bmatrix}$.

A7.44 $\mathbf{A} = \begin{bmatrix} -11 & 6 & -4 & 2 \\ 3 & -9 & 8 & -4 \\ 18 & -19 & 16 & -7 \\ 2 & -2 & 2 & 1 \end{bmatrix}$.

A7.45 $\mathbf{A} = \begin{bmatrix} -16 & 18 & -12 & 6 \\ -39 & 38 & -24 & 12 \\ -18 & 15 & -7 & 3 \\ 6 & -6 & 6 & -4 \end{bmatrix}$.

A7.46 $\mathbf{A} = \begin{bmatrix} -24 & 24 & -16 & 8 \\ -50 & 46 & -30 & 15 \\ -22 & 18 & -10 & 4 \\ 6 & -6 & 6 & -5 \end{bmatrix}$.

$$\textbf{A7.47} \quad \mathbf{A} = \begin{bmatrix} -36 & 30 & -20 & 10 \\ -61 & 50 & -36 & 18 \\ -34 & 29 & -25 & 13 \\ -10 & 10 & -10 & 6 \end{bmatrix}.$$

$$\textbf{A7.49} \quad \mathbf{A} = \begin{bmatrix} -9 & 6 & -4 & 2 \\ -7 & 3 & -2 & 1 \\ 6 & -7 & 6 & -5 \\ 8 & -8 & 8 & -8 \end{bmatrix}.$$

$$\textbf{A7.48} \quad \mathbf{A} = \begin{bmatrix} 30 & -24 & 16 & -8 \\ 38 & -28 & 18 & -9 \\ 6 & -2 & 0 & 0 \\ -2 & 2 & -2 & 1 \end{bmatrix}.$$

$$\textbf{A7.50} \quad \mathbf{A} = \begin{bmatrix} -28 & 24 & -16 & 8 \\ -42 & 34 & -22 & 11 \\ -10 & 6 & -2 & 0 \\ 6 & -6 & 6 & -5 \end{bmatrix}.$$

EXTEND YOUR UNDERSTANDING

U7.1 Compare the number of iterations required in using QR to find the eigenvalues of

$$\mathbf{F} = \begin{bmatrix} -631 & 316 & -156 & 144 & -36 \\ -798 & 400 & -195 & 180 & -45 \\ 900 & -450 & 227 & -204 & 51 \\ -28 & 14 & -7 & 12 & -1 \\ 96 & -48 & 24 & -24 & 14 \end{bmatrix}$$

with the number needed when $\mathbf{F}$ is preprocessed to Hessenberg form. Consider a reasonable test for convergence. The exact eigenvalues are

$$\text{eig(F)} = 1 \ \ 2 \ \ 5 \ \ 8 \ \ 6.$$

U7.2 The rate of convergence of the power method is influenced by the separation between the largest eigenvalue and the next largest. Compare the performance of the power method in finding the dominant eigenvalue for the matrices that follow. Use a reasonable test for convergence. The exact eigenvalues are given for comparison.

$$\mathbf{F} = \begin{bmatrix} -631 & 316 & -156 & 144 & -36 \\ -798 & 400 & -195 & 180 & -45 \\ 900 & -450 & 227 & -204 & 51 \\ -28 & 14 & -7 & 12 & -1 \\ 96 & -48 & 24 & -24 & 14 \end{bmatrix}.$$

The exact eigenvalues are

$$\text{eig(F)} = 1 \ \ 2 \ \ 5 \ \ 8 \ \ 6.$$

$$\mathbf{E} = \begin{bmatrix} -101 & 51 & -12 & 0 & 0 \\ -174 & 88 & -20 & 0 & 0 \\ 136 & -68 & 19 & 0 & 0 \\ 840 & -420 & 105 & -32 & 18 \\ 2016 & -1008 & 252 & -84 & 46 \end{bmatrix}.$$

The exact eigenvalues are

$$\text{eig(E)} = 10 \ \ 1 \ \ 2 \ \ 3 \ \ 4.$$

U7.3 Compare QR for matrix $\mathbf{A}$ and for the pre-processed matrix $\mathbf{T}$:

$$\mathbf{A} = \begin{bmatrix} 2 & 0 & 0 & 0 \\ -4 & 4 & 0 & 0 \\ 12 & -6 & 6 & 0 \\ -48 & 24 & -8 & 8 \end{bmatrix},$$

$$\mathbf{T} = \begin{bmatrix} 2 & 0 & 0 & 0 \\ 49.639 & 11.714 & -19.21 & -16.187 \\ 0 & 1.1265 & 3.3383 & -0.78038 \\ 0 & 0 & -1.425 & 2.9474 \end{bmatrix}.$$

U7.4 Find the eigenvalues of each of the following Jacobi iteration matrices for the indicated exercise:

$$\mathbf{T} = \begin{bmatrix} 0.0 & 0.2 & -0.1 \\ 0.2 & 0.0 & 0.2 \\ 0.2 & 0.5 & 0.0 \end{bmatrix} \text{ (Exercise 4.1);}$$

$$\mathbf{T} = \begin{bmatrix} 0.0 & 0.2 & 0.0 \\ 0.2 & 0.0 & 0.2 \\ 0.0 & 0.5 & 0.0 \end{bmatrix} \text{ (Exercise 4.3);}$$

$$\mathbf{T} = \begin{bmatrix} 0 & -1/4 & 0 \\ -1/3 & 0 & 1/3 \\ 0 & 1/4 & 0 \end{bmatrix} \text{(Exercise 4.5)};$$

$$\mathbf{T} = \begin{bmatrix} 0 & 1/2 & 0 & 0 \\ 1/2 & 0 & 1/2 & 0 \\ 0 & 1/2 & 0 & 1/2 \\ 0 & 0 & 1/2 & 0 \end{bmatrix} \text{(Exercise 4.6)};$$

$$\mathbf{T} = \begin{bmatrix} 0 & -1/5 & 0 & 0 \\ -1/5 & 0 & -1/5 & 0 \\ 0 & -1/5 & 0 & -1/5 \\ 0 & 0 & -1/5 & 0 \end{bmatrix} \text{(Exercise 4.7)}.$$

U7.5 Write an improved MATLAB function for the inverse power method to handle the case when zero is an eigenvalue. A small shift in the matrix will avoid the divide by zero difficulties.

U7.6 Modify the MATLAB function for Householder transformations to handle the case when $s = 0$.

U7.7 Compare the computational effort required for finding one, several, or all eigenvalues of a matrix for the different methods described in this chapter, including MATLAB's built-in function eig.

Interpolation

In this chapter, we study methods for representing a function based on knowledge of its behavior at certain discrete points. From this information, we may wish to obtain estimates of function values at other points, or we may need to use the closed-form representation of the function as the basis for other numerical techniques, such as numerical differentiation or integration, which we consider in Chapter 11.

Interpolation produces a function that matches the given data exactly; we seek a function that also provides a good approximation to the (unknown) data values at intermediate points. The data may come from measured experimental values or computed values from other numerical methods, such as the solution of differential equations (Chapters 12–15).

Our first interpolation methods provide a polynomial of an appropriate degree to exactly match a given set of data. The two standard forms for the polynomial (Lagrange and Newton) are presented with MATLAB functions and examples. It is also possible to interpolate not only function values, but derivative values. Hermite interpolation is included as the simplest example of "osculatory interpolation" for function and first-derivative values.

For some functions that are not well approximated by polynomial interpolation, rational function interpolation gives better results. In this chapter, we consider the problem of interpolating a set of data values with a rational function. In the next chapter, we present a method for finding a rational function to match the function and derivative values at a single point.

Finally, we investigate piecewise polynomial interpolation. This technique allows us to produce a smooth curve without too many "wiggles" through a large number of data points. After a brief presentation of piecewise linear and piecewise quadratic interpolation, we focus on one of the most important piecewise polynomial interpolation techniques, that of cubic splines.

Interpolation may be needed in any field in which measured data are important; the technique may be used to generate function values at points intermediate between those for which measurements are available. Interpolation may also be used to produce a smooth graph of a function for which values are known only at discrete points, either from measurements or calculations.

Example 8-A Chemical Reaction Product

Consider the observed concentration of the product of a simple chemical reaction, as a function of time:

Time:	0.0	0.5	1.0	1.5	2.0
Product:	0.0	0.19	0.26	0.29	0.31

In this chapter, we discuss several techniques for approximating the concentration of the product at other times. The data are illustrated in Fig. 8.1.

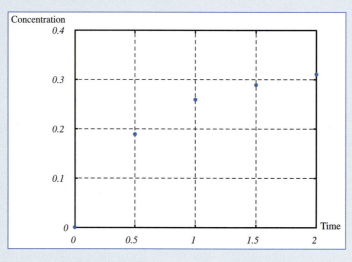

FIGURE 8.1   Chemical reaction product data.

Besides interpolating the data shown above, we also consider the effect of utilizing a more extensive set of data.

Time:

0.00	0.10	0.40	0.50	0.60	0.90	1.00	1.10	1.40	1.50	1.60	1.90	2.00

Product:

0.00	0.06	0.17	0.19	0.21	0.25	0.26	0.27	0.29	0.29	0.30	0.31	0.31

One possibility is to use these data directly in the interpolation. Another approach is to use the data to estimate the first derivative of the desired interpolation function by means of the techniques discussed in Chapter 11.

Example 8-B

Spline interpolation is used in computer graphics to represent smooth curves (in parametric form). Several points are chosen along the curve and are indexed in terms of a parameter, t. Interpolation is performed on the x and y coordinates separately (each as a function of t). The resulting parametric plot, $(x(t), y(t))$ gives the interpolated curve. For example, we take the points shown in Figure 8.2 as the data, which gives

```
t = [ 1    2    3    4    5    6    7    8    9   10   11   12 ]
x = [ 0    1    2    2    1    1    2    3    3    3    4    5 ]
y = [ 0    0    0    1    1    2    2    2    1    0    0    0 ]
```

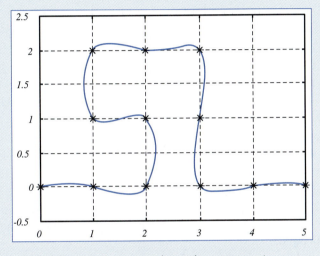

FIGURE 8.2 Spline interpolation for a parametric curve.

Data for several other curves are given in the exercises.

Although the uniform spacing used for the parameter values in this example is probably appropriate, it is not required. For figures in which consecutive pairs of points are not all the same Euclidean distance apart, the parameter values are sometimes adjusted to reflect the distance between the points. It is easy to experiment with the effect of different choices of the parameter t using the MATLAB spline function given in this chapter. For a discussion of the use of splines in computer graphics, see Bartels, Beatty, and Barsky, 1987.

The two most common forms of polynomial interpolation are Lagrangian interpolation and Newton interpolation. Of course, since the polynomial determined by a set of points is unique, the differences in these forms occur in the process of finding the polynomial (and the form in which it is expressed), not in the resulting function. Each approach has its advantages in different circumstances.

8.1.1 Lagrange Interpolation Polynomials

The Lagrange form of the equation of the straight line passing through two points (x_1, y_1) and (x_2, y_2) is

$$p(x) = \frac{(x - x_2)}{(x_1 - x_2)} y_1 + \frac{(x - x_1)}{(x_2 - x_1)} y_2.$$

It is easy to verify that this equation represents a line and that the given points are on the line.

The Lagrange form of the equation of the parabola passing through three points (x_1, y_1), (x_2, y_2), and (x_3, y_3) is

$$p(x) = \frac{(x - x_2)(x - x_3)}{(x_1 - x_2)(x_1 - x_3)} y_1 + \frac{(x - x_1)(x - x_3)}{(x_2 - x_1)(x_2 - x_3)} y_2 + \frac{(x - x_1)(x - x_2)}{(x_3 - x_1)(x_3 - x_2)} y_3,$$

which can also be checked directly.

The general form of the polynomial passing through the n data points $(x_1, y_1), \ldots, (x_n, y_n)$ has n terms on the right-hand side, one corresponding to each data point:

$$p(x) = L_1 y_1 + L_2 y_2 + \ldots + L_n y_n.$$

The kth term is the product of the kth data value and the $(n - 1)$st-degree polynomial:

$$L_k(x) = \frac{(x - x_1) \ldots (x - x_{k-1})(x - x_{k+1}) \ldots (x - x_n)}{(x_k - x_1) \ldots (x_k - x_{k-1})(x_k - x_{k+1}) \ldots (x_k - x_n)}.$$

The numerator is the product

$$N_k(x) = (x - x_1) \ldots (x - x_{k-1})(x - x_{k+1}) \ldots (x - x_n),$$

and the denominator is of the same form, but with the variable x replaced by the given value x_k:

$$D_k = N_k(x_k) = (x_k - x_1) \ldots (x_k - x_{k-1})(x_k - x_{k+1}) \ldots (x_k - x_n).$$

Thus, $L_k(x_k)$ is 1 and $L_k(x)$ is 0 when x is one of the other specified values of the independent variable, i.e., when $x = x_j$ for $j \neq k$.

Example 8.1 Lagrange Interpolation Parabola

We can find a quadratic polynomial using the three given points

$$(x_1, y_1) = (-2, 4), \ (x_2, y_2) = (0, 2), \ (x_3, y_3) = (2, 8),$$

by substituting into the general formula, which gives

$$p(x) = \frac{(x - 0)(x - 2)}{(-2 - 0)(-2 - 2)} 4 + \frac{(x - (-2))(x - 2)}{(0 - (-2))(0 - 2)} 2 + \frac{(x - (-2))(x - 0)}{(2 - (-2))(2 - 0)} 8.$$

This simplifies to

$$p(x) = \frac{x(x - 2)}{8} 4 + \frac{(x + 2)(x - 2)}{-4} 2 + \frac{x(x + 2)}{8} 8 = x^2 + x + 2.$$

The data points and the interpolation polynomial are illustrated in Fig. 8.3.

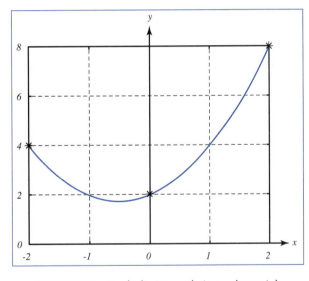

FIGURE 8.3   Parabolic interpolation polynomial.

The coefficients of the Lagrange interpolation polynomial can be found using the following MATLAB function. This function finds the coefficients c_k used in expressing the polynomial in the form

$$p(x) = c_1 N_1 + c_2 N_2 + \ldots + c_n N_n,$$

where

$$c_k = \frac{y_k}{D_k} = \frac{y_k}{(x_k - x_1) \ldots (x_k - x_{k-1})(x_k - x_{k+1}) \ldots (x_k - x_n)}$$

and

$$N_k(x) = (x - x_1) \ldots (x - x_{k-1})(x - x_{k+1}) \ldots (x - x_n).$$

MATLAB Functions for Lagrange Interpolation Polynomial

```
function c = Lagrange_coef(x, y)
% Calculate coefficients of Lagrange functions
n = length(x);
for k = 1 : n
    d(k) = 1;
    for i = 1 : n
        if i ~= k
            d(k) = d(k)*(x(k) - x(i));
        end
        c(k) = y(k)/d(k);
    end
end
```

The evaluation of the Lagrange polynomial at $x = t$ is done in a separate function that uses the x-coordinates of the original data points and the computed coefficients:

```
function p = Lagrange_Eval(t, x, c)
% Evaluate Lagrange interpolation polynomial at x = t
m = length(x);
for i = 1 : length(t) ,
    p(i) = 0 ;
    for j = 1 : m
        N(j) = 1 ;
        for k = 1 : m
            if ( j ~= k)
                N(j) = N(j) * (t(i) - x(k));
            end
        end
        p(i) = p(i) + N(j) * c(j);
    end
end
```

Example 8.2 Additional Data Points

If we add two more data points to those that we previously interpolated in Example 8.1, we must rework the problem. Suppose that the new data vectors are

$$\mathbf{x} = [-2 \quad 0 \quad -1 \quad 1 \quad 2],$$
$$\mathbf{y} = [\ 4 \quad 2 \quad -1 \quad 1 \quad 8].$$

Then the coefficients computed by the MATLAB function presented previously are

$$\mathbf{c} = [0.1667 \quad 0.5000 \quad 0.1667 \quad -0.1667 \quad 0.3333].$$

The resulting Lagrange interpolation polynomial is

$$p(x) = \frac{1}{6}(x)(x + 1)(x - 1)(x - 2) + \frac{1}{2}(x + 2)(x + 1)(x - 1)(x - 2)$$

$$+ \frac{1}{6}\left(1(x + 2)(x)(x - 1)(x - 2) - \frac{1}{6}(x + 2)(x)(x + 1)(x - 2)\right)$$

$$+ \frac{1}{3}(x + 2)(x)(x + 1)(x - 1).$$

The polynomial and the data points are illustrated in Fig. 8.4.

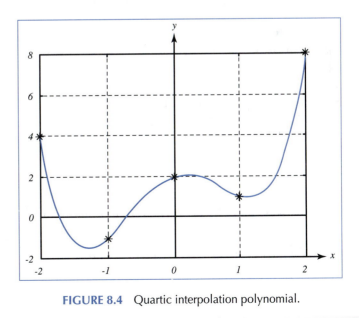

FIGURE 8.4 Quartic interpolation polynomial.

Example 8.3 Chemical Reaction Product Data

The interpolation polynomial and the data points for the observed product concentration data given in Example 8-A are shown in Fig. 8.5.

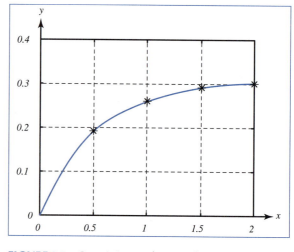

FIGURE 8.5   Quartic interpolation polynomial for chemical reaction product data.

Suppose now that we use the additional data given in Example 8-A to attempt to improve the nice-looking production curve. The graph of the new interpolation polynomial, shown in Fig. 8.6, demonstrates the difficulties resulting from using a polynomial of very high degree for interpolation.

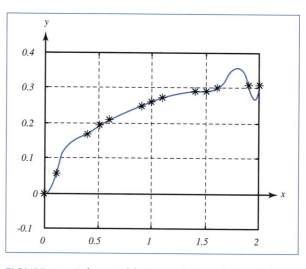

FIGURE 8.6   Polynomial for interpolating additional chemical reaction data.

We note that, in addition to not improving the appearance of the curve, it is necessary to completely rework the problem with the new, expanded data set when one uses the Lagrange form of interpolation.

The next example shows that the (apparent) degree of the Lagrange interpolation polynomial is determined by the number of data points. In fact, the data points all fall on a cubic polynomial, which would be evident if the Lagrange polynomial were simplified.

Example 8.4 Higher Order Interpolation Polynomials

Consider the following data:

$$\mathbf{x} = [\ -2 \quad -1 \quad 0 \quad 1 \quad 2 \quad 3 \quad 4],$$
$$\mathbf{y} = [-15 \quad 0 \quad 3 \quad 0 \quad -3 \quad 0 \quad 15].$$

The MATLAB function presented earlier produces the coefficients for the polynomial, which appears to be of sixth degree (as is expected for seven data points). The data and polynomial are shown in Fig. 8.7. This example will be revisited in the next section in Example 8.8. The equation of the polynomial is

$$p(x) = -0.0208(x+1)(x)(x-1)(x-2)(x-3)(x-4)$$
$$+ 0.0625(x+2)(x+1)(x-1)(x-2)(x-3)(x-4)$$
$$- 0.0625(x+2)(x+1)(x)(x-1)(x-3)(x-4)$$
$$+ 0.0208(x+2)(x+1)(x)(x-1)(x-2)(x-3).$$

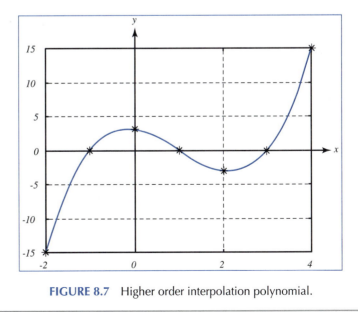

FIGURE 8.7 Higher order interpolation polynomial.

Discussion

Consider first of all the problem of writing the equation of a line that goes through two points (x_1, y_1) and (x_2, y_2). It is easy to see that

$$p(x) = \frac{(x - x_2)}{(x_1 - x_2)}\, y_1 + \frac{(x - x_1)}{(x_2 - x_1)}\, y_2$$

has the desired properties:

1. It is the equation of a straight line. (The highest power of the independent variable x is the first power.)
2. If $x = x_1$, then the coefficient of y_1 is 1 and the coefficient of y_2 is 0, so $y = y_1$.
3. If $x = x_2$, then the coefficient of y_1 is 0 and the coefficient of y_2 is 1, so $y = y_2$.

Geometrically this corresponds to determining two straight lines, one of which (call it L_1) is 1 at x_1 and 0 at x_2; the other (call it L_2) is 1 at x_2 and 0 at x_1. These lines are determined by the abscissas of the data points. The final interpolating polynomial is a linear combination of the two lines. Thus, we have

$$L_1: \quad y = \frac{x - x_2}{x_1 - x_2}, \qquad L_2: \quad y = \frac{x - x_1}{x_2 - x_1}; \qquad L(x) = L_1 y_1 + L_2 y_2.$$

The lines L_1 and L_2 are illustrated in Fig. 8.8 for $x_1 = 0$ and $x_2 = 1$. For these particular values of x_1 and x_2, the basis lines are

$$L_1: \quad y = -x + 1, \qquad L_2: \quad y = x.$$

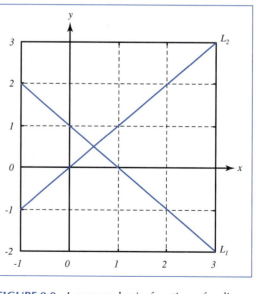

FIGURE 8.8 Lagrange basis functions for linear interpolation polynomial.

Now let us use the same idea on the problem of writing the equation of a quadratic polynomial through three points: (x_1, y_1), (x_2, y_2), and (x_3, y_3). We see that

$$p(x) = \frac{(x - x_2)(x - x_3)}{(x_1 - x_2)(x_1 - x_3)}\, y_1 + \frac{(x - x_1)(x - x_3)}{(x_2 - x_1)(x_2 - x_3)}\, y_2 + \frac{(x - x_1)(x - x_2)}{(x_3 - x_1)(x_3 - x_2)}\, y_3$$

has the desired properties:

1. It is the equation of a parabola. (The highest power of the independent variable x is the second power.)
2. If $x = x_1$, then $y = y_1$. (The coefficient of y_1 is 1, the coefficient of y_2 is 0, and the coefficient of y_3 is 0.)
3. If $x = x_2$, then $y = y_2$. (The coefficient of y_1 is 0, the coefficient of y_2 is 1, and the coefficient of y_3 is 0.)
4. If $x = x_3$, then $y = y_3$. (The coefficient of y_1 is 0, the coefficient of y_2 is 0, and the coefficient of y_3 is 1.)

The basis polynomials $P_1 = (x - 1)(x - 2)/2$, $P_2 = x(2 - x)$, and $P_3 = x(x - 1)/2$ are illustrated in Fig. 8.9 for $x_1 = 0$, $x_2 = 1$, and $x_3 = 2$.

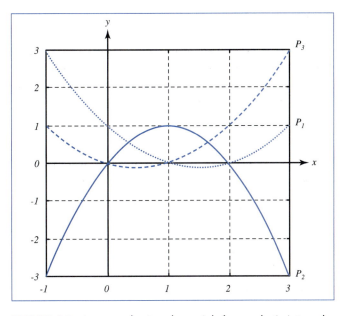

FIGURE 8.9 Lagrange basis polynomials for quadratic interpolation polynomial.

In general, there are as many terms on the right-hand side as there are data points; the coefficient of the kth term is a fraction whose numerator is the product $(x - x_1) \ldots$ $(x - x_{k-1})(x - x_{k+1}) \ldots (x - x_n)$ and whose denominator is of the same form with x replaced by x_k. This gives a fraction that is 1 when $x = x_k$ and is 0 when x equals any of the other specified values of the independent variable.

The Lagrange form of polynomial interpolation is particularly convenient when the same abscissas (values of the independent variable x) may occur in different applications (with only the corresponding y values changed). This form is less convenient than the Newton form (discussed in the next section) when additional data points may be added to the problem or when the appropriate degree of the interpolating polynomial is unknown (i.e., when it might be better to use less than the full set of available data).

Let I be the smallest interval containing $x_1, \ldots, x_n$, and t. Then if $f(x)$ has n continuous derivatives, the error in computing $f(x)$ at $x = t$ using the polynomial that interpolates $f(x)$ at $x_1, \ldots, x_n$, is $\dfrac{(t - x_1) \ldots (t - x_n)}{n!} f^{(n)}(\eta)$, for some η in I. (See Atkinson, 1989, pp. 134–135.)

8.1.2 Newton Interpolation Polynomials

The Newton form of the equation of a straight line passing through two points (x_1, y_1) and (x_2, y_2) is

$$p(x) = a_1 + a_2(x - x_1).$$

The Newton form of the equation of a parabola passing through three points (x_1, y_1), (x_2, y_2), and (x_3, y_3) is

$$p(x) = a_1 + a_2(x - x_1) + a_3(x - x_1)(x - x_2),$$

and the general form of the polynomial passing through n points $(x_1, y_1), \ldots, (x_n, y_n)$ is

$$p(x) = a_1 + a_2(x - x_1) + a_3(x - x_1)(x - x_2) + \ldots + a_n(x - x_1) \ldots (x - x_{n-1}).$$

To illustrate the method for finding the coefficients, consider the problem of finding the values of a_1, a_2, and a_3 for the parabola passing through the points (x_1, y_1), (x_2, y_2) and (x_3, y_3).

Substituting (x_1, y_1) into $y = a_1 + a_2(x - x_1) + a_3(x - x_1)(x - x_2)$ gives

$$a_1 = y_1.$$

Substituting (x_2, y_2) into $y = a_1 + a_2(x - x_1) + a_3(x - x_1)(x - x_2)$ gives $y_2 = a_1 + a_2(x_2 - x_1)$, or

$$a_2 = \frac{y_2 - y_1}{x_2 - x_1}.$$

Substituting (x_3, y_3) into $y = a_1 + a_2(x - x_1) + a_3(x - x_1)(x - x_2)$ gives $y_3 = a_1 + a_2(x_3 - x_1) + a_3(x_3 - x_1)(x_3 - x_2)$, or (after a little algebra)

$$a_3 = \frac{\dfrac{y_3 - y_2}{x_3 - x_2} - \dfrac{y_2 - y_1}{x_2 - x_1}}{x_3 - x_1}.$$

The calculations can be performed in a systematic manner by using the "divided differences" of the function values, as illustrated in Examples 8.5–8.7.

Example 8.5 Newton Interpolation Parabola

Consider again the data from Example 8.1. We can find a quadratic polynomial passing through the points $(x_1, y_1) = (-2, 4)$, $(x_2, y_2) = (0, 2)$, and $(x_3, y_3) = (2, 8)$. The Newton form of the equation is

$$p(x) = a_1 + a_2(x - (-2)) + a_3(x - (-2))(x - 0),$$

where the coefficients are

$$a_1 = y_1 = 4,$$

$$a_2 = \frac{y_2 - y_1}{x_2 - x_1} = \frac{2 - 4}{0 - (-2)} = -1,$$

and

$$a_3 = \frac{\dfrac{y_3 - y_2}{x_3 - x_2} - \dfrac{y_2 - y_1}{x_2 - x_1}}{x_3 - x_0} = \frac{\dfrac{8 - 2}{2 - 0} - \dfrac{2 - 4}{0 - (-2)}}{2 - (-2)} = 1.$$

Thus,

$$p(x) = 4 - (x + 2) + x(x + 2) = x^2 + x + 2,$$

as before.

The calculations can be performed in a systematic manner, using a "divided-difference table":

x_i	y_i	$d_i = \dfrac{y_{i+1} - y_i}{x_{i+1} - x_i}$	$dd_i = \dfrac{d_{i+1} - d_i}{x_{i+2} - x_i}$
-2	$\boxed{4}$		
		$\dfrac{y_2 - y_1}{x_2 - x_1} = \dfrac{2 - 4}{0 - (-2)} = \boxed{-1}$	
0	2		$\dfrac{d_2 - d_1}{x_3 - x_1} = \dfrac{3 - (-1)}{2 - (-2)} = \boxed{1}$
		$\dfrac{y_3 - y_2}{x_3 - x_2} = \dfrac{8 - 2}{2 - 0} = 3$	
2	8		

The coefficients of the Newton polynomial are the top entries in this table.

The graph of the interpolation polynomial is shown in Fig. 8.3.

Example 8.6 Additional Data Points

One of the advantages of the Newton form of polynomial interpolation is that it is easy to add more data points and try a higher order polynomial. If we extend the previous example, adding the points $(x_4, y_4) = (-1, -1)$ and $(x_5, y_5) = (1, 1)$, the polynomial has the form

$$p(x) = a_1 + a_2(x - x_1) + a_3(x - x_1)(x - x_2) + a_4(x - x_1)(x - x_2)(x - x_3)$$
$$+ a_5(x - x_1)(x - x_2)(x - x_3)(x - x_4).$$

The divided-difference table becomes (with new entries shown in bold)

x_i	y_i	d_i	dd_i	ddd_i	$dddd_i$
-2	$\boxed{4}$				
		$\dfrac{(2-4)}{(0+2)} = \boxed{-1}$			
0	2		$\dfrac{(3+1)}{(2+2)} = \boxed{1}$		
		$\dfrac{(8-2)}{(2-0)} = 3$		$\dfrac{(0-1)}{(-1+2)} = \boxed{-1}$	
2	8		$\dfrac{(3-3)}{(-1-0)} = 0$		$\dfrac{(2+1)}{(1+2)} = \boxed{1}$
		$\dfrac{(-1-8)}{(-1-2)} = 3$		$\dfrac{(2-0)}{(1-0)} = 2$	
-1	-1		$\dfrac{(1-3)}{(1-2)} = 2$		
		$\dfrac{(1+1)}{(1+1)} = 1$			
1	1				

The Newton interpolation polynomial is

$$p(x) = 4 - (x+2) + (x+2)(x) - (x+2)(x)(x-2) + (x+2)(x)(x-2)(x+1).$$

This expression looks quite different from that obtained for the Lagrange interpolation polynomial in Example 8.2; however, the two polynomials are equivalent. The graph of the interpolation polynomial is shown in Fig. 8.4.

Example 8.7 Higher Order Interpolation Polynomials

Consider again the data from Example 8.4, shown in the first two columns of the following divided-difference table.

The fact that the last three columns are zeros means that the degree of the interpolation polynomial is three less than it could have been based on the number of data points. The entry at the top of each column is the coefficient of the corresponding term in the Newton interpolation polynomial:

$$N(x) = -15 + 15(x+2) - 6(x+2)(x+1) + (x+2)(x+1)x.$$

This shows one advantage of the Newton form of the interpolation polynomial: That the polynomial is cubic is clear. (It was not clear from the Lagrange form.) The interpolation polynomial and the data are shown in Fig. 8.7.

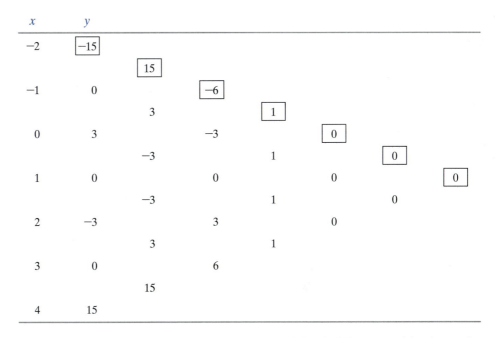

If the y values are modified slightly, the divided-difference table shows the small contribution from the higher degree terms:

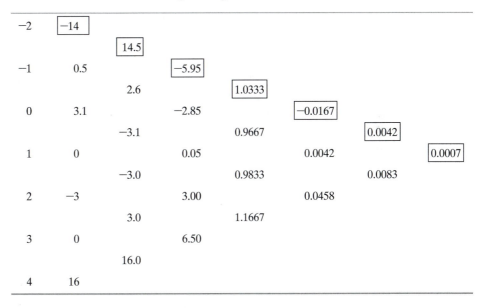

The Newton interpolation polynomial is

$$N(x) = -14 + 14.5(x+2) - 5.95(x+2)(x+1) + 1.0333(x+2)(x+1)x$$
$$- 0.0167(x+2)(x+1)x(x-1) + 0.0042(x+2)(x+1)x(x-1)(x-2)$$
$$+ 0.0007(x+2)(x+1)x(x-1)(x-2)(x-3).$$

MATLAB Functions for Newton Interpolation Polynomial

```
function a = Newton_Coef(x, y)
n = length(x);
% Calculate coefficients of Newton interpolating polynomial
a(1) = y(1);
for k = 1 : n-1
    d(k , 1) = (y(k+1) - y(k))/(x(k+1) - x(k));
                                          % 1st divided diff
end
for j = 2 : n-1
    for k = 1 : n-j
        d(k, j) = (d(k+1,j-1) - d(k,j-1))/(x(k+j) - x(k));
                                          % jth divided diff
    end
end
d
for j = 2 : n
    a(j) = d(1, j-1);
end
```

The divided-difference table is displayed in the preceding function; the original data could also be included as the first two columns, if desired, by forming the array [*x'* *y'* *d*]. The function to evaluate the polynomial is as follows:

```
function p = Newton_Eval(t, x, a)
n = length(x);
for i = 1 : length(t) ,
    ddd(1) = 1;                           % Compute first term
    c(1) = a(1) ;
    for j = 2 : n
        ddd(j) = (t(i) - x(j-1)).*ddd(j-1);
                                          % Compute jth term
        c(j) = a(j).*ddd(j);
    end ;
    p(i) = sum(c);
end
```

Discussion

The polynomial to interpolate the single point (x_1, y_1) is the constant function

$$N_1(x) = a_1,$$

where $a_1 = y_1$.

The polynomial to interpolate the points (x_1, y_1) and (x_2, y_2) is of the form

$$N_2(x) = a_1 + a_2(x - x_1) = N_1(x) + a_2(x - x_1).$$

We require that $N_2(x_2) = y_2 = a_1 + a_2(x_2 - x_1)$; solving for a_2 yields

$$a_2 = \frac{y_2 - y_1}{x_2 - x_1}.$$

The polynomial to interpolate the points $(x_1, y_1), (x_2, y_2),$ and (x_3, y_3) is of the form

$$N_3(x) = a_1 + a_2(x - x_1) + a_3(x - x_1)(x - x_2) = N_2(x) + a_3(x - x_1)(x - x_2),$$

where we determine a_3 so that

$N_3(x_3) = y_3 = a_1 + a_2(x_3 - x_1) + a_3(x_3 - x_1)(x_3 - x_2)$. After some algebra, we obtain

$$a_3 = \frac{\dfrac{y_3 - y_2}{x_3 - x_2} - \dfrac{y_2 - y_1}{x_2 - x_1}}{x_3 - x_1}.$$

Rather than continuing in this direct computation manner, we wish to find a more general iterative approach. Writing the polynomial to interpolate the points $(x_1, y_1), (x_2, y_2),$ and (x_3, y_3) in the form

$$N_3(x) = a_1 + a_2(x - x_1) + a_3(x - x_1)(x - x_2) = N_2(x) + a_3(x - x_1)(x - x_2)$$

suggests that $N_3(x)$ is formed as an extension of the polynomial (call it $N_2(x)$) that interpolates the points (x_1, y_1) and (x_2, y_2) by adding the point (x_3, y_3). On the other hand, we could just as well have supposed that we already had a polynomial (call it $M_2(x)$) that interpolates the points (x_2, y_2) and (x_3, y_3) that we extended by adding the point (x_1, y_1). From this point of view, we would write

$$M_3(x) = b_1 + b_2(x - x_2) + b_3(x - x_2)(x - x_3) = M_2(x) + b_3(x - x_2)(x - x_3).$$

However, these polynomials are simply different expressions for the same function. Comparing them, we see that the coefficient of the highest power of x must be the same, so $a_3 = b_3$. We now proceed to find an expression for a_3. Setting $N_3(x) = M_3(x)$, we have

$$N_2(x) + a_3(x - x_1)(x - x_2) = M_2(x) + a_3(x - x_2)(x - x_3),$$

so rearranging terms and factoring out the common factor a_3 yields

$$M_2(x) - N_2(x) = a_3 [\, (x - x_1)(x - x_2) - (x - x_2)(x - x_3) \,]$$
$$= a_3 (x - x_2)(x_3 - x_1).$$

The coefficient of x on the left-hand side of the equation is $b_2 - a_2$; the coefficient of x on the right-hand side is $a_3(x_3 - x_1)$. Solving $b_2 - a_2 = a_3(x_3 - x_1)$ for a_3 gives

$$a_3 = \frac{b_2 - a_2}{x_3 - x_1},$$

where

$$b_2 = \frac{y_3 - y_2}{x_3 - x_2}$$

and

$$a_2 = \frac{y_2 - y_1}{x_2 - x_1}.$$

For the general case, assume that $P_{k-1}(x)$ interpolates $f(x)$ at $x_1, \ldots, x_{k-1}$ and $Q_{k-1}(x)$ interpolates $f(x)$ at $x_2, \ldots, x_k$. Denote the leading coefficient of $P_{k-1}(x)$ as p; this coefficient is the $(k-1)$st divided difference formed using the points $(x_1, y_1), \ldots, (x_{k-1}, y_{k-1})$. Similarly, let q be the leading coefficient of $Q_{k-1}(x)$; then q is the $(k-1)$st divided difference formed using the points $(x_2, y_2), \ldots, (x_k, y_k)$. We can write the polynomial interpolating $f(x)$ at $x_1, \ldots, x_k$ in two ways: Viewed as $P_{k-1}(x)$ with the addition of x_k, the polynomial is written

$$N(x) = P_{k-1}(x) + a(x - x_1) \ldots (x - x_{k-1});$$

viewed as $Q_{k-1}(x)$ with the addition of x_1, the polynomial is written

$$N(x) = Q_{k-1}(x) + a(x - x_2) \ldots (x - x_k).$$

As before, the coefficient a that we seek to find must be the same in each of these expressions, because it is the coefficient of the highest power of x and the interpolation polynomial is unique.

Equating the two expressions for $N(x)$ and rearranging terms, we have

$$Q_{k-1}(x) + a(x - x_2) \ldots (x - x_k) = P_{k-1}(x) + a(x - x_1) \ldots (x - x_{k-1}),$$
$$Q_{k-1}(x) - P_{k-1}(x) = a(x - x_1) \ldots (x - x_{k-1}) - a(x - x_2) \ldots (x - x_k)$$
$$= a(x - x_2) \ldots (x - x_{k-1})[(x - x_1) - (x - x_k)]$$
$$= a(x - x_2) \ldots (x - x_{k-1})(x_k - x_1).$$

Equating the coefficients of x^{k-1} gives $q - p = a(x_k - x_1)$, so

$$a = \frac{q - p}{x_k - x_1}.$$

The standard notation for the divided differences is illustrated in the following table, but it is not particularly convenient for computation:

x_1	$f[x_1]$		
		$f[x_1;x_2] = \dfrac{f[x_2] - f[x_1]}{x_2 - x_1}$	
x_2	$f[x_2]$		$f[x_1;x_2;x_3] = \dfrac{f[x_2;x_3] - f[x_1;x_2]}{x_3 - x_1}$
		$f[x_2;x_3] = \dfrac{f[x_3] - f[x_2]}{x_3 - x_2}$	
x_3	$f[x_3]$		

The Newton form of polynomial interpolation is especially convenient when the spacing between the x values of the data is constant. The spacing would have been constant in Example 8.6 if we had taken the points in order. However, instead, we placed the additional points at the bottom of the table to emphasize the primary advantage of Newton interpolation, which is that more data points can be incorporated and a higher degree polynomial generated without repeating the calculations used for the lower order polynomial. This is in contrast to Lagrange interpolation, where the work to generate a higher degree polynomial does not make use of calculations to form lower order functions.

Geometrically, Newton's form of the interpolating polynomial starts with a constant function that has the correct value at $x = x_1$. The next term is a linear function that is 0 at x_1 and has the desired value at x_2, i.e., the value such that the sum of the linear and constant parts is y_2. The three terms in the Newton form of the quadratic passing through the points $(0, 1)$, $(1, 3)$, and $(2, 6)$ are illustrated in Fig. 8.10. These points are

$$P_1(x) = 1,$$

$$P_2(x) = x,$$

and

$$P_3(x) = x(x - 1).$$

The interpolation polynomial is $N(x) = 1 + 2(x - 0) + 0.5x(x - 1)$.

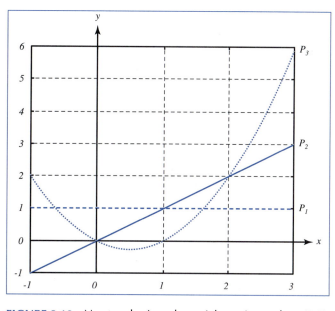

FIGURE 8.10 Newton basis polynomials to interpolate (0,1), (1,3), and (2,6).

8.1.3 Difficulties with Polynomial Interpolation

There are many types of problems in which polynomial interpolation through a moderate number of data points works very poorly. We illustrate three well-known cases in Examples 8.8 to 8.10. The first is an example of a function that varies over part of its domain, but is essentially constant over other portions of the domain. The second example is a function that is essentially a straight line. The third is a classic example due to Runge.

Example 8.8 Humped and Flat Data

The data

$$\mathbf{x} = [-2 \quad -1.5 \quad -1 \quad -0.5 \quad 0 \quad 0.5 \quad 1 \quad 1.5 \quad 2],$$
$$\mathbf{y} = [\ 0 \quad \ 0 \quad \ \ 0 \quad 0.87 \quad 1 \quad 0.87 \quad 0 \quad 0 \quad \ 0],$$

illustrate the difficulty with using higher order polynomials to interpolate a moderately large number of points, especially when the curve changes shape significantly over the interval, being flat in some regions and not in others. (See Fig. 8.11.)

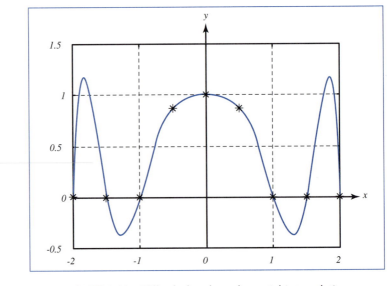

FIGURE 8.11   Difficult data for polynomial interpolation.

Example 8.9 Noisy Straight Line

Another example of data to which polynomial interpolation is not well suited is a noisy straight line, with y values given at unevenly spaced x values, like the following data:

$$\mathbf{x} = [0.00 \quad 0.20 \quad 0.80 \quad 1.00 \quad 1.20 \quad 1.90 \quad 2.00 \quad 2.10 \quad 2.95 \quad 3.00],$$
$$\mathbf{y} = [0.01 \quad 0.22 \quad 0.76 \quad 1.03 \quad 1.18 \quad 1.94 \quad 2.01 \quad 2.08 \quad 2.90 \quad 2.95].$$

The following divided-difference table is in the form produced by the MATLAB function for Newton interpolation; the data are not shown. The top row of the array gives the coefficients of the interpolation polynomial, which is shown in Fig. 8.11.

1.0500	−0.1875	0.7500	−2.3438	2.3993	−2.4070	2.4061	−1.3332	0.7254
0.9000	0.5625	−2.0625	2.2148	−2.4147	2.6458	−1.5270	0.8429	
1.3500	−1.5000	1.7027	−2.1316	2.6123	−1.5535	0.8331		
0.7500	0.3730	−0.8552	1.2644	−0.7276	0.2793			
1.0857	−0.4821	0.5357	−0.1545	−0.1691				
0.7000	0.0000	0.2654	−0.4589					
0.7000	0.2786	−0.2394						
0.9647	0.0392							
1.0000								

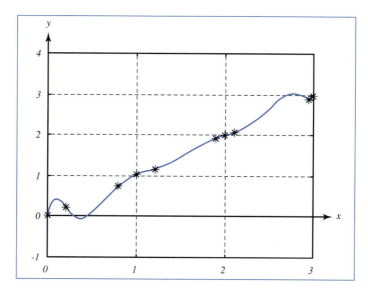

FIGURE 8.12 Noisy data for a straight line.

Example 8.10 Runge Function

The function

$$f(x) = \frac{1}{1 + 25x^2}$$

is a famous example of the fact that polynomial interpolation does not produce a good approximation for some functions and that using more function values (at evenly spaced x values) does not necessarily improve the situation. This example is widely known in the literature as *Runge's example*, or the *Runge function*.

First, we interpolate using five equally spaced points in the interval $[-1, 1]$:

$$\mathbf{x} = [-1 \qquad -0.5 \qquad 0.0 \qquad 0.5 \qquad 1.0],$$
$$\mathbf{y} = [\ 0.0385 \qquad 0.1379 \quad 1.0000 \quad 0.1379 \quad 0.0385].$$

The divided-difference table, with data values, is as follows:

x	y	d	dd	ddd	dddd
−1	0.0385				
		0.1989			
−0.5	0.1379		1.5252		
		1.7241		−3.3156	
0.0	1.0000		−3.4483		3.3156
		−1.7241		3.3156	
0.5	0.1379		1.5252		
		−0.1989			
1	0.0385				

The interpolation polynomial (blue line) and the original function (dashed black line) are shown in Fig. 8.13.

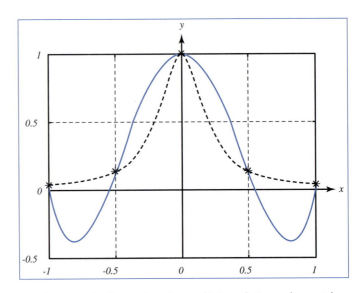

FIGURE 8.13   Runge function and interpolation polynomial.

If we use nine equally spaced data points for the interpolation, e.g.,

$$\mathbf{x} = [-1.000 \qquad -0.750 \quad -0.500 \quad -0.250 \quad 0.000 \quad 0.250 \quad 0.500 \quad 0.750 \quad 1.000],$$
$$\mathbf{y} = [\ 0.0385 \qquad 0.0664 \quad 0.138 \quad 0.3902 \quad 1.000 \quad 0.3902 \quad 0.138 \quad 0.0664 \quad 0.0385],$$

then the divided-difference table (without the data) is as follows:

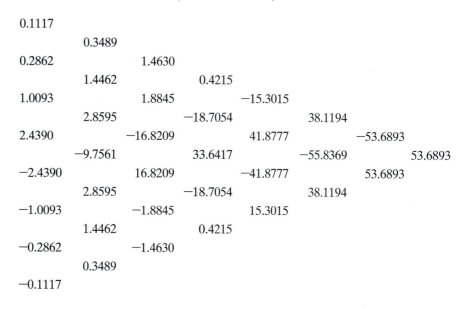

0.1117

    0.3489

0.2862

    1.4462   1.4630

1.0093   1.8845   0.4215

    2.8595   −18.7054   −15.3015

2.4390   −16.8209   41.8777   38.1194

    −9.7561   33.6417   −55.8369   −53.6893

−2.4390   16.8209   −41.8777   53.6893   53.6893

    2.8595   −18.7054   38.1194

−1.0093   −1.8845   15.3015

    1.4462   0.4215

−0.2862   −1.4630

    0.3489

−0.1117

The interpolation polynomial overshoots the true polynomial much *more* severely than the polynomial formed by using only five points; note the change of vertical scale in Fig. 8.14, compared with Fig. 8.13.

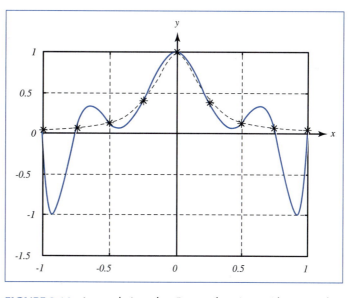

FIGURE 8.14 Interpolating the Runge function with more data points is worse!

Hermite interpolation allows us to find a polynomial that matches both function values and some of the derivative values at specified values of the independent variable; it includes both Taylor polynomials and Lagrange and Newton interpolation as special cases. In this section, we consider the simplest case of Hermite interpolation, that in which function values and first-derivative values are given at each point. A classic example would be data for the position and velocity of a vehicle at several different times; instead, we use the data from two of our previous examples to estimate the desired derivative value at several data points.

Suppose we have data measurements representing the values of a function and its first derivative at several values of the independent variable. The computationally most efficient form of Hermite interpolation is based on the Newton divided-difference tables. However, we require the interpolating polynomial to match each data point twice. For two data points, we obtain a cubic polynomial. The divided-difference table is of the same format as for Newton, except that each data point is entered twice, with values supplied for the first derivative at points where the denominators of the difference quotients would be zero, i.e., between repeated data points:

z_i x_i	w_i y_i	$d_i = \dfrac{w_{i+1} - w_i}{z_{i+1} - z_i}$	$dd_i = \dfrac{d_{i+1} - d_i}{z_{i+2} - z_i}$	$ddd_i = \dfrac{dd_{i+1} - dd_i}{z_{i+3} - z_i}$
$z_1 = x_1$ $w_1 = y_1$				
		$d_1 = y_1'$		
$z_2 = x_1$ $w_2 = y_1$			$dd_1 = \dfrac{d_2 - d_1}{z_3 - z_1}$	
		$d_2 = \dfrac{w_3 - w_2}{z_3 - z_2}$		$\dfrac{dd_2 - dd_1}{z_4 - z_1}$
$z_3 = x_2$ $w_3 = y_2$			$dd_2 = \dfrac{d_3 - d_2}{z_4 - z_2}$	
		$d_3 = y_2'$		
$z_4 = x_2$ $w_4 = y_2$				

Example 8.11 More Data for Product Concentration

Consider again the product concentration data introduced in Example 8-A. This time, instead of using all the data as separate points, we estimate the values for the derivative (using techniques from Chapter 11). The divided-difference table is as follows, with the data shown in bold:

```
x_i    y_i    dy
0      0
              0.6
0      0      −0.44
       0.38          0.16
0.5    0.19   −0.36         0.08
       0.2           0.24         −0.24
0.5    0.19   −0.12         −0.16         0.1956
       0.14          0.08         0.0533         −0.0652
1.00   0.26   −0.08         −0.08         0.0978         −0.0519
       0.1           −0.00         0.20          −0.1689         0.1259
1.00   0.26   −0.08         0.12          −0.24          0.2000
       0.06          0.12          −0.16          0.2311
1.50   0.29   −0.02         −0.12         0.1067
       0.05          −0.00         0.00
1.50   0.29   −0.02         −0.12
       0.04          −0.12
2.00   0.31   −0.08
       0.00
2.00   0.31
```

The resulting polynomial is illustrated in Fig. 8.15.

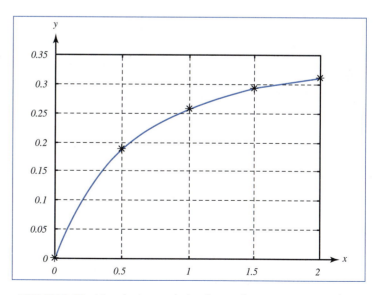

FIGURE 8.15   Hermite interpolation for product concentration data.

The following MATLAB function finds the coefficients of the Hermite interpolation polynomial, for data given in the arrays **x**, **y**, and **dy**. The process is essentially the same as for Newton interpolation.

MATLAB Functions for Hermite Interpolation Polynomial

```
function a = Hermite_coef(x, y, dy)
n = length(x);
a(1) = y(1);
for i = 1 : n
    xx(2*i-1) = x(i);
    yy(2*i-1) = y(i);
    xx(2*i) = x(i);
    yy(2*i) = y(i);
end
xx
yy
for k = 1 : n-1                          % 1st divided diff
    d(2*k-1, 1) = dy(k);
    d(2*k,1) = (yy(2*k+1) - yy(2*k))/(xx(2*k+1) - xx(2*k));
end
d(2*n-1,1) = dy(n);
for j = 2:2*(n-1)
    for k = 1:2*n-j                     % jth divided diff
        d(k,j) = (d(k+1,j-1) - d(k,j-1))/(xx(k+j) - xx(k));
    end
end
d(1,2*n-1) = (d(2, 2*(n-1)) -d(1,2*(n-1)))/(xx(2*n)- xx(1));
d                                       % display divided diff
for j = 2:2*n
    a(j) = d(1,j-1);
end
```

The following MATLAB function evaluates a Hermite interpolation polynomial at $x = t$. The data values used to find the coefficients are given in array **x**, and the coefficients are given in array **a**.

```
function p = Hermite_eval(t, x, a)
n = length(x);
for i = 1 : n
    xx(2*i-1) = x(i);
    xx(2*i) = x(i);
end
for i = 1 : length(t)              % Evaluate at t
    ddd(1) = 1;                    % Compute first term
    c(1) = a(1) ;
    for j = 2 : 2*n                % Compute jth term
        ddd(j) = (t(i) - xx(j-1)).*ddd(j-1);
        c(j) = a(j).*ddd(j);
    end
    p(i) = sum(c);
end
```

Example 8.12 Difficult Data

If we use the data from Example 8.8 to estimate both the function values and first derivative values at seven points, we have

$$\mathbf{x} = \begin{bmatrix} -2 & -1 & -0.5 & 0 & 0.5 & 1 & 2 \end{bmatrix},$$

$$\mathbf{y} = \begin{bmatrix} 0 & 0 & 0.87 & 1 & 0.87 & 0 & 0 \end{bmatrix},$$

$$\mathbf{dy} = \begin{bmatrix} 0 & 0 & 0.5 & 0 & -0.5 & 0 & 0 \end{bmatrix}.$$

As with lower order polynomial interpolation, trying to interpolate in humped and flat regions (see Fig. 8.16) causes overshoots.

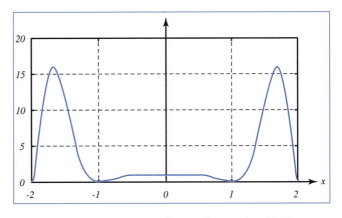

FIGURE 8.16 Hermite interpolation of humped and flat function.

8.3 RATIONAL-FUNCTION INTERPOLATION

Polynomials are not always the most effective form of representation of a function or a set of data. A *rational function* (a ratio of two polynomials) may be a better choice, especially if the function to be approximated has a pole (zero of the denominator) in the region of interest. Difficulties occur with polynomial interpolation even if the pole occurs in the complex plane, unless it is far removed from the data being interpolated. The Runge function introduced in Example 8.10, when viewed as a function of the complex variable $z = x + yi$, becomes $f(z) = 1/(1 + 25z^2)$; its poles at $z = \pm 0.2i$ are too close to the region of interest, namely, the real interval $[-1, 1]$.

In this section, we present a brief description of rational-function interpolation. The Bulirsch–Stoer algorithm produces a "diagonal" rational function, i.e., a rational function in which the degree of the numerator is either the same as, or one less than, the degree of the denominator. The approach is recursive, based on tabulated data (in a manner similar to that for the Newton form of polynomial interpolation). In the next chapter we consider Padé approximation, which seeks to find a rational function to fit the function value and derivative values at a given point x_0, in a manner more reminiscent of Taylor polynomials.

Given a set of k data points $(x_1, y_1), \ldots, (x_k, y_k)$, we seek an interpolation function of the form

$$r(x) = \frac{p_m(x)}{q_n(x)} = \frac{a_m x^m + \ldots + a_0}{b_n x^n + \ldots + b_0}.$$

In general, we would need to specify the degree of the numerator and the degree of the denominator. However, for the Bulirsch–Stoer method, $r(x)$ will have either $m = n$ or $m = n - 1$ (depending on whether the number of data points, k, is even or odd). The algorithm can be described recursively; we begin by showing the steps for $k = 3$ in some detail.

The following table shows the Bulirsch–Stoer method for three data points:

Data	First stage	Second stage	Third stage
$x_1\ y_1$	$R_1 = y_1$		
		$R_{12} = R_2 + \dfrac{R_2 - R_1}{\dfrac{x - x_1}{x - x_2}\left[1 - \dfrac{R_2 - R_1}{R_2}\right] - 1}$	
$x_2\ y_2$	$R_2 = y_2$		$R_{123} = R_{23} + \dfrac{R_{23} - R_{12}}{\dfrac{x - x_1}{x - x_3}\left[1 - \dfrac{R_{23} - R_{12}}{R_{23} - R_2}\right] - 1}$
		$R_{23} = R_3 + \dfrac{R_3 - R_2}{\dfrac{x - x_2}{x - x_3}\left[1 - \dfrac{R_3 - R_2}{R_3}\right] - 1}$	
$x_3\ y_3$	$R_3 = y_3$		

The general pattern is established by the third stage. The rational function $R_{123\ldots k}$ to interpolate k points $(x_1, y_1), \ldots, (x_k, y_k)$ is formed from the function $R_{23\ldots k}$ to interpolate the $(k-1)$ points $(x_2, y_2), \ldots, (x_k, y_k)$, the function $R_{123\ldots(k-1)}$ to interpolate the $(k-1)$ points $(x_1, y_1), \ldots, (x_{k-1}, y_{k-1})$, and the function $R_{23\ldots(k-1)}$ to interpolate the $(k-2)$ points $(x_2, y_2), \ldots, (x_{k-1}, y_{k-1})$, as follows:

$$R_{123\ldots k} = R_{23\ldots(k-1)} + \frac{R_{23\ldots k} - R_{123\ldots(k-1)}}{\dfrac{x - x_1}{x - x_k}\left[1 - \dfrac{R_{23\ldots k} - R_{12\ldots(k-1)}}{R_{23\ldots k} - R_{23\ldots(k-1)}}\right] - 1}.$$

The computation at the second stage follows this form also, with the understanding that the rational function to interpolate the $k-2$ points is zero at that stage.

It is fairly easy to verify that the expressions at the second stage, i.e., the result of interpolating two data points, have the expected form. However, the algorithm does not yield a simple algebraic expression for the rational function to interpolate several points; rather, it provides a systematic method of computing the interpolated value at specified points. (See Press et al., 1986, and Stoer and Bulirsch, 1980, for further discussion.)

The MATLAB function that follows implements the Bulirsch–Stoer process. The function treats interpolation at the data points separately, to save computational effort and to avoid many possible divisions by zero. The general expression for the entries in the jth column (the computation of R at the jth stage) has been rewritten to reduce the number of divisions that could lead to the indeterminant form 0/0, which MATLAB expresses as NaN. If an NaN does occur for some computed value of y, MATLAB skips that point in plotting the interpolated data.

MATLAB Function for Bulirsch–Stoer Rational Function Interpolation

```
function yy = rat_interp(x, y, xx)
% given k data in row vectors x and y
% find interpolated values yy at points xx
% using Bulirsch-Stoer rational function interpolation
[k1,k] = size(x);   [kk1,kk] = size(xx);
test = 0;
for h = 1:kk
    for i = 1:k                    % xx(h) is data point
        dd = (xx(h)-x(i));
        if dd == 0
            yy(h) = y(i);
            test = 1;
        end
    end
end
```

```
    if test == 0  % xx(h) is not data point
        R = zeros(k);
        R(:,1) = y(:);
        for i = 1:k-1
            D = R(i+1,1)-R(i,1);
            rr = (xx(h)-x(i))/(xx(h)-x(i+1));
            denom = rr*(1-D/R(i+1,1)) - 1;
            R(i,2) = R(i+1,1) + D/denom;
        end
        for j = 3:k
            for i = 1:k-j+1
                D = R(i+1,j-1) - R(i,j-1);
                rr = (xx(h) - x(i))/(xx(h) - x(i+j-1));
                if D == 0
                    R(i,j) = R(i+1,j-1);
                else
                    DD = R(i+1,j-1) - R(i+1,j-2);
                    denom = rr*(DD-D)-DD;
                    R(i,j) = R(i+1,j-1) + D*DD/denom;
                end
            end
        end
        yy(h) = R(1,k);
    end
    test = 0;
end
```

Example 8.13 Rational-Function Interpolation

We illustrate the use of the MATLAB function for Bulirsch–Stoer rational-function interpolation by considering the data for the Runge function introduced in Example 8.10:

$$\mathbf{x} = \begin{bmatrix} -1 & -0.5 & 0.0 & 0.5 & 1.0 \end{bmatrix},$$
$$\mathbf{y} = \begin{bmatrix} 0.0385 & 0.1379 & 1.0000 & 0.1379 & 0.0385 \end{bmatrix}.$$

The data and the interpolated results are shown in Fig. 8.17. The interpolated values are indistinguishable from the actual function values.

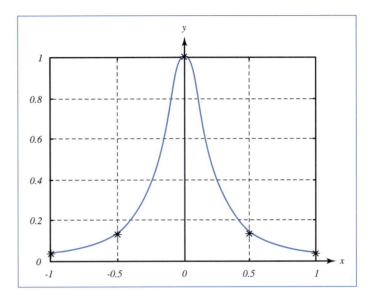

FIGURE 8.17   Data and interpolated values for Runge function.

Using more data for the interpolation does not materially change the results. Certainly, using more data does not cause difficulty, as it did for polynomial interpolation.

8.4   SPLINE INTERPOLATION

The disadvantage of using a single polynomial (of high degree) to interpolate a large number of data points is illustrated in Example 8.10. To avoid these problems, we can use piecewise polynomials. Historically, the design and construction of a ship or aircraft involved the use of full-sized models. One method of forming a smooth curve passing through specified points was to take a thin, flexible metal or wooden lath and bend it around pegs set at the required points. The resulting curve was traced out and used in the design process. Curves generated in this manner were known as *splines* (as were the thin laths used in their construction). Spline curves represent the curve of minimum strain energy; they are also aesthetically pleasing. These physical splines assume the shape of a piecewise cubic polynomial. After a brief discussion of piecewise linear and quadratic interpolation, we consider cubic spline interpolation. Other basis functions are also used for spline interpolation. (See the references at the end of the chapter.)

8.4.1 Piecewise Linear Interpolation

To illustrate the simplest form of piecewise polynomial interpolation, namely, piecewise linear interpolation, consider a set of four data points

$$(x_1, y_1), (x_2, y_2), (x_3, y_3), (x_4, y_4)$$

with $x_1 < x_2 < x_3 < x_4$. These points define three subintervals of the x-axis:

$$I_1 = [x_1, x_2], I_2 = [x_2, x_3], I_3 = [x_3, x_4].$$

If we use a straight line on each subinterval, we can interpolate the data with the piecewise linear function

$$P(x) = \begin{cases} \dfrac{(x - x_2)}{(x_1 - x_2)} y_1 + \dfrac{(x - x_1)}{(x_2 - x_1)} y_2, & x_1 \leq x \leq x_2; \\[2ex] \dfrac{(x - x_3)}{(x_2 - x_3)} y_2 + \dfrac{(x - x_2)}{(x_3 - x_2)} y_3, & x_2 \leq x \leq x_3, \\[2ex] \dfrac{(x - x_4)}{(x_3 - x_4)} y_3 + \dfrac{(x - x_3)}{(x_4 - x_3)} y_4, & x_3 \leq x \leq x_4. \end{cases}$$

Example 8.14 Piecewise Linear Interpolation

Using $\mathbf{x} = [\,0 \quad 1 \quad 2 \quad 3\,]$ and $\mathbf{y} = [\,0 \quad 1 \quad 4 \quad 3\,]$, we find the piecewise linear interpolation function illustrated in Fig. 8.18. The function is continuous, but not smooth.

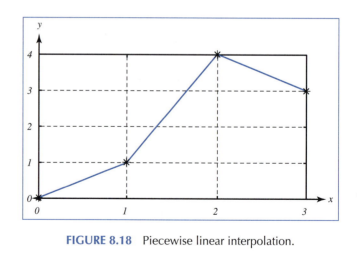

FIGURE 8.18   Piecewise linear interpolation.

8.4.2 Piecewise Quadratic Interpolation

We could use quadratic functions on each subinterval and try to make the first derivatives, as well as the function values, agree at the data points. For $n + 1$ data points, there are n intervals. Also, there are three unknowns to determine for each quadratic polynomial, so we have $3n$ unknowns. Further, there are two equations for each interval, corresponding to specified values for the quadratic function at the interval endpoints. (That is, (x_1, y_1) and (x_2, y_2) must satisfy the quadratic equation on the first interval, etc.) In addition, there are $n-1$ points at which the intervals meet; we require that the first derivatives of the parabolas on the adjacent intervals be continuous. This gives $2n + n - 1$ equations for the $3n$ unknowns. We have one free parameter; it is not clear how to best define one additional condition.

In order to have a more useful interpolation scheme based on piecewise quadratics, we define the "knots" where the intervals meet to be the midpoints between the data points where the function values are given. We illustrate the process for four data points (x_1, y_1), (x_2, y_2), (x_3, y_3), and (x_4, y_4), with $x_1 < x_2 < x_3 < x_4$.

We define the node points

$$z_1 = x_1, \quad z_2 = (x_1 + x_2)/2, \quad z_3 = (x_2 + x_3)/2, \quad z_4 = (x_3 + x_4)/2, \quad z_5 = x_4$$

and the spacings between consecutive data points by

$$h_1 = x_2 - x_1, \quad h_2 = x_3 - x_2, \quad h_3 = x_4 - x_3,$$

then

$$z_2 - x_1 = h_1/2, \quad z_3 - x_2 = h_2/2, \quad z_4 - x_3 = h_3/2,$$

and

$$z_2 - x_2 = -h_1/2, \quad z_3 - x_3 = -h_2/2, \quad z_4 - x_4 = -h_3/2.$$

Now we define

$$P_1 \text{ on } [z_1, z_2]: \quad P_1(x) = a_1(x - x_1)^2 + b_1(x - x_1) + c_1;$$
$$P_2 \text{ on } [z_2, z_3]: \quad P_2(x) = a_2(x - x_2)^2 + b_2(x - x_2) + c_2;$$
$$P_3 \text{ on } [z_3, z_4]: \quad P_3(x) = a_3(x - x_3)^2 + b_3(x - x_3) + c_3;$$
$$P_4 \text{ on } [z_4, z_5]: \quad P_4(x) = a_4(x - x_4)^2 + b_4(x - x_4) + c_4.$$

Since $P_k(x_k) = c_k$, imposing the interpolation condition that $P_k(x_k) = y_k$ immediately yields $c_k = y_k$ for $k = 1, 2, 3, 4$. Now if we impose continuity conditions on the polynomials at the interior nodes, we obtain the following three equations:

$$P_1(z_2) = P_2(z_2): \quad h_1^2 a_1 - h_1^2 a_2 + 2h_1 b_1 + 2h_1 b_2 = 4(y_2 - y_1);$$
$$P_2(z_3) = P_3(z_3): \quad h_2^2 a_2 - h_2^2 a_3 + 2h_2 b_2 + 2h_2 b_3 = 4(y_3 - y_2);$$
$$P_3(z_4) = P_4(z_4): \quad h_3^2 a_3 - h_3^2 a_4 + 2h_3 b_3 + 2h_3 b_4 = 4(y_4 - y_3).$$

Similarly, if we impose continuity conditions on the first derivatives of the polynomials at the interior nodes, we obtain another three equations:

$$P_1'(z_2) = P_2'(z_2): \quad h_1 a_1 + h_1 a_2 + b_1 - b_2 = 0;$$
$$P_2'(z_3) = P_3'(z_3): \quad h_2 a_2 + h_2 a_3 + b_2 - b_3 = 0;$$
$$P_3'(z_4) = P_4'(z_4): \quad h_3 a_3 + h_2 a_4 + b_3 - b_4 = 0.$$

At this stage, we have a system of six equations for the eight unknown coefficients (a_1, a_2, a_3, a_4, b_1, b_2, b_3, and b_4). Since $P_k'(x) = 2a_k(x - x_k) + b_k$, we can determine

b_1 and b_4 by imposing conditions on the derivative values at the interval endpoints, x_1 and x_4. Setting $P_1'(x_1) = 0$ gives $b_1 = 0$, and setting $P_4'(x_4) = 0$ gives $b_4 = 0$.

With these zero-slope conditions at the endpoints of the interval, the equations for the coefficients become

$$
\begin{aligned}
a_1 h_1^2 - a_2 h_1^2 \quad\quad\quad\quad\quad\quad + 2b_2 h_1 \quad\quad\quad &= 4(y_2 - y_1), \\
+ a_2 h_2^2 - a_3 h_2^2 \quad\quad\quad + 2b_2 h_2 + 2b_3 h_2 &= 4(y_3 - y_2), \\
+ a_3 h_3^2 - a_4 h_3^2 \quad\quad\quad\quad\quad + 2b_3 h_3 &= 4(y_4 - y_3), \\
a_1 h_1 + a_2 h_1 \quad\quad\quad\quad\quad - b_2 \quad\quad\quad &= 0, \\
+ a_2 h_2 + a_3 h_2 \quad\quad + b_2 \quad - b_3 \quad &= 0, \\
+ a_3 h_3 + a_4 h_3 \quad\quad\quad + b_3 \quad &= 0.
\end{aligned}
$$

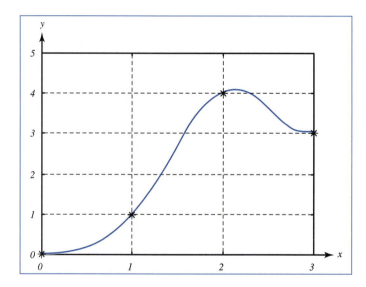

FIGURE 8.19 Piecewise quadratic interpolation of four data points.

Although there are circumstances in which piecewise quadratic interpolation has some theoretical advantages, compared with cubic spline interpolation, we illustrate the former in a simple example and then proceed to the more popular cubic spline interpolation in the next section.

Example 8.15 Piecewise Quadratic Interpolation

Consider the data points (0,0), (1,1), (2,4), and (3,3). The linear system of equations for the coefficients can be solved using the MATLAB function for Gaussian elimination from Chapter 3. The matrix $\mathbf{A}$ and right-hand side $\mathbf{r}$, are, respectively,

$$\mathbf{A} = \begin{bmatrix} 1 & -1 & 0 & 0 & 2 & 0 \\ 0 & 1 & -1 & 0 & 2 & 2 \\ 0 & 0 & 1 & -1 & 0 & 2 \\ 1 & 1 & 0 & 0 & -1 & 0 \\ 0 & 1 & 1 & 0 & 1 & -1 \\ 0 & 0 & 1 & 1 & 0 & 1 \end{bmatrix},$$

$$\mathbf{r} = \begin{bmatrix} 4 & 12 & -4 & 0 & 0 & 0 \end{bmatrix}'.$$

The solution vector gives the coefficients $a_1, a_2, a_3, a_4, b_2,$ and b_3:

$$\mathbf{x} = \begin{bmatrix} 0.7429 & 1.7714 & -3.3714 & 2.4571 & 2.5143 & 0.9143 \end{bmatrix}'$$

The piecewise interpolating polynomial is illustrated in Fig. 8.19 and is given by

$$P_1(x) = 0.7429(x-0)^2 \qquad\qquad \text{on } [0.0, 0.5],$$
$$P_2(x) = 1.7714(x-1)^2 + 2.5143(x-1) + 1 \quad \text{on } [0.5, 1.5],$$
$$P_3(x) = -3.3714(x-2)^2 + 0.9143(x-2) + 4 \text{ on } [1.5, 2.5],$$
$$P_4(x) = 2.4571(x-3)^2 + 3 \qquad\qquad \text{on } [2.5, 3.0].$$

8.4.3 Piecewise Cubic Interpolation

We can do better, without much more work, if we use cubic splines (i.e., a piecewise cubic polynomial). A simple calculation shows that we have enough information to require continuity of the function and its first and second derivatives at each of the "node points," i.e., the boundaries of the subintervals.

The calculation of the coefficients of the cubic polynomials on each subinterval is simplified by a suitable choice of the algebraic representation of the equations. The n given points $(x_1, y_1), (x_2, y_2), \ldots, (x_i, y_i), \ldots, (x_n, y_n)$ define $n-1$ subintervals. Since the spacing between the x values is not required to be uniform, let $h_i = x_{i+1} - x_i$. We are looking for a spline function

$$S(x) = \begin{cases} P_1(x), & x_1 \le x \le x_2, \\ P_i(x), & x_i \le x \le x_{i+1}, \\ P_{n-1}(x), & x_{n-1} \le x \le x_n, \end{cases}$$

that is a piecewise cubic with continuous derivatives up to order 2.

For $i = 1, \ldots, n-1$, we write

$$P_i(x) = a_{i-1}\frac{(x_{i+1} - x)^3}{6h_i} + a_i\frac{(x - x_i)^3}{6h_i} + b_i(x_{i+1} - x) + c_i(x - x_i).$$

The motivation for this form of the cubic and the derivation of the equations for the coefficients a_i, b_i, and c_i are given in the discussion at the end of this section. First we illustrate the method with several examples and a MATLAB function for generating cubic splines. The $n-2$ equations for the n unknowns $a_0, \ldots, a_{n-1}$ have the form

$$\frac{h_i}{6}a_{i-1} + \frac{h_i + h_{i+1}}{3}a_i + \frac{h_{i+1}}{6}a_{i+1} = \frac{y_{i+2} - y_{i+1}}{h_{i+1}} - \frac{y_{i+1} - y_i}{h_i} \quad (i = 1, \ldots, n-2).$$

There are several possible choices for the conditions on the second derivatives at the endpoints, which provide the additional conditions to determine all of the unknowns. The simplest choice, the natural cubic spline, assigns values of zero to the second derivatives at x_1 and x_n. The values of b_i and c_i ($i = 1, \ldots, n - 1$) are expressed in terms of the a_i coefficients as follows:

$$b_i = \frac{y_i}{h_i} - \frac{a_{i-1}h_i}{6}, \quad c_i = \frac{y_{i+1}}{h_i} - \frac{a_i h_i}{6}.$$

Example 8.16 Natural Cubic Spline Interpolation

Consider the data points $(-2, 4), (-1, -1), (0, 2), (1, 1),$ and $(2, 8)$. We have $h_i = 1$ for all intervals, and $a_0 = a_4 = 0$ for a natural cubic spline. The equations for $a_1, a_2,$ and a_3 are as follows:

$$i = 1: \quad \frac{1}{6}a_0 + \frac{2}{3}a_1 + \frac{1}{6}a_2 \qquad\qquad = (y_3 - y_2) - (y_2 - y_1);$$

$$i = 2: \qquad\quad \frac{1}{6}a_1 + \frac{2}{3}a_2 + \frac{1}{6}a_3 \qquad = (y_4 - y_3) - (y_3 - y_2);$$

$$i = 3: \qquad\qquad\quad \frac{1}{6}a_2 + \frac{2}{3}a_3 + \frac{1}{6}a_4 = (y_5 - y_4) - (y_4 - y_3).$$

Substituting in the values for $a_0, a_4,$ and y_i ($i = 1, \ldots, 5$) and simplifying, we obtain

$$4a_1 + a_2 \qquad\quad = 48,$$

$$a_1 + 4a_2 + a_3 = -24,$$

$$a_2 + 4a_3 = 48.$$

This gives a tridiagonal system that can be solved as in Chapter 3. We find that

$$a_1 = 15.4286, \quad a_2 = -13.7143, \quad a_3 = 15.4286.$$

Solving for the b_i gives

$$b_1 = y_1 - a_0/6 = 4, \qquad b_2 = y_2 - a_1/6 = -3.5714,$$

$$b_3 = y_3 - a_2/6 = 4.2857, \quad b_4 = y_4 - a_3/6 = -1.5714,$$

and for the c_i gives

$$c_1 = y_2 - a_1/6 = -3.5714, \quad c_2 = y_3 - a_2/6 = 4.2857,$$

$$c_3 = y_4 - a_3/6 = -1.5714, \quad c_4 = y_5 - a_4/6 = 8.$$

The cubic spline is illustrated in Fig. 8.20; it simplifies to

$S(x) =$

$$\begin{cases} 2.57(x + 2)^3 & - 4(x + 1) & - 3.57(x + 2), & -2 \le x \le -1, \\ -2.57x^3 & - 2.29(x + 1)^3 + 3.57x & + 4.29(x + 1), & -1 \le x \le 0, \\ -2.29(1 - x)^3 + 2.57x^3 & + 4.29(1 - x) - 1.57x, & & 0 \le x \le 1, \\ 2.57(2 - x)^3 & - 1.57(2 - x) + 8(x - 1), & & 1 \le x \le 2. \end{cases}$$

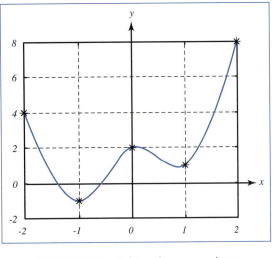

FIGURE 8.20 Cubic spline interpolant.

Example 8.17 Runge Function

Consider again the Runge function $f(x) = 1/(1 + 25x^2)$, introduced in Example 8.10.

$$x = [-1 \quad -0.5 \quad 0.0 \quad 0.5 \quad 1.0],$$
$$y = [\ 0.0385 \quad 0.1379 \quad 1.0000 \quad 0.1379 \quad 0.0385].$$

The data are shown in Fig. 8.21, together with the spline function (solid) and the actual Runge function (dashed). The agreement is much better than that found previously using polynomial interpolation, but is not as good as that with rational-function interpolation.

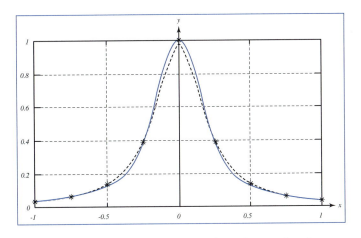

FIGURE 8.21 Cubic spline interpolant of Runge function.

```
function s = Spline(xx,yy)
n = length(xx);                    % this function requires n >= 4
h(1:n-1) = xx(2:n) - xx(1:n-1);
T(1:n-1) = (yy(2 : n) - yy(1 : n-1))./h(1:n-1);
R(1:n-2) = T(2:n-1) - T(1:n-2);
U(1:n-3) = h(2:n-2)/6;
D(1:n-2) = (h(1:n-2) + h(2:n-1))/3;
L(1:n-3) = h(2:n-2)/6;
a = tridiag(U, D, L, R);
b(1) = yy(1)/h(1);
c(1) = yy(2)/h(1) - a(1)*h(1)/6;
b(2:n-2) = yy(2:n-2)./h(2:n-2) - a(1:n-3).*h(2:n-2)/6;
c(2:n-2) = yy(3:n-1)./h(2:n-2) - a(2:n-2).*h(2:n-2)/6;
b(n-1) = yy(n-1)/h(n-1) - a(n-2)*h(n-1)/6;
c(n-1) = yy(n)/h(n-1);
                              %print piecewise function and plot it
fprintf('\nResulting piecewise function:\n\n');
s1 = [sprintf('(%f)*(x-(%f)).^3/(%f)',a(1),xx(1),6*h(1))]
s2 = [sprintf('(%f)*((%f)-x)',b(1),xx(2))]
s3 = [sprintf('(%f)*(x-(%f))',c(1),xx(1))]
x = xx(1): (xx(2)-xx(1))/10 : xx(2);
y = eval(s1) + eval(s2) + eval(s3);
xxx = x;     yyy = y;
for i = 2:n-2
   s1 = [];    s2 = []; s3 = []; s4 = [];
   fprintf(\nResulting piecewise function:\n\n');
   s1 = [sprintf('(%f)*((%f)-x).^3/(%f)',a(i-1),xx(i+1),6*h(i))]
   s2 = [sprintf('(%f)*(x-(%f)).^3/(%f)',a(i),xx(i),6*h(i))]
   s3 = [sprintf('(%f)*((%f)-x)',b(i),xx(i+1))]
   s4 = [sprintf('(%f)*(x-(%f))',c(i),xx(i))]
   x = xx(i): (xx(i+1)-xx(i))/10 : xx(i+1);
   y = eval(s1) + eval(s2) + eval(s3) + eval(s4);
   xxx = [ xxx x];    yyy = [ yyy y];
end
```

```
s1 = [];    s2 = [];    s3 = [];
fprintf(\nResulting piecewise function:\n\n');
s1 = [sprintf('(%f)*((%f)-x).^3/(%f)',a(n-2),xx(n),6*h(n-1))]
s2 = [sprintf('(%f)*((%f)-x)',b(n-1),xx(n))]
s3 = [sprintf('(%f)*(x-(%f))',c(n-1),xx(n-1))]
x = xx(n-1): (xx(n)-xx(n-1))/10 : xx(n);
y = eval(s1) + eval(s2) + eval(s3);
xxx = [ xxx x];    yyy = [ yyy y];
plot(xxx, yyy);
hold on;
plot(xx, yy,'r*');                          %  plot data points
hold off
```

Example 8.18 Chemical Reaction Product Data

Consider again the (additional) data presented in Example 8-A for product concentration as a function of time in a chemical reaction:

$\mathbf{x} = [0.00\ \ 0.10\ \ 0.40\ \ 0.50\ \ 0.60\ \ 0.90\ \ 1.00\ \ 1.10\ \ 1.40\ \ 1.50\ \ 1.60\ \ 1.90\ \ 2.00]$

$\mathbf{y} = [0.00\ \ 0.06\ \ 0.17\ \ 0.19\ \ 0.21\ \ 0.25\ \ 0.26\ \ 0.27\ \ 0.29\ \ 0.29\ \ 0.30\ \ 0.31\ \ 0.31]$

Figure 8.22 shows that the curve is smoother than the high-degree polynomial (Fig. 8.6) necessary to interpolate all of the points with a single polynomial. However, the limited precision of the data means that especially around $x = 1.5$ and $x = 2.0$, the additional data points do not really improve the appearance of the original curve (Fig. 8.5) based on five data points.

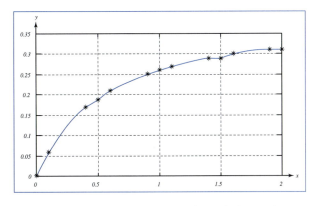

FIGURE 8.22 Cubic spline interpolant of chemical reaction data.

Example 8.19 Difficult Data

Consider again the data presented in Example 8.8 for the humped and flat function:

$$\mathbf{x} = \begin{bmatrix} -2 & -1.5 & -1 & -0.5 & 0 & 0.5 & 1 & 1.5 & 2 \end{bmatrix}$$

$$\mathbf{y} = \begin{bmatrix} 0 & 0 & 0 & 0.87 & 1 & 0.87 & 0 & 0 & 0 \end{bmatrix}$$

The resulting piecewise function is made up of the following polynomials given over each subinterval:

$$P_1 = -0.61(x+2)^3 + 0.15(x+2), \qquad\qquad -2.0 \le x \le -1.5,$$

$$P_2 = -0.61(-1-x)^3 + 2.45(x+1.5)^3 + 0.15(-10-x) - 0.61(x+1.5),$$
$$-1.5 \le x \le -1.0,$$

$$P_3 = 2.45(-0.5-x)^3 - 2.24(x+1)^3 - 0.61(-0.5-x) + 2.30(x+1),$$
$$-1.0 \le x \le -0.5,$$

$$P_4 = -2.24(-x)^3 + 0.60(x+0.5)^3 + 2.30(-x) + 1.85(x+0.5), \qquad -0.5 \le x \le 0.0,$$

$$P_5 = 0.60(0.5-x)^3 - 2.24(x)^3 + 1.85(0.5-x) + 2.30x, \qquad\qquad 0.0 \le x \le 0.5,$$

$$P_6 = -2.24(1-x)^3 + 7.36(x-0.5)^3/3 + 2.30(1-x) - 0.61(x-0.5), \qquad 0.5 \le x \le 1.0,$$

$$P_7 = 7.36(1.5-x)^3/3 - 1.84(x-1)^3/3 - 0.61(1.5-x) + 0.15(x-1), \qquad 1.0 \le x \le 1.5,$$

$$P_8 = -1.84(2-x)^3/3 + 0.15(2-x) + 0(x-1.5), \qquad\qquad 1.5 \le x \le 2.0.$$

Figure 8.23 shows that the curve is still oscillating in the flat region, as well as near the peak of the hump. It is likely that setting the first derivative, instead of the second, equal to zero at the endpoints of the interval would improve the results obtained.

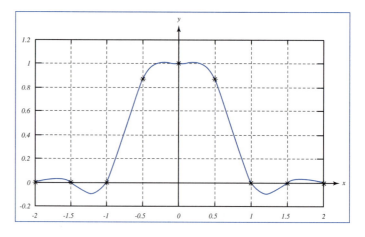

FIGURE 8.23   Cubic spline interpolation of humped and flat data.

Discussion

To see that we can require continuity of the cubic polynomials and their first and second derivatives at the node points, assume that we have n data points $(x_1, y_1), \ldots,$ (x_n, y_n). In other words, the node points coincide with the data points in this case. We have $n - 1$ intervals and 4 unknowns to determine a cubic polynomial on each interval; thus, we have $4(n - 1)$ unknowns. Now, two data points must lie on the curve of each cubic polynomial, so there are $2(n - 1)$ equations for the given data. In addition, there are $n - 2$ values of x at which we must have continuity of the first and second derivatives. This gives $2(n - 2)$ more equations, so altogether we have $4n - 6$ equations for $4n - 4$ unknowns. We can obtain two more equations by specifying the value of either the first or the second derivative at each of the two endpoints of the interval (i.e., at x_1 and x_n).

The actual derivation of the spline interpolation formulas is simplified by a suitable choice of the algebraic representation of the equations. Since the spacing between the x values of the data is not required to be uniform, we let $h_i = x_{i+1} - x_i$. We are looking for a spline function of the form

$$S(x) = \begin{cases} P_1(x), & x_1 \leq x \leq x_2, \\ P_i(x), & x_i \leq x \leq x_{i+1}, \\ P_{n-1}(x), & x_{n-1} \leq x \leq x_n. \end{cases}$$

For $i = 1, \ldots, n - 1$, we write

$$P_i(x) = a_{i-1} \frac{(x_{i+1} - x)^3}{6h_i} + a_i \frac{(x - x_i)^3}{6h_i} + b_i(x_{i+1} - x) + c_i(x - x_i).$$

This form of the cubic is motivated by the fact that the second derivatives of the polynomials on adjacent subintervals must be equal at the common node between the two subintervals. Using the definition of h_i, we easily see that $P_i''(x_{i+1}) = a_i$ and that $P_{i+1}''(x_{i+1}) = a_i$ also. Thus, the form of the expression for $P_i(x)$ ensures that the second derivatives are continuous at the interior nodes.

By integrating $P_i''(x) = a_{i-1} \dfrac{(x_{i+1} - x)}{h_i} + a_i \dfrac{(x - x_i)}{h_i}$ twice and imposing the requirements that $P_i(x_i) = y_i$ and $P_i(x_{i+1}) = y_{i+1}$, we can determine values for the coefficients b_i and c_i, to obtain the expression

$$P_i(x) = a_{i-1} \frac{(x_{i+1} - x)^3}{6h_i} + a_i \frac{(x - x_i)^3}{6h_i}$$

$$+ \left[y_i - \frac{a_{i-1}h_i^2}{6} \right] \frac{(x_{i+1} - x)}{h_i} + \left[y_{i+1} - \frac{a_i h_i^2}{6} \right] \frac{(x - x_i)}{h_i}.$$

We now apply the requirement that the first derivatives of P_i and P_{i+1} must agree at x_{i+1}. After some algebra, we find that

$$\frac{h_i}{6}a_{i-1} + \frac{h_i + h_{i+1}}{3}a_i + \frac{h_{i+1}}{6}a_{i+1} = \frac{y_{i+2} - y_{i+1}}{h_{i+1}} - \frac{y_{i+1} - y_i}{h_i} \quad (i = 1, 2, \ldots, n-2).$$

We thus have $n-2$ equations, but n unknowns $(a_0, \ldots, a_{n-1})$.

There are several possible choices for specifying two additional conditions. The natural cubic spline assigns values of zero for both a_0 and a_{n-1}; thus, the second derivative is zero at the endpoints. A clamped spline specifies the value of the first derivative at the endpoints.

The error is using cubic spline interpolation is $|S(x) - g(x)|$, where $S(x)$ is the spline interpolation function and $g(x)$ is the function that generated the data. Let h be the maximum spacing between node points, and $G = \max |g^{(4)}(x)|$. Then as long as reasonable choices are made for the two additional conditions,

$$|S(x) - g(x)| < kh^4 G = O(h^4).$$

(See Kahaner et al., 1989, for futher discussion.)

8.5 MATLAB's INTERPOLATION FUNCTIONS

MATLAB has several built-in functions that perform interpolation. In this section, we summarize the characteristics of the functions `interp1` and `interp2`.

8.5.1 Interpolation in One Dimension

For one-dimensional data, the vector of values of the independent variable x must be monotonically increasing or decreasing. The MATLAB function `interp1` finds the interpolated value yy for the specified value xx, based on data given in the vectors **x** and **y**. (xx and yy may be vectors also.) The default method is linear interpolation; the calling syntax is

```
yy = interp1(x, y, xx).
```

Other methods include cubic, spline (cubic spline), and nearest value methods; the corresponding function calls are

```
yy = interp1(x, y, xx, 'cubic' ),
yy = interp1(x, y, xx, 'spline' ),
yy = interp1(x, y, xx, 'nearest' ).
```

The vectors **x**, **y**, and **xx** are mapped onto an equally spaced domain before the appropriate interpolation is performed. If the data are given at equally spaced intervals (i.e., if x is equally spaced and monotonic), the faster methods `'*linear'`, `'*cubic'`, `'*nearest'`, or `'*spline'` may be used. For faster linear interpolation on data that are not uniformly spaced, the function `interp1q` may be used.

Note also that the `plot` function uses linear interpolation.

8.5.2 Interpolation in Two Dimensions

The general interpolation problem for two (or more) independent variables is much more difficult than for a single variable. One reason is that, unless the function values are known on a rectangular grid of points, it is not easy either to order the data points or to determine which of them should be used to find the interpolated value at any particular point in the region. Let us consider MATLAB's built-in function `interp2` for interpolation of data defined on a rectangular grid:

$$(x_1, y_1) \quad (x_1, y_2) \quad (x_3, y_3) \quad \ldots \quad (x_1, y_m)$$
$$(x_2, y_1) \quad (x_2, y_2) \quad (x_3, y_3) \quad \ldots \quad (x_2, y_m)$$
$$\vdots \qquad \quad \vdots \qquad \quad \vdots \qquad \qquad \vdots$$
$$(x_n, y_1) \quad (x_n, y_2) \quad (x_n, y_3) \quad \ldots \quad (x_n, y_m)$$

In other words, the data are of the form $z(i,j) = f(x(i),y(j))$.

We next examine three ways in which the function `interp2` can be used. The first two simplified forms rely on specific assumptions about either the points at which interpolated values are desired or the form of the arrays **x** and **y** in which the original data are given. The most general form allows interpolation on a rectangular grid given by user-specified vectors **xx** and **yy**; it also allows the original data to be given on a rectangular grid specified by the vectors **x** and **y**. It is possible as well to specify cubic interpolation, rather than the default bilinear interpolation.

The simplest form of interpolation in two dimensions expands the data matrix **z** by interleaving interpolanes between every element. If **z** is defined on the grid given by the vectors $\mathbf{x} = [x_1, x_2, \ldots, x_n]$ and $\mathbf{y} = [y_1, y_2, \ldots, y_m]$, then interpolated values are found on the grid defined by the vectors

$$\mathbf{xx} = [x_1, (x_1 + x_2)/2, x_2, \ldots, (x_{n-1} + x_n)/2, x_n]$$

and

$$\mathbf{yy} = [y_1, (y_1 + y_2)/2, y_2, \ldots, (y_{m-1} + y_m)/2, y_m].$$

The function call is `zz = interp2(z); zz = interp2(z, k)` performs the expansion recursively k times. Thus, `zz = interp2(z)` is the same as `zz = interp2(z, 1)`, which performs the expansion once. In this form, neither the vectors forming the grid for the data matrix **z** nor the vectors defining the grid for the interpolated data are supplied as input to the function.

Example 8.20 Simple Interpolation in Two-Dimensions

Let $\mathbf{x} = [\, 2, 4 \,]$, $\mathbf{y} = [\, 3, 5, 7 \,]$, and $\mathbf{z} = \mathbf{x}'\mathbf{y}$. The data array is

$$z = \begin{bmatrix} 6 & 10 & 14 \\ 12 & 20 & 28 \end{bmatrix}.$$

Figure 8.24 shows the data, plotted using the function call `mesh(x,y,z')`; the interpolated points found by zz = `interp2(z)` are shown in blue. Note that

$$zz = \begin{bmatrix} 6 & 8 & 10 & 12 & 14 \\ 9 & 12 & 15 & 18 & 21 \\ 12 & 16 & 20 & 24 & 28 \end{bmatrix}$$

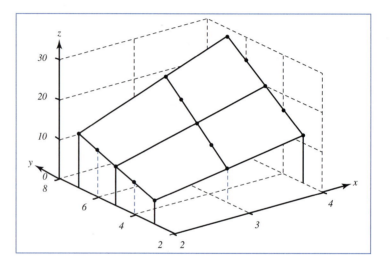

FIGURE 8.24 Data and interpolated points.

The second special form in which the function `interp2` can be used assumes that the data values being interpolated are defined on a mesh given by the vectors $\mathbf{x} = 1{:}n$ and $\mathbf{y} = 1{:}m$, where $[m, n] = \text{size}(\mathbf{z})$; note that the vector $\mathbf{y}$ gives the rows of the grid, and $\mathbf{x}$ gives the columns. We illustrate this form in the next example.

Example 8.21 Data on a Special Grid

We generate a grid of data values z = `x'*y`, with

$$\mathbf{x} = \begin{bmatrix} 1 & 2 & 3 \end{bmatrix}$$
$$\mathbf{y} = \begin{bmatrix} 1 & 2 & 3 & 4 & 5 \end{bmatrix}$$

so that

$$\mathbf{z} = \begin{bmatrix} 1 & 2 & 3 & 4 & 5 \\ 2 & 4 & 6 & 8 & 10 \\ 3 & 6 & 9 & 12 & 15 \end{bmatrix}$$

For data values given at the points $\mathbf{x} = 1{:}n$, $\mathbf{y} = 1{:}m$, the surface can be plotted using the simplified call to the mesh function, `mesh(z')`; that is, the vectors $\mathbf{x}$ and $\mathbf{y}$ do not need to be given.

   Now suppose we would like to interpolate this data on a mesh defined by the vectors $\mathbf{xx} = [\ 1, 1.2, 2, 2.2, 3]$ and $\mathbf{yy} = [\ 1, 1.8, 2, 4, 4.8, 5]$. We find `zz = interp2(z', xx, yy')`, or

$$zz = \begin{bmatrix} 1.00 & 1.20 & 2.00 & 3.00 \\ 1.80 & 2.16 & 3.96 & 5.40 \\ 2.00 & 2.40 & 4.40 & 6.00 \\ 4.00 & 4.80 & 8.80 & 12.00 \\ 4.80 & 5.76 & 10.56 & 14.40 \\ 5.00 & 6.00 & 11.00 & 15.00 \end{bmatrix}$$

The interpolated data, plotted using the function `mesh(xx,yy,zz)`, are shown in Fig. 8.25.

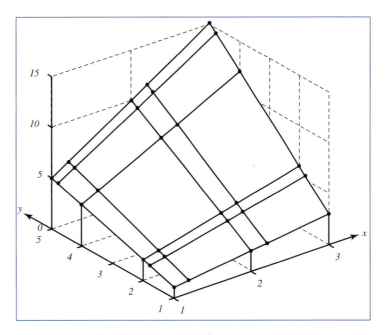

FIGURE 8.25 Interpolated data points.

The previous examples illustrated the use of MATLAB's two-dimensional interpolation function in two of its simplified forms. We now show that **z** can be given on a fairly general rectangular grid $(x(i), y(j))$.

Example 8.22 Interpolation on a Rectangular Grid in Two Dimensions

Let $\mathbf{x} = [\,2, 4\,]$ and $\mathbf{y} = [\,3, 5, 7\,]$; define $\mathbf{z} = \mathbf{x}'\mathbf{y}$ as in Example 8.20, so that

$$
\mathbf{z} = \begin{bmatrix} 6 & 10 & 14 \\ 12 & 20 & 28 \end{bmatrix}
$$

We now wish to interpolate **z** on the grid defined by

$$\mathbf{xx} = [2, 2.4, 2.6, 2.8, 3, 3.5, 4]$$

and

$$\mathbf{yy} = [3, 3.5, 5, 7].$$

Since the original vectors **x** and **y** are not of the form $\mathbf{x} = 1{:}n$ and $\mathbf{y} = 1{:}m$, we must include **x** and **y** as input to the function `interp2`:

```
zz = interp2( x, y', z', xx, yy' )
```
```
zz =
```
$$
\begin{bmatrix}
6.00 & 7.20 & 7.80 & 8.40 & 9.00 & 10.50 & 12.00 \\
7.00 & 8.40 & 9.10 & 9.80 & 10.50 & 12.25 & 14.00 \\
10.00 & 12.00 & 13.00 & 14.00 & 15.00 & 17.50 & 20.00 \\
14.00 & 16.80 & 18.20 & 19.60 & 21.00 & 24.50 & 28.00
\end{bmatrix}
$$

The interpolated function, plotted using `mesh(xx,yy,zz)`, is shown in Fig. 8.26.

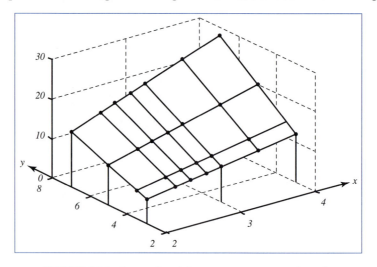

FIGURE 8.26   Interpolated data on a more general mesh.

The linear interpolation in two dimensions used in MATLAB's `interp2` functions is more properly known as *bilinear interpolation.* On each rectangular subregion, the interpolation is based on a bilinear function (linear in either x or y) of the form

$$z = a + bx + cy + dxy,$$

using the data values at the four corners of the region. Thus, for region R_{ij}, with data values (x_i, y_j), (x_i, y_{j+1}), (x_{i+1}, y_j), (x_{i+1}, y_{j+1}), there are four equations for the four unknowns a_{ij}, b_{ij}, c_{ij}, and d_{ij}:

$$z(i,j) = a_{ij} + b_{ij}x(i) + c_{ij}y(j) + d_{ij}x(i)y(j),$$

$$z(i,j+1) = a_{ij} + b_{ij}x(i) + c_{ij}y(j+1) + d_{ij}x(i)y(j+1),$$

$$z(i+1,j) = a_{ij} + b_{ij}x(i+1) + c_{ij}y(j) + d_{ij}x(i+1)y(j),$$

$$z(i+1,j+1) = a_{ij} + b_{ij}x(i+1) + c_{ij}y(j+1) + d_{ij}x(i+1)y(j+1).$$

Additional options for using `interp2` allow the user to specify the form of the interpolation, including 'cubic' (bicubic interpolation), 'nearest' (nearest neighbor interpolation), 'linear' (bilinear interpolation). Faster methods for data that are equally spaced are indicated as for `interp1`.

MATLAB also provides functions for interpolation (or lookup tables) in higher dimensions. For details, use the `help` command to read the comments at the beginning of the functions `interp3` and `interpn`.

SUMMARY

Polynomial Interpolation

The *Lagrange form* of the equation of the parabola passing through three points (x_1, y_1), (x_2, y_2), and (x_3, y_3) is

$$p(x) = \frac{(x - x_2)(x - x_3)}{(x_1 - x_2)(x_1 - x_3)} y_1 + \frac{(x - x_1)(x - x_3)}{(x_2 - x_1)(x_2 - x_3)} y_2 + \frac{(x - x_1)(x - x_2)}{(x_3 - x_1)(x_3 - x_2)} y_3.$$

The *Newton form* of the equation is

$$p(x) = a_1 + a_2(x - x_1) + a_3(x - x_1)(x - x_2),$$

where the coefficients are

$$a_1 = y_1, a_2 = \frac{y_2 - y_1}{x_2 - x_1}, a_3 \frac{\dfrac{y_3 - y_2}{x_3 - x_2} - \dfrac{y_2 - y_1}{x_2 - x_1}}{x_3 - x_0}.$$

The calculations can be performed using a "divided-difference table":

x_i	y_i	$d_i = \dfrac{y_{i+1} - y_i}{x_{i+1} - x_i}$	$dd_i = \dfrac{d_{i+1} - d_i}{x_{i+2} - x_i}$
x_1	y_1		
		$\dfrac{y_2 - y_1}{x_2 - x_1}$	
x_2	y_2		$\dfrac{d_2 - d_1}{x_3 - x_1}$
		$\dfrac{y_3 - y_2}{x_3 - x_2}$	
x_3	y_3		

Hermite interpolation finds a polynomial that agrees with function values and first-derivative values at the node points:

z_i	x_i	w_i	y_i	$d_i = \dfrac{w_{i+1} - w_i}{z_{i+1} - z_i}$	$dd_i = \dfrac{d_{i+1} - d_i}{z_{i+2} - z_i}$	$ddd_i = \dfrac{dd_{i+1} - dd_i}{z_{i+3} - z_i}$
$z_1 = x_1$		$w_1 = y_1$				
				$d_1 = y_1'$		
$z_2 = x_1$		$w_2 = y_1$			$dd_1 = \dfrac{d_2 - d_1}{z_3 - z_1}$	
				$d_2 = \dfrac{w_3 - w_2}{z_3 - z_2}$		$\dfrac{dd_2 - dd_1}{z_4 - z_1}$
$z_3 = x_2$		$w_3 = y_2$			$dd_2 = \dfrac{d_3 - d_2}{z_4 - z_2}$	
				$d_3 = y_2'$		
$z_4 = x_2$		$w_4 = y_2$				

Rational function interpolation is discussed in Section 8.3. The equations are not repeated here.

Piecewise polynomial interpolation is discussed in Section 8.4. The equations for piecewise linear and piecewise quadratic interpolation are not repeated here.

Cubic Spline Interpolation: Let $h_i = x_{i+1} - x_i$. We are looking for a spline function

$$S(x) = \begin{cases} P_1(x), & x_1 \le x \le x_2, \\ P_i(x), & x_i \le x \le x_{i+1}, \\ P_{n-1}(x), & x_{n-1} \le x \le x_n, \end{cases}$$

that is a piecewise cubic with continuous derivatives up to order 2. For $i = 1, \ldots, n - 1$, we write

$$P_i(x) = a_{i-1} \frac{(x_{i+1} - x)^3}{6h_i} + a_i \frac{(x - x_i)^3}{6h_i} + b_i(x_{i+1} - x) + c_i(x - x_i).$$

The $n - 2$ equations for the n unknowns $a_0, \ldots, a_{n-1}$ have the form

$$\frac{h_i}{6} a_{i-1} + \frac{h_i + h_{i+1}}{3} a_i + \frac{h_{i+1}}{6} a_{i+1} = \frac{y_{i+2} - y_{i+1}}{h_{i+1}} - \frac{y_{i+1} - y_i}{h_i} \qquad (i - 1, \ldots, n - 2).$$

The natural cubic spline sets $a_0 = a_{n-1} = 0$. The other coefficients are

$$b_i = \frac{y_i}{h_i} - \frac{a_{i-1}h_i}{6}, \qquad c_i = \frac{y_{i+1}}{h_i} - \frac{a_i h_i}{6}.$$

SUGGESTIONS FOR FURTHER READING

For a more extensive discussion of interpolation, see any of the following three sources:

Kahaner, D., C. Moler, and S. Nash, *Numerical Methods and Software,* Prentice Hall, Englewood Cliffs, NJ, 1989, Chapter 4.

Press, W. H., B. P. Flannery, S. A. Teukolsky, and W. T. Vetterling, *Numerical Recipes,* Cambridge University Press, Cambridge, U.K., 1986, see especially Sections 3.2 and 3.3.

Stoer, J., and R. Bulirsch, *Introduction to Numerical Analysis,* Springer Verlag, New York, 1980 (especially rational function interpolation.)

An excellent description of spline interpolation is given in

deBoor, C., *A Practical Guide to Splines,* Springer-Verlag, New York, 1978.

Applications of spline interpolation for computer graphics are presented in the following two sources:

Bartels, R. H., J. C. Beatty, and B. A. Barsky, *An Introduction to Splines for Use in Computer Graphics and Geometric Modeling,* Morgan Kaufmann, Los Altos, CA, 1987.

Farin, G., *Curves and Surfaces for Computer Aided Geometric Design: A Practical Guide* (2d ed.), Academic Press, Boston, 1990.

Quadratic spline interpolation is discussed in

Kammer, W. J., G. W. Reddien, and R. S. Varga, "Quadratic Splines," *Numerische Mathematik,* vol. 22, 1974, pp. 241–259.

For further discussion of interpolation in two dimensions, see

Lancaster, P., and K. Salkauskas, *Curve and Surface Fitting: An Introduction,* Academic Press, Boston, 1986.

For a more mathematically advanced treatment of interpolation and approximation, see

Davis, P. J., *Interpolation and Approximation,* Dover, New York, 1975. (Originally published by Blaisdell Publishing in 1963.)

PRACTICE THE TECHNIQUES

For Problems P8.1–P8.10, find the

    a. *interpolating polynomial in Lagrange form.*
    b. *interpolating polynomial in Newton form.*
    c. *piecewise linear interpolating function.*

P8.1 $x = [1 \quad 2 \quad 3]$,
        $y = [1 \quad 4 \quad 8]$.

P8.2 $x = [1 \quad 4 \quad 9]$,
        $y = [1 \quad 2 \quad 3]$.

P8.3 $x = [4 \quad 9 \quad 16]$,
        $y = [2 \quad 3 \quad 4]$.

P8.4 $x = [-1 \quad 0 \quad 1]$,
        $y = [-2 \quad 3 \quad 2]$.

P8.5 $x = [0 \quad 1 \quad 2]$,
        $y = [1 \quad 2 \quad 4]$.

P8.6 $x = [0 \quad 1 \quad 2 \quad 4]$,
        $y = [1 \quad 1 \quad 2 \quad 5]$.

P8.7 $x = [-1 \quad 0 \quad 1 \quad 2]$,
        $y = [1/3 \quad 1 \quad 3 \quad 9]$.

P8.8 $x = [0 \quad 1 \quad 2 \quad 3]$,
        $y = [1 \quad 2 \quad 4 \quad 8]$.

P8.9 $x = [0 \quad 1 \quad 2 \quad 3]$,
        $y = [0 \quad 1 \quad 0 \quad -1]$.

P8.10 $x = [0 \quad 1 \quad 2 \quad 3]$,
         $y = [0 \quad 1 \quad 0 \quad -1]$.

For P8.11–P8.15, find the

    a. *interpolating polynomial in Lagrange form.*
    b. *interpolating polynomial in Newton form.*
    c. *piecewise linear interpolating function.*
    d. *piecewise quadratic interpolating function (with knots midway between data points).*
    e. *cubic spline interpolating function.*

P8.11 $x = [0 \quad 2/3 \quad 1 \quad 2]$,
         $y = [2 \quad -2 \quad -1 \quad -1/2]$.

P8.12 $x = [0 \quad 2/3 \quad 1 \quad 2]$,
         $y = [4 \quad -4 \quad -2 \quad -1/2]$.

P8.13 $x = [0 \quad 2/3 \quad 1 \quad 2]$,
         $y = [4 \quad -4 \quad -7/2 \quad -1/2]$.

P8.14 $x = [1 \quad 2 \quad 3 \quad 4]$,
         $y = [2 \quad 4 \quad 8 \quad 16]$.

P8.15 $x = [0 \quad 1/2 \quad 1 \quad 3/2]$,
         $y = [1 \quad 2 \quad 1 \quad 0]$.

For P8.16–P8.20 find the

    a. *interpolation polynomial (either form).*
    b. *cubic spline interpolation function.*

P8.16 $x = [0 \quad 1 \quad 8 \quad 27]$,
         $y = [0 \quad 1 \quad 2 \quad 3]$.

Compare the interpolated values at $x = 0.5, 3.5$, and 18 with the corresponding values of $f(x) = \sqrt[3]{x}$.

P8.17 $x = [0 \quad 1 \quad 4 \quad 9]$,
         $y = [0 \quad 1 \quad 2 \quad 3]$.

Compare the interpolated values at $x = 0.5, 2.5$, and 6.5 with the corresponding values of $f(x) = \sqrt{x}$.

P8.18 $x = [-1 \quad -0.75 \quad -0.25 \quad 0.25 \quad 0.75 \quad 1]$,
         $y = [0 \quad -0.7 \quad -0.7 \quad 0.7 \quad 0.7 \quad 0]$.

Compare the interpolated values at $x = -0.5, 0$, and 0.5 with the corresponding values of $f(x) = \sin(\pi x)$.

P8.19 $x = [-2 \quad -1 \quad 0 \quad 1 \quad 2 \quad 3 \quad 4]$,
         $y = [-14 \quad 0.5 \quad 3.1 \quad 0 \quad -3 \quad 0 \quad 16]$.

Compare your results with Examples 8.4 and 8.7.

P8.20 $x = [0 \quad 0.5 \quad 1.0 \quad 1.5 \quad 2.0 \quad 2.5 \quad 3.0]$,
         $y = [4.0 \quad 0 \quad -2.0 \quad 0 \quad 1.0 \quad 0 \quad -0.5]$.

Compare the interpolated values with the corresponding values of the function $y = 2^{(2-x)} \cos(\pi x)$.

For P8.21–P8.30 find

    a. *the interpolation polynomial (either form).*
    b. *the cubic spline interpolation function.*
    c. *the Bulirsch–Stoer rational interpolation function.*

P8.21 $x = [0 \quad 1 \quad 2 \quad\quad 3 \quad 4 \quad\quad 5 \quad 6 \quad\quad 7 \quad 8 \quad\quad 9 \quad 10 \quad\quad]$,
$y = [2.0 \quad 0 \quad 0.6667 \quad 0 \quad 0.40 \quad 0 \quad 0.2857 \quad 0 \quad 0.2222 \quad 0 \quad 0.1818]$.

Compare the interpolated values with the corresponding values of $y = \dfrac{1 + \cos(\pi x)}{1 + x}$.

P8.22 $x = [0 \quad 1 \quad\quad 2 \quad\quad 3 \quad\quad 4 \quad\quad 5 \quad\quad 6 \quad\quad 7 \quad\quad 8 \quad\quad 9 \quad\quad 10 \quad]$,
$y = [2.0 \quad 0.7702 \quad 0.1946 \quad 0.0025 \quad 0.0693 \quad 0.2139 \quad 0.280 \quad 0.2192 \quad 0.0949 \quad 0.0089 \quad 0.0]$.

Compare the interpolated values with the corresponding values of $z = \dfrac{1 + \cos(x)}{1 + x}$.

P8.23 $x = [0 \quad 1 \quad 2 \quad 3 \quad\quad 4 \quad\quad 5 \quad\quad 6 \quad\quad 7 \quad\quad 8 \quad\quad 9 \quad\quad 10 \quad]$,
$y = [0 \quad 0.5 \quad 0.5 \quad 0.375 \quad 0.25 \quad 0.1562 \quad 0.0938 \quad 0.0547 \quad 0.0312 \quad 0.0176 \quad 0.0098]$.

Compare the interpolated values with the corresponding values of $w = x2^{-x}$.

P8.24 $x = [1 \quad 2 \quad\quad 3 \quad\quad 4 \quad\quad 5 \quad\quad 6 \quad\quad 7 \quad\quad 8 \quad\quad 9 \quad\quad 10 \quad]$,
$y = [0 \quad 0.3466 \quad 0.3662 \quad 0.3466 \quad 0.3219 \quad 0.2986 \quad 0.2780 \quad 0.2599 \quad 0.2441 \quad 0.2303]$.

Compare the interpolated values with the corresponding values of $y = \dfrac{\log(x)}{x}$.

P8.25 $x = [\quad 0 \quad\quad 0.50 \quad\quad 1.00 \quad\quad 1.50 \quad\quad 2.00 \quad\quad 2.50 \quad\quad 3.00]$,
$y = [-0.3333 \quad -0.2703 \quad -0.2000 \quad -0.1333 \quad -0.0769 \quad -0.0328 \quad 0 \quad]$.

Compare the interpolated values with the corresponding values of $y = \dfrac{x - 3}{x^2 + 9}$.

P8.26 $x = [\quad 0.0 \quad\quad 1.00 \quad\quad 2.00 \quad 3.00 \quad 4.00 \quad 5.00 \quad 6.00]$,
$y = [-0.33 \quad -0.20 \quad -0.08 \quad 0.00 \quad 0.04 \quad 0.06 \quad 0.07]$.

Compare the interpolated values with the corresponding values of $y = \dfrac{x - 3}{x^2 + 9}$.

P8.27 $x = [\quad 0 \quad\quad 5 \quad\quad 10 \quad\quad 15 \quad\quad 20 \quad\quad 25 \quad\quad 30 \quad\quad 35 \quad\quad 40 \quad\quad]$,
$y = [-0.3333 \quad 0.0588 \quad 0.0642 \quad 0.0513 \quad 0.0416 \quad 0.0347 \quad 0.0297 \quad 0.0259 \quad 0.0230]$.

Compare the interpolated values with the corresponding values of $y = \dfrac{x - 3}{x^2 + 9}$.

P8.28 Interpolate

$x = [-5 \quad\quad -4 \quad\quad -3 \quad\quad -2 \quad\quad -1 \quad\quad 0 \quad\quad 1 \quad\quad 2 \quad\quad 3 \quad\quad 4 \quad\quad 5 \quad\quad]$,
$y = [-0.1923 \quad -0.2353 \quad -0.30 \quad -0.40 \quad -0.50 \quad 0.00 \quad 0.50 \quad 0.40 \quad 0.30 \quad 0.2353 \quad 0.1923]$.

Compare the interpolated values at $x = -4.5, -3.5, \ldots, 3.5, 4.5$ with the corresponding values of the exact function
$w = \dfrac{x}{x^2 + 1}$.

P8.29 $x = [0 \quad 1 \quad 2 \quad\quad 3 \quad\quad 4 \quad\quad 5 \quad\quad 6 \quad\quad 7 \quad\quad 8 \quad\quad 9 \quad\quad 10 \quad]$,
$y = [1.0 \quad 1.0 \quad 0.5556 \quad 0.3571 \quad 0.2615 \quad 0.2063 \quad 0.1705 \quad 0.1453 \quad 0.1267 \quad 0.1123 \quad 0.100]$.

Compare the interpolated values with the corresponding values of $y = \dfrac{x^2 + 1}{x^3 + 1}$.

P8.30 $x = [0 \quad 1 \quad 2 \quad 3 \quad 4 \quad 5 \quad 6 \quad 7 \quad 8 \quad 9 \quad 10 \quad]$,
$y = [0.5 \quad 1.0 \quad 1.7 \quad 1.8966 \quad 1.9545 \quad 1.9764 \quad 1.9862 \quad 1.9913 \quad 1.9942 \quad 1.9959 \quad 1.9970]$.

Compare the interpolated values with the corresponding values of $y = \dfrac{2x^3 + 1}{x^3 + 2}$.

Problems P8.31–P8.35 provide practice in the use of Hermite interpolation.
  a. *Find the interpolation polynomial using the given data.*
  b. *Find the Hermite interpolation polynomial using the given values of the function and the derivative.*
  c. *Compare the interpolated values (at some intermediate values of x) from Parts a and b with the corresponding values of the specified function.*

P8.31 Interpolate:

$x = [-5 \quad -4 \quad -3 \quad -2 \quad -1 \quad 0 \quad 1 \quad 2 \quad 3 \quad 4 \quad 5 \quad]$,
$y = [\ 0.0385 \quad 0.588 \quad 0.10 \quad 0.20 \quad 0.50 \quad 1.00 \quad 0.50 \quad 0.20 \quad 0.10 \quad 0.588 \quad 0.0385]$.

For Hermite interpolation,

$x = [-5 \quad -3 \quad -1 \quad 1 \quad 3 \quad 5 \quad]$
$w = [\ 0.0385 \quad 0.10 \quad 0.50 \quad 0.50 \quad 0.10 \quad 0.0385]$
$dw = [\ 0.0148 \quad 0.06 \quad 0.50 \quad -0.50 \quad -0.06 \quad -0.0148]$

or

$x = [-4 \quad -2 \quad 0 \quad 2 \quad 4 \quad]$
$w = [\ 0.0588 \quad 0.20 \quad 1.00 \quad 0.20 \quad 0.0588]$
$dw = [\ 0.0277 \quad 0.1600 \quad 0 \quad -0.1600 \quad -0.0277]$

or

$x = [0 \quad 1 \quad 2 \quad 3 \quad 4 \quad 5 \quad]$
$w = [1.00 \quad 0.50 \quad 0.20 \quad 0.10 \quad 0.0588 \quad 0.0385]$
$dw = [0 \quad -0.5000 \quad -0.1600 \quad -0.0600 \quad -0.0277 \quad -0.0148]$

The function for comparison is $w = \dfrac{1}{x^2 + 1}$.

P8.32 Interpolate:

$x = [1 \quad 2 \quad 3 \quad 4 \quad 5 \quad 6 \quad 7 \quad 8 \quad 9 \quad 10 \quad]$,
$y = [0 \quad 0.6931 \quad 1.0986 \quad 1.3863 \quad 1.6094 \quad 1.7918 \quad 1.9459 \quad 2.0794 \quad 2.1972 \quad 2.3026]$.

For Hermite interpolation,

$x = [1 \quad 3 \quad 5 \quad 7 \quad 9 \quad]$
$w = [0 \quad 1.0986 \quad 1.6094 \quad 1.9459 \quad 2.1972]$
$dw = [1.0 \quad 0.3333 \quad 0.20 \quad 0.1429 \quad 0.1111]$

or

$x = [2 \quad 4 \quad 6 \quad 8 \quad 10 \quad]$
$w = [0.6931 \quad 1.3863 \quad 1.7918 \quad 2.0794 \quad 2.3026]$
$dw = [0.50 \quad 0.25 \quad 0.1667 \quad 0.1250 \quad 0.1000]$

The function for comparison is $\log(x)$ (the natural logarithm).

P8.33 $x = \begin{bmatrix} 0 & 1 & 2 & 3 & 4 & 5 & 6 & 7 & 8 & 9 & 10 \end{bmatrix}$,
$y = \begin{bmatrix} 0.50 & 0.7311 & 0.8808 & 0.9526 & 0.9820 & 0.993 & 0.9975 & 0.9991 & 0.9997 & 0.9999 & 1 \end{bmatrix}$.

For Hermite interpolation, use half of the preceding data, together with the following corresponding values of the derivative:

$$dy = \begin{bmatrix} 0.25 & 0.1966 & 0.1050 & 0.045 & 20.0177 & 0.0066 & 0.0025 & 0.0009 & 0.0003 & 0.001 & 0 \end{bmatrix}$$

The function for comparison is $y = \dfrac{1}{1 + \exp(-x)}$.

P8.34 $x = \begin{bmatrix} 0 & 1 & 2 & 3 & 4 & 5 & 6 & 7 & 8 & 9 & 10 \end{bmatrix}$
$y = \begin{bmatrix} 0 & 0.5000 & 0.6667 & 0.7500 & 0.8000 & 0.8333 & 0.8571 & 0.8750 & 0.8889 & 0.9000 & 0.9 \end{bmatrix}$

For Hermite interpolation, use half of the preceding data, together with the following corresponding values of the derivative:
$dy = \begin{bmatrix} 1 & 0.2500 & 0.1111 & 0.0625 & 0.0400 & 0.0278 & 0.0204 & 0.0156 & 0.0123 & 0.0100 & 0.0 \end{bmatrix}$

The function for comparison is $y = \dfrac{x}{1 + x}$.

P8.35 $x = \begin{bmatrix} 0.0100 & 1.0000 & 4.0000 & 9.0000 & 16.0000 & 25.0000 & 36.0000 \end{bmatrix}$
$y = \begin{bmatrix} 0.1000 & 1.0000 & 2.0000 & 3.0000 & 4.0000 & 5.0000 & 6.0000 \end{bmatrix}$
$dy = \begin{bmatrix} 5.0000 & 0.5000 & 0.2500 & 0.1667 & 0.1250 & 0.1000 & 0.0833 \end{bmatrix}$

The function for comparison is $y = \sqrt{x}$.

Problems P8.36–P8.40 provide practice in using the MATLAB two-dimensional interpolation functions.

P8.36 Let

$$x = \begin{bmatrix} 0 & 0.2 & 0.4 & 0.6 & 0.8 & 1.0 \end{bmatrix}$$
$$y = \begin{bmatrix} 0 & 0.2 & 0.4 & 0.6 & 0.8 & 1.0 \end{bmatrix}$$
$$z = \begin{bmatrix} 0 & 0 & 0 & 0 & 0 & 0 \\ 0 & 0.0047 & 0.0374 & 0.1263 & 0.2994 & 0.5848 \\ 0 & 0.0059 & 0.0472 & 0.1592 & 0.3772 & 0.7368 \\ 0 & 0.0067 & 0.0540 & 0.1822 & 0.4318 & 0.8434 \\ 0 & 0.0074 & 0.0594 & 0.2005 & 0.4753 & 0.9283 \\ 0 & 0.0080 & 0.0640 & 0.2160 & 0.5120 & 1.0000 \end{bmatrix}$$

Use $zz = \text{interp2(z)}$ to find the interpolated values on the mesh defined by

$$xx = \begin{bmatrix} 0 & 0.1 & 0.2 & 0.3 & 0.4 & 0.5 & 0.6 & 0.7 & 0.8 & 0.9 & 1.0 \end{bmatrix}$$
$$yy = \begin{bmatrix} 0 & 0.1 & 0.2 & 0.3 & 0.4 & 0.5 & 0.6 & 0.7 & 0.8 & 0.9 & 1.0 \end{bmatrix}$$

Compare the interpolated results with those found from the function that generated the data, namely, $z = \text{x'.^(1/3)} * \text{y.^(3)}$.

P8.37 Let

$$x = \begin{bmatrix} 0 & 0.1000 & 0.2000 & 0.4000 & 0.7000 & 1.0000 \end{bmatrix}$$
$$y = \begin{bmatrix} 0 & 0.1000 & 0.2000 & 0.4000 & 0.7000 & 1.0000 \end{bmatrix}$$
$$z = \begin{bmatrix} 0 & 0 & 0 & 0 & 0 & 0 \\ 0 & 0.0005 & 0.0037 & 0.0297 & 0.1592 & 0.4642 \\ 0 & 0.0006 & 0.0047 & 0.0374 & 0.2006 & 0.5848 \\ 0 & 0.0007 & 0.0059 & 0.0472 & 0.2527 & 0.7368 \\ 0 & 0.0009 & 0.0071 & 0.0568 & 0.3046 & 0.8879 \\ 0 & 0.0010 & 0.0080 & 0.0640 & 0.3430 & 1.0000 \end{bmatrix}$$

Interpolate these data on a mesh defined by the vectors

$$xx = [0 \quad 0.10 \quad 0.20 \quad 0.30 \quad 0.40 \quad 0.50 \quad 0.60 \quad 0.70 \quad 0.80 \quad 0.90 \quad 1.00]$$
$$yy = [0 \quad 0.10 \quad 0.20 \quad 0.30 \quad 0.40 \quad 0.50 \quad 0.60 \quad 0.70 \quad 0.80 \quad 0.90 \quad 1.00]$$

```
zz = interp2( x, y', z', xx, yy' ).
```

Compare the interpolated results with those found from the function that generated the data, namely,

$$z = x'.\hat{}(1/3) * y.\hat{}(3)$$

P8.38 Let

$$x = [0 \quad 0.2 \quad 0.4 \quad 0.6 \quad 0.8 \quad 1.0]$$
$$y = [0 \quad 0.2 \quad 0.4 \quad 0.6 \quad 0.8 \quad 1.0]$$

$$z = \begin{bmatrix} 0 & 0.0400 & 0.1600 & 0.3600 & 0.6400 & 1.0000 \\ 0.4472 & 0.4872 & 0.6072 & 0.8072 & 1.0872 & 1.4472 \\ 0.6325 & 0.6725 & 0.7925 & 0.9925 & 1.2725 & 1.6325 \\ 0.7746 & 0.8146 & 0.9346 & 1.1346 & 1.4146 & 1.7746 \\ 0.8944 & 0.9344 & 1.0544 & 1.2544 & 1.5344 & 1.8944 \\ 1.0000 & 1.0400 & 1.1600 & 1.3600 & 1.6400 & 2.0000 \end{bmatrix}$$

Use `zz = interp2(z)` to interpolate.

P8.39 Let

$$x = [0 \quad 0.2 \quad 0.4 \quad 0.6 \quad 0.8 \quad 1.0]$$
$$y = [0 \quad 0.2 \quad 0.4 \quad 0.6 \quad 0.8 \quad 1.0]$$

$$z = \begin{bmatrix} 1.0000 & 1.2214 & 1.4918 & 1.8221 & 2.2255 & 2.7183 \\ 1.7878 & 2.0092 & 2.2796 & 2.6099 & 3.0133 & 3.5061 \\ 2.3511 & 2.5725 & 2.8429 & 3.1732 & 3.5766 & 4.0693 \\ 2.5511 & 2.7725 & 3.0429 & 3.3732 & 3.7766 & 4.2693 \\ 2.3878 & 2.6092 & 2.8796 & 3.2099 & 3.6133 & 4.1061 \\ 2.0000 & 2.2214 & 2.4918 & 2.8221 & 3.2255 & 3.7183 \end{bmatrix}$$

$$xx = [0 \quad 0.10 \quad 0.20 \quad 0.30 \quad 0.40 \quad 0.50 \quad 0.60 \quad 0.70 \quad 0.80 \quad 0.90 \quad 1.00]$$
$$yy = [0 \quad 0.10 \quad 0.20 \quad 0.30 \quad 0.40 \quad 0.50 \quad 0.60 \quad 0.70 \quad 0.80 \quad 0.90 \quad 1.00]$$

Interpolate using

a. `zz = interp2( x, y', z', xx, yy' )`
b. `zz = interp2( x, y', z', xx, yy', 'cubic')`

Compare your results from Parts a and b.

P8.40

$$x = [0 \quad 0.2 \quad 0.4 \quad 0.6 \quad 0.8 \quad 1.0]$$
$$y = [0 \quad 0.2 \quad 0.4 \quad 0.6 \quad 0.8 \quad 1.0]$$

$$z = \begin{bmatrix} 0 & 0 & 0 & 0 & 0 & 0 \\ 0.7878 & 0.9622 & 1.1752 & 1.4354 & 1.7532 & 2.1414 \\ 1.3511 & 1.6502 & 2.0155 & 2.4618 & 3.0068 & 3.6726 \\ 1.5511 & 1.8945 & 2.3139 & 2.8262 & 3.4519 & 4.2162 \\ 1.3878 & 1.6950 & 2.0703 & 2.5287 & 3.0886 & 3.7724 \\ 1.0000 & 1.2214 & 1.4918 & 1.8221 & 2.2255 & 2.7183 \end{bmatrix}$$

$$xx = [0 \quad 0.10 \quad 0.20 \quad 0.30 \quad 0.40 \quad 0.50 \quad 0.60 \quad 0.70 \quad 0.80 \quad 0.90 \quad 1.00]$$
$$yy = [0 \quad 0.10 \quad 0.20 \quad 0.30 \quad 0.40 \quad 0.50 \quad 0.60 \quad 0.70 \quad 0.80 \quad 0.90 \quad 1.00]$$

Interpolate using

    a. `zz = interp2( x, y', z', xx, yy' ).`

    b. `zz = interp2( x, y', z', xx, yy', 'cubic').`

Compare your results from Parts a and b. Then, compare the interpolated values with the corresponding values of z = `(x + sin(pi*x))'*exp(y)`.

Problems P8.41–P8.50 provide practice in using spline interpolation for parametric curves. Modify the spline interpolation function given in Section 8.4.3 so that it does not print the interpolated function or the original data. Then use spline interpolation to find `xx = spline(t, x)` *and* `yy = spline(t, y)`, *and plot the curve with plot* `(xx, yy)` *and the data with plot* `(x, y, '*')`.

P8.41 $t = [1\ \ 2\ \ 3\ \ 4\ \ \ 5\ \ \ 6\ \ \ 7\ \ \ 8\ \ \ 9\ \ \ 10\ \ \ 11\ \ \ 12\ \ 13]$

        $x = [7\ \ 4\ \ 3\ \ 0\ \ -3\ \ -4\ \ -7\ \ -4\ \ -3\ \ \ \ 0\ \ \ \ 3\ \ \ \ 4\ \ \ \ 7]$

        $y = [0\ \ 2\ \ 5\ \ 8\ \ \ \ 5\ \ \ \ 2\ \ \ \ 0\ \ -2\ \ -5\ \ -8\ \ -5\ \ -2\ \ \ \ 0]$

P8.42 $t = [1\ \ 2\ \ 3\ \ 4\ \ 5\ \ 6\ \ \ 7\ \ \ 8\ \ \ 9\ \ \ 10\ \ \ 11\ \ \ 12\ \ \ 13\ \ \ 14\ \ \ 15\ \ \ 16\ \ \ 17\ \ \ 18\ \ \ 19\ \ \ 20\ \ \ 21]$

        $x = [3\ \ 4\ \ 3\ \ 2\ \ 1\ \ 0\ -1\ -2\ -3\ -4\ -3\ -4\ -3\ -2\ -1\ \ \ \ 0\ \ \ \ 1\ \ \ \ 2\ \ \ \ 3\ \ \ \ 4\ \ \ \ 3]$

        $y = [0\ \ 1\ \ 2\ \ 3\ \ 4\ \ 4\ \ \ 4\ \ \ 3\ \ \ 2\ \ \ \ 1\ \ \ \ 0\ -1\ -2\ -3\ -4\ -4\ -4\ -3\ -2\ -1\ \ \ \ 0]$

P8.43 $t = [1\ \ 2\ \ \ \ 3\ \ 4\ \ \ 5\ \ \ \ 6\ \ 7]$

        $x = [0\ \ 1.5\ \ 3\ \ 0\ -3\ -1.5\ \ 0]$

        $y = [0\ \ 1.5\ \ 6\ \ 4\ \ \ 6\ \ \ 1.5\ \ 0]$

Investigate the effect of taking the same points, but starting at a different point; e.g. use

        $t = [1\ \ \ \ 2\ \ \ \ \ 3\ \ 4\ \ 5\ \ \ \ 6\ \ 7]$

        $x = [0\ -3\ -1.5\ \ 0\ \ 1.5\ \ 3\ \ 0]$

        $y = [4\ \ \ 6\ \ \ 1.5\ \ 0\ \ 1.5\ \ 6\ \ 4]$

P8.44 $t = [1\ \ 2\ \ 3\ \ 4\ \ \ 5\ \ \ 6\ \ \ 7\ \ \ 8\ \ \ \ 9\ \ \ 10\ \ \ 11]$

        $x = [0\ \ 2\ \ 5\ \ 2\ \ \ 4\ \ \ 0\ -4\ -2\ -5\ -2\ \ \ 0]$

        $y = [5\ \ 3\ \ 3\ \ 1\ -2\ -1\ -2\ \ \ 1\ \ \ 3\ \ \ 3\ \ \ 5]$

P8.45 $t = [1\ \ 2\ \ 3\ \ \ 4\ \ \ 5\ \ \ 6\ \ \ 7\ \ \ 8\ \ 9]$

        $x = [5\ \ 1\ \ 0\ -1\ -5\ -1\ \ \ 0\ \ \ 1\ \ 5]$

        $y = [0\ \ 2\ \ 5\ \ \ 2\ \ \ 0\ -1\ -5\ -1\ \ 0]$

P8.46 $t = [\ 1\ \ \ \ 2\ \ 3\ \ 4\ \ 5\ \ 6\ \ \ 7\ \ \ 8\ \ 9\ \ 10\ \ \ 11\ \ \ 12]$

        $x = [-2\ -1\ \ 0\ \ 1\ \ 1\ \ 0\ -1\ -1\ \ 0\ \ \ 1\ \ \ \ 2\ \ \ \ 3]$

        $y = [\ 0\ \ \ \ 0\ \ 0\ \ 1\ \ 2\ \ 3\ \ \ 2\ \ \ 1\ \ 0\ \ \ 0\ \ \ \ 0\ \ \ \ 0]$

P8.47 $t = [1\ \ \ \ 2\ \ \ \ \ 3\ \ \ \ \ 4\ \ \ \ \ \ 5\ \ \ \ \ \ 6\ \ \ \ \ \ 7\ \ \ \ \ \ 8\ \ \ \ \ 9\ ]$

        $x = [0.9\ \ 0.25\ \ 0\ \ \ \ \ -0.25\ \ -0.9\ \ -0.25\ \ \ \ 0\ \ \ \ \ \ 0.25\ \ 0.9]$

        $y = [0\ \ \ \ \ 0.25\ \ 0.9\ \ \ \ 0.25\ \ \ \ 0\ \ \ \ -0.25\ \ -0.9\ \ -0.25\ \ 0\ ]$

P8.48 $t = [1\ \ \ \ 2\ \ \ \ \ 3\ \ \ \ \ 4\ \ \ \ \ \ 5\ \ \ \ \ \ 6\ \ \ \ \ \ 7\ \ \ \ 8\ \ \ \ 9\ ]$

        $x = [0.9\ \ 0.25\ \ 0\ \ \ \ \ -0.25\ \ -0.9\ \ -0.25\ \ \ \ 0\ \ \ \ \ 0.25\ \ 0.9]$

        $y = [0\ \ \ \ \ 0.25\ \ 0.9\ \ -0.25\ \ \ \ \ 0\ \ \ \ -0.25\ \ -0.9\ \ \ 0.25\ \ 0\ ]$

P8.49 $t = [\ 1\ \ \ \ \ 2\ \ \ \ 3\ \ \ \ 4\ \ \ 5\ \ \ \ \ \ 6\ \ \ \ 7\ \ \ 8\ \ \ \ \ 9\ \ \ \ \ 10\ \ \ \ 11\ \ \ \ \ 12\,]$

        $x = [\ 1\ \ \ \ \ \ 1\ \ \ \ 1/4\ \ 1/4\ \ -1/4\ \ -1/4\ \ -1\ \ \ -1\ \ \ \ -1/4\ \ \ \ 0\ \ \ \ 1/4\ \ \ \ \ 1\,]$

        $y = [-1/4\ \ 1/4\ \ 1/4\ \ \ \ 1\ \ \ \ \ 1\ \ \ \ \ 1/4\ \ 1/4\ \ -1/4\ \ -1/4\ \ -1\ \ -1/4\ \ -1/4]$

Investigate the effect of taking the same points in a different order.

P8.50 Many of the previous problems on spline interpolation for parametric curves were designed by the author's students. Draw an interesting figure, find the coordinates of some points on it, and use spline interpolation to find the interpolated parametric curve. Compare it with your original curve.

EXPLORE SOME APPLICATIONS

A8.1 Using the following data for the heat capacity C_p (kJ/kg °K) of methylcyclohexane C_7H_{14} as a function of temperature (°K), interpolate to estimate the heat capacity at 175, 225, and 275°K.

T	150	200	250	300
C_p	1.43	1.54	1.70	1.89

(These data are adapted from Vargaftik, 1975.)

A8.2 The drag coefficient C_d for a baseball is a function of velocity (mph) in accordance with the following tabulation:

v	0	50	75	100	125
C_d	0.5	0.5	0.4	0.28	0.23

Approximate the drag coefficient for a baseball at 90 mph (data adapted from Garcia, 1994, p. 42).

A8.3 Use interpolation on data for Bessel functions J_0, J_1, and J_2. The following are the data for J_0:

$x = \begin{bmatrix} 0 & 1 & 2 & 3 & 4 & 5 & 6 & 7 & 8 & 9 & 10 \end{bmatrix}$
$y = \begin{bmatrix} 1.00 & 0.77 & 0.22 & -0.26 & -0.40 & -0.18 & 0.15 & 0.30 & 0.17 & -0.09 & -0.25 \end{bmatrix}$

Compare your interpolated values at $x = 0.5, 1.5, \ldots, 9.5$ with those found from the MATLAB function besselj $(0, x)$; also, compare the interpolation polynomial with the function $P(x) = 1 - x^2/4 + x^4/64 - x^6/2304$, which is the first four terms of the series expansion for J_0.

The Data for Bessel function J_1 are as follows:

$x = \begin{bmatrix} 0 & 1 & 2 & 3 & 4 & 5 & 6 & 7 & 8 & 9 & 10 \end{bmatrix}$
$y = \begin{bmatrix} 0 & 0.44 & 0.58 & 0.34 & -0.07 & -0.33 & -0.28 & -0.0047 & 0.23 & 0.25 & 0.0435 \end{bmatrix}$

Compare your interpolated values at $x = 0.5, 1.5, \ldots, 9.5$ with those found from the MATLAB function besselj$(1, x)$.

A8.4 The viscosity μ of a fluid depends on the temperatures T of the fluid according to a relationship represented by the following data:

T(°C)	5	20	30	50	55
μ (N-sec/m²)	0.08	0.015	0.009	0.006	0.0055

Use interpolation to find an estimate for the viscosity at $T = 25$ and $T = 40$
(Data adapted from Ayyub and McCuen, 1996, p. 174.)

A8.5 Using the following tabulated data for the specific enthalpy h (Btu/lb) of superheated steam as a function of temperature T (at a constant pressure of 2500 lb/in²), find an interpolating polynomial and estimate the enthalpy at 1100°F:

T	800	1000	1200	1400	1600
h	1303.6	1458.4	1585.3	1706.1	1826.2

(Data adapted from Ayyub and McCuen, 1996, p. 176.)

A8.6 Using the following tabulated data for the short-wave radiation flux (in gram-calories per cm² per day for September) at the outer limit of the atmosphere, estimate the flux at a latitude of 35°:

Latitude	0	20	40	60	80
Flux	891	856	719	494	219

(Data adapted from Ayyub and McCuen, 1996, p. 176.)

A8.7 Using the following tabulated data for the vapor pressure P (mm Hg) of water as a function of temperature T (°C), find an interpolating polynomial and estimate the pressure at $T = 50$.

T	40	48	56	64	72
P	55.3	83.7	123.8	179.2	254.5

(Data adapted from Ayyub and McCuen, 1996, p. 151.)

A8.8 Using the following tabulated data for the saturation values of dissolved oxygen concentration D (mg/L) as a function of temperature T (°C), find an interpolating polynomial:

$$T = [0 \quad 5 \quad 10 \quad 15 \quad 20 \quad 25 \ ]$$
$$D = [14.6 \quad 12.8 \quad 11.3 \quad 10.2 \quad 9.2 \quad 8.4]$$

(Data adapted from Ayyub and McCuen, 1996, p. 159.)

A8.9 Let

$$K(m) = \int_0^{\pi/2} \frac{dt}{\sqrt{1 - m\sin^2 t}},$$

$$E(m) = \int_0^{\circ/2} \sqrt{1 - m\sin^2 t}\ dt.$$

Given the following tabulated values (truncated to two decimal places) for the elliptic integrals of the first and second kinds, (Abramowitz and Stegun, 19 , pp. 608–609), use interpolation to find values for $m = 0.1, 0.3, 0.5, 0.7, 0.9$:

$$m = [0.00 \quad 0.20 \quad 0.40 \quad 0.60 \quad 0.80 \quad 1.00]$$
$$K = [1.57 \quad 1.66 \quad 1.78 \quad 1.95 \quad 2.26 \quad \infty \ ]$$
$$E = [1.57 \quad 1.49 \quad 1.40 \quad 1.30 \quad 1.18 \quad 1.00]$$

A8.10 Let

$$C(x) = \int_0^x \cos\left(\frac{\pi}{2}t^2\right) dt, \quad S(x) = \int_0^x \sin\left(\frac{\pi}{2}t^2\right) dt.$$

Given the following tabulated values (truncated to three decimal places) for the Fresnel integrals, (adapted from Abramowitz and Stegun, 1, pp. 321–322), use interpolation to find the values for $m = 0.5, 1.5, 2.5, 3.5$, and 4.5:

$$x = [0.00 \quad 1.00 \quad 2.00 \quad 3.00 \quad 4.00 \quad 5.00 \ ]$$
$$C = [0.000 \quad 0.780 \quad 0.488 \quad 0.606 \quad 0.498 \quad 0.564]$$
$$S = [0.000 \quad 0.438 \quad 0.343 \quad 0.496 \quad 0.421 \quad 0.499]$$

A8.11 In modeling a combustion process, it is required to find the enthalpy E as a function of the temperature T. Find an interpolation polynomial or a spline or rational-function interpolation for the following data, and compare the interpolated values with the following tabulated values:

$$T = [60 \quad 80 \quad 100 \quad 120 \quad 140 \quad 160 \quad 180 \quad 200 \ ]$$
$$E = [\ 0.0 \quad 17.2 \quad 45.2 \quad 92.9 \quad 178.8 \quad 349.4 \quad 764.3 \quad 2648.4]$$

Data adapted from the Handbook of Hazardous Waste Incineration, Tab professional and reference books, 1989.

A8.12 Use the following data on annual building permits issued (in millions of permits) to estimate the number of permits issued in 1982, 1988, 1993, and 1996:

$$Y = [1980 \quad 1985 \quad 1990 \quad 1995]$$
$$P = [1.19 \quad 1.73 \quad 1.11 \quad 1.33\,]$$

(Data adapted from the U. S. Bureau of the Census Web page.)

A8.13 Use the following data (adapted from the U.S. Bureau of the Census Web page) to estimate the average (mean) annual earnings for workers in 1978, 1983, 1988, and 1993 for workers with the following levels of education: HS (workers who are high school graduates), AA (workers with associate degree), BA (workers with bachelor's degree), AD (workers with advanced degree).

year	1975	1980	1985	1990	1995
HS	7,843	11,314	14,457	17,820	21,431
AA	8,388	12,409	16,349	20,694	23,862
BA	12,332	18,075	24,877	31,112	36,980
AD	16,725	23,308	32,909	41,458	56,667

A8.14 Use the following data on enrollments (in millions) to estimate the school enrollments in 1978, 1983, 1988, and 1993 for students in kindergarten (K), elementary school (E), high school (H), or college (C). The data are adapted from the U.S. Bureau of the Census Web page).

year	1955	1960	1965	1970	1975	1980	1985	1990	1995
K	1.6	2.1	3.1	3.2	3.4	3.2	3.8	4.0	3.9
E	25.5	30.3	32.5	33.9	30.5	27.5	26.9	29.2	31.8

EXTEND YOUR UNDERSTANDING

U8.1 The MATLAB functions `Newton_coef` and `Newton_eval` do not make as extensive a use of MATLAB's vector capabilities as they could. Replace the loops by the appropriate vector operations; compare the computational efficiency of the two approaches.

U8.2 Investigate the difficulties in interpolating a "noisy line" by generating some data as follows:

$$x = [0 \quad 1 \quad 2 \quad 34 \quad 5 \quad 6]$$
$$y = x + 0.1*\text{rand}(1,7) - 0.05$$

Show that even if the interpolating polynomial appears to fit the data well, extrapolating beyond the data is not a good idea.

U8.3 Show that the difficulties in interpolating a "noisy line" are much more severe when the data are not evenly spaced; e.g., generate some data of the form

$$x = [0 \quad 0.2 \quad 0.4 \quad 2 \quad 4 \quad 4.2 \quad 4.4]$$
$$y = x + 0.1*\text{rand}(1,7) - 0.05$$

or

$$x = [0 \quad 0.1 \quad 0.2 \quad 2 \quad 4.1 \quad 4.2 \quad 4.3]$$
$$y = x + 0.1*\text{rand}(1,7) - 0.05$$

U8.4 Show that for a cubic spline, specifying the value of $P_1'(x_1) = 0$ gives the following equation relating a_0 and a_1:

$$\frac{a_0 h_1}{3} + \frac{a_1 h_1}{6} = \frac{y_2 - y_1}{h_1} - P_1'(x_1).$$

U8.5 Modify to MATLAB function for the natural cubic spline by adding the equation from U8.4 to the system of equations for $a_0, \ldots, a_{n-1}$ given in Section 8.4.3, to form a function for a spline that is clamped at x_1.

U8.6 Use the function from U8.5 to repeat some of the exercises P8.16–P8.25.

U8.7 Show that the equation describing a clamped boundary at x_n (see U8.4) is

$$\frac{a_{n-2} h_{n-1}}{6} + \frac{a_{n-1} h_{n-1}}{3} = P_{n-1}'(x_n) - \frac{y_n - y_{n-1}}{h_{n-1}}.$$

U8.8 Use Hermite cubic polynomials for piecewise cubic interpolation by specifying the function value and derivative value at each node point. Use the data from Example 8.12.

U8.9 Use Hermite cubic polynomials for piecewise cubic interpolation by specifying the function value and derivative value at each node point. Compare your results using the following dat to the results of Example 8.10.

$$x = [\begin{matrix} -1 & -0.5 & 0 & 0.5 & 1. \end{matrix}],$$

$$y = [\begin{matrix} 0.0385 & 0.1379 & 1.00 & 0.1379 & 0.0385 \end{matrix}],$$

$$dy = [\begin{matrix} 0.074 & 0.4756 & 0.00 & -0.4756 & -0.074 \end{matrix}].$$

U8.10 The error bound formula for cubic spline interpolation given in the discussion at the end of Section 8.4.3 does not state the proportionality constant, since it depends on the choice of endpoint conditions. With clamped boundary conditions, it is

$$|S(x) - g(x)| < (5/384)h^4 G.$$

(See deBoor, 1978.)

Use $g(x) = \cos(x)$ to generate evenly spaced data on $[0, \pi]$ for different values of h. Find the cubic spline interpolation function $S(x)$, the actual error $|S(x) - g(x)|$, and the error bound $(5/384) h^4 G$.

9 Function Approximation

Function approximation is closely related to the idea of function interpolation, discussed in the previous chapter. In function approximation, we do not require the approximating function to match the given data exactly. This avoids some of the difficulties demonstrated previously in regard to trying to match a moderate-to-large amount of data, especially if noise (such as errors in measurement) is present. There are also many applications in which a theoretical functional form is known and the "best" function of that form is required.

The most common approach to "best fit" approximation is to minimize the sum of the squares of the differences between the data values and the values of the approximating function; this is the *method of least squares*. We first investigate *linear least squares* approximation, also known as linear regression (especially in statistics). The same approach is used to find the *quadratic least squares* function or a polynomial of some other (specified) degree. For data that appear to follow an exponential function, the standard approach is to find a linear function that fits the natural logarithm of the data. This gives a close approximation to the "best fit" exponential (but with much less effort).

It may also be desirable in some applications to approximate a given function by the best function of a specified form, on a given interval. This leads to the topic of *continuous least squares* approximation.

In certain situations, a function may be better represented by a rational function than by a polynomial. *Padé approximation* is the rational-function analog of Taylor polynomial approximation. In these cases, knowledge of the function and its derivatives at a single point is used to construct the best local representation of the function.

In the next chapter, we consider fitting periodic data with trigonometric polynomials. In that case, the appropriate function for approximation or interpolation of a given set of data can be found by the least squares approach.

Example 9-A Oil Reservoir Modeling

In modeling an oil reservoir, it may be necessary to find a relationship between the equilibrium constant of a reaction and the pressure, at constant temperature. The data shown in Table 9.1 relate equilibrium constants (K-values) to pressure (expressed in terms of 1000 PSIA) and were obtained from an experimental PVT analysis. Fig. 9.1 is a plot of these data.

Table 9.1 Oil reservoir data.

Pressure	K-value
0.635	7.5
1.035	5.58
1.435	4.35
1.835	3.55
2.235	2.97
2.635	2.53
3.035	2.2
3.435	1.93
3.835	1.7
4.235	1.46
4.635	1.28
5.035	1.11
5.435	1.0

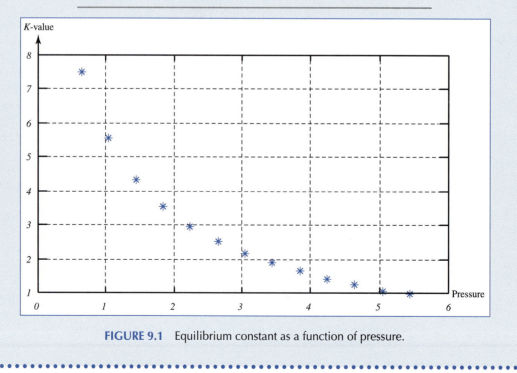

FIGURE 9.1 Equilibrium constant as a function of pressure.

Example 9-B Logistic Population Growth

The data in Fig. 9.2 describe the growth of a population following a logistic model. The plot could also represent a uniform sampling from a cumulative distribution. Several kinds of functions can be used to fit data that display this "s-shaped" form; the appropriate choice depends on the particular application.

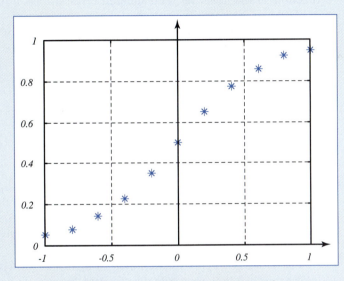

FIGURE 9.2   Logistic population growth.

We see in Example 9.7 that a cubic polynomial provides a reasonable fit to the given data.

On the other hand, if we wish to obtain an approximating function of the appropriate form for the solution of a logistic differential equation, we may look for a function of the form $y = 1/(1 + \exp(ax + b))$.

We transform the given data:

$x =$	-1.0	-0.8	-0.6	-0.4	-0.2	0.0	0.2	0.4	0.6	0.8	1.0
$y =$	0.05	0.08	0.14	0.23	0.35	0.50	0.65	0.77	0.86	0.92	0.95

to form $z = 1/y - 1$

$z =$	19.00	11.50	6.143	3.348	1.857	1.00	0.539	0.299	0.163	0.087	0.053

We then find the coefficients a and b for the exponential function to fit z.

Some of the most common methods of approximating data are based on the desire to minimize some measure of the difference between the approximating function and the given data points. The method of least squares seeks to minimize the sum (over all data points) of the squares of the differences between the function value and the data value. The method is based on results from calculus demonstrating that a function, in this case the total squared error, attains a minimum value when its partial derivatives are zero.

There are several advantages to using the square of the differences at each point, rather than the difference, or the absolute value of the difference, or some other measure of the error. By squaring the difference,

1. positive differences do not cancel negative differences;
2. differentiation is not difficult; and
3. small differences become smaller and large differences are magnified.

We begin with an example in which the data can be approximated nicely by a straight line. We then consider several variations, in which the appropriate choice of approximating function is a higher degree polynomial, an exponential function, or the reciprocal of a polynomial. The choice depends to a large extent on the general characteristics of the data.

For data to be approximated by a straight line, we wish to find the best function $f(x) = ax + b$ that approximates the data. In order to find the coefficients a and b, we must define what we mean by the "best fit" of a function to some data. Of course, we want to minimize the difference between the data points and the points on our approximating function, in some sense. The most common method is to minimize the sum of the squares of the differences between the given data values y_i and the computed function values $f_i = ax_i + b$. Another approach, known as total least squares, minimizes the distance from each data point to the straight line, where distance is measured perpendicular to the line, not in the vertical direction. This leads to a much more difficult mathematical problem, which is beyond the scope of our discussion.

9.1.1 Linear Least Squares Approximation

Example 9.1 Linear Approximation to Four Points

Consider the data $(1, 2.1)$, $(2, 2.9)$, $(5, 6.1)$, and $(7, 8.3)$, as shown in Fig. 9.3.

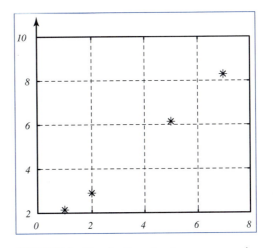

FIGURE 9.3 Data for linear least squares example.

If we approximate the data by the straight line $f(x) = 0.9x + 1.4$, as shown in Fig. 9.4, the squared errors are as follows:

$$\text{At } x_1 = 1: \quad f(1) = 2.3, \quad y_1 = 2.1, \quad e_1 = (2.3 - 2.1)^2 = 0.04;$$

$$\text{At } x_2 = 2: \quad f(2) = 3.2, \quad y_2 = 2.9, \quad e_2 = (3.2 - 2.9)^2 = 0.09;$$

$$\text{At } x_3 = 5: \quad f(5) = 5.9, \quad y_3 = 6.1, \quad e_3 = (5.9 - 6.1)^2 = 0.04;$$

$$\text{At } x_4 = 7: \quad f(7) = 7.7, \quad y_4 = 8.3, \quad e_4 = (7.7 - 8.3)^2 = 0.36.$$

The total squared error is $0.04 + 0.09 + 0.04 + 0.36 = 0.53$. By finding better values for the coefficients of the straight line, we can make this number smaller.

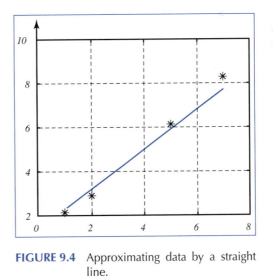

FIGURE 9.4 Approximating data by a straight line.

Let us consider a systematic way of finding the coefficients of the "best fit" straight line to approximate data; we illustrate the process for four data points.

The best coefficients for the straight line are those that minimize the total-squared-error function

$$E = [f(x_1) - y_1]^2 \quad + [f(x_2) - y_2]^2 \quad + [f(x_3) - y_3]^2 \quad + [f(x_4) - y_4]^2$$
$$= [ax_1 + b - y_1]^2 + [ax_2 + b - y_2]^2 + [ax_3 + b - y_3]^2 + [ax_4 + b - y_4]^2.$$

The minimum of a function of several variables (two in this case, the coefficients a and b) occurs when the partial derivatives of the function with respect to each of the variables are equal to zero. Here, we have the system of equations $\dfrac{\partial E}{\partial a} = 0$ and $\dfrac{\partial E}{\partial b} = 0$.

The solution depends on several quantities that can be computed from the data. The required four summations can be denoted as

$$S_{xx} = \sum_{i=1}^{4} x_i^2, \quad S_x = \sum_{i=1}^{4} x_i, \quad S_{xy} = \sum_{i=1}^{4} x_i y_i, \quad S_y = \sum_{i=1}^{4} y_i.$$

The unknowns (a and b) can be found from the following system of equations, known as the normal equations:

$$aS_{xx} + bS_x = S_{xy},$$
$$aS_x + b(4) = S_y.$$

The solution to the system of equations is

$$a = \frac{4S_{xy} - S_x S_y}{4S_{xx} - S_x S_x}, \quad b = \frac{S_{xx} S_y - S_{xy} S_x}{4S_{xx} - S_x S_x}.$$

The MATLAB function Lin_LS (x, y) gives the linear least squares approximation to the data in arrays **x** and **y**.

MATLAB Function for Linear Least Squares Approximation

```
function s = Lin_LS(x, y)
% linear regression function,
% input x and y as row or column vectors
% (they are converted to column form if necessary)
m = length(x);   x = x(:);  y = y(:);
sx = sum(x);  sy = sum(y);
sxx = sum(x.*x);  sxy = sum(x.*y);
a = ( m*sxy - sx*sy) / (m*sxx - sx^2)
b = ( sxx*sy - sxy*sx) / (m*sxx - sx^2)
table = [x    y       (a*x+b)         (y - (a*x+b))];
disp('        x         y          (a*x+b)      (y - (a*x+b))')
disp(table), err = sum(table( : , 4) .^ 2)
s(1) = a;   s(2) = b;
```

Example 9.2 Least Squares Straight Line to Fit Four Data Points

For our previous example with the data points $(1, 2.1), (2, 2.9), (5, 6.1),$ and $(7, 8.3),$ the system of equations for a and b is

$$79a + 15b = 96.5,$$

$$15a + 4b = 19.4.$$

The solution is $a = 1.0440, b = 0.9352.$

Using the preceding MATLAB function, Table 9.2 gives the difference between the data and the computed values. The total squared error is

$$d_1^2 + d_2^2 + d_3^2 + d_4^2 = 0.0360.$$

Figure 9.5 shows the plot of the linear least squares line with the data.

Table 9.2 Linear least squares straight line

x_i	y_i	$ax_i + b$	$d_i = y_i - ax_i - b$
1	2.1	1.9791	0.1209
2	2.9	3.0231	−0.1231
5	6.1	6.1549	−0.0549
7	8.3	8.2429	0.0571

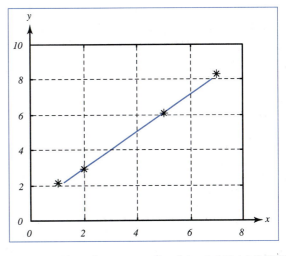

FIGURE 9.5   Linear least squares line $f(x) = 1.044x + 0.9352.$

Example 9.3 Noisy Straight-Line Data

Let us revisit the data introduced in Example 8.9:

$$\mathbf{x} = [0.00 \quad 0.20 \quad 0.80 \quad 1.00 \quad 1.20 \quad 1.90 \quad 2.00 \quad 2.10 \quad 2.95 \quad 3.00],$$
$$\mathbf{y} = [0.01 \quad 0.22 \quad 0.76 \quad 1.03 \quad 1.18 \quad 1.94 \quad 2.01 \quad 2.08 \quad 2.90 \quad 2.95].$$

Using the MATLAB function for linear least squares approximation, we find that

$$a = 0.9839, \qquad b = 0.0174.$$

In other words, the linear function that best fits the data (in the least squares sense) is

$$y(x) = 0.9839x + 0.0174.$$

The data values (x_i and y_i), computed function values $y(x_i)$, and actual difference at each x_i are shown in Table 9.3. The line is plotted in Fig. 9.6.

Table 9.3 Data and linear fit for noisy straight line

x_i	y_i	$ax_i + b$	$d_i = y_i - ax_i - b$
0.00	0.01	0.0174	−0.0074
0.20	0.22	0.2142	0.0058
0.80	0.76	0.8045	−0.0445
1.00	1.03	1.0013	0.0287
1.20	1.18	1.1981	−0.0181
1.90	1.94	1.8868	0.0532
2.00	2.01	1.9852	0.0248
2.10	2.08	2.0836	−0.0036
2.95	2.90	2.9199	−0.0199
3.00	2.95	2.9691	−0.0191

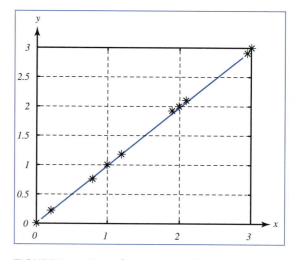

FIGURE 9.6 Linear least squares line and data for noisy straight line.

Discussion

We now consider in a little more detail how the normal equations for linear least square approximation arise, illustrating the derivation for four arbitrary data points, namely, $(x_1, y_1), (x_2, y_2), (x_3, y_3), (x_4, y_4)$, that we wish to approximate by the linear function $f(x) = ax + b$. We want to find those values of a and b that minimize the total squared error E over the data points; that is, we have

$$E = [f(x_1) - y_1]^2 + [f(x_2) - y_2]^2 + [f(x_3) - y_3]^2 + [f(x_2) - y_4]^2$$
$$= [ax_1 + b - y_1]^2 + [ax_2 + b - y_2]^2 + [ax_3 + b - y_3]^2 + [ax_4 + b - y_4]^2.$$

Setting $\dfrac{\partial E}{\partial a} = 0$ and $\dfrac{\partial E}{\partial b} = 0$ gives

$$[ax_1 + b - y_1]x_1 + [ax_2 + b - y_2]x_2 + [ax_3 + b - y_3]x_3 + [ax_4 + b - y_4]x_4 = 0,$$

and

$$[ax_1 + b - y_1] + [ax_2 + b - y_2] + [ax_3 + b - y_3] + [ax_4 + b - y_4] = 0,$$

Simplifying gives

$$a[x_1^2 + x_2^2 + x_3^2 + x_4^2] + b[x_1 + x_2 + x_3 + x_4] = x_1 y_1 + x_2 y_2 + x_3 y_3 + x_4 y_4,$$

and

$$a[x_1 + x_2 + x_3 + x_4] + b[1 + 1 + 1 + 1] = y_1 + y_2 + y_3 + y_4.$$

We see that no matter how many data points we have, if we want a straight line to minimize the error in the y-coordinate, we get two equations in two unknowns. In general form, the equations are

$$a \sum_{i=1}^{n} x_i^2 + b \sum_{i=1}^{n} x_i = \sum_{i=1}^{n} x_i y_i,$$

$$a \sum_{i=1}^{n} x_i + b \sum_{i=1}^{n} 1 = \sum_{i=1}^{n} y_i.$$

Of course, $\sum_{i=1}^{n} 1 = n$, so there are only four summations that must be calculated. For simplicity, they can be denoted as

$$S_{xx} = \sum_{i=1}^{n} x_i^2, \quad S_x = \sum_{i=1}^{n} x_i, \quad S_{xy} = \sum_{i=1}^{n} x_i y_i, \quad S_y = \sum_{i=1}^{n} y_i.$$

The solution of the system of equations (the normal equations) is

$$a = \frac{nS_{xy} - S_x S_y}{nS_{xx} - S_x S_x}, \quad b = \frac{S_{xx} S_y - S_{xy} S_x}{nS_{xx} - S_x S_x}.$$

9.1.2 Quadratic Least Squares Approximation

Using the same approach as before, let us now approximate our data with a quadratic function $f(x) = ax^2 + bx + c$. The error function is

$$E = \sum_{i=1}^{n} [f(x_i) - y_1]^2.$$

By equating the partial derivatives of E with respect to a, b, and c to zero, we obtain the normal equations for a, b, and c:

$$a \sum_{i=1}^{n} x_i^4 + b \sum_{i=1}^{n} x_i^3 + c \sum_{i=1}^{n} x_i^2 = \sum_{i=1}^{n} x_i^2 y_i,$$

$$a \sum_{i=1}^{n} x_i^3 + b \sum_{i=1}^{n} x_i^2 + c \sum_{i=1}^{n} x_i = \sum_{i=1}^{n} x_i y_i,$$

$$a \sum_{i=1}^{n} x_i^2 + b \sum_{i=1}^{n} x_i + c[n] = \sum_{i=1}^{n} y_i.$$

The required summations are computed and the resulting system solved in the next MATLAB program.

MATLAB Function for Quadratic Least Squares Approximation

```
function z = Quad_LS(x,y)
% quadratic regression, input x and y as row or column vectors
n = length(x);   x = x(:);   y = y(:);
sx  = sum(x);      sx2 = sum(x.^2);
sx3 = sum(x.^3); sx4 = sum(x.^4);
sy = sum(y);       sxy = sum(x.* y);
sx2y = sum(x.*x.*y);
  A = [     sx4          sx3          sx2,
            sx3          sx2          sx,
            sx2          sx           n]
r = [sx2y       sxy        sy]'
z = A\r;
a = z(1),        b = z(2),        c = z(3)
table = [x     y    (a*x.^2 + b*x + c)    (y - (a*x.^2 + b*x + c))];
disp('  x      y    (a*x.^2 + b*x + c)    (y - (a*x.^2 + b*x + c))')
disp(table)
err = sum(table( : , 4) .^ 2)
```

Example 9.4 Chemical Reaction Data

Consider again the product data from a simple chemical reaction (see Chapter 8), shown in Table 9.4.

The normal equations to find the quadratic least squares polynomial can be written as $\mathbf{Ax} = \mathbf{b}$, with

$$\mathbf{A} = \begin{bmatrix} 22.125 & 12.500 & 7.500 \\ 12.500 & 7.500 & 5.000 \\ 7.500 & 5.000 & 5.000 \end{bmatrix} \quad \text{and} \quad \mathbf{b} = \begin{bmatrix} 2.20 \\ 1.41 \\ 1.05 \end{bmatrix}.$$

The least squares quadratic function for these points is

$$p(x) = -0.1086x^2 + 0.3611x + 0.0117.$$

The data points, corresponding approximations from $p(x)$, and differences are presented in Table 9.4. The data and the least squares parabola are shown in Fig. 9.7. The total squared error is 0.0012.

Table 9.4 Data and least squares quadratic approximation for chemical reaction data.

x_i	y_i	p_i	$d_i = y_i - p_i$
0.0000	0.0000	0.0117	−0.0117
0.5000	0.1900	0.1651	0.0249
1.0000	0.2600	0.2643	−0.0043
1.5000	0.2900	0.3091	−0.0191
2.0000	0.3100	0.2997	0.0103

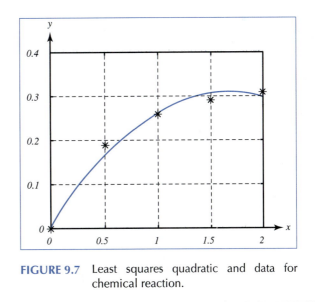

FIGURE 9.7 Least squares quadratic and data for chemical reaction.

Example 9.5 Gompertz Growth Curve

Consider the problem of fitting a quadratic function to data generated from the Gompertz growth curve, $y = \exp(-2\exp(-x))$. The vectors

$$\mathbf{x} = \begin{bmatrix} 0 & 1 & 2 & 3 & 4 & 5 & 6 \end{bmatrix},$$

$$\mathbf{y} = \begin{bmatrix} 0.135 & 0.479 & 0.763 & 0.905 & 0.964 & 0.987 & 0.995 \end{bmatrix}.$$

are input to the MATLAB function Quad_LS. The linear system for the coefficients is

$$\begin{bmatrix} 2275 & 441 & 91 \\ 441 & 91 & 21 \\ 91 & 21 & 7 \end{bmatrix} \begin{bmatrix} z_1 \\ z_2 \\ z_3 \end{bmatrix} = \begin{bmatrix} 87.5895 \\ 19.4801 \\ 5.2283 \end{bmatrix}.$$

The data, approximations, and errors are listed in Table 9.5. The total squared error is 0.0047. The least squares parabola is shown, together with the data, in Fig. 9.8.

$$p(x) = -0.0375x^2 + 0.3605x + 0.1528$$

Table 9.5 Least squares parabola and data for Gompertz growth curve.

x_i	y_i	p_i	d_i
0.0000	0.1353	0.1528	−0.0174
1.0000	0.4791	0.4758	0.0033
2.0000	0.7629	0.7238	0.0390
3.0000	0.9052	0.8969	0.0083
4.0000	0.9640	0.9949	−0.0309
5.0000	0.9866	1.0180	−0.0314
6.0000	0.9951	0.9661	0.0290

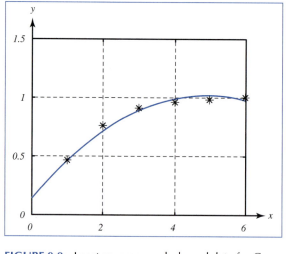

FIGURE 9.8 Least squares parabola and data for Gompertz growth curve.

Example 9.6 Oil Reservoir

Let us consider the problem of finding the least squares quadratic function to approximate a subset of the experimental data introduced in Example 9-A. The data represent the relationship between pressure x and reaction rate y for an oil reservoir modeling problem are shown in Table 9.6.

Using the MATLAB function for quadratic least squares, we find that the normal equations are $\mathbf{Az} = \mathbf{b}$, with

$$\mathbf{A} = \begin{bmatrix} 1668.9 & 360.3 & 82.8 \\ 360.3 & 82.8 & 21.3 \\ 82.8 & 21.3 & 7.0 \end{bmatrix} \quad \text{and} \quad \mathbf{b} = \begin{bmatrix} 130.3413 \\ 42.4743 \\ 21.0000 \end{bmatrix}$$

The solution is $\mathbf{z} = [9.0748, -3.3833, 0.3582]$, so the desired quadratic function is

$$p(x) = 0.3582x^2 - 3.3833x + 9.0748.$$

The total squared error is $E = \sum_{i=1}^{n} [d_i]^2 = 0.8110$.

Table 9.6 lists the data, approximations, and errors for this problem. The data and the least squares parabola are plotted in Fig. 9.9.

Table 9.6 Data and least squares parabola for oil reservoir example.

x_i	y_i	p_i	d_i
5.4350	1.0000	1.2664	−0.2664
4.6350	1.2800	1.0877	0.1923
3.8350	1.7000	1.3674	0.3326
3.0350	2.2000	2.1056	0.0944
2.3250	2.9700	3.1447	−0.1747
1.4350	4.3500	4.9573	−0.6073
0.6350	7.5000	7.0708	0.4292

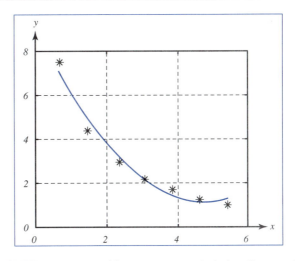

FIGURE 9.9 Data and least squares parabola for oil reservoir.

Discussion

For n data points, $(x_1, y_1), \ldots, (x_n, y_n)$ we wish to minimize

$$E = [a(x_1)^2 + b(x_1) + c - y_1]^2 + \ldots + [a(x_n)^2 + b(x_n) + c - y_n]^2.$$

Setting $\dfrac{\partial E}{\partial a} = 0$ gives

$$[a(x_1)^2 + b(x_1) + c - y_1](x_1)^2 + \ldots + [a(x_n)^2 + b(x_n) + c - y_n](x_n)^2 = 0,$$

and similarly, setting $\dfrac{\partial E}{\partial b} = 0$ yields

$$[a(x_1)^2 + b(x_1) + c - y_1](x_1) + \ldots + [a(x_n)^2 + b(x_n) + c - y_n](x_n) = 0,$$

while setting $\dfrac{\partial E}{\partial c} = 0$ gives

$$[a(x_1)^2 + b(x_1) + c - y_1] + \ldots + [a(x_n)^2 + b(x_n) + c - y_n] = 0.$$

These equations simplify to

$$a \sum_{i=1}^{n} x_i^4 + b \sum_{i=1}^{n} x_i^3 + b \sum_{i=1}^{n} x_i^2 = \sum_{i=1}^{n} x_i^2 y_i,$$

$$a \sum_{i=1}^{n} x_i^3 + b \sum_{i=1}^{n} x_i^2 + c \sum_{i=1}^{n} x_i = \sum_{i=1}^{n} x_i y_i,$$

and

$$a \sum_{i=1}^{n} x_i^2 + b \sum_{i=1}^{n} x_i + c[n] = \sum_{i=1}^{n} y_i.$$

9.1.3 Cubic Least Squares Approximation

Proceeding in a manner analogous to that of quadratic least squares approximation, we find that the system of linear equations to determine the coefficients for the "best fit" cubic function

$$f(x) = ax^3 + bx^2 + cx + d$$

is

$$a\sum_{i=1}^{n} x_i^6 + b\sum_{i=1}^{n} x_i^5 + c\sum_{i=1}^{n} x_i^4 + d\sum_{i=1}^{n} x_i^3 = \sum_{i=1}^{n} x_i^3 y_i,$$

$$a\sum_{i=1}^{n} x_i^5 + b\sum_{i=1}^{n} x_i^4 + c\sum_{i=1}^{n} x_i^3 + d\sum_{i=1}^{n} x_i^2 = \sum_{i=1}^{n} x_i^2 y_i,$$

$$a\sum_{i=1}^{n} x_i^4 + b\sum_{i=1}^{n} x_i^3 + c\sum_{i=1}^{n} x_i^2 + d\sum_{i=1}^{n} x_i = \sum_{i=1}^{n} x_i y_i,$$

$$a\sum_{i=1}^{n} x_i^3 + b\sum_{i=1}^{n} x_i^2 + c\sum_{i=1}^{n} x_i + d\sum_{i=1}^{n} 1 = \sum_{i=1}^{n} y_i.$$

MATLAB Function for Cubic Least Squares Approximation

```
function z = Cubic_LS(x,y)
% cubic regression, input x and y as row or column vectors
 n = length(x);      x = x(:);   y = y(:);
 sx = sum(x);        sx2 = sum(x .^2);
 sx3 = sum(x .^3);   sx4 = sum(x .^4);
 sx5 = sum(x .^5);   sx6 = sum(x .^6);
 sy = sum(y);        syx = sum(y.* x);
 syx2 = sum(y.*x.^2); syx3 = sum(y.*x.^3);
 A = [     sx6     sx5     sx4     sx3
           sx5     sx4     sx3     sx2
           sx4     sx3     sx2     sx,
           sx3     sx2     sx      n]
 r = [syx3    syx2     syx      sy]'
 z = A\r;
 a = z(1);      b = z(2);     c = z(3);     d = z(4);
 p = a*x.^3 + b*x.^2 + c*x + d;
 table = [x    y    p    (y - p)];
 disp('  x       y    p(x) = a x^3 + b x^2 + c x + d y - p(x)')
 disp(table)
 err = sum(table( : , 4) .^ 2)
```

Example 9.7 Cubic Least Squares

The data introduced in Example 9-B look like they might be approximated reasonably by a cubic equation. Using the preceding MATLAB function for cubic least squares, we find that the linear system for the coefficients is $\mathbf{Az} = \mathbf{r}$, with

$$\mathbf{A} = \begin{bmatrix} 2.6259 & 0.0000 & 3.1328 & 0.0 \\ 0.0000 & 3.1328 & 0.0000 & 4.4 \\ 3.1328 & 0.0000 & 4.4000 & 0.0 \\ 0.0000 & 4.4000 & 0.0000 & 11.0 \end{bmatrix} \quad \text{and} \quad \mathbf{r} = \begin{bmatrix} 1.5226 \\ 2.2000 \\ 2.2800 \\ 5.5000 \end{bmatrix}.$$

The least squares cubic function is

$$p(x) = ax^3 + bx^2 + cx + d,$$

with the computed coefficients:

$$a = -0.2550, \quad b = 0.0000, \quad c = 0.6997, \quad d = 0.5$$

The data, approximated function values, and differences are shown in Table 9.7. The data and the cubic function are plotted in Fig. 9.10. The total squared error is 0.000646.

Table 9.7   Cubic least squares data and approximated values

x	y	$p(x)$	$y - p(x)$
−1.0	0.05	0.0552	−0.0052
−0.8	0.08	0.0708	0.0092
−0.6	0.14	0.1352	0.0048
−0.4	0.23	0.2364	−0.0064
−0.2	0.35	0.3621	−0.0121
0	0.50	0.5000	−0.0000
0.2	0.65	0.6379	0.0121
0.4	0.77	0.7636	0.0064
0.6	0.86	0.8648	−0.0048
0.8	0.92	0.9292	−0.0092
1.0	0.95	0.9448	0.0052

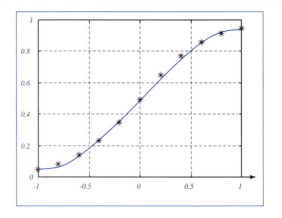

FIGURE 9.10   Data and cubic least squares function.

Example 9.8 Cubic Least Squares, Continued

We now consider the cubic approximation function found by using only a portion of the data in Example 9-B—specifically, the data on the interval $[0, 1]$. The linear system of equations for the coefficients is $\mathbf{Az} = \mathbf{r}$, with

$$\mathbf{A} = \begin{bmatrix} 1.3130 & 1.4160 & 1.5664 & 1.8 \\ 1.4160 & 1.5664 & 1.8000 & 2.2 \\ 1.5664 & 1.8000 & 2.2000 & 3.0 \\ 1.8000 & 2.2000 & 3.0000 & 6.0 \end{bmatrix}$$

and

$$\mathbf{r} = \begin{bmatrix} 1.6613 \\ 1.9976 \\ 2.6400 \\ 4.6500 \end{bmatrix}$$

The cubic approximation function is $p(x) = ax^3 + bx^2 + cx + d$, with

$$a = 0.00, \quad b = -0.375, \quad c = 0.825, \quad d = 0.500$$

The resulting function is actually a quadratic for this data, which is quite different than what we found in Example 9.7. The total squared error is computed by MATLAB to be 6.8902e-30, so we have essentially a perfect fit, on $[0, 1]$.

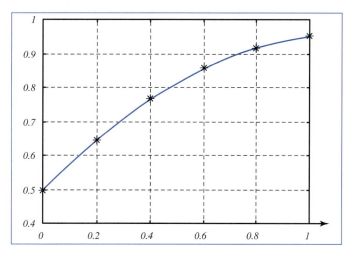

FIGURE 9.11 Cubic least squares approximation on $[0, 1]$.

The coefficient matrix for this example has a condition number of 8358, which indicates that the problem is very ill conditioned.

We illustrate the use of higher order polynomial least squares in Section 9.4, using MATLAB's built-in functions.

9.1.4 Least Squares Approximation for Other Functional Forms

If the data are best fit by an exponential function, it is convenient instead to fit the logarithm of the data by a straight line. This gives a very close approximation to the best fit exponential. (The natural logarithm is denoted log in MATLAB). The following MATLAB function performs the transformation on the data, finds the linear least squares fit to the logarithmic data, and displays the data, approximating function value, and difference in a table. The function also plots the data and the approximating exponential function.

MATLAB Function for Linear Least Squares Fit to Log y

```
function s = Log_Linear_LS(x,y)
m = length(x) ;
yy = log(y)
sx = sum(x);
sy = sum(yy);
sxx = sum(x.^2);
sxy = sum(x .* yy);
a = ( m * sxy - sx * sy) / (m *sxx - sx^2)
b = ( sxx * sy - sxy * sx) / (m * sxx - sx^2)
table = [x      y      exp(a*x+b)      (y - exp(a*x+b))]
err = sum(table(:,4) .^ 2)
plot(x, y,'r*', x, exp(a*x+b), 'b-')
```

We illustrate the use of the function Log_Linear_LS in the next example.

Example 9.9 Oil Reservoir Data

Consider the data introduced in Example 9-A. We find an approximating function of the form $y = \exp(ax + b)$ by finding the linear least squares fit to $\log(y)$. The transformed function values are

$$\mathbf{yy} = \log(y) = [0 \quad 0.2469 \quad 0.5306 \quad 0.7885 \quad 1.0886 \quad 1.4702 \quad 2.0149]'.$$

The computed coefficients are $a = -0.4060$ and $b = 2.1146$. The results are summarized in Table 9.8 and illustrated in Figures 9.12 and 9.13. The total squared error for the linear approximation and the logarithm of the data is 0.0538; the total squared error for the exponential function and the original data is 71.4017.

Table 9.8 Data and best fit exponential for oil reservoir

x_i	$\log y_i$	$ax_i + b$	d_i	y_i	$\exp(ax_i + b)$	e_i
5.435	0.0000	−0.0922	0.0922	1.00	0.9120	0.0880
4.635	0.2469	0.2327	0.0142	1.28	1.2619	0.0181
3.835	0.5306	0.5575	0.0269	1.70	1.7463	−0.0463
3.035	0.7885	0.8823	−0.0938	2.20	2.4165	−0.2165
2.325	1.0886	1.1706	−0.0820	2.97	3.2239	−0.2539
1.435	1.4702	1.5320	−0.0618	4.35	4.6272	−0.2772
0.635	2.0149	1.8568	0.1581	7.50	6.4030	1.0970

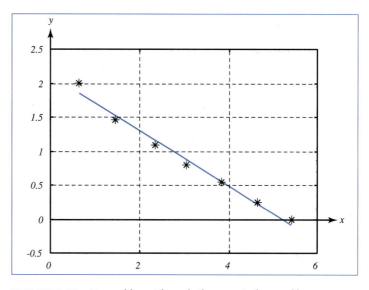

FIGURE 9.12   Natural logarithm of oil reservoir data and least squares straight line.

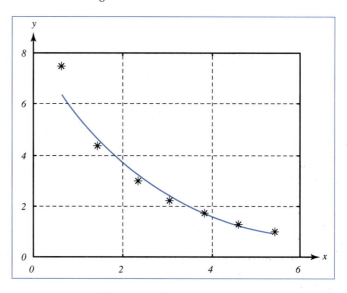

FIGURE 9.13   Oil reservoir data and exponential equation from linear least squares fit to log(y_i).

Transformations of the original data may be helpful in other settings also. For example, if the data seem to describe an inverse relation, it may be appropriate to perform a least squares approximation to the reciprocal of the original data.

Example 9.10 Least-Squares Approximation of a Reciprocal Relation

The plot (see Fig. 9.14) of the following data suggests that they could be fit by a function of the form $y = 1/(ax + b)$:

$$\mathbf{x} = \begin{bmatrix} 0 & 0.5 & 1 & 1.5 & 2 \end{bmatrix},$$
$$\mathbf{y} = \begin{bmatrix} 1.00 & 0.50 & 0.30 & 0.20 & 0.20 \end{bmatrix}.$$

To find such a function, we consider the reciprocal of the original data and perform a linear least squares approximation to the data given by x and $z = 1/y = [1.00\ 2.00\ 3.3333\ 5.00\ 5.00]$. The computed coefficients are $a = 2.2$ and $b = 1.0667$. Figure 9.14 shows the data and the linear least squares fit to the reciprocal of the data.

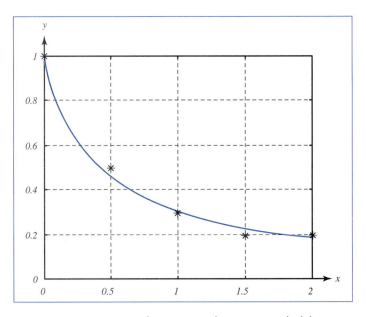

FIGURE 9.14 Linear least squares fit to reciprocal of data.

Example 9.11 Light Intensity

The following data on the intensity of light as a function of the distance from the light source were obtained from measurments in a classroom experiment:

$$\mathbf{d} = \begin{bmatrix} 30 & 35 & 40 & 45 & 50 & 55 & 60 & 65 & 70 & 75 \end{bmatrix}$$
$$\mathbf{i} = \begin{bmatrix} 0.85 & 0.67 & 0.52 & 0.42 & 0.34 & 0.28 & 0.24 & 0.21 & 0.18 & 0.15 \end{bmatrix}.$$

The inverse nature of the relationship is evident from a plot of the data (see Fig. 9.15). We thus consider several least squares approximations to the reciprocal of the data.

Figure 9.15 illustrates the linear least squares fit (dashed) and the quadratic least squares fit (solid) to the reciprocal of the data. The agreement between the data and the computed function,

$$z = \frac{1}{0.0013d^2 - 0.0208d + 0.6161},$$

is quite good.

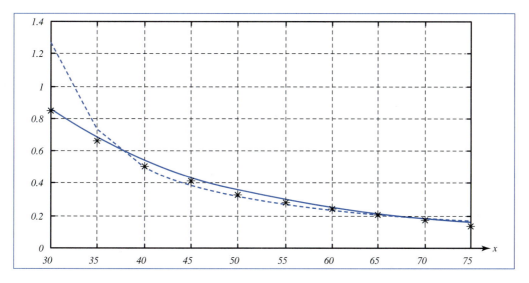

FIGURE 9.15 Linear and quadratic least squares fit to reciprocal of light-intensity data.

9.2 CONTINUOUS LEAST SQUARES

Suppose that instead of just knowing the value of the function we wish to approximate at some specific points, we know the exact value of the function for all points in an interval—say, for all x in $[0, 1]$. We can then find the best fit linear, quadratic, or other given form of function, by minimizing the error over the entire interval. The summations are replaced by the corresponding integrals. To approximate a given function $s(x)$ with a quadratic function $p(x) = ax^2 + bx + c$ on the interval $[0, 1]$, we wish to minimize

$$E = \int_0^1 [ax^2 + bx + c - s(x)]^2 \, dx.$$

The resulting equations for a, b, and c are

$$\frac{a}{5} + \frac{b}{4} + \frac{c}{3} = \int_0^1 x^2 s(x)\, dx,$$

$$\frac{a}{4} + \frac{b}{3} + \frac{c}{2} = \int_0^1 x s(x)\, dx,$$

$$\frac{a}{3} + \frac{b}{2} + c = \int_0^1 s(x)\, dx.$$

To approximate a given function $s(x)$ with a quadratic function $p(x) = ax^2 + bx + c$ on the interval $[-1, 1]$, we wish to minimize

$$E = \int_{-1}^1 [ax^2 + bx + c - s(x)]^2\, dx.$$

The resulting equations for a, b, and c are

$$\frac{2}{5} a + 0 + \frac{2}{3} c = \int_{-1}^1 x^2 s(x)\, dx,$$

$$0 + \frac{2}{3} b + 0 = \int_{-1}^1 x s(x)\, dx,$$

$$\frac{2}{3} a + 0 + 2c = \int_{-1}^1 s(x)\, dx.$$

Example 9.12 Continuous Least Squares

To find the continuous least squares quadratic approximation to the exponential function on $[-1, 1]$, we have the coefficient matrix

$$\mathbf{A} = \begin{bmatrix} 2/5 & 0 & 2/3 \\ 0 & 2/3 & 0 \\ 2/3 & 0 & 2 \end{bmatrix}.$$

To find the right-hand side of the linear system, we use the following results from calculus:

$$\int x^2 e^x\, dx = x^2 e^x - 2 \int x e^x\, dx = x^2 e^x - 2(x e^x - e^x) = e^x(x^2 - 2x + 2);$$

$$\int x e^x\, dx = x^2 e^x - e^x;$$

$$\int e^x\, dx = e^x.$$

Then

$$\int_{-1}^1 x^2 e^x\, dx = e - \frac{5}{e} \approx 0.8789$$

$$\int_{-1}^1 x e^x\, dx = \frac{2}{e} \approx 0.7358,$$

and

$$\int_{-1}^{1} e^x \, dx = e - \frac{1}{e} \approx 2.3504.$$

Thus, the right-hand side of the system is $\mathbf{r} = [0.8789 \quad 0.7358 \quad 2.3504]'$, and solving the linear system gives $\mathbf{z} = [0.5368 \quad 1.1037 \quad 0.9963]'$. Figure 9.16 shows the exponential function (blue-solid), the quadratic approximation $p = 0.5368x^2 + 1.1037x + 0.9963$ (black-dashed), and the Taylor polynomial for the exponential function, $t(x) = 0.5x^2 + x + 1$ (black-dotted).

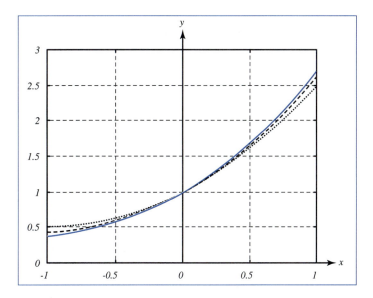

FIGURE 9.16 Exponential function, least squares approximation, and Taylor polynomial.

Discussion

We wish to minimize $E = \int_{0}^{1} [ax^2 + bx + c - s(x)]^2 \, dx.$

Setting $\dfrac{\partial E}{\partial a} = 0$ gives

$$\int_{0}^{1} x^2 [ax^2 + bx + c - s(x)] \, dx = 0,$$

$$a \int_{0}^{1} x^4 \, dx + b \int_{0}^{1} x^3 \, dx + c \int_{0}^{1} x^2 \, dx = \int_{0}^{1} x^2 s(x) \, dx,$$

$$\frac{1}{5} a + \frac{1}{4} b + \frac{1}{3} c = \int_{0}^{1} x^2 s(x) \, dx.$$

Setting $\dfrac{\partial E}{\partial b} = 0$ gives

$$\int_0^1 x[ax^2 + bx + c - s(x)] \, dx = 0,$$

$$a \int_0^1 x^3 \, dx + b \int_0^1 x^2 \, dx + c \int_0^1 x \, dx = \int_0^1 xs(x) \, dx,$$

$$\frac{1}{4}a + \frac{1}{3}b + \frac{1}{2} = \int_0^1 xs(x) \, dx.$$

And setting $\dfrac{\partial E}{\partial c} = 0$ gives

$$\int_0^1 [ax^2 + bx + c - s(x)] \, dx = 0,$$

$$a \int_0^1 x^2 \, dx + b \int_0^1 x \, dx + c \int_0^1 dx = \int_0^1 s(x) \, dx,$$

$$\frac{1}{3}a + \frac{1}{2}b + c = \int_0^1 s(x) \, dx.$$

The coefficient matrix is the three-by-three Hilbert matrix, which is notoriously ill conditioned. If we continue this approach with higher degree polynomial approximations, we find that the coefficient matrix is the correspondingly larger Hilbert matrix. The larger the Hilbert matrix, the worse is the conditioning. The computations for continuous least squares approximation on $[-1, 1]$ are completely analogous. Here, the coefficient matrix is not as ill conditioned as the Hilbert matrix, but its conditioning does become increasingly worse for higher order polynomials.

To utilize continuous least squares for higher degree polynomials, it is better to use a basis of polynomials that are orthogonal on the interval over which the approximation is desired. In addition to reducing the computational difficulties encountered in solving a linear system with an ill-conditioned coefficient matrix, the use of orthogonal polynomials allows us to progress easily from a lower degree approximation to the next higher degree polynomial.

9.2.1 Continuous Least Squares with Orthogonal Polynomials

We say that a set of functions $\{f_0, f_1, f_2, \dots, f_n\}$ is linearly independent on the interval $[a, b]$ if a linear combination of the functions is the zero function only if all of the coefficients are zero. In other words, if $c_0 f_0(x) + c_1 f_1(x) + c_2 f_2(x) + \dots + c_n f_n(x) = 0$ for all x in $[a, b]$, then $c_0 = c_1 = c_2 = \dots = c_n = 0$. The functions $f_0 = 1$, $f_1 = x$, $f_2 = x^2, \dots, f_n = x^n$, are linearly independent on any interval $[a, b]$, but in fact, any set of functions $\{p_0, p_1, p_2, \dots, p_n\}$, where p_j is a polynomial of degree j, is linearly independent. Another important set of linearly independent functions, which we will use in the next chapter, is the set of trigonometric functions $\{1, \sin(x), \cos(x), \sin(2x), \cos(2x), \dots, \sin(nx), \cos(nx)\}$.

The set of functions $\{f_0, f_1, f_2, \ldots, f_n\}$ is said to be orthogonal on $[a, b]$ if

$$\int_a^b f_i(x)f_j(x)\,dx = \begin{cases} 0 & \text{if } i \neq j \\ d_j > 0 & \text{if } i = j \end{cases}.$$

A more general concept of orthogonality includes a weighting function w in the integral, but we restrict our investigations to the case where $w = 1$.

If the functions are orthogonal and $d_j = 1$ for all j, the functions are called *orthonormal*.

9.2.2 Gram–Schmidt Process

We now show how we can construct a sequence of polynomials that are orthogonal on the interval $[a, b]$. For $n = 0, 1, 2, \ldots$, we require that

1. p_n be a polynomial of degree n,

2. $\displaystyle\int_a^b p_n(x)p_m(x)\,dx = 0$ if $n \neq m$,

3. $\displaystyle\int_a^b p_n(x)p_n(x)\,dx = 1$.

4. the coefficient of x^n in p_n be positive.

We start by taking $p_0(x) = c > 0$.

To satisfy condition 3, we must have

$$\int_a^b c^2\,dx = 1 \Rightarrow (b - a)c^2 = 1, \text{ so } c = \frac{1}{\sqrt{b - a}}.$$

To construct $p_1(x)$, we begin by letting $q_1(x) = x + c_{1,0}p_0$.

We first require that $q_1(x)$ be orthogonal to p_0:

$$\int_a^b p_0(x + c_{1,0}p_0)\,dx = 0 \Rightarrow \int_a^b xp_0\,dx + c_{1,0}\int_a^b p_0 p_0\,dx = 0.$$

Since $\displaystyle\int_a^b p_0 p_0\,dx = 1$, we have, by construction

$$c_{1,0} = -\int_a^b xp_0\,dx.$$

With this choice of $c_{1,0}$, $q_1(x) = x + c_{1,0}p_0$ is orthogonal to p_0.

To satisfy condition 3, we normalize $q_1(x)$ to get

$$p_1(x) = \frac{q_1(x)}{\displaystyle\int_a^b q_1(x)q_1(x)\,dx}.$$

To construct $p_2(x)$, we begin by letting $q_2(x) = x^2 + c_{2,1}\,p_1(x) + c_{2,0}\,p_0(x)$.

We first require that $q_2(x)$ be orthogonal to $p_1(x)$:

$$\int_a^b p_1(x)(x^2 + c_{2,1}p_1(x) + c_{2,0}p_0(x))\,dx = 0 \Rightarrow$$

$$\int_a^b x^2 p_1(x)\,dx + c_{2,1}\int_a^b p_1(x)p_1(x)\,dx + c_{2,0}\int_a^b p_1(x)\,p_0(x)\,dx = 0.$$

Because p_1 is orthogonal to p_0, the third integral is zero; the second integral evaluates to one, so we have

$$c_{2,1} = -\int_a^b x^2 p_1(x)\,dx.$$

Similarly, we require that $q_2(x)$ be orthogonal to $p_0(x)$:

$$\int_a^b p_0(x)(x^2 + c_{2,1}p_1(x) + c_{2,0}p_0(x))\,dx = 0 \Rightarrow$$

$$\int_a^b x^2 p_0(x)\,dx + c_{2,1}\int_a^b p_0(x)p_1(x)\,dx + c_{2,0}\int_a^b p_0(x)p_0(x)\,dx = 0.$$

And before, since p_1 is orthogonal to p_0, the second integral is zero and the third integral is one, so we have

$$c_{2,0} = -\int_a^b x^2 p_0(x)\,dx.$$

We complete this step by normalizing $q_2(x)$ to form $p_2(x)$:

$$p_2(x) = \frac{q_2(x)}{\displaystyle\int_a^b q_2(x)q_2(x)\,dx}.$$

The process continues in the same manner, as we construct each higher degree polynomial in turn. The polynomial $p_n(x)$ is formed from

$$q_n(x) = x^n + c_{n,0}p_0(x) + c_{n,1}p_1(x) + \ldots + c_{n,n-1}p_{n-1}(x),$$

by normalization. (The coefficients $c_{n,0}, \ldots, c_{n,n-1}$ are found so that $q_n(x)$ is orthogonal to each of the previously generated polynomials.)

9.2.3 Legendre Polynomials

Although the difficulties with forming and solving a linear system of equations for the coefficients of the continuous least squares approximation problem are most severe on $[0, 1]$, the situation is not good on any other finite interval. The most convenient interval for finding a continuous least squares approximating function using orthogonal polynomials is $[-1, 1]$. A function of x defined on any finite interval $a \le x \le b$ can be transformed to a function of t defined for $-1 \le t \le 1$ by the change of variables $x = \dfrac{b-a}{2}t + \dfrac{b+a}{2}$.

The functions known as *Legendre polynomials* form an orthogonal set on $[-1, 1]$; they are useful for continuous least squares function approximation on a finite interval (transformed, if necessary, to $[-1, 1]$). We will encounter them again in Chapter 11 when we discuss Gaussian quadrature. We list the first few Legendre polynomials here, normalized so that the coefficient of the leading term is unity:

$$P_0(x) = 1, \qquad\qquad P_1(x) = x,$$

$$P_2(x) = x^2 - \frac{1}{3}, \qquad\qquad P_3(x) = x^3 - \frac{3}{5}x,$$

$$P_4(x) = x^4 - \frac{6}{7}x^2 - \frac{3}{35}, \quad P_5(x) = x^5 - \frac{10}{9}x^3 - \frac{5}{21}.$$

For this normalization, we have

$$\int_{-1}^{1} P_0(x)P_0(x)\, dx = 2,$$

$$\int_{-1}^{1} P_1(x)P_1(x)\, dx = \int_{-1}^{1} x^2\, dx = \frac{2}{3},$$

$$\int_{-1}^{1} P_2(x)P_2(x)\, dx = \int_{-1}^{1} x^4 - \frac{2}{3}x^2 + \frac{1}{9}\, dx = \frac{8}{45}.$$

An alternative definition of the Legendre polynomials gives

$$p_0(x) = 1 \quad \text{and} \quad p_n(x) = \frac{(-1)^n}{2^n n!} \frac{d^n}{dx^n}[(1 - x^2)^n], \quad \text{for } n \geq 1.$$

The polynomials defined in this way are normalized so that $p_n(1) = 1$ and

$$\int_{-1}^{1} p_n(x)p_n(x)\, dx = \frac{2}{2n + 1}.$$

We turn our attention next to illustrating how the property of orthogonality can be used for finding a continuous least squares approximation function.

9.2.4 Least Squares Approximation with Legendre Polynomials

To find the quadratic least squares approximation to $f(x)$ on the interval $[-1, 1]$ in terms of the Legendre polynomials, we need to determine the coefficients c_0, c_1, c_2 that minimize

$$E = \int_{-1}^{1} [c_0 P_0(x) + c_1 P_1(x) + c_2 P_2(x) - f(x)]^2\, dx.$$

The normal equations are found as before, by setting the partial derivatives of E equal to zero. Setting $\frac{\partial E}{\partial c_0} = 0$ yields

$$\int_{-1}^{1} 2[c_0 P_0(x) + c_1 P_1(x) + c_2 P_2(x) - f(x)]P_0(x)\, dx = 0,$$

which, after dividing out the common factor of 2, expands to give

$$\int_{-1}^{1} c_0 P_0(x) P_0(x)\, dx + \int_{-1}^{1} c_1 P_1(x) P_0(x)\, dx$$

$$+ \int_{-1}^{1} c_2 P_2(x) P_0(x)\, dx = \int_{-1}^{1} f(x) P_0(x)\, dx.$$

Now, because the Legendre polynomials are orthogonal, the second and third integrals on the left side of the equations are zero, so we have

$$c_0 \int_{-1}^{1} P_0(x) P_0(x)\, dx = \int_{-1}^{1} f(x) P_0(x)\, dx.$$

In a similar manner, the equations formed by setting $\dfrac{\partial E}{\partial c_1} = 0$ and $\dfrac{\partial E}{\partial c_2} = 0$ give

$$c_1 \int_{-1}^{1} P_1(x) P_1(x)\, dx = \int_{-1}^{1} f(x) P_1(x)\, dx$$

and

$$c_2 \int_{-1}^{1} P_2(x) P_2(x)\, dx = \int_{-1}^{1} f(x) P_2(x)\, dx.$$

The integrations on the left were performed earlier; the result is

$$c_0 = \frac{1}{2} \int_{-1}^{1} f(x) P_0(x)\, dx, \quad c_1 = \frac{3}{2} \int_{-1}^{1} f(x) P_1(x)\, dx, \quad c_2 = \frac{45}{8} \int_{-1}^{1} f(x) P_2(x)\, dx.$$

If we wish a higher order approximation, we have only to compute the additional integrals; this is in contrast to the system-of-linear-equations approach, in which the entire problem must be reworked if the order of the approximating polynomial is to be increased.

Example 9.13 Least Squares Approximation Using Legendre Polynomials

To find the quadratic least squares approximation to $f(x) = e^x$ on the interval $[-1, 1]$ in terms of the Legendre polynomials, we write

$$g(x) = c_0\, P_0(x) + c_1 P_1(x) + c_2 P_2(x),$$

where $P_0(x) = 1$, $P_1(x) = x$, and $P_2(x) = x^2 - \dfrac{1}{3}$. We determine the coefficients c_0, c_1, and c_2 as described previously. We will need the values of the following integrals, found in Example 9.12:

$$\int_{-1}^{1} x^2 e^x\, dx \approx 0.8789, \qquad \int_{-1}^{1} x e^x\, dx \approx 0.7358, \qquad \int_{-1}^{1} e^x\, dx \approx 2.3504;$$

$$c_0 = \frac{1}{2} \int_{-1}^{1} e^x P_0(x)\, dx = \frac{1}{2} \int_{-1}^{1} e^x\, dx \approx \frac{1}{2}(2.3504) \approx 1.1752;$$

$$c_1 = \frac{3}{2} \int_{-1}^{1} f(x) P_1(x)\, dx = \frac{3}{2} \int_{-1}^{1} xe^x\, dx \approx \frac{3}{2}(0.7358) \approx 1.1037;$$

$$c_2 = \frac{45}{8} \int_{-1}^{1} f(x) P_2(x)\, dx = \frac{45}{8} \int_{-1}^{1} e^x\left(x^2 - \frac{1}{3}\right) dx = \approx 0.5368.$$

We thus have $g(x) = c_0 P_0(x) + c_1 P_1(x) + c_2 P_2(x) = c_0 + c_1 x + c_2\left(x^2 - \frac{1}{3}\right)$; the plot of $g(x)$ and $f(x)$ shown in Fig. 9.17 strongly suggests what we could verify algebraically if we desire, namely, that this is the same quadratic approximation function as that found in Example 9.12.

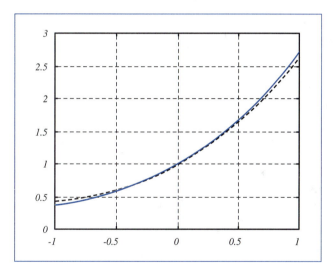

FIGURE 9.17 Exponential and least squares approximation function.

9.3 FUNCTION APPROXIMATION AT A POINT

In this section, we consider two important methods of approximating a function $f(x)$ at a specific value of x: Taylor polynomial approximation and Padé rational function approximation.

9.3.1 Taylor Approximation

For a polynomial approximation, the Taylor polynomial (of degree n) gives the highest possible order of contact between the function and the polynomial. That is, the Taylor polynomial agrees with the function and its first n derivatives at $x = a$; the formula is

$$p(x) = f(a) + f'(a)(x - a) + \frac{f''(a)}{2!}(x - a)^2 + \ldots + \frac{f^{(n)}(a)}{n!}(x - a)^n.$$

The Taylor polynomial was included in Example 9.12 for comparison with the exponential function and its least squares approximation.

The Taylor polynomial is widely used in the analysis of numerical techniques. (It was introduced in Chapter 1 in the discussion of truncation error.) The error incurred in using $p(x)$ to approximate the actual value of the function $f(x)$ is given by

$$\frac{f^{(n+1)}(\eta)}{(n+1)!}(x - a)^{n+1},$$

for some η between x and a. Taylor's formula is derived in most standard calculus texts.

We next present a method for finding a rational function that agrees with the values of a given function and its derivatives at a specific point.

9.3.2 Padé Approximation

Padé approximation seeks to approximate a function $f(x)$ by finding a rational function that fits the values of the function and its derivatives at a given point x_0. The desired rational function has the form

$$r(x) = \frac{p_m(x)}{q_n(x)} = \frac{a_m x^m + \ldots + a_0}{b_n x^n + \ldots + b_0}.$$

We assume that $f(x_0), f'(x_0), \ldots, f^{(k)}(x_0)$ are given for $k = m + n$, and, in the discussion that follows, we assume, for simplicity, that $x_0 = 0$.

Let $t(x)$ be the Taylor polynomial for the given function $f(x)$. We write

$$t(x) = c_k x^k + \ldots + c_2 x^2 + c_1 x + c_0.$$

In terms of information about the derivatives of $f(x)$, we have $c_k = \dfrac{f^{(k)}(0)}{k!}$. We want $r(x)$ to be the same as $t(x)$—to have the same value at $x = 0$ and the same derivatives of all orders up to, and including, $k = m + n$. Our basic approach is to use the equivalence of the expressions

$$t(x) = r(x) = \frac{p_m(x)}{q_n(x)} \quad \text{and} \quad q_n(x)t(x) = p_m(x).$$

Thus, we work with the relationship

$$(b_n x^n + \ldots + b_0)(c_k x^k + \ldots + c_2 x^2 + c_1 x + c_0) = a_m x^m + \ldots + a_0. \tag{9.1}$$

We begin by considering the requirement that $q_n(0)t(0) = p_m(0)$; this gives

$$b_0 c_0 = a_0.$$

The preceding rational function $r(x)$ is determined only up to a scale factor. We choose $b_0 = 1$. With this convention, we have an equation for determining a_0.

Taking the first derivative of eq. (9.1), we find that

$$(b_n x^n + \ldots + b_0)(c_1 + 2c_2 x + \ldots + kc_k x^{k-1}) + (nb_n x^{n-1} + \ldots + b_1)(c_0 + c_1 x + \ldots + c_k x^k)$$
$$= ma_m x^{m-1} + \ldots + a_1.$$

We require that this equation be satisfied when $x = 0$, so we have $b_0 c_1 + b_1 c_0 = a_1$. This gives us an equation relating the unknown coefficients a_1 and b_1 to the known quantities c_0, c_1, and b_0. We rewrite the equation as

$$a_1 - b_1 c_0 = c_1.$$

To continue the process of finding higher derivatives of the product $g(x) = q(x)t(x)$ efficiently, we note the following formulae, which can be found by repeated applications of the product rule:

$$g'(x) = q(x)t'(x) + q'(x)t(x),$$
$$g''(x) = q(x)t''(x) + 2q'(x)t'(x) + q''(x)t(x),$$
$$\vdots$$
$$g^{(n)}(x) = \sum_{j=0}^{n} \frac{n!}{j!(n-j)!} q^{(j)}(x)t^{(n-j)}(x).$$

We are interested in the value of the derivative at $x = 0$, so we have

$$g^{(n)}(0) = \sum_{j=0}^{n} \frac{n!}{j!(n-j)!} q^{(j)}(0)t^{(n-j)}(0).$$

Taking the second derivative of eq. (9.1) at $x = 0$, we find that

$$q(0)t''(0) + 2q'(0)t'(0) + q''(0)t(0) = p''(0).$$

Substituting in the values of these derivatives (in terms of the coefficients), we have

$$2b_0 c_2 + 2b_1 c_1 + 2b_2 c_0 = 2a_2,$$

or, after simplifying,

$$a_2 - b_1 c_1 - b_2 c_0 = c_2.$$

We continue in this manner until all required equations are specified (depending on the degrees of the polynomials p_m and q_n).

If we define $a_j = 0$ for $j > m$ and $b_j = 0$ for $j > n$, then the unknowns a_k and b_k can be found from the general relationship

$$a_k - \sum_{i=0}^{k-1} c_i b_{k-i} = c_k, \qquad k = 0, 1, \ldots, m + n.$$

Example 9.14 Padé Approximation of the Runge Function

The values of the Runge function

$$f(x) = \frac{1}{1 + 25x^2}$$

and its first three derivatives at $x = 0$ are

$$f(0) = 1, \quad f'(0) = 0, \quad f''(0) = -50, \quad f'''(0) = 0.$$

The Taylor polynomial of the function (at $x = 0$) is

$$t(x) = 1 + 0x - 25x^2 + 0x^3.$$

We seek a rational-function representation, using $k = 3$, $m = 1$, and $n = 2$. That is, we want

$$r(x) = \frac{a_1 x + a_0}{b_2 x^2 + b_1 x + 1}.$$

For $k = 3$, the linear system of equations is

$$a_0 = c_0,$$
$$a_1 - c_0 b_1 = c_1,$$
$$a_2 - c_0 b_2 - c_1 b_1 = c_2,$$
$$a_3 - c_0 b_3 - c_1 b_2 - c_2 b_1 = c_3.$$

In this particular problem, we have

$$c_0 = 1, c_1 = 0, c_2 = -25, \text{ and } c_3 = 1.$$

The solution of the linear system is found to be

$$a_0 = 1, a_1 = b_1 = 0, b_2 = 25,$$

so

$$r(x) = \frac{1}{1 + 25x^2}.$$

Thus, the Padé approximation has given us the exact representation of the Runge function in this example.

In general, errors for Padé approximates are less when the degree of the numerator and the degree of the denominator are the same or when the degree of the numerator is one larger than the denominator. (See Ralston & Rabinowitz, 1978, p. 295.) It is desired to have the polynomial in the denominator of sufficiently high degree to account for any poles that the original function may have in the complex plane (since such poles are often the cause of the difficulties that arise with polynomial interpolation, even when our interest is restricted to real variables only.)

9.4   USING MATLAB's FUNCTIONS

The MATLAB function polyfit finds the coefficients of the polynomial of specified degree that best fits a set of data, in a least squares sense. The function is called as [p,S] = polyfit(x,y,n), where **x** and **y** are vectors containing the data and n is the degree of the polynomial desired. The function returns the coefficients of the polynomial in the vector **p**. The returned structure S can be used with the function polyval to obtain error bounds on the predictions. As described in the comments at the beginning of the function polyfit, if the errors in **y** are independent random variables, normally distributed with constant variance, polyval will produce error bounds that contain at least 50% of the predictions.

The polynomial coefficients are a row vector by convention, with the coefficient of the highest power of the independent variable given first.

```
% script for polynomial regression
% generate data
x = -3 : 0.1 : 3;
y1 = sin(x);
y2 = cos(2*x);
yy = y1 + y2;
y = 0.01*round(100*yy);
% find least squares 6th-degree polynomial to fit data
z = polyfit(x,y,6)
% evaluate the polynomial
p = polyval(z,x);
% plot the polynomial
plot(x,p)
hold on
% plot the data
plot(x,y,'+')
hold off
```

Example 9.15 Higher Order Least Squares Polynomial Approximation

Let us illustrate the use of higher degree polynomials for a least squares fit to data. The data are illustrated in Figs. 9.18–9.20, together with the fourth-, fifth-, and sixth-degree polynomials found by MATLAB's built-in function polyfit. The polynomial is evaluated using the function polyval. The data are generated and fitted with a sixth-degree polynomial using the previous MATLAB script.

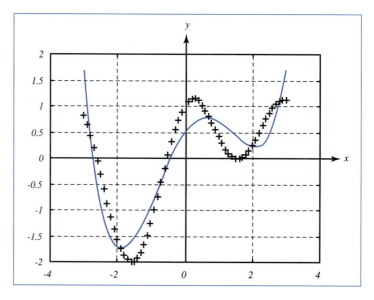

FIGURE 9.18 Data and fourth-degree polynomial approximation.

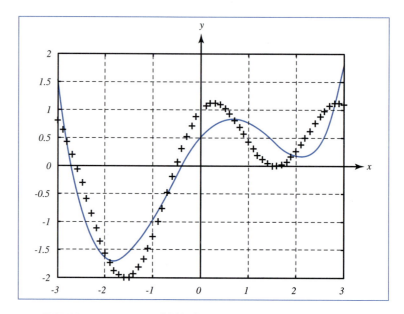

FIGURE 9.19 Data and fifth-degree polynomial approximation.

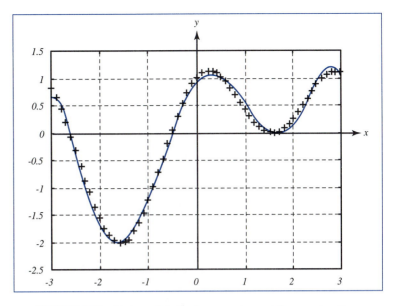

FIGURE 9.20 Data and sixth-degree polynomial approximation.

Using fewer data points (10 rather than 61), so that it is more convenient to display the data explicitly, yields

$$\mathbf{x} = [-3 \quad -2.33 \quad -1.67 \quad -1 \quad -0.33 \quad 0.33 \quad 1 \quad 1.67 \quad 2.33 \quad 3],$$

$$\mathbf{y} = [0.82 \quad -0.77 \quad -1.98 \quad -1.26 \quad 0.46 \quad 1.11 \quad 0.43 \quad 0.01 \quad 0.68 \quad 1.1].$$

The coefficients are computed as

$$\mathbf{z} = [-0.02412 \quad 0.0057 \quad 0.398 \quad -0.156 \quad -1.627 \quad 0.991 \quad 0.9199],$$

so the approximation polynomial is

$$p(x) = -0.02412x^6 + 0.0057x^5 + 0.398x^4 - 0.156x^3 - 1.627x^2 + 0.991x + 0.9199.$$

SUMMARY

Linear least squares approximation: To approximate the data

$$x = [x_1, x_2, \ldots, x_n], \quad y = [y_1, y_2, \ldots, y_n],$$

the coefficients a and b for the straight line $y = ax + b$ can be found from the system of equations

$$aS_{xx} + bS_x = S_{xy},$$
$$aS_x + bn = S_y,$$

where

$$S_{xx} = \sum_{i=1}^{n} x_i^2, \quad S_x = \sum_{i=1}^{n} x_i, \quad S_{xy} = \sum_{i=1}^{n} x_i y_i, \quad \text{and} \quad S_y = \sum_{i=1}^{n} y_i.$$

The solution to the system of equations is

$$a = \frac{nS_{xy} - S_x S_y}{nS_{xx} - S_x S_x}, \quad b = \frac{S_{xx} S_y - S_{xy} S_x}{nS_{xx} - S_x S_x}.$$

Quadratic least squares approximation: The coefficients of the quadratic function $f(x) = ax^2 + bx + c$ that best fit the data are found by solving the system of equations

$$a \sum_{i=1}^{n} x_i^4 + b \sum_{i-1}^{n} x_i^3 + c \sum_{i=1}^{n} x_i^2 = \sum_{i=1}^{n} x_i^2 y_i,$$

$$a \sum_{i=1}^{n} x_i^3 + b \sum_{i-1}^{n} x_i^2 + c \sum_{i=1}^{n} x_i = \sum_{i=1}^{n} x_i y_i,$$

$$a \sum_{i=1}^{n} x_i^2 + b \sum_{i=1}^{n} x_i + c[n] = \sum_{i=1}^{n} y_i.$$

To find an **exponential function approximation** of the form $y = \exp(ax + b)$ to fit a set of data, we first find a linear fit to the logarithm of the data.

Continuous least squares approximation may be obtained in an analogous manner, with integrals replacing summations. To approximate a given function $s(x)$ with a quadratic function $p(x) = ax^2 + bx + c$ on the interval $[-1, 1]$, the resulting equations for a, b, and c are

$$\frac{2}{5} a + 0 + \frac{2}{3} c = \int_{-1}^{1} x^2 s(x) \, dx,$$

$$0 + \frac{2}{3} b + 0 = \int_{-1}^{1} x s(x) \, dx,$$

$$\frac{2}{3} a + 0 + 2c = \int_{-1}^{1} s(x) \, dx.$$

Since the coefficient matrix of the linear system is ill conditioned, it is better to use orthogonal polynomials, rather than powers of x, as the basis functions for the approximation. The quadratic least squares approximation to $f(x)$ in terms of the Legendre polynomials (on $[-1, 1]$) is $c_0 P_0(x) + c_1 P_1(x) + c_2 P_2(x)$; the coefficients are

$$c_0 = \frac{1}{2} \int_{-1}^{1} f(x) P_0(x) \, dx, \quad c_1 = \frac{3}{2} \int_{-1}^{1} f(x) P_1(x) \, dx, \quad c_2 = \frac{45}{8} \int_{-1}^{1} f(x) P_2(x) \, dx.$$

Padé Approximation:

The desired rational function has the form

$$r(x) = \frac{p_m(x)}{q_n(x)} = \frac{a_m x^m + \ldots + a_0}{b_n x^n + \ldots + b_0}.$$

Given $f(0), f'(0), \ldots, f^{(k)}(0)$ for $k = m + n$, the Taylor polynomial for $f(x)$ is

$$t(x) = c_k x^k + \ldots + c_2 x^2 + c_1 x + c_0, \quad \text{where } c_k = \frac{f^{(k)}(0)}{k!}.$$

We choose $b_0 = 1$; then the coefficients are

$$b_0 c_0 = a_0,$$
$$a_1 - b_1 c_0 = c_1,$$
$$a_2 - b_1 c_1 - b_2 c_0 = c_2.$$

If we define $a_j = 0$ for $j > m$ and $b_j = 0$ for $j > n$, then the unknowns a_k and b_k can be found from the general relationship

$$a_k - \sum_{i=0}^{k-1} c_i b_{k-i} = c_k, \quad k = 0, 1, \ldots, m + n.$$

SUGGESTIONS FOR FURTHER READING

The following are standard texts on approximation of functions:

Achieser, N. I., *Theory of Approximation*, Dover, New York, 1993.

Cheney, E. W., *Introduction to Approximation Theory*, McGraw-Hill, New York, 1966.

Rivlin, T. J., *An Introduction to the Approximation of Functions*, Dover, New York, 1981. (Originally published by Blaisdell Publishing, 1969.)

Timan, A. F. , C. J. Hyman, and N. I. Achieser, *Theory of Approximation*, Dover, New York, 1993.

For further discussion of Padé approximation, see the following two sources:

Jensen, J. A., and J. H. Rowland, *Methods of Computation*, Scott, Foresman and Company, Glenview, IL, 1975.

Brezinski, C., *History of Continued Fractions and Padé Approximants*, Springer-Verlag, Berlin, 1991.

PRACTICE THE TECHNIQUES

For Problems P9.1–P9.5, find the linear least squares approximation to the points.

P9.1 $x = [1 \quad 2 \quad 3]$,
$y = [1 \quad 4 \quad 8]$.

P9.2 $x = [1 \quad 4 \quad 9]$,
$y = [1 \quad 2 \quad 3]$.

P9.3 $x = [4\ 9\ 16]$,
$y = [2\ 3\ 4]$.

P9.4 $x = [-1 \quad 0 \quad 1]$,
$y = [-2 \quad 3 \quad -2]$.

P9.5 $x = [0 \quad 1 \quad 2]$,
$y = [1 \quad 2 \quad 4]$.

For Problems P9.6–P9.15:
  a. Find the linear least squares approximation to the data.
  b. Find the quadratic least squares approximation to the data.

P9.6 $x = [0 \quad 1 \quad 2 \quad 4]$,
$y = [1 \quad 1 \quad 2 \quad 5]$.

P9.7 $x = [-1 \quad 0 \quad 1 \quad 2]$,
$y = [1/3 \quad 1 \quad 3 \quad 9]$.

P9.8 $x = [0 \quad 1 \quad 2 \quad 3]$,
$y = [1 \quad 2 \quad 4 \quad 8]$.

P9.9 $x = [0 \quad 1 \quad 2 \quad 3]$,
$y = [1 \quad 2 \quad 4 \quad 8]$.

P9.10 $x = [-1 \quad 0 \quad 1 \quad 2]$,
$y = [0 \quad 1 \quad 2 \quad 9]$.

P9.11 $x = [0 \quad 2/3 \quad 1 \quad 2]$,
$y = [2 \quad -2 \quad -1 \quad -1/2]$.

P9.12 $x = [0 \quad 2/3 \quad 1 \quad 2]$,
$y = [4 \quad -4 \quad -2 \quad -1/2]$.

P9.13 $x = [0 \quad 2/3 \quad 1 \quad 2]$,
$y = [4 \quad -4 \quad -3.5 \quad -0.5]$.

P9.14 $x = [1 \quad 2 \quad 3 \quad 4]$,
$y = [2 \quad 4 \quad 8 \quad 16]$.

P9.15 $x = [0 \quad 1/2 \quad 1 \quad 3/2]$,
$y = [1 \quad 2 \quad 1 \quad 0]$.

For Problems P9.16–P 9.20:
  a. Find the linear least squares approximation to the data.
  b. Find the quadratic least squares approximation to the data.
  c. Find the cubic least squares approximation to the data.

P9.16 $x = [0 \quad 1 \quad 2 \quad 3 \quad 4]$,
$y = [0 \quad 1 \quad 4 \quad 8 \quad 16]$.

P9.17 $x = [0 \quad 1 \quad 4 \quad 9 \quad 16]$,
$y = [0 \quad 1 \quad 2 \quad 3 \quad 4]$.

P9.18 $x = [-1 \quad -0.75 \quad -0.25 \quad 0.25 \quad 0.75 \quad 1]$,
$y = [0 \quad -0.7 \quad -0.7 \quad 0.7 \quad 0.7 \quad 0]$.

P9.19 $x = [-1 \quad -0.5 \quad 0.0 \quad 0.5 \quad 0.75 \quad 1]$,
$y = [0.4 \quad 0.6 \quad 1.0 \quad 1.6 \quad 2.1 \quad 2.7]$.

P9.20 $x = [0.5 \quad 0.75 \quad 1.0 \quad 1.25 \quad 1.5 \quad 1.75]$,
$y = [-0.7 \quad -0.3 \quad 0.0 \quad 0.2 \quad 0.4 \quad 0.6]$.

For Problems P9.21–P 9.25, find the linear least squares approximation to the data.

P9.21 $x = [1 \quad 2 \quad 3 \quad 4 \quad 5 \quad 6 \quad 7 \quad 8 \quad 9 \quad 10 \ ]$
$y = [6.0 \quad 9.2 \quad 13.0 \quad 14.7 \quad 19.7 \quad 21.8 \quad 22.8 \quad 29.1 \quad 30.2 \quad 32.2]$

P9.22 $x = [1 \quad 2 \quad 3 \quad 4 \quad 5 \quad 6 \quad 7 \quad 8 \quad 9 \quad 10 \ ]$
$y = [5.7 \quad 8.9 \quad 15.2 \quad 16.6 \quad 20.9 \quad 26.7 \quad 28.6 \quad 34.0 \quad 34.1 \quad 47.0]$

P9.23 $x = [\ 1 \quad 2 \quad 3 \quad 4 \quad 5 \quad 6 \quad 7 \quad 8 \quad 9 \quad 10 \ ]$
$y = [-3.3 \quad -7.1 \quad -9.8 \quad -12.3 \quad -14.0 \quad -21.4 \quad -21.3 \quad -28.6 \quad -29.0 \quad -32.8]$

P9.24 $x = [1 \quad 2 \quad 3 \quad 4 \quad 5 \quad 6 \quad 7 \quad 8 \quad 9 \quad 10 \ ]$
$y = [2.9 \quad 0.5 \quad -0.2 \quad -3.8 \quad -5.4 \quad -4.3 \quad -7.8 \quad -13.8 \quad -10.4 \quad -13.9]$

P9.25 $x = [\ 4.6 \quad 8.7 \quad 9.3 \quad 2.6 \quad 1.6 \quad 8.7 \quad 2.4 \quad 6.5 \quad 9.7 \quad 6.6]$
$y = [16.5 \quad 35.8 \quad 31.6 \quad 6.6 \quad 2.5 \quad 28.0 \quad 6.8 \quad 21.1 \quad 38.8 \quad 20.8]$

For Problems P9.26–P9.30, find the quadratic least squares approximation to the data.

P9.26 $x = [1 \quad 2 \quad 3 \quad 4 \quad 5 \quad 6 \quad 7 \quad 8 \quad 9 \quad 10 \ ]$
$y = [2.9 \quad 4.8 \quad 6.0 \quad 18.9 \quad 8.7 \quad 30.7 \quad 25.7 \quad 77.7 \quad 55.8 \quad 104.8]$

P9.27 $x = [\ 1 \quad 2 \quad 3 \quad 4 \quad 5 \quad 6 \quad 7 \quad 8 \quad 9 \quad 10 \ ]$
$y = [-0.4 \quad -4.1 \quad -7.4 \quad -21.5 \quad -21.3 \quad -45.2 \quad -44.7 \quad -62.8 \quad -80.6 \quad -96.5]$

P9.28 $x = [-4 \quad -3 \quad -2 \quad -1 \quad 0 \quad 1 \quad 2 \quad 3 \quad 4 \quad 5 \ ]$
$y = [\ 8.0 \quad 9.9 \quad 1.8 \quad 1.4 \quad 1.7 \quad 3.6 \quad 7.5 \quad 16.8 \quad 14.1 \quad 27.2]$

P9.29 $x = [-3.2 \quad -0.0 \quad -0.8 \quad 1.6 \quad 1.7 \quad 4.6 \quad -3.1 \quad -3.9 \quad 0.7 \quad 4.7]$
$y = [\ 57.7 \quad 4.4 \quad 6.4 \quad 17.6 \quad 19.6 \quad 101.6 \quad 49.8 \quad 86.2 \quad 6.7 \quad 117.1]$

P9.30 $x = [-3.8 \quad -4.3 \quad 3.5 \quad -3.2 \quad -4.7 \quad 2.3 \quad 0.4 \quad -2.2 \quad -1.3 \quad -4.9]$
$y = [-91.8 \quad -120.5 \quad -50.4 \quad -70.2 \quad -125.1 \quad -23.5 \quad -4.1 \quad -36.1 \quad -18.1 \quad -150.7]$

For Problems P9.31–P9.50, plot the data, choose an appropriate form for the least squares approximation function (linear, quadratic, cubic, exponential, reciprocal of linear, or reciprocal of quadratic), and then determine the best fit function of the chosen form.

P9.31 $x = [3.0 \quad 0.5 \quad 6.9 \quad 6.5 \quad 9.8 \quad 5.5 \quad 4.0 \quad 2.0 \quad 6.3 \quad 7.3]$
$y = [5.8 \quad -2.5 \quad 22.1 \quad 23.9 \quad 36.5 \quad 18.0 \quad 10.3 \quad 2.2 \quad 18.4 \quad 21.5]$

P9.32 $x = [\ 5.80 \quad 1.40 \quad 8.70 \quad 3.30 \quad 4.90 \quad 4.30 \quad 2.60 \quad 9.80 \quad 9.70 \quad 9.50]$
$y = [10.90 \quad 1.40 \quad 15.30 \quad 5.90 \quad 11.10 \quad 9.20 \quad 3.30 \quad 14.50 \quad 17.00 \quad 14.00]$

P9.33 $x = [-3.5 \quad -1.2 \quad -1.9 \quad -3.3 \quad 4.0 \quad -1.8 \quad 2.3 \quad -0.9 \quad -1.0 \quad 0.1]$
$y = [32.2 \quad -0.9 \quad 4.9 \quad 25.7 \quad 81.2 \quad 4.8 \quad 28.5 \quad -2.0 \quad -2.3 \quad -1.2]$

P9.34 $x = [\ -2.5 \quad 3.0 \quad 1.7 \quad -4.9 \quad 0.6 \quad -0.5 \quad 4.0 \quad -2.2 \quad -4.3 \quad -0.2]$
$y = [-20.1 \quad -21.8 \quad -6.0 \quad -65.4 \quad 0.2 \quad 0.6 \quad -41.3 \quad -15.4 \quad -56.1 \quad 0.5]$

P9.35 $x = [3.00 \quad 1.80 \quad 6.90 \quad 2.60 \quad 4.60 \quad 8.40 \quad 8.80 \quad 7.00 \quad 7.60 \quad 9.70]$
$y = [0.08 \quad 0.14 \quad 0.03 \quad 0.10 \quad 0.05 \quad 0.03 \quad 0.02 \quad 0.03 \quad 0.03 \quad 0.02]$

P9.36 $x = [4.70 \quad 2.30 \quad 3.20 \quad 7.90 \quad 6.30 \quad 6.60 \quad 5.40 \quad 9.20 \quad 7.80 \quad 3.30]$
$y = [0.13 \quad 0.33 \quad 0.18 \quad 0.10 \quad 0.13 \quad 0.07 \quad 0.13 \quad 0.08 \quad 0.08 \quad 0.17]$

P9.37 $x = [0.70 \quad 3.10 \quad 9.40 \quad 9.80 \quad 5.60 \quad 9.90 \quad 6.90 \quad 2.40 \quad 8.10 \quad 9.30]$
$y = [0.36 \quad 0.07 \quad 0.02 \quad 0.02 \quad 0.04 \quad 0.02 \quad 0.03 \quad 0.09 \quad 0.03 \quad 0.02]$

P9.38 $x = [\ 8.80 \quad 4.90 \quad 8.90 \quad 7.60 \quad 6.60 \quad 9.70 \quad 1.70 \quad 1.40 \quad 7.60 \quad 3.10]$
$y = [-0.02 \quad -0.04 \quad -0.02 \quad -0.02 \quad -0.03 \quad -0.02 \quad -0.11 \quad -0.13 \quad -0.03 \quad -0.06]$

P9.39 $x = [-0.20 \quad 0.00 \quad -2.10 \quad -4.40 \quad -2.40 \quad -3.10 \quad 4.20 \quad -3.80 \quad -4.90 \quad -1.30]$
$y = [\ 0.42 \quad 0.63 \quad 0.05 \quad 0.01 \quad 0.04 \quad 0.02 \quad 0.02 \quad 0.01 \quad 0.01 \quad 0.10]$

P9.40 $x = [4.40 \quad -0.10 \quad -4.10 \quad 1.70 \quad 0.10 \quad -2.80 \quad 2.30 \quad -4.30 \quad 4.60 \quad -2.90]$
$y = [0.02 \quad 1.23 \quad 0.07 \quad 0.08 \quad 0.70 \quad 0.18 \quad 0.05 \quad 0.04 \quad 0.01 \quad 0.14]$

P9.41 $x = [4.20 \quad 0.20 \quad -4.10 \quad 2.40 \quad -5.00 \quad 1.00 \quad 4.60 \quad -1.00 \quad 2.30 \quad 1.80]$
$y = [0.01 \quad 0.20 \quad 0.01 \quad 0.04 \quad 0.01 \quad 0.11 \quad 0.01 \quad 0.11 \quad 0.04 \quad 0.05]$

P9.42 $x = [-0.90 \quad 0.30 \quad 4.20 \quad -1.20 \quad 1.40 \quad -3.30 \quad 2.90 \quad -1.30 \quad 2.80 \quad -1.60]$
$y = [\ 1.10 \quad 1.70 \quad 6.40 \quad 0.90 \quad 2.60 \quad 0.50 \quad 4.80 \quad 0.90 \quad 4.80 \quad 0.80]$

P9.43 $x = [0.30 \quad 0.00 \quad -0.20 \quad -1.20 \quad 0.20 \quad 3.20 \quad -2.90 \quad -1.10 \quad -4.50 \quad -2.00]$
$y = [0.80 \quad 0.70 \quad 0.70 \quad 0.50 \quad 0.70 \quad 1.60 \quad 0.30 \quad 0.50 \quad .30 \quad 0.40]$

P9.44 $x = [-4.90 \quad 1.40 \quad -3.90 \quad -2.80 \quad 4.10 \quad -3.60 \quad -2.90 \quad 3.50 \quad 2.10 \quad -4.20]$
$y = [\ 0.20 \quad 1.70 \quad 0.30 \quad 0.50 \quad 3.90 \quad 0.30 \quad 0.50 \quad 3.40 \quad 2.60 \quad 0.40]$

P9.45 $x = [-2.00 \quad 1.00 \quad -3.20 \quad 2.30 \quad 0.50 \quad -3.40 \quad 4.30 \quad -3.00 \quad -4.90 \quad 1.90]$
$y = [\ 0.50 \quad 1.20 \quad 0.30 \quad 1.80 \quad 1.00 \quad 0.30 \quad 2.80 \quad 0.30 \quad 0.10 \quad 1.40]$

P9.46 $x = [\ -2.60 \quad 4.40 \quad -4.10 \quad 0.40 \quad 4.00 \quad 3.60 \quad 1.30 \quad -2.40 \quad -1.20 \quad -1.60]$
$y = [-11.70 \quad 380.40 \quad -119.20 \quad 2.80 \quad 260.70 \quad 188.90 \quad 14.00 \quad -15.40 \quad 5.10 \quad 4.60]$

P9.47 $x = [-0.40 \quad 3.30 \quad -2.00 \quad 2.10 \quad -4.30 \quad 2.50 \quad -0.30 \quad 4.40 \quad -4.90 \quad -4.50]$
$y = [-1.20 \quad 145.10 \quad -1.90 \quad 32.10 \quad -144.10 \quad 54.50 \quad -1.60 \quad 307.70 \quad -236.30 \quad -146.10]$

P9.48 $x = [\ 4.80 \quad 4.00 \quad -4.70 \quad -2.20 \quad -3.10 \quad 1.10 \quad -2.90 \quad 5.00 \quad -4.80 \quad -0.60]$
$y = [262.00 \quad 156.10 \quad -200.60 \quad -27.00 \quad -75.20 \quad 9.10 \quad -62.40 \quad 331.30 \quad -262.70 \quad -2.60]$

P9.49 $x = [\ 3.10 \quad 2.60 \quad 3.10 \quad 1.80 \quad 1.20 \quad -1.30 \quad -3.00 \quad -2.20 \quad -0.20 \quad -1.00 \ ]$
$y = [-33.90 \quad -20.00 \quad -33.70 \quad -9.70 \quad -0.40 \quad -4.90 \quad -34.50 \quad -20.80 \quad 2.20 \quad -1.60 \ ]$

P9.50 $x = [\ 1.10 \quad -1.30 \quad -3.00 \quad 4.00 \quad 4.90 \quad 4.20 \quad -1.10 \quad 1.60 \quad 0.40 \quad -2.90]$
$y = [-4.60 \quad 0.70 \quad 14.60 \quad 20.50 \quad 40.80 \quad 22.00 \quad -0.40 \quad -2.20 \quad -6.10 \quad 23.00]$

EXPLORE SOME APPLICATIONS

A9.1

The following data describe the product of a chemical reaction as a function of time:

$$t = [0.00 \quad 0.10 \quad 0.40 \quad 0.50 \quad 0.60 \quad 0.90 \quad 1.00 \quad 1.10 \quad 1.40 \quad 1.50 \quad 1.60 \quad 1.90 \quad 2.00]$$
$$y = [0.00 \quad 0.06 \quad 0.17 \quad 0.19 \quad 0.21 \quad 0.25 \quad 0.26 \quad 0.27 \quad 0.29 \quad 0.29 \quad 0.30 \quad 0.31 \quad 0.31]$$

Find a least squares approximating function for the data. Compare your function with the functions found in Examples 8.3 and 8.11, in which interpolation was used on a subset of these data.

A9.2

Use the following rounded data to find the linear relationship between C and F:

$$C = [\ 50 \quad 45 \quad 40 \quad 35 \quad 30 \quad 25 \quad 20 \quad 15 \quad 10 \quad 5 \quad 0 \quad -5 \quad -10]$$
$$F = [122 \quad 113 \quad 104 \quad 95 \quad 86 \quad 77 \quad 68 \quad 59 \quad 50 \quad 41 \quad 32 \quad 23 \quad 14]$$

A9.3

A laboratory experiment measured the height of a bouncing ball; the following data give the time and height of the peak of each bounce:

$$t = [0.43 \quad 0.989 \quad 1.462 \quad 1.892 \quad 2.279 \quad 2.623 \quad 2.924 \quad 3.182]$$
$$h = [0.428 \quad 0.308 \quad 0.239 \quad 0.19 \quad 0.153 \quad 0.121 \quad 0.097 \quad 0.079]$$

Find the best fit function of the form suggested by a plot of the data.

A9.4

According to Newton's law of cooling, the rate of change of the temperature of a cup of hot liquid (such as coffee) is proportional to the difference between the temperature and the surrounding air. The following data were obtained from a simple classroom laboratory experiment:

$t = [\ 0$	5	10	15	20	25	30	$\ldots$
35	40	45	50	55	60		$\ldots$
65	70	75	80	85	90	95];	

$d = [88.266$	75.072	66.144	60.204	54.912	50.43	46.398	$\ldots$
42.51	38.748	35.562	32.646	29.802	27.228		$\ldots$
24.906	22.602	20.514	18.678	16.626	15.006	13.584];	

Using `Log_Lin_LS`, find the coefficients in the "best fit" exponential function.

A9.5

An experiment was conducted to measure the weight of the water in a cylindrical can. The water drained out through a small hole in the bottom of the can. Find the quadratic best fit to the following data obtained from the experiment:

time (in seconds)

1.00 6.06 11.12 16.18 21.23 26.29 31.35 36.41 41.47 46.53 51.59 56.64

weight of water (in Newtons).

2.85 2.74 2.63 2.46 2.35 2.24 2.14 2.03 1.97 1.92 1.81 1.81

A9.6

An experiment that involved rolling a can up an inclined plane produced the following data for the distance of the can from the measuring device as a function of time:

$$t = [0.00 \quad 0.27 \quad 0.54 \quad 0.81 \quad 1.08 \quad 1.34 \quad 1.61 \quad 1.88 \quad 2.15 \quad 2.42 \quad 2.69 \quad 2.96 \quad 3.23 \quad 3.49 \quad 3.76 \quad 4.03 \quad 4.30 \quad 4.57 \quad 4.84]$$
$$d = [1.91 \quad 1.82 \quad 1.61 \quad 1.43 \quad 1.28 \quad 1.18 \quad 1.10 \quad 1.04 \quad 1.00 \quad 0.99 \quad 1.00 \quad 1.03 \quad 1.08 \quad 1.15 \quad 1.24 \quad 1.34 \quad 1.48 \quad 1.66 \quad 1.86]$$

Find the best fit quadratic function.

A9.7

An experiment to measure the intensity of light as a function of the distance from the source of the light produced the following data:

$$d = [\ 30 \quad 35 \quad 40 \quad 45 \quad 50 \quad 55 \quad 60 \quad 65 \quad 70 \quad 75\ ];$$
$$i = [\ 0.85 \quad 0.67 \quad 0.52 \quad 0.42 \quad 0.34 \quad 0.28 \quad 0.24 \quad 0.21 \quad 0.18 \quad 0.15\ ];$$

Find the best fit exponential function and the best fit quadratic function.

EXTEND YOUR UNDERSTANDING

U9.1 Show that the functions $P_2 = x^2 - (1/3)$ and $P_3 = x^3 - (3/5)x$ are orthogonal on $[-1,1]$ with respect to the weight function $w(x) = 1$. Are the two functions orthonormal? Why or why not?

U9.2 Use the Gram–Schmidt process to construct the first four Legendre polynomials.

U9.3 Use the Gram–Schmidt process to construct the first four polynomials that are orthonomal on the interval $[0, 4]$.

For Problems U9.4–U9.8, find the Padé approximation function with $k = 6$.

  a.   *Take $m = 2$ and $n = 4$; that is, find the best approximation function of the form*

$$\frac{a_2 x^2 + a_1 x + a_0}{b_4 x^4 + b_3 x^3 + b_2 x^2 + b_1 x + 1}.$$

  b.   *Take $m = 3$ and $n = 3$; that is, find the best approximation function of the form*

$$\frac{a_3 x^3 + a_2 x^2 + a_1 x + a_0}{b_3 x^3 + b_2 x^2 + b_1 x + 1}.$$

  c.   *Take $m = 4$ and $n = 2$; that is, find the best approximation function of the form*

$$\frac{a_4 x^4 + a_3 x^3 + a_2 x^2 + a_1 x + a_0}{b_2 x^2 + b_1 x + 1}.$$

  d.   *Compare the errors incurred in using the approximations from Parts a, b, and c on the interval $[-1, 1]$.*

U9.4 $f(x) = \sin(x)$.

U9.5 $f(x) = \cos(x)$.

U9.6 $f(x) = \tan(x)$.

U9.7 $f(x) = e^x$.

U9.8 $f(x) = \log(x + 1)$.

10

Fourier Methods

In the previous two chapters, we interpolated data by polynomials and approximated data by polynomials, exponential functions, or rational functions, depending on the general characteristics of the data. However, for periodic data, it is more appropriate to use sine and cosine functions for the approximation or interpolation.

We begin this chapter with an investigation into data approximation and interpolation using trigonometric polynomials, also known as (finite) Fourier series. The approach is the same as that discussed previously, namely, we seek to minimize the total squared error by setting the partial derivatives of the error equal to zero. The formulas for the coefficients are found by using the appropriate orthogonality results for the sine and cosine functions. The coefficients are given by sums of the form

$$a_j = \frac{2}{n} \sum_{k=0}^{n-1} x_k \cos(jt_k)$$

or

$$b_j = \frac{2}{n} \sum_{k=0}^{n-1} x_k \sin(jt_k).$$

If we form a single complex quantity, $c_j = a_j + ib_j$, these summations can be combined to give one example of the discrete Fourier transform, which maps the data x_k to the transformed data c_j.

The *fast Fourier transform* (FFT), a computationally efficient method of computing the discrete Fourier transform, has greatly increased the feasibility of using this transform for large sets of data. In Section 10.2, we introduce the FFT in its most common setting, the case in which n is a power of 2; this is called a *radix-2* FFT. The method is presented in both matrix and algebraic forms for $n = 4$, and a MATLAB function is also given. For higher powers of 2, we use MATLAB's built-in function fft.

In Section 10.3, we describe the general FFT for the case when n is not a power of 2. The process is a generalization of the algebraic approach for the radix-2 transform.

Example 10-A Waveforms for Musical Instruments

The characteristic sound of different instruments playing the same pitch can be shown by the vibrational waveform of the sound. (See Fig. 10.1.) Such periodic vibrations are often analyzed by Fourier transform methods.

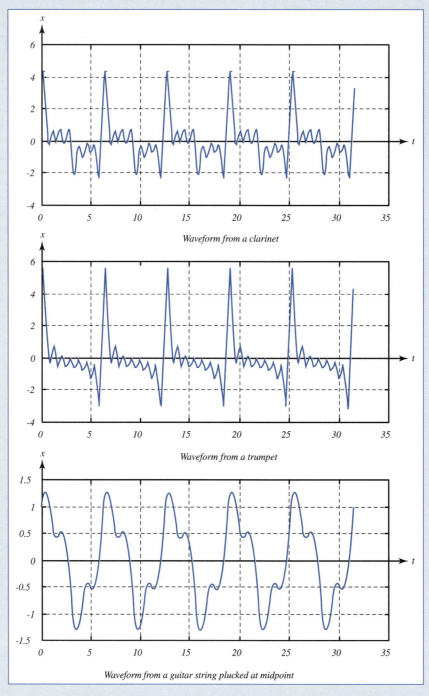

Waveform from a clarinet

Waveform from a trumpet

Waveform from a guitar string plucked at midpoint

FIGURE 10.1 Waveforms from musical instruments.

Example 10-B Geometric Figures

Fourier transforms may be used to remove angular dependence in data. Consider, for example, describing various geometric figures, centered at the origin, by measuring the distance from the origin to the boundary of the figure at certain (evenly spaced) angles. (See Fig. 10.2.) In different rotations, a square is distinguishable from a triangle or a cross.

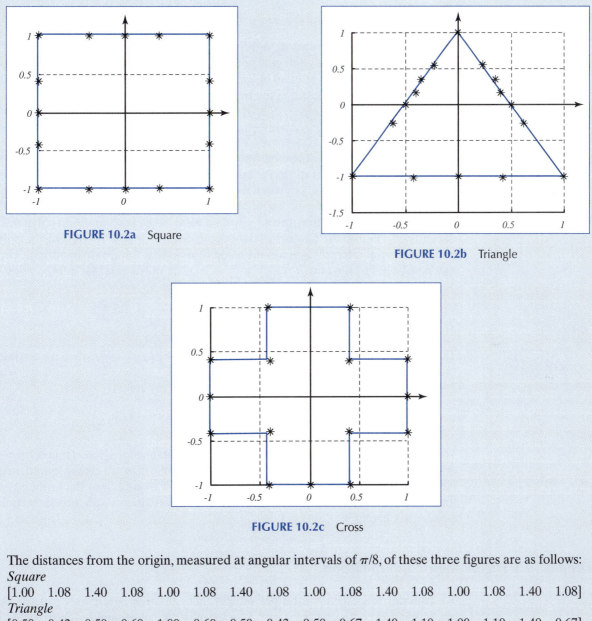

FIGURE 10.2a Square

FIGURE 10.2b Triangle

FIGURE 10.2c Cross

The distances from the origin, measured at angular intervals of $\pi/8$, of these three figures are as follows:
Square
[1.00 1.08 1.40 1.08 1.00 1.08 1.40 1.08 1.00 1.08 1.40 1.08 1.00 1.08 1.40 1.08]
Triangle
[0.50 0.43 0.50 0.60 1.00 0.60 0.50 0.43 0.50 0.67 1.40 1.10 1.00 1.10 1.40 0.67]
Cross
[1.00 1.08 0.56 1.08 1.00 1.08 0.56 1.08 1.00 1.08 0.56 1.08 1.00 1.08 0.56 1.08]

In order to approximate or interpolate a set of data using a trigonometric polynomial, i.e., a function of the form

$$f(t) = \frac{a_0}{2} + a_1 \cos t + a_2 \cos 2t + \ldots + a_m \cos mt$$
$$+ b_1 \sin t + b_2 \sin 2t + \ldots + b_m \sin mt.$$

we must find the coefficients $a_0, a_1, \ldots, a_m$, and $b_1, \ldots, b_m$. The function $f(t)$ is a trigonometric polynomial of degree m if a_m and b_m are not both zero.

We assume that the interval $[0, 2\pi)$ is divided into n equal subintervals and that we have the data values given at the points

$$t_0 = 0, \quad t_1 = \frac{2\pi}{n}, \quad t_2 = 2\frac{2\pi}{n}, \ldots, t_k = k\frac{2\pi}{n}, \ldots, t_{n-1} = (n-1)\frac{2\pi}{n}.$$

We denote the corresponding data values as $x_0, x_1, \ldots, x_{n-1}$.

The functional form for $f(t)$ is appropriate for a least squares approximation problem when $2m + 1 < n$, i.e., when we have more data points than there are coefficients to be determined.

For exact interpolation, the appropriate form of the trigonometric polynomial depends on whether the number of data points is even or odd. If n is odd, the polynomial for exact interpolation has the same form as that for approximation (except that $n = 2m + 1$). However, if n is even ($n = 2m$), the polynomial for interpolation is

$$f(t) = \frac{a_0}{2} + a_1 \cos t + a_2 \cos 2t + \ldots + \frac{a_m}{2} \cos mt$$
$$+ b_1 \sin t + b_2 \sin 2t + \ldots + b_{m-1} \sin(m-1)t.$$

The reason for the difference in functional form will be made clear when we consider the derivation of the formulas for the coefficients.

The formulas for the coefficients ($j = 0, 1, \ldots, m$) are

$$a_j = \frac{2}{n} \sum_{k=0}^{n-1} x_k \cos(j t_k), \qquad b_j = \frac{2}{n} \sum_{k=0}^{n-1} x_k \sin(j t_k).$$

We do not have to solve a linear system, since the set of functions $\{1, \cos(t), \cos(2t), \ldots, \cos(mt), \sin(t), \ldots, \sin(mt)\}$ are orthogonal as long as the data are evenly spaced on an interval of length 2π; we assume that the data are given on $[0, 2\pi)$. The formulas are found in a manner analogous to that for continuous least squares with orthogonal polynomials in Chapter 9.

Example 10.1 Trigonometric Interpolation

We consider the trigonometric polynomial that fits three data points exactly. The maximum degree we can use is $m = 1$, so we must find a_0, a_1, and b_1. The data for k, t, and x are as shown in the following table:

	$k = 0$	1	2
t	0	$\dfrac{2\pi}{3}$	$\dfrac{4\pi}{3}$
x	0	$\dfrac{8\pi^3}{27}$	$\dfrac{-8\pi^3}{27}$

Also,

$$a_0 = \frac{2}{3}\left[x_0 \cos(0t_0) + x_1 \cos(0t_1) + x_2 \cos(0t_2) = \frac{2}{3}[x_0 + x_1 + x_2] = 0,\right.$$

$$a_1 = \frac{2}{3}[x_0 \cos(t_0) + x_1 \cos(t_1) + x_2 \cos(t_2)]$$

$$= \frac{2}{3}\left[0\cos(0) + \frac{8\pi^3}{27}\cos\left(\frac{2\pi}{3}\right) + \frac{-8\pi^3}{27}\cos\left(\frac{4\pi}{3}\right)\right] = 0,$$

$$b_1 = \frac{2}{3}[x_0 \sin(t_0) + x_1 \sin(t_1) + x_2 \sin(t_2)]$$

$$= \frac{2}{3}\left[0\sin(1x_0) + \frac{8\pi^3}{27}\sin\left(\frac{2\pi}{3}\right) + \frac{-8\pi^3}{28}\sin\left(\frac{4\pi}{3}\right)\right] = \frac{16\pi^3\sqrt{3}}{81}.$$

The interpolating polynomial is $x(t) = \dfrac{16\pi^3\sqrt{3}}{81}\sin t$, shown in Fig. 10.3.

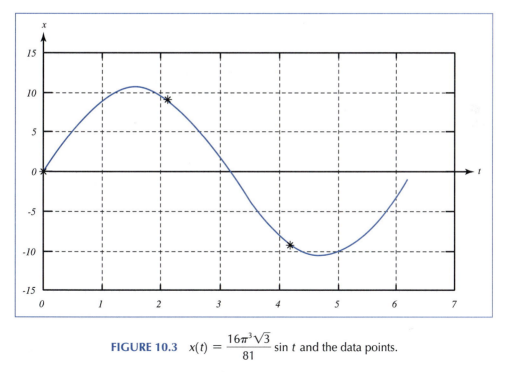

FIGURE 10.3 $x(t) = \dfrac{16\pi^3\sqrt{3}}{81}\sin t$ and the data points.

Example 10.2 Trigonometric Approximation

We seek the least squares trigonometric polynomial, with $m = 1$, for the five data points shown here:

$$k = [0 \quad 1 \quad 2 \quad 3 \quad 4 \quad]$$
$$t = [0 \quad 2\pi/5 \quad 4\pi/5 \quad 6\pi/5 \quad 8\pi/5 \quad]$$
$$x = [0 \quad 48\pi^3/125 \quad 24\pi^3/125 \quad -24\pi^3/125 \quad -48\pi^3/125]$$

The formulas for the coefficients,

$$a_0 = \frac{2}{5} \sum_{k=0}^{4} x_k, \qquad a_1 = \frac{2}{5} \sum_{k=0}^{4} x_k \cos(t_k), \qquad b_1 = \frac{2}{5} \sum_{k=0}^{4} x_k \sin(t_k),$$

make use of the following sine and cosine values

$$\cos(t_k) = [1 \quad 0.3090 \quad -0.8090 \quad -0.8090 \quad 0.3090]$$
$$\sin(t_k) = [0 \quad 0.9511 \quad 0.5878 \quad -0.5878 \quad 0.9511]$$

The coefficients are

$$a_0 = \frac{2}{5}[x_0 + x_1 + x_2 + x_3 + x_4] = 0,$$

$$a_1 = \frac{2}{5}\left[0\cos(t_0) + \frac{48\pi^3}{125}\cos(t_1) + \frac{24\pi^3}{125}\cos(t_2) + \frac{-24\pi^3}{125}\cos(t_3) + \frac{-48\pi^3}{125}\cos(t_4)\right] = 0,$$

$$b_1 = \frac{2}{5}\left[0\sin(t_0) + \frac{48\pi^3}{125}\sin(t_1) + \frac{24\pi^3}{125}\sin(t_2) + \frac{-24\pi^3}{125}\sin(t_3) + \frac{-48\pi^3}{125}\sin(t_4)\right] = 11.8584.$$

Figure 10.4 shows the approximating function.

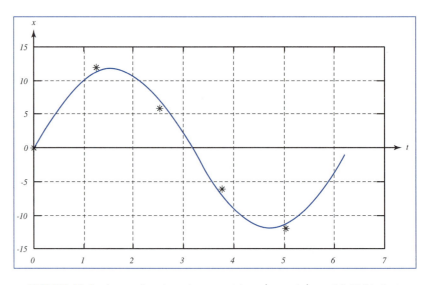

FIGURE 10.4 Approximating trigonometric polynomial $y = 11.8584 \sin t$.

The previous examples show that for more data points, we have more terms in each summation. For exact-fit trigonometric polynomials, we have as many coefficients to be determined as there are data points.

In the following MATLAB function, the coefficients a_0 and (if necessary) a_m have been divided by 2. The coefficient a_0 is treated separately to avoid having to shift indices on the vector **a**, since MATLAB does not accept an index value of zero. The data values are input as a row vector.

10.1.1 MATLAB Function for Fourier Interpolation or Approximation

```
function [a, b] = Trig_poly(x, m)
% approximate or interpolate n data points
% at t = 0, 2pi/n, . . . , 2 k pi/n, . . . , 2(n-1)pi/n
% use trigonometric polynomial of degree m, with
%      2 m + 1 < n                    for approximation
%      2 m + 1 = n  or 2 m = n        for interpolation
n = length(x);          w = 2*pi/n;
t = 0 : w : (2*pi - w);     t = t';
a = zeros(m, 1);        b = a;
% find coefficients (summation included in vector product)
for j = 1 : m
      a(j) = x*cos(j*t);
      b(j) = x*sin(j*t);
end
a = 2*a/n;              b = 2*b/n;
a0 = sum(x)/n;
if n == 2*m
      a(m) = a(m)/2;
end
% evaluate trig polynomial on [0,2*pi]
tt = 0 : 0.1 : 2*pi;
xx = a0 + a(1)*cos(tt) + b(1)*sin(tt);
for j = 2 : m
      xx = xx + a(j)*cos(j*tt) + b(j)*sin(j*tt);
end
% plot function and data
plot( tt,  xx,  t,  x,  '*')
% display coefficients, including a0 and b0 (which is 0)
a = [ a0,
          a]
b = [ 0,
          b]
```

Example 10.3 A Step Function

To illustrate the use of the foregoing MATLAB function, consider the problem of interpolating a step function with eight data points. A short script includes the data and the function call:

```
% script for Fourier example
z = [ 1  1  1  1  0  0  0  0 ]
m = 4
[a, b] = Trig_poly(z, m)
```

The output consists of the coefficients (including a_0 and b_0 as the respective first elements of the vectors **a** and **b**) and a plot of the data and the interpolation function (see Fig. 10.5):

$$a = [0.5 \quad 0.25 \quad 0 \quad 0.25 \quad 0]$$

$$b = [0 \quad 0.6036 \quad 0 \quad 0.1036 \quad 0]$$

The coefficients b_0 and b_4 are included for completeness, even though they are always zero for $n = 8$. In fact, b_0 is always zero; b_m is zero for m even.

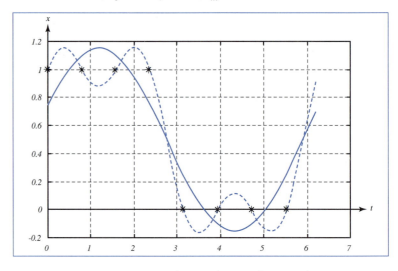

FIGURE 10.5 Trigonometric polynomial interpolation and approximation.

Since $a_4 = b_4 = 0$ in this example, it should not be surprising that the approximation function found with $m = 3$ is identical to the interpolation function. For $m = 2$, the approximation function is

$$f(t) = \frac{a_0}{2} + a_1 \cos t + \frac{a_2}{2} \cos 2t + b_1 \sin t,$$

with $a_0 = 0.5$, $a_1 = 0.25$, $a_2 = 0$, and $b_1 = 0.6036$.

10.1.2 Discussion

Derivation of Fourier Approximation and Interpolation Formulas

Fourier approximation and interpolation formulas can be derived in the same manner as polynomial and other least squares approximation formulas were in the previous chapter. However, the special properties of the sine and cosine functions at evenly spaced data points lead to simplifications that make the calculation of the coefficients more manageable.

Given n data at evenly spaced points in $[0, 2\pi)$, viz.,

$$\mathbf{t} = \left[0, \frac{2\pi}{n}, 2\frac{2\pi}{n}, \ldots, k\frac{2\pi}{n}, \ldots, (n-1)\frac{2\pi}{n} \right],$$

$$\mathbf{x} = [x_0, x_1, x_2, \ldots, \quad x_k, \ldots, \quad x_{n-1}],$$

we consider the trigonometric polynomial

$$p(t) = \frac{a_0}{2} + a_1 \cos t + a_2 \cos 2t + \ldots + a_m \cos mt + b_1 \sin t$$

$$+ b_2 \sin 2t + \ldots + b_m \sin mt$$

$$= \frac{a_0}{2} + \sum_{j=1}^{m} a_j \cos(jt_k) + \sum_{j=1}^{m} b_j \sin(jt_k),$$

where $2m + 1 \leq n$. We wish to minimize

$$E = \sum_{k=0}^{n-1} \left[\frac{a_0}{2} + \sum_{j=1}^{m} a_j \cos(tj_k) + \sum_{j=1}^{m} b_j \sin(jt_k) - x_k \right]^2.$$

We proceed by setting the partial derivatives of E with respect to each of the unknown coefficients to zero. We use the index J to denote the generic coefficient a_J or b_J during this derivation, to distinguish it from the index of summation. We will return to the more common lowercase later. Because of the restriction that $2m + 1 \leq n$, we only need to consider $J \leq n/2$.

Setting $\partial E/\partial a_0 = 0$ results in

$$\sum_{k=0}^{n-1} \left[\frac{a_0}{2} + \sum_{j=1}^{m} a_j \cos(jt_k) + \sum_{j=1}^{m} b_j \sin(jt_k) - x_k \right] = 0. \qquad (10.1)$$

Setting $\partial E/\partial a_J = 0$ yields

$$\sum_{k=0}^{n-1} \left[\frac{a_0}{2} + \sum_{j=1}^{m} a_j \cos(jt_k) + \sum_{j=1}^{m} b_j \sin(jt_k) - x_k \right] \cos(Jt_k) = 0. \qquad (10.2)$$

And setting $\partial E/\partial b_J = 0$ gives

$$\sum_{k=0}^{n-1} \left[\frac{a_0}{2} + \sum_{j=1}^{m} a_j \cos(jt_k) + \sum_{j=1}^{m} b_j \sin(jt_k) - x_k \right] \sin(Jt_k) = 0. \qquad (10.3)$$

Equation (10.1) can be written as

$$\frac{n}{2}a_0 + \sum_{k=0}^{n-1}\sum_{j=1}^{m} a_j \cos(jt_k) + \sum_{k=0}^{n-1}\sum_{j=1}^{m} b_j \sin(jt_k) = \sum_{k=0}^{n-1} x_k,$$

which, after interchanging the order of the summations, becomes

$$\frac{n}{2}a_0 + \sum_{j=1}^{m} a_j \sum_{k=0}^{n-1} \cos(jt_k) + \sum_{j=1}^{m} b_j \sum_{k=0}^{n-1} \sin(jt_k) = \sum_{k=0}^{n-1} x_k.$$

However, since the data are evenly spaced, we have, for each j,

$$\sum_{k=0}^{n-1} \cos(jt_k) = 0$$

and

$$\sum_{k=0}^{n-1} \sin(jt_k) = 0,$$

so that

$$\frac{n}{2}a_0 = \sum_{k=0}^{n-1} x_k,$$

which gives

$$a_0 = \frac{2}{n}\sum_{k=0}^{n-1} x_k$$

The analysis of eqs. (10.2) and (10.3) makes use of the fact that the functions

$$1, \cos t, \cos 2t, \ldots, \cos(n-1)t, \sin t, \ldots, \sin(n-1)t$$

are orthogonal with respect to n evenly spaced data points in $[0, 2\pi)$, which gives the following results:

$$\sum_{k=0}^{n-1} \cos(Jt_k)\cos(jt_k) = \begin{cases} 0, & \text{for } j \neq J, \\ n/2, & \text{for } j = J < n/2, \\ n, & \text{for } j = J = n/2, \end{cases}$$

$$\sum_{k=0}^{n-1} \cos(Jt_k)\sin(jt_k) = 0,$$

$$\sum_{k=0}^{n-1} \sin(Jt_k)\sin(jt_k) = \begin{cases} 0, & \text{for } j \neq J, \\ n/2, & \text{for } j = J < n/2, \\ 0, & \text{for } j = J = n/2. \end{cases}$$

The summations that are equal to zero for $j \neq J$ may be verified using the following basic trigonometric identities:

$$\cos j \cos J = (\cos(j-J) + \cos(j+J))/2;$$

$$\cos j \sin J = (\sin(j+J) - \sin(j-J))/2;$$

$$\sin j \sin J = (\cos(j-J) - \cos(j+J))/2.$$

When $j = J < n/2$, we use the half-angle formulas

$$(\sin j)^2 = (1 - \cos(2j))/2 \quad \text{and} \quad (\cos j)^2 = (1 + \cos(2j))/2.$$

Finally, in the case of $j = J = n/2$ (which occurs only for the exact interpolation of an even number of data points),

$$\sum_{k=0}^{n-1} \cos^2(jt_k) = \sum_{k=0}^{n-1} \cos^2\left(\frac{n}{2} k \frac{2\pi}{n}\right) = \sum_{k=0}^{n-1} \cos^2(k\pi) = n.$$

On the other hand,

$$\sum_{k=0}^{n-1} \sin(Jt_k) \sin(jt_k) = 0,$$

since all terms in the summation involve $\sin(k\pi)$, which is zero.

We now consider eq. (10.2) in some detail; the simplification of (10.3) follows in a similar manner. Rearranging the terms in eq. (10.2) yields

$$\sum_{k=0}^{n-1} \frac{a_0}{2} \cos(Jt_k) + \sum_{k=0}^{n-1} \cos(Jt_k) \sum_{j=0}^{m} a_j \cos(jt_k)$$

$$+ \sum_{k=0}^{n-1} \cos(Jt_k) \sum_{j=0}^{m} b_j \sin(jt_k) = \sum_{k=0}^{n-1} \cos(jt_k) x_k$$

We simplify each summation on the left-hand side of the equation separately:

$$\sum_{k=0}^{n-1} \frac{a_0}{2} \cos(Jt_k) = \frac{a_0}{2} \sum_{k=0}^{n-1} \cos(Jt_k) = 0,$$

$$\sum_{k=0}^{n-1} \cos(Jt_k) \sum_{j=0}^{m} a_j \cos(jt_k) = \sum_{j=0}^{m} a_j \sum_{k=0}^{n-1} \cos(jt_k) \cos(Jt_k))$$

$$= \begin{cases} 0, & \text{for } j \neq J, \\ \dfrac{a_J n}{2}, & \text{for } j = J < n/2, \\ a_J n, & \text{for } j = J = n/2, \end{cases}$$

$$\sum_{k=0}^{n-1} \cos(Jt_k) \sum_{j=0}^{m} b_j \sin(jt_k) = \sum_{j=0}^{m} b_j \sum_{k=0}^{n-1} \sin(jt_k) \cos(Jt_k) = 0.$$

Thus, for $J < n/2$, eq. (10.2) gives us

$$\frac{n}{2} a_J = \sum_{k=0}^{n-1} \cos(Jt_k) x_k,$$

or

$$a_J = \frac{2}{n} \sum_{k=0}^{n-1} \cos(Jt_k) x_k.$$

For exact interpolation with an even number of data points, we have $n = 2m$. Rather than using a different formula for a_m in this case (which would be required by the difference in the value of the summation of $\cos(Jt_k)^2$ when $J = n/2$), we choose, for $n = 2m$, to define the interpolating polynomial as

$$p(t) = \frac{a_0}{2} + a_1 \cos t + a_2 \cos 2t + \ldots + \frac{a_m}{2} \cos mt$$

$$+ b_1 \sin t + b_2 \sin 2t + \ldots + b_{m-1} \sin(m-1)t$$

$$= \frac{a_0}{2} + \sum_{j=1}^{m-1} a_j \cos(jt_k) + \frac{a_m}{2} \cos mt + \sum_{j=1}^{m-1} b_j \sin(jt_k).$$

Using this form, we find that all of the coefficients follow the same formulas:

$$a_j = \frac{2}{n} \sum_{k=0}^{n-1} \cos(jt_k)x_k, \qquad b_j = \frac{2}{n} \sum_{k=0}^{n-1} \sin(jt_k)x_k, \qquad j = 0, \ldots, m.$$

Note that the formula for b_j can be included for $j = 0$; however, b_0 is always zero, so it is not necessary to compute it. Similarly, for $n = 2m$ (interpolation of an even number of data points), we always have $b_m = 0$, since all terms in the summation are of the form $\sin(k\pi)$.

Data on Other Intervals

If the given data are evenly spaced on $[-\pi, \pi]$, the formulas for a_j and b_j in terms of t_k remain the same; however, the t_k change. Although the form of the polynomial and the formulas for the coefficients are the same, the values of the coefficients will be different because the t_k are different.

Data on any other interval may be transformed to $[0, 2\pi]$ or $[-\pi, \pi]$ by a linear transformation; the process is similar to that for Gaussian integration (discussed in Chapter 11), or orthogonal polynomials (Section 9.2.3).

The MATLAB function for Fourier interpolation or approximation may be modified to use data that are evenly distributed on any interval of length 2π by giving the left-hand end of the interval, t_0, and defining $t = t0:w:(t0 + 2*pi - w)$.

Example 10.4 Geometric Figures

The following data represent the distance from the origin to the perimeter of a square (shown in Figure 10.2a), measured at evenly spaced angular intervals t_k:

$$\mathbf{t} = [0 \quad \pi/4 \quad \pi/2 \quad 3\pi/4 \quad \pi \quad 5\pi/4 \quad 3\pi/2 \quad 7\pi/4],$$

$$\mathbf{x} = [1.0 \quad 1.4 \quad 1.0 \quad 1.4 \quad 1.0 \quad 1.4 \quad 1.0 \quad 1.4 \ ].$$

With the use of the MATLAB function `Trig_poly(x, m)`, the coefficients are found to be

$$\mathbf{a} = [1.2 \quad 0 \quad 0 \quad 0 \quad -0.2],$$

$$\mathbf{b} = [0 \quad 0 \quad 0 \quad 0 \quad 0 \ ].$$

We denote the interpolation function as $r(t)$ because it represents radial distance from the origin:

$$r(t) = 1.2 - 0.2 \cos(4t).$$

We can reconstruct a rough approximation of the original figure by plotting $x = r \cos(t)$, $y = r \sin(t)$, as shown in Fig. 10.6.

For the triangle shown in Figure 10.2b, (sampled at angular intervals of $\pi/4$), the data are $\mathbf{d} = [0.5 \quad 0.5 \quad 1.0 \quad 0.5 \quad 0.5 \quad 1.4 \quad 1.0 \quad 1.4]$.

The coefficients are

$$\mathbf{a} = [0.85 \quad 0.00 \quad -0.25 \quad 0.00 \quad -0.1],$$

$$\mathbf{b} = [0.00 \quad -0.3182 \quad 0.00 \quad -0.3182 \quad 0.0],$$

so the interpolation function for the radial distance is

$$r(t) = 0.85 - 0.25 \cos(2t) - 0.1 \cos(4t) - 0.3182 \sin(t) - 0.3182 \sin(3t).$$

The reconstructed triangle is shown in Fig. 10.7. Using more data points improves the figures, as we shall see later.

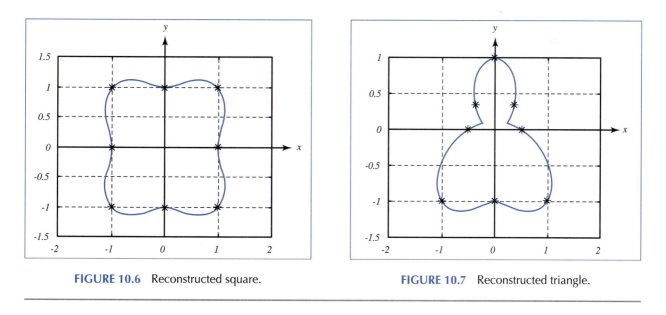

FIGURE 10.6 Reconstructed square.

FIGURE 10.7 Reconstructed triangle.

Finding the coefficients of a Fourier polynomial leads to the problem of computing, for $j = 0, \ldots, m$,

$$a_j = \frac{2}{n} \sum_{k=0}^{n-1} x_k \cos(jt_k),$$

$$b_j = \frac{2}{n} \sum_{k=0}^{n-1} x_k \sin(jt_k).$$

The a_j and b_j can be combined into a single complex quantity

$$c_j = a_j + ib_j = \frac{2}{n} \sum_{k=0}^{n-1} x_k [\cos(jt_k) + i \sin(jt_k)], \qquad \text{where } i = \sqrt{-1}.$$

These computations can be carried our more conveniently by working in the complex domain. Using Euler's formula relating the trigonometric and exponential functions for complex variables, we may write

$$c_j = \frac{2}{n} \sum_{k=0}^{n-1} x_k \exp(ijt_k).$$

Recalling that the points t_k are evenly spaced on $[0, 2\pi)$, we define $\omega = \dfrac{2\pi}{n}$ and write t_k as $k\omega$ to obtain

$$c_j = \frac{2}{n} \sum_{k=0}^{n-1} x_k \exp(ijk\omega).$$

The coefficients of the Fourier polynomial are the scaled real and imaginary parts of the discrete Fourier transform of the data, which we consider in the remainder of this section.

10.2.1 Discrete Fourier Transform

The discrete Fourier transform of a set of n complex data values z_k evenly spaced on $[0, 2\pi)$ is the set of complex numbers

$$g_j = \sum_{k=0}^{n-1} z_k \exp(ijk\omega), \qquad \text{for } j = 0, \ldots, n - 1.$$

This transformation has a wide range of applications beyond just the computation of interpolating coefficients discussed in the previous section.

Since $e^{i\theta} = \cos\theta + i \sin\theta$, the periodicity of $\cos\theta$ and $\sin\theta$ cause the complex exponential to be periodic also. Direct computation of the g_j requires $O(n^2)$ operations. However, by exploiting the efficiencies of the fast Fourier transform, the numbers can be reduced to $O(n \log n)$ operations.

10.2.2 Fast Fourier Transform

We begin by considering the FFT when n is a power of 2, i.e., $n = 2^r$; this is the case to which the FFT is most often applied. The basic idea in the FFT is to make use of the periodic nature of the complex exponential function and clever reordering of the computations, in order to reduce the total effort required to find the transform.

We define $w = \exp(i\omega)$ (with $\omega = \dfrac{2\pi}{n}$, as before). With this notation, we write

$$g_j = \sum_{k=0}^{n-1} z_k w^{jk}, \qquad \text{for } j = 0, \dots, n-1. \tag{10.4}$$

Note that $w^n = 1$, so that some simplifications can be achieved in some of the equations for the g_j.

The cleverness in the computations results from the fact that the index on the components of the transform and the index on the summation both run from 0 to $n-1$. Each value of j ($0 \le j \le n-1$) can be written in binary form as $j = 2^{r-1} j_r + \dots + 2^2 j_3 + 2 j_2 + j_1$, where each of the numbers $j_1, j_2, \dots, j_r$ is either 0 or 1.

For example, if $n = 4$, we express the numbers $0, 1, \dots, 3$ as $j = 2 j_2 + j_1$:

i	i_2	i_1
0	0	0
1	0	1
2	1	0
3	1	1

We also write the numbers $k = 0, 1, \dots, 3$ in binary form, but as $k = 2 k_1 + k_2$. If we keep the values of k_1 and k_2 in the same order as for j_1 and j_2, the values of k appear in a scrambled form, which is useful for the FFT. Combining the representations of j and k in a single table, such as Table 10.1, clarifies the relationship between the binary coefficients. This reordering of the k values relative to the j values is called *bit reversal*.

Table 10.1 Binary coefficients in natural and scrambled order

j	j_2	j_1	k_2	k_1	k
0	0	0	0	0	0
1	0	1	0	1	2
2	1	0	1	0	1
3	1	1	1	1	3

There are several equivalent methods of presenting the FFT method. We first consider the matrix form, which we illustrate for $n = 4$. The resulting computations are shown schematically. Finally, the FFT method for $n = 4$ is developed from a more algebraic point of view, which allows generalization to the case when n has prime factors other than 2.

10.2.3 Matrix Form of FFT

We begin by writing out the linear system of equations for the Fourier transform components for the case $n = 4$:

$$w^0 z_0 + w^0 z_1 + w^0 z_2 + w^0 z_3 = g_0,$$

$$w^0 z_0 + w^1 z_1 + w^2 z_2 + w^3 z_3 = g_1,$$

$$w^0 z_0 + w^2 z_1 + w^4 z_2 + w^6 z_3 = g_2,$$

$$w^0 z_0 + w^3 z_1 + w^6 z_2 + w^9 z_3 = g_3.$$

Making use of the fact that $w^4 = w^0 = 1$, to simplify the equations, and interchanging the order of the second and third equations (which corresponds to the previous interchange in the order of the j and k indices) gives the system

$$1 z_0 + 1 z_1 + 1 z_2 + 1 z_3 = g_0,$$

$$1 z_0 + w^2 z_1 + 1 z_2 + w^2 z_3 = g_2,$$

$$1 z_0 + w^1 z_1 + w^2 z_2 + w^3 z_3 = g_1,$$

$$1 z_0 + w^3 z_1 + w^2 z_2 + w^1 z_3 = g_3.$$

Writing these equations in matrix form, we have

$$
\begin{bmatrix}
1 & 1 & 1 & 1 \\
1 & w^2 & 1 & w^2 \\
1 & w & w^2 & w^3 \\
1 & w^3 & w^2 & w
\end{bmatrix}
\begin{bmatrix}
z_0 \\
z_1 \\
z_2 \\
z_3
\end{bmatrix}
=
\begin{bmatrix}
g_0 \\
g_2 \\
g_1 \\
g_3
\end{bmatrix}.
\tag{10.5}
$$

We now factor the coefficient matrix:

$$
\begin{bmatrix}
1 & 1 & 0 & 0 \\
1 & w^2 & 0 & 0 \\
0 & 0 & 1 & w \\
0 & 0 & 1 & w^3
\end{bmatrix}
\begin{bmatrix}
1 & 0 & 1 & 0 \\
0 & 1 & 0 & 1 \\
1 & 0 & w^2 & 0 \\
0 & 1 & 0 & w^2
\end{bmatrix}
=
\begin{bmatrix}
1 & 1 & 1 & 1 \\
1 & w^2 & 1 & w^2 \\
1 & w & w^2 & w^3 \\
1 & w^3 & w^2 & w
\end{bmatrix}.
$$

Next, we carry out the computation of the g's in two steps. Substituting the factored form of the coefficient matrix into eq. (10.5), we obtain

$$
\begin{bmatrix}
1 & 1 & 0 & 0 \\
1 & w^2 & 0 & 0 \\
0 & 0 & 1 & w \\
0 & 0 & 1 & w^3
\end{bmatrix}
\begin{bmatrix}
1 & 0 & 1 & 0 \\
0 & 1 & 0 & 1 \\
1 & 0 & w^2 & 0 \\
0 & 1 & 0 & w^2
\end{bmatrix}
\begin{bmatrix}
z_0 \\
z_1 \\
z_2 \\
z_3
\end{bmatrix}
=
\begin{bmatrix}
g_0 \\
g_1 \\
g_2 \\
g_3
\end{bmatrix}.
\tag{10.6}
$$

First we find the product

$$\begin{bmatrix} 1 & 0 & 1 & 0 \\ 0 & 1 & 0 & 1 \\ 1 & 0 & w^2 & 0 \\ 0 & 1 & 0 & w^2 \end{bmatrix} \begin{bmatrix} z_0 \\ z_1 \\ z_2 \\ z_3 \end{bmatrix} = \begin{bmatrix} z_0 + z_2 \\ z_1 + z_3 \\ z_0 + w^2 z_2 \\ z_1 + w^2 z_3 \end{bmatrix} = \begin{bmatrix} s_0 \\ s_1 \\ s_2 \\ s_3 \end{bmatrix}.$$

Then we form the second product

$$\begin{bmatrix} 1 & 1 & 0 & 0 \\ 1 & w^2 & 0 & 0 \\ 0 & 0 & 1 & w \\ 0 & 0 & 1 & w^3 \end{bmatrix} \begin{bmatrix} s_0 \\ s_1 \\ s_2 \\ s_3 \end{bmatrix} = \begin{bmatrix} s_0 + s_1 \\ s_0 + w^2 s_1 \\ s_2 + w s_3 \\ s_2 + w^3 s_3 \end{bmatrix} = \begin{bmatrix} g_0 \\ g_1 \\ g_2 \\ g_3 \end{bmatrix}.$$

The efficiencies in this computation result from the structure of the matrices that are employed in the two stages. The method is implemented not by using general matrix multiplication, but by performing only the necessary mutiplications and additions.

The computations are shown schematically in Figure 10.8. Pathways with powers of w on them indicate that the quantity on the left is multiplied by that amount.

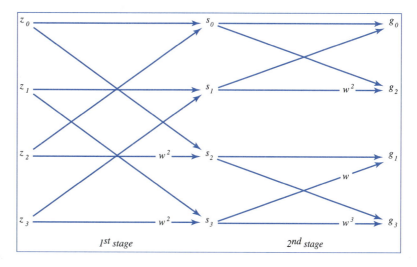

FIGURE 10.8 Two-stage computational procedure.

10.2.4 Algebraic Form of FFT

We now consider an alternative approach to the FFT for $n = 2^r$. As before, each value of j $(0 \leq j \leq n-1)$ is written in binary form, and each value of k is written in binary form with the bits reversed. For example, if $n = 4$, the binary coefficients are given in Table 10.1.

To calculate the discrete Fourier transform of the data z_k, i.e.,

$$g_j = \sum_{k=0}^{3} z_k \exp(ijk\omega), \qquad \text{for } j = 0, \ldots, 3,$$

we write $w = \exp(i\omega) = \exp\left(i\dfrac{\pi}{2}\right)$. Then the sum is given (as in eq. 10.4) by

$$g_j = \sum_{k=0}^{3} z_k w^{jk}.$$

Note that $w^4 = 1$, and therefore, $w^{4a} = 1$ for any integer a. Using the binary factorizations of j and k, we have

$$g_j = g(j_1 + 2j_2) = \sum_{k=0}^{3} z(k_2 + 2k_1) w^{(j_1 + 2j_2)(k_2 + 2k_1)}$$

$$= \sum_{k=0}^{3} z(k_2 + 2k_1) w^{(j_1 + 2j_2)k_2} w^{(j_1 + 2j_2)2k_1}$$

$$= \sum_{k_2=0}^{1} \sum_{k_1=0}^{1} z(k_2 + 2k_1) w^{(j_1 + 2j_2)2k_1} w^{(j_1 + 2j_2)k_2}$$

$$= \sum_{k_2=0}^{1} \left[\sum_{k_1=0}^{1} z(k_2 + 2k_1) w^{(j_1)(2)(k_1)} \right] w^{(j_1 + 2j_2)k_2}.$$

Since $w = \exp\left(i\dfrac{2\pi}{4}\right) = \exp\left(i\dfrac{\pi}{2}\right) = \cos\dfrac{\pi}{2} + i\sin\dfrac{\pi}{2}$, we have

$$w^0 = 1; \qquad w = 0 + i(1/2);$$
$$w^2 = -1; \qquad w^3 = 0 - i(1/2).$$

We can use these results to simplify our final calculations, but first we observe that the way in which the original summation over all data points has been decomposed into two nested summations forms the basis for the FFT.

We first compute the inner summation, $\left[\displaystyle\sum_{k_1=0}^{1} z(k_2 + 2k_1) w^{(j_1)(2)(k_1)} \right]$, for each value of j, but we do so by using each possible value of j_1 (0 or 1) and each possible value of j_2 (0 or 1).

Writing the digits so that j is in natural order, we have $k = k_2 + 2k_1$ and $j = j_1 + 2j_2$; the first stage produces the values of $s(j_1 + 2k_2)$:

$$s(j_1 + 2k_2) = \sum_{k_1=0}^{1} z(k_2 + 2k_1)w^{(j_1)(2)(k_1)}$$
$$= z(k_2 + 0)w^{(j_1)(2)(0)} + z(k_2 + 2)w^{(j_1)(2)(1)}.$$

These values are summarized in the following table:

$z(k_2 + 2k_1)$	k_1	k_2	j_1	j_2	$s(j_1 + 2k_2)$
z_0	0	0	0	0	$z_0 w^{(0)(2)(0)} + z_2 w^{(0)(2)(1)} = s_0$
z_3	1	0	1	0	$z_0 w^{(1)(2)(0)} + z_2 w^{(1)(2)(1)} = s_1$
z_1	0	1	0	1	$z_1 w^{(0)(2)(0)} + z_3 w^{(0)(2)(1)} = s_2$
z_4	1	1	1	1	$z_1 w^{(1)(2)(0)} + z_3 w^{(1)(2)(1)} = s_3$

The results of this first summation are expressed in terms of the digits j_1 and k_2, since the summation over the possible values of k_1 has been performed, but the second summation, over k_2, remains to be done.

We now compute the outer summation,

$$g(j_1 + 2j_2) = \sum_{k_2=0}^{1} s(j_1 + 2k_2)w^{(j_1 + 2j_2)k_2}$$
$$= s(j_1 + 2(0))w^{(j_1 + 2j_2)(0)} + s(j_1 + 2(1))w^{(j_1 + 2j_2)(1)},$$

and its corresponding table of values:

s	k_1	k_2	j_1	j_2	g
s_0	0	0	0	0	$s_0 w^{(0+2(0))0} + s_2 w^{(0+2(0))1} = s_0 w^0 + s_2 w^0$
s_1	1	0	1	0	$s_1 w^{(1+2(0))0} + s_3 w^{(1+2(0))1} = s_1 w^0 + s_3 w^1$
s_2	0	1	0	1	$s_0 w^{(0+2(1))0} + s_2 w^{(0+2(1))1} = s_0 w^0 + s_2 w^2$
s_3	1	1	1	1	$s_1 w^{(1+2(1))0} + s_3 w^{(1+2(1))1} = s_1 w^0 + s_3 w^3$

The foregoing computations are implemented in the MATLAB function for calculating the fast Fourier transform on four data points:

10.2.5 Matlab Function for FFT with $n = 4$

```matlab
function g = FFT_4(z)
% FFT for n = 4
n = length(z);
for h = 0:8
  w(h+1) = exp(i*pi*h/2);
end
for k2 = 0 : 1                                    % perform bit reversal
  for k1 = 0 : 1
    zz(2*k2+k1+1) = z(2*k1+k2+1);
  end
end
s = zeros(1, 4);
for k2 = 0 : 1
  for j1 = 0 : 1
    for k1 = 0 : 1
      s(2*k2+j1+1) = s(2*k2+j1+1)+ zz(2*k2+k1+1)*w(j1*2*k1+1);
    end
  end
end
g = zeros(1,4);
for j2 = 0 : 1
  for j1 = 0 : 1
    for k2 = 0 : 1
      g(2*j2+j1+1) = g(2*j2+j1+1)+s(2*k2+j1+1)*w((j1+2*j2)*k2+1);
    end
  end
end
```

Example 10.5 FFT with Four Points

The script that follows illustrates the use of the function FFT_4. The coefficients for the Fourier interpolation function are the real and imaginary parts of the Fourier transform data, scaled by $2/n$ (except for a_0 and a_2, which are scaled by $1/n$). The data and the interpolation function are shown in Figure 10.9.

```
% script for fft example
z = [ 1  1  0  0 ];
g = FFT_4(z)
a0 = real(g(1))/n;
a(1) = 2*real(g(2))/n;
a(2) = real(g(3))/n;
b(1) = 2*imag(g(2))/n;
tt = 0 : 0.1 : 2*pi;
yy = a0 + a(1)*cos(tt) + b(1)*sin(tt) + a(2)*cos(2*tt);
t = 0 : pi/2 : (2*pi - pi/2);
plot(tt, yy, t, z, '*')
grid on
```

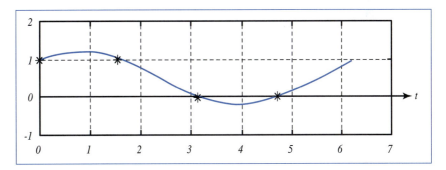

FIGURE 10.9 Fourier interpolation function found from FFT.

Although the FFT is most often applied for $n = 2^r$, the general FFT does not require the factorization of n to have any specific form. We designate the prime factorization of n as $n = r_1 r_2 \ldots r_t$, where we assume that $r_1 \le r_2 \le \ldots \le r_t$. In a generalization of the binary representation of a number, each value of $j(0 \le j \le n - 1)$ can be written in terms of the prime factors of n as $j = r_1 \ldots r_{t-1} j_t + \ldots + r_1 r_2 j_3 + r_1 j_2 + j_1$. The possible values for j_1 are $0, 1, \ldots, r_1 - 1$; for j_2 are $0, 1, \ldots, r_2 - 1$; and for j_t are $0, 1, \ldots, r_t - 1$.

We also write the numbers $k = 0, 1, \ldots, n - 1$ in terms of the factors of n, but as $k = r_t \ldots r_2 k_1 + \ldots + r_t r_{t-1} k_{t-2} + r_t k_{t-1} + k_t$. The coefficient k_s can take on values $0, 1, \ldots, r_s - 1$.

For example, if $n = 6$, we have $r_1 = 2$ and $r_2 = 3$. We express the numbers $0, 1, \ldots, 5$ as $j = r_1 j_2 + j_1 = 2 j_2 + j_1$; j_1 is 0 or 1, and j_2 is 0, 1, or 2. The following table gives j in terms of j_2 and j_1:

j	j_2	j_1
0	0	0
1	0	1
2	1	0
3	1	1
4	2	0
5	2	1

For this example, $k = r_2 k_1 + k_2 = 3 k_1 + k_2$; k_1 is 0 or 1, k_2 is 0, 1, or 2, and the table is as follows:

k	k_1	k_2
0	0	0
1	0	1
2	0	2
3	1	0
4	1	1
5	1	2

Note that the possible values for k_1 and j_1 are the same, for k_2 and j_2 are the same, etc. However, k_2 is the lowest order digit in the representation of k, whereas j_2 is the *highest* order digit in the representation of j. In what follows, we perform the operations in each computation by letting j_1 and j_2 run through all possible values. We also let k_1 and k_2 run through their range of values, in the same order as j_1 and j_2; this generates all possible values of k also, but in a scrambled order, as shown in Table 10.2.

Table 10.2 The integers 0, ... 5 expressed in terms of prime factors.

$j = 2j_2 + j_1$	j_2	j_1	k_1	k_2	$k = 3k_1 + k_2$
0	0	0	0	0	0
1	0	1	1	0	3
2	1	0	0	1	1
3	1	1	1	1	4
4	2	0	0	2	2
5	2	1	1	2	5

Now let us consider the calculation of the discrete Fourier transform of the data z_k, where $w = \exp(i\omega) = \exp\left(i\,\dfrac{2\pi}{n}\right)$, in which $n = r_1 r_2$. We have

$$g_j = \sum_{k=0}^{n-1} z_k \exp(ijk\omega) = \sum_{k=0}^{n-1} z_k w^{ik}, \qquad \text{for } j = 0, \ldots, n-1.$$

Since $w^n = 1$, any term of the form $w^{r_1 r_2 a}$ is equal to unity and can be dropped from the calculations in the formulas that follow. Using the preceding factorization of j and k, we have

$$g_j = g(r_1 j_2 + j_1) = \sum_{k=0}^{n-1} z(r_2 k_1 + k_2) w^{(j_1 + r_1 j_2)(k_2 + r_2 k_1)}$$

$$= \sum_{k=0}^{n-1} z(r_2 k_1 + k_2) w^{(j_1 + r_1 j_2)k_2} w^{(j_1 + r_1 j_2)r_2 k_1}$$

$$= \sum_{k_2=0}^{r_2-1} \sum_{k_1=0}^{r_1-1} z(r_2 k_1 + k_2) w^{(j_1 + r_1 j_2)r_2 k_1} w^{(j_1 + r_1 j_2)k_2}$$

$$= \sum_{k_2=0}^{r_2-1} \left[\sum_{k_1=0}^{r_1-1} z(r_2 k_1 + k_2) w^{j_1 r_2 k_1} \right] w^{(j_1 + r_1 j_2)k_2}$$

The result of first stage is

$$s(2k_2 + j_1) = \sum_{k_1=0}^{1} z(3k_1 + k_2) w^{3j_1 k_1} = z(3(0) + k_2) w^{3j_1(0)} + z(3(1) + k_2) w^{3j_1(1)},$$

so that we have the following table:

$z(k_2 + 3k_1)$	k_1	k_2	j_1	j_2	$s(2k_2 + j_1)$
z_0	0	0	0	0	$z_0 w^{(0)(3)(0)} + z_3 w^{(0)(3)(1)} = s_0$
z_3	1	0	1	0	$z_0 w^{(1)(3)(0)} + z_3 w^{(1)(3)(1)} = s_1$
z_1	0	1	0	1	$z_1 w^{(0)(3)(0)} + z_4 w^{(0)(3)(1)} = s_2$
z_4	1	1	1	1	$z_1 w^{(1)(3)(0)} + z_4 w^{(1)(3)(1)} = s_3$
z_2	0	2	0	2	$z_2 w^{(0)(3)(0)} + z_5 w^{(0)(3)(1)} = s_4$
z_5	1	2	1	2	$z_2 w^{(1)(3)(0)} + z_5 w^{(1)(3)(1)} = s_5$

We next compute the outer summation,

$$g(2j_2 + j_1) = \sum_{k_2=0}^{3-1} s(2k_2 + j_1)w^{(j_1+2j_2)k_2}$$

$$= s(2(0) + j_1)w^{(j_1+2j_2)0} + s(2(1) + j_1)w^{(j_1+2j_2)1} + s(2(2) + j_1)w^{(j_1+2j_2)2},$$

yielding the following table:

j	k_1	k_2	j_1	j_2	s	g
0	0	0	0	0	s_0	$s_0 w^{(0+2(0))0} + s_2 w^{(0+2(0))1} + s_4 w^{(0+2(0))2}$
1	1	0	1	0	s_3	$s_1 w^{(1+2(0))0} + s_3 w^{(1+2(0))1} + s_5 w^{(1+2(0))2}$
2	0	1	0	1	s_1	$s_0 w^{(0+2(1))0} + s_2 w^{(0+2(1))1} + s_4 w^{(0+2(1))2}$
3	1	1	1	1	s_4	$s_1 w^{(1+2(1))0} + s_3 w^{(1+2(1))1} + s_5 w^{(1+2(1))2}$
4	0	2	0	2	s_2	$s_0 w^{(0+2(2))0} + s_2 w^{(0+2(2))1} + s_4 w^{(0+2(2))2}$
5	1	2	1	2	s_5	$s_1 w^{(1+2(2))0} + s_3 w^{(1+2(2))1} + s_5 w^{(1+2(2))2}$

Simplifying, we obtain the final table:

j	k_1	k_2	j_1	j_2	s	g
0	0	0	0	0	s_0	$s_0 w^0 + s_2 w^{0} + s_4 w^0$
1	1	0	1	0	s_3	$s_1 w^0 + s_3 w^1 + s_5 w^2$
2	0	1	0	1	s_1	$s_0 w^0 + s_2 w^2 + s_4 w^4$
3	1	1	1	1	s_4	$s_1 w^0 + s_3 w^3 + s_5 w^6$
4	0	2	0	2	s_2	$s_0 w^0 + s_2 w^4 + s_4 w^8$
5	1	2	1	2	s_5	$s_1 w^0 + s_3 w^5 + s_5 w^{10}$

Since

$$w = \exp\left(i\frac{2\pi}{n}\right) = \exp\left(i\frac{2\pi}{3}\right)$$

we have

$$w^0 = 1 = w^6 = \exp\left(i\frac{6\pi}{3}\right) = 1,$$

$$w = \exp\left(i\frac{\pi}{3}\right) = \cos\frac{\pi}{3} + i\sin\frac{\pi}{3} = 1/2 + i\sqrt{3}/2,$$

$$w^2 = \exp\left(i\frac{2\pi}{3}\right) = \cos\frac{2\pi}{3} + i\sin\frac{2\pi}{3} = -1/2 + i\sqrt{3}/2 = w^8,$$

$$w^3 = \exp(i\pi) = -1,$$

$$w^4 = \exp\left(i\frac{4\pi}{3}\right) = \cos\frac{4\pi}{3} + i\sin\frac{4\pi}{3} = -1/2 - i\sqrt{3}/2 = w^{10},$$

$$w^5 = \exp\left(i\frac{5\pi}{3}\right) = \cos\frac{5\pi}{3} + i\sin\frac{5\pi}{3} = 1/2 - i\sqrt{3}/2.$$

Note that powers of w up to and including $w^{(n-1)(n-1)}$ appear in the summations, although powers above $w^{(n-1)}$ can be simplified and expressed in terms of lower powers if desired.

Example 10.6 FFT for Six Data Points

We illustrate the use of the FFT for six data points by finding the interpolation function for the data $\mathbf{z} = [0 \ \ 1 \ \ 2 \ \ 3 \ \ 2 \ \ 1]$. From before, for $n = 6$, $k = 3k_1 + k_2$ and $j = 3j_2 + j_1$. The data are listed in scrambled order so that the final results (the g's) are in natural order.

First, we compute the inner sum for each pair of values of j_1 and k_2:

$$s(2k_2 + j_1) = \sum_{k_1=0}^{2-1} z(3k_1 + k_2)w^{j_1(3)k_1}$$

$$= z(0 + k_2)w^{j_1(3)(0)} + z(3 + k_2)w^{j_1(3)(1)}.$$

This yields the following table:

z	k	j	k_1	k_2	j_1	j_2	$s(2k_2 + j_1)$
0	0	0	0	0	0	0	$0w^0 + 3w^0 = 3 = s_0$
3	3	1	1	0	1	0	$0w^0 + 3w^3 = -3 = s_1$
1	1	2	0	1	0	1	$1w^0 + 2w^0 = 3 = s_2$
2	4	3	1	1	1	1	$1w^0 + 2w^3 = -1 = s_3$
2	2	4	0	2	0	2	$2w^0 + 1w^0 = 3 = s_4$
1	5	5	1	2	1	2	$2w^0 + 1w^3 = 1 = s_5$

Next, we compute the outer sum:

$$g_j = \sum_{k_2=0}^{3-1} s(2k_2 + j_1)w^{(j_1+2j_2)(k_2)}$$

$$= s(0 + j_1)(w^{(j_1+2j_2)(0)} + s(2 + j_1)w^{(j_1+2j_2)(1)} + s(4 + j_1)w^{(j_1+2j_2)(2)}.$$

The associated table is as follows:

j	k_1	k_2	j_1	j_2	$g(2j_2 + j_1)$	
0	0	0	0	0	$s_0w^0 + s_2w^0 + s_4w^0,$	$g_0 = 9$
1	1	0	1	0	$s_1w^0 + s_3w^1 + s_5w^2,$	$g_1 = -4$
2	0	1	0	1	$s_0w^0 + s_2w^2 + s_4w^4,$	$g_2 = 0$
3	1	1	1	1	$s_1w^0 + s_3w^3 + s_5w^6,$	$g_3 = -1$
4	0	2	0	2	$s_0w^0 + s_2w^4 + s_4w^8,$	$g_4 = 0$
5	1	2	1	2	$s_1w^0 + s_3w^5 + s_5w^{10},$	$g_5 = -4$

To use these results to find the interpolating trigonometric polynomial, we note that, in general, $a = 2\text{Re}(g)/n$; in addition, a_0 (and a_m when $n = 2m$) is divided by 2. In this example, all g's are real, so all b's are zero. We have $a_0 = g_0/6 = 3/2$, $a_1 = g_1/3 = -4/3$, $a_2 = g_2/3 = 0$, $a_3 = g_3/6 = -1/6$. The data and the interpolation function are shown in Figure 10.10.

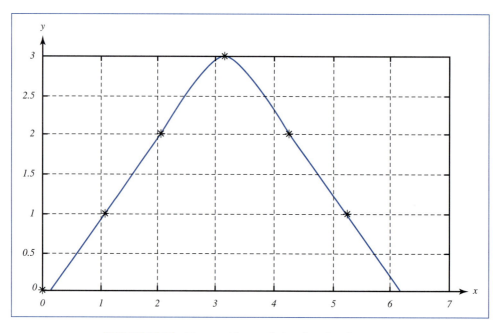

FIGURE 10.10   Data and interpolation function for $n = 6$.

10.3.1 MATLAB Function for FFT with $n = rs$ (Data Evenly Spaced on $[0, 2\pi)$)

```
function g = FFT2(z, r, s)
n = length(z);          % r = r(1), s = r(2)
for h = 0 : 2*n
    w(h+1) = exp(i*2*pi*h/n);
end
for k2 = 0 : s-1
    for k1 = 0 : r-1
        zz(r*k2 + k1 + 1) = z(s*k1 + k2 + 1);
    end
end
end
```

```
ss = zeros(1,n);
for k2 = 0 : s-1
  for j1 = 0 : r-1
    for k1 = 0 : r-1
        ss(r*k2+j1+1)=ss(r*k2+j1+1)+zz(r*k2+k1+1)*w(j1*s*k1+1);
    end
  end
end
g = zeros(1,n);
for j2 = 0 : s-1
  for j1 = 0 : r-1
    for k2 = 0 : s-1
      g(r*j2 +j1+1)=g(r*j2+j1+1)+ s(r*k2+j1+1)*w((j1+r*j2)*k2+1);
    end
  end
end
```

10.4 USING MATLAB's FUNCTIONS

MATLAB has built-in functions for computing continuous and discrete Fourier transforms. We limit our description to the use of the function fft, which finds the discrete Fourier transform of a vector **x**. If the length of **x** is a power of two, a fast radix-2 FFT algorithm is used. If the length of **x** is not a power of two, a slower, non-power-of-two algorithm is employed. The MATLAB function fft uses the following definition of the discrete Fourier transform:

$$g_j = \sum_{k=0}^{n-1} x_k \exp(-ijk\omega), \qquad \text{for } j = 0, \ldots, n-1.$$

Examples 10.7 and 10.8 use MATLAB's function fft. Since this function uses a convention opposite from the one we have been using on the sign of the exponential function, we reverse the sign of k in constructing the interpolation function.

Example 10.7 Waveform of a Clarinet

We sample the waveform of a clarinet over one period, at 16 evenly spaced points (from 0 to $2\pi - \pi/8$), and use the data together with the MATLAB function fft to find the interpolation function as shown in Figure 10.11.

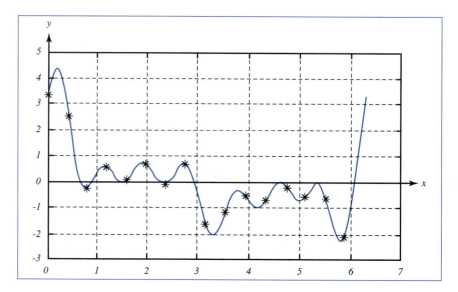

FIGURE 10.11 Waveform of a clarinet.

We apply the function fft to the data representing the amplitude of the wave; i.e.,

$yy =$ 3.304   2.5535 −0.22396   0.56711   0.067979 0.69711 −0.14572   0.70309

   −1.635 −1.1464 −0.55064 −0.70925 −0.18781 −0.55497 −0.62887 −2.1101

and obtain the transformed data

$$
\begin{array}{lll}
z = -1.1102\text{e-}15 & 5.6569 & -5.6569\,i \\
1.7889 - 1.7889\,i & 5.3666 & -5.3666\,i \\
3.0984 - 3.0984\,i & 3564.7329 - 4.7329\,i \\
1.7889 - 1.7889\,i & 4 & -4i \\
1.6653\text{e-}14 & 4 & +4i \\
1.7889 + 1.7889\,i & 4.7329 & +4.7329\,i \\
3.0984 = 3.0984\,i & 5.3666 & +5.3666\,i \\
1.7889 + 1.7889\,i & 5.6569 & +5.6569\,i
\end{array}
$$

The original waveform can be reconstructed from the transformed data as follows:

```
yyy = z(1)/2;
for k + 1 : n/2
    yyy = yyy + real(z(k + 1))*cos(k*x) + imag(z(k + 1))*sin(-k*x);
end
yyy = yyy*(2/n);
```

The absolute value of z (defined as z*conj(z) and computed in MATLAB either by the definition or by abs(z)) contains much of the important information about the waveform, including the power spectrum of the waveform, which is a common method of describing a musical sound. As with the reconstruction of the waveform itself, only the first $n/2$ terms are relevant. We have

$$2*z*\text{conj}(z)/n =$$

1.3878e-16	1	0.31623	0.94868
0.54772	0.83666	0.31623	0.70711
2.0817e-15	0.70711	0.31623	0.83666
0.54772	0.94868	0.31623	1

Example 10.8 Rotation-Invariant Figures

We conclude our investigation of the FFT by illustrating its use in pattern recognition, where the figures we wish to identify may appear in different orientations. Using the data from Example 10-B, we can reconstruct a reasonable approximation to the original figures. (See Fig. 10.12.)

The power spectrum for the square does not change when it is rotated:

ps = 332.7   0   0   0   2.56   0   0   0.

Not only does the power spectrum for the triangle not change when the figure is rotated, but it is significantly different from that of the square:

ps = 153.76 5.6661 3.4171 1.7784 0.64   1.469   0.022944 0.027299.

The power spectrum for the cross does not change when the figure is rotated; it is much more similar to that of the square than that of the triangle:

ps = 221.41 0   0   0   3.0976 0   0   0.

The computations for the triangle are given in the following MATLAB script:

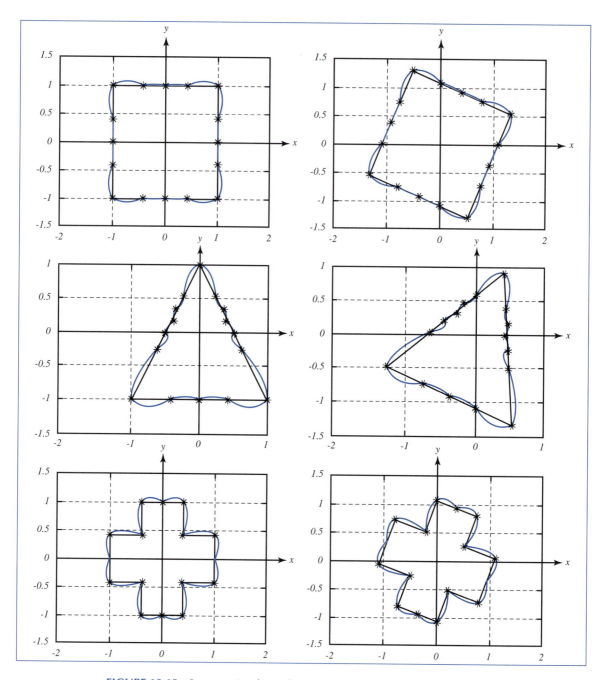

FIGURE 10.12 Square, triangle, and cross reconstructed from measured data.

```
% S_triangle
% script for triangle fft
y = [.5  .43  .5  .6  1  .6  .5  .43  .5  .67  1.4  1.1  1  1.1  1.4  .67]
n = length(y);  nn = n/2;  z = fft(y);  zz = z/nn;
a0 = real(zz(1))/2;              a(1:nn) = real(zz(2:nn+1));
b(1:nn) = imag(zz(2:nn+1));  a(nn) = a(nn)/2;
r = a0*ones(1,100);    t=linspace(0, 2*pi);
for k = 1:nn
  r = r + a(k)*cos(k*t) - b(k)*sin(k*t);
end
xx = r.*cos(t);  yy = r.*sin(t);
plot(xx,yy)
grid on
hold on
s = 2*pi/n;  tt = 0:s:2*pi-s;  d1 = y.*cos(tt);  d2 = y.*sin(tt);
plot(d1, d2, '*')
% find power spectrum
ps = z.*conj(z)
hold off
```

Consider data values $x_0, x_1, \ldots, x_{n-1}$ given at points evenly spaced on $[0, 2\pi)$—i.e., at

$$t_0 = 0, t_1 = \frac{2\pi}{n}, \ldots, t_k = k\frac{2\pi}{n}, \ldots, t_{n-1} = (n-1)\frac{2\pi}{n}.$$

If $n > 2m + 1$, the trigonometric polynomial

$$f(t) = \frac{a_0}{2} + a_1 \cos t + a_2 \cos 2t + \ldots + a_m \cos mt$$

$$+ b_1 \sin t + b_2 \sin 2t + \ldots + b_m \sin mt,$$

with coefficients

$$a_j = \frac{2}{n} \sum_{k=0}^{n-1} x_k \cos(jt_k) \quad \text{and} \quad b_j = \frac{2}{n} \sum_{k=0}^{n-1} x_k \sin(jt_k),$$

gives the least squares approximation to the data.

If $n = 2m + 1$, the polynomial for exact interpolation has the same form as that for approximation. If $n = 2m$, the trigonometric polynomial for interpolation is

$$f(t) = \frac{a_0}{2} + a_1 \cos t + a_2 \cos 2t + \ldots + \frac{a_m}{2} \cos mt$$

$$+ b_1 \sin t + b_2 \sin 2t + \ldots + b_{m-1} \sin (m-1)t.$$

The formulas for the coefficients are the same as those in the case of approximation.

SUGGESTIONS FOR FURTHER READING

The following books are recommended for additional discussion of trigonometric interpolation, approximation, and the use of the FFT:

Briggs, W. L., and V. E. Henson, *The DFT: An Owner's Manual for the Discrete Fourier Transform*, SIAM, Philadelphia, 1995.

Golub, G. H., and C. F. Van Loan, *Matrix Computations* (3d ed.), Johns Hopkins University Press, Baltimore, 1996.

Ralston, A., and P. Rabinowitz, *A First Course in Numerical Analysis* (2d ed.), McGraw-Hill, New York, 1978.

PRACTICE THE TECHNIQUES

In Problems P10.1–P10.5, assume that the data are evenly distributed on $[0, 2\pi)$.

    a. Find the best fit trigonometric polymonial of degree $m = 1$.

    b. Find the trigonometric interpolating polymonial.

P10.1 $x = [\,1\ 1\ 0\ 0\,]$

P10.2 $x = [\,0\ 1\ 0\ -1\,]$

P10.3 $x = [\,0\ 1\ 1\ 0\,]$

P10.4 $x = [\,0\ 1/2\ 1\ 1/2\,]$

P10.5 $x = [\,0\ 1/3\ 2/3\ 1\,]$

In Problems P10.6–P10.10, assume that the data are evenly distributed on $[0, 2\pi)$.

    a. Find the best fit trigonometric polymonial of degrees $m = 1$ and $m = 2$.

    b. Find the trigonometric interpolating polymonial.

P10.6 $x = [\,1\ 1\ 1\ 0\ 0\ 0\,]$

P10.7 $x = [\,0\ 1/3\ 2/3\ 1\ 2/3\ 1/3\,]$

P10.8 $x = [\,0\ 1/2\ 1\ 0\ -1\ -1/2\,]$

P10.9 $x = [\,1\ 1\ 1\ 1\ 0\ 0\ 0\ 0\,]$

P10.10 $x = [\,0\ 1/2\ 1\ 1/2\ 0\ -1/2\ -1\ -1/2\,]$

Problems P10.11–P10.20: Use the data values from Problems P10.1–P10.10, but assume that the data are evenly distributed on $[-\pi, \pi)$.

Problems P10.21–P10.30: Find the FFT of the data in Problems P10.1–P10.10, evenly distributed on the interval $[0, 2\pi)$.

EXPLORE SOME APPLICATIONS

A10.1 Find the best fit trigonometric polynomial of degree $m = 1$ for the following data, which give the monthly (average daily) high temperature at various locations (such data are available from the Internet, travel brochures, and a variety of other sources):

	Jan	Feb	Mar	Apr	May	Jun	Jul	Aug	Sep	Oct	Nov	Dec
Paris	43	45	54	60	68	73	76	75	70	60	50	44
Amsterdam	40	42	49	56	64	70	72	71	67	57	48	42
Prague	31	34	44	54	64	70	73	72	65	53	42	34
St. Petersburg, Russia	19	22	32	46	59	68	70	69	60	48	35	26
Rome	52	55	59	66	74	82	87	86	79	71	61	55
Madrid	47	52	59	65	70	80	87	85	77	65	55	48
Marrakesh, Morocco	65	68	74	79	84	92	101	100	92	83	73	66
Palermo, Sicily	60	62	63	68	74	81	85	86	83	77	71	64
Ankara, Turkey	39	42	51	63	73	78	86	87	78	69	57	43
Shanghai	46	47	55	66	77	82	90	90	82	74	63	53
Reykjavik, Iceland	35	37	39	43	50	54	57	56	52	45	39	36
Edinburgh	42	43	46	51	56	62	65	64	60	54	48	44
London	43	44	50	56	62	69	71	71	65	58	50	45
Toronto	30	30	37	50	63	73	79	77	69	56	43	33
Santa Fe, NM	40	43	51	59	68	78	80	79	73	62	50	40
Melbourne, FL	73	73	75	79	83	86	89	90	89	86	80	74
Aiken, SC	58	61	65	74	82	88	92	91	89	81	72	62

A10.2 Find the waveform and power spectrum for the following sounds:

　　a.　A guitar string plucked at the midpoint;

y = [2.2118　2.1734　1.1321　1.2247　0.8702　0.9085
　　0.6849　0.5923　2.2118　2.1734　1.1321　1.2247
　　0.8702　0.9085　0.6849　0.5923].

　　b.　A guitar string plucked one-fourth of the way from one end of the string;

y = [　3.0572　3.2011　2.0739　2.3860　1.7887　0.9738
　　0.7410　0.5787　1.1081　0.9605　0.4487　0.1454
　　−0.1605　0.6580　0.7410　0.8945].

　　c.　A guitar string plucked fairly close to one end;

y = [4.6101　5.3621　2.6796　1.3951　1.4639　0.9843
　　0.9115　1.0058　0.4658　0.4313　0.6075　0.1599
　　0.1480　−0.0899　−1.0885　0.5493].

　　d.　A trumpet;

y = [3.9408　3.8613　1.1210　1.0305　0.5567　0.7601
　　0.4008　0.6906　0.0800　0.2362　0.2165　0.1217
　　0.0398　−0.2403　−0.6988　−0.8033]

The data in Problems A10.3–A10.20 give the radial distance from the origin to the perimeter of a geometric figure. For each problem:

　　a.　Find the power spectrum of the data.
　　b.　Reconstruct the figure represented by each set of data.

A10.3

y = [1.40　1.08　1.00　1.08　1.40　1.08　1.00　1.08　1.40
　　1.08　1.00　1.08　1.40　1.08　1.00　1.08]

A10.4

y = [1.00　1.08　1.40　1.08　1.00　1.08　1.40　1.08　1.00
　　1.08　1.40　1.08　1.00　1.08　1.40　1.08]

A10.5

y = [0.5　0.6　1.0　0.6　0.5　0.43　0.5　0.67　1.4　1.1　1.0　1.1
　　1.4　0.67　0.5　0.43]

A10.6

y = [1.0　0.6　0.5　0.43　0.5　0.67　1.4　1.1　1.0　1.1　1.4
　　0.67　0.5　0.43　0.5　0.6]

A10.7

y = [0.56　1.08　1.00　1.08　0.56　1.08　1.00　1.08　0.56
　　1.08　1.00　1.08　0.56　1.08　1.00　1.08]

A10.8

y = [1.00　1.08　0.56　1.08　1.00　1.08　0.56　1.08　1.00
　　1.08　0.56　1.08　1.00　1.08　0.56　1.08]

A10.9

y = [2.83　2.16　2.00　1.18　0.94　0.90　1.00　1.36　2.83
　　2.16　2.00　1.18　0.94　0.90　1.00　1.36]

A10.10

y = [1.26　1.06　1.00　1.06　1.26　1.67　2.00　1.67　1.26
　　1.06　1.00　1.06　1.26　1.67　2.00　1.67]

A10.11

y = [2.00　0.81　0.57　0.81　2.00　0.81　0.57　0.81　2.00
　　0.81　0.57　0.81　2.00　0.81　0.57　0.81]

A10.12

y = [0.57　0.81　2.00　0.81　0.57　0.81　2.00　0.81　0.57
　　0.81　2.00　0.81　0.57　0.81　2.00　0.81]

A10.13

y = [1.08　1.00　1.08　1.40　1.08　1.00　1.08　1.40　1.08
　　1.00　1.08　1.40　1.08　1.00　1.08　1.40]

A10.14

y = [1.08　1.00　1.08　0.56　1.08　1.00　1.08　0.56　1.08
　　1.00　1.08　0.56　1.08　1.00　1.08　0.56]

A10.15

y = [1.67　1.26　1.06　1.00　1.06　1.26　1.67　2.00　1.67
　　1.26　1.06　1.00　1.06　1.26　1.67　2.00]

A10.16

y = [1.36　2.83　2.16　2.00　1.18　0.94　0.90　1.00　1.36
　　2.83　2.16　2.00　1.18　0.94　0.90　1.00]

A10.17

y = [0.81　0.57　0.81　2.00　0.81　0.57　0.81　2.00　0.81
　　0.57　0.81　2.00　0.81　0.57　0.81　2.00]

A10.18

$\mathbf{y} = [2.00\ 1.67\ 1.26\ 1.06\ 1.00\ 1.06\ 1.26\ 1.67\ 2.00$
$\quad 1.67\ 1.26\ 1.06\ 1.00\ 1.06\ 1.26\ 1.67]$

A10.19

$\mathbf{y} = [1.00\ 1.36\ 2.83\ 2.16\ 2.00\ 1.18\ 0.94\ 0.90\ 1.00$
$\quad 1.36\ 2.83\ 2.16\ 2.00\ 1.18\ 0.94\ 0.90]$

A10.20

$\mathbf{y} = [0.6\ 1.0\ 0.6\ 0.5\ 0.43\ 0.5\ 0.67\ 1.4\ 1.1\ 1.0\ 1.1\ 1.4$
$\quad 0.67\ 0.5\ 0.43\ 0.5]$

A10.21 Using your results from Part a of Problems A10.3–A10.20, determine which data represent the same figure (in different rotations).

EXTEND YOUR UNDERSTANDING

U10.1 Modify the MATLAB function `trig_poly` to use n data points evenly spaced on an arbitrary interval of length 2π (i.e., on $[t_0, t_0 + 2\pi)$).

U10.2 Write a script to transform (evenly spaced) data on $[a, b)$, use the MATLAB function `trig_poly` to find the coefficients for the best fit trigonometric polynomial, and display the plot in terms of the original independent variable.

U10.3 Write a MATLAB function `FFT8` to implement the FFT for $n = 8$.

U10.4 Write an algorithmic description of the process for Fourier least squares approximation and interpolation.

U10.5 Construct the table showing the bit-reversal scheme for $n = 8$.

U10.6 Write a MATLAB function `FFT_R3` for the case in which $n = r_1 r_2 r_3$.

In Problems U10.7–U10.10, use your MATLAB function `FFT8` *or MATLAB's built-in function* `fft` *to find the interpolative trigonometric polynomial for the given data.*

U10.7 $\mathbf{z} = [0\ 0.5\ 1\ 0.5\ 0\ -0.5\ -1\ -0.5]$

U10.8 $\mathbf{z} = [1\ \sqrt{2}/2\ 1\ \sqrt{2}/2\ 1\ \sqrt{2}\ 1\ \sqrt{2}\,]$

U10.9 $\mathbf{z} = [0\ 1/4\ 1/2\ 3/4\ 1\ 3/4\ 1/2\ 1/4]$

U10.10 $\mathbf{z} = [0\ 0\ 1\ 1\ 1\ 1\ 0\ 0]$

U10.11 Show that the matrix form of the FFT can be applied with the order of the data shuffled, so that the transform components appear in natural order. Use the factorization of the coefficient matrix to create a schematic diagram for the two-stage computations.

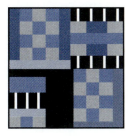

11

Numerical Differentiation and Integration

We now turn our attention to the use of numerical methods for solving problems from calculus and differential equations. In this chapter, we investigate numerical techniques for finding derivatives and definite integrals. Several formulas for approximating a first or second derivative by a difference quotient are given. These formulas can be found with the use of Taylor polynomials or Lagrange interpolation polynomials.

Numerical methods approximate the definite integral of a given function by a weighted sum of function values at specified points. We first consider several methods, known as Newton–Cotes formulas, that use evenly spaced data points. These methods are based on the integral of a simple interpolating polynomial. The trapezoid rule uses the function values at the ends of the interval of integration; Simpson's rule is based on a parabola through the ends of the interval and the midpoint of the interval. Improved accuracy can be obtained by subdividing the interval of integration and applying one of these simple techniques on each subinterval. Finally, we present a powerful integration technique, Gaussian quadrature, in which the points used in evaluating a function are chosen to provide the best possible result for a certain class of functions.

Applications of numerical differentiation are especially common in converting differential equations into difference equations for numerical solution. One must be very careful when using numerical techniques to estimate the rate of change of measured data, since small errors are exaggerated by differentiation. Integration, on the other hand, tends to smooth out errors. Numerical integration is widely used in applications, because some simple functions are difficult or impossible to integrate exactly. We present a few representative problems and use them, together with other examples, to illustrate the techniques of the chapter. We consider techniques for ordinary differential equations in Chapters 12–14 and for partial differential equations in Chapter 15.

Example 11-A Simple Functions That Do Not Have Simple Antiderivatives

The normal distribution is a very important function in statistics. Gaussian noise is one of many ways in which this function is used in engineering and science. The normal distribution function is a scaled form of the function $f(x) = e^{-x^2}$, shown in Fig. 11.1.

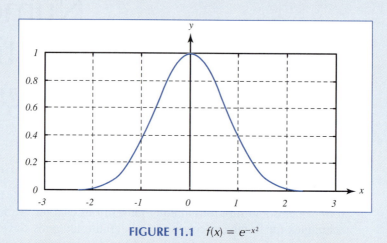

FIGURE 11.1 $f(x) = e^{-x^2}$

The indefinite integral of this function cannot be represented as a simple function. Instead, we find numerical approximations to the area under the graph of the function between any two finite values of x (say, $x = a$ and $x = b$); that is,

$$A = \int_a^b e^{-x^2} \, dx.$$

Another function that is important in optics and other applications, but does not have a simple antiderivative, is $f(x) = \sin(x)/x$; its graph is illustrated in Fig. 11.2.

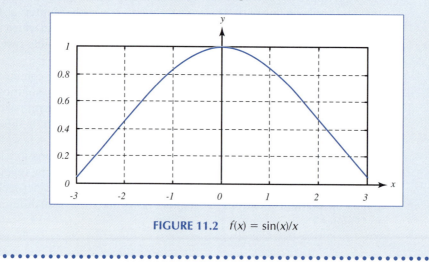

FIGURE 11.2 $f(x) = \sin(x)/x$

Example 11-B Length of an Elliptical Orbit

The simplest form of planetary orbit is an ellipse. Example 2-B in Chapter 2 describes the motion of a planet in an elliptical orbit with an eccentricity of 0.5 according to Kepler's law. If, instead of wishing to find the position of the planet at certain times, we desire to find the length of the orbit or the distance traveled between certain positions (measured by the central angle), we are faced with an example of the difficulty of calculating arc length, even for fairly simple functions. The well-known formula for the arc length of a curve described parametrically as $x(r), y(r)$ is

$$L = \int_a^b \sqrt{(x')^2 + (y')^2}\, dr.$$

If $x(r) = \cos(r)$ and $y(r) = \dfrac{3}{4}\sin(r)$, the function to be integrated is

$$f(r) = 0.25\sqrt{16\sin^2(r) + 9\cos^2(r)}.$$

We will find approximate values for the length of this ellipse using several different techniques.

For example, we may wish to compare the length of the arc traversed from $t = 0$ to $t = 10$ with the arc from $t = 60$ to $t = 70$. (See Fig. 11.3.) The central angles at 10-day intervals were found in Chapter 2 to be

$$\mathbf{r} = [0.00 \quad 1.07 \quad 1.75 \quad 2.27 \quad 2.72 \quad 3.14 \quad 3.56 \quad 4.01 \quad 4.53 \quad 5.22 \quad 6.28],$$

so we are interested in the arc length from $r = 0.00$ to $r = 1.07$ and the length from $r = 3.56$ to $r = 4.01$.

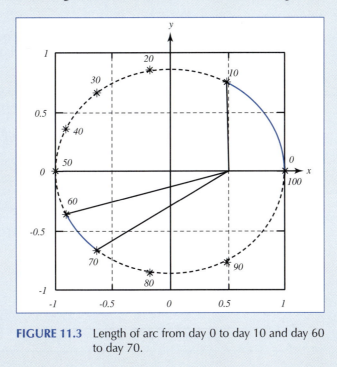

FIGURE 11.3 Length of arc from day 0 to day 10 and day 60 to day 70.

Numerical differentiation requires us to find estimates for the derivative or slope of a function by using the function values at only a set of discrete points. We begin by considering methods of approximating a first derivative. We then present formulas for second and higher derivatives. The final topic in our treatment of numerical differentiation is the use of acceleration (introduced in Chapter 1) to improve an approximate derivative value.

11.1.1 First Derivatives

The simplest difference formulas are based on using a straight line to interpolate the given data; that is, they use two data points to estimate the derivative. We assume that we have function values at x_{i-1}, x_i, and x_{i+1}; we let $f(x_{i-1}) = y_{i-1}$, $f(x_i) = y_i$, and $f(x_{i+1}) = y_{i+1}$. The spacing between the values of x is constant, so that $h = x_{i+1} - x_i = x_i - x_{i-1}$. Then we have the standard two-point formulas:

Forward difference formula

$$f'(x_i) \approx \frac{f(x_{i+1}) - f(x_i)}{x_{i+1} - x_i} = \frac{y_{i+1} - y_i}{x_{i+1} - x_i}.$$

Backward difference formula

$$f'(x_i) \approx \frac{f(x_i) - f(x_{i-1})}{x_i - x_{i-1}} = \frac{y_i - y_{i-1}}{x_i - x_{i-1}}.$$

A more balanced approach gives an approximation to the derivative at x_i using function values $f(x_{i-1})$ and $f(x_{i+1})$. Taking the average of the approximations from the forward and backward difference formulas gives the central difference formula.

Central difference formula

$$f'(x_i) \approx \frac{f(x_{i+1}) - f(x_{i-1})}{x_{i+1} - x_{i-1}} = \frac{y_{i+1} - y_{i-1}}{x_{i+1} - x_{i-1}}.$$

The three kinds of difference formula are shown in Fig. 11.4.

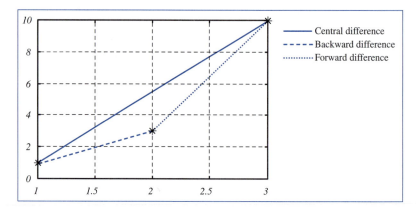

FIGURE 11.4 Three difference approximations to $f'(x_i)$.

Example 11.1 Forward, Backward, and Central Differences

To illustrate the three kinds of difference formula, consider the data points $(x_0, y_0) = (1, 2), (x_1, y_1) = (2, 4), (x_2, y_2) = (3, 8), (x_3, y_3) = (4, 16)$, and $(x_4, y_4) = (5, 32)$. Using the forward difference formula, we estimate $f'(x_2) = f'(3)$, with $h = 1$, as

$$f'(x_2) \approx \frac{f(x_3) - f(x_2)}{x_3 - x_2} = \frac{y_3 - y_2}{1} = 16 - 8 = 8.$$

Using the backward difference formula, we find that

$$f'(x_2) \approx \frac{f(x_2) - f(x_1)}{x_2 - x_1} = \frac{y_2 - y_1}{1} = 8 - 4 = 4.$$

With the central difference formula, the estimate for $f'(x_2)$, with $h = 1$, is

$$f'(x_2) \approx \frac{f(x_3) - f(x_1)}{x_3 - x_1} = \frac{y_3 - y_1}{2} = \frac{16 - 4}{2} = 6.$$

We also observe that we can use any of these formulas with the given data and $h = 2$. For example, the central difference formula estimate for $f'(x_2)$ with $h = 2$ is

$$f'(x_2) \approx \frac{f(x_4) - f(x_0)}{x_4 - x_0} = \frac{y_4 - y_0}{4} = \frac{32 - 2}{4} = 7.5.$$

Although it may seem surprising that we would want to use a larger step size (like $h = 2$), we will use this result in Example 11.4.

The data are taken from the function $y = f(x) = 2^x$, so we can compare estimates of the derivative with the true value, found by evaluating $f'(x) = 2^x (\ln 2)$ at $x = 3$. The result is $f'(3) \approx 2^3 (0.693) = 5.544$.

Interpolating the data by a polynomial rather than a straight line gives a difference formula that makes use of more than two data points. The forward and backward three-point formulas are given next.

Three-point forward difference formula

$$f'(x_i) \approx \frac{-f(x_{i+2}) + 4f(x_{i+1}) - 3f(x_i)}{x_{i+2} - x_i} = \frac{-y_{i+2} + 4y_{i+1} - 3y_i}{x_{i+2} - x_i}.$$

Three-point backward difference formula

$$f'(x_i) \approx \frac{3f(x_i) - 4f(x_{i-1}) + f(x_{i-2})}{x_i - x_{i-2}} = \frac{3y_i - 4y_{i-1} + y_{i-2}}{x_i - x_{i-2}}.$$

Example 11.2 Three-Point Difference Formulas

We illustrate these difference formulas by using the data from Example 11.1. Using the three point forward difference formula, we find that

$$f'(x_2) \approx \frac{-y_4 + 4y_3 - 3y_2}{2} = \frac{-32 + 4(16) - 3(8)}{2} = 4.$$

Using the three-point backward difference formula, we find that

$$f'(x_2) \approx \frac{3y_2 - 4y_1 + y_0}{2} = \frac{3(8) - 4(4) + 2}{2} = 5.$$

Discussion

The forward difference formula can be found from the Taylor polynomial with remainder:

$$f(x + h) = f(x) + hf'(x) + \frac{h^2}{2} f''(\eta). \tag{11.1}$$

For $h = x_{i+1} - x_i$, this gives

$$f'(x_i) = \frac{f(x_{i+1}) - f(x_i)}{h} - \frac{h}{2} f''(\eta),$$

for some $x_i \leq \eta \leq x_{i+1}$. Thus, the truncation error for the forward difference formula is $O(h)$. The formula can also be obtained by considering the Lagrange interpolating polynomial for the points (x_i, y_i) and (x_{i+1}, y_{i+1}).

Similarly, the backward difference formula can be found from eq. (11.1) by letting $h = x_{i-1} - x_i$. This gives $f(x_{i-1}) = f(x_i) + hf'(x_i) + \frac{h^2}{2} f''(\eta)$, or

$$f'(x_i) = \frac{f(x_{i-1}) - f(x_i)}{h} - \frac{h}{2} f''(\eta), \qquad \text{for some } x_{i-1} \leq \eta \leq x_i.$$

The central difference formula for the first derivative of f at the point x_i can be found from the next higher order Taylor polynomial, with $h = x_{i+1} - x_i = x_i - x_{i-1}$:

$$f(x_{i+1}) = f(x_i + h) = f(x_i) + hf'(x_i) + \frac{h^2}{2!} f''(x_i) + \frac{h^3}{3!} f'''(\eta_1),$$

$$f(x_{i-1}) = f(x_i - h) = f(x_i) - hf'(x_i) + \frac{h^2}{2!} f''(x_i) - \frac{h^3}{3!} f'''(\eta_2),$$

where $x \leq \eta_1 \leq x + h$ and $x - h \leq \eta_2 \leq x$. Although the error term involves the third derivative at two unknown points in two different intervals, if we assume that the third derivative is continuous on $[x - h, x + h]$, we can write the central difference formula with the error term as

$$f'(x_i) = \frac{f(x_{i+1}) - f(x_{i-1})}{2h} + \frac{h^2}{6} f'''(\eta), \qquad \text{for some point } x_{i-1} \leq \eta \leq x_{i+1}.$$

The central difference formula can also be found from the three-point Lagrange interpolating polynomial and is therefore known as a three-point formula (although $f(x_i)$ does not appear in it).

General Three-Point Formulas

Three-point approximation formulas for the first derivative, based on the Lagrange interpolation polynomial, do not require that the data points be equally spaced; given the three points, (x_1, y_1), (x_2, y_2), and (x_3, y_3), with $x_1 < x_2 < x_3$, the formula that follows can be used to approximate the derivative at any point in the interval $[x_1, x_3]$. The first derivative at each of the data points is given by

$$f'(x_1) \approx \frac{2x_1 - x_2 - x_3}{(x_1 - x_2)(x_1 - x_3)} y_1 + \frac{x_1 - x_3}{(x_2 - x_1)(x_2 - x_3)} y_2$$

$$+ \frac{x_1 - x_2}{(x_3 - x_1)(x_3 - x_2)} y_3,$$

$$f'(x_2) \approx \frac{x_2 - x_3}{(x_1 - x_2)(x_1 - x_3)} y_1 + \frac{2x_2 - x_1 - x_3}{(x_2 - x_1)(x_2 - x_3)} y_2$$

$$+ \frac{x_2 - x_1}{(x_3 - x_1)(x_3 - x_2)} y_3,$$

$$f'(x_3) \approx \frac{x_3 - x_2}{(x_1 - x_2)(x_1 - x_3)} y_1 + \frac{x_3 - x_1}{(x_2 - x_1)(x_2 - x_3)} y_2$$

$$+ \frac{2x_3 - x_1 - x_2}{(x_3 - x_1)(x_3 - x_2)} y_3.$$

For evenly spaced data, the formula for $f'(x_2)$ reduces to the central difference formula presented earlier.

As discussed in Chapter 8, the Lagrange interpolation polynomial for the points (x_1, y_1), (x_2, y_2), and (x_3, y_3) can be written as

$$L(x) = L_1(x)y_1 + L_2(x)y_2 + L_3(x)y_3,$$

where

$$L_1(x) = \frac{(x - x_2)(x - x_3)}{(x_1 - x_2)(x_1 - x_3)}, \quad L_2(x) = \frac{(x - x_1)(x - x_3)}{(x_2 - x_1)(x_2 - x_3)},$$

$$L_3(x) = \frac{(x - x_1)(x - x_2)}{(x_3 - x_1)(x_3 - x_2)}.$$

The approximation to the first derivative of f comes from $f'(x) \approx L'(x)$, which can be written as

$$L'(x) = L_1'(x)y_1 + L_2'(x)y_2 + L_3'(x)y_3,$$

where

$$L_1'(x) = \frac{2x - x_2 - x_3}{(x_1 - x_2)(x_1 - x_3)}, \quad L_2'(x) = \frac{2x - x_1 - x_3}{(x_2 - x_1)(x_2 - x_3)},$$

$$L_3'(x) = \frac{2x - x_1 - x_2}{(x_3 - x_1)(x_3 - x_2)}.$$

Thus,

$$f'(x) \approx \frac{2x - x_2 - x_3}{(x_1 - x_2)(x_1 - x_3)} y_1 + \frac{2x - x_1 - x_3}{(x_2 - x_1)(x_2 - x_3)} y_2$$

$$+ \frac{2x - x_1 - x_2}{(x_3 - x_1)(x_3 - x_2)} y_3.$$

11.1.2 Higher Derivatives

Formulas for higher derivatives can be found by differentiating the interpolating polynomial repeatedly or by using Taylor expansions. For example, given data at three equally spaced abscissas x_{i-1}, x_i, and x_{i+1}, the formula for the second derivative is

$$f''(x_i) \approx \frac{1}{h^2} [f(x_{i+1}) - 2f(x_i) + f(x_{i-1})], \qquad \text{with truncation error } O(h^2).$$

Example 11.3 Second Derivative

Using the data given in Example 11.1, we estimate the second derivative at $x_2 = 3$, using the points $(x_1, y_1) = (2, 4)$, $(x_2, y_2) = (3, 8)$, and $(x_3, y_3) = (4, 16)$; for this example, $h = 1$, so we have

$$f''(3) \approx [f(4) - 2f(3) + f(2)] = [16 - 2(8) + 4] = 4.$$

Derivation of Second-Derivative Formula

From the Taylor polynomial with remainder, we find that

$$f(x + h) = f(x) + hf'(x) + \frac{h^2}{2!} f''(x) + \frac{h^3}{3!} f'''(x) + \frac{h^4}{4!} f^{(4)}(\eta_1),$$

$$f(x - h) = f(x) - hf'(x) + \frac{h^2}{2!} f''(x) - \frac{h^3}{3!} f'''(x) + \frac{h^4}{4!} f^{(4)}(\eta_2),$$

where $x \le \eta_1 \le x + h$ and $x - h \le \eta_2 \le x$. Adding gives

$$f(x + h) + f(x - h) = 2f(x) + h^2 f''(x) + \frac{h^4}{4!} [f^{(4)}(\eta_1) + f^{(4)}(\eta_2)],$$

or $f''(x) \approx \frac{1}{h^2} [f(x + h) - 2f(x) + f(x - h)]$, with truncation error $O(h^4)$. The error depends on even powers of h. If we assume that the fourth derivative is continuous on $[x - h, x + h]$, we can write the error term as $-\frac{h^2}{12} f^{(4)}(\eta)$ for some point $x - h \le \eta \le x + h$.

To find formulas for the third and fourth derivatives, we seek a linear combination of the Taylor expansions for $f(x + 2h), f(x + h), f(x - h)$, and $f(x - 2h)$ so that all derivatives below the desired derivative cancel. Table 11.1 gives these formulas.

Table 11.1   Centered difference formulas, all $O(h^2)$.

$$f'(x_i) \approx \frac{1}{2h} [f(x_{i+1}) - f(x_{i-1})]$$

$$f''(x_i) \approx \frac{1}{h^2} [f(x_{i+1}) - 2f(x_i) + f(x_{i-1})]$$

$$f'''(x_i) \approx \frac{1}{2h^3} [f(x_{i+2}) - 2f(x_{i+1}) + 2f(x_{i-1}) - f(x_{i-2})]$$

$$f''''(x_i) \approx \frac{1}{h^4} [f(x_{i+2}) - 4f(x_{i+1}) + 6f(x_i) - 4f(x_{i-1}) + f(x_{i-2})]$$

Partial Derivatives

Finite-difference approximations for partial derivatives of a function of two variables are based on a discrete mesh of points for both variables. We denote a general point as (x_i, y_j) and the value of the function $u(x, y)$ at that point as $u_{i,j}$; the spacing in the x and y directions is the same, h. The simplest partial-derivative formulas are direct analogs of the preceding ordinary-derivative formulas; we use subscripts to indicate partial differentiation. Also, each formula is given in a schematic form, indicating only the coefficients on each function value. All of the following formulas are $O(h^2)$; the approximation to each partial derivative is given at (x_i, y_j):

$$u_x \approx \frac{1}{2h}[-u_{i-1,j} + u_{i+1,j}] \approx \frac{1}{2h} \{ \, \boxed{-1} \!-\!\!-\!\!-\! \boxed{0} \!-\!\!-\!\!-\! \boxed{1} \, \} \qquad j;$$

$$ i-1 \qquad i \qquad i+1$$

$$u_{xx} \approx \frac{1}{h^2}[u_{i-1,j} - 2u_{i,j} + u_{i+1,j}] \approx \frac{1}{h^2} \{ \, \boxed{1} \!-\!\!-\!\!-\! \boxed{-2} \!-\!\!-\!\!-\! \boxed{1} \, \} \qquad j.$$

$$\phantom{u_{xx} \approx} i-1 \qquad i \qquad i+1$$

For the mixed second partial derivative and higher derivatives, the schematic form is especially convenient. The Laplacian operator is $\nabla^2 u = u_{xx} + u_{yy}$, and the biharmonic operator is $\nabla^4 u = u_{xxxx} + 2u_{xxyy} + u_{yyyy}$. We thus have

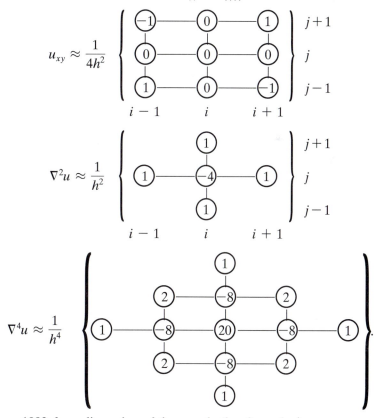

(See Ames, 1992, for a discussion of these and other formulas.)

11.1.3 Richardson Extrapolation

The technique known as Richardson extrapolation, introduced in Chapter 1, provides a method of improving the accuracy of a low-order approximation formula $A(h)$ whose error can be expressed as

$$A - A(h) = a_2h^2 + a_4h^4 + \ldots,$$

where A is the true (unknown) value of the quantity being approximated by $A(h)$ and the coefficients of the error terms do not depend on the step size h. To apply Richardson extrapolation, we form approximations to A separately using the step sizes h and $h/2$. These are combined to give an $O(h^4)$ approximation to A by means of two applications of an $O(h^2)$ formula:

$$A = \frac{4A(h/2) - A(h)}{3}.$$

To continue the extrapolation process, consider

$$A = B(h) + b_4h^4 + b_6h^6 + b_8h^8 + \ldots,$$

where $B(h)$ is simply the extrapolated approximation to A, using step sizes h and $h/2$. If we can also find an approximation to A using step sizes $h/2$ and $h/4$, this would correspond to $B(h/2)$. If we extrapolate using $B(h)$ and $B(h/2)$, we get

$$C(h) \approx \frac{16B(h/2) - B(h)}{15},$$

which has error $O(h^6)$.

The central difference formula can be written as

$$D(h) = f'(x) = \frac{1}{2h}[f(x + h) - f(x - h)] - \frac{h^2}{6}f'''(x) + O(h^4).$$

We can also find $f'(x)$ using one-half the previous value of h (whatever it may have been):

$$D(h/2) = f'(x) = \frac{1}{h}[f(x + h/2) - f(x - h/2)] - \frac{h^2}{24}f'''(x) + O(h^4).$$

Since the coefficient of the h^2 term does not change (although we do not, in general, know its value), the two estimates can be combined to give

$$D = \frac{4D(h/2) - D(h)}{3}.$$

Example 11.4 Improved Estimate of the Derivative

We illustrate the use of Richardson extrapolation with the values from Example 11.1. The value of h is 2, and the approximation to $f'(x_2)$ is based on $D(h) = 7.5$ and $D(h/2)$. We have

$$D = \frac{4(6) - 7.5}{3} = \frac{16.5}{3} \approx 5.5.$$

The data in the example are points on the curve $f(x) = 2^x$. The actual value of $f'(x)$ is $(\ln 2)2^x$, which gives $f'(3) \approx 5.54$.

Discussion

Richardson extrapolation forms a linear combination of approximations $A(h)$ and $A(h/2)$, the first using a step size h, the second based on half the original step size; the combination is chosen so that the dominant error term, which depends on h^2, cancels. Representing A in terms of the approximation and the error terms, we have

$$A = A(h) + a_2 h^2 + a_4 h^4 + \ldots. \tag{11.2}$$

If the same approximation formula is used with step size $h/2$ in place of h, the true value can be expressed as

$$A = A(h/2) + a_2 \frac{h^2}{4} + a_4 \frac{h^4}{16} + \ldots,$$

or

$$4A = 4A(h/2) + a_2 h^2 + a_4 \frac{h^4}{4} + \ldots. \tag{11.3}$$

Subtracting eq. (11.2) from eq. (11.3) gives

$$3A = 4A(h/2) - A(h) + O(h^4),$$

or

$$A = \frac{1}{3}\left[4A(h/2) - A(h)\right] + O(h^4).$$

The h^2 error terms cancel, although the higher order terms do not. However, we now have an $O(h^4)$ approximation to A derived by using two applications of an $O(h^2)$ formula.

To continue the extrapolation, we write
$$A = B(h) + b_4 h^4 + b_6 h^6 + b_8 h^8 + \ldots, \qquad (11.4)$$
where $B(h)$ is simply the extrapolated approximation to A, using step sizes h and $h/2$. If we can also find an approximation to A using step sizes $h/2$ and $h/4$, this would correspond to $B(h/2)$. We begin with $B(h/2)$
$$A = B(h/2) + b_4 (h^4/16) + b_6 (h^6/64) + b_8(h^8/2^8) + \ldots. \qquad (11.5)$$
Multiplying eq. (11.5) by 16 and subtracting eq. (11.4) from the result, so that the h^4 terms cancel, yields
$$15A = 16B(h/2) - B(h) + c_6 h^6 + c_8 h^8 + \ldots.$$
Now we define the second-level extrapolated approximation to A as
$$C(h) \approx (16B(h/2) - B(h))/15.$$

11.2 BASIC NUMERICAL INTEGRATION

Numerical integration (quadrature) rules are very important because even simple functions may not have exact formulas for their antiderivatives (indefinite integrals). Even when an exact formula for the antiderivative does exist, it may be difficult to find.

In general, a numerical integration formula approximates a definite integral by a weighted sum of function values at points within the interval of integration. A numerical integration rule has the form
$$\int_a^b f(x) \, dx \approx \sum_{i=0}^{n} c_i f(x_i),$$
where the coefficients c_i depend on the particular method. In this section, we consider the most common numerical integration formulas that are based on equally spaced data points; these are known as Newton–Cotes formulas. We first present the most basic formulas, namely, the trapezoid, Simpson, and the midpoint rules. In the next section we consider two methods of improving these simple formulas: composite quadrature and extrapolation. In Section 11.4, we present Gaussian quadrature, which is an effective method of obtaining more accurate results (for a given number of function evaluations) if the function to be integrated may be evaluated at any desired points.

We start by investigating several basic quadrature formulas that use function values at equally spaced points. There are two basic types of Newton–Cotes formulas, depending on whether or not the function values at the ends of the interval of integration are used. In this section, we consider the trapezoid and Simpson rules, "closed" formulas in which the endpoint values *are* used, and the midpoint rule, an "open" formula in which the endpoints are not used. Each of these formulas can be derived by approximating the function to be integrated by its Lagrange interpolating polynomial (different methods use polynomials of different degree) and then integrating the polynomial exactly. Since the interpolation polynomials also have an explicit formula for the error bound, error bounds can be obtained for the numerical integration formulas.

One way to achieve greater accuracy in numerical integration might be to use a method based on a higher order interpolating polynomial; however, interpolation with higher degree polynomials is not generally a good idea. We next consider integration formulas derived from linear and quadratic interpolation of $f(x)$. Later, more accurate methods based on subdivision of the original interval of integration are presented.

11.2.1 Trapezoid Rule

One of the simplest ways to approximate the area under a curve is to approximate the curve by a straight line. The trapezoid rule approximates the curve by the straight line that passes through the points $(a, f(a))$ and $(b, f(b))$, the two ends of the interval of interest. We have $x_0 = a$, $x_1 = b$, and $h = b - a$, and then

$$\int_a^b f(x)\, dx \approx \frac{h}{2}[f(x_0) + f(x_1)].$$

Example 11.5 Integral of e^{-x^2} Using the Trapezoid Rule

Consider now a very important function for which the exact value of the integral is not known:

$$f(x) = \exp(-x^2), \quad x_0 = a = 0, \quad x_1 = b = 2.$$

Using the trapezoid rule, we find (since $(b - a)/2 = 1$ for this example) that

$$\int_0^2 \exp(-x^2)\, dx \approx [\exp(-0^2) + \exp(-2^2)] = 1 + \exp(-4) = 1.0183.$$

The function and the straight-line approximation are shown in Fig. 11.5.

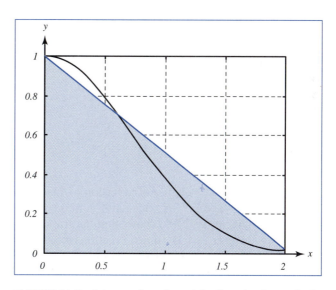

FIGURE 11.5 $f(x) = e^{-x^2}$ and straight line for integral obtained by means of the trapezoid rule.

Discussion

The trapezoid rule can be derived from the foregoing geometric reasoning or, more formally, from the Lagrange form of linear interpolation of $f(x)$ using the endpoints of the interval of integration. To demonstrate the latter method, we define $h = b - a = x_1 - x_0$ and let

$$L(x) = L_0(x)y_0 + L_1(x)y_1 = \frac{(x - x_1)}{(x_0 - x_1)} f(x_0) + \frac{(x - x_0)}{(x_1 - x_0)} f(x_1).$$

Then

$$\int_a^b f(x)\, dx \approx \int_a^b \frac{(x - x_1)}{(x_0 - x_1)} f(x_0) + \frac{(x - x_0)}{(x_1 - x_0)} f(x_1)\, dx.$$

$$= \int_a^b \frac{(x_1 - x)}{h} f(x_0) + \frac{(x - x_0)}{h} f(x_1)\, dx$$

$$= \frac{1}{h} \int_a^b x_1 f(x_0) - x_0 f(x_1) + x[f(x_1) - f(x_0)]\, dx$$

$$= x_1 f(x_0) - x_0 f(x_1) + \frac{1}{h} \int_a^b x[f(x_1) - f(x_0)]\, dx$$

$$= x_1 f(x_0) - x_0 f(x_1) + \frac{b^2 - a^2}{2h} [f(x_1) - f(x_0)]$$

$$= bf(x_0) - af(x_1) + \frac{b + a}{2} [f(x_1) - f(x_0)]$$

$$= \frac{b - a}{2} f(x_0) + \frac{b - a}{2} f(x_1)$$

$$= \frac{h}{2} [f(x_0) + f(x_1)].$$

The degree of precision r of an integration formula is the (highest) degree of polynomial for which the method gives an exact result. Error analysis (see, e.g., Atkinson, 1989) shows that the trapezoid rule gives exact results for polynomials of degree ≤ 1, i.e., linear functions for which the interpolating polynomial is exact. Thus, the trapezoid rule has a degree of precision, $r = 1$. In general, if we assume that $f(x)$ is twice continuously differentiable on $[a, b]$, then

$$\int_a^b f(x)\, dx = \frac{b - a}{2} [f(a) + f(b)] - \frac{(b - a)^3}{12} f''(\eta), \qquad \text{for some } \eta \in [a, b].$$

$$(11.6)$$

11.2.2 Simpson Rule

Approximating the function to be integrated by a quadratic polynomial leads to the basic Simpson rule:

$$h = \frac{b - a}{2}, \qquad x_0 = a, \qquad x_1 = x_0 + h = \frac{b + a}{2}, \qquad x_2 = b.$$

The approximate integral is given by

$$\int_a^b f(x)\,dx \approx \frac{h}{3}[f(x_0) + 4f(x_1) + f(x_2)] = \frac{b - a}{6}\left[f(a) + 4f\left(\frac{b + a}{2}\right) + f(b)\right].$$

Example 11.6 Integral Using Simpson's Rule

Consider the problem of finding $\displaystyle\int_0^1 \frac{1}{1 + x^2}\,dx$ numerically. Using Simpson's rule with $f(x) = 1/(1 + x^2)$, $a = 0$, and $b = 1$ gives $h = 1/2$, and

$$\int_0^1 \frac{1}{1 + x^2}\,dx \approx \frac{1}{6}[f(0) + 4f(1/2) + f(1)] = \frac{1}{6}\left[\frac{1}{1} + (4)\frac{4}{5} + \frac{1}{2}\right] = \frac{47}{60} \approx 0.78333.$$

The exact value of the integral is $\arctan(1) = \pi/4 \approx 0.7853.\dots$ The graphs of $f(x) = 1/(1 + x^2)$ and the quadratic polynomial that passes through the points $(0, 1)$, $(1/2, 4/5)$, and $(1, 1/2)$ are shown in Fig. 11.6. It is not surprising that the approximate value of the integral from Simpson's rule is quite good, because the two functions are very similar.

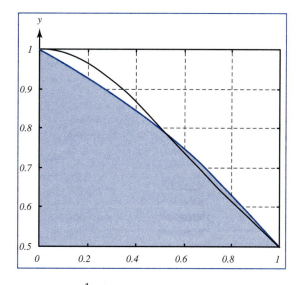

FIGURE 11.6 $f(x) = \dfrac{1}{1 + x^2}$ and parabolic approximation for Simpson's rule.

Example 11.7 Integral of e^{-x^2} Using Simpson's Rule

Consider the problem of finding the integral of $f(x) = \exp(-x^2)$ on $[0, 2]$. The required values for applying Simpson's rule are

$$h = \frac{b-a}{2} = 1, \qquad x_0 = a = 0, \qquad x_1 = (2+0)/2 = 1, \qquad x_2 = b = 2,$$

which gives

$$\int_0^2 \exp(-x^2)\, dx \approx \frac{1}{3}\left[\exp(-0^2) + 4\exp(-1^2) + \exp(-2^2)\right] = .8299.$$

The graphs of $f(x) = \exp(-x^2)$ and the quadratic polynomial passing through the points $(0, 1), (1, \exp(-1))$, and $(2, \exp(-4))$ are shown in Fig. 11.7.

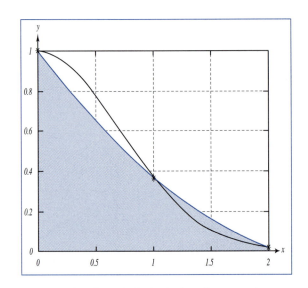

FIGURE 11.7 $f(x) = e^{-x^2}$ and parabola for finding the integral using Simpson's rule.

Discussion

Simpson's rule is found by integrating the Lagrange interpolating polynomial for $f(x)$, viz.,

$$L(x) = \frac{(x - x_1)(x - x_2)}{(x_0 - x_1)(x_0 - x_2)} f(x_0) + \frac{(x - x_0)(x - x_2)}{(x_1 - x_0)(x_1 - x_2)} f(x_1)$$

$$+ \frac{(x - x_0)(x - x_1)}{(x_2 - x_0)(x_2 - x_1)} f(x_2),$$

where

$$x_0 = a, \qquad x_1 = x_0 + h = \frac{b + a}{2}, \qquad x_2 = b, \qquad h = \frac{b - a}{2}.$$

Integrating, we obtain

$$\int_a^b f(x)\, dx \approx \int_a^b \frac{(x - x_1)(x - x_2)}{2h^2} f(x_0)\, dx$$

$$- \int_a^b \frac{(x - x_0)(x - x_2)}{h^2} f(x_1)\, dx$$

$$+ \int_a^b \frac{(x - x_0)(x - x_1)}{2h^2} f(x_2)\, dx = I_1 - I_2 + I_3.$$

We show the computations for I_1; the other terms in the formula can be derived from I_2 and I_3 in a similar manner. For I_1, we have

$$I_1 = \int_a^b \frac{(x - x_1)(x - x_2)}{2h^2} f(x_0)\, dx$$

$$= \frac{f(x_0)}{2h^2} \int_a^b x^2 - (x_1 + x_2)x + x_1 x_2\, dx$$

$$= \frac{f(x_0)}{2h^2} \left[\frac{b^3 - a^3}{3} - (x_1 + x_2)\frac{b^2 - a^2}{2} + x_1 x_2 (b - a) \right]$$

$$= \frac{f(x_0)}{12h} [b^2 - 2ba + a^2] = \frac{h}{3} f(x_0).$$

Error analysis shows that Simpson's rule gives the exact value of the integral for polynomials of degree ≤ 3, even though quadratic interpolation is exact only if $f(x)$ is a polynomial of degree ≤ 2. This surprising result indicates that Simpson's rule is significantly more accurate than the trapezoid rule. The degree of precision for Simpson's rule is $r = 3$. If $f(x)$ is four times continuously differentiable on $[a, b]$, then

$$\int_a^b f(x)\, dx = \frac{h}{3} \left[f(a) + 4f\left(\frac{a + b}{2} \right) + f(b) \right] - \frac{h^5}{90} f^{(4)}(\eta), \qquad (11.7)$$

for some $\eta \in [a, b]$. (See Atkinson, 1989, for details.)

11.2.3 Midpoint Rule

The trapezoid and Simpson rules are the simplest examples of Newton–Cotes closed formulas; that is, they use function evaluations at the endpoints of the interval of integration. If we use only function evaluations at points within the interval, the simplest formula (a Newton–Cotes *open* formula) is the midpoint rule. This formula uses only one function evaluation (so $n = 1$), at the midpoint of the interval, $x_m = (a + b)/2$. Interpolating the function by the constant value $f(x_m)$, we get the midpoint rule:

$$\int_a^b f(x)dx \approx (b - a)f\left(\frac{a + b}{2}\right).$$

Assuming that f is twice continuously differentiable yields

$$\int_a^b f(x)\, dx = (b - a)f\left(\frac{a + b}{2}\right) + \frac{(b - a)^3}{24} f''(\eta), \qquad \text{for some } \eta \in [a, b].$$

Example 11.8 The Midpoint Rule

Using the midpoint rule to approximate the integral

$$S = \int_0^\pi \frac{\sin(x)}{x}\, dx,$$

we find that

$$\int_0^\pi \frac{\sin(x)}{x}\, dx \approx \pi \frac{\sin(\pi/2)}{\pi/2} = \pi \frac{1}{\pi/2} = 2.$$

Figure 11.8 compares the actual value of the area with that found by using the midpoint rule.

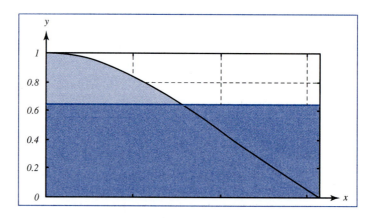

FIGURE 11.8   The area given by the integral S, and the approximation using the midpoint rule.

11.2.4 Other Newton–Cotes Open Formulas

The Newton–Cotes open formula that uses two function evaluations is given by

$$x_0 = a, \qquad x_1 = \frac{2a + b}{3}, \qquad x_2 = \frac{a + 2b}{3}, \qquad f_1 = f(x_1), \qquad f_2 = f(x_2),$$

$$\int_a^b f(x)\, dx = \frac{b - a}{2}[f_1 + f_2] + \frac{(b - a)^3}{108} f''(\eta), \qquad \text{for some } \eta \in [a, b].$$

$$(11.8)$$

The coefficient of the error term is smaller than that in the trapezoid rule (eq. (11.6)), which uses the same number of function evaluations. (See Isaacson and Keller, 1994, p. 316.)

For the Newton–Cotes open formula using three functions evaluations, we define $f_1 = f(x_1), f_2 = f(x_2)$, and $f_3 = f(x_3)$, where

$$x_o = a, \qquad x_1 = \frac{3a + b}{4}, \qquad x_2 = \frac{2a + 2b}{4}, \qquad x_3 = \frac{a + 3b}{4}.$$

Then, taking $h = \dfrac{b - a}{4}$, we have

$$\int_a^b f(x)\, dx = \frac{4h}{3}[2f_1 - f_2 + 2f_3] + \frac{14h^5}{45} f^{(4)}(\eta), \quad \text{for some } \eta \in [a, b]. \quad (11.9)$$

The coefficient of the error term is smaller than that in Simpson's rule (eq. (11.7)), which uses the same number of function evaluations. (Note the difference in the definition of h in eqs. (11.7) and (11.9)); (see Isaacson and Keller, 1994, p. 316.)

Care must be taken in comparing open and closed formulas, since a comparison can be made on the number of nodes or on the number of function evaluations. Issacson and Keller define the number of nodes to be the number of subintervals used, so that closed formulas use $n + 1$ function evaluations and open formulas use $n - 1$ evaluations, for a given number of subintervals.

Rather than continuing to use quadrature formulas based on interpolating polynomials of ever higher order, we now consider three more effective methods of improving the accuracy of integration. The first two of these improvements are based (as are all our formulas so far) on function evaluations at evenly spaced points. Composite integration formulas, which we examine in the next section, are based on subdividing the interval of integration into subintervals and applying the basic integration rule in each subinterval. The formal statement of the algorithm and MATLAB function for each rule is presented for the more general, composite, form of the method.

The easiest method of improving the accuracy of numerical integration is to apply one of the lower order methods presented in the previous section repeatedly on several subintervals. This is known as *composite integration*.

11.3.1 Composite Trapezoid Rule

If we divide the interval of integration, $[a, b]$, into two or more subintervals and use the trapezoid rule on each subinterval, we obtain the composite trapezoid rule. For the simplest case, which uses the same number of function evaluations (at the same points) as the Simpson rule, consider two subintervals $[a, x_1]$ and $[x_1, b]$, where $x_1 = (b + a)/2$. The value of h is the same for each subinterval, namely, $h = (b - a)/2$. Then

$$\int_a^b f(x)\, dx = \int_a^{x_1} f(x)\, dx + \int_{x_1}^b f(x)\, dx \approx$$

$$\frac{h}{2}[f(a) + f(x_1)] + \frac{h}{2}[f(x_1) + f(b)],$$

or

$$\int_a^b f(x)\, dx \approx \frac{h}{2}[f(a) + 2f(x_1) + f(b)] = \frac{b - a}{4}[f(a) + 2f(x_1) + f(b)].$$

If we divide the interval into n subintervals, we get $h = \dfrac{b - a}{n}$, and

$$\int_a^b f(x)\, dx = \int_a^{x_1} f(x)\, dx + \ldots + \int_{x_{n-1}}^b f(x)\, dx$$

$$\approx \frac{h}{2}[f(a) + f(x_1)] + \ldots + \frac{h}{2}[f(x_{n-1} + f(b)],$$

so that

$$\int_a^b f(x)\, dx \approx \frac{b - a}{2n}[f(a) + 2f(x_1) + \ldots + 2f(x_{n-1}) + f(b)].$$

MATLAB Function for Trapezoid Rule

```
function I = Trap( f, a, b, n)
%    find integral of f using composite trapezoid rule
h = (b-a)/n; S = feval(f, a);
for i = 1 : n-1
    x(i) = a + h*i
    S = S + 2*feval(f, x(i))
end
S = S + feval(f, b); I = h*S/2
```

Example 11.9 Integral of 1/x Using the Composite Trapezoid Rule

Consider the problem of finding

$$\int_1^2 \frac{dx}{x} \approx \frac{h}{2}[f(a) + 2f(x_1) + \ldots + 2f(x_{n-1}) + f(b)].$$

For $n = 2$ subintervals, $h = (2-1)/2 = 1/2$, and the composite trapezoid rule gives

$$I_1 = \frac{1}{4}[f(1) + 2f(1.5) + f(2)] = \frac{1}{4}\left[\frac{1}{1} + \frac{2}{1.5} + \frac{1}{2}\right] = \frac{17}{24} \approx 0.7083.$$

The function and the two straight-line approximations are shown in Fig. 11.9.

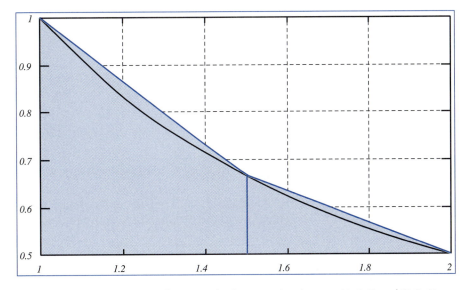

FIGURE 11.9 $y = 1/x$ and trapezoid rule approximations on [1, 1.5] and [1.5, 2].

For $n = 2^2 = 4$ subintervals, $h = 1/4$, and the composite trapezoid rule gives

$$I_2 = \frac{1}{8}[f(1) + 2f(5/4) + 2f(3/2) + 2f(7/4) + f(2)]$$

$$= \frac{1}{8}\left[1 + \frac{8}{5} + \frac{4}{3} + \frac{8}{7} + \frac{1}{2}\right] = 0.6970\ldots.$$

For $n = 2^3 = 8$ subintervals, $h = 1/8$, and the composite trapezoid rule yields

$$I_3 = \frac{1}{16}[f(1) + 2f(9/8) + 2f(5/4) + 2f(11/8) + 2f(3/2)$$

$$+ 2f(13/8) + 2f(7/4) + 2f(15/8) + f(2)]$$

$$= 0.6941\ldots.$$

The exact value of the integral is $\ln(2) \approx 0.693147\ldots.$

11.3.2 Composite Simpson's Rule

Applying the same idea of subdivision of intervals to Simpson's rule and requiring that n be even gives the composite Simpson rule. If we divide the interval of integration $[a, b]$ into two subintervals, we have $n = 4$, and we can apply Simpsons's rule twice. Accordingly, consider the two subintervals $[a, x_2]$ and $[x_2, b]$, where $x_2 = (b + a)/2$ and $h = (b - a)/4$. Then

$$\int_a^b f(x)\, dx = \int_a^{x_2} f(x)\, dx + \int_{x_2}^b f(x)\, dx$$

$$\approx \frac{h}{3}[f(a) + 4f(x_1) + f(x_2)] + \frac{h}{3}[f(x_2) + 4f(x_3) + f(b)],$$

or

$$\int_a^b f(x)\, dx \approx \frac{h}{3}[f(a) + 4f(x_1) + 2f(x_2) + 4f(x_3) + f(b)].$$

In general, for n even, we have $h = (b - a)/n$, and Simpson's rule is

$$\int_a^b f(x)\, dx \approx \frac{h}{3}[f(a) + 4f(x_1) + 2f(x_2) + 4f(x_3) + 2f(x_4)$$
$$+ \ldots + 2f(x_{n-2}) + 4f(x_{n-1}) + f(b)].$$

Example 11.10 Integral of exp(−x²) Using Composite Simpson's Rule

For $n = 4$ and $f(x) = \exp(-x^2)$, the approximate value of the integral of f is 0.84232. The function and the two quadratic approximations are illustrated in Fig. 11.10.

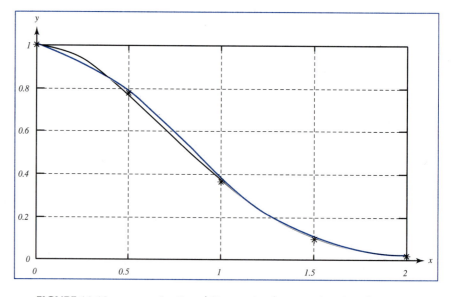

FIGURE 11.10 $y = \exp(-x^2)$ and Simpson's rule approximations for $n = 4$.

MATLAB Function for Simpson's Rule

```
function I = Simp(f, a, b, n)
%    integral of f using composite Simpson rule
%    n must be even
h = (b-a)/n;
S = feval(f, a);
for i = 1 : 2 : n-1
        x(i) = a + h*i;
        S = S + 4*feval(f, x(i));
end
for i = 2 : 2 : n-2
        x(i) = a + h*i;
        S = S + 2*feval(f, x(i));
end
S = S + feval(f, b);
I = h*S/3
```

Example 11.11 Length of Elliptical Orbit

Consider the problem of finding the length of an elliptical orbit, where the ellipse is described parametrically as $x(r) = \cos(r)$ and $y(r) = \dfrac{3}{4}\sin(r)$. The length of the orbit is

$$L = \int_a^b \sqrt{(x')^2 + (y')^2}\, dr = 0.25 \int_a^b \sqrt{16\sin^2(r) + 9\cos^2(r)}\, dr.$$

We can approximate the entire length of the orbit by using the preceding Simpson integration function, with $a = 0$ and $b = 2\pi$. If we use $n = 4$, the approximate value of the integral is $I = 4.4506$; using $n = 20$ gives $I = 5.3688$.

As described in Example 11-B, we can estimate the difference in the speed of the orbiting object when it is close to the planet (say, between day 0 and day 10) and the speed when it is further away (say, between day 60 and day 70). The arc length covered from day 0 to day 10 is approximately $I = 0.8556$; the arc length covered from day 60 to day 70 is approximately $I = 0.3702$. Thus, during the 10 days that the orbiting object is closest to the object it is revolving around, it is traveling more than twice as fast as it travels during days 60 to 70 (not quite the time it is farthest away).

11.3.3 Extrapolation Methods for Quadrature

As we saw earlier, an approximation formula whose error can be expressed as even powers of the step size may be extrapolated by using results from two step sizes (h and $h/2$) to obtain an estimate that is more accurate than either of the original results. The extrapolated form of the trapezoid rule is known as *Romberg integration*. The midpoint rule is also suitable for extrapolation.

The composite trapezoid rule can be expressed as

$$\int_a^b f(x)\, dx = \frac{h}{2}[f(a) + 2f(x_1) + \ldots + 2f(x_{n-1}) + f(b)] + \sum_{j=1}^{\infty} c_j h^{2j},$$

which indicates that we can apply Richardson extrapolation. We start with a simple example.

Example 11.12 Integral of 1/x Using Romberg Integration

Consider the problem of finding $\int_1^2 \frac{dx}{x}$ using the trapezoid rule. We start with one subinterval, so $h = 1$, and the trapezoid rule gives

$$\int_1^2 \frac{dx}{x} \approx I_0 = \frac{1}{2}[f(1) + f(2)] = \frac{1}{2}\left[\frac{1}{1} + \frac{1}{2}\right] = \frac{3}{4} = 0.75.$$

For two subintervals, $h = 1/2$, and the composite trapezoid rule gives

$$I_1 = \frac{1}{4}[f(1) + 2f(1.5) + f(2)] = \frac{1}{4}\left[\frac{1}{1} + \frac{2}{1.5} + \frac{1}{2}\right] = \frac{17}{24} \approx 0.7083.$$

To apply Richardson extrapolation, we use the formula

$$A \approx \frac{1}{3}\left[4A\left(\frac{h}{2}\right) - A(h)\right];$$

we let I_0 be $A(h)$ and I_1 be $A\left(\frac{h}{2}\right)$ to give the extrapolated value

$$I \approx \frac{1}{3}[4I_1 - I_0] = [4(0.7083) - 0.7500]/3 = 0.6944.$$

The exact value of the integral is $\ln(2) \approx 0.693147\ldots$.

It is convenient to form a table of the approximations; Column I gives the result from the composite trapezoid rule, and column II gives the extrapolated approximation:

	I	II
$h = 1$	0.7500	
		0.6944
$h = 1/2$	0.7083	

We extend this process by applying the composite trapezoid rule several times, using twice as many subintervals each time. This produces a corresponding succession of values of h. We denote the approximation formed using $n = 2^k$ subintervals as I_k. Note that each time we increase k by 1, we double the number of points at which the function is evaluated and half the value of h (as is required for Richardson extrapolation). Furthermore, the function values that were used for a previous estimate appear again on each refinement. Before giving the general formulas, we continue our previous example.

Example 11.12, continued

Continue the problem of finding

$$\int_1^2 \frac{dx}{x} \approx \frac{h}{2}[f(a) + 2f(x_1) + \ldots + 2f(x_{n-1}) + f(b)].$$

For $k = 0$, we found that $I_0 = 0.75$.
For $k = 1$, we found that $I_1 = 0.7083$.
For $k = 2$, we have $n = 2^2 = 4$ subintervals; so $h = 1/4$ and

$$I_2 = \frac{1}{8}\left[1 + \frac{8}{5} + \frac{4}{3} + \frac{8}{7} + \frac{1}{2}\right] \approx 0.6970.$$

For $k = 3$, we have $n = 2^3 = 8$ subintervals; so $h = 1/8$ and

$$I_3 \approx 0.6941.$$

To apply Richardson extrapolation to the sequence we have generated, we have several approximations that can play the role of $A(h/2)$ and $A(h)$ in the basic formula,

$$A \approx \frac{1}{3}\left[4A\left(\frac{h}{2}\right) - A(h)\right].$$

First, we could let I_0 be $A(h)$ and I_1 be $A(h/2)$, as we did previously. Then

$$I \approx \frac{1}{3}[4I_1 - I_0] = [4(0.7083) - 0.7500]/3 = 0.6944.$$

Or we could use I_1 as $A(h)$ and I_2 as $A(h/2)$, yielding

$$I \approx \frac{1}{3}[4I_2 - I_1].$$

Extending the previous table of the approximations, with the first column giving the values computed by the composite trapezoid rule and the second column giving the extrapolated approximation, results in the following new table:

	I	II
$h = 1$	0.7500	
		0.6944
$h = 1/2$	0.7083	
		0.6933
$h = 1/4$	0.6970	
		0.6932
$h = 1/8$	0.6941	

If we use the fact that the error term in the composite trapezoid rule can be represented as a series with only even powers of h (see, e.g., Ralston and Rabinowitz, 1978), the extrapolation can be extended for as many levels as is desired. For the second level of extrapolation, we have

$$C(h) \approx \frac{16}{15} B\left(\frac{h}{2}\right) - \frac{1}{15} B(h)$$

and the following table:

	I	II	III
$h = 1$	0.7500		
		0.6944	
$h = 1/2$	0.7083		$[16(0.6933) - 0.6944]/15$
		0.6933	
$h = 1/4$	0.6970		

For the kth level of extrapolation, the appropriate formula is

$$D(h) \approx \frac{4^k C(h/2) - C(h)}{4^k - 1}.$$

Allowing for five levels of extrapolation in the MATLAB function presented shortly, we find the following table of values for $\int_1^2 \frac{dx}{x}$:

0.7500	0.6944	0.6932	0.6931	0.6931	0.6931
0.7083	0.6933	0.6931	0.6931	0.6931	0
0.6970	0.6932	0.6931	0.6931	0	0
0.6941	0.6931	0.6931	0	0	0
0.6934	0.6931	0	0	0	0
0.6932	0	0	0	0	0

The full algorithm for Romberg integration makes use of the fact that the same function evaluations that were used in the previous approximation are needed (along with some additional ones) in the current approximation, to achieve further efficiencies that are not included in the MATLAB function that follows. We choose instead to rely on repeated calls to the function for the trapezoid rule given earlier.

MATLAB Function for Romberg Integration

```
function Q = Romberg(f, a, b, kmax)
%   find integral of function f on the interval [a, b]
%   using kmax steps of Romberg integration (accelerated trapezoid rule)
Q(1, 1) = trap(f, a, b, 1);
Q(2, 1) = trap(f, a, b, 2);
Q(1, 2)  = (4*Q(2, 1) - Q(1, 1))/3;
for k = 2 : kmax
    n = 2^k;
    Q(k+1, 1) = trap(f, a, b, n);  % one more entry in col 1
    for j = 2 : k+1
        c = 4^(j-1);
        Q(k-j+2, j)  = (c*Q(k-j+3, j-1) - Q(k-j+2, j-1))/(c-1);
                                    %   one more extrapolated value

    end
end
```

11.4 GAUSSIAN QUADRATURE

The Newton–Cotes formulas are based on evaluations of a function at equally spaced values of the independent variable. Gaussian integration formulas evaluate functions at points which are chosen so that the formula is exact for polynomials of as high a degree as possible. Gaussian integration formulas are usually expressed in terms of the interval of integration $[-1, 1]$. For other intervals, a change of variable is used to transform the problem so that it utilizes the interval $[-1, 1]$.

11.4.1 Gaussian Quadrature on $[-1, 1]$

The basic form of a Gaussian quadrature formula is

$$\int_{-1}^{1} f(x)\, dx \approx \sum_{i=1}^{n} c_i f(x_i),$$

where the appropriate values of the points x_i and the coefficients c_i depend on the choice of n.

By choosing the quadrature points $x_1, \ldots, x_n$ as the n zeros of the nth-degree Legendre polynomial, and by using the appropriate coefficients, the integration formula is exact for polynomials of degree up to $2n-1$.

For example, the Gauss–Legendre quadrature rule for two evaluation points, which is exact for polynomials up to and including degree 3, has the form

$$\int_{-1}^{1} f(x)\, dx \approx c_1 f(x_1) + c_2 f(x_2) = f(-1/\sqrt{3}) + f(1/\sqrt{3})$$

$$\approx f(-0.577) + f(0.577).$$

Similarly, the Gauss–Legendre quadrature rule for $n = 3$ evaluation points, which is exact for polynomials up to and including degree 5, has the form

$$\int_{-1}^{1} f(x)\, dx \approx c_1 f(x_1) + c_2 f(x_2) + c_3 f(x_3) = \frac{5}{9} f(-\sqrt{3/5}) + \frac{8}{9} f(0) + \frac{5}{9} f(\sqrt{3/5})$$

$$\approx \frac{5}{9} f(-0.775) + \frac{8}{9} f(0) + \frac{5}{9} f(0.775).$$

Example 11.13 Integral of $\exp(-x^2)$ on $[-1, 1]$ Using Gaussian Quadrature

Consider now the integral

$$\int_{-1}^{1} \exp(-x^2)\, dx \approx c_1 f(x_1) + c_2 f(x_2) = f(-1/\sqrt{3}) + f(1/\sqrt{3})$$

$$= \exp[-(-1/\sqrt{3})^2] + \exp[-(1/\sqrt{3})^2]$$

$$= \exp[-(1/3)] + \exp[-(1/3)] \approx 2(0.7165) \approx 1.433.$$

Table 11.2 gives values of the Gaussian quadrature parameters x_i and c_i for values of $n = 2, \ldots, 4$.

Table 11.2 Parameters for Gaussian quadrature

n	x_i	c_i
2	± 0.57735	1
3	0	8/9
	± 0.77459	5/9
4	± 0.861136	0.34785
	± 0.339981	0.652145

11.4.2 Gaussian Quadrature on $[a, b]$

If we have an integral on an interval $[a, b]$ that is not $[-1, 1]$, we must make a change of variable to transform the integral to the required interval. We start by writing the desired integral in terms of some variable other than x, say, t:

$$\int_a^b f(t)\, dt.$$

The change of variable that is required to convert an integral on the interval $t \in [a, b]$ to the required interval $x \in [-1, 1]$ for Gaussian quadrature is simply the linear transformation

$$t = \frac{(b - a)x + b + a}{2},$$

or

$$\frac{2t - b - a}{b - a} = x.$$

Thus, the integral from a to b of the function $f(t)$ is changed into the integral from -1 to 1 of the function

$$f\left[\frac{(b - a)x + b + a}{2}\right]\frac{b - a}{2},$$

where the factor $\dfrac{b - a}{2}$ comes from the conversion from dt to dx. Accordingly, we now apply Gaussian quadrature to the integral

$$\int_{-1}^1 f\left[\frac{(b - a)x + b + a}{2}\right]\frac{b - a}{2}\, dx.$$

Example 11.14 Integral of exp(−x²) on [0, 2] Using Gaussian Quadrature

Consider again the integral

$$f(t) = \exp(-t^2), \qquad t_0 = a = 0, \qquad t_1 = b = 2.$$

The required change of variable gives

$$t = \frac{(b-a)x + b + a}{2} = \frac{(2-0)x + 2 + 0}{2} = x + 1,$$

or

$$x = \frac{2t - b - a}{b - a} = \frac{2t - 2 - 0}{2 - 0} = t - 1.$$

Thus, the integral from a to b of the function $f(t)$ is changed into the integral from -1 to 1 of the function

$$\exp[-(x + 1)^2].$$

We now apply Gaussian quadrature to the integral $\displaystyle\int_{-1}^{1} \exp[-(x + 1)^2]\, dx$:

$$\int_{-1}^{1} f(x)\, dx \approx c_1 f(x_1) + c_2 f(x_2) = \exp[-(1.5774)^2] + \exp[-(0.4226)^2] \approx 0.9195.$$

MATLAB Function for Gaussian Quadrature

```
function I = Gauss_quad( f, a, b, k)
% find integral of function f on [ a, b]
% using Gaussian quadrature at k (k = 2, ... 5) points
 t = [-0.5773502692    -0.7745966692    -0.8611363116    -0.9061798459;
      0.5773502692     0.0000000000     -0.3399810436    -0.5384693101;
      0.0              0.7745966692     0.3399810436     0.0000000000;
      0.0              0.0              0.8611363116     0.5384693101;
      0.0              0.0              0.0              0.9061798459]
 c = [1.0              0.5555555556     0.3478548451     0.2369268850;
      1.0              0.8888888889     0.6521451549     0.4786286705;
      0.0              0.5555555556     0.6521451549     0.5688888889;
      0.0              0.0              0.3478548451     0.4786286705;
      0.0              0.0              0.0              0.2369268850]
 x(1:k) = 0.5*((b - a).*t(1:k,k-1) + b + a)
 y = feval(f, x)
 cc(1 : k) = c(1 : k, k-1)
 cd = cc'
int = y*cd
I = int*(b-a)/2
```

Discussion

It is fairly simple to directly derive the coefficients for the case of $n = 2$ by requiring that the integration formula give the exact result for the polynomials $f_0 = 1$, $f_1 = x$, $f_2 = x^2$, and $f_3 = x^3$. For $f_0 = 1$, we require that

$$\int_{-1}^{1} 1 \, dx = 2 = c_1 + c_1;$$

for $f_1 = x$, we require that

$$\int_{-1}^{1} x \, dx = 0 = c_1 x_1 + c_1 x_2;$$

for $f_2 = x^2$, we require that

$$\int_{-1}^{1} x^2 \, dx = \frac{2}{3} = c_1 x_1^2 + c_1 x_2^2;$$

and for $f_3 = x^3$, we require that

$$\int_{-1}^{1} x^3 \, dx = 0 = c_1 x_1^3 + c_1 x_2^3.$$

These four equations must be solved for the points x_1 and x_2 and the coefficients c_1 and c_2. First, we observe that none of the unknowns can be zero. Then, solving the second equation for c_1 and substituting into the fourth equation gives $x_1^2 = x_2^2$. Since we assume that $x_1 \neq x_2$, we must have $x_1 = -x_2$. Substituting the expressions for c_1 and x_1 into the first equation gives $c_2 = c_1 = 1$. Finally, using the third equation gives $x_1 = -1/\sqrt{3}$ and $x_2 = +1/\sqrt{3}$.

Using a direct algebraic approach to derive higher degree Gaussian quadrature is not practical. Instead, the analysis utilizes the orthogonality of the Legendre polynomials (introduced in Chapter 9). The best approximation to the integral is obtained when the function is evaluated at the zeros of the appropriate Legendre polynomial. (See Atkinson, 1989, for details.)

The n-point Gauss–Legendre quadrature rule evaluates a function at the n zeros of the nth-degree Legendre polynomial; the quadrature rule has a degree of precision of at least $2n - 1$ (i.e., it is exact for polynomials of degree at least $2n - 1$).

The coefficients are

$$c_i = \frac{-2}{(n + 1)P_n'(x_i)P_{n+1}(x_i)}.$$

(See Atkinson, 1989, p. 276; Ralston and Rabinowitz, 1978, p. 105.)

The error in Gaussian quadrature goes to zero more rapidly for integrands that are smoother, whereas the composite trapezoid rule converges as h^2, regardless of the smoothness of $f(x)$. (See Atkinson, 1989.)

11.5 MATLAB's Methods

11.5.1 Differentiation

Since small changes in a function can create large changes in its slope, numerical differentiation is much more difficult than numerical integration. Especially if the data to be differentiated are obtained experimentally, the best approach may be to find a least squares fit to the data and then differentiate the approximating function. MATLAB's function p = polyfit(x, y, n) will find the coefficients of the polynomial of degree n that best fits the data in the least squares sense. The resulting polynomial (with coefficients given in the vector **p**) can be evaluated using polyfit(p, x) and differentiated with polyder(p).

MATLAB can also provide the forward or backward difference approximation to dy/dx, by using the function diff. For $x = [x(1), x(2), \ldots, x(n)]$, diff(x) gives a vector, of length $n-1$, consisting of the differences between successive elements of x; i.e., diff(x) = $[x(2) - x(1), x(3) - x(2), \ldots, x(n) - x(n-1)]$. Thus, the ith element of dy = diff(y)./diff(x) is the forward difference approximation to dy/dx at $x(i)$ and is also the backward difference approximation to dy/dx at $x(i+1)$.

11.5.2 Integration

MATLAB has three built-in functions for numerically computing a definite integral (over a finite range). The function traps(x, y) uses the composite trapezoid rule for the data points given in the vectors **x** and **y**. Vector **y** gives the function values at **x**.

The functions Q = quad('f', xmin, xmax) and Q = quad8('f', xmin, xmax) evaluate the function f at whatever points are necessary to achieve accurate results; 'f' is a string containing the name of the function. The function f must return a vector of output values if it is given a vector of input values. Q = quad('f', xmin, xmax) approximates the integral of $f(x)$ from xmin to xmax to within a relative error of 0.001 using an adaptive recursive Simpson's rule. Q = quad8('f', xmin, xmax) approximates the integral of $f(x)$ from xmin to xmax to within a relative error of 0.001, using an adaptive recursive Newton–Cotes eight-panel rule.

For both quad and quad8, Q = Inf is returned if an excessive recursion level is reached, indicating a possibly singular integral. Additional optional parameters may be passed to the quad function, allowing the user to specify the desired tolerance (either relative or a combination of relative and absolute). A trace of the function evaluations with a point plot of the integrand, as well as coefficients to be passed to the function f, may also be specified. The documentation for implementing these options is included in the comments at the beginning of the function.

First derivatives:

Forward difference formula

$$f'(x_i) \approx \frac{y_{i+1} - y_i}{x_{i+1} - x_i}.$$

Backward difference formula

$$f'(x_i) \approx \frac{y_i - y_{i-1}}{x_i - x_{i-1}}.$$

Central difference formula

$$f'(x_i) \approx \frac{y_{i+1} - y_{i-1}}{x_{i+1} - x_{i-1}}.$$

Second derivative:

$$f''(x_i) \approx \frac{1}{h^2} [f(x_{i+1}) - 2f(x_i) + f(x_{i-1})].$$

Integration:

Trapezoid rule

$$\int_a^b f(x)\, dx \approx \frac{b - a}{2n} [f(a) + 2f(x_1) + \ldots + 2f(x_{n-1}) + f(b)].$$

Simpson's rule (n must be even)

$$\int_a^b f(x)\, dx \approx \frac{b - a}{3n} [f(a) + 4f(x_1) + 2f(x_2) + 4f(x_3) + 2f(x_4) + \ldots$$

$$+ 2f(x_{n-2}) + 4f(x_{n-1}) + f(b)].$$

Midpoint rule

$$\int_a^b f(x)\, dx \approx \frac{b - a}{n} \sum_{j=1}^n f(x_j), \qquad x_j = a + \left(j - \frac{1}{2} \right)h.$$

Gaussian quadrature

$$\int_{-1}^1 f(x)\, dx \approx \sum_{i=1}^n c_i f(x_i).$$

n	x_i	c_i
2	$\pm 1/\sqrt{3} \approx \pm 0.57735$	1
3	0	8/9
	$\pm \sqrt{3/5} \approx \pm 0.77459$	5/9

SUGGESTIONS FOR FURTHER READING

Basic formulas

Ames, W. F., *Numerical Methods for Partial Differential Equations*, 3rd ed., Academic Press, Boston, 1992.

Atkinson, K. E., *An Introduction to Numerical Analysis*, 2d ed., John Wiley & Sons, New York, 1989.

Isaacson, E., and H. B. Keller, *Analysis of Numerical Methods*, Dover, New York, 1994 (originally published by John Wiley & Sons, 1966).

Ralston, A., and P. Rabinowitz, *A First Course in Numerical Analysis*, 2d ed., McGraw-Hill, New York, 1978. (discussion of Richardson extrapolation, p. 124.)

Applications

Ayyub, B. M., and R. H. McCuen, *Numerical Methods for Engineers*, Prentice Hall, Upper Saddle River, NJ, 1996.

Abramowitz, M., and I. A. Stegun (eds.), *Handbook of Mathematical Functions, with Formulas, Graphs, and Mathematical Tables*, Dover, New York, 1965.

Ritger, P. D., and N. J. Rose, *Differential Equations with Applications*, McGraw-Hill, New York, 1968.

Jensen, J. A., and J. H. Rowland, *Methods of Computation*, Scott, Foresman and Company, Glenview, IL, 1975.

PRACTICE THE TECHNIQUES

In these problems, we follow the MATLAB *convention and denote the natural logarithm function as log(x). For problems P11.1–P11.5, approximate the specified derivative*

a. *Using the forward difference formula.*
b. *Using the backward difference formula.*
c. *Using the central difference formula.*
d. *Using Richardson extrapolation to improve your answer to Part c.*

P11.1 Approximate $y'(1.0)$ if

$\mathbf{x} = [0.8 \quad 0.9 \quad 1.0 \quad 1.1 \quad 1.2]$

$\mathbf{y} = [0.992 \quad 0.999 \quad 1.000 \quad 1.001 \quad 1.008]$

P11.2 Approximate $y'(2)$ if

$\mathbf{x} = [0 \quad 1 \quad 2 \quad 3 \quad 4]$

$\mathbf{y} = [0 \quad 1 \quad 4 \quad 9 \quad 16]$

P11.3 Approximate $y'(1)$ if

$\mathbf{x} = [-1 \quad 0 \quad 1 \quad 2 \quad 3]$

$\mathbf{y} = [1/3 \quad 1 \quad 3 \quad 9 \quad 27]$

P11.4 Approximate $y'(1)$ if

$\mathbf{x} = [-1 \quad 0 \quad 1 \quad 2 \quad 3]$

$\mathbf{y} = [1/2 \quad 1 \quad 2 \quad 4 \quad 8]$

P11.5 Approximate $y'(4)$ if

$\mathbf{x} = [0 \quad 1 \quad 4 \quad 9 \quad 16]$

$\mathbf{y} = [0 \quad 1 \quad 2 \quad 3 \quad 4]$

For Problems P11.6–P11.15, approximate the specified integral

a. *Using the composite trapezoid method with 2 subintervals.*

b. Using the composite trapezoid method with 10 subintervals.
c. Using Simpson's rule with 2 subintervals.
d. Using the composite Simpson's rule with 10 subintervals.
e. Using Gaussian quadrature with $n = 2$.
f. Using Romberg integration.

P11.6 $\int_0^1 x \sin(\pi x) \, dx.$

P11.7 $\int_0^4 2^x \, dx.$

P11.8 $\int_0^2 \sqrt{x} \, dx.$

P11.9 $\int_1^2 \frac{dx}{1 + x}.$

P11.10 $\int_1^2 \frac{dx}{x}.$

P11.11 $\int_{-1}^1 \frac{dx}{1 + x^2}.$

P11.12 $\int_0^2 e^x \, dx.$

P11.13 $\int_0^1 \frac{1 + x}{1 + x^3} \, dx.$

P11.14 $\int_1^2 \sqrt{x^3 - 1} \, dx.$

P11.15 $\int_2^3 \sqrt{x^2 - 4} \, dx.$

P11.16 $\int_0^\pi x^2 \sin(2x) \, dx.$

P11.17 $\int_0^3 \frac{1}{\sqrt{x^3 + 1}} \, dx.$

P11.18 $\int_0^\pi x^3 \sin(x^2) \, dx.$

P11.19 $\int_0^3 \sqrt[3]{x^3 + 1} \, dx.$

P11.20 $\int_0^2 \log(x^3 + 1) \, dx.$

EXPLORE SOME APPLICATIONS

A11.1 The flow rate of an incompressible fluid in a pipe of radius 1 is given by

$$Q = \int_0^1 2\pi r V \, dr,$$

where r is the distance from the center of the pipe and V is the velocity of the fluid. Find Q if only the following tabulated velocity measurements V are available:

$$r = [0.0 \quad 0.1 \quad 0.2 \quad 0.3 \quad 0.4 \quad 0.5 \quad 0.6 \quad 0.7 \quad 0.8 \quad 0.9 \quad 1.0]$$

$$V = [1.0 \quad 0.99 \quad 0.96 \quad 0.91 \quad 0.84 \quad 0.75 \quad 0.64 \quad 0.51 \quad 0.36 \quad 0.19 \quad 0.0]$$

Compare your result with the value obtained by using $V = 1 - r^2$. (See Ayyub and McCuen, 1996, for a discussion of similar problems.)

Problems A11.2–A11.7 investigate some important nonelementary functions that are defined by integrals. Tabulated values are available for these functions in many reference books.

A11.2 The error function is defined as

$$\text{Erf}(x) = \frac{2}{\sqrt{\pi}} \int_0^x e^{-t^2} \, dt.$$

Find Erf(2).

A11.3 The sine-integral is defined as

$$\text{Si}(x) = \int_0^x \frac{\sin t}{t} \, dt.$$

Find Si(2).

A11.4 The cosine-integral is defined as

$$\text{Ci}(x) = \int_1^x \frac{\cos t}{t} \, dt.$$

Find Ci(2).

A11.5 The exponential-integral is defined as

$$\text{Ei}(x) = \int_1^x \frac{e^{-t}}{t}\, dt.$$

Find Ei(2).

A11.6 The Fresnel integrals are defined as

$$C(x) = \int_0^x \cos\left(\frac{\pi}{2} t^2\right) dt \quad \text{and}$$

$$S(x) = \int_0^x \sin\left(\frac{\pi}{2} t^2\right) dt.$$

Find C(2) and S(2).

A11.7 There are several forms of elliptic integrals.

a. The complete elliptic integral of the first kind is defined as

$$K(m) = \int_0^{\pi/2} \frac{dt}{\sqrt{1 - m \sin^2 t}}.$$

Find K(1) and K(4).

b. The complete elliptic integral of the second kind is defined as

$$E(m) = \int_0^{\pi/2} \sqrt{1 - m \sin^2 t}\, dt.$$

Find E(1) and E(4).

c. The elliptic integral of the first kind is

$$K(k, x) = \int_0^x \frac{dt}{\sqrt{1 - k^2 \sin^2 t}}.$$

Find K(1,1) and K(2,1).

d. The elliptic integral of the second kind is

$$E(k, x) = \int_0^x \sqrt{1 - k^2 \sin^2 t}\, dt.$$

Find E(1, 1) and E(2, 1).
(See Ritger and Rose, 1968, or Abramowitz and Stegun, 1965, for tabulated values.)

Problems A11.8–A11.15 illustrate some integrals that arise in the measurement of arc length. For many functions, the integral that measures the length cannot be evaluated exactly.

A11.8 Find the arc length of the curve described by the function $y = x^2, 0 < x < 2$; the length is given by the integral

$$\int_0^2 \sqrt{1 + 4x^2}\, dx.$$

A11.9 Find the arc length of the curve described by the function $y = x^3, 0 < x < 2$; the length is given by the integral

$$\int_0^2 \sqrt{1 + 9x^4}\, dx.$$

A11.10 Find the arc length of the curve described by the function $y = x^{-1}, 1 < x < 2$; the length is given by the integral

$$\int_1^2 \sqrt{1 + x^{-4}}\, dx.$$

A11.11 Find the arc length of the curve described by the function $y = \sqrt{x}, 1 < x < 2$; the length is given by the integral

$$\int_1^2 \sqrt{1 + (1/4)x^{-1}}\, dx.$$

A11.12 Find the arc length of the curve described by the function $y = \sin(x), 0 < x < \pi$; the length is given by the integral

$$\int_0^\pi \sqrt{1 + \cos^2(x)}\, dx.$$

A11.13 Find the arc length of the curve described by the function $y = \tan(x), 0 < x < \pi/4$; the length is given by the integral

$$\int_0^{\pi/4} \sqrt{1 + \sec^4(x)}\, dx.$$

A11.14 Find the arc length of the curve described by the function $y = e^x, 0 < x < 2$; the length is given by the integral

$$\int_0^2 \sqrt{1 + (e^x)^2}\, dx = \int_0^2 \sqrt{1 + e^{2x}}\, dx.$$

A11.15 Find the arc length of the curve described by the function $y = \log(x), 1 < x < 2$; the length is given by the integral

$$\int_1^2 \sqrt{1 + x^{-2}}\, dx.$$

EXTEND YOUR UNDERSTANDING

U11.1 Use the definition of the Legendre polynomial,

$$P_n(x) = \frac{(-1)^n}{2^n n!} \frac{d^n}{dx^n} [(1 - x^2)^n], \qquad n \geq 1,$$

to find a relationship between $P_n'(x)$ and $P_{n+1}(x)$, and then show the equivalence of the following expressions for the coefficients for Gaussian quadrature:

$$c_i = \frac{-2}{(n + 1)P_n'(x_i)P_{n+1}(x_i)} \quad \text{and}$$

$$c_i = \frac{2(1 - x_i^2)}{(n + 1)^2 P_{n+1}^2(x_i)}.$$

U11.2 The coefficients for Gauss–Legendre quadrature can be given by the integral of the Lagrange interpolating polynomial (Jensen and Rowland, 1975, p. 225) as follows:

$$c_j = \int_{-1}^{1} \frac{(x - x_1) \dots (x - x_{j-1})(x - x_{j+1}) \dots (x - x_n)}{(x_j - x_1) \dots (x_j - x_{j-1})(x_j - x_{j+1}) \dots (x_j - x_n)} dx.$$

Use this form to compute the c_j for $n = 1, 2,$ and 3.

U11.3 Use Gaussian quadrature with $n = 3$ and exact arithmetic to approximate $\int_{-1}^{1} x^4 \, dx$.

Compare your results to the exact value of the integral, and discuss the two.

U11.4 Consider again the computations for I_0, I_1, and I_2 in Romberg integration, but now pay special attention to the function evaluations that can be reused at each stage. Since the value of h changes at each stage, it may be helpful to denote the value at stage i as h_i.

$$\int_a^b f(x) \, dx \approx$$

$$\frac{h}{2} [f(a) + 2f(x_1) + \dots + 2f(x_{n-1}) + f(b)]$$

$$h = \frac{b - a}{n}, \qquad n \text{ subintervals}$$

First take 1 subinterval, i.e., $n = 1$, $h_0 = b - a$:

$$I_0 \approx \frac{b - a}{2} [f(a) + f(b)].$$

Next, 2 subintervals, $n = 2$, $h_1 = \dfrac{b - a}{2}$

$$I_1 \approx \frac{b - a}{4} \left[f(a) + 2f\left(\frac{a + b}{2}\right) + f(b) \right]$$

$$= \frac{b - a}{4} [f(a) + f(b)] + \frac{b - a}{4} 2f\left(\frac{a + b}{2}\right)$$

$$= \frac{1}{2} I_0 + h_1 f\left(\frac{a + b}{2}\right).$$

Subdividing again, 4 subintervals, $n = 4$, $h_2 = \dfrac{b - a}{4}$.

$$I_2 \approx \frac{b - a}{8} \left[f(a) + 2f\left(\frac{3a + b}{4}\right) + 2f\left(\frac{a + b}{2}\right) \right.$$

$$\left. + 2f\left(\frac{a + 3b}{4}\right) + f(b) \right]$$

$$= \frac{b - a}{8} \left[f(a) + 2f\left(\frac{a + b}{2}\right) + f(b) \right]$$

$$+ \frac{b - a}{8} \left[2f\left(\frac{3a + b}{4}\right) + 2f\left(\frac{a + 3b}{4}\right) \right]$$

$$= \frac{1}{2} I_1 + h_2 \left[f\left(\frac{3a + b}{4}\right) + f\left(\frac{a + 3b}{4}\right) \right].$$

Expand the algorithm and MATLAB functions for Romberg integration to minimize the number of function evaluations required by replacing the calls to the trapezoid function by the computation shown here. Compare the compuational effort and the clarity of the process for the two forms.

U11.5 Show that the first extrapolated value obtained in Romberg integration is identical to that found by Simpson's rule.

U11.6 The error incurred in using the composite trapezoid rule to integrate $f(x)$ for $a \leq x \leq b$, with n subdivisions and $h = (b - a)/n$, is

$$E_T = \frac{-1}{12} (b - a)h^2 f''(\eta), \qquad \text{for some } \eta \in [a, b].$$

Use this formula to find a bound on the error in the results obtained for Problems 11.6, 11.8, 11.10, 11.12, and 11.15.

Now, find the actual error for each of the preceding integrals—i.e., the difference between the exact value and the approximate value of the given integral. Compare the actual error with the error bound.

U11.7 The error incurred in using the composite Simpson rule to integrate $f(x)$ for $a \le x \le b$, with n subdivisions and $h = (b-a)/n$, is

$$E_S = \frac{-1}{180}(b-a)h^4 f^{(4)}(\eta),$$

for some $\eta \in [a, b]$.

Use this formula to find a bound on the error in the results obtained for Problems 11.6, 11.8, 11.10, 11.12, and 11.15.

Now, find the actual error for each of the preceding integrals—i.e., the difference between the exact value and the approximate value of the given integral. Compare the actual error with the error bound.

U11.8 The error incurred in using the composite midpoint rule to integrate $f(x)$ for $a \le x \le b$, with n subdivisions and $h = (b-a)/n$, is

$$E_M = \frac{1}{24}(b-a)h^2 f''(\eta), \qquad \text{for some } \eta \in [a, b].$$

Use this formula to find a bound on the error in the results obtained for Problems 11.6, 11.8, 11.10, 11.12, and 11.15.

Now, find the actual error for each of the preceding integrals—i.e., the difference between the exact value and the approximate value of the given integral. Compare the actual error with the error bound.

12

Ordinary Differential Equations: Initial-Value Problems

The numerical differentiation formulas presented in the previous chapter are used extensively in the numerical solution of ordinary and partial differential equations; techniques for solving first-order ordinary differential equations are the subject of this chapter. We assume that the differential equation is written in the form $y' = f(x, y)$ with the value of the function $y(x)$ given at x_0, i.e., $y(x_0) = y_0$. The basic idea is to divide the interval of interest into discrete steps (of fixed width h) and find approximations to the function y at those values of x. In other words, we find solutions at $x_1, x_2, x_3, \ldots, x_n$.

The first methods we consider are based on the Taylor polynomial representation of the unknown function $y(x)$. The simplest method, Euler's, retains only the first-derivative term in the Taylor expansion. In order to use higher order Taylor polynomials, it is necessary to find higher derivatives of the function $f(x, y)$ that defines the slope of the unknown function $y(x)$. The Runge–Kutta method achieves a more accurate solution than Euler's method does, without computing higher derivatives of f. Each step of a Runge–Kutta method involves evaluating $f(x, y)$ at several different values of x and y and combining the results to form the approximation to y at the next x.

The third group of techniques that we study are the "multistep methods," which include both explicit and implicit forms. The term "multi-step" refers to the fact that these methods make use of the computed value of the solution at several previous points. Implicit methods have superior stability characteristics, but are more difficult to solve than the explicit methods. An implicit and an explicit method are often combined to form a predictor–corrector formula.

In the next chapter, we investigate techniques for solving higher order ordinary differential equation initial-value problems (ODE IVPs) and systems of first order ODE-IVPs. In Chapter 14, we consider techniques for solving ODE boundary-value problems (BVPs). Finally, Chapter 15 presents an introduction to methods for numerically solving partial differential equations.

Example 12-A Motion of a Falling Body

The motion of a falling body is described by Newton's second law, $F = ma$. The acceleration a is the rate of change of the velocity of the body with respect to time. The forces acting on the body may include, in addition to gravity, air resistance that is proportional to a power of the velocity. Empirical studies suggest that air resistance can be modeled as

$$F = kv^p,$$

where $1 \leq p \leq 2$ and the value of the proportionality constant k depends on the size and shape of the body, as well as the density and viscosity of the air. Typically, $p = 1$ for relatively slow velocities and $p = 2$ for high velocities. For intermediate velocities (with $0 < p < 1$), numerical methods may be especially appropriate.

For $p = 1$, the differential equation takes the form

$$m\frac{dv}{dt} = -kv - mg,$$

with the positive y-direction upward and $y = 0$ at ground level. Thus, when the body is falling ($v < 0$), the resistance force is positive (upward); when the body is rising ($v > 0$), the resistance acts in the downward direction.

Using separation of variables, we find that $v(t) = Ce^{-\rho t} - g/\rho$, where $\rho = k/m$. The terminal velocity, $v_f = \lim_{t \to \infty} v(t) = -g/\rho = -gm/k$.

The ratio k/m is known as the drag coefficient; for a parachutist, a typical value is $k/m \approx 1.5$; the terminal velocity is on the order of 21 ft/s. (See Edwards and Penney, 1996.)

For resistance proportional to the square of the velocity, we must distinguish between upward and downward motion, to be sure that the resistance force is acting opposite to the motion of the object. If we leave our coordinate axis as before (with up positive), we have

$$m\frac{dv}{dt} = -kv^2 - mg \quad \text{(for a body moving upward)}$$

or

$$m\frac{dv}{dt} = kv^2 - mg \quad \text{(for a body moving downward)}.$$

The velocity for downward motion with air resistance proportional to velocity squared is

$$v(t) = b\frac{1 + C\,e^{pt}}{1 - C\,e^{pt}},$$

where $p = 2\sqrt{gk/m}$ and $b = \sqrt{gm/k}$. Ther terminal velocity is $v_f = -b$.

In this section, we consider two methods that are based on the Taylor series representation of the unknown function $y(x)$. We first discuss Euler's method, which uses only the first term in the Taylor series; we then present a higher order Taylor method.

12.1.1 Euler's Method

The simplest method of approximating the solution of the differential equation

$$y' = f(x, y)$$

is to start by treating the function as a constant, $f(x_0, y_0)$, and replace the derivative y' by the forward difference quotient. This gives

$$y_1 - y_0 = f(x_0, y_0)(x_1 - x_0),$$

or

$$y_1 = y_0 + h f(x_0, y_0),$$

where $h = (b - a)/n$, in which n is the number of values of the independent variable where we wish to calculate the approximate solution. Geometrically, this corresponds to using the line tangent to the true solution curve $y(x)$ to find the value of y_1, the approximation to the value of y at x_1.

In general, Euler's method gives

$$y_i = y_{i-1} + h f(x_{i-1}, y_{i-1}), \qquad \text{for } i = 1, \ldots, n.$$

If we take $f(x, y) = x + y$, $x_0 = 0$, $y_0 = 2$, and $h = 1/2$, the first step of Euler's method proceeds along the straight line shown in Fig. 12.1.

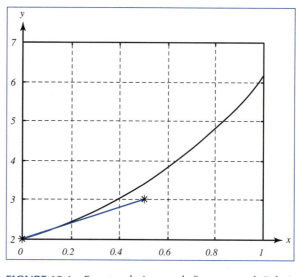

FIGURE 12.1 Exact solution and first step of Euler's method for $y' = x + y$.

Example 12.1 Solving a Simple ODE with Euler's Method

Consider the differential equation $y' = f(x, y)$ on $a \leq x \leq b$.

$$y' = x + y, \qquad 0 \leq x \leq 1 \quad (\text{i.e., } a = 0, b = 1), \qquad y(0) = 2.$$

First, we find the approximate solution for $h = 0.5$ ($n = 2$), a very large step size. The approximation at $x_1 = 0.5$ is

$$y_1 = y_0 + h(x_0 + y_0) = 2.0 + 0.5(0.0 + 2.0) = 3.0.$$

Next, we find the approximate solution y_2 at $x_2 = 0.0 + 2h = 1.0$:

$$y_2 = y_1 + h(x_1 + y_1) = 3.0 + 0.5(0.5 + 3.0) = 4.75.$$

To find a better approximate solution, we use $n = 10$ intervals, so that $h = 0.1$. We find the approximate solution at the points

$$x_0 = 0.0, \quad x_1 = 0.1, \quad x_2 = 0.2, \quad x_3 = 0.3, \quad x_4 = 0.4, \ldots, \quad x_{10} = 1.0.$$

Rather than continuing by hand, let us use the MATLAB function for Euler's method; the solution at the mesh points are shown in Table 12.1. The computed and exact solutions for $n = 20$ are illustrated in Fig. 12.2.

Table 12.1 $y' = x + y$, using Euler's method ($n = 10$)

x	Exact solution	Approximate solution	Absolute error
0.1	2.2155	2.2000	0.01551
0.2	2.4642	2.4300	0.034201
0.3	2.7496	2.6930	0.05658
0.4	3.0755	2.9923	0.08317
0.5	3.4462	3.3315	0.11463
0.6	3.8664	3.7147	0.15167
0.7	4.3413	4.1462	0.19511
0.8	4.8766	4.6308	0.24586
0.9	5.4788	5.1738	0.30497
1.0	6.1548	5.7812	0.37362

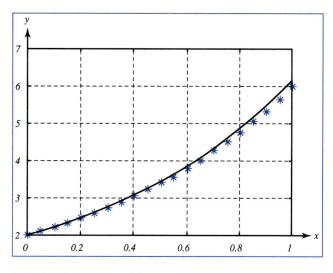

FIGURE 12.2 Exact solution $y = 3e^x - x - 1$ and Euler solution for $n = 20$.

MATLAB Function for Euler's Method

```
function [x , y]  = Euler( f, tspan, y0, n )
% solve y' = f(x,y) with initial condition y(a) = y0
% using n steps of Euler's method; step size h = (b-a)/n
a = tspan(1); b = tspan(2); h = (b-a) / n;
x = (a+h : h : b);
y(1) = y0 + h*feval( f, a, y0);
for i = 2 : n
    y(i) = y(i-1) + h* feval(f, x(i-1), y(i-1));
end
x = [ a   x ];
y = [ y0  y ];
```

Example 12.2 Another Example of the Use of Euler's Method

Consider the differential equation

$$y' = f(x, y) = \begin{cases} y\left(-2x + \dfrac{1}{x}\right), & x \neq 0, \\ 1, & x = 0, \end{cases}$$

on the interval $0 \leq x \leq 2$ with initial value $y(0) = 0.0$. With $n = 10$ intervals, the step size $h = (b - a)/n = 0.2$. The approximate and exact solutions are graphed in Fig. 12.3. The exact solution is $y = x \exp(-x^2)$.

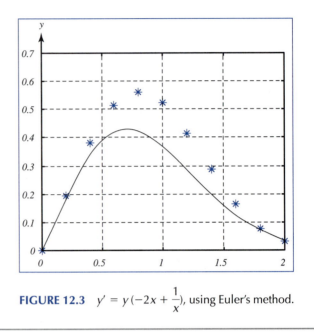

FIGURE 12.3 $y' = y(-2x + \dfrac{1}{x})$, using Euler's method.

Discussion

The question of how well a numerical technique for solving an initial-value ordinary differential equation works is closely related to the truncation error of the method. This is a measure of the error introduced by the approximation to the first derivative of y that is used in deriving the method. Euler's method employs only the first term in the Taylor expansion of the unknown function $y(x)$; that is,

$$y(x + h) = y(x) + hy'(x) + O(h^2),$$

with $y(x + h) = y_{i+1}$, $y(x) = y_i$, and $y'(x) = f(x_i, y_i)$. Thus the *local truncation error* is $O(h^2)$. Local error is also described in terms of the *local discretization error*, $L(x, h) = \dfrac{1}{h}[y(x + h) - y(x)] - f(x, y(x))$. The local discretization error for Euler's method is $O(h)$.

Of course, the actual error also depends on the higher derivatives of y, so if, in fact, y is linear, there will be no error. However, since the actual form of y is, in general, unknown, the dependence of the error on the step size is the most direct way to compare methods.

The total truncation error ε_n in going from x_0 to $x_0 + nh$ is bounded by an expression that depends on the Lipschitz constant for f, the bound for f', and the step size h. If f satisfies the Lipschitz condition $|f(x, y_2) - f(x, y_1)| < L|y_2 - y_1|$ and the second derivative of y is bounded $(|y''(\eta)| \le N)$, then

$$|\varepsilon_n| \le \frac{h}{2} N \frac{\exp(L(x - x_0)) - 1}{L}.$$

Thus, the total truncation error for Euler's method is $O(h)$ and Euler's method is a first order method. The total truncation error can also be expressed as a series (in powers of h) with coefficients that depend on x and $f(x, y)$. [See Froberg, 1985, p. 323.]

The usefulness of Euler's method is primarily a result of its simplicity, which makes it convenient for hand calculations. It may be used to provide a very few starting values for a multistep method (Section 12.3), although the Runge–Kutta methods presented in Section 12.2 give more accurate results for only slightly more computational effort.

The results of the basic Euler's method can be improved by using it with Richardson extrapolation. We sketch the process here, following the discussion in Jain (1976, pp. 57–58). For a given value of h, the value of y at x_{i+1} is

$$y_{i+1} = y_i + \sum_{j=1}^{\infty} c_j h^j.$$

If we denote the computed value as $Y(h)$, we can also find y_{i+1} by taking two steps with $h/2$ or by taking four steps with $h/4$, etc. Because the error expansion includes all powers of h, rather than only even powers, as we saw before, the extrapolation formula is

$$Y_m(k) = \frac{2^m Y_{m-1}(k + 1) - Y_{m-1}(k)}{2^m - 1},$$

where k designates the step size. ($k = 0, 1, \ldots, r$ correspond to step sizes of $h/2^0, h/2, h/2^2, \ldots, h/2$.) The parameter m gives the extrapolation level, with Y_0 $(m = 1)$ being the values computed directly from Euler's method.

12.1.2 Higher Order Taylor Methods

The discussion in the previous section suggests that one way to obtain a better solution technique is to use more terms in the Taylor series for y, in order to obtain a higher order truncation error. For example, a second order Taylor method uses

$$y(x + h) = y(x) + hy'(x) + \frac{h^2}{2} y''(x) + O(h^3).$$

However, we do not have a formula for $y''(x)$. If $y'(x) = f(x, y)$ is not too complicated, it may be practical to differentiate f with respect to x (using the chain rule, since y is a function of x) to find a representation for $y''(x)$.

Example 12.3 Solving a Simple ODE with Taylor's Method

Consider again the differential equation

$$y' = x + y, \quad 0 \le x \le 1, \quad \text{with initial condition } y(0) = 2.$$

To apply the second-order Taylor method to the equation, we find

$$y'' = \frac{d}{dx}(x + y) = 1 + y' = 1 + x + y.$$

This gives the approximation formula

$$y(x + h) = y(x) + hy'(x) + \frac{h^2}{2} y''(x),$$

or

$$y_{i+1} = y_i + h(x_i + y_i) + \frac{h^2}{2}(1 + x_i + y_i).$$

For $n = 2$ $(h = 0.5)$, we find

$$y_1 = y_0 + h(x_0 + y_0) + \frac{h^2}{2}(1 + x_0 + y_0) = 2 + \frac{0 + 2}{2} + \frac{1 + 0 + 2}{8} = \frac{27}{8},$$

$$y_2 = y_1 + h(x_1 + y_1) + \frac{h^2}{2}(1 + x_1 + y_1) =$$

$$\frac{27}{8} + \frac{1}{2} \cdot \frac{27}{8} + \frac{1}{8}\left(1 + \frac{1}{2} + \frac{1}{8}\right) = 5.9219.$$

The exact solution and the approximate solution using $n = 10$ are illustrated in Fig. 12.4.

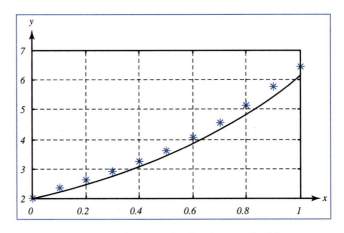

FIGURE 12.4 Simple example of Taylor's method for ODEs.

A minor modification to the MATLAB function given for Euler's method produces the second-order Taylor approximation; in addition to the function $y' = f(x, y)$, the function for y'' must be provided.

```
function [x , y]  = Taylor(f, g, tspan, y0, n)
% solve y' = f(x, y) with initial condition y(a) = y0
% using n steps of the 2nd order Taylor's method;
% function g(x, y) = f_x + f_y  y' = f_x + f * f_y
a = tspan(1);    b = tspan(2);    h = (b-a)/n;  hh = h*h/2;
x = (a+h : h : b);
y(1) = y0 + h*feval( f, a, y0) + 0.5*h*feval( g, a, y0);
for i = 1 : n-1
    y(i+1) = y(i) + h* feval(f,x(i),y(i)) + hh*feval(g,x(i),y(i));
end
x = [a    x];    y = [y0    y];
```

12.2 RUNGE–KUTTA METHODS

In the previous section, we saw that using more terms in the Taylor series representation for the unknown function y gives more accurate results, but the necessity of computing derivatives of $f(x, y)$ is often too difficult to make the higher order Taylor methods attractive.

In this section, we consider several forms of a method of obtaining estimates for the slope of our unknown function y that do not require differentiating $f(x, y)$ in order to use higher order Taylor series expansions, but that still improve on the accuracy we can obtain from Euler's method. For example, if we could use the slope of y (i.e., the value of f) at the midpoint of the interval, it would seem to be a more balanced approximation than relying only on information at the left end of the interval. We do not know the value of y at the midpoint, but we can estimate it, as we shall see.

12.2.1 Midpoint Method

The simplest Runge–Kutta method is based on approximating the value of y at $x_i + h/2$ by taking one-half of the change in y that is given by Euler's method and adding that on to the current value y_i. This method is known as the midpoint method. The formulas are

$$k_1 = h f(x_i, y_i) \qquad \text{(change in } y \text{ given by Euler's method),}$$

$$k_2 = h f\left(x_i + \frac{1}{2}h, y_i + \frac{1}{2}k_1\right) \text{ (change in } y \text{ using estimate of slope at midpoint),}$$

$$y_{i+1} = y_i + k_2.$$

Although the geometric interpretation helps the method seem more intuitively plausible, the derivation of a Runge–Kutta method depends on finding ways of approximating the slope of y, using the function f evaluated at various points in the interval, so that the accuracy agrees with that obtained from Taylor series approximations. Not too surprisingly, using more involved approximations gives higher order (more accurate) methods.

Example 12.4 Solving a Simple ODE with the Midpoint Method

Consider the differential equation $y' = f(x,y)$ on $a \le x \le b$, where

$$y' = x + y, \qquad 0 \le x \le 1, \qquad y(0) = 2.$$

First, we find the approximate solution for $h = 0.5$ ($n = 2$), a very large step size. The approximation at $x_1 = 0.5$ is

$$k_1 = h f(x_0, y_0) \qquad\qquad = 0.5(x_0 + y_0) \qquad\qquad = 1.0,$$

$$k_2 = h f\left(x_0 + \frac{h}{2}, y_0 + \frac{k_1}{2}\right) = 0.5(x_0 + 0.25 + y_0 + 0.5) = 1.375,$$

$$y_1 = y_0 + k_2 \qquad\qquad\qquad\qquad = 3.375.$$

Next, we find the approximate solution y_2 at point $x_2 = 0.0 + 2h = 1.0$:

$$k_1 = h f(x_1, y_1) = 0.5(x_1 + y_1) = 0.5(0.5 + 3.375) \qquad = 1.9375,$$

$$k_2 = h f\left(x_1 + \frac{h}{2}, y_1 + \frac{k_1}{2}\right) \quad = 0.5(0.5 + 0.25 + 3.375 + 0.97) = 2.547,$$

$$y_2 = y_1 + k_2 \qquad\qquad\qquad = 3.375 + 2.547 \qquad\qquad = 5.922.$$

The computed points and the exact solution, $y = 3e^x - x - 1$, are shown in Fig. 12.5.

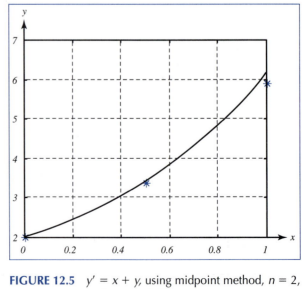

FIGURE 12.5 $y' = x + y$, using midpoint method, $n = 2$, and exact solution.

With $n = 10$, the computed values appear to fall directly on the graph of the exact solution. For comparison, the midpoint method with $n = 10$ requires approximately the same number of function evaluations as does Euler's method with $n = 20$ (Fig. 12.2) and the fourth-order Runge–Kutta method presented in the next section, with $n = 5$.

MATLAB Function for the Midpoint Method

```
function [x , y]  = RK2(f, tspan, y0, n)
% function [x , y]  = RK2(f, y0, a, b, n)
% solve y' = f(x,y)
% with initial condition y(a) = y0
% using n steps of the midpoint (RK2) method;
a = tspan(1); b = tspan(2); h = (b-a) / n;
x = (a+h : h : b);
k1 = h*feval(f, a, y0 );
k2 = h*feval(f,  a + h / 2, y0 + k1 / 2 );
y(1) = y0 + k2;
for i = 1 : n-1
    k1 = h*feval(f, x(i), y(i) );
    k2 = h*feval(f, x(i) + h / 2, y(i) + k1 / 2 );
    y(i+1) = y(i) + k2;
end
x = [ a    x ];
y = [ y0   y ];
```

Example 12.5 ODE for Dawson's Integral

Let

$$y' = 1 - 2xy, \quad y(0) = 0, \quad a = 0, \quad b = 1, \quad n = 10.$$

The computed points, shown in Fig. 12.6, are as follows:

$x = 0.00 \quad 0.10 \quad 0.20 \quad 0.30 \quad 0.40 \quad 0.50 \quad 0.60 \quad 0.70 \quad 0.80 \quad 0.90 \quad 1.000,$

$y = 0.00 \quad 0.099 \quad 0.19 \quad 0.28 \quad 0.36 \quad 0.42 \quad 0.47 \quad 0.51 \quad 0.53 \quad 0.54 \quad 0.54.$

The exact solution is $y = \exp(-x^2) \int_0^x \exp(t^2)$, which is known as Dawson's Integral.

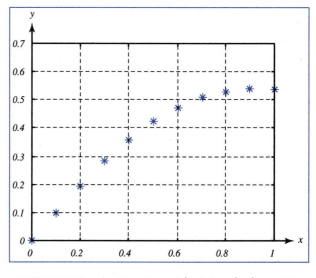

FIGURE 12.6 $y' = 1 - 2xy$, midpoint method, $n = 10$.

12.2.2 Other Second-Order Runge–Kutta Methods

The general form for a second-order Runge–Kutta method is

$$k_1 = h f(x_n, y_n),$$
$$k_2 = h f(x_n + c_2 h, y_n + a_{21} k_1),$$
$$y_{n+1} = y_n + w_1 k_1 + w_2 k_2.$$

We can summarize any such method by listing its parameters in an array whose standard form is as follows:

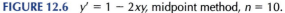

A parameter array is even more useful for higher order methods, which we consider shortly.

The modified Euler's (or Euler–Cauchy) method is given by the formulas

$$k_1 = h f(x_n, y_n),$$
$$k_2 = h f(x_n + h, y_n + k_1),$$
$$y_{n+1} = y_n + \frac{1}{2} k_1 + \frac{1}{2} k_2.$$

The parameter array for the modified Euler method is as follows:

$$
\begin{array}{c|cc}
1 & 1 & \\
\hline
& 1/2 & 1/2
\end{array}
$$

Heun's method, with

$$k_1 = hf(x_n, y_n),$$

$$k_2 = hf\left(x_n + \frac{2}{3}h, y_n + \frac{2}{3}k_1\right),$$

$$y_{n+1} = y_n + \frac{1}{4}k_1 + \frac{3}{4}k_2,$$

has the following parameter array:

$$
\begin{array}{c|cc}
2/3 & 2/3 & \\
\hline
& 1/4 & 3/4
\end{array}
$$

For comparison, the formulas for the midpoint method are

$$k_1 = hf(x_n, y_n), \qquad k_2 = hf\left(x_n + \frac{1}{2}h, y_n + \frac{1}{2}k_1\right), \qquad y_{n+1} = y_n + k_2.$$

The parameters for the midpoint method are as follows:

$$
\begin{array}{c|cc}
1/2 & 1/2 & \\
\hline
& 0 & 1
\end{array}
$$

Discussion

To derive the second-order Runge–Kutta formulas, we write them as

$$y(x + h) = y(x) + h[w_1 f(x, y) + w_2 f(x + c_2 h, y + a_{21} k_1)],$$

form the Taylor expansion of $f(x + c_2 h, y + a_{21} k_1)$, and find values of the parameters w_1, w_2, c_2, and a_{21}, so that the method agrees with the second-order Taylor method. The Taylor expansion for $f(x + c_2 h, y + a_{21} k_1)$ is

$$f(x + c_2 h, y + a_{21} k_1) = f(x, y) + c_2 h f_x(x, y) + a_{21} k_1 f_y(x, y).$$

Thus, we want the Runge–Kutta formula

$$y(x + h) = y(x) + h w_1 f + h w_2 f + w_2 c_2 h^2 f_x + w_2 a_{21} k_1 h f_y \qquad (12.1)$$

to agree with the second order Taylor formula

$$y(x + h) = y(x) + hf + \frac{h^2}{2}[f_x + f_y f], \qquad (12.2)$$

where $f, f_x,$ and f_y are all evaluated at (x, y).

Matching the terms involving f in eqs. (12.1) and (12.2) gives

$$w_1 + w_2 = 1.$$

Matching the terms with f_x gives $w_2 c_2 h^2 = \frac{h^2}{2}$, so

$$w_2 c_2 = \frac{1}{2}.$$

Matching the terms with f_y gives $w_2 a_{21} k_1 h = \frac{h^2}{2} f$; since $k_1 = hf$, we have

$$w_2 a_{21} = \frac{1}{2}.$$

The midpoint method is obtained by taking $w_1 = 0$ and $w_2 = 1$; this then requires that $c_2 = \frac{1}{2}$ and $a_{21} = \frac{1}{2}$. The modified Euler method is obtained by taking $w_1 = \frac{1}{2}$ and $w_2 = \frac{1}{2}$; this then requires that $c_2 = 1$ and $a_{21} = 1$. The Heun method is obtained by taking $w_1 = \frac{1}{4}$ and $w_2 = \frac{3}{4}$; this then requires that $c_2 = \frac{2}{3}$ and $a_{21} = \frac{2}{3}$.

12.2.3 Third-Order Runge–Kutta Methods

The general form for a third-order Runge–Kutta method is

$$k_1 = hf(x_n, y_n),$$
$$k_2 = hf(x_n + c_2 h, y_n + a_{21} k_1),$$
$$k_3 = hf(x_n + c_3 h, y_n + a_{31} k_1 + a_{32} k_2),$$
$$y_{n+1} = y_n + w_1 k_1 + w_2 k_2 + w_3 k_3.$$

The array of parameters has the following form:

c_2		a_{21}	
c_3		a_{31}	a_{32}
		w_1	w_2	w_3

The parameters for four well-known third-order methods are as follows (see Jain, 1979 for further discussion):

2/3		2/3		
2/3		0	2/3	
		2/8	3/8	3/8

Nystrom

1/2		1/2		
3/4		0	3/4	
		2/9	3/9	4/9

Nearly Optimal

1/2		1/2		
1		−1	2	
		1/6	4/6	1/6

Classical

1/3		1/3		
2/3		0	2/3	
		1/4	0	3/4

Heun

A combination of a second-order method and a third-order method forms the basis for MATLAB's function `ode23`.

12.2.4 Classic Runge–Kutta Method

Probably the most common form of the Runge–Kutta method is the classic fourth-order method, which uses a linear combination of four function evaluations:

$$k_1 = hf(x_i, y_i),$$

$$k_2 = hf\left(x_i + \frac{1}{2}h, y_i + \frac{1}{2}k_1\right),$$

$$k_3 = hf\left(x_i + \frac{1}{2}h, y_i + \frac{1}{2}k_2\right),$$

$$k_4 = hf(x_i + h, y_i + k_3).$$

These four equations, together with the recursion equation

$$y_{i+1} = y_i + \frac{1}{6}k_1 + \frac{1}{3}k_2 + \frac{1}{3}k_3 + \frac{1}{6}k_4,$$

make up the method. The classic fourth-order Runge–Kutta method is implemented in the following MATLAB function.

MATLAB Function for Classic Runge–Kutta Method

```
function [x , y]  = RK4(f, tspan, y0, n)
% solve y' = f(x,y) with initial condition y(a) = y0
% using n steps of the classic 4th order Runge-Kutta method;
a = tspan(1); b = tspan(2); h = (b-a)/n;
x = (a+h : h : b);
k1 = h *feval( f, a, y0 );
k2 = h *feval( f, a + h / 2 , y0 +  k1 / 2 );
k3 =  h *feval( f, a + h / 2  , y0 + k2 / 2 );
k4 = h *feval( f, a +  h , y0 + k3 );
y(1) = y0 + k1 / 6 + k2 / 3 + k3 / 3 + k4 / 6;
for i = 1 : n-1
        k1 = h *feval( f, x(i), y(i) );
        k2 = h *feval( f, x(i) + h / 2, y(i) + k1 / 2 );
        k3 =  h *feval( f, x(i) + h / 2 , y(i) + k2 / 2 );
        k4 = h *feval( f, x(i) + h , y(i) + k3 );
        y(i+1) = y(i) + k1 / 6 + k2 / 3 + k3 / 3 + k4 / 6;
end
x = [  a    x ];
y = [  y0   y ];
```

Example 12.6 Solving a Simple ODE with the Classic Runge–Kutta Method

Consider again the differential equation

$$y' = f(x, y) = x + y, \quad y(0) = 2, \quad a = 0, \quad b = 1, \quad n = 5, \quad h = 0.2$$

For comparison with the results of Euler's method, observe that this choice of n will require approximately the same number of evaluations of $f(x, y)$ as are used in Euler's method with $n = 20$.

The graph of the approximate and exact solutions are almost indistinguishable. The table of values shows that the error is much less than for Euler's method. The computed points and the exact solution, $y = 3e^x - x - 1$, are shown in Fig. 12.7 and tabulated in Table 12.2.

Table 12.2 Solving $y' = x + y$ with classic fourth-order Runge–Kutta method.

x	Exact solution	Approximate solution	Absolute error
0.2	2.4642	2.4642	8.2745e-06
0.4	3.0755	3.0755	2.0213e-05
0.6	3.8664	3.8663	3.7032e-05
0.8	4.8766	4.8766	6.0308e-05
1.0	6.1548	6.1548	9.2076e-05

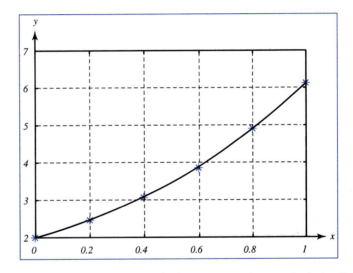

FIGURE 12.7 $y' = x + y$ with classic Runge–Kutta method, $n = 5$.

Example 12.7 Another Example of the Use of Runge–Kutta Method

Consider once more the differential equation

$$y' = f(x, y) = \begin{cases} y\left(-2x + \dfrac{1}{x}\right), & x \neq 0, \\ 1, & x = 0, \end{cases}$$

on the interval $0 \leq x \leq 2$ with initial value $y(0) = 0.0$. The values of the exact solution, $y = x \exp(-x^2)$ and the approximate solution at the mesh points (with $n = 10$) are shown in Table 12.3 and graphed in Figure 12.8.

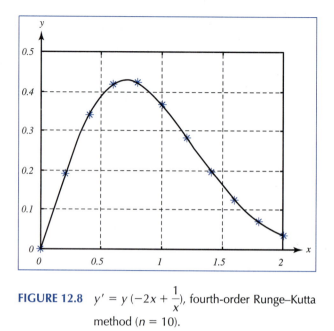

FIGURE 12.8 $y' = y\left(-2x + \dfrac{1}{x}\right)$, fourth-order Runge–Kutta method ($n = 10$).

x	Exact solution	Approximate solution	Absolute error
0.2	0.19216	0.19215	1.2288e-05
0.4	0.34086	0.34093	7.1314e-05
0.6	0.41861	0.41872	1.1072e-04
0.8	0.42183	0.42195	1.1763e-04
1.0	0.36788	0.36798	1.0280e-04
1.2	0.28431	0.28439	7.9678e-05
1.4	0.19720	0.19727	6.5398e-05
1.6	0.12369	0.12376	7.0105e-05
1.8	0.070495	0.070584	8.9035e-05
2.0	0.036631	0.036738	1.0716e-04

Table 12.3 $y' = y\left(-2x + \dfrac{1}{x}\right)$, fourth order Runge–Kutta method ($n = 10$).

12.2.5 Other Runge–Kutta Methods

The Runge–Kutta methods described in the previous sections are only the most common, simple forms of a very extensive field of study. We write a general Runge–Kutta method as

$$k_1 = h f(x_n, y_n),$$

$$k_2 = h f(x_n + c_2 h, y_n + a_{21}k_1),$$

$$k_3 = h f(x_n + c_3 h, y_n + a_{31}k_1 + a_{32}k_2),$$

Chapter 12   Ordinary Differential Equations: Initial-Value Problems

$$k_4 = h\,f(x_n + c_4 h, y_n + a_{41}k_1 + a_{42}k_2 + a_{43}k_3),$$
$$\vdots$$
$$k_m = h\,f(x_n + c_m h, y_n + a_{m1}k_1 + a_{m2}k_2 + \ldots + a_{m,m-1}k_{m-1}),$$
$$y_{n+1} = y_n + w_1 k_1 + w_2 k_2 + \ldots + w_m k_m.$$

Thus, to describe a Runge–Kutta method, we need to specify the parameters $c_2, \ldots, c_m, a_{21}, \ldots, a_{m,m-1}$, and $w_1, \ldots, w_m$.

For fourth-order methods,

$$k_1 = h\,f(x_n, y_n),$$
$$k_2 = h\,f(x_n + c_2 h, y_n + a_{21}k_1),$$
$$k_3 = h\,f(x_n + c_3 h, y_n + a_{31}k_1 + a_{32}k_2),$$
$$k_4 = h\,f(x_n + c_4 h, y_n + a_{41}k_1 + a_{42}k_2 + a_{43}k_3),$$
$$y_{n+1} = y_n + w_1 k_1 + w_2 k_2 + w_3 k_3 + w_4 k_4,$$

and the array of parameters has the form

c_2	a_{21}		
c_3	a_{31}	a_{32}	
c_4	a_{41}	a_{42}	a_{43}
	w_1	w_2	w_3	w_4

The parameter arrays for two fourth-order methods are as follows:

1/2	1/2		
1/2	0	1/2	
1	0	0	1
	1/6	2/6	2/6	1/6

Classic fourth-order Runge–Kutta

1/3	1/3		
2/3	−1/3	1	
1	1	−1	1
	1/8	3/8	3/8	1/8

Kutta's method

Higher order Runge–Kutta methods are described in a similar manner; the parameters for a fifth-order method and a sixth-order method are given in the following tables (see Jain, 1979 for further discusssion):

1/2	1/2				
1/4	3/16	1/16			
1/2	0	0	1/2		
3/4	0	−3/16	6/16	9/16	
1	1/7	4/7	6/7	−12/7	8/7
	7/90	0	32/90	12/90	32/90	7/90

Lawson's fifth-order Runge–Kutta method

1/3	1/3					
2/3	0	2/3				
1/3	1/12	1/3	−1/12			
1/2	−1/16	9/8	−3/16	−3/8		
1/2	0	9/8	−3/8	−3/4	1/2	
1	9/44	−9/11	63/44	18/11	0	−16/11
	11/120	0	27/40	27/40	−4/15	−4/15	11/120

Butcher's sixth-order Runge–Kutta method

12.2.6 Runge–Kutta–Fehlberg Methods

The Runge–Kutta–Fehlberg methods use a pair of Runge–Kutta methods to obtain both the computed solution and an estimate of the truncation error. The estimate of the error can be used in programs of variable step size to decide when to adjust the step size. We outline here the most well-known Runge–Kutta–Fehlberg formulas, which combine Runge–Kutta formulas of orders 4 and 5. In general, six function evaluations are required for a method of order 5; Fehlberg developed a fourth-order method which uses five of the function evaluations that are used in the higher order method, so the extra computational burden is slight. The parameters for the fourth- and fifth-order methods are given in the following two tables:

$$
\begin{array}{c|ccccc}
\dfrac{1}{4} & \dfrac{1}{4} \\[2mm]
\dfrac{3}{8} & \dfrac{3}{32} & \dfrac{9}{32} \\[2mm]
\dfrac{12}{13} & \dfrac{1932}{2197} & \dfrac{-7200}{2197} & \dfrac{7296}{2197} \\[2mm]
1 & \dfrac{439}{216} & -8 & \dfrac{3680}{513} & \dfrac{-845}{4104} \\[2mm]
\hline
& \dfrac{25}{216} & 0 & \dfrac{1408}{2565} & \dfrac{2197}{4104} & \dfrac{-1}{5}
\end{array}
$$

Fourth-order Runge–Kutta–Fehlberg method

$$
\begin{array}{c|cccccc}
\dfrac{1}{4} & \dfrac{1}{4} \\[2mm]
\dfrac{3}{8} & \dfrac{3}{32} & \dfrac{9}{32} \\[2mm]
\dfrac{12}{13} & \dfrac{1932}{2197} & \dfrac{-7200}{2197} & \dfrac{7296}{2197} \\[2mm]
1 & \dfrac{439}{216} & -8 & \dfrac{3680}{513} & \dfrac{-845}{4104} \\[2mm]
\dfrac{1}{2} & \dfrac{-8}{27} & 2 & \dfrac{-3544}{2565} & \dfrac{1859}{4104} & \dfrac{-11}{40} \\[2mm]
\hline
& \dfrac{16}{135} & 0 & \dfrac{6656}{12,825} & \dfrac{28,561}{56,430} & \dfrac{-9}{50} & \dfrac{2}{55}
\end{array}
$$

Fifth-order Runge–Kutta–Fehlberg method

The estimated error is the value computed from the fifth-order method minus the value computed from the fourth-order method; it can be expressed directly as

$$\text{error} = \frac{1}{360} k_1 + 0 k_2 + \frac{-128}{4275} k_3 + \frac{-2197}{75,240} k_4 + \frac{1}{50} k_5 + \frac{2}{55} k_6.$$

(See Atkinson, 1989, for further discussion.)

12.3 MULTISTEP METHODS

Many approximation methods use more than one previous approximate solution value or function evaluation (of the right-hand side of the differential equation) involving approximate solution values at several previous points; such methods are known as *multistep methods*. The methods we have discussed so far use only one previous approximation and are therefore known as *one-step methods*. The general form of a two-step method is

$$y_{i+1} = a_1 y_i + a_2 y_{i-1} + h[b_0 f(x_{i+1}, y_{i+1}) + b_1 f(x_i, y_i) + b_2 f(x_{i-1}, y_{i-1})],$$

where the coefficients $a_1, a_2, b_0, b_1,$ and b_2 depend on the particular method. We use the notation

$$f_{i+1} = f(x_{i+1}, y_{i+1}), \qquad f_i = f(x_i, y_i), \qquad f_{i-1} = f(x_{i-1}, y_{i-1}), \qquad h = \frac{b-a}{n}.$$

Multistep methods are further distinguished according to whether the coefficient of the $f(x_{i+1}, y_{i+1})$ term is zero. If the coefficient is not zero, then the unknown y_{i+1} appears on the right-hand side of the equation, necessitating an iterative solution procedure, in general. Such methods are called *implicit*. Not too surprisingly, they have some nice properties that make them important techniques and that compensate for the apparent disadvantages of the difficulty of their solution. Multistep methods in which the coefficient of the $f(x_{i+1}, y_{i+1})$ term is zero are known as *explicit* methods.

Multistep methods require starting values, in addition to the initial condition specified for the differential equation. For a two-step method, y_1 must be found by some other method, such as a Runge–Kutta solution; for an n-step method, the first $n-1$ values must be computed by another method.

12.3.1 Adams–Bashforth Methods

Among the most popular explicit multistep methods are the Adams–Bashforth methods.

The formulas for the Adams–Bashforth two-step method are as follows:
y_0 is given by the initial condition for the differential equation.
y_1 is found from a one-step method, such as a Runge–Kutta technique. Then

$$y_{i+1} = y_i + \frac{h}{2}[3f_i - f_{i-1}], \qquad \text{for } i = 1, \ldots, n-1.$$

Comparing this formula with the general form of a two-step method, we see that

$$a_1 = 1, \quad a_2 = 0, \quad b_0 = 0, \quad b_1 = 3/2, \quad \text{and} \quad b_2 = -1/2.$$

It is quite common to have $a_2 = 0$. Because the method is explicit, $b_0 = 0$. This is a second-order method with local truncation error $O(h^3)$.

Following are the formulas for higher order Adams–Bashforth methods:

Adams–Bashforth three-step method
y_0 is given.
y_1 and y_2 are found from a one-step method. Then

$$y_{i+1} = y_i + \frac{h}{12}[23f_i - 16f_{i-1} + 5f_{i-2}], \qquad \text{for } i = 2, \ldots, n-1.$$

This a third-order method with truncation error $O(h^4)$.

Adams–Bashforth four-step method
y_0 is given.
$y_1, y_2,$ and y_3 are found from a one-step method. Then

$$y_{i+1} = y_i + \frac{h}{24}[55f_i - 59f_{i-1} + 37f_{i-2} - 9f_{i-3}], \qquad \text{for } i = 3, \ldots, n-1.$$

This is a fourth-order method with truncation error $O(h^5)$.

Adams–Bashforth five-step method
y_0 is given.
y_1 through y_4 are found from a one-step method. Then

$$y_{i+1} = y_i + \frac{h}{720} [1901f_i - 2774f_{i-1} + 2616f_{i-2} - 1274f_{i-3} + 251f_{i-4}].$$

This is a fifth-order method with truncation error $O(h^6)$.

The primary use of the explicit Adams–Bashforth methods presented in this section is in conjunction with the implicit Adams–Moulton methods that we consider next. Especially for the higher order Adams–Bashforth methods, stability requirements severely limit the step size for which the method gives reasonable results. The large negative coefficients appearing in the formula for the fifth-order Adams–Bashforth method are one indication that the method may have difficulty.

MATLAB Function for Adams–Bashforth Third-Order Method

```
function [x, y]  = AB3(f, tspan, y0, n)
a = tspan(1);       b = tspan(2);
h = (b-a) / n;      hh = h/12;
x = (a+h : h : b);
                    %  Use midpoint method to start
z0 = feval(f, a, y0 );
k1 = h*z0;    k2 = h*feval(f,  a + h/2, y0 + k1/2 );
y(1) = y0 + k2;
z(1) = feval(f, x(1), y(1));
k1 = h*z(1);    k2 = h*feval(f,  x(1) + h/2, y(1) + k1/2 );
y(2) = y(1) + k2;
                    %  Use 3rd order AB method to continue
z(2) = feval(f, x(2), y(2));
y(3) = y(2) + hh*(23*z(2) - 16*z(1) + 5*feval(f, a, y0));
for i = 3 : n-1
        z(i) = feval(f, x(i), y(i));
        y(i+1) = y(i) + hh*(23*z(i) - 16*z(i-1) + 5*z(i-2));
end
x = [ a    x ];
y = [ y0    y ];
```

Example 12.8 Solving a Simple ODE with an Adams–Bashford Method

Using the preceding MATLAB function for the Adams–Bashforth three-step method to solve the simple ODE $y' = x + y$, $y(0) = 2$, gives the following computed values:

$x =$	0	0.2	0.4	0.6	0.8	1
$y =$	2	2.46	3.0652	3.8509	4.8546	6.1241

For comparison, the exact solution, to five digits, is:

$y =$	2	2.4642	3.0755	3.8664	4.8766	6.1548

The computed values are graphed, together with the exact solution, $y = 3e^x - x - 1$, in Fig. 12.9.

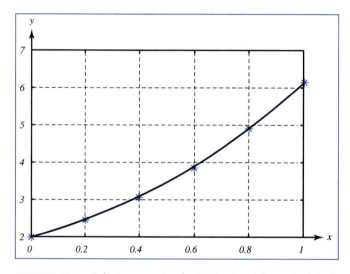

FIGURE 12.9 Solution to a simple ODE using Adams–Bashforth third-order method.

12.3.2 Adams–Moulton Methods

Among the most popular *implicit* multistep methods are the Adams–Moulton methods. We first give the formulas for the Adams–Moulton two-, three-, and four-step methods. We then show how these are used together with the Adams–Bashforth methods in practice.

Adams–Moulton two-step method

y_0 is given; y_1 is found from a one-step method, such as a Runge–Kutta technique. Then

$$y_{i+1} = y_i + \frac{h}{12}[5f_{i+1} + 8f_i - f_{i-1}], \qquad \text{for } i = 1, \ldots, n-1.$$

This is a third-order method with local truncation error $O(h^4)$.

Comparing this formula with the general form of a two-step method, we see that

$$a_1 = 1, \qquad a_2 = 0, \qquad b_0 = 5/12, \qquad b_1 = 8/12, \quad \text{and} \quad b_2 = -1/12.$$

As with the two-step Adams–Bashforth method, $a_0 = 0$. Also, note that $b_0 \neq 0$, because this method is implicit. The coefficients of the error term are, in general, smaller for implicit methods than for the corresponding explicit method of the same order. (See summary at end of chapter.) Thus, implicit methods have less round-off error than do explicit methods.

Adams–Moulton three-step method

y_0 is given by the initial condition; y_1 and y_2 are found from a one-step method. Then

$$y_{i+1} = y_i + \frac{h}{24}[9f_{i+1} + 19f_i - 5f_{i-1} + f_{i-2}], \qquad \text{for } i = 2, \ldots, n-1.$$

This is a fourth-order method with local truncation error $O(h^5)$.

Adams–Moulton four-step method

y_0 is given by the initial condition; y_1, y_2, and y_3 are found from a one-step method. Then

$$y_{i+1} = y_i + \frac{h}{720}[251f_{i+1} + 646f_i - 264f_{i-1} + 106f_{i-2} - 19f_{i-3}].$$

This is a fifth-order method with local truncation error $O(h^6)$.

12.3.3 Predictor–Corrector Methods

In order to take advantage of the beneficial properties of the implicit multistep methods while avoiding the difficulties inherent in solving the implicit equation, an explicit and implicit method can be combined. The explicit method is used to predict a value of y_{i+1}, which we denote y^*_{i+1}. This value is then used in the right-hand side of the implicit method, which produces an improved, or corrected, value of y_{i+1}.

Adams Third-Order Predictor–Corrector Method

As a simple example, we use the third-order Adams–Bashforth three-step method as a predictor, with the third-order Adams–Moulton two-step method as a corrector.

y_0 is given by the initial condition; y_1 and y_2 are found from a one-step method.

Then for $i = 2, \ldots, n-1$

$$y_{i+1}^* = y_i + \frac{h}{12}[23f(x_i, y_i) - 16f(x_{i-1}, y_{i-1}) + 5f(x_{i-2}, y_{i-2})],$$

$$y_{i+1} = y_i + \frac{h}{12}[5f(x_{i+1}, y_{i+1}^*) + 8f(x_i, y_i) - f(x_{i-1}, y_{i-1})].$$

Since the local truncation error is $O(h^4)$ for each of these methods, the combination is also $O(h^4)$.

Example 12.9 Solving a Simple ODE with the Adams Predictor–Corrector Method

Consider again the differential equation

$$y' = f(x, y) = x + y, \qquad y(0) = 2.$$

The approximate solution was computed using the third-order Adams–Bashforth–Moulton predictor–corrector equations, with the midpoint method to start. Since the exact solution is $y = 3e^x - x - 1$, we can find the error at each value of x where the solution has been approximated. In order to demonstrate the benefit derived from using the corrector, we also show the results we computed earlier using the Adams–Bashforth third-order method (see Fig. 12.10 as well):

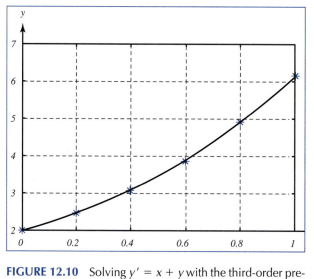

FIGURE 12.10 Solving $y' = x + y$ with the third-order predictor–corrector method.

$$x = \quad 0 \quad 0.2 \quad 0.4 \quad 0.6 \quad 0.8 \quad 1$$

Computed results using Adams–Bashforth–Moulton third-order predictor–corrector method:

$$y = \quad 2 \quad 2.46 \quad 3.0652 \quad 3.8538 \quad 4.8614 \quad 6.1365$$

Values of exact solution (to five digits):

$$y = \quad 2 \quad 2.4642 \quad 3.0755 \quad 3.8664 \quad 4.8766 \quad 6.1548$$

Computed result from third-order method without corrector (see Ex. 12.8)

$$y = \quad 2 \quad 2.46 \quad 3.0652 \quad 3.8509 \quad 4.8546 \quad 6.1241$$

For variety, we illustrate the use of the third-order predictor–corrector method in the following MATLAB script, which includes the definition of the problem in Example 12.9:

```
% S_ABM3_12_9

% script for Adams-Bashford-Moulton 3rd order method

clear all

% solve y' = f(x,y); y(a) = ya, on  [ a, b]

a = 0;  b = 1;  n = 5;

f = 'x+y';

ya = 2;

% end problem definition

h = (b-a) / n;      hh = h/12;

xx = (a+h:h:b);

                    %  midpoint method to start

x = a;        y = ya;      z0 = eval(f); k1 = h*z0;

x = a + h/2; y = ya + k1/2; zz = eval(f); k2 = h*zz;

yy(1) = ya + k2;

x = xx(1);      y = yy(1);       z(1) = eval(f); k1 = h*z(1);

x = xx(1)+h/2; y = yy(1) + k1/2; zz = eval(f);   k2 = h*zz;
```

```
yy(2) = yy(1) + k2;
                                % 3rd order A-B/A-M      method
x = xx(2);  y = yy(2);  z(2) = eval(f);
yy(3) = yy(2) + hh*(23*z(2) - 16*z(1) + 5*z0);
x = xx(3);  y = yy(3);  zz = eval(f);
yy(3) = yy(2) + hh*(5*zz + 8*z(2) - z(1));
for i = 3 : n-1
        x = xx(i);  y = yy(i);  z(i) = eval(f);
        yy(i+1) = yy(i) + hh*(23*z(i) - 16*z(i-1) + 5*z(i-2));
        x = xx(i+1);  y = yy(i+1);  zz = eval(f);
        yy(i+1) = yy(i) + hh*(5*zz + 8*z(i) - z(i-1));
end
xx = [ a    xx ]
yy = [ ya   yy ]
plot(xx, yy, '*' )
grid on
% plot exact solution if known
hold on
yyy = 3*exp(xx) - xx - 1
plot(xx, yyy )
hold off
```

Example 12.10 Velocity of Falling Parachutist

Consider the situation described in Example 12-A, in which the velocity of a parachutist with drag coefficient $k/m = 1.5, g = 32$, and $v_0 = 0$ is given by

$$m \frac{dv}{dt} = k(-v) - mg.$$

The parachutist reaches a terminal velocity of approximately 21 ft/sec after only about 3 seconds.

If we modify the model slightly, so that

$$m \frac{dv}{dt} = k(-v)^{1.1} - mg,$$

we find that the terminal velocity is somewhat slower. Figure 12.11 shows the velocity of the parachutist under both models of air resistance.

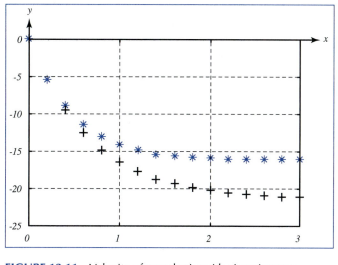

FIGURE 12.11 Velocity of parachutist with air resistance:
+ denotes resistance proportional to v;
* denotes resistance proportional to $v^{1.1}$.

12.4 STABILITY

The term *stability* is used in a variety of ways in the description of differential equations and, in particular, numerical methods for solving differential equations. For some differential equations, any errors that occur in computation will be magnified regardless of the numerical method. Such problems are called *ill conditioned*. Other differential equations require extremely small step sizes to achieve accurate results; these problems are called *stiff*. Since both types of difficulties occur more often with higher order ODEs, or systems of ODEs, we postpone our discussion of stiff and ill-conditioned problems until Chapter 13.

We now consider the stability of the numerical methods presented in the previous sections. We call a numerical method *stable* if errors incurred at one stage of the process do not tend to be magnified at later stages. The analysis of the stability of a method often involves the investigation of the error for a simple problem such as $y' = \lambda y$. If the method is unstable for the model equation, it is likely to behave badly for other problems as well, and the method is unstable in general. If $\lambda > 0$, the true solution grows exponentially, and it is not reasonable to expect the error to remain small as x increases. The most we could hope for is that the error remain small relative to the solution. On the other hand, for $\lambda < 0$, the exact solution is a decaying exponential, and we would like the error also to go to zero as $x \to \infty$.

If we apply Euler's method to the model equation with initial condition $y(0) = y_0$ and to the same equation with error introduced in the form of a perturbation of the initial condition to $y(0) = y_0 + \varepsilon$, we find that the difference of the two solutions, $z(x)$, satisfies the differential equation $z' = \lambda z$ with $z(0) = \varepsilon$. Applying Euler's method (with step size h) to this equation leads to the stability requirement $-2 < h\lambda < 0$, which gives the *region of absolute stability*.

In general, a method with a larger region of absolute stability will impose less of a restriction on the step size h. A similar analysis applied to the Adams–Bashforth second-order method shows that the region of absolute stability is $-1 < h\lambda < 0$. Note that although this is a smaller region than that for Euler's method, the fact that the Adams–Bashforth method is of a higher order than Euler's method gives it some advantage. The second-order Adams–Moulton method, an implicit method, is absolutely stable for $-\infty < h\lambda < 0$. (See Atkinson, 1993, for further details.)

The stability results summarized in the previous paragraphs give some indication of the restrictions on the step size that may be necessary to achieve a stable numerical solution. We now consider more directly the stability of the difference equation that defines a numerical method. We generalize the notation introduced in Section 12.3 for a two-step method to represent an *m*-step method:

$$y_{i+1} = a_1 y_i + a_2 y_{i-1} + \ldots + a_m y_{i+1-m} + h(b_0 f_{i+1} + b_1 f_i + \ldots + b_m f_{i+1-m}).$$

The method is stable if all roots of the characteristic polynomial

$$p(\lambda) = \lambda^m - (a_1 \lambda^{m-1} + a_2 \lambda^{m-2} + \ldots + a_m)$$

satisfy $|\lambda_k| \leq 1$ and any root with $|\lambda_k| = 1$ is simple. It can be shown that, for any method that is at least first-order accurate, we must have $a_1 + a_2 + \ldots + a_m = 1$, so $\lambda_k = 1$ is a root. If the other $m - 1$ roots satisfy $|\lambda_k| < 1$, the method is called *strongly stable*. If the method is stable, but not strongly stable, it is called *weakly stable*. A strongly stable method is stable for $y' = \lambda y$ regardless of the sign of λ; a method that is only weakly stable can yield unstable numerical solutions when $\lambda < 0$, as the next example illustrates. The stability analysis based on the roots of the characteristic polynomial reveals the behavior of the method in the limit as the step size becomes arbitrarily small. Even a stable method can exhibit unstable behavior if the step size is too large.

Example 12.11 A Weakly Stable Method

Consider the simple two-step method

$$y_{i+1} = y_{i-1} + 2hf(x_i, y_i)$$

and the differential equation

$$y' = -4y, \qquad y(0) = 1,$$

for which the exact solution is $y = e^{-4x}$. If we perturb the initial condition slightly, to $y(0) = 1 + \varepsilon$, the solution becomes $y = (1 + \varepsilon)e^{-4x}$.

However, the numerical method is only weakly stable: The characteristic polynomial is $\lambda^2 - 1 = 0$, which has roots $\lambda = 1$ and $\lambda = -1$. The numerical results for $h = 0.1$ are illustrated, in Fig. 12.12. Figure 12.13 indicates that a smaller step size ($h = 0.02$) delays the onset of the instability, but does not prevent it from occurring.

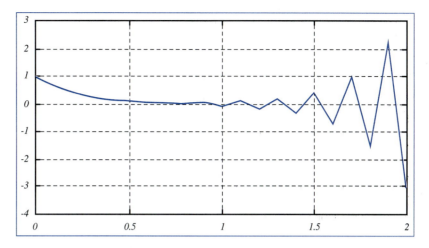

FIGURE 12.12 The solution of $y' = -4y$ with a weakly stable numerical method and $h = 0.1$.

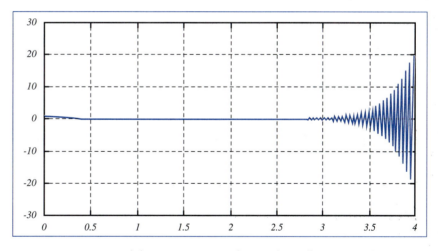

FIGURE 12.13 Instability occurs even with a much smaller step size $h = 0.02$.

On the other hand, for the differential equation

$$y' = 4y, \qquad y(0) = 1,$$

the weakly stable method yields acceptable results, even for $h = 0.1$, as illustrated in Fig. 12.14.

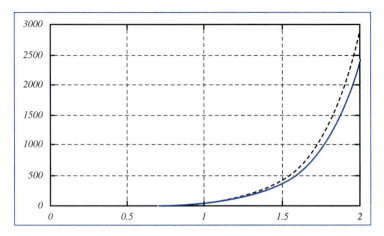

FIGURE 12.14 The solution of $y' = 4y$ with a weakly stable numerical method and $h = 0.1$.

12.5 MATLAB's METHODS

MATLAB includes three functions—ode23, ode45, and ode113—for solving non-stiff ODEs. The functions ode23 and ode45 implement a pair of explicit Runge–Kutta methods, second and third order, and fourth and fifth order, respectively. The function ode113 is a fully variable step-size ODE solver based on the Adams–Bashforth–Moulton family of formulas of orders 1–12.

The syntax for the function call to each of the ODE solvers is the same; we illustrate it here for ode23. For that function, we have

$$[t, y] = \text{ode23}(`F\text{'}, \text{tspan}, y0), \qquad \text{where tspan} = [\ t0 \ \ t\_final\ ].$$

'F' is a string containing the name of an ODE file. The function $F(t, y)$ must return a column vector of values. Each row in the solution array y corresponds to a time returned in column vector t. To obtain solutions at specific times t0, t1, ... , t_final (all increasing or all decreasing), use tspan = [t0, t1, ... , t_final]. The initial conditions are given in the vector y0. There are several variations for input and also for output. More details are available in the on-line help provided with each function.

The use of these functions is illustrated in the next chapter.

SUMMARY

Explicit 1-Step Methods: *Euler* (first order with local truncation error $O(h^2)$):

$$y_{i+1} = y_i + hf_i + \frac{h^2}{2} y''(\eta_i).$$

Taylor method (second order with local truncation error $O(h^3)$):

$$y_{i+1} = y_i + hf_i + \frac{h^2}{2} g_i + O(h^3), \quad \text{where } g_i = \frac{d}{dx} f(x_i, y_i) = y''(x).$$

Runge–Kutta
Midpoint (second order):

$$y_{i+1} = y_i + hf\left(x_i + \frac{h}{2}, y_i + \frac{h}{2} f(x_i, y_i)\right) + O(h^3).$$

(This can also be viewed as an explicit two-step method with step size $H = 2h$.)

Modified Euler's method (second order):

$$y_{i+1} = y_i + \frac{h}{2} [f(x_i, y_i) + f(x_i + h, y_i + hf(x_i, y_i))] + O(h^3).$$

Heun's method (second order):

$$y_{i+1} = y_i + \frac{h}{4}\left[f(x_i, y_i) + 3f\left(x_i + \frac{2h}{3}, y_i + \frac{2h}{3} f(x_i, y_i)\right)\right] + O(h^3).$$

Classic Runge–Kutta (fourth order):

$$k_1 = hf(x_i, y_i), \qquad\qquad k_2 = hf\left(x_i + \frac{1}{2} h, y_i + \frac{1}{2} k_1\right),$$

$$k_3 = hf\left(x_i + \frac{1}{2} h, y_i + \frac{1}{2} k_2\right), \quad k_4 = hf(x_i + h, y_i + k_3),$$

$$y_{i+1} = y_1 + \frac{1}{6} k_1 + \frac{1}{3} k_2 + \frac{1}{3} k_3 + \frac{1}{6} k_4.$$

Implicit One-Step Methods: *Trapezoid* method (second order; see Atkinson, 1989, p. 366):

$$y_{i+1} = y_i + \frac{h}{2} [f_{i+1} + f_i] - \frac{h^3}{12} y^{(3)}(\eta_i).$$

(This method can also be viewed as the second-order Adams–Moulton method.)

Explicit Multistep Methods: *Midpoint* (two steps, second order):

$$y_{i+1} = y_{i-1} + 2hf_i + \frac{h^3}{3} y^{(3)}(\eta_i).$$

General form of two-step, second-order methods (see Atkinson, 1989, p. 382):

$$y_{i+1} = a_1 y_i + a_2 y_{i-1} + h[b_0 f_{i+1} + b_1 f_i + b_2 f_{i-1}],$$

with $a_1 = 1 - a_2,$ $\quad b_0 = 1 - \dfrac{1}{4}a_2 - \dfrac{1}{2}b_1,$ $\quad b_2 = 1 - \dfrac{3}{4}a_2 - \dfrac{1}{2}b_1.$

Adams–Bashforth (see Atkinson, 1989, p. 387):
Two steps, second order, local truncation error $O(h^3)$:

$$y_{i+1} = y_i + \frac{h}{2}[3f_i - f_{i-1}] + \frac{5}{12}h^3 y^{(3)}(\eta_i).$$

Three steps, third order, local truncation error $O(h^4)$:

$$y_{i+1} = y_i + \frac{h}{12}[23f_i - 16f_{i-1} + 5f_{i-2}] + \frac{3}{8}h^4 y^{(4)}(\eta_i).$$

Four steps, fourth order, local truncation error $O(h^5)$:

$$y_{i+1} = y_i + \frac{h}{24}[55f_i - 59f_{i-1} + 37f_{i-2} - 9f_{i-3}] + \frac{251}{720}h^5 y^{(5)}(\eta_i).$$

Five steps, fifth order, local truncation error $O(h^6)$:

$$y_{i+1} = y_i + \frac{h}{720}[1901f_i - 2774f_{i-1} + 2616f_{i-2} - 1274f_{i-3} + 251f_{i-4}].$$

Implicit Multistep Methods: *Adams–Moulton* (see Atkinson, 1989, p. 388):
Two steps, third order, local truncation error $O(h^4)$:

$$y_{i+1} = y_i + \frac{h}{12}[5f_{i+1} + 8f_i - f_{i-1}] - \frac{1}{24}h^4 y^{(4)}(\eta_i).$$

Three steps, fourth order, local truncation error $O(h^5)$:

$$y_{i+1} = y_i + \frac{h}{24}[9f_{i+1} + 19f_i - 5f_{i-1} + f_{i-2}] + \frac{19}{720}h^5 y^{(5)}(\eta_i).$$

Four steps, fifth order, local truncation error $O(h^6)$:

$$y_{i+1} = y_i + \frac{h}{720}[251f_{i+1} + 646f_i - 264f_{i-1} + 106f_{i-2} - 19f_{i-3}].$$

Adams–Bashforth Predictor–Corrector Methods: $f^*_{i+1} = f(x_{i+1}, y^*_{i+1})$
Second order:

$$y^*_{i+1} = y_i + \frac{h}{2}[3f_i - f_{i-1}] + \frac{5}{12}h^3 y^{(3)}(\eta_1),$$

$$y_{i+1} = y_i + \frac{h}{2}[f^*_{i+1} + f_i] - \frac{1}{12}h^3 y^{(3)}(\eta_2).$$

Third order:

$$y_{i+1}^* = y_i + \frac{h}{12}[23f_i - 16f_{i-1} + 5f_{i-2}] + \frac{3}{8}h^4 y^{(4)}(\eta_1),$$

$$y_{i+1} = y_i + \frac{h}{12}[5f_{i+1}^* + 8f_i - f_{i-1}] - \frac{1}{24}h^4 y^{(4)}(\eta_2).$$

Fourth order:

$$y_{i+1}^* = y_i + \frac{h}{24}[55f_i - 59f_{i-1} + 37f_{i-2} - 9f_{i-3}] + \frac{251}{720}h^5 y^{(5)}(\eta_1),$$

$$y_{i+1} = y_i + \frac{h}{24}[9f_{i+1}^* + 19f_i - 5f_{i-1} + f_{i-2}] + \frac{19}{720}h^5 y^{(5)}(\eta_2).$$

SUGGESTIONS FOR FURTHER READING

Edwards, C. H., Jr., and D. E. Penney, *Differential Equations and Boundary Value Problems: Computing and Modeling*, Prentice Hall, Englewood Cliffs, NJ, 1996.

Edwards C. H., Jr., and D. E. Penney, *Elementary Differential Equations with Boundary Value Problems*, 3d ed., Prentice Hall, Englewood Cliffs, NJ, 1993.

Finizio, N., and G. Ladas, *An Introduction to Differential Equations, with Difference Equations, Fourier Series, and Partial Differential Equations*, Wadsworth Publishing, Belmont, CA, 1982.

Froberg, C. E., *Numerical Mathematics: Theory and Computer Applications*, Benjamin/Cummings, Menlo Park, CA, 1985.

Garcia, A. L., *Numerical Methods for Physics*, Prentice Hall, Englewood Cliffs, NJ, 1994.

Gear, C. W., *Numerical Initial Value Problems in Ordinary Differential Equations*, Prentice-Hall, Englewood Cliffs, NJ, 1971.

Golub, G. H., and J. M. Ortega, *Scientific Computing and Differential Equations: An Introduction to Numerical Methods*, Academic Press, Boston, 1992.

Hanna, O. T., and O. C. Sandall, *Computational Methods in Chemical Engineering*, Prentice Hall, Upper Saddle River, NJ, 1995.

Jain, M. K., *Numerical Solution of Differential Equations*, John Wiley & Sons, New York, 1979.

Ortega, J. M., and W. G. Poole, *An Introduction to Numerical Methods for Differential Equations*, Pitman Publishing, Marshfield, MA, 1981.

Ritger, P. D., and N. J. Rose, *Differential Equations with Applications*, McGraw-Hill, New York, 1968.

Roberts, C. E., *Ordinary Differential Equations: A Computational Approach*, Prentice-Hall, Englewood Cliffs, NJ, 1979.

Shampine, L. F., and M. W. Reichelt, "The MATLAB ODE Suite," *SIAM Journal on Scientific Computing*, vol. 18, no. 1, 1997.

Zill, D. G., *Differential Equations with Boundary-Value Problems*, Prindle, Weber, & Schmidt, Boston, 1986.

PRACTICE THE TECHNIQUES

In Problems P12.1–P12.10, solve the initial-value problem and compare your results with the exact solution given. Problems with $h = 0.5$ are suggested for hand calculation; smaller values of h are more appropriate with MATLAB programs.

  a. Use Euler's method with $h = 0.5$ or $h = 0.1$.
  b. Use the second-order Taylor method with $h = 0.5$ or $h = 0.1$.
  c. Use the midpoint method with $h = 0.5$ or $h = 0.1$.
  d. Use the classic Runge–Kutta method with $h = 0.5$ or $h = 0.1$.

P12.1 Solve $y' = y$, $y(0) = 2$, on $[0, 1]$.
The exact solution is $y = 2e^x$.

P12.2 Solve $y' = x + y$, $y(0) = 2$, on $[0, 1]$.
The exact solution is $y = 3e^x - x - 1$.

P12.3 Solve $y' = -y^2$, $y(0) = 1$, on $[0, 1]$.
The exact solution is $y = 1/(x + 1)$.

P12.4 Solve $y' = 1 + x - y - xy$, $y(0) = 2$, on $[0, 1]$.
The exact solution is
$$y = 1 + \exp\left(-x - \frac{x^2}{2}\right).$$

P12.5 Solve $y' = y\,x^{-2}$, $y(1) = 2$, on $[1, 2]$.
The exact solution is $y = 2\exp((x - 1)/x)$.

P12.6 Solve $y' = xy + x$, $y(0) = 0$, on $[0, 1]$.
The exact solution is
$$y = -1 + \exp\left(\frac{x^2}{2}\right).$$

P12.7 Solve $y' = -2xy$, $y(0) = 2$, on $[0, 1]$.
The exact solution is $y = 2\exp(-x^2)$.

P12.8 Solve $y' = x + 4yx^{-1}$, $y(1) = 1/2$, on $[1, 2]$.
The exact solution is $y = -\frac{1}{2}x^2 + x^4$.

P12.9 Solve $y' = 3x^2y$, $y(0) = 1$, on $[0, 1]$.
The exact solution is $y = \exp(x^3)$.

P12.10 Solve $y' = y\cos(x)$, $y(0) = 1$, on $[0, 1]$.
The exact solution is $y = e^{\sin x}$.

In Problems P12.11–P12.20, solve the initial-value problem and compare your results with the exact solution given. Investigate the effect of using different step sizes.

  a. Use Euler's method.
  b. Use the midpoint method.
  c. Use the classic Runge–Kutta method.
  d. Use the Adams–Bashforth–Moulton predictor–corrector method.

P12.11 Solve $y' = -y + \sin(x)$, $y(0) = 1$, on $[0, \pi]$.
(Compare the results using $n = 10, 20$, and 40.)
The exact solution is
$y = 1.5e^{-x} + 0.5\sin(x) - 0.5\cos(x)$.

P12.12 Solve $y' = y\tan(x) + x$, $y(0) = 3$, on $[0, \pi/4]$.
The exact solution is
$y = x\tan(x) + 2\sec(x) + 1$.

P12.13 Solve $y' = \dfrac{x^2 + y^2}{2xy}$, $y(1) = 2$, on $[1, 2]$.
The exact solution is $y^2 = x(x + 3)$.

P12.14 Solve $y' = -y\ \tan(x) + \sec(x)$, $y(0) = 2$ on $[0, \pi/4]$.
The exact solution is $y = \sin(x) + 2\cos(x)$.

P12.15 Solve $y' = -2\sqrt{y - 1}$, $y(0) = 5$ on $[0, 2]$.
The exact solution is $y = 1 + (x - 2)^2$.

P12.16 Solve $y' = x + 2yx^{-1}$, $y(1) = 1$, on $[1, 2]$.
The exact solution is $y = x^2\log(x) + x^2$.

P12.17 Solve $y' = 4xy^{-1} - xy$, $y(0) = 3$, on $[0, 2]$.
The exact solution is
$y = \sqrt{4 + 5\exp(-x^2)}$.

P12.18 Solve $y' = xy^{-1} - xy$, $y(0) = 2$, on $[0, 2]$.
The exact solution is
$y = \sqrt{1 + 3\exp(-x^2)}$.

P12.19 $y' = (y + x)^2$, $y(0) = -1$, on $[0, \pi/2]$.
The exact solution is
$y = -x + \tan(x - \pi/4)$.

P12.20 Solve $y' = \dfrac{3x}{y} - xy$, $y(0) = 2$, on $[0, 2]$.
The exact solution is
$y = \sqrt{3 + \exp(-x^2)}$.

In Problems P12.21–P12.25, solve the initial-value problem. Investigate the effect of using different step sizes and intervals of different lengths.

P12.21 $y' = y + x^2$, $y(0) = 1$.
P12.22 $y' = y + \cos(x)$, $y(0) = 1$.
P12.23 $y' = y + \log(x + 1)$, $y(0) = 1$.
P12.24 $y' = y + x^{-1}$, $y(1) = 1$.
P12.25 $y' = y\tan(x)$, $y(0) = 1$.

EXPLORE SOME APPLICATIONS

A12.1 The concentration of a chemical in a batch reactor can be modeled by the differential equation

$$\frac{dC}{dt} = \frac{-k_1 C}{1 + k_2 C}.$$

Find a numerical solution for $0 \le x \le 1$.

a. Use $k_1 = 2$, $k_2 = 0.1$, and $C(0) = 1$.

b. Use $k_1 = 1$, $k_2 = 0.3$, and $C(0) = 0.8$.

(See Hanna and Sandall, 1995, for a discussion of similar problems.)

A12.2 Solve the Ginzburg–Landau equation

$$\frac{dx}{dt} = k^2 x^3 - x$$

on the interval $[0,3]$ for the given values of the parameter k and the given initial condition.

a. $k = 1$, $x(0) = 0.7$.

b. $k = -0.1$, $x(0) = 0.9$.

c. $k = -0.8$, $x(0) = 0.9$.

d. $k = 0.5$, $x(0) = 1.2$.

(Adapted from Garcia, 1994.)

A12.3 The velocity of a body subject to the force of gravity and air resistance proportional to v is given by the differential equation

$$\frac{dv}{dt} = g - pv,$$

where g represents the acceleration due to gravity (32 ft/sec) and p is the drag coefficient.

a. Find the velocity of an arrow with initial velocity $v_0 = 300$ ft/sec and drag coefficient $p = 0.05$.

b. Find the velocity of a parachutist with $v_0 = 0$ ft/sec and drag coefficient $p = 1.5$. (See Edwards and Penney, 1993, for a discussion of similar problems.)

A12.4 According to Torricelli's law, the depth y of the water in a tank with a hole in the bottom changes according to the differential equation

$$\frac{dy}{dt} = -k\sqrt{y}\, A(y),$$

where $A(y)$ is the cross-sectional area of the tank at depth y. The parameter k is equal to $a\sqrt{2g}$, where g is the acceleration due to gravity (32 ft/sec) and a is the area of the hole. (See Edwards and Penney, 1996, for a derivation of this equation.)

a. Find the water depth in a tank with cross-sectional area $A(y) = \pi y$; that is, the tank is formed by rotating the curve $y = x^2$ around the y-axis. Let the initial water depth be 2 ft and the area of the hole be 0.01. When is the tank empty?

b. Find the water depth in a tank with cross-sectional area $A(y) = \pi y^{2/3}$; that is, the tank is formed by rotating the curve $y = x^3$ around the y-axis. Take the initial water depth to be 2 ft and the area of the hole be 0.01. When is the tank empty?

A12.5 A simple model of the spread of disease is $P' = kP(C - P)$, where $P(t)$ represents the number of individuals in the population that are infected and C is the constant size of the total population. The solution of this differential equation is the logistic function. Suppose now that the parameter k fluctuates (perhaps because the population is more susceptible during certain seasons). Solve the modified problem and compare your results with those obtained from the original model. The new model is

$$P' = (k + 0.1\sin(t))\, P(C - P),$$

$$k = 2, C = 2000, P(0) = 10.$$

A12.6 The balance in a bank account in which interest is being earned at the rate of 5%, compounded continuously and reinvested, obeys the differential equation

$$B' = 0.05\, B, B(0) = B_0.$$

Suppose now that additional deposits are made on a regular basis, but with larger deposits made during certain months. The change in the bank balance could then be modeled by the ODE

$$B' = 0.05B + C(\sin(2\pi t))^4, B(0) = B_0.$$

Take an initial deposit of $B_0 = 1000$ and a deposit schedule of $2(\sin(2\pi t))^4$. Compare the balance in the account after two years with that given by the initial deposit and reinvestment only.

Problems A12.7–A12.13 explore some Riccati differential equations, i.e., differential equations of the form $y' = P(x)y + Q(x)y^2 + R(x)$.

A12.7 Solve $y' = xy + y^2 + x^2$, $y(0) = 1$, on $[0, 0.5]$.

A12.8 Solve $y' = \dfrac{-1}{x}y - y^2 + \dfrac{1}{x^2}$, $y(1) = -1/3$, on $[1, 2]$.

A12.9 Solve $y' = \dfrac{1}{x}y + \dfrac{1}{x}y^2 + \dfrac{-2}{x^2}$, $y(0.1) = 1$, on $[0.1, 1]$.

A12.10 Solve $y' = \dfrac{1}{x}y + \dfrac{1}{x}y^2 + \dfrac{-2}{x}$, $y(2) = -3$, on $[2, 3]$.

A12.11 Solve $y' = y^2 + x^{-4}$, $y(1) = 0.1$, on $[1, 2]$.

A12.12 Solve $y' = y^2 + x^{-8/5}$, $y(1) = 0.1$, on $[1, 2]$.

A12.13 Solve $y' = y^2 + x^{-8/3}$, $y(1) = 0.1$, on $[1, 3]$.

Problems A12.14–A12.16 explore some Bernoulli differential equations, i.e., differential equations of the form $y' = -P(x)y + Q(x)y^n$.

A12.14 Solve $y' = 1.5x^{-1}y + 2xy^{-1}$, $y(1) = 0$, on $[1, 3]$.

A12.15 Solve $y' = 6x^{-1}y + 3y^{4/3}$, $y(1) = 1/8$, on $[1, 3]$.

A12.16 Solve $y' = xy + y^2$, $y(1) = 0.1$, on $[0, 2]$.

EXTEND YOUR UNDERSTANDING

U12.1 Solve $y' = x^2 + y^2$, $y(0) = 1$, on $[0, 0.9]$.
Discuss what happens if you try to extend the interval to $[0, 1]$.

U12.2 Solve $y' = -x^2 + y^2$, $y(0) = 1$, on $[0, 1]$.

U12.3 Solve $y' = x^2 - y^2$, $y(0) = 1$, on $[0, 1]$.

U12.4 Solve $y' = 1 - y^2$,
   a. $y(0) = 0$, on $[0, 5]$.
   b. $y(1) = 4$, on $[1, 5]$.

U12.5 Solve $y' = 4y - 2x^2$, $y(0) = 1/16$, on $[0,3]$.
Compae your results with the exact solution, $y = (1/2)x^2 + (1/4)x + 1/16$.

Problems U12.6–U12.9 explore the application of numerical methods to differential equations for which the solution may not be unique. (See a standard differential equations text, e.g., Edwards and Penney, 1996, for a discussion of the conditions that guarantee the existence and uniqueness of the solution of a first-order ODE initial-value problem.

U12.6 Solve $y' = y - \sin x$, $y(-\pi) = -0.5$, on $[-\pi, \pi]$.

U12.7 Solve $y' = 2yx^{-1}$, $y(-1) = 1$, on $[-1, 1]$.

U12.8 Solve $y' = 2\sqrt{y}$, $y(0) = 0$, on $[0, 1]$. Compare your solution with that for $y(0) = 0.001$ on $[0, 1]$.

U12.9 Solve $y' = y^2$, $y(0) = 1$, on $[0, 0.5]$. Compare your solution with that for $y(2) = -0.5$ on $[2, 3]$.

U12.10 Investigate the stability of the predictor and corrector formulas for Milne's (fourth-order) method. The predictor is given by

$$y^*_{i+1} = y_{i-3} + \frac{4h}{3}[2f_i - f_{i-1} + 2f_{i-2}]$$

$$+ \frac{14}{45}h^5 y^{(5)}(\eta_1),$$

and the corrector is

$$y_{i+1} = y_{i-1} + \frac{h}{3}[f^*_{i+1} + 4f_i + f_{i-1}]$$

$$- \frac{1}{90}h^5 y^{(5)}(\eta_2).$$

(See Froberg, 1985, p. 338 for a further discussion of the topic.)

13

Systems of Ordinary Differential Equations

In this chapter, we extend the techniques presented in the previous chapter to higher order ODEs and systems of first-order ODEs. We begin by showing how a higher order ODE can be converted into a system of first- order ODEs. In the second section, we treat the Euler and midpoint methods for second-order ODEs and systems of two first-order ODEs in some detail in order to emphasize the direct relationship between each of the methods for a single ODE and the corresponding method for a system of ODEs.

For larger first-order systems, we can update all components of the solution very easily by utilizing MATLAB's vector capabilities. The function for each of the methods presented in the previous chapter can be applied to systems of arbitrary size with only minor modifications. Although the methods presented in this chapter are direct extensions of those seen in the last chapter, the variety of applications that can be solved is greatly expanded. We illustrate the methods using simple examples and problems, including the motion of a nonlinear pendulum, a spring–mass system, and a two-link robot arm. Sample problems describing chemical reactions are also solved.

Ordinary differential equations can be used to describe a wide variety of processes. Population growth models, predator–prey models, radioactive carbon dating, combat models, traffic flow models, and mechanical and electrical vibrations are a few of the most common applications; the list of possibilities is almost endless.

The solution of ODE initial-value problems forms the basis for the shooting method, one of the approaches to solving boundary-value problems for ordinary differential equations. The study of numerical methods for ODE–BVPs is the subject of the next chapter.

Example 13-A Motion of a Nonlinear Pendulum

The motion of a pendulum of length L subject to damping can be described by the angular displacement of the pendulum from the vertical, θ, as a function of time. (See Fig. 13.1.) If we let m be the mass of the pendulum, g the gravitational constant, and c the damping coefficient (i.e., the damping force is $F = -c\theta'$), then the ODE initial-value problem describing this motion is

$$\theta'' + \frac{c}{mL}\theta' + \frac{g}{L}\sin\theta = 0.$$

The initial conditions give the angular displacement and velocity at time zero; for example, if $\theta(0) = a$ and $\theta'(0) = 0$, the pendulum has an initial displacement, but is released with 0 initial velocity.

   Analytic (closed-form) solutions rely on approximating $\sin\theta$; the exact solutions to this approximated system do not have the characteristics of the physical pendulum, namely, a decreasing amplitude and a decreasing period. (See Greenspan, 1974, for further discussion.)

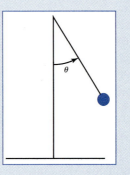

FIGURE 13.1a   Simple pendulum.

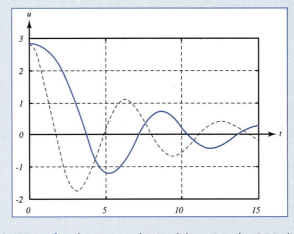

FIGURE 13.1b   The motion of a pendulum given by ODE above
(solid line) and linearized ODE (dashed line).

Example 13-B Chemical Flow

A *circular reaction* involving three chemical reactions can be described as

$$A + A' \xrightarrow{\;\;k_1\;\;} B,$$

$$B + B' \xrightarrow{\;\;k_2\;\;} C,$$

$$C + C' \xrightarrow{\;\;k_3\;\;} A.$$

We assume that compounds A', B' and C' are present in excess, so that changes in their quantities can be neglected, and we simplify the notation by defining $r_1 = k_1 A'$, $r_2 = k_2 B'$, and $r_3 = k_3 C'$; the differential equations can be written as

$$\frac{dA}{dt} = r_3 C - r_1 A,$$

$$\frac{dB}{dt} = r_1 A - r_2 B,$$

$$\frac{dC}{dt} = r_2 B - r_3 C.$$

If the reaction rates are constants, the solution can be found from the eigenvalues and eigenvectors of the coefficient matrix R when the differential equation is written in matrix-vector form, $\mathbf{x}' = \mathbf{R}\mathbf{x}$, with $\mathbf{x} = [A, B, C]'$ and

$$\mathbf{R} = \begin{bmatrix} -r_1 & 0 & r_3 \\ r_1 & -r_2 & 0 \\ 0 & r_2 & -r_3 \end{bmatrix}$$

This is discussed briefly in problems A7.27–A7.50. On the other hand, if the reaction rates are not constant, numerical methods may be especially useful. For example, we can take $r_2 = 2, r_3 = 1$, and r_1 changing from 0.1 to 10. (The units for these parameters are sec^{-1}.) The appropriate initial values of the unknown functions A, B, and C depend on the total amount of the three chemicals that is present ($Q = A + B + C$) and the rate constants; the initial values are chosen to be consistent with the equilibrium values, which are

$$A = \frac{Q}{1 + r_1/r_2 + r_1/r_3}, \qquad B = \frac{r_1}{r_2} A, \qquad C = \frac{r_1}{r_3} A.$$

(For further discussion, see Simon, 1986, p. 118.)

13.1 HIGHER ORDER ODEs

A second-order ODE of the form

$$y'' = g(x, y, y')$$

can be converted to a system of two first-order ODEs by a simple change of variables:

$$u = y,$$
$$v = y'.$$

The differential equations relating these variables (functions) are

$$u' = v = f(x, u, v),$$
$$v' = g(x, u, v).$$

The initial conditions for the original ODE,

$$y(0) = \alpha_0, \qquad y'(0) = \alpha_1,$$

become the initial conditions for the system, i. e.,

$$u(0) = \alpha_0, \qquad v(0) = \alpha_1.$$

Example 13.1 Nonlinear Pendulum

Consider the nonlinear pendulum described in Example 13-A, with angular displacement $y(x)$ given by

$$y'' + \frac{c}{mL} y' + \frac{g}{L} \sin y = 0, \qquad y(0) = a, \qquad y'(0) = b.$$

Choosing $g/L = 1$ and $c/(mL) = 0.3$, $a = \pi/2$, and $b = 0$, we get the second-order ODE–IVP

$$y'' = -0.3y' - \sin y,$$

which can be converted to a system of first-order ODEs by means of the change of variables

$$u = y,$$
$$v = y'.$$

The differential equations relating these variables are

$$u' = v = f(x, u, v),$$
$$v' = -0.3v - \sin u = g(x,u,v),$$

with initial conditions $u(0) = \pi/2, v(0) = 0$.

We investigate the application of Euler's method and the midpoint method to this and other systems of two first-order ODEs in the next section.

A higher order ODE may be converted to a system of first-order ODEs by a similar change of variables. The nth-order ODE

$$y^{(n)} = f(x, y, y', y'', \ldots, y^{(n-1)}),$$

$$y(0) = \alpha_0, \quad y'(0) = \alpha_1, \quad y''(0) = \alpha_2, \ldots, \quad y^{(n-1)}(0) = \alpha_{n-1},$$

becomes a system of first-order ODEs by the following change of variables:

$$u_1 = y,$$
$$u_2 = y',$$
$$u_3 = y'',$$
$$\vdots$$
$$u_n = y^{(n-1)}.$$

The differential equations relating these variables are

$$u_1' = u_2,$$
$$u_2' = u_3,$$
$$u_3' = u_4,$$
$$\vdots$$
$$u_n' = f(x, u_1, u_2, u_3, \ldots, u_n),$$

with the initial conditions

$$u_1(0) = \alpha_0, \quad u_2(0) = \alpha_1, \quad u_3(0) = \alpha_2, \quad \ldots, \quad u_n(0) = \alpha_{n-1}.$$

We investigate the application of several of the methods from Chapter 12 to general systems of ODEs in Section 13.3. By utilizing MATLAB's vector capabilities, only minor changes are required to the functions presented in Chapter 12.

13.2 SYSTEMS OF TWO FIRST-ORDER ODEs

Any of the methods for solving ODE–IVPs discussed in Chapter 12 can be generalized to apply to systems of equations. In this section, we consider systems of two first-order ODEs in detail, using the Euler and Runge–Kutta methods. In Section 13.3, we treat systems of arbitrary size, using MATLAB's vector capabilities extensively.

13.2.1 Euler's Method for Solving Two ODE–IVPs

To apply the basic Euler's method

$$y_{i+1} = y_i + h f(x_i, y_i)$$

to the system of ODEs

$$u' = f(x, u, v), \qquad v' = g(x, u, v),$$

we update the function u using $f(x, u, v)$ and update v using $g(x, u, v)$. The same step size h is used for each function (since that refers to the spacing of the independent variable x):

$$u(i + 1) = u(i) + h f(x(i), u(i), v(i)),$$

$$v(i + 1) = v(i) + h g(x(i), u(i), v(i)).$$

Example 13.2 Nonlinear Pendulum using Euler's Method

Consider the system of ODEs obtained from the second-order ODE for the motion of the nonlinear pendulum described in Examples 13-A and 13.1:

$$u' = v = f(x, u, v), \qquad v' = -0.3v - \sin u = g(x, u, v).$$

The initial conditions are $u_0 = \pi/2, v_0 = 0$.

In order to get accurate results, we must take a fairly small step size, e.g., $n = 200$. The motion for the first 15 seconds is shown in Fig. 13.2 for $n = 50, n = 100$, and $n = 200$.

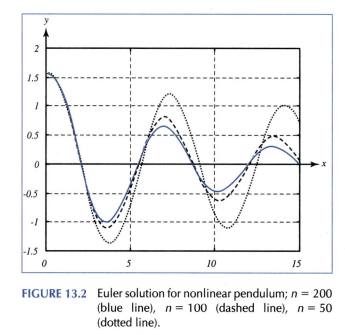

FIGURE 13.2 Euler solution for nonlinear pendulum; $n = 200$ (blue line), $n = 100$ (dashed line), $n = 50$ (dotted line).

MATLAB Function for Euler's Method for Solving a System of Two First-Order ODEs

```
function [x, u, v] = Euler_sys2(f, g, a, b, u0, v0, n)
h = (b-a)/n;
x = (a+h : h : b);
u(1) = u0 + h*feval( f, a, u0, v0);
```

```
v(1) = v0 + h*feval( g, a, u0, v0);
for i = 2 : n
    u(i) = u(i-1) + h*feval(f, x(i-1), u(i-1), v(i-1));
    v(i) = v(i-1) + h*feval(g, x(i-1), u(i-1), v(i-1));
end
x = [ a    x ];      u = [ u0    u ];       v = [ v0    v];
```

Example 13.3 Series Dilution Problem using Euler's Method

To illustrate the use of Euler's method for a system of two ODEs, consider the concentration of a dye in a two-compartment dilution process. A pure substance flows into the first tank at the same rate that a mixture leaves the first tank and flows into the second tank; the dye leaves the first tank at a rate that is proportional to the concentration. The loss from the first tank becomes the influx to the second tank, which in turn loses fluid at the same rate; thus, the volume of fluid in each tank is constant. The differential equations describing the concentration of dye in the two tanks are

$$\frac{dC_1}{dt} = -\frac{L}{V_1} C_1, \qquad \frac{dC_2}{dt} = -\frac{L}{V_2} [C_2 - C_1].$$

Taking $C_1(0) = 0.3$ moles/liter, $C_2(0) = 0$, $L = 2$ liters/min, $V_1 = 10$ liters, and $V_2 = 5$ liters, we find the concentration in the two tanks for the first 10 minutes of the process. The computed values of C_1 and C_2 are plotted in Fig. 13.3. The exact solutions are also shown for comparison; the equations are given in Example 13.5.

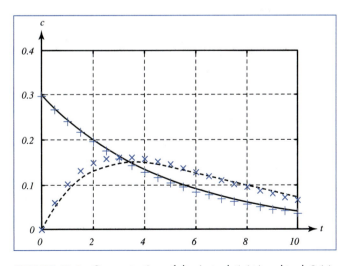

FIGURE 13.3   Concentration of dye in tank 1 (+) and tank 2 (x).

13.2.2 Midpoint Method for Solving Two ODE–IVPs

The idea in generalizing Runge–Kutta methods to systems of two equations is the same as for Euler's method; that is, we update each unknown function u and v, using the basic Runge–Kutta formulas and the appropriate right-hand-side function, f or g, from the differential equation for the unknown:

$$u' = f(x, u, v),$$
$$v' = g(x, u, v).$$

We rewrite the basic second-order Runge–Kutta formulas (the midpoint method),

$$k_1 = h f(x_i, y_i),$$
$$k_2 = h f\left(x_i + \frac{1}{2}h, y_i + \frac{1}{2}k_1\right),$$
$$y_{i+1} = y_i + k_2,$$

using k_1 and k_2 to represent the update quantities for the unknown function u and calling the corresponding quantities for the function v, m_1 and m_2. We must remember to update function f by the appropriate multiple of k_1 or k_2 and function g by the corresponding amount of m_1 or m_2. This means that k_1 and m_1 must be computed before k_2 and m_2 can be found. Thus,

$$k_1 = h f(x_i, u_i, v_i),$$
$$m_1 = h g(x_i, u_i, v_i),$$
$$k_2 = h f\left(x_i + \frac{1}{2}h, u_i + \frac{1}{2}k_1, v_i + \frac{1}{2}m_1\right),$$
$$m_2 = h g\left(x_i + \frac{1}{2}h, u_i + \frac{1}{2}k_1, v_i + \frac{1}{2}m_1\right),$$
$$u_{i+1} = u_i + k_2,$$
$$v_{i+1} = v_i + m_2.$$

MATLAB Function for Runge–Kutta Two-Step Method for Solving Two ODEs

```
function [ x, u, v ] = RK2_sys( f, g, a, b, u0, v0, n )
h = (b-a)/n;    hh = h/2;
x = (a+h : h : b);
k1 = h*feval( f, a, u0, v0 );
m1 = h*feval( g, a, u0, v0 );
k2 = h*feval( f, a + hh, u0 +0.5*k1, v0 +0.5*m1);
m2 = h*feval( g, a + hh, u0 +0.5*k1, v0 +0.5*m1);
u(1) = u0 + k2;
v(1) = v0 + m2;
```

```
for i = 1 : n-1
    k1 = h*feval(f, x(i), u(i), v(i) );
    m1 = h*feval(g, x(i), u(i), v(i) );
    k2 = h*feval(f, x(i) + hh, u(i) +0.5*k1, v(i) +0.5*m1);
    m2 = h*feval(g, x(i) + hh, u(i) +0.5*k1, v(i) +0.5*m1);
    u(i+1) = u(i) + k2;
    v(i+1) = v(i) + m2;
end
x = [a    x];       u = [ u0    u ];    v = [ v0    v ];
```

Example 13.4 Nonlinear Pendulum using Runge–Kutta Method

Consider again the system of ODEs obtained from the second-order ODE for the motion of the nonlinear pendulum described in Examples 13-A, 13.1, and 13.2, i.e.,

$$u' = v = f(x, u, v),$$

$$v' = -0.3v - \sin u = g(x, u, v),$$

with initial conditions

$$u_0 = \pi/2; \qquad v_0 = 0.$$

The motion for the first 15 seconds is shown in Fig. 13.4. The computed solutions for $n = 50, n = 100,$ and $n = 200$ are indistinguishable. The motion of a linear pendulum and a nonlinear pendulum is illustrated in Fig. 13.5 for a larger initial displacement.

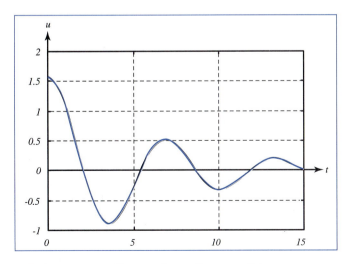

FIGURE 13.4   Oscillations of a nonlinear pendulum.

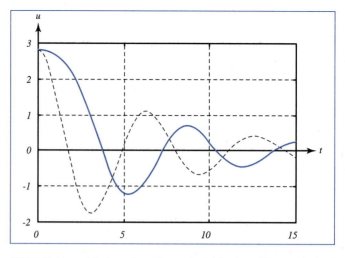

FIGURE 13.5 Motion of nonlinear (solid line) and linear (dashed line) pendulum; $u_0 = 0.9\pi$, $v_0 = 0$.

Example 13.5 Series Dilution using a Runge–Kutta Technique

We consider a two-tank dilution process and model the concentration of a dye (or other tracer) in each of the tanks as a function of time (as in Example 13.3). If water flows into the first tank at the same rate that the mixture flows from the first tank into the second, and the second tank loses its mixture at the same rate L, then the volume of solution in each tank remains constant. The concentrations of the dye in the two tanks satisfy the following differential equations:

$$\frac{dC_1}{dt} = -\frac{L}{V_1} C_1,$$

$$\frac{dC_2}{dt} = -\frac{L}{V_2} [C_1 - C_2].$$

Taking $C_1(0) = 0.3$, $C_2(0) = 0$, $L = 2$, $V_1 = 10$, $V_2 = 5$, and $n = 20$, the computed results are shown in Fig. 13.6, together with the exact solutions, viz.,

$$C_1(t) = C_1(0) \exp[(-L/V_1)t]$$

$$= 0.3 \exp(-0.2t);$$

$$C_2(t) = \frac{V_1 C_1(0)}{V_1 - V_2} [\exp[-(L/V_1)t - \exp[-(L/V_2)t]]$$

$$= 0.6[\exp(-0.2t) - \exp(-0.4t)].$$

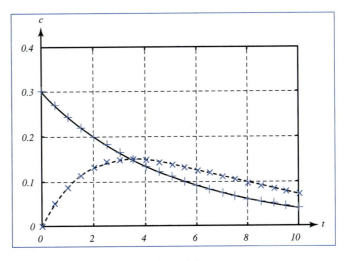

FIGURE 13.6 Concentration of dye in two compartments.

13.3 SYSTEMS OF FIRST-ORDER ODE–IVPs

Systems of ODEs may arise directly from applications such as chemical reactions, predator–prey models, and many others. They also come from the conversion of higher order ODEs into system form.

Example 13.6 A Higher Order System of ODEs

Consider the equation

$$y''' = f(x, y, y', y'') = x + 2y - 3y' + 4y''$$

with initial conditions

$$y(0) = 4, \quad y'(0) = 3, \quad y''(0) = 2.$$

The system of ODEs is

$$u_1' = f_1(x, u_1, u_2, u_3) = u_2,$$

$$u_2' = f_2(x, u_1, u_2, u_3) = u_3,$$

$$u_3' = f_3(x, u_1, u_2, u_3) = x + 2u_1 - 3u_2 + 4u_3.$$

For systems that come from a single higher order ODE, this structure for the right hand side is a direct result of the definitions of the transformed functions. For systems of ODEs in general, each of the right-hand-side functions $f_1, f_2, \ldots$ may contain any or all of the indicated variables.

A system of ODEs can be expressed compactly in vector notation as

$$\mathbf{u}' = \mathbf{f}(x, \mathbf{u}).$$

Since the components of the vectors, $\mathbf{u}$ and $\mathbf{f}$, are denoted by subscripts, we indicate the approximate solutions at the grid points as $u_1(i)$, etc.

13.3.1 Euler's Method for Solving Systems of ODEs

To apply the basic Euler method, $y_{i+1} = y_i + h f(x_i, y_i)$, to the system of ODEs

$$u_1' = f_1(x, u_1, u_2, u_3),$$

$$u_2' = f_2(x, u_1, u_2, u_3),$$

$$u_3' = f_3(x, u_1, u_2, u_3),$$

we update the function u_1 using f_1, u_2 using f_2, and u_3 using f_3. The same step size h is used for each function. We have

$$u_1(i+1) = u_1(i) + h f_1(x(i), u_1(i), u_2(i), u_3(i)),$$

$$u_2(i+1) = u_2(i) + h f_2(x(i), u_1(i), u_2(i), u_3(i)),$$

$$u_3(i+1) = u_3(i) + h f_3(x(i), u_1(i), u_2(i), u_3(i)).$$

Example 13.7 Solving a Higher Order System using Euler's Method

We apply Euler's method with $n = 2$ to find an approximate solution of the system of ODEs

$$u_1' = u_2,$$

$$u_2' = u_3,$$

$$u_3' = x + 2u_1 - 3u_2 + 4u_3,$$

with initial conditions $u_1(0) = 4$, $u_2(0) = 3$, and $u_3(0) = 2$ on $[0, 1]$. The solution at $i = 1$ corresponds to $x(i = 1) = 0.5$:

$$u_1(1) = u_1(0) + 0.5u_2(0) = 4 + 0.5(3) = 5.5,$$

$$u_2(1) = u_2(0) + 0.5u_3(0) = 3 + 0.5(2) = 4,$$

$$u_3(1) = u_3(0) + 0.5(x(0) + 2u_1(0) - 3u_2(0) + 4u_3(0))$$

$$= 2 + 0.5(0 \quad + 2(4) \quad - 3(3) \quad + 4(2)) \quad = 5.5.$$

The solution at $i = 2$ corresponds to $x(i = 2) = 1.0$:

$$u_1(2) = u_1(1) + 0.5u_2(1) = 5.5 + 0.5(4) = 7.5,$$

$$u_2(2) = u_2(1) + 0.5u_3(1) = 4 + 0.5(5.5) = 6.75,$$

$$u_3(2) = u_3(1) + 0.5(x(1) + 2u_1(1) - 3u_2(1) + 4u_3(1))$$

$$= 5.5 \quad + 0.5(0.5 \quad + 2(5.5) - 3(4) \quad + 4(5.5)) = 11.25.$$

Example 13.8 Solving Another Higher Order System using Euler's Method

Consider the system

$$u_1' = u_2, \qquad u_2' = \frac{-2}{x}u_2, \qquad u_3' = u_4, \qquad u_4' = \frac{-2}{x}u_4,$$

with initial conditions

$$u_1(1) = 10, \qquad u_2(1) = 0, \qquad u_3(1) = 0, \qquad u_4(1) = 1,$$

on $[1, 2]$ with $n = 2$ ($h = 0.5$). The following calculations show the values of each component of the solution as a function of x (not the mesh index); at $x = 3/2$:

$$u_1(3/2) = 10 + 0.5(0) = 10, \quad u_2(3/2) = 0 + 0.5(0) = 0,$$

$$u_3(3/2) = 0 + 0.5(1) = 0.5, \quad u_4(3/2) = 1 + 0.5(-2/1) = 0;$$

and at $x = 2$:

$$u_1(2) = 10 + 0.5(0) = 10, \quad u_2(2) = 0 + 0.5(0) = 0,$$

$$u_3(2) = 1/2 + 0.5(0) = 0.5, \quad u_4(2) = 0 + 0.5(0) = 0.$$

These equations occur as part of the shooting method for solving the problem of finding the electrostatic potential between two concentric spheres, Example 14.1 in the next chapter.

13.3.2 Runge–Kutta Methods for Solving Systems of ODEs

The idea in generalizing Runge–Kutta methods for use on systems of equations is the same as for Euler's method; that is, we update each unknown function $u_1, u_2, \ldots$, using the basic Runge–Kutta formulas and the appropriate right-hand-side function $f_1, f_2, \ldots$, from the differential equation for the unknown. We denote the two update parameters for a second order Runge–Kutta method as k and m.

The basic second-order Runge–Kutta formulas (the midpoint method) are

$$k = h f(x_i, y_i), \qquad m = h f\left(x_i + \frac{1}{2}h, y_i + \frac{1}{2}k\right),$$

$$y_{i+1} = y_i + m.$$

To apply these formulas to a system, we must compute k and m for each unknown function (i.e., for each component of the unknown vector $\mathbf{u}$). In fact, k must be computed for each unknown before m can be found.

We illustrate the process for a system of three ODEs:

$$u_1' = f_1(x, u_1, u_2, u_3), \qquad u_2' = f_2(x, u_1, u_2, u_3), \qquad u_3' = f_3(x, u_1, u_2, u_3).$$

The values of the parameter k for the unknown functions $u_1, u_2,$ and u_3 are

$$k_1 = h f_1(x(i), u_1(i), u_2(i), u_3(i)),$$
$$k_2 = h f_2(x(i), u_1(i), u_2(i), u_3(i)),$$
$$k_3 = h f_3(x(i), u_1(i), u_2(i), u_3(i)).$$

Similarly, the values of m are $m_1, m_2,$ and m_3. Of course, to find the value of m for the first ODE, we use f_1; however, we must evaluate f_1 at the appropriate values of $x, u_1, u_2,$ and u_3. Remembering that we are approximating the value of the unknown function employed in evaluating f makes it clear that we approximate each u using its value of k:

$$m_1 = h f_1\left(x(i) + \frac{1}{2}h, u_1(i) + \frac{1}{2}k_1, u_2(i) + \frac{1}{2}k_2, u_3(i) + \frac{1}{2}k_3\right),$$

$$m_2 = h f_2\left(x(i) + \frac{1}{2}h, u_1(i) + \frac{1}{2}k_1, u_2(i) + \frac{1}{2}k_2, u_3(i) + \frac{1}{2}k_3\right),$$

$$m_3 = h f_3\left(x(i) + \frac{1}{2}h, u_1(i) + \frac{1}{2}k_1, u_2(i) + \frac{1}{2}k_2, u_3(i) + \frac{1}{2}k_3\right).$$

Finally, the values of the unknown functions at the next grid point are found:

$$u_1(i+1) = u_1(i) + m_1,$$
$$u_2(i+1) = u_2(i) + m_2,$$
$$u_3(i+1) = u_3(i) + m_3.$$

Example 13.9 Solving a Higher Order System using a Runge–Kutta Method

Let us use a Runge–Kutta method to find an approximate solution on the interval $[0, 1]$ of the system of ODEs

$$u_1' = u_2, \qquad u_2' = u_3, \qquad u_3' = x + 2u_1 - 3u_2 + 4u_3,$$

with initial conditions

$$u_1(0) = 4, \qquad u_2(0) = 3, \qquad u_3(0) = 2.$$

With $n = 2$, we find the following values for $x, u_1, u_2,$ and u_3:

x	u_1	u_2	u_3
0.0	4.0000	3.0000	2.0000
0.5	5.7500	4.8750	9.1250
1.0	9.7656	11.9844	32.8594

The following MATLAB function for the two-step Runge–Kutta method for systems relies on MATLAB's characteristic of treating all variables as vectors. Thus, the only changes from the two-step Runge–Kutta program (midpoint method) in Chapter 12 that are required are the indexing of the matrix for the solution u at each step.

MATLAB Function for Systems Using a Second-Order Runge–Kutta Method

```
function [ x , u ]  = RK2_sys( f, tspan, u0, n)
% solve ODE-IVP using midpoint method (RK2)
%   u' = f(x, u)    a ≤ x ≤ b
% interval of interest is given as tspan = [ a, b ]
% function f(x, u) returns a column vector of values
a = tspan(1);
b = tspan(2);
h = (b-a)/n;
x = (a+h : h : b);
k = h*feval( f, a, u0 )';
m = h*feval( f, a + h/2, u0 + k/2)';
u(1, : ) = u0 + m;
for i = 1 : n-1
        k = h*feval(f, x(i), u(i, : ) )';
        m = h*feval(f, x(i) + h/2, u(i, :) + k/2 )';
        u(i+1, : ) = u(i, : ) + m;
end
x = [a    x];
u = [ u0,
      u ];
```

Example 13.10 Solving a Higher Order System using a Runge–Kutta Method

The system

$$u_1' = u_2, \qquad u_2' = \frac{-2}{x} u_2, \qquad u_3' = u_4, \qquad u_4' = \frac{-2}{x} u_4,$$

with initial conditions

$$u_1(1) = 10, \qquad u_2(1) = 0, \qquad u_3(1) = 0, \qquad u_4(1) = 1,$$

on the interval $[1, 2]$, arises in the solution of the differential equation describing the electrostatic potential between two concentric spheres, one of radius 1 and the other of radius 2.

Using $n = 2$ (and $h = 0.5$), we calculate the values of each component of the solution as a function of x (not the mesh index). First, we find k for each component:

$$k_1 = 0.5(u_2(1)) = 0, \qquad k_2 = 0.5\left(\frac{-2}{x} u_2(1)\right) = 0,$$

$$k_3 = 0.5(u_4(1)) = 0.5, \qquad k_4 = 0.5\left(\frac{-2}{x} u_4(1)\right) = -1,$$

Next, we find m for each component:

$$m_1 = 0.5(u_2(1) + 0.5k_2) = 0,$$

$$m_2 = 0.5\left(\frac{-2}{1.25}\right)(u_2(1) + 0.5k_2) = 0,$$

$$m_3 = 0.5(u_4(1) + 0.5(k_4) = 0.25,$$

$$m_4 = 0.5\left(\frac{-2}{1.25}\right)(u_4(1) + 0.5k_4) = -0.4.$$

The approximate solution at $x = 1.5$ is

$$u_1(1.5) = 10 + 0 = 10, \qquad u_2(1.5) = 0 + 0 = 0,$$
$$u_3(1.5) = 0 + 0.25 = 0.25, \qquad u_4(1.5) = 1 - 0.4 = 0.6.$$

Now we again find k for each component:

$$k_1 = 0.5(u_2(1.5)) = 0, \qquad k_2 = 0.5\left(\frac{-2}{1.5} u_2(1.5)\right) = 0,$$

$$k_3 = 0.5(u_4(1.5)) = 0.3, \qquad k_4 = 0.5\left(\frac{-2}{1.5} u_4(1.5)\right) = -0.4.$$

Next, we again find m for each component:

$$m_1 = 0.5(u_2(1.5) + 0.5k_2) = 0,$$

$$m_2 = 0.5\left(\frac{-2}{1.75}\right)(u_2(1.5) + 0.5k_2) = 0,$$

$$m_3 = 0.5(u_4(1.5) + 0.5k_4) = 0.2,$$

$$m_4 = 0.5\left(\frac{-2}{1.75}\right)(u_4(1.5) + 0.5k_4) = -0.2286.$$

The approximate solution at $x = 1.0$ is

$$u_1(1.0) = 10 + 0 = 10, \qquad u_2(1.0) = 0 + 0 = 0,$$
$$u_3(1.0) = 0.25 + 0.2 = 0.45, \qquad u_4(1.0) = 0.6 - 0.2286 = 0.3714.$$

Using $n = 20$, the foregoing MATLAB function gives the results summarized in Table 13.1.

Table 13.1 ODE–IVP system for electrostatic potential problem.

x	u_1	u_2	u_3	u_4
1.00	10.0000	0.0000	0.0000	1.0000
1.10	10.0000	0.0000	0.0907	0.8269
1.20	10.0000	0.0000	0.1664	0.6952
1.30	10.0000	0.0000	0.2304	0.5925
1.40	10.0000	0.0000	0.2854	0.5110
1.50	10.0000	0.0000	0.3330	0.4453
1.60	10.0000	0.0000	0.3747	0.3914
1.70	10.0000	0.0000	0.4115	0.3468
1.80	10.0000	0.0000	0.4443	0.3094
1.90	10.0000	0.0000	0.4735	0.2777
2.00	10.0000	0.0000	0.4999	0.2506

MATLAB Function for Systems Using a Fourth-Order Runge–Kutta Method

```
% function f(x, u):
%     input:    column vector x and row vector u
%     return:   column vector of values for u'
a = tspan(1); b = tspan(2); h = (b-a) / n;
x = (a+h : h : b)';
k1 = h *feval( f, a,      u0       )';
k2 = h *feval( f, a+h/2, u0+k1/2 )';
k3 = h *feval( f, a+h/2, u0+k2/2 )';
k4 = h *feval( f, a+h ,  u0+k3    )';
u(1, : ) = u0 + k1/6 + k2/3 + k3/3 + k4/6;
for i = 1 : n-1
    k1 = h *feval( f, x(i),      u(i,:)      )';
    k2 = h *feval( f, x(i)+h/2, u(i,:)+k1/2 )';
    k3 = h *feval( f, x(i)+h/2, u(i,:)+k2/2 )';
    k4 = h *feval( f, x(i)+h,   u(i,:)+k3    )';
    u(i+1, : ) = u(i, : ) + k1/6 + k2/3 + k3/3 + k4/6;
end
x = [a
     x];
u = [u0
     u];
```

Example 13.11 Solving a Circular Chemical Reaction Using a Runge–Kutta Method

Consider the circular reaction involving three chemical reactions described in Example 13-B; the differential equations are

$$\frac{dA}{dt} = r_3 C - r_1 A, \qquad \frac{dB}{dt} = r_1 A - r_2 B, \qquad \frac{dC}{dt} = r_2 B - r_3 C.$$

We assume that the total quantity of the chemicals is $A + B + C = Q = 1$; the initial values of A, B, and C are chosen to satisfy the relations

$$A = \frac{1}{1 + r_1/r_2 + r_1/r_3}, \qquad B = \frac{r_1}{r_2} A, \qquad C = \frac{r_1}{r_3} A$$

for the initial rate parameters r_1, r_2, and r_3. We let $r_2 = 2$, let $r_3 = 1$, and allow r_1 to change slowly from an initial value of 0.1 according to the linear equation $r_1 = 0.1(t + 1)$. The initial values of A, B, and C are

$$A(0) = \frac{1}{1.15} = 0.8696, \qquad B(0) = \frac{0.05}{1.15} = 0.0435, \qquad C(0) = \frac{0.1}{1.15} = 0.0870.$$

Taking $n = 100$ subdivisions gives the concentrations illustrated in Figure 13.7.

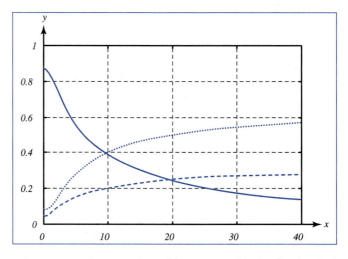

FIGURE 13.7 Concentrations of three reactants in circular chemical reaction. A = solid, B = dashed, C = dotted.

13.3.3 Multistep Methods for Systems

The basic two-step Adams–Bashforth method, in which y_0 is given by the initial condition for the differential equation, y_1 is found from a one-step method, such as a Runge–Kutta technique, and for $i = 1, \ldots, n-1$ and $h = \dfrac{b-a}{n}$,

$$y_{i+1} = y_i + \frac{h}{2}[3f(x_i, y_i) - f(x_{i-1}, y_{i-1})],$$

can be extended for use with a system of three ODEs

$$u_1' = f_1(x, u_1, u_2, u_3),$$

$$u_2' = f_2(x, u_1, u_2, u_3),$$

$$u_3' = f_3(x, u_1, u_2, u_3),$$

in a similarly straightforward manner. That is, $u_1(i=0)$, $u_2(i=0)$, $u_3(i=0)$ are given by the initial condition, $u_1(i=1)$, $u_2(i=1)$, $u_3(i=1)$ are found from a one-step method, and for $i = 1, \ldots, n-1$ and $h = \dfrac{b-a}{n}$,

$$u_1(i+1) = u_1(i) + \frac{h}{2}\,[3f_1(x(i), u_1(i), u_2(i), u_3(i))$$

$$- f_1(x(i-1), u_1(i-1), u_2(i-1), u_3(i-1))],$$

$$u_2(i+1) = u_2(i) + \frac{h}{2}\,[3f_2(x(i), u_1(i), u_2(i), u_3(i))$$

$$- f_2(x(i-1), u_1(i-1), u_2(i-1), u_3(i-1))],$$

$$u_3(i+1) = u_3(i) + \frac{h}{2}\,[3f_3(x(i), u_1(i), u_2(i), u_3(i))$$

$$- f_3(x(i-1), u_1(i-1), u_2(i-1), u_3(i-1))].$$

The Adams-Bashforth-Moulton predictor-corrector methods are extended for use with systems of ODEs in a similar manner. The third-order method is implemented in the MATLAB function ABM3_sys that follows (on p.468). The dimesions of the vectors **u**, **u**0, and tspan depend on the ODE system being solved, as illustrated in Examples 13.12 and 13.13.

Example 13.12 Mass-and-Spring System

The vertical displacements of two masses m_1 and m_2 suspended in series by springs with spring constants s_1 and s_2 are given by Hooke's law as a system of two second-order ODEs. The displacements are x_1 and x_2. (See Fig. 13.8; the displacement of each mass is measured from its equilibrium position, with the positive direction downward.) The ODEs are

$$m_1 x_1'' = -s_1 x_1 + s_2(x_2 - x_1), \qquad m_2 x_2'' = -s_2(x_2 - x_1).$$

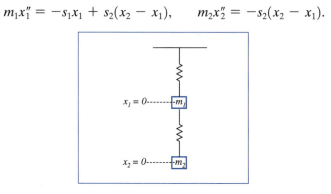

FIGURE 13.8   Two-mass system

The differential equations relating these variables (functions) are

$$u_1' = u_2, \qquad u_2' = -\frac{s_1}{m_1} u_1 + \frac{s_2}{m_1}(u_3 - u_1),$$

$$u_3' = u_4, \qquad u_4' = -\frac{s_2}{m_2}(u_3 - u_1),$$

with the initial conditions

$$u_1(0) = \alpha_1, \qquad u_2(0) = \alpha_2, \qquad u_3(0) = \alpha_3, \qquad u_4(0) = \alpha_4$$

The displacement profiles of a 10-kg mass and a 2-kg mass, are illustrated in Fig. 13.9. The spring constants are 100 and 120, respectively. A script for this example and the function defining the ODEs are given after the figure.

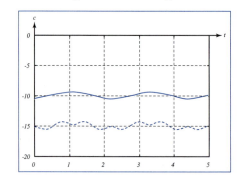

FIGURE 13.9   Displacement profiles of two masses connected by springs.

```
% S_13_12
a = 0;    b = 5;  tspan = [ a b];    n = 100;
y0 = [ 0.5  0  0.25  0 ];
% measurements in kg, meters, Newtons, etc.
% static deflection: mass*(9.81)/(spring constant in N/m)
% actual position depends on length of springs also,
% so we take r1 and r2 to include both deflection and length
global  s1   m1   s2   m2
s1 = 100; m1 = 10; s2 = 120; m2 = 2; r1 = 10; r2 = 15;
[t, y] = ABM3_sys( 'f_13_12', tspan, y0, n);
[ nn, mm] = size(y);   out = [ t  y ];
% down is positive direction, so we plot -y
plot(t(1:nn), -(r1+y(1:nn,1)), '-' )
hold on
plot(t(1:nn), -(r2+y(1:nn, 3)), '-.' )
grid on
plot([a  b], [0  0])
hold off
```

```
function du = f_13_12(t, u)
global s1   m1   s2   m2
  du = [   u(2);
          (-s1*u(1) + s2*(u(3) - u(1)))/m1;
           u(4);
          - s2*(u(3) - u(1))/m2   ];
```

Example 13.13 Motion of a Baseball

Air resistance is one of the factors influencing how far a fly ball travels. In this example, we illustrate the effect of changing assumptions about the form of the air resistance. If a ball is hit with an initial velocity of $[100, 45]$ and is subject to air resistance proportional to its velocity (acting on the horizontal component only), the motion can be found by the MATLAB script that follows. The functions for four variations on the air resistance assumptions are given; the results are shown in Figs. 13.10 and 13.11.

```
%  S_13_13
a = 0; b = 3; tspan = [a  b]; n = 100; y0 = [ 0  100  3  45 ];
[t, y] = ABM3_sys( 'f_bb', tspan, y0, n);
[ nn, mm] = size(y);  out = [ t  y ];
plot(y(1:nn,1),y(1:nn,3), '-')
```

MATLAB Function for Air Resistance Proportional to Velocity in *x* Direction

```
function dz = f_bb_1(x, z)
dz = [z(2);   -0.1*z(2);     z(4);    -32];
```

MATLAB Function for Air Resistance Proportional to Velocity

```
function dz = f_bb_2(x, z)
dz = [z(2); -0.1*sqrt(z(2)^2+z(4)^2);
       z(4); -32-0.1*sqrt(z(2)^2+z(4)^2)*sign(z(4))];
```

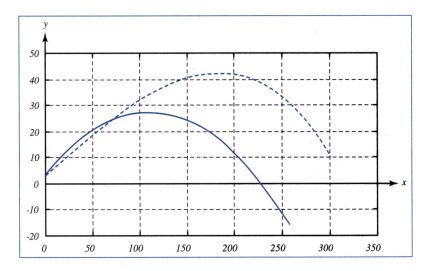

FIGURE 13.10 Flight of a baseball. Dashed line presupposes air resistance proportional to velocity in *x* direction. Solid line presupposes air resistance proportional to velocity.

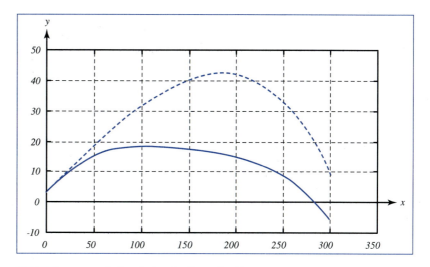

FIGURE 13.11   Flight of a baseball. Dashed line presupposes air resistance proportional to velocity squared in x-direction. Solid line presupposes air resistance proportional to velocity squared.

To take air resistance proportional to the velocity squared, we take a larger initial velocity so that the ball goes a comparable distance. We use $y_0 = [0\ 150\ 3\ 50]$.

MATLAB Function for Air Resistance Proportional to Velocity in Squared x Direction

```
function dz = f_bb_21(x, z)
dz = [z(2);       -0.0025*z(2)^2;      z(4);      -32];
```

MATLAB Function for Air Resistance Proportional to Velocity Squared

```
function dz = f_bb_22(x, z)
dz = [z(2);      -0.0025*(z(2)^2 + z(4)^2)
      z(4);      -32-0.0025*(z(2)^2 + z(4)^2)*sign(z(4))];
```

MATLAB Function for Predictor-Corrector Method for Solving Systems of ODEs

```
function [x, u]  = ABM3_sys(f, tspan, u0, n)
a = tspan(1);
b = tspan(2);
h = (b-a)/n;
hh = h/12;
x = (a+h : h : b)';
%  Use the midpoint method to find the first two points
k = h*feval(f,a,u0)';          m = h*feval(f,a+h/2,u0+k/2)';
u(1, : ) = u0 + m;
k = h*feval(f,x(1),u(1,:))';  m = h*feval(f,x(1)+h/2,u(1,:)+k/2)';
u(2, : ) = u(1, : ) + m;
%  Now use the 3rd order A-B/A-M method for the remaining points
z(2, : ) = feval(f, x(2), u(2, : ))';
uu(3,:) = u(2,:) + hh*(23*z(2,:) - 16*z(1,:) + 5*feval(f, a, u0)');
zz = feval(f, x(3), uu(3, : ))' ;
u(3,:) = u(2,:) + hh*(5*zz + 8*z(2,:) - z(1,:));
for i = 3 : n-1
    z(i, : ) = feval(f, x(i), u(i, : ))';
    uu(i+1,:) = u(i,:) + hh*(23*z(i,:) - 16*z(i-1,:) + 5*z(i-2,:));
    zz = feval(f, x(i+1), uu(i+1, : ))';
    u(i+1,:) = u(i,:) + hh*(5*zz + 8*z(i,:) - z(i-1,:));
end
x = [ a
      x];
u = [ u0,
      u];
```

13.4 STIFF ODE AND ILL-CONDITIONED PROBLEMS

There are ODE for which any error that occurs will increase, regardless of the numerical method employed. Such problems are called *ill conditioned*. As an illustration, consider the system

$$u_1' = 2u_2$$
$$u_2' = 2u_1$$

for which the general solution is

$$u_1 = a\,e^{2x} + b\,e^{-2x}$$
$$u_2 = a\,e^{2x} - b\,e^{-2x}$$

With the initial conditions

$$u_1(0) = 3$$
$$u_2(0) = -3$$

we have $a = 0$, $b = 3$. However, for any numerical error that occurs, a component of the positive exponential will be introduced and will eventually dominate the true solution.

Ill conditioning can also occur for a single first-order ODE, as the following problem shows. Consider the ODE

$$y' = 3y - t^2$$

for which the general solution is

$$y = Ce^{3t} + \frac{1}{3}t^2 + \frac{2}{9}t + \frac{2}{27}.$$

If we take the initial condition as $y(0) = \dfrac{2}{27}$, the exact solution is

$$y = \frac{1}{3}t^2 + \frac{2}{9}t + \frac{2}{27}.$$

However, any error in the numerical solution process will introduce the exponential component which will eventually dominate the true solution. The exponential term is known as a *parasitic solution*.

An ODE in which there is a rapidly decaying transient solution also causes difficulties for numerical solution, requiring an extremely small step size in order to obtain an accurate solution. One source of such equations is in the description of a spring-mass system with large spring constants, hence these problems are known as *stiff ODE*. Stiff ODEs are very common in chemical kinetic studies, and also occur in many network analysis and simulation problems.

As an illustration, consider the system

$$u' = \quad 98u + 198v,$$

$$v' = -99u + 199v,$$

with initial conditions $u(0) = 1$, $v(0) = 0$.
The exact solution is

$$u(t) = 2\,e^{-t} - e^{-100t},$$

$$v(t) = -e^{-t} + e^{-100t}.$$

It is also possible for a single first-order ODE to be stiff, as the following problem shows. Consider the ODE

$$y' = \lambda(y - g(t)) + g'(t)$$

with $\lambda \ll 0$ and $g(t)$ a smooth, slowly varying function. The solution is

$$y = (y_0 - g(0))\,e^{\lambda t} + g(t).$$

The first term in the solution will soon be insignificant compared with $g(t)$, but stability will continue to be governed by $h\lambda$, necessitating a very small step size.
For a system of equations

$$\mathbf{y}' = \mathbf{A}(\mathbf{y} - \mathbf{g}(t)) + \mathbf{g}'(t)$$

the eigenvalues of $\mathbf{A}$ correspond to λ; if all of the eigenvalues have negative real parts, the solution will converge towards $\mathbf{g}(t)$ as $t \to \infty$.
The simplest method for stiff problems is the backward Euler method

$$y_{i+1} = y_i + h\,f(t_{i+1}, y_{i+1}).$$

The error is amplified by $(1 - h\lambda)^{-1}$ at each step, which is less than one if $Re(\lambda) < 0$. Thus, the backward Euler's method is *A*-stable, according to the following definition.

A method is called *A-stable* if any solution produced when the method is applied (with fixed step size $h > 0$) to the problem $y' = \lambda y$ (with $\lambda = \alpha + \beta i$ and $\alpha < 0$) tends to zero as $n \to \infty$.

Dahlquist (1963) showed that a multistep method that is *A*-stable cannot have order greater than two. The trapezoid method is the second-order multistep method with the smallest error constant (see summary for Chapter 12).

Since *A*-stability is difficult to achieve, a somewhat less restrictive stability condition, known as stiff-stability is often sufficient. Methods for stiff ODE are implicit and often require iterative techniques for their solution. Newton's method may be used, with the required Jacobian either supplied by the user, or generated numerically. (See Gear, 1971 for further discussion.)

The M**ATLAB** functions for solving the ODE described at the end of the previous chapter are directly applicable to systems of ODEs. We illustrate the use of the function `ode23` to solve the problem of simulating the motion of a two-link planar robot arm. This is an example of a forward dynamics problem—i.e., given the applied joint torques, we solve for the resulting motion of the system. Attaining a solution involves integrating the equations of motion, which are two nonlinear coupled ODEs. (See Spong and Vidyasagar, *Robot Dynamics and Control*, John Wiley & Sons, Inc., New York, 1989, for a derivation of the equations; the coordinate convention is taken from Fig. 6-3 in that work.) Figure 13.12 shows the motion of the arm.

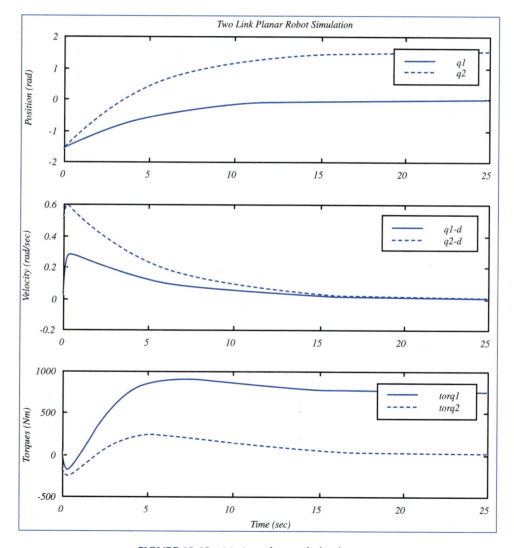

FIGURE 13.12 Motion of a two-link robot arm.

```
function ydot = robot2(t,y);
% Calculate the accelerations for a two-link planar robot
% Equations of motion [Spong, p 145, ex. 6.4.2]
% This example was contributed by
% Pierre Larochelle, Florida Institute of Technology, 5-12-97
% make sure this function has access to the global variables
global L1  Lc1  L2  Lc2  m1  m2  g
global I1  I2  q1_goal  q2_goal  K_p  K_v
% Use aliases for input states to match standard robotics notation
q1  = y(1);   q2  = y(2);   q1d = y(3);   q2d = y(4);
% Calculate the mass matrix [M]
d11 = m1*Lc1^2 + m2*(L1^2 + Lc2^2 + 2*L1*Lc2*cos(q2)) + I1 + I2;
d12 = m2*(Lc2^2 + L1*Lc2*cos(q2)) + I2;
d21 = d12;   d22 = m2*Lc2^2 + I2;   M = [d11 d12; d21 d22];
% Calculate the Christoffel matrix
h = -m2*L1*Lc2*sin(q2);
C = h * [q2d  q2d+q1d   ;
          -q1d      0     ];
% Calculate the gravity vector
phi1 = (m1*Lc1 + m2*L1)*g*cos(q1) + m2*Lc2*g*cos(q1 + q2);
phi2 = m2*Lc2*g*cos(q1 + q2);
phi = [phi1  phi2]';
% Calculate the error vectors
e = [(q1 - q1_goal)  (q2 - q2_goal)]';   ed = [q1d  q2d]';
% Calculate control torque vector; P-D Control with gravity compensation
tau = -K_p*e - K_v*ed + phi;
% Calculate the generalized accelerations
qd = [q1d   q2d]';   qdd = inv(M)*(tau - C*qd - phi);
% Generate the change in the state vector
ydott(1) = q1d;  ydott(2) = q2d;  ydott(3) = qdd(1);  ydott(4) = qdd(2);
ydot = ydott';
```

```
% S_robot_motion

% Make sure the function robot2.m can see the preset values
global L1  Lc1  L2  Lc2  m1  m2  g
global I1  I2  q1_goal  q2_goal  K_p  K_v

% Set up parameters (in metric units)
L1 = 1.0;    Lc1 = 0.5;    L2 = 1.0;    Lc2 = 0.5;    % meters
m1 = 50.0;    m2  = 50.0;                             % kilograms
g  = 9.81;                                            % gravity

% Set up control parameters (in metric units)
q1_start = -pi/2;      q2_start = -pi/2;
q1_goal = -0.0;        q2_goal = pi/2;
K_p = 200.0*eye(2);    K_v = 1000.0*eye(2);

% Calculate moment of inertia for long, slender rod
I1 = m1*L1^2 / 12;    I2 = m2*L2^2 / 12;
% Set up values for ode23 call
t0 = 0;    tf = 25.0;  tspan = [ t0 tf];    y0 = [q1_start   q2_start   0   0]';
[T, Y] = ode23('robot2',tspan, y0);

% make the output easy to look at
t = T;    q1  = y(:,1);    q2  = y(:,2);    q1d = y(:,3);    q2d = y(:,4);

% Find the required torques for each instant of time(t)
imax = max(size(t));
for i = 1:1:imax,
    phi1 = (m1*Lc1 + m2*L1)*g*cos(q1(i)) + m2*Lc2*g*cos(q1(i) + q2(i));
    phi2 = m2*Lc2*g*cos(q1(i) + q2(i));
    phi = [phi1 phi2]';    q_dot = [q1d(i) q2d(i)]';
    e = [q1(i)-q1_goal q2(i)-q2_goal]';    ed = q_dot;
    torq = -K_p*e - K_v*ed + phi;    torq1(i) = torq(1);    torq2(i) = torq(2);
end
% plot position vs time for both link coordinates
subplot(3,1,1); plot(t,q1,'-',t,q2,':');  legend('q1','q2');
ylabel('Position (rad)');  title('Two Link Planar Robot Simulation')
% plot velocity vs time for both link coordinates
subplot(3,1,2); plot(t,q1d,'-',t,q2d,':');  legend('q1-d','q2-d');
ylabel('Velocity (rad/sec)')
% plot torques vs time for both link coordinates
subplot(3,1,3); plot(t,torq1,'-',t,torq2,':');legend('torq1','torq2');
ylabel('Torques (Nm)'); xlabel('Time (sec)')
```

Convert Higher Order ODE to System of First-Order ODE: The nth-order ODE

$$y^{(n)} = f(x, y, y', y'', \ldots, y^{(n-1)}),$$

$$y(0) = \alpha_0, \quad y'(0) = \alpha_1, \quad y''(0) = \alpha_2, \quad \ldots, \quad y^{(n-1)}(0) = \alpha_{n-1},$$

becomes a system of first-order ODEs by the following change of variables:

$$u_1 = y, \quad u_2 = y', \quad u_3 = y'', \quad \ldots, \quad u_n = y^{(n-1)}.$$

The differential equations relating these variables are

$$u_1' = u_2, \quad u_2' = u_3, \quad u_3' = u_4, \quad \ldots, \quad u_n' = f(x, u_1, u_2, u_3, \ldots, u_n),$$

with the initial conditions: $u_1(0) = \alpha_0, u_2(0) = \alpha_1, u_3(0) = \alpha_2, \ldots, u_n(0) = \alpha_{n-1}$.

Solve a System of Two First-Order ODEs $u' = f(x, u, v)$, $v' = g(x, u, v)$:

Euler's method updates u using $f(x, u, v)$ and updates v using $g(x, u, v)$:

$$u_{i+1} = u_i + hf(x_i, u_i, v_i), \qquad v_{i+1} = v_i + h\, g(x_i, u_i, v_i).$$

The midpoint method can be written using
k_1 and k_2 to represent the update quantities for the unknown function u, m_1 and m_2 give the corresponding quantities for function v. We have

$$k_1 = hf(x_i, u_i, v_i), \qquad\qquad m_1 = hg(x_i, u_i, v_i).$$

$$k_2 = hf\left(x_i + \frac{h}{2}, u_i + \frac{1}{2}k_1, v_i + \frac{1}{2}m_1\right), \qquad m_2 = hg\left(x_i + \frac{h}{2}, u_i + \frac{1}{2}k_1, v_i + \frac{1}{2}m_1\right).$$

$$u_{i+1} = u_i + k_2, \qquad\qquad v_{i+1} = v_i + m_2.$$

Solve a System of Three First-Order ODEs

The basic two-step Adams-Bashforth method for a system of three ODEs

$$u_1' = f_1(x, u_1, u_2, u_3), \qquad u_2' = f_2(x, u_1, u_2, u_3), \qquad u_3' = f_3(x, u_1, u_2, u_3),$$

is described as follows:

$u_1(i = 0), u_2(i = 0), u_3(i = 0)$ are given by the initial condition, $u_1(i = 1), u_2(i = 1)$, $u_3(i = 1)$ are found from a 1-step method, and for $i = 1, \ldots, n - 1$, and $h = \dfrac{b - a}{n}$:

$$u_1(i + 1) = u_1(i) + \frac{h}{2} \; [3f_1(x(i), u_1(i), u_2(i), u_3(i)$$

$$- f_1(x(i - 1), u_1(i - 1), u_2(i - 1), u_3(i - 1))],$$

$$u_2(i + 1) = u_2(i) + \frac{h}{2} \; [3f_2(x(i), u_1(i), u_2(i), u_3(i))$$

$$- f_2(x(i - 1), u_1(i - 1), u_2(i - 1), u_3(i - 1))],$$

$$u_3(i + 1) = u_3(i) + \frac{h}{2} \; [3f_3(x(i), u_1(i), u_2(i), u_3(i))$$

$$- f_3(x(i - 1), u_1(i - 1), u_2(i - 1), u_3(i - 1))],$$

SUGGESTIONS FOR FURTHER READING

The suggested readings for Chapter 12 are also excellent references for the topics in this chapter. In addition, the following texts include discussion of applications of ODEs:

Ayyub, B. M. and R. H. McCuen, *Numerical Methods for Engineers,* Prentice Hall, Upper Saddle River, NJ, 1996.

Greenberg, M. D., *Advanced Engineering Mathematics,* 2d ed., Prentice Hall, Upper Saddle River, NJ, 1998.

Greenberg, M. D., *Foundations of Applied Mathematics,* Prentice-Hall, Englewood Cliffs, NJ, 1978.

Grossman, S. I., and W. R. Derrick, *Advanced Engineering Mathematics,* Harper & Row, New York, 1988.

Hanna, O. T., and O. C. Sandall, *Computational Methods In Chemical Engineering,* Prentice Hall, Upper Saddle River, NJ, 1995.

Hildebrand, F. B., *Advanced Calculus for Applications,* 2d ed., Prentice-Hall, Englewood Cliffs, NJ, 1976.

Thomson, W. T., *Theory of Vibrations with Applications,* Prentice Hall, Englewood Cliff, NJ, 1993.

Inman, D. J., *Engineering Vibration,* Prentice Hall, Englewood Cliffs, NJ, 1996.

Simon, W., *Mathematical Techniques for Biology and Medicine,* Dover, New York, 1986.

Spong and Vidyasagar, *Robot Dynamics and Control,* John Wiley & Sons, New York, 1989. (See p. 145, ex. 6.4.2.)

PRACTICE THE TECHNIQUES

For Problems P13.1–P13.10 solve the initial value problem by first converting the problem to a system of first-order ODE. For each solution method, investigate the effect of increasing n (decreasing the step size).

   a. *Solve the system using Euler's method.*
   b. *Solve the system using the midpoint method.*
   c. *Solve the system using the classic Runge–Kutta method.*
   d. *Solve the system using the Adams-Bashforth-Moulton method.*
   e. *Solve the system using the built-in MATLAB function* ode23.

P13.1 $y'' = y + x$, $y(0) = 2$, $y'(0) = 0$, on $[0, 2]$.

P13.2 $y'' = y' + y + x$, $y(0) = 1$, $y'(0) = 0.5$, on $[0, 2]$.

P13.3 $y'' = -2y' - y + x^2$, $y(0) = 7$, $y'(0) = -4$, on $[0, 2]$.

P13.4 $y'' = -4y' - 4y$, $y(0) = 1$, $y'(0) = 8$, on $[0, 4]$.

P13.5 $y'' = y + x^2 - 4x$, $y(0) = -2$, $y'(0) = 2$, on $[0, 4]$.

P13.6 $y'' = 5y' - 6y$, $y(0) = 2$, $y'(0) = 5$, on $[0, 1]$.

P13.7 $y'' = -7' - 6y$, $y(0) = 2$, $y'(0) = -2$, on $[0, 1]$.

P13.8 $y'' = -9y$, $y(0) = 1$, $y'(0) = 6$, on $[0, 2\pi]$.

P13.9 $y'' + \dfrac{-1}{1 + x} y' + \dfrac{-3}{1 + x} y = 0$, $y(0) = 1$, $y'(0) = -1$, on $[0, 2]$.

P13.10 $y'' + \dfrac{4}{1 + x^2} y' + \dfrac{2}{1 + x^2} y = 0$, $y(0) = 1$, $y'(0) = 0$, on $[0, 2]$.

For Problems P13.11–P13.20 solve the initial value problem by the numerical method of your choice. Investigate the effect of modifying the initial conditions (for either y or y').

P13.11 $y'' + \dfrac{-6x^2}{1 + x^3} y' + \dfrac{-6x}{1 + x^3} y = 0$, $y(0) = 1$, $y'(0) = 0$, on $[0, 1]$.

P13.12 $y'' + y' - y^2 = 0$, $y(0) = 1$, $y'(0) = 0$, on $[0, 2]$.

P13.13 $y'' + y + y^3 = 0$, $y(0) = 2$, $y'(0) = 0$, on $[0, 10]$.

P13.14 $y'' = -2yy'$, $y(1) = 1$, $y'(1) = -1$, on $[1, 5]$.

P13.15 $y'' = -2(y + x)(y' + 1)$, $y(1) = 0$, $y'(1) = -2$, on $[1, 5]$.

P13.16 $y'' = \dfrac{6x^4}{y}$, $y(1) = 1$, $y'(1) = 3$, on $[1, 2]$.

P13.17 $y y'' + (y')^2 = 0$, $y(1) = 2$, $y'(1) = 1/2$, on $[1, 2]$.

P13.18 $y'' + 4x^{-1} y' + 2x^{-2} y = 0$, $y(1) = 2$; $y'(1) = -3$, on $[1, 2]$.

P13.19 $y'' - 4x^{-1} y' + 6x^{-2} y = 0$, $y(1) = 5$, $y'(1) = 13$, on $[1, 2]$.

P13.20 $x^2 y'' + 4xy' + 2y = x$, $y(1) = 1/6$, $y'(1) = -5/6$, on $[1, 2]$.

P13.21 $y'' - 2x^{-2} y = 0$, $y(1) = 3$, $y'(1) = 3$, on $[1, 2]$.

P13.22 $x^2 y'' - xy' + y = 0$, $y(1) = 1$, $y'(1) = 2$, on $[1, 2]$.

P13.23 $x^2 y'' + xy' + y = 0$, $y(1) = 0$, $y'(1) = 3$, on $[1, 3]$.

P13.24 Solve the Bessel equation of order zero

$$x^2 y'' + xy' + x^2 y = 0, \ y(1) = 1, \ y'(1) = 0, \text{ on } [1, 4].$$

P13.25 Solve the Bessel equation of order one

$$x^2 y'' + xy' + (x^2 - 1)y = 0, \ y(1) = 1, \ y'(1) = 0, \text{ on } [1, 4].$$

P13.26 Solve Legendre's equation for $\alpha = 1, 2$, or 3.

$$(1-x^2) y'' - 2xy' + \alpha(\alpha + 1)y = 0, \ y(0) = 1,$$
$$y'(0) = 1, \text{ on } [0, 0.9].$$

P13.27 Solve the Chebyshev equation for $\alpha = 1, 2$, or 3.

$$(1 - x^2) y'' - xy' + \alpha^2 y = 0, \ y(0) = 1, \ y'(0) = 1,$$
$$\text{on } [0, 0.9].$$

P13.28 Solve Airy's equation

$$y'' - xy = 0, \ y(0) = 1, \ y'(0) = 1, \text{ on } [0, 5].$$

P13.29 Solve the Hermite equation for $\lambda = 1, 2, 3$, or 4.

$$y'' - 2xy' + \lambda y = 0, \ y(1) = 1, \ y'(1) = 0, \text{ on } [1, 3].$$

P13.30 Solve the Laguerre equation for $\lambda = 1, 2, 3$, or 4.

$$x y' + (1 - x) y' + \lambda y = 0, \ y(1) = 1, \ y'(1) = 0, \text{ on } [1, 4].$$

For problems P13.31–P13.40, solve the initial value problem $\mathbf{x}' = A\mathbf{x}$.

P13.31

$$A = \begin{bmatrix} 3 & -3 & 2 & -1 \\ 12 & -12 & 10 & -5 \\ 15 & -15 & 14 & -7 \\ 6 & -6 & 6 & -3 \end{bmatrix}$$

   a. $x0 = \begin{bmatrix} 1 & 0 & 0 & 0 \end{bmatrix}'$ b. $x0 = \begin{bmatrix} 0 & 1 & 0 & 0 \end{bmatrix}'$
   c. $x0 = \begin{bmatrix} 0 & 0 & 1 & 0 \end{bmatrix}'$ d. $x0 = \begin{bmatrix} 0 & 0 & 0 & 1 \end{bmatrix}'$

P13.32

$$A = \begin{bmatrix} 1 & -3 & 2 & -1 \\ 4 & -6 & 2 & -1 \\ -5 & 5 & -8 & 5 \\ -10 & 10 & -10 & 7 \end{bmatrix}$$

a. $x0 = \begin{bmatrix} 1 & 0 & 0 & 0 \end{bmatrix}'$ b. $x0 = \begin{bmatrix} 0 & 1 & 0 & 0 \end{bmatrix}'$
c. $x0 = \begin{bmatrix} 0 & 0 & 1 & 0 \end{bmatrix}'$ d. $x0 = \begin{bmatrix} 0 & 0 & 0 & 1 \end{bmatrix}'$

P13.33

$$A = \begin{bmatrix} 3 & -3 & 2 & -1 \\ 10 & -10 & 8 & -4 \\ 10 & -10 & 9 & -4 \\ 2 & -2 & 2 & 0 \end{bmatrix}$$

a. $x0 = \begin{bmatrix} 1 & 0 & 0 & 0 \end{bmatrix}'$ b. $x0 = \begin{bmatrix} 0 & 1 & 0 & 0 \end{bmatrix}'$
c. $x0 = \begin{bmatrix} 0 & 0 & 1 & 0 \end{bmatrix}'$ d. $x0 = \begin{bmatrix} 0 & 0 & 0 & 1 \end{bmatrix}'$

P13.34

$$A = \begin{bmatrix} -9 & 9 & -6 & 3 \\ -10 & 11 & -6 & 3 \\ 3 & -2 & 4 & -2 \\ 4 & -4 & 4 & -2 \end{bmatrix}$$

a. $x0 = \begin{bmatrix} 1 & 0 & 0 & 0 \end{bmatrix}'$ b. $x0 = \begin{bmatrix} 0 & 1 & 0 & 0 \end{bmatrix}'$
c. $x0 = \begin{bmatrix} 0 & 0 & 1 & 0 \end{bmatrix}'$ d. $x0 = \begin{bmatrix} 0 & 0 & 0 & 1 \end{bmatrix}'$

P13.35

$$A = \begin{bmatrix} -2 & 3 & -2 & 1 \\ 1 & 1 & 2 & -1 \\ 10 & -9 & 12 & -7 \\ 9 & -9 & 10 & -7 \end{bmatrix}$$

a. $x0 = \begin{bmatrix} 1 & 0 & 0 & 0 \end{bmatrix}'$ b. $x0 = \begin{bmatrix} 0 & 1 & 0 & 0 \end{bmatrix}'$
c. $x0 = \begin{bmatrix} 0 & 0 & 1 & 0 \end{bmatrix}'$ d. $x0 = \begin{bmatrix} 0 & 0 & 0 & 1 \end{bmatrix}'$

P13.36

$$A = \begin{bmatrix} -13 & 12 & -8 & 4 \\ -24 & 21 & -14 & 7 \\ -14 & 12 & -9 & 6 \\ -6 & 6 & -6 & 6 \end{bmatrix}$$

a. $x0 = \begin{bmatrix} 1 & 0 & 0 & 0 \end{bmatrix}'$ b. $x0 = \begin{bmatrix} 0 & 1 & 0 & 0 \end{bmatrix}'$
c. $x0 = \begin{bmatrix} 0 & 0 & 1 & 0 \end{bmatrix}'$ d. $x0 = \begin{bmatrix} 0 & 0 & 0 & 1 \end{bmatrix}'$

P13.37

$$A = \begin{bmatrix} -11 & 6 & -4 & 2 \\ 3 & -9 & 8 & -4 \\ 18 & -19 & 16 & -7 \\ 2 & -2 & 2 & 1 \end{bmatrix}$$

a. $x0 = \begin{bmatrix} 1 & 0 & 0 & 0 \end{bmatrix}'$ b. $x0 = \begin{bmatrix} 0 & 1 & 0 & 0 \end{bmatrix}'$
c. $x0 = \begin{bmatrix} 0 & 0 & 1 & 0 \end{bmatrix}'$ d. $x0 = \begin{bmatrix} 0 & 0 & 0 & 1 \end{bmatrix}'$

P13.38

$$A = \begin{bmatrix} -36 & 30 & -20 & 10 \\ -61 & 50 & -36 & 18 \\ -34 & 29 & -25 & 13 \\ -10 & 10 & -10 & 6 \end{bmatrix}$$

a. $x0 = \begin{bmatrix} 1 & 0 & 0 & 0 \end{bmatrix}'$ b. $x0 = \begin{bmatrix} 0 & 1 & 0 & 0 \end{bmatrix}'$
c. $x0 = \begin{bmatrix} 0 & 0 & 1 & 0 \end{bmatrix}'$ d. $x0 = \begin{bmatrix} 0 & 0 & 0 & 1 \end{bmatrix}'$

P13.39

$$A = \begin{bmatrix} 30 & -24 & 16 & -8 \\ 38 & -28 & 18 & -9 \\ 6 & -2 & 0 & 0 \\ -2 & 2 & -2 & 1 \end{bmatrix}$$

a. $x0 = \begin{bmatrix} 1 & 0 & 0 & 0 \end{bmatrix}'$ b. $x0 = \begin{bmatrix} 0 & 1 & 0 & 0 \end{bmatrix}'$
c. $x0 = \begin{bmatrix} 0 & 0 & 1 & 0 \end{bmatrix}'$ d. $x0 = \begin{bmatrix} 0 & 0 & 0 & 1 \end{bmatrix}'$

P13.40

$$A = \begin{bmatrix} -28 & 24 & -16 & 8 \\ -42 & 34 & -22 & 11 \\ -10 & 6 & -2 & 0 \\ 6 & -6 & 6 & -5 \end{bmatrix}$$

a. $x0 = \begin{bmatrix} 1 & 0 & 0 & 0 \end{bmatrix}'$ b. $x0 = \begin{bmatrix} 0 & 1 & 0 & 0 \end{bmatrix}'$
c. $x0 = \begin{bmatrix} 0 & 0 & 1 & 0 \end{bmatrix}'$ d. $x0 = \begin{bmatrix} 0 & 0 & 0 & 1 \end{bmatrix}'$

EXPLORE SOME APPLICATIONS

A13.1 The motion $x(t)$, $y(t)$ of an object (such as a baseball), subject to the forces of gravity and air resistance proportional to velocity, can be described by the system of second-order ODEs

$$x'' = -c\,v\,x', \qquad y'' = -c\,v\,y' - g,$$

where the speed of the object is $v = \sqrt{(x')^2 + (y')^2}$, $g = 32$ ft/s^2, and $c = 0.002$ is a typical value for a baseball. (In mks units, $g = 9.81$ m/s^2, and $c = 0.006$.) Solve with initial conditions $x(0) = 0$; $y(0) = 0$; $x'(0) = 100$ ft/s; $y'(0) = 100$ ft/s. Does the ball clear a fence which is 400 ft from home plate and 10 ft tall? Investigate other initial conditions for the velocity of the ball.

A13.2 The motion of one body around another, such as a comet orbiting around the sun, can be described by the system of ODEs

$$x'' = -K\,x/r^3, \qquad y'' = -K\,y/r^3,$$

where $r = \sqrt{x^2 + y^2}$. With distance measured in AU ($1\,AU = 1.496 \times 10^{11}$ m) and time measured in years, we have $K \approx 40$ (for an object rotating around the sun). Take as initial conditions, $x(0) = 1$, $x'(0) = 0$, $y(0) = 0$, $y'(0) = 2$, and solve for $0 \le t \le 4$; investigate the effect of different values of $y'(0)$. (For further discussion, see Garcia, 1994, or Greenberg, 1978.)

A13.3 The motion of a spherical pendulum of length L can be described, in terms of its angular displacement from the vertical ϕ and its angular dispacement from the positive x-axis θ, by the ODEs

$$\phi'' = -2\,\phi'\,\theta'\,\cot(\theta),$$

$$\theta'' = (\phi')^2 \sin(\theta) \cos(\theta) - (g/L) \sin(\theta).$$

Find the motion for the following sets of initial conditions

a.	$\phi = 0,$	$\theta = 0.2,$	$\phi' = 0,$	$\theta' = 0.2.$
b.	$\phi = 0,$	$\theta = 0,$	$\phi' = 0.2,$	$\theta' = 0.$
c.	$\phi = 0,$	$\theta = 0.2,$	$\phi' = 0.2,$	$\theta' = 0.2.$
d.	$\phi = 0,$	$\theta = 0.2,$	$\phi' = 0.01,$	$\theta' = 0.2.$
e.	$\phi = 0,$	$\theta = 0.2,$	$\phi' = 0.2,$	$\theta' = 0.$

(See Thomson, 1986, p. 275.)

A13.4 Consider a system of four blocks coupled by springs, between two walls a distance L_w apart, as introduced in Chapter 3 (A3.6). Let the unstretched lengths of the springs be $L_1, \ldots, L_5$, the spring constants be $k_1, \ldots, k_5$, and the masses of the blocks be $m_1, \ldots m_4$. The equations of motion for each block ($i = 1, \ldots, 4$) are

$$\frac{dx_i}{dt} = v_i \qquad \frac{dv_i}{dt} = \frac{F_i}{m_i}$$

where
$$F_1 = -k_1(x_1 - L_1) + k_2(x_2 - x_1 - L_2)$$
$$F_2 = -k_2(x_2 - x_1 - L_2) + k_3(x_3 - x_2 - L_3)$$
$$F_3 = -k_3(x_3 - x_2 - L_3) + k_4(x_4 - x_3 - L_4)$$
$$F_4 = -k_4(x_4 - x_3 - L_4) + k_5(L_w - x_4 - L_5)$$

Solve the system for

$$L_1 = 2; L_2 = 2; L_3 = 2; L_4 = 2; L_5 = 2; L_w = 8.$$

$$k_1 = 1; k_2 = 1; k_3 = 1; k_4 = 1; k_5 = 5, m_1 = \ldots = m_4 = 4.$$

Investigate the effect of changing various parameter values, including making the blocks of different masses. (See Garcia, 1994, p. 103 for further discussion.)

A13.5 The time-evolution of the concentrations of two components (A and C) in a nonlinear chemical reaction of the form $A + B \leftrightarrow C \to D + E$, occuring in a constant volume batch reactor, can be modeled by the equations

$$\frac{dy_1}{dt} = -r_1\,y_1\,(y_1 - K) + r_2\,y_2, \qquad y_1(0) = 1,$$

$$\frac{dy_2}{dt} = -(r_2 + r_3)\,y_2 + r_1\,y_1\,(y_1 - K), \quad y_2(0) = 0.$$

where y_1 is the concentration of A, y_2 is the concentration of C, r_1, r_2, and r_3 are rate constants, and the parameter K depends on the initial composition of the mixture. Solve using $r_1 = r_2 = r_3 = 1$, $K = 0$; investigate the effect of modifying these values. (See Hanna and Sandall, 1995, p. 285 for further discussion.)

A13.6 The time evolution of the concentration of two chemical species in an oscillatory chemical system such as the Belousov-Zhabotinski reaction can be described by the Brusselator model:

$$\frac{dx}{dt} = A + x^2 y - (B + 1)x, \qquad \frac{dy}{dt} = Bx - x^2 y.$$

The parameters A and B are positive, as are the initial conditions for x and y; investigate the solutions for various choices of $A, B, x(0)$ and $y(0)$. Consider cases where $B/(1 + A^2) < 1; B/(1 + A^2) > 1$; and $B/(1 + A^2) = 1$. (See Garcia, 1994, p. 98 for further discussion; the original reference is Nicolis and Prigogine, 1977.)

A13.7 A fairly general two-compartment chemical flow problem describes the concentration of two chemicals, C_1 and C_2, in two compartments with volumes V_1 and V_2 respectively. The concentrations change with time as a result of concentration-independent input into each compartment, I_1 and I_2, concentration-dependent output (L_1C_1 and L_2C_2) and diffusion from V_1 into V_2, $K(C_1 - C_2)$. Any of the inputs or outputs can be taken to be negative to represent flow in the opposite direction. The system of differential equations is

$$\frac{dC_1}{dt} = \frac{1}{V_1}[I_1 - L_1C_1 - K(C_1 - C_2)]$$

$$\frac{dC_2}{dt} = \frac{1}{V_2}[I_2 - L_2C_2 - K(C_2 - C_1)]$$

The behavior of the system depends on the relative values of the various rates and volumes. For example, let $C_1(0) = C_2(0) = 0$, $I_1 = 1$, $I_2 = 0$, $V_1 = 10$, $V_2 = 5$, and investigate the following flows:

   a. $L_1 = 2, L_2 = 2, K = 10$;
   b. $L_1 = 2, L_2 = 3, K = 20$;

find the concentration in the two tanks for the first 10 minutes of the process. (See Simon, 1986, p. 88, for further discussion.)

A13.8 For a mother-daughter radioactive decay process, we assume that for each mother atom that decays, a daughter atom is produced; daughter atoms are in turn lost at a rate proportional to their quantity. This process is described by the equations

$$\frac{dM}{dt} = -L_1 M, \quad \frac{dD}{dt} = -L_2 D + L_1 M.$$

Find the amount of each substance as a function of time if $M(0) = 10$, $D(0) = 0$, $L_1 = 2$, $L_2 = 0.1$. Investigate the effect of varying any of these values. (See Simon, 1986, p. 37 for further discussion.)

A13.9 The Lorenz equations

$$\frac{dx}{dt} = p\,(y - x) \quad \frac{dy}{dt} = rx - y - xz \quad \frac{dz}{dt} = xy - qz$$

are a well known example of a system with chaotic behavior for certain values of the parameters. The system was studied by Lorenz in connection with the problem of finding the effect of heating a horizontal fluid layer from below. Investigate the solutions for the following values of the parameters and initial conditions.

   a. $p = 10$, $q = 8/3$, $r = 28$, $[x\ y\ z] = [1\ 1\ 2]$
   b. $p = 10$, $q = 8/3$, $r = 28$, $[x\ y\ z] = [1\ 2\ 2]$
   c. $p = 10$, $q = 8/3$, $r = 28$, $[x\ y\ z] = [2\ 2\ 2]$
   d. $p = 10$, $q = 3$, $\quad r = 18$, $[x\ y\ z] = [1\ 1\ 2]$

   e. $p = 10$, $q = 3$, $r = 18$, $[x\ y\ z] = [1\ 2\ 2]$
   f. $p = 10$, $q = 3$, $r = 18$, $[x\ y\ z] = [2\ 2\ 2]$
   g. $p = 10$, $q = 8$, $r = 18$, $[x\ y\ z] = [1\ 1\ 2]$
   h. $p = 10$, $q = 8$, $r = 18$, $[x\ y\ z] = [1\ 2\ 2]$
   i. $p = 10$, $q = 8$, $r = 18$, $[x\ y\ z] = [2\ 2\ 2]$

The solutions are often plotted in the x-y plane or the y-z plane.

A13.10 Solve the classical Van der Pol differential equation for an oscillator

$$\frac{d^2x}{dt^2} - \mu(1 - x^2)\frac{dx}{dt} + x = 0,$$

for a variety of values of the parameter μ and the initial conditions.

   a. $\mu = 0.4, x(0) = 0.1, x'(0) = 0.$
   b. $\mu = 1, \quad x(0) = 0.5, x'(0) = 0.$
   c. $\mu = 2, \quad x(0) = 1, \quad x'(0) = 1.$
   d. $\mu = 5, \quad x(0) = 1, \quad x'(0) = 0.$
   e. $\mu = 5, \quad x(0) = 1, \quad x'(0) = 1.$

A13.11 A simple predator-prey relationship is described by the Lotka-Volterra model, which we write in terms of a fox population $f(t)$, with birth rate b_f and death rate d_f and a geese population $g(t)$ with birth rate b_g and death rate d_g.

$$\frac{df}{dt} = f(t)\,(b_f g(t) - d_f) \qquad \frac{dg}{dt} = g(t)\,(b_g - d_g\,f(t))$$

Find the populations as a function of time for the following initial conditions and parameter values.

   a. $b_f = 1, d_f = 1, b_g = 1, d_g = 1, f(0) = 2, g(0) = 2.$
   b. $b_f = 1, d_f = 1, b_g = 1, d_g = 1, f(0) = 10, g(0) = 2.$
   c. $b_f = 1, d_f = 1, b_g = 1, d_g = 1, f(0) = 2, g(0) = 10.$
   d. $b_f = 1, d_f = 1, b_g = 1, d_g = 1, f(0) = 2, g(0) = 2.$
   e. $b_f = 1, d_f = 1, b_g = 1, d_g = 1, f(0) = 10, g(0) = 2.$
   f. $b_f = 1, \quad d_f = 0.5, \quad b_g = 1, \quad d_g = 0.5, \quad f(0) = 2,$
      $g(0) = 10.$

A13.12 If two species compete for food but do not prey on each other, the populations can be described by the equations

$$\frac{dx}{dt} = x(a_1 - b_1\,x - c_1\,y) \qquad \frac{dy}{dt} = y\,(a_2 - b_2\,y - c_2\,x)$$

where all constants are positive; each population would have logistic growth if the other were not present. Find the solutions for the following combinations of parameter values and initial conditions.

   a. $a_1 = 2;\ b_1 = 1;\ c_1 = 1;\ a_2 = 10;\ b_2 = 10;\ c_2 = 1;$
      $x(0) = 4;\ y(0) = 2.$
   b. try other combinations of parameters for which $a_2/c_2 > a_1/b_1$ and $a_1/c_1 > a_2/b_2$

c. $a_1 = 2$, $b_1 = 1$, $c_1 = 1$, $a_2 = 10$, $b_2 = 1$, $c_2 = 1$, $x(0) = 4$; $y(0) = 2$.

d. try other combinations of parameters for which $a_2/c_2 > a_1/b_1$ and $a_2/b_2 > a_1/c_1$

e. $a_1 = 2$, $b_1 = 1$, $c_1 = 1$, $a_2 = 10$, $b_2 = 1$, $c_2 = 10$, $x(0) = 4$; $y(0) = 2$.

f. try other combinations of parameters for which $a_1/b_1 > a_2/c_2$ and $a_2/b_2 > a_1/c_1$

A13.13 The equations for the deflection y and rotation z of a simply supported beam with a uniformly distributed load of intensity 2 kips/ft and bending moment $M(x) = 10\,x - x^2$, can be expressed as

$$\frac{dz}{dx} = \frac{M}{EI} = \frac{10x - x^2}{EI} \qquad \frac{dy}{dt} = z$$

where E is the modulus of elasticity, and I is the moment of inertia of the cross section of the beam. Taking $EI = 3600$ kip/ft, $y(0) = 0$ and $z(0) = -0.02$, find y and z

(for $0 \le x \le 10$). (See Ayyub and McCuen, 1996, p. 239 for further discussion.)

A13.14 The shape of a cantilever beam with a uniformly distributed load of intensity w kips/ft can be expressed in terms of the deflection y, the slope of the tangent to deflected shape of the beam s, the bending moment m, and the shear force v by the following system of ODEs:

$$\frac{dy}{dx} = s; \qquad \frac{ds}{dx} = \frac{m}{EI}; \qquad \frac{dm}{dx} = v; \qquad \frac{dv}{dx} = -w.$$

Taking $EI = 3600$ kip/ft, $w = 1.5$ kips/ft, and initial conditions

$$y(0) = 0,\ s(0) = 0,\ v(0) = 20 \text{ kips},\ m(0) = -100 \text{ kip-ft}$$

find y and z (for $0 \le x \le 10$). (See Ayyub and McCuen, 1996, p. 260 for a discussion of a similar problem.)

EXTEND YOUR UNDERSTANDING

U13.1 Investigate the numerical solution of the ODE $y'' = 16\,y$, $y(0) = 1$, $y'\ (0) = -4$; using the techniques discussed in this chapter, including MATLAB's built-in functions. Compare each numerical solution to the exact solution. What is the nature of the difficulty displayed by this problem?

U13.2 Compare the computational effort required in using the fourth-order Runge–Kutta method with that for the third-order Adams-Bashforth-Moulton method; use several of the previous problems to investigate these two methods.

14

Ordinary Differential Equations: Boundary Value Problems

For the higher order ordinary differential equations considered in the previous chapter, all of the required information about the solution is specified at the same point, say, $x = a$, and the solution function is sought on an interval $a \leq x \leq b$. In many important applications, the information that is known about the desired solution is given at the endpoints of the interval. Such problems are called *ordinary differential equation boundary-value problems* (ODE–BVPs).

In this chapter, we consider two standard approaches to solving ODE–BVPs, the shooting method and the finite-difference method. The shooting method is motivated by the example of trying to hit a target at a specified distance. In the initial-value problem for the motion of an object, both the initial position and the initial velocity are given. From the solution, the location at which the object lands can be determined. In an experimental setting, one could try different velocities, observe the landing points, and eventually make the necessary adjustments to hit the target. Fortunately, for a linear problem, this basic idea leads to a numerical method that does not rely on repeated trial-and-error corrections. For a nonlinear ODE, we obtain an iterative technique analogous to the secant method or Newton's method from Chapter 2.

The finite-difference method is based on dividing the interval of interest into a number of subintervals and replacing the derivatives by the appropriate finite-difference approximations, as discussed in Chapter 11. If the differential equation is linear, it is transformed into a system of linear algebraic equations, which can be solved by the techniques investigated in previous chapters. For a nonlinear ODE, the system of algebraic equations is nonlinear, and the methods of Chapter 5 may be used. The finite-difference approach is also very important for partial differential equations, which are the subject of the next chapter.

Example 14-A Deflection of a Beam

Several boundary-value problems arise in the study of the deflection of a horizontal beam. For example, we consider a beam (see Fig. 14.1) that is freely hinged at its ends (i.e., at $x = 0$ and $x = L$), with a uniform transverse load w and tension T. In this case, the deflection, $y(x)$, is described by the ODE boundary-value problem

$$y'' - \frac{T}{EI} y = \frac{wx(x - L)}{2EI}, \qquad 0 \le x \le L.$$

The physical parameters of the beam are the modulus of elasticity, E, and the central moment of inertia, I. We assume that the beam is of uniform thickness, so that the product EI is a constant. For convenience, the downward direction is taken as positive.

The boundary conditions state that the beam is supported, and therefore has no deflection, at $x = 0$ and $x = L$; i.e.,

$$y(0) = y(L) = 0.$$

The exact solution of the ODE is

$$y(x) = A \sinh(\alpha x) + B \sinh(\alpha(L - x)) - \frac{w}{\alpha^2 T} + \frac{wLx}{2T} - \frac{wx^2}{2T},$$

with $\alpha^2 = T/(EI)$ and $A \sinh(\alpha L) = B \sinh(\alpha L) = w/(\alpha^2 T)$.

However, the ODE is based on the assumption that y' is small, so that $(y')^2$ is negligible and $1/R \approx y''$. In general, the radius of curvature, R, is related to the deflection by

$$\frac{1}{R} = \frac{y''}{[1 + (y')^2]^{3/2}},$$

which leads to the differential equation

$$\frac{y''}{[1 + (y')^2]^{3/2}} - \frac{T}{EI} y = \frac{wx(x - L)}{2EI}, \qquad 0 \le x \le L,$$

for which numerical methods are important. (See Jaeger, 1951, for discussion.)

FIGURE 14.1 Bending of a beam.

Example 14-B A Well-Hit Ball

Many factors influence the path of a baseball after it is hit. As an example, we consider a ball hit so that it lands 300 feet from home plate after 3 seconds. We assume that air resistance acts only against the horizontal component of the flight and is proportional to the horizontal velocity, so that the motion of the ball is given by

$$\frac{d^2x}{dt^2} = -c\frac{dx}{dt}$$

and

$$\frac{d^2y}{dt^2} = -g.$$

The initial position is $x(0) = 0$, $y(0) = 3$, and the desired landing time is $t_f = 3$, so that $x(3) = 300$, $y(3) = 0$. We take the drag coefficient $c = 0.5$. The vertical component of the motion can be found directly by

$$y(t) = -16t^2 + 47t + 3.$$

The solution for $x(t)$ can be found by the methods of this chapter. Plotting y versus x gives the path of the ball, as illustrated in Fig. 14.2.

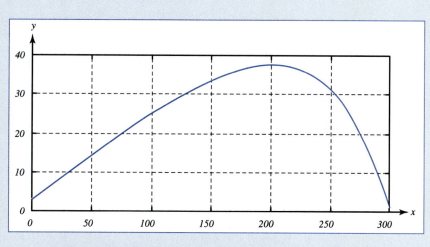

FIGURE 14.2 Flight of a baseball subject to some air resistance.

Higher order ODEs do not necessarily have all of the information about the solution given at the same (initial) point. Problems in which the value of the unknown function or its derivative is given at two different points are known as *boundary-value problems*. In particular, we investigate the second-order, two-point boundary-value problem of the form

$$y'' = f(x, y, y'), \quad a \le x \le b$$

with Dirichlet boundary conditions

$$y(a) = \alpha, \quad y(b) = \beta,$$

or Neuman boundary conditions

$$y'(a) = \alpha, \quad y'(b) = \beta,$$

or mixed boundary conditions

$$y'(a) + c_1 y(a) = \alpha, \quad y'(b) + c_2 y(b) = \beta.$$

The first method we consider is based on the techniques presented in Chapter 13 for IVPs. The idea is to guess an initial-value for $y'(a)$, generate a solution, and then adjust the solution so that it matches the specified value for $y(b)$. This is known as the *shooting method*. If the ODE is linear, we can solve two IVPs and form a linear combination of the solutions that will solve the BVP. If the ODE is nonlinear, an iterative process can be used. The linear case is described in the next section.

14.1   SHOOTING METHOD FOR SOLVING LINEAR BVPs

A linear two-point boundary value problem can be solved by forming a linear combination of the solutions to two initial-value problems. The form of the IVP depends on the form of the boundary conditions. We begin with the simplest case, Dirichlet boundary conditions, in which the value of the function is given at each end of the interval. We then consider some more general boundary conditions.

14.1.1 Simple Boundary Conditions

Suppose the two-point boundary-value problem is linear, i.e., of the form $y'' = p(x)y' + q(x)y + r(x), a \le x \le b$, with boundary conditions $y(a) = y_a, y(b) = y_b$. The approach is to solve the two IVPs

$$u'' = p(x)u' + q(x)u + r(x), \quad u(a) = y_a, \quad u'(a) = 0,$$
$$v'' = p(x)v' + q(x)v, \quad v(a) = 0, \quad v'(a) = 1.$$

If $v(b) \ne 0$, the solution of the original two-point BVP is given by

$$y(x) = u(x) + \frac{y_b - u(b)}{v(b)} v(x).$$

This solution is based on the standard technique of solving a linear ODE by finding a general solution of the homogeneous equation (expressed as the ODE for v) and a particular solution of the nonhomogeneous equation (expressed as the ODE for u). The arbitrary constant A that would appear in the solution $y(x) = u(x) + A v(x)$ is found from the requirement that $y(b) = u(b) + Av(b) = y_b$, which yields $A = \dfrac{y_b - u(b)}{v(b)}$.

Example 14.1 Electrostatic Potential Between Two Spheres

The electrostatic potential between two concentric spheres can be represented by the second-order ODE

$$y'' = \frac{-2}{x} y'.$$

If we assume that the radius of the inner sphere is one and its potential is 10, while the radius of the outer sphere is two and its potential is zero, then

$$y(1) = 10, \quad y(2) = 0.$$

This equation can be converted to the pair of initial-value problems

$$u'' = \frac{-2}{x} u, \quad u(1) = 10, \quad u'(1) = 0,$$

$$v'' = \frac{-2}{x} v, \quad v(1) = 0, \quad v(1) = 1,$$

which becomes a system of four first-order initial-value problems by defining the variables $w_1, \ldots, w_4$ as $w_1 = u$, $w_2 = u'$, $w_3 = v$, $w_4 = v'$. The differential equations become

$$w_1' = w_2, \quad w_2' = \frac{-2}{x} w_2, \quad w_3' = w_4, \quad w_4' = \frac{-2}{x} w_4,$$

with initial conditions

$$w_1(1) = 10, \quad w_2(1) = 0, \quad w_3(1) = 0, \quad w_4(1) = 1.$$

The solution of the original ODE is the linear combination of the solutions u and v, or, in terms of our system,

$$y(x) = w_1(x) + \frac{0 - w_1(b)}{w_3(b)} w_3(x).$$

Example 14.2 A Simple Linear Shooting Problem

Consider the ODE

$$y'' = \frac{2x}{x^2 + 1} y' - \frac{2}{x^2 + 1} y + x^2 + 1,$$

with boundary conditions $y(0) = 2$, $y(1) = 5/3$. For reference, we note that the general solution of the ODE is

$$y(x) = d_1 x + d_2(x^2 - 1) + x^4/6 + x^2/2.$$

The exact solution of the BVP is $y = x^4/6 - 3x^2/2 + x + 2$. The following MATLAB script and function generate the solution shown in Fig. 14.3:

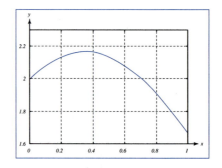

FIGURE 14.3 Solution of a simple linear shooting problem.

MATLAB Script and Function for Linear Shooting Example

```
% S_14_2
clear all
ya = 2; yb = 5/3; z0 = [ ya   0   0   1];
a = 0; b = 1; tspan = [ 0  1];
[ x  z ] = RK4_sys('f_14_2', tspan, z0, 10)
[ n  m ] = size(z)
y(1:n,1) = z(1:n,1) + (yb - z(n,1))*z(1:n,3)./z(n,3)
plot(x, y),        grid on


function dz = f_14_2(x, z)
dz = [z(2)
      z(2).*2.*x./(x.^2 + 1) - z(1).*2/(x.^2 + 1) + x.^2 + 1
      z(4)
      z(4).*2.*x./(x.^2 + 1) - z(3).*2/(x.^2 + 1)];
```

Example 14.3 Deflection of a Simply Supported Beam

As described in Example 14-A, the deflection of a beam supported at both ends, subject to uniform loading along its length, is described by the ODE–BVP

$$y'' = \frac{T}{EI}y + \frac{wx(x - L)}{2EI}, \quad 0 \leq x \leq L, \quad y(0) = y(L) = 0.$$

We illustrate the problem for the following parameter values:

$$L = 100, \quad w = 100, \quad E = 10^7, \quad T = 500, \quad I = 500.$$

The problem is linear, of the form

$$y'' = p(x)y' + q(x)y + r(x), \quad a \leq x \leq b,$$

with $a = 0$, $b = L = 100$, $p(x) = 0$, $q(x) = T/EI = 10^{-7}$, and $r(x) = 10^{-8}[x(x - L)]$; the boundary conditions are $y(a) = 0$, and $y(b) = 0$.

The solution can be obtained by solving the following IVPs over $a \leq x \leq b$:

$$u'' = q(x)u + r(x), \quad u(a) = 0, \quad u'(a) = 0,$$
$$v'' = q(x)v, \quad v(a) = 0, \quad v'(a) = 1.$$

The solution of the two-point BVP is given by

$$y(x) = u(x) - \frac{u(b)}{v(b)}v(x).$$

The two second-order IVPs are converted to a system of four first-order IVPs by the change of variables

$$u_1 = u, \quad u_2 = u', \quad u_3 = v, \quad u_4 = v'.$$

The differential equations relating these variables are

$$u_1' = u_2, \quad u_2' = 10^{-7}u_1 + 10^{-8}[x(x - L)],$$
$$u_3' = u_4, \quad u_4' = 10^{-7}u_3,$$

with the initial conditions $u_1(0) = 0, u_2(0) = 0, u_3(0) = 0, u_4(0) = 1$. The computed solution is illustrated in Fig. 14.4.

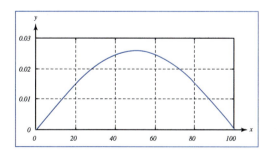

FIGURE 14.4   Deflection of a simply supported beam with uniform loading.

14.1.2 General Boundary Condition at $x = b$

Suppose that the linear ODE

$$y'' = p(x)y' + q(x)y + r(x)$$

has boundary conditions consisting of the value of y given at $x = a$, but the condition at $x = b$ involves a linear combination of $y(b)$ and $y'(b)$, i.e.,

$$y(a) = y_a, \qquad y'(b) + c\,y(b) = y_b.$$

As in the previous discussion, the approach is to solve the two IVPs

$$u'' = p(x)u' + q(x)u + r(x), \qquad u(a) = y_a, \qquad u'(a) = 0,$$
$$v'' = p(x)v' + q(x)v, \qquad\qquad v(a) = 0, \qquad v'(a) = 1.$$

The linear combination $y = u + d\,v$ satisfies the conditions at $x = a$, since $y(a) = y_a$. We now need to find d (if possible) such that y satisfies

$$y'(b) + cy(b) = y_b.$$

If $v'(b) + cv(b) \neq 0$, there is a unique solution, given by

$$y(x) = u(x) + \frac{y_b - u'(b) - c\,u(b)}{v'(b) + c\,v(b)}\,v(x).$$

Example 14.4 More General Boundary Conditions

Consider the ODE from Example 14.2, i.e.,

$$y'' = \frac{2x}{x^2 + 1}y' - \frac{2}{x^2 + 1}y + x^2 + 1,$$

but with the boundary conditions $y(0) = 1$, $y'(1) + y(1) = 0$. The exact solution, $y = (x^4 - 3x^2 - x + 6)/6$, and the computed solution are indistinguishable in Fig. 14.5.

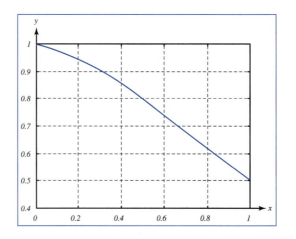

FIGURE 14.5   A BVP with a mixed boundary condition at $x = b$.

14.1.3 General Boundary Conditions at Both Ends of the Interval

Suppose that the linear ODE $y'' = p(x)y' + q(x)y + r(x)$ has mixed boundary conditions at both $x = a$ and $x = b$, i.e.,

$$y'(a) + c_1 y(a) = y_a, \qquad y'(b) + c_2 y(b) = y_b.$$

As in the previous discussion, the approach is to solve two IVPs, however, the appropriate forms are now

$$u'' = p(x)u' + q(x)u + r(x), \qquad u(a) = 0, \qquad u'(a) = y_a,$$

and

$$v'' = p(x)v' + q(x)v, \qquad v(a) = 1, \qquad v'(a) = -c_1.$$

The linear combination $y = u + dv$ satisfies $y'(a) + c_1 y(a) = y_a$; we need to find d (if possible) such that y satisfies $y'(b) + c_2 y(b) = y_b$. If $v'(b) + c_2 v(b) \neq 0$, there is a unique solution, given by

$$y(x) = u(x) + \frac{y_b - u'(b) - c_2 u(b)}{v'(b) + c_2 v(b)} v(x).$$

Example 14.5 Linear Shooting with Mixed Boundary Conditions

Consider again the ODE from Examples 14.2 and 14.4, i.e.,

$$y'' = \frac{2x}{x^2 + 1} y' - \frac{2}{x^2 - 1} y + x^2 + 1,$$

but with the boundary conditions

$$y'(0) + y(0) = 0, \qquad y'(1) - y(1) = 3.$$

The exact solution of the BVP, $y = x^4/6 + 3x^2/2 + x - 1$, and the computed solution appear as a single curve in Fig. 14.6.

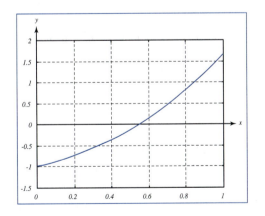

FIGURE 14.6   Solution to linear shooting problem with mixed boundary conditions.

14.2 SHOOTING METHOD FOR SOLVING NONLINEAR BVPs

We now consider the shooting method for nonlinear problems of the form $y'' = f(x, y, y')$ on the interval $[a, b]$. We assume that $y(a)$ is given and that some condition on the solution is also given at $x = b$. The idea is the same as for linear problems, namely, to solve the appropriate initial-value problems and use the results to find a solution to the nonlinear problem. However, for a nonlinear BVP, we have an iterative procedure rather than a simple formula for combining the solutions of two IVPs. In both the linear and the nonlinear case, we need to find a zero of the function representing the error—that is, the amount by which the solution to the IVP fails to satisfy the boundary condition at $x = b$. We assume the continuity of f, f_x, and f_y on an appropriate domain, to ensure that the initial-value problems have unique solutions. We begin by solving the initial-value problem

$$u'' = f(x, u, u'), \qquad u(a) = y_a, \qquad u'(a) = t, \qquad (14.1)$$

for some particular value of t. We then find the error associated with this solution; that is, we evaluate the boundary condition at $x = b$ using $u(b)$ and $u'(b)$. Unless it happens that $u(x)$ satisfies the boundary condition at $x = b$, we take a different initial-value for $u'(a)$ and solve the resulting IVP. Thus, the error (the amount by which our shot misses its mark) is a function of our choice for the initial slope. We denote this function as $m(t)$.

The first approach we consider uses the secant method to find the zero of the error function. This allows us to treat a fairly general boundary condition at $x = b$. The second approach is based on Newton's method.

14.2.1 Nonlinear Shooting Based on the Secant Method

To solve a nonlinear BVP of the form

$$y'' = f(x, y, y'), \qquad y(a) = y_a, \qquad h(y(b), y'(b)) = 0,$$

we may use an iterative process based on the secant method presented in Chapter 2. We need to find a value of t, the initial slope, so that solving eq. (14.1) gives a solution that is within a specified tolerance of the boundary condition at $x = b$. We begin by solving the equation with $u'(a) = t(1) = 0$; the corresponding error is $m(1)$. Unless the absolute value of $m(1)$ is less than the tolerance, we continue by solving eq. (14.1) with $u'(a) = t(2) = 1$. If this solution does not happen to satisfy the boundary condition (at $x = b$) either, we continue by updating our initial slopes according to the secant rule (until our stopping condition is satisfied), i. e.,

$$t(i) = t(i - 1) - \frac{t(i - 1) - t(i - 2)}{m(i - 1) - m(i - 2)} m(i - 1).$$

Example 14.6 Nonlinear Shooting Method

We illustrate the nonlinear shooting method in the MATLAB script that follows. The BVP is

$$y'' = -2y\, y', \qquad y(0) = 1, \qquad y(1) + y'(1) - 0.25 = 0.$$

The exact solution is $y = 1/(x + 1)$. The computed solution, $u(x)$, and $u'(x)$ are shown in Fig. 14.7. For the given tolerance, tol $= 0.00001$, the process converges in eight iterations.

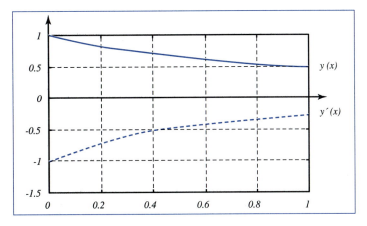

FIGURE 14.7 Solution $y(x)$ and $y'(x)$ for nonlinear shooting problem.

MATLAB Script for Nonlinear Shooting Using Secant Method

```
% S_nonlinear_shoot
%  nonlinear shooting method based on secant method
%  convert BVP  y'' = f(x, y, y');  y(a) = ya;  h(y(b),y'(b)) = 0
%  into IVP     u'' = f(x, u, u');  u(a) = ya;  u'(a) = t
%  update t by secant rule to find zero of the error function:
%    m(t) = h(u(b),u'(b))
% stop when abs(m(t)) < tol or after max_it iterations
clear all
%***************Define problem
ya = 1;  a = 0;  b = 1;  max_it = 10;  tol = 0.00001;
h = 'z1 + z2 - 0.25';
%*****************
t(1) = 0; t(2) = 1;          % start with t = 0 and t = 1
test = 1;   i = 1;   tspan = [ a   b];   hold on
while (test>tol)&(i<=max_it)
    if i > 2
        t(i) = t(i-1) - (t(i-1) - t(i-2))*m(i-1)/(m(i-1) - m(i-2))
    end
    z0 = [ya   t(i)];    [ x,  z ] = ode23( 'f_ns_1', tspan, z0);
    [ n  nn]  = size(z); z1 = z(n,1); z2 = z(n,2);
    m(i) = eval(h);    plot(x,z),    test = abs(m(i));   i = i+1;
end
hold off
```

Example 14.7 Flight of a Baseball

Let us now investigate the effect of air resistance on the flight of a baseball if the resistance is proportional to the square of the velocity. As in Example 14-B, we neglect the effect of the air resistance on the vertical component of the motion. With a small drag coefficient $c = -0.0025$, the path is not dissimilar to that found for the linear BVP, as illustrated in Fig. 14. 8.

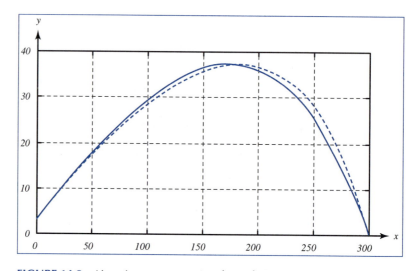

FIGURE 14.8 Air resistance proportional to velocity squared (solid line), and proportional to velocity (dashed line), each acting on x component only.

14.2.2 Nonlinear Shooting Using Newton's Method

We next illustrate how Newton's method can be used to find the value of $y'(a) = t$ in the initial-value problem for nonlinear shooting. We consider the following nonlinear BVP with simple boundary conditions at $x = a$ and $x = b$:

$$y'' = f(x, y, y'), \qquad y(a) = y_a, \qquad y(b) = y_b.$$

We begin by solving the initial-value problem

$$u'' = f(x, u, u'), \qquad u(a) = y_a, \qquad u'(a) = t.$$

The error in this solution is the amount by which $y(b)$ misses the desired value, y_b. For different choices of t, we get different errors, so we define

$$m(t) = u(b, t) - y_b.$$

We need to find t such that $m(t) = 0$ (or $m(t)$ is as close to zero as we wish to continue the process). In the previous section, we found a sequence of t using linear interpolation between the two previous solutions; in order to use Newton's method, we need to have the derivative of the function whose zero is required, namely, $m(t)$. Although we do not have an explicit formula for $m(t)$, we can construct an additional differential equation whose solution allows us to update t at each iteration. The solution process is outlined in the algorithm that follows. The derivation of the auxiliary ODE is given in the discussion at the end of the section.

Algorithm for nonlinear shooting using Newton's method:
Given an estimate for t, t_k, solve

$$u'' = f(x, u, u'),$$

$$u(a) = y_a, \qquad u'(a) = t_k,$$

$$v'' = v f_u(x, u, u') + v' f_{u'}(x, u, u'),$$

$$v(a) = 0, \qquad v'(a) = 1.$$

Check for convergence:

$$m = u(b, t_k) - y_b;$$
$$\text{if } |m| < \text{tol, stop};$$

Otherwise, update t:

$$t_{k+1} = t_k - m/v(b, t_k).$$

Example 14.8 Nonlinear Shooting with Newton's Method

Let

$$y'' = -\frac{[y']^2}{y}, \qquad y(0) = 1, \qquad y(1) = 2.$$

The exact solution of this ODE is $y = \sqrt{3x + 1}$.

The initial-value problem consists of two second-order ODEs. The first corresponds to the original problem, but with the boundary condition replaced by an initial condition on the first derivative, $u'(0) = t_k$. The second ODE is an auxiliary equation that allows us to update the value of the parameter t_k. The first ODE is

$$u'' = -[u']^2 u^{-1}, \qquad u(0) = 1, \qquad u'(0) = t_k.$$

To construct the auxiliary ODE, we need the following partial derivatives:

$$f_u(x, u, u') = -[u']^2(-1)u^{-2},$$
$$f_{u'}(x, u, u') = -2[u']u^{-1}.$$

Thus, the auxiliary ODE is

$$v'' = v[u']^2 u^{-2} - v'2[u']u^{-1}, \qquad v(0) = 0, \qquad v'(0) = 1.$$

Writing this as a system of four first-order ODEs, we define the components of our unknown function z as follows:

$$z_1 = u, \qquad z_2 = u', \qquad z_3 = v, \qquad z_4 = v'.$$

The ODEs are

$$z_1' = z_2, \qquad z_2' = -\frac{z_2^2}{z_1},$$

$$z_3' = z_4, \qquad z_4' = z_3\left(\frac{z_2}{z_1}\right)^2 - \frac{2z_4 z_2}{z_1}.$$

The graph of the solution found using the MATLAB script that follows is shown in Fig. 14.9.

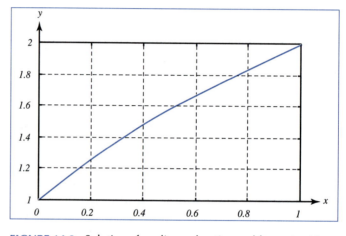

FIGURE 14.9 Solution of nonlinear shooting problem using Newton's method.

MATLAB Script for Nonlinear Shooting Using Newton's Method

```
% S_nonlin_shoot_Newton
% nonlinear shooting method based on Newton's method
%  convert y'' = f(x, y, y'); y(a) = ya; y(b) = yb
% into ODE-IVP
%       u'' =  f(x, u, u');    u(a) = ya;  u'(a) = t
%       v'' = v*f_u(x, u, u') + v'*f_u'(x, u, u')
%              v(a) = 0;  v'(a) = 1
clear all
%****************
ya = 1; yb = 2; a = 0; b = 1;  max_it = 5; tol = 0.00001;
```

```
%****************
t(1) = 0; test = 1;   i = 1;    tspan = [ a    b];
while (test>tol)&(i<=max_it)
   z0 = [ya   t(i)  0  1 ];
   [ x , z ] = ode23( 'f_ns_newt',tspan,z0);
   [ n   nn ] = size(z);  m(i) = z(n,1)-yb;   test = abs(m(i));
   t(i+1) = t(i) - m(i) / z(n,3);
   i = i+1;
end
plot(x, z(:,1))
```

MATLAB Function for Example 14.8

```
function dz = f_ns_newt(x, z)
dz = [z(2)
      -(z(2).^2)./z(1)
      z(4)
      z(3).*(z(2)./z(1)).^2 - 2*z(4).*z(2)./z(1) ];
```

Discussion

In order to use Newton's method to find the value of the parameter t so that the amount by which the solution to the initial-value problem

$$u'' = f(x, u, u'), \qquad u(a) = y_a, \qquad u'(a) = t$$

misses the solution to the original boundary-value problem

$$y'' = f(x, y, y'), \qquad y(a) = y_a, \qquad y(b) = y_b,$$

we need to know how the error function, $m(t) = u(b, t) - y_b$, varies with t. Newton's method updates t as

$$t_i = t_{i-1} - \frac{m(t_{i-1})}{m_t(t_{i-1})}.$$

We continue to use a prime to denote differentiation with respect to x, and we use a subscript to denote a partial derivative. In order to find an expression for m_t, we make use of the fact that, for the given form of boundary condition, we have $m_t(t) = u_t(b, t)$. To find u_t, we use the chain rule for partial derivatives to differentiate $u'' = f(x, u, u')$:

$$(u'')_t = f_t(x, u, u') = f_x x_t + f_u u_t + f_{u'}(u')_t.$$

Since x and t are independent, $x_t = 0$, so we have

$$(u'')_t = f_u u_t + f_{u'}(u')_t.$$

We introduce a new variable $v = u_t$ and assume sufficient continuity that we can interchange the order of differentiation with respect to x and t, so that $(u'')_t = (u_t)''$ and $(u')_t = (u_t)'$. This gives the linear ODE for v:

$$v'' = f_u v + f_{u'} v'.$$

The initial conditions $u(a, t) = ya$ and $u'(a) = t$ yield the initial conditions for v, namely, $v(a) = 0$ and $v'(a) = 1$. Thus, solving the ODE–IVP for v allows us to use the fact that $v = u_t = m_t$ to update t in the formula for Newton's method.

Shooting methods can suffer from instabilities in the IVP; however, for a nonlinear second-order ODE–BVP, the resulting nonlinear zero-finding problem depends on only one variable. Newton's method generalizes to systems more easily than the secant method does and may converge more rapidly, but requires solving twice as many ODEs. In the next sections, we investigate an alternative approach to solving ODE–BVPs.

14.3   FINITE-DIFFERENCE METHOD FOR SOLVING LINEAR BVPs

The second type of solution technique we consider for ODE–BVPs is based on replacing the derivatives in the differential equation by finite-difference approximations (discussed in Chapter 11). The interval of interest, $[a, b]$, is divided into n subintervals by specifying evenly spaced values of the independent variable, $x_0, x_1, x_2, \ldots, x_n$, with $x_0 = a$ and $x_n = b$. The length of each subinterval is $h = x_{i+1} - x_i$. The approximate solution at x_i is denoted y_i. We first illustrate the finite-difference method with a simple example.

Example 14.9 A Finite-Difference Problem

Use the finite-difference method to solve the problem

$$y'' = y + x(x - 4), \qquad 0 \le x \le 4,$$

with $y(0) = y(4) = 0$ and $n = 4$ subintervals. The finite-difference method will find an approximate solution at the points $x_1 = 1, x_2 = 2$, and $x_3 = 3$. Using the central difference formula for the second derviative, we find that the differential equation becomes the system

$$y''(x_i) \approx \frac{y_{i+1} - 2y_i + y_{i-1}}{h^2} = y_i + x_i(x_i - 4), \qquad i = 1, 2, 3.$$

For this example, $h = 1$. In writing out the system of algebraic equations, we make use of the fact that at $i = 1, y_0 = 0$ (from the boundary condition at $x = 0$), and similarly, at $i = 3, y_4 = 0$. Substituting in the values of x_1, x_2, and x_3, we obtain

$$y_2 - 2y_1 + 0 = y_1 + 1(1 - 4),$$
$$y_3 - 2y_2 + y_1 = y_2 + 2(2 - 4),$$
$$0 - 2y_3 + y_2 = y_3 + 3(3 - 4).$$

Combining like terms and simplifying gives

$$-3y_1 + \ y_2 \qquad\quad = -3,$$
$$y_1 - 3y_2 + \ y_3 = -4,$$
$$y_2 - 3y_3 = -3.$$

Solving, we find that $y_1 = 13/7$, $y_2 = 18/7$, and $y_3 = 13/7$.

We note for comparison that the exact solution of this problem is

$$y = \frac{2(1-e^4)}{e^{-4}-e^4}e^{-x} - \frac{2(1-e^{-4})}{e^{-4}-e^4}e^x - x^2 + 4x - 2.$$

At $x = 1$, the exact solution is 1.8341 (to four decimal places); the finite-difference solution is $y_1 = 13/7 = 1.8571$. (See Fig. 14.10.)

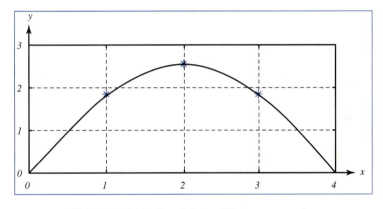

FIGURE 14.10 Small finite-difference example.

We now consider the general linear two-point boundary-value problem

$$y'' = p(x)y' + q(x)y + r(x), \qquad a \le x \le b,$$

with boundary conditions

$$y(a) = \alpha, \qquad y(b) = \beta.$$

To solve this problem using finite-differences, we divide the interval $[a, b]$ into n subintervals, so that $h = (b-a)/n$. To approximate the function $y(x)$ at the points $x_1 = a + h, \ldots, x_{n-1} = a + (n-1)h$, we use the central difference formulas from Chapter 11:

$$y''(x_i) \approx \frac{y_{i+1} - 2y_i + y_{i-1}}{h^2}, \qquad y'(x_i) \approx \frac{y_{i+1} - y_{i-1}}{2h}.$$

Substituting these expressions into the BVP and writing $p(x_i)$ as p_i, $q(x_i)$ as q_i, and $r(x_i)$ as r_i gives

$$\frac{y_{i+1} - 2y_i + y_{i-1}}{h^2} = p_i \frac{y_{i+1} - y_{i-1}}{2h} + q_i y_i + r_i.$$

Further algebraic simplification leads to a tridiagonal system for the unknowns $y_1, \ldots, y_{n-1}$, viz.,

$$\left(1 + p_i \frac{h}{2}\right)y_{i-1} - (2 + h^2 q_i)y_i + \left(1 - p_i \frac{h}{2}\right)y_{i+1} = h^2 r_i, \qquad i = 1, \ldots, n - 1,$$

where $y_0 = y(a) = \alpha$ and $y_n = y(b) = \beta$

Expanding this expression into the full system gives

$$-(2 + h^2 q_1)y_1 + \left(1 - p_1 \frac{h}{2}\right)y_2 = h^2 r_1 - \left(1 + p_1 \frac{h}{2}\right)\alpha,$$

$$\left(1 + p_1 \frac{h}{2}\right)y_1 - (2 + h^2 q_2)y_2 + \left(1 - p_2 \frac{h}{2}\right)y_3 = h^2 r_2,$$

$$\vdots$$

$$\left(1 + p_i \frac{h}{2}\right)y_{i-1} - (2 + h^2 q_i)y_i + \left(1 - p_i \frac{h}{2}\right)y_{i+1} = h^2 r_i,$$

$$\vdots$$

$$\left(1 + p_{n-2} \frac{h}{2}\right)y_{n-3} - (2 + h^2 q_{n-2})y_{n-2} + \left(1 - p_{n-2} \frac{h}{2}\right)y_{n-1} = h^2 r_{n-2},$$

$$\left(1 + p_{n-1} \frac{h}{2}\right)y_{n-2} - (2 + h^2 q_{n-1})y_{n-1} = h^2 r_{n-1} - \left(1 - p_{n-1} \frac{h}{2}\right)\beta.$$

Example14.10 A MATLAB Script for a Linear Finite-Difference Problem

The MATLAB script that follows solves the BVP

$$y_{xx} = 2y, \qquad y(0) = 0.1, \qquad y(3) = 0.1e^3 \cos(3).$$

The solution is shown in Fig. 14.11.

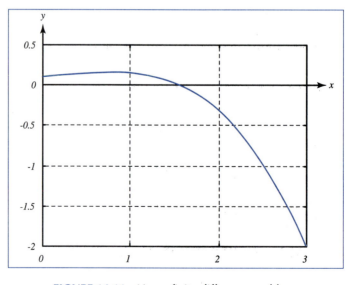

FIGURE 14.11 Linear finite-difference problem.

Matlab Script for Finite-Difference Method for Linear BVP

```
%  S_linear_FD
%  script for finite-difference ODE-BVP
%   y_xx = p(x) y_x  +  q(x) y  +  r(x)        aa ≤ x ≤ bb
%   y(aa) = ya; y(bb) = yb.
%*********************** begin problem definition
%   this example is y_xx = 2 y_x  -2 y  +  0
aa = 0;      bb = 3;            n = 300;
%   define p(x), q(x), r(x)
p = 2*ones(1,n-1);   q = -2*ones(1,n-1);   r = zeros(1,n-1);
ya = 0.1;  yb = 0.1*exp(3)*cos(3);     % boundary conditions
%*************************** end problem definition
h = (bb-aa)/n;   h2 = h/2;   hh = h*h;  % define parameters
x = linspace(aa+h, bb, n);              % grid points, x(1), ... x(n-1)
%  upper diagonal (a), diagonal (d), lower diagonal (b)
a = zeros(1,n-1); b = a;
a(1:n-2) = 1 - p(1,1:n-2)*h2;  d = -(2 + hh*q);
b(2:n-1) = 1 + p(1,2:n-1)*h2;
c(1) = hh*r(1) - ( 1 + p(1)*h2 )*ya;   % right-hand side (c)
c(2:n-2) = hh*r(2:n-2);
c(n-1) =  hh*r(n-1) - ( 1- p(n-1)*h2 )*yb;
y = Thomas(a, d, b, c);
xx = [aa     x]; yy = [ya  y  yb];
out = [xx'  yy']; disp(out)
plot(xx,yy), grid on, hold on
% ******************** plot exact solution if known
plot(xx,0.1*exp(xx).*cos(xx))
% ********************
hold off
```

Example 14.11 Deflection of a Beam, Using Finite-Differences

Consider again the deflection of a simply supported beam, described by the ODE boundary-value problem

$$y'' = \frac{T}{EI}y = \frac{wx(x - L)}{2EI}, \qquad 0 \le x \le L,$$

where we use the specific parameter values given in Example 14.3:

$$L = 100, \quad w = 100, \quad E = 10^7, \quad T = 500, \quad I = 500.$$

Thus, the problem reduces to $y'' = 10^{-7}y + 10^{-8}[x(x - L)], 0 \le x \le 100$, with

$$y(0) = y(100) = 0,$$

$$p(x) = 0, \quad q(x) = 10^{-7}, \quad r(x) = 10^{-8}[x(x - L)].$$

We let $n = 20$ be the number of subintervals.

The only portion of the script S_linear_FD that must be changed for this example is the section on the definition of the problem given here, and the plot of the exact solution (which we omit):

```
%*********************** begin problem definition
%    this example is y_xx = 10^(-7)*y  +  10^(-8)*x.*(x-100)
aa = 0;      bb = 100;      n = 20;      h = (bb-aa)/n
x = h:h:bb
%    define p(x), q(x), r(x)
p = zeros(1,n-1); q = 10^(-7)*ones(1,n-1);
r = 10^(-8)*x.*(x-100);
ya = 0;   yb = 0;              % boundary conditions
%*********************** end problem definition
```

The solution is shown in Fig. 14.12.

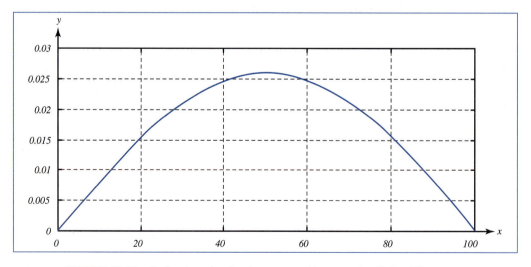

FIGURE 14.12   Deflection of a simply supported beam, using finite-differences.

We next discuss briefly the use of finite-differences in nonlinear boundary-value problems. As has been remarked earlier, nonlinear problems are, in general, significantly more difficult than linear problems. We consider the nonlinear ODE–BVP of the form

$$y'' = f(x, y, y'), \qquad y(a) = \alpha, \qquad y(b) = \beta.$$

We assume that $f(x, y, y')$ has continuous derivatives that satisfy

$$0 < Q_* \le f_y(x, y, y') \le Q^* \quad \text{and} \quad |f_{y'}(x, y, y')| \le P^*$$

for some constants $Q_*, Q^*,$ and P^*.

We use a finite-difference grid with spacing $h \le 2/P^*$. Let us apply the central difference formula for y' and y'' to obtain a nonlinear system of equations. We denote the result of evaluating f at x_i using $(y_{i+1} - y_{i-1})/(2h)$ for y' as f_i. The ODE then becomes the system

$$\frac{y_{i+1} - 2y_i + y_{i-1}}{h^2} - f_i = 0.$$

An explicit iteration scheme, analogous to the SOR method, is given by

$$y_i = \frac{1}{2(1 + \omega)}[y_{i-1} + 2\omega y_i + y_{i+1} - h^2 f_i],$$

where $y_0 = \alpha$ and $y_n = \beta$.

The remarkable result is that, for $\omega \ge h^2 Q^*/2$, the process will converge. (See Keller, 1968, Section 3.2.) We illustrate the process for the nonlinear BVP introduced in Example 14.8.

Example 14.12 Solving a Nonlinear BVP by Using Finite-Differences

Consider again the nonlinear BVP

$$y'' = \frac{[y']^2}{y}, \qquad y(0) = 1, \qquad y(1) = 2.$$

We illustrate the use of the iterative procedure just outlined by taking a grid with $h = 1/4$, so that $x_0 = 0, x_1 = 0.25, x_2 = 0.5, x_3 = 0.75,$ and $x_4 = 1$. The general form of the difference equation is

$$y_i = \frac{1}{2(1 + \omega)}[y_{i-1} + 2\omega y_i + y_{i+1} - h^2 f_i],$$

where

$$f_i = -\frac{[(y_{i+1} - y_{i-1})/(2h)]^2}{y_i} = -\frac{y_{i+1}^2 - 2y_{i+1}y_{i-1} + y_{i-1}^2}{4h^2 y_i}.$$

Substituting the rightmost expression for f_i into the equation for y_i, we obtain

$$y_i = \frac{1}{2(1+\omega)}\left[y_{i-1} + 2\omega y_i + y_{i+1} + \frac{y_{i+1}^2 - 2y_{i+1}y_{i-1} + y_{i-1}^2}{4y_i} \right].$$

The computed solution after 10 iterations agrees very closely with the exact solution, as is shown in Fig. 14.13. The MATLAB script to solve this problem is presented after the figure; to use a finer grid, a loop can be added to generate the equations for $i = 2, \ldots, n-1$, since only the first and last equations have a special form to accommodate the boundary conditions.

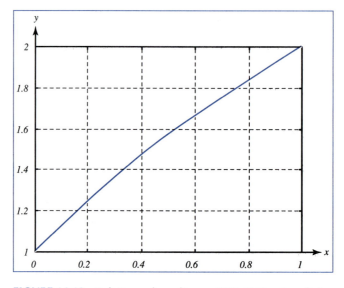

FIGURE 14.13 Solution of nonlinear ODE–BVP using finite-differences.

MATLAB Script for Finite-Difference Method for Nonlinear BVP

```
% S_nonlinear_FD
%*****************
ya = 1;        yb = 2; a = 0;    b = 1;
max_it = 10;   n = 4; w = 0.1;   ww = 1/(2*(1+w)); h = (b-a)/n
%*****************
y(1:n-1) = 1
for k = 1:max_it
    y(1) = ww*(ya+2*w*y(1)+y(2)+(ya^2-2*ya*y(2)+y(2)^2)/(4*y(1)));
    y(2) = ww*(y(1)+2*w*y(2)+y(3)+(y(1)^2-2*y(1)*y(3)+ y(3)^2)/(4*y(2)));
    y(3) = ww*(y(2)+2*w*y(3)+ yb+(y(2)^2-2*y(2)*yb + yb^2)/(4*y(3)));
end
x = [ a  a+h  a+2*h  a+3*h  b]; z = [ ya  y  yb];
plot(x, z), hold on, zz = sqrt(3*x+1); plot(x,zz), hold off
```

Linear Shooting:

$$y'' = p(x)y' + q(x)y + r(x), \qquad y(a) = \alpha, \qquad y(b) = \beta.$$

Solve the IVP $u'' = p(x)u' + q(x)u + r(x), u(a) = \alpha, u'(a) = 0,$ and (assuming $u(b) \neq \beta$)

$$v'' = p(x)v' + q(x)v, \qquad v(a) = 0, \qquad v'(a) = 1.$$

If $v(b) \neq 0$, the solution of the original two-point BVP is given by

$$y(x) = u(x) + \frac{\beta - u(b)}{v(b)} v(x).$$

Nonlinear Shooting:

$$y'' = f(x, y, y'), \qquad y(a) = y_a, \qquad h(y(b), y'(b))0 = y_b.$$

Solve the IVP $u'' = f(x, u, u'), u(a) = y_a, u'(a) = 0$.
　　Calculate $h_1 = h(u(b), u'(b))$ and $m_1 = y_b - h_1$ (the error at $x = b$).
　　If $|m_1| <$ tol, accept $u(x)$ as the solution; otherwise, continue.
Solve the IVP $v'' = f(x, v, v'), v(a) = y_a, v'(a) = 1$.
　　Find $h_2 = h(v(b), v'(b))$, and $m_2 = y_b - h_2$ (error at $x = b$).
　　If $|m_2| <$ tol, accept $v(x)$ as the solution; otherwise, continue.
Form a new initial guess for $y'(a)$:

$$t = u'(a) + \frac{[v'(a) - u'(a)]m_1}{h_2 - h_1}.$$

Solve $w'' = f(x, y, y'), w(a) = y_a, w'(a) = t$.
　　Find $h_3 = h(w(b), w'(b))$, and $m_3 = y_b - h_3$ (error at $x = b$).
　　If $|m_3| <$ tol, accept $w(x)$ as the solution;
　　otherwise, continue with linear interpolation to refine the value of t.

Finite-Difference Method for Linear BVP:

$$y'' = p(x)y' + q(x)y + r(x) \qquad a \leq x \leq b$$

$$\frac{y_{i+1} - 2y_i + y_{i-1}}{h^2} = p(x_i) \frac{y_{i+1} - y_{i-1}}{2h} + q(x_i)y_i + r(x_i).$$

$$y_{i+1} - 2y_i + y_{i-1} = (y_{i+1} - y_{i-1})p(x_i)\frac{h}{2} + h^2 q(x_i)y_i + h^2 r(x_i).$$

$$\left(1 + p(x_i)\frac{h}{2}\right)y_{i-1} - (2 + h^2 q(x_i))y_i + \left(1 - p(x_i)\frac{h}{2}\right)y_{i+1} = h^2 r(x_i).$$

Finite-Difference Method for Nonlinear BVP:

$$y'' = f(x, y, y'), \qquad y(a) = \alpha, \qquad y(b) = \beta.$$

Assume that there are constants Q_*, Q^*, and P^* such that

$$0 < Q^* \le f_y(x, y, y') \quad \text{and} \quad |f_{y'}(x, y, y')| \le P^*$$

Use a finite-difference grid with spacing $h = 2/P^*$, and let f_i denote the result of evaluating f at x_i using $(y_{i+1} - y_{i-1})/(2h)$ for y'. The ODE then becomes the system $\frac{y_{i+1} - 2y_i + y_{i-1}}{h^2} - f_i = 0$.

An explicit iteration scheme, analogous to the SOR method, is given by

$$y_i = \frac{1}{2(1 + \omega)} [y_{i-1} + 2\omega y_i + y_{i+1} - h^2 f_i],$$

where $y_0 = \alpha$, and $y_n = \beta$. The process will converge for $\omega \ge h^2 Q^*/2$.

SUGGESTIONS FOR FURTHER READING

For the basic theory, see suggestions from Chapter 12. In addition, see

Ascher, U. M., R. M. M. Mattheij, and R. D. Russell, *Numerical Solution of Boundary Value Problems for Ordinary Differential Equations*, SIAM, Philadelphia, 1995.

Fox, L., *Numerical Solution of Two-Point Boundary Value Problems in Ordinary Differential Equations*, Dover, New York, 1990.

Keller, H. B., *Numerical Methods for Two-point Boundary-value Problems*, Blaisdell, Waltham, MA, 1968.

Troutman, J. L., and M. Bautista, *Boundary Value Problems of Applied Mathematics*, Prindle, Weber & Schmidt Publishing, Boston 1994.

For further discussion of applications of two-point boundary value problems, see

Haberman, R., *Elementary Applied Partial Differential Equations, with Fourier Series and Boundary Value Problems*, Prentice-Hall, Englewood Cliffs, NJ, 1983.

Hanna, O. T., and O. C. Sandall, *Computational Methods In Chemical Engineering*, Prentice Hall, Upper Saddle River, NJ, 1995.

Hornbeck, R. W., *Numerical Methods*, Prentice-Hall, Englewood Cliffs, NJ, 1975.

Inman, D. J. *Engineering Vibration*, Prentice Hall, Upper Saddle River, NJ, 1996.

Jaeger, J. C., *An Introduction to Applied Mathematics*, Clarenden Press, Oxford, U. K., 1951.

Roberts, C. E., *Ordinary Differential Equations: A Computational Approach*, Prentice-Hall, Englewood Cliffs, NJ, 1979.

PRACTICE THE TECHNIQUES

For Problems P14.1–P14.14, solve the boundary value problem

   a.   *Using the linear shooting method.*
   b.   *Using the finite-difference method.*

P14.1 $y'' = -y$, $y(0) = 1$, $y(\pi) = -1$.

P14.2 $y'' = y + x$, $y(0) = 2$, $y(1) = 2.5$.

P14.3 $y'' = -2y' - y + x^2$, $y(0) = 10$, $y(1) = 2$.

P14.4 $y'' = y/(e^x + 1)$, $y(0) = 1$, $y(1) = 5$.

P14.5 $y'' = -2y' - 4y$, $y(0) = 2$, $y(1) = 2$.

P14.6 $y'' = -9y$, $y(0) = 0$, $y(\pi/6) = 1$.

P14.7 $y'' = y/4 + 8$, $y(0) = 0$, $y(\pi) = 2$.

P14.8 $y'' = -2xy'$, $y(0) = 1$, $y(10) = 0$.

P14.9 $x^2y'' + xy' + x^2y = 0$, $y(1) = 1$, $y(8) = 0$.

P14.10 $x^2y'' - xy' + y = 0$, $y(1) = 1$, $y(3) = 4$.

P14.11 $x^2y'' + xy' + y = 0$, $y(1) = 0$, $y(10) = 1/2$.

P14.12 $6x^2y'' + xy' + y = 0$, $y(1) = 2$, $y(64) = 12$.

P14.13 $xy'' - y' - x^5 = 0$, $y(1) = 1/2$, $y(2) = 4$.

P14.14 $xy'' + y' + x = 0$, $y(2) = -1$, $y(4) = 15$.

For Problems P14.15–P14.25, solve the boundary value problem

   a.   *Using the nonlinear shooting method.*
   b.   *Using the finite-difference method.*

P14.15 $y'' + y' - y^2 = 0$ $y(0) = 1, y(1) = 2$.

P14.16 $y'' = 2y\,y'$, $y(1) = 1, y(2) = 1/2$.

P14.17 $y'' = -2\,(y + x)(y' + 1)$, $y(1) = 0, y(2) = -2$.

P14.18 $y'' = -x\,(y')^2 - x^2y$, $y(0) = 1, y(1) = -1$.

P14.19 $y'' = e^y$, $y(0) = 1, y(1) = 0$.

P14.20 $2yy'' = (y')^2 - 4y^2$, $y(\pi/6) = 1/4, y(\pi/2) = 1$.

P14.21 $y'' = 2y^3$, $y(1) = 1, y(2) = 1/2$.

P14.22 $yy'' = -(y')^2 - 1$, $y(1) = 1, y(1/2) = \sqrt{3/4}$.

P14.23 $(1 + x^2)\,y'' = 4xy' - 6y$, $y(0) = 1, y(1) = -4/3$.

P14.24 $x^3y'' = x^2y' + 3 - x^2$, $y(1) = 4, y(1) = 15/2$.

P14.25 $y'' = -x(y')^3$, $y(0) = 0, y(1) = \pi/2$.

EXPLORE SOME APPLICATIONS

A14.1 The steady state temperature distribution for a rod of length L, with source term $Q(x)$, and temperatures given at the two ends of the rod, is described by the BVP:

$$u_{xx} + Q(x) = 0; \quad u(0) = A, \quad u(L) = B.$$

Solve for $Q(x) = 1$, $A = 0, B = 100$.

A14.2 To find the steady state temperature distribution for a rod of length L, with source term $Q(x) = \sin(2\pi x/L)$, and insulated ends, solve the BVP:

$$u_{xx} + Q(x) = 0; \quad u_x(0) = 0, \quad u_x(L) = 0.$$

A14.3 The steady state temperature distribution for a rod of length L, with source term $Q(x) = x^2$, temperature fixed at $x = 0$, and the end of the rod at $x = L$ insulted, is described by the BVP:

$$u_{xx} + Q(x) = 0, \quad u(0) = T, \quad u_x(L) = 0.$$

Solve for $T = 100, L = 1$.

A14.4 The steady state temperature distribution between two concentric spheres, with fixed temperature at $r = a$ and $r = b$, is given by the BVP:

$$r\,u_{rr} + 2\,u_r = 0; \quad u(a) = T_1, \quad u(b) = T_2.$$

Solve for $a = 1, u(1) = 0, b = 4, u(4) = 80$.

A14.4 The steady state temperature distribution of a rod with heat source $Q > 0$ proportional to temperature, and with the temperature at the ends of the rod fixed at 0, is given by the BVP:

$$u_{xx} + Qu = 0; \quad u(0) = 0, \quad u(L) = 0.$$

Solve for $L = 10, Q = (\pi/L)^2$

A14.5 Modeling a second-order chemical flow reactor with axial dispersion leads to the ODE–BVP:

$$eP_{zz} - P_z - BP^2 = 0; \quad eP_z(0) = P(0) - 1; \quad P_z(1) = 0.$$

Solve for $B = 7.5$, and $e = 0.1$ to find P(1). (See Hanna and Sandall, 1995, p. 16–18.)

A14.6 The Blasius equation describes laminar boundary layer flow on a flat plate

$$f_{xxx} + f f_{xx} = 0; \quad f(0) = 0; \quad f_x(0) = 0; \quad f_x(\infty) = 1.$$

Investigate a numerical solution by approximating ∞ by some large value of x. (See Hanna and Sandall, 1995, p. 256, for discussion of a series approach to the solution).

A14.7 A simple model of pseudo-homogeneous, iso-thermal chemical reaction and diffusion in a cylindrical catalyst pellet with irreversible first-order reaction kinetics can be written (in terms of dimensionless variables) as

$$y_{xx} + \frac{1}{x} y_x = By \quad y_x(0) = 0 \quad y(1) = 1$$

Investigate the numerical solution of this problem for $B = 1, 10$, and 100. (see Hanna and Sandall, pp. 257–258, for discussion of a series approach to the solution).

A14.8 Equations for the deflection (y) and rotation (z) of a simply supported beam with a uniformly distributed load of intensity 2 kips/ft and bending moment $M(x) = 10x - x^2$ can expressed as

$$\frac{dz}{dx} = \frac{M}{EI} = \frac{10x - x^2}{EI}, \quad \frac{dy}{dx} = z,$$

where E is the modulus of elasticity and I is the moment of inertia of the cross section of the beam. Taking $EI = 3600$ kip/ft, $y(0) = 0$, and $y(10) = 0$, find y and z for $0 \le x \le 10$. (See Ayyub and McCuen, 1996, p. 239)

A14.9 The deflection of a uniform beam of length L, with both ends fixed, subject to a load proportional to the distance from one end, i.e., $w = bx$, is described by the ODE–BVP

$$EI \frac{d^4 y}{dx^4} = w(x) = bx, \quad y(0) = y'(0) = 0,$$
$$y(L) = y'(L) = 0.$$

Solve using $EI = 3600$ kip/ft, $L = 10, b = 2$.

A14.10 To find the deflection of a cantilever beam of unit length, with a distributed load, $w(x) = x$, solve the BVP

$$u_{xxxx} = x$$

with the boundary conditions

$$u(0) = u'(0) = u''(1) = u'''(1) = 0.$$

The conditions at $x = 1$ correspond to no bending moment and no shear there.

A14.11 To find the deflection of a simply supported beam of unit length, with a point load P at the midpoint, $w(x) = \delta(x - 1/2)$, solve the BVP

$$u_{xxxx} = w(x)$$

with the boundary conditions

$$u(0) = u'(0) = u(1) = u'(1) = 0.$$

EXTEND YOUR UNDERSTANDING

U14.1 Consider the numerical solutions to the BVP

$$y'' = -y; \quad y(0) = 0; \quad y(\pi) = 0.$$

The exact solution is $y = A \sin(x)$ for any constant A. How do the shooting method and the finite-difference method respond to the nonunique solution?

U14.2 Consider the numerical solutions to the BVP

$$y'' = -y; \quad y(0) = 0; \quad y(\pi) = 1.$$

The general solution is $y = A \sin(x) + B \cos(x)$, but no choice of A and B will satisfy these boundary conditions. How do the shooting method and the finite-difference method repsond to this situation?

U14.3 $y'' = \dfrac{2x}{x^2 + 1} y' - \dfrac{2}{x^2 + 1} y + x^2 + 1;$
$$y(0) = 2; y'(1) - y(1) = -3$$

This BVP has infinitely many solutions (See Roberts, 1979, p. 347)

U14.4 $y'' = \dfrac{2x}{x^2 + 1} y' - \dfrac{2}{x^2 + 1} y + x^2 + 1;$
$$y(0) = 2; y'(1) - y(1) = -1$$

U14.5 The finite-difference method presented in the text uses the central difference approximation for y'. The linear system that is obtained in using the finite-difference method is guaranteed to be diagonally dominant if the step size $\Delta x < 2/M$, where M is an upper bound on $|p(x)|$. Consider the problem:

$$y'' = -2 x y', \quad y(0) = 1, \quad y(10) = 0.$$

Investigate the solution of this problem using finite-differences with different values of Δx, both larger and smaller than 0.1.

U14.6 Forward differences may be preferable for the first derivative approximation in cases where $p(x) \le 0$. Develop a program implementing this method and compare the results to those found in U14.5.

15

Partial Differential Equations

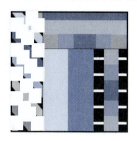

We conclude our investigation into numerical methods for solving differential equations with an introduction to some numerical techniques for solving linear second-order partial differential equations (PDEs) with constant coefficients. These equations fall into three basic categories: parabolic, hyperbolic, and elliptic. As an example of a parabolic PDE, we consider the heat equation, which describes the temperature distribution in a slender rod. A hyperbolic PDE is illustrated by the wave equation for a vibrating string. To illustrate numerical methods for elliptic PDEs, we investigate the Laplace (potential) and Poisson equations for steady-state temperature distribution in a two-dimensional region.

Numerical techniques for solving partial differential equations are primarily of two types: finite-difference methods and finite-element methods. In the first three sections of the chapter, we investigate finite-difference methods for parabolic, hyperbolic, and elliptic equations, using the heat equation, wave equation, and Poisson equation as examples. These techniques are a direct extension of the ideas presented in the previous two chapters. Replacing the partial derivatives by finite-difference approximations leads to a system of algebraic equations for the values of the unknown function at the grid points. Depending on the type of PDE and the choice of difference approximation (forward, backward, or central), the resulting equations may be solved directly or may require iterative techniques. Stability issues restrict the choice of mesh spacing for some types of problems also.

The final section of the chapter provides an introduction to finite-element methods for dealing with elliptic problems. The finite-element approach seeks to find a solution as a linear combination of relatively simple basis functions. For many elliptic problems, the solution of the PDE is equivalent to minimizing an integral over the relevant domain or, for certain problems with derivative boundary conditions, a combination of an integral over the region and an integral along the boundary. Finite-element methods are especially suitable for regions that are not rectangular. We illustrate the process using triangular subregions and basis functions that are piecewise linear on the subregions. The use of MATLAB's functions for graphing a surface defined on a triangular mesh is illustrated in the notes at the end of the chapter, which makes the visualization of finite-element solutions quite convenient.

Example 15-A Heat Equation

The temperature in a thin rod can be described by the one-dimensional heat equation

$$u_t = c\,u_{xx}, \qquad \text{for } 0 < x < a, \qquad 0 < t.$$

The initial temperature is given for each point in the rod:

$$u(x, 0) = f(x), \qquad 0 < x < a.$$

In addition, information must be supplied describing what happens at each end of the rod. If the ends of the rod are kept at specified temperatures (by immersing each end in a fluid bath with a temperature that fluctuates with time, for example), then the boundary conditions are

$$u(0, t) = g_1(t), \qquad u(a, t) = g_2(t), \qquad 0 < t.$$

Other physical situations give different forms for the boundary conditions. For example, keeping an end of the rod insulated corresponds to specifying that the partial derivative u_x is zero at that end of the rod:

$$u_x(0, t) = 0 \quad \text{or} \quad u_x(a, t) = 0.$$

A third possibility is that an end of the rod is subject to convective cooling (a warm rod exposed to cooler air, for example). The corresponding boundary condition involves a combination of u and u_x at the appropriate end.

This combination of PDE, initial condition, and boundary conditions is a standard example of a parabolic PDE. (See Fig. 15.1.)

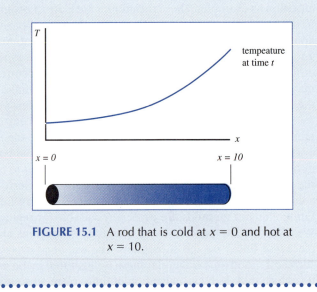

FIGURE 15.1 A rod that is cold at $x = 0$ and hot at $x = 10$.

Example 15-B Wave Equation

The motion of a vibrating string can be described by the one-dimensional wave equation

$$u_{tt} - c^2 u_{xx} = 0, \qquad \text{for } 0 < x < a \text{ and } 0 < t.$$

The initial displacement $u(x, 0)$ and initial velocity $u_t(x, 0)$ are given for each point in the string:

$$u(x, 0) = f_1(x), \qquad u_t(x, 0) = f_2(x), \qquad \text{for } 0 < x < a.$$

In addition, information must be supplied about the motion of the ends of the string. The string may be fixed at each end (with zero displacement), which gives the boundary conditions

$$u(0, t) = 0, \qquad u(a, t) = 0, \qquad 0 < t.$$

If the ends of the string are allowed to move in a prescribed manner, the boundary conditions have the more general form

$$u(0, t) = g_1(t), \qquad u(a, t) = g_2(t), \qquad 0 < t,$$

where either g_1 or g_2 could be the zero function.

   If an end of the string is attached to a frictionless vertical track, the appropriate boundary condition specifies that, at $x = 0$ or $x = a$,

$$u_x = 0;$$

this corresponds to the insulated boundary condition for the one-dimensional heat equation.

   More complicated boundary conditions result when an end of the string is attached to a spring–mass system. For example, the so-called elastic boundary condition is analogous to the Newton-cooling boundary condition for the one-dimensional heat equation.

   This combination of PDE, initial conditions and boundary conditions, is a standard example of a hyperbolic PDE. (See Fig. 15.2.)

   Although the one-dimensional wave equation does not usually require a numerical solution, an example will serve as an introduction to higher dimensional wave equations, wherein numerical methods are more likely to be worthwhile.

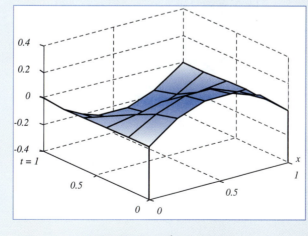

FIGURE 15.2   Vibrating string.

Example 15-C Poisson's Equation

The steady-state temperature distribution in a rectangular plate can be described by the Poisson equation

$$u_{xx} + u_{yy} = f(x, y), \qquad 0 \le x \le a, \qquad 0 \le y \le b.$$

If there are no heat sources (i.e., if $f(x, y) = 0$), the equation is known as Laplace's equation. Gravitational and electrostatic potentials also satisfy the Poisson equation (or the Laplace or potential equation if there are no sources).

The temperature may be prescribed along each boundary:

$$u(0, y) = g_1(y), \qquad u(a, y) = g_2(y), \qquad 0 < y < b;$$
$$u(x, 0) = g_3(x), \qquad u(x, b) = g_4(x), \qquad 0 < x < a.$$

As with the one-dimensional heat equation, other possible boundary conditions include having the boundary or part of the boundary insulated, so that the directional derivative of u in the outward normal direction is zero along that part of the boundary:

$$u_x(0, y) = 0, \quad \text{or } u_x(a, y) = 0, \quad \text{or } u_y(x, 0) = 0, \quad \text{or } u_y(x, b) = 0.$$

The Newton cooling boundary condition corresponds to heat flowing out at a rate proportional to the difference between the temperature of the plate and that of the surrounding medium.

The Poisson equation is a standard example of an elliptic PDE. (See Fig. 15.3.)

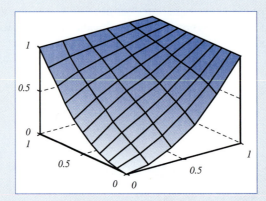

FIGURE 15.3   Steady-state temperature in a plate.

Although the theory of solutions of PDEs and many of the techniques for numerical solutions of PDEs are beyond the scope of this book, we examine several standard techniques for the numerical solution of linear second-order PDEs involving two independent variables—either spatial variables x and y or a single spatial variable and a time variable. The general form of PDE we consider is

$$a\,u_{xx} + b\,u_{xy} + c\,u_{yy} + d\,u_x + e\,u_y + fu + g = 0$$

or

$$a\,u_{xx} + b\,u_{xt} + c\,u_{tt} + d\,u_x + e\,u_t + fu + g = 0.$$

The coefficients $a, b, \ldots, g$ may depend on the independent variables (but not on the unknown function u).

PDEs of the preceding form are normally classified into three types—parabolic, hyperbolic, and elliptic—depending on the sign of $b^2 - 4ac$. The PDE is

$$\text{parabolic} \quad \text{if} \quad b^2 - 4ac = 0,$$

$$\text{hyperbolic} \quad \text{if} \quad b^2 - 4ac > 0,$$

$$\text{elliptic} \quad \text{if} \quad b^2 - 4ac < 0.$$

Of course, if the coefficients are not constants, the PDE may have a different classification in different parts of the solution domain.

The most widespread numerical techniques for solving PDEs are finite-difference methods and finite-element methods. Finite differences are based on subdividing the domain of the problem by introducing a mesh of discrete points for each of the independent variables. Derivatives are replaced by the appropriate difference quotients (see Chapter 11), and the resulting system of algebraic equations is solved by methods presented in previous chapters. Finite-element methods are based on restricting the form of the functions used (rather than the points at which the solution is sought) and finding a linear combination of these simple functions that minimizes the appropriate integral functional (which includes information from both the differential equation and the boundary conditions). For finite elements, the simple functions are required to be zero except on a small subregion of the problem domain. Finite-element methods are especially popular for elliptic problems.

15.1 HEAT EQUATION: PARABOLIC PDE

A finite-difference solution of the one-dimensional heat equation

$$u_t = c\,u_{xx}, \qquad \text{for } 0 < x < a, \qquad 0 < t \le T,$$

with initial conditions

$$u(x, 0) = f(x), \qquad 0 < x < a,$$

and boundary conditions of

$$u(0, t) = g_1(t), \qquad u(a, t) = g_2(t), \qquad 0 < t \leq T,$$

at $x = 0$ and $x = a$ begins with the definition of a mesh of points at which the solution is sought. We divide the interval $[0, a]$ into n pieces, each of length $h = \Delta x = a/n$. The corresponding points are denoted x_i, for $i = 0, \ldots, n$. The ends of the interval are at $x_0 = 0$ and $x_n = a$; the interior points are $x_i = ih$, for $i = 1, \ldots, n - 1$. (See Fig. 15.4.)

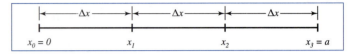

FIGURE 15.4 Spatial mesh, $n = 3$.

In a similar manner, we define a mesh for the time interval, with m subdivisions with $k = \Delta t = T/m$ and $t_j = jk, j = 0, 1, \ldots, m$. As with the variable x, the ends of the time interval are $t_0 = 0$ and $t_m = T$. (See Fig. 15.5.)

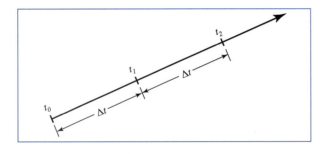

FIGURE 15.5 Temporal mesh, $m = 2$.

The solution at a grid point $u(x_i, t_j)$ is denoted u_{ij}. Similarly, values of the initial condition $f(x)$ at grid points are abbreviated as f_i, and values of the boundary conditions are either g_{1j} or g_{2j}. Finite-difference techniques replace the partial derivatives in the PDE with difference quotients.

For the heat equation, we use the forward difference formula for u_t:

$$u_t \Rightarrow \frac{1}{k} [u_{i,j+1} - u_{i,j}].$$

Similarly, we replace the second derivative (with respect to the spatial variable) by the finite-difference formula from Chapter 11, using the fact that the spacing between points in the x direction is h. If this difference formula is applied at the jth time step, we have

$$c\, u_{xx} \Rightarrow \frac{c}{h^2} [u_{i-1,j} - 2u_{i,j} + u_{i+1,j}].$$

This expression yields an explicit method that is easy to solve, but imposes restrictions on the relative values of the mesh spacing in the x and t directions (to maintain stability of the solution, i.e., to prevent the inevitable errors in the solution from becoming larger as the calculations proceed from $t = 0$ to $t = T$).

The points that are involved in the calculations at time steps j and $j + 1$ with the explicit method are shown schematically in Fig. 15.6.

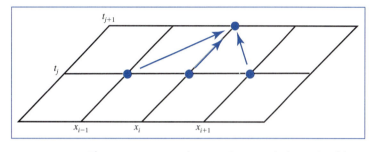

FIGURE 15.6 The temperature at the next time step is determined from information at the previous time step.

On the other hand, if the difference is used at the $(j + 1)$st time step, we have

$$c\,u_{xx} \Rightarrow \frac{c}{h^2}\left[u_{i-1,j+1} - 2u_{i,j+1} + u_{i+1,j+1}\right].$$

This expression gives an implicit method that is somewhat more difficult to solve, but that is stable without placing any restrictions on the mesh spacing.

Finally, we consider the Crank–Nicolson method, which averages the second-derivative difference formulas at the jth and $(j + 1)$st time steps; this gives a stable method with better truncation error than the simple implicit method.

15.1.1 Explicit Method for Solving Heat Equation

Replacing the space derivative by the difference formula at the jth time step and the time derivative by a forward difference gives a linear system of equations for the temperature u at the grid points:

$$\frac{1}{k}\left[u_{i,j+1} - u_{i,j}\right] = \frac{c}{h^2}\left[u_{i-1,j} - 2u_{i,j} + u_{i+1,j}\right].$$

This equation can be simplified by introducing the parameter $r = \dfrac{ck}{h^2}$; solving for $u_{i,j+1}$, we have

$$u_{i,j+1} = r\,u_{i-1,j} + (1 - 2r)u_{i,j} + r\,u_{i+1,j}, \qquad \text{for } i = 1, \ldots, n - 1.$$

Since the solution is known for $t = 0$, we can solve explicitly for the first time step and proceed from there in a step-by-step manner.

The x and t meshes must be chosen so that $0 < r \le 0.5$ in order to ensure stability. This requirement is discussed further following an example.

MATLAB Function for Solving Heat Equation

```
function w = Heat( f, g1, g2, L, T, n, m, a)
% solve u_t = a u_xx              for 0 ≤ x ≤ L,  0 ≤ t ≤ T
%      BC:   u(0, t) = g1(t);    u(L, t) = g2(t)      0 < t
%      IC:   u(x, 0) = f(x)       0 ≤ x ≤ L
%      n = number of subintervals for x
%      m = number of subintervals for t
h = L/n;                 k = T/m;
r = a*k/h^2;             rr = 1 - 2*r;
x = h:h:(n-1)*h;         t = k:k:m*k;
% evaluate initial conditions
      y0 = feval(f, 0);    y = feval(f, x);    yL = feval(f, L);
% evaluate boundary conditions
      g1k = feval(g1, t); g2k = feval(g2,t);
% find solution at first time step
      u(1, 1) = r*y0 + rr*y(1) + r*y(2);
      u(2:n-2,1) = r*y(1:n-3)' + rr*y(2:n-2)' + r*y(3:n-1)';
      u(n-1, 1) = r*y(n-2) + rr*y(n-1) + r*yL;
% find solution at remaining time steps
for j = 2:m
    u(1, j) = r*g1k(j-1) + rr*u(1, j-1) + r*u(2, j-1);
    u(2:n-2,j) = r*u(1:n-3,j-1) + rr*u(2:n-2,j-1) + r*u(3:n-1,j-1);
    u(n-1,j) = r*u(n-2,j-1) + rr*u(n-1,j-1) + r*g2k(j-1);
end
w =[ y0    y    yL
     g1k   u'   g2k];
```

Example 15.1 Temperature in a Rod, Explicit Method, Stable Solution

Consider the temperature in a rod of unit length, given by the PDE

$$u_t - u_{xx} = 0, \qquad \text{for } 0 < x < 1, \qquad 0 < t.$$

The initial temperature of the rod is

$$u(x,0) = x^4, \qquad 0 < x < 1,$$

and the temperatures at $x = 0$ and $x = 1$ are, respectively,

$$u(0, t) = 0, \qquad u(1, t) = 1, \qquad 0 < t.$$

Taking a fairly coarse mesh with $h = \Delta x = 0.2$ and the largest time step allowed for stability (so that $\Delta t = 0.02$ and $r = 0.5$) results in a simplification of the general forward difference equation

$$u_{i,j+1} = r u_{i-1,j} + (1 - 2r) u_{i,j} + r u_{i+1,j}$$

to the form

$$u_{i,j+1} = 0.5 u_{i-1,j} + 0.5 u_{i+1,j}.$$

It is convenient to display the solution in an array with the rod extending from left to right and time progressing down the page. The values of the independent variables (x and t) at the mesh points are shown across the top of the array and down the left-hand side; the corresponding mesh index values at these points are also shown for reference. The initial and boundary conditions are shown in bold. The solution is shown in Fig. 15.7.

The solution at the first time step is as follows:

	$x =$	0.0	0.2	0.4	0.6	0.8	1.0
t	$j\backslash i$	0	1	2	3	4	5
0.00	0	**0**	**0.0016**	**0.0256**	**0.1296**	**0.4096**	**1**
0.02	1	**0.0**	0.0128	0.0656	0.2176	0.5648	**1.0**
0.04	2	**0.0**					**1.0**

Continuing the solution for several more time steps yields the following tabulation:

	$x =$	0.0	0.2	0.4	0.6	0.8	1.0
t	$j\backslash i$	0	1	2	3	4	5
0.00	0	**0.0**	**0.0016**	**0.0256**	**0.1296**	**0.4096**	**1.0**
0.02	1	**0.0**	0.0128	0.0656	0.2176	0.5648	**1.0**
0.04	2	**0.0**	0.0328	0.1152	0.3152	0.6088	**1.0**
0.06	3	**0.0**	0.0576	0.174	0.362	0.6576	**1.0**
0.08	4	**0.0**	0.087	0.2098	0.4158	0.681	**1.0**
0.10	5	**0.0**	0.1049	0.2514	0.4454	0.7079	**1.0**

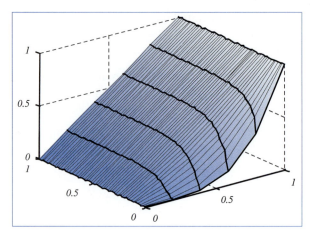

FIGURE 15.7   Temperature in a rod.

Discussion

The finite-difference representations of the partial derivatives in the heat equation are based on the Taylor series formulas developed in Chapter 11. The partial derivative of u with respect to t is

$$u_t(x_i, t_j) = \frac{u(x_i, t_{j+1}) - u(x_i, t_j)}{k} + O(k) = \frac{1}{k}[u_{i,j+1} - u_{i,j}] + O(k).$$

Similarly,

$$u_{xx}(x_i, t_j) = \frac{1}{h^2}[u_{i-1,j} - 2u_{i,j} + u_{i+1,j}] + O(h^2).$$

Substituting into the PDE gives

$$\frac{1}{k}[u_{i,j+1} - u_{i,j}] + O(k) = \frac{c}{h^2}[u_{i-1,j} - 2u_{i,j} + u_{i+1,j}] + O(h^2).$$

Combining the two expressions for the truncation error shows that the truncation error for the explicit method is $O(h^2 + k)$:

$$\frac{1}{k}[u_{ij+1} - u_{i,j}] = \frac{c}{h^2}[u_{i-1,j} - 2u_{i,j} + u_{i+1,j}] + O(h^2) + O(k).$$

If we make use of the actual form of the first term of the error, we find that

$$\frac{1}{k}[u_{i,j+1} - u_{i,j}] = \frac{c}{h^2}[u_{i-1,j} - 2u_{i,j} + u_{i+1,j}] + \frac{ch^2}{12}u_{xxxx} - \frac{k}{2}u_{tt}$$

$$+ \text{ higher order terms.}$$

Since u satisfies the PDE $u_t = cu_{xx}$, assuming sufficient continuity for the derivatives, we find by calculus that $u_{tt} = cu_{xxxx}$. Thus, we can obtain a method with truncation error $O(k^2)$ if we choose h and k so that

$$\frac{ch^2}{12} u_{xxxx} - \frac{k}{2} u_{tt} = \frac{h^2}{12} u_{tt} - \frac{k}{2} u_{tt} = \frac{1}{2}\left(\frac{h^2}{6} - k\right) u_{tt} = 0.$$

Hence, for $\dfrac{k}{h^2} = \dfrac{1}{6}$, the truncation error is $O(k^2) = O(h^4)$.

The primary difficulty with the explicit method is the stability condition, which requires that

$$r = \frac{ck}{h^2} \le \frac{1}{2}.$$

A numerical method is stable if errors that may be present at one stage of the computation do not grow as the process proceeds. To consider the stability of the forward difference solution of the heat equation, it is useful to express the computation in matrix-vector form. The solution at time step $j+1$, which we denote by the column vector $\mathbf{u}(:, j+1)$, is found by multiplying the tridiagonal matrix $\mathbf{A}$ by the solution at the jth time step:

$$
\begin{bmatrix}
1-2r & r & & & \\
r & 1-2r & r & & \\
 & . & \vdots & . & \\
 & & r & 1-2r & r \\
 & & & r & 1-2r
\end{bmatrix}
\begin{bmatrix}
u(1,j) \\
\vdots \\
\\
u(n,j)
\end{bmatrix}
=
\begin{bmatrix}
u(1,j+1) \\
\vdots \\
\\
u(n,j+1)
\end{bmatrix}
$$

Suppose the true solution of the PDE at time step j is $\mathbf{U}(:, j)$ and the computed solution is $\mathbf{u}(:, j) = \mathbf{U}(:, j) + \mathbf{E}$. Then the computed solution at step $j+1$ is

$$\mathbf{A}(:, j) = \mathbf{A}\{\mathbf{U}(:, j) + \mathbf{E}\} = \mathbf{A}\mathbf{U}(:, j) + \mathbf{A}\mathbf{E}.$$

After m time steps, the effect of the error $\mathbf{E}$ has become $\mathbf{A}^m\mathbf{E}$. From matrix algebra, it follows that

$$\|\mathbf{A}^m\,\mathbf{E}\| \le |\lambda|^m\,\|\mathbf{E}\|,$$

where λ is the dominant eigenvalue of $\mathbf{A}$. Stability is assured if $|\lambda| \le 1$. The Gerschgorin theorem (Chapter 1) bounds the eigenvalues of $\mathbf{A}$ inside circles centered at $1-2r$; the radius of each of the largest circles is $2r$, so any eigenvalue μ satisfies $(1-2r) - 2r \le \mu \le (1-2r) + 2r$; thus, we are guaranteed that $-1 \le \lambda \le 1$ if $-1 \le 1 - 4r$, or $r \le \dfrac{1}{2}$.

Example 15.2 Temperature in a Rod, Explicit Method, Unstable Solution

Using $h = 0.2$, but disregarding the stability requirement by taking $k = 0.04$ so that $r = 1.0$, results in the update equation

$$u_{i,j+1} = u_{i-1,j} - u_{i,j} + u_{i+1,j}.$$

The wild oscillations in the computed solution are evidence of the numerical instability of the method, with an inappropriate ratio of step sizes. The temperature is plotted in Fig. 15.8; distance along the rod goes from left to right, and time goes from front to back. The following tabulation shows the computed solution for the first six time steps.

$x = 0.0$	0.2	0.4	0.6	0.8	1.0
0	0.0016	0.0256	0.1296	0.4096	1
0	0.024	0.1056	0.3056	0.72	1
0	0.0816	0.224	0.52	0.5856	1
0	0.1424	0.3776	0.2896	0.9344	1
0	0.2352	0.0544	1.0224	0.3552	1
0	−0.1808	1.2032	−0.6128	1.6672	1

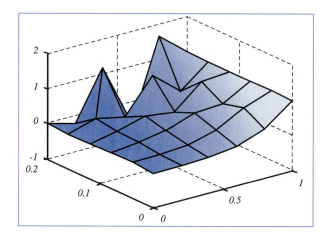

FIGURE 15.8 Unstable solution of heat equation.

15.1.2 Implicit Method for Solving Heat Equation

Consider again the PDE

$$u_t = c\, u_{xx}, \qquad \text{for } 0 < x < a, \qquad 0 < t \le T.$$

Replacing the space derivative by a centered difference at the *forward* time step $j + 1$ and the time derivative by a *forward* difference gives

$$\frac{1}{k}\left[u_{i,j+1} - u_{i,j}\right] = \frac{c}{h^2}\left[u_{i-1,j+1} - 2u_{i,j+1} + u_{i+1,j+1}\right],$$

or

$$u_{i,j} = (-r)u_{i-1,j+1} + (1 + 2r)\, u_{i,j+1} + (-r)u_{i+1,j+1},$$

where $r = \dfrac{ck}{h^2}$. This method is unconditionally stable.

The points involved in the calculations are illustrated in Fig. 15.9. Unlike calculations in the explicit method, calculations for a point at the $j + 1$ time level depend

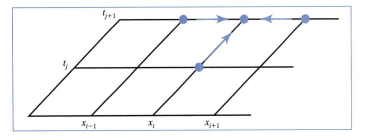

FIGURE 15.9 Values needed for computation at time $j + 1$.

both on the results from one point at the jth time level and on other points at the $(j+1)$th level. The resulting system of equations can be solved by techniques discussed in Chapter 6. The tridiagonal system must be solved at each time step, with a different right-hand side, so LU factorization of the tridiagonal system is an efficient approach, as given in the MATLAB function that follows Example 15.3.

Example 15.3 Temperature in a Rod, Implicit Method

Let the temperature in a rod (of unit length) be given by the PDE

$$u_t - u_{xx} = 0, \qquad \text{for } 0 < x < 1, \qquad 0 < t < T.$$

The initial conditions are

$$u(x, 0) = x^4, \qquad 0 \le x \le 1,$$

and the boundary conditions are

$$u(0, t) = 0, \qquad u(1, t) = 1, \qquad 0 < t < T.$$

Consider a fairly coarse mesh, with $n = 5$, so that $h = \Delta x = 0.2$, and take $m = 5$ and $T = 0.2$, so that $k = \Delta t = 0.04$. With these parameter values, we get

$$r = \frac{ck}{h^2} = \frac{\Delta t}{(\Delta x)^2} = 1.0, \text{ and the general equation}$$

$$u_{i,j} = -r u_{i-1,j+1} + (1 + 2r)u_{i,j+1} - r u_{i+1,j+1}$$

simplifies to

$$-u_{i-1,j+1} + 3u_{i,j+1} - u_{i+1,j+1} = u_{i,j}.$$

We must find values of u at the node points $i = 1, 2, 3$, and 4 for each time step; u is given by the boundary conditions for $i = 0$ and $i = 5$. To go from the initial conditions ($t = 0$) to the solution at the first time step ($t = 0.04$) requires that the following tridiagonal system be solved:

$$
\begin{aligned}
3u_{1,1} - u_{2,1} &&&= u_{1,0} + u_{0,1} = 0.0016 + 0.0, \\
-u_{1,1} + 3u_{2,1} - u_{3,1} &&&= u_{2,0} = 0.0256, \\
-u_{2,1} + 3u_{3,1} - u_{4,1} &&= u_{3,0} &= 0.1296, \\
-u_{3,1} + 3u_{4,1} &&= u_{4,0} + u_{5,1} &= 0.4096 + 1.0.
\end{aligned}
$$

The computed values are

$$u_{11} = 0.037033, \qquad u_{21} = 0.1095, \qquad u_{31} = 0.26586, \qquad u_{41} = 0.55849.$$

The right-hand side for the second time step is

$$(0.037033, 0.1095, 0.26586, 1.55849).$$

Repeating the calculations, using the right-hand side found from the solution at the previous time step, gives the solution illustrated in Fig. 15.10 and with values listed in Table 15.1.

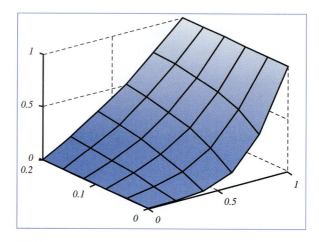

FIGURE 15.10 Temperature in a rod, found by implicit method.

Table 15.1 Temperature in a rod; solution for $t = 0.00$ to $t = 0.32$.

0	0.0016	0.0256	0.1296	0.4096	1
0	0.037033	0.1095	0.26586	0.55849	1
0	0.072904	0.18168	0.36264	0.64038	1
0	0.10387	0.2387	0.43055	0.69031	1
0	0.1286	0.28192	0.47846	0.72292	1
0	0.14753	0.314	0.51254	0.74515	1

MATLAB Function for Solving Heat Equation, Implicit Method

```
function zz = Heat_Imp(f,  g1,  g2,  a,  T,  n,  m,  c)
%   to solve w_t = c w_xx              on  0 ≤ x ≤ a, 0 ≤ t ≤ T.
%   initial condition   w(x, 0) = f(x)       0 ≤ x ≤ a
%   boundary conditions w(0, t) = g1(t)    w(a, t) = g2(t)    0 < t
%   define mesh:   n = subdivisions for x, m = subdivisions for t
```

```
%    define mesh spacing and parameters
     h = a/n;      k = T/m;     r = c*k/h^2;
     x = h : h : h*(n-1);       t = k : k: k*m;
     w00 = feval(f, 0);         wx0 = feval(f, x);     wa0 = feval(f, a);
     w0t = feval(g1, t);        wat = feval(g2, t);
%    Solve w(i, j) = (-r)w(i-1, j+1) + (1+ 2r) w(i,j+1) + (-r)w(i+1,j+1)
     d = (1+2*r)*ones(1 : n-1);            %  Define tridiagonal system
     aa = -r*ones(1 : n-2);   aa(n-1) = 0;
     b = -r*ones(1 : n-1);     b(1) = 0;
     [dd, bb] = LU_tridiag(aa, d, b);              % Factor system
%    Solution for first time step
       cc(1) = r*w0t(1) + wx0(1);                      % form right-hand side
       cc(2 : n-2) = wx0(2 : n-2);
       cc(n-1) = r*wat(1) + wx0(n-1);
       x = LU_tridiag_solve(aa, dd, bb, cc);
       w(1 : n-1, 1) = x(1 : n-1)';                    % store solution in w
%    for time steps, j = 2 . . . m
       for j = 2 : m
           cc(1) = r*w0t(j) + w(1,j-1);                % form right-hand side
           cc(2 : n-2) = w(2 : n-2, j-1);
           cc(n-1) = r*wat(j) + w(n-1, j-1);
           x = LU_tridiag_solve(aa, dd, bb, cc);
           w(1 : n-1, j) = x(1 : n-1)';                % store solution in w
       end
% Display solution with I.C. and B.C.; x from left to right
     zz = w';    zz = [ w0t        zz         wat];
     ww = [ w00        wx0        wa0];
     zz = [ ww,
           zz];
```

Discussion

The finite-difference representations of the partial derivatives in the heat equation are as given for the explicit method, except that the second derivative is approximated at step $j+1$, rather than at step j. Thus, we have

$$u_t(x_i, t_j) = \frac{1}{k}[u_{i,j+1} - u_{i,j}] + O(k)$$

and

$$u_{xx}(x_i, t_{j+1}) = \frac{1}{h^2}[u_{i-1,j+1} - 2u_{i,j+1} + u_{i+1,j+1}] + O(h^2).$$

Substituting into the PDE and simplifying shows that the truncation error for the implicit method is the same as for the explicit method, i.e., $O(h^2 + k)$.

To show that the implicit method is unconditionally stable, consider the matrix-vector form of the process, viz.,

$$\begin{bmatrix} 1+2r & -r & & & \\ -r & 1+2r & -r & & \\ & \cdot & \vdots & \cdot & \\ & & -r & 1+2r & -r \\ & & & -r & 1+2r \end{bmatrix} \begin{bmatrix} u(1, j+1) \\ \vdots \\ u(n, j+1) \end{bmatrix} = \begin{bmatrix} u(1, j) \\ \vdots \\ u(n, j) \end{bmatrix},$$

or

$$\mathbf{A}\mathbf{u}(:, j+1) = \mathbf{u}(:j).$$

For analysis (but not for actual computation!), we write the latter equation as

$$\mathbf{A}^{-1}\mathbf{u}(:, j) = \mathbf{u}(:j+1),$$

so that, by the same reasoning as for the explicit method, stability is assured if λ, the dominant eigenvalue of $\mathbf{A}^{-1}$, satisfies $|\lambda| = 1$. In terms of the eigenvalues of $\mathbf{A}$, the condition becomes

$$|\mu| \geq 1,$$

where μ is the eigenvalue of $\mathbf{A}$ with the smallest magnitude. By the Gerschgorin theorem, this condition is true regardless of the value of r.

15.1.3 Crank–Nicolson Method for Solving Heat Equation

Using the average of the centered difference at the forward time step $j+1$ and the current time step j gives

$$\frac{1}{k}[u_{i,j+1} - u_{i,j}] = \frac{c}{2h^2}[u_{i-1,j} - 2u_{i,j} + u_{i+1,j}] + \frac{c}{2h^2}[u_{i-1,j+1} - 2u_{i,j+1} + u_{i+1,j+1}].$$

Defining $r = \dfrac{ck}{h^2}$ as before, we can write the equations as

$$-\frac{r}{2}u_{i-1,j+1} + (1+r)u_{i,j+1} - \frac{r}{2}u_{i+1,j+1} = \frac{r}{2}u_{i-1,j} + (1-r)u_{i,j} + \frac{r}{2}u_{i+1,j}.$$

A general two-stage method with weighting factor λ, for $0 \le \lambda \le 1$, gives

$$\frac{1}{k}[u_{i,j+1} - u_{i,j}] = \frac{\lambda}{h^2}[u_{i+1,j} - 2u_{i,j} + u_{i-1,j}]$$

$$+ \frac{1-\lambda}{h^2}[u_{i+1,j+1} - 2u_{i,j+1} + u_{i-1,j+1}],$$

or, in terms of r and λ,

$$-r\lambda u_{i-1,j+1} + (1+2r\lambda)u_{i,j+1} - r\lambda u_{i+1,j+1} =$$
$$r(1-\lambda)u_{i-1,j} + (1-2r(1-\lambda))u_{i,j} + r(1-\lambda)u_{i+1,j}.$$

The resulting system of equations can be solved by techniques discussed in Chapter 6.

The Crank–Nicolson method is unconditionally stable and has better trunca-tion error, $O(h^2 + k^2)$, than the basic implicit method. For the appropriate choice of λ, the truncation error for the general two-stage method is $O(h^4)$; this occurs when $2r\lambda = r - 1/6$. The truncation error is reduced to $O(h^6)$ if the step sizes are chosen so that $r = \frac{\sqrt{5}}{10}$ and $\lambda = \frac{3-\sqrt{5}}{6}$. (See Ames, 1992, p. 65, for further discussion.)

Example 15.4 Temperature in a Rod, Crank–Nicolson Method

Consider again the temperature of a rod of unit length, given by the PDE

$$u_t - u_{xx} = 0, \qquad \text{for } 0 < x < 1, \qquad 0 < t,$$

with initial temperature

$$u(x, 0) = x^4, \qquad 0 < x < 1,$$

and temperatures of

$$u(0, t) = 0, \qquad u(1, t) = 1, \qquad 0 < t,$$

at $x = 0$ and $x = 1$, respectively. Take a fairly coarse mesh, with $h = 0.2$ and $k = 0.04$, so that $r = \frac{ck}{h^2} = 1$. In this case, the general equation

$$-\frac{r}{2}u_{i-1,j+1} + (1+r)u_{i,j+1} - \frac{r}{2}u_{i+1,j+1} = \frac{r}{2}u_{i-1,j} + (1-r)u_{i,j} + \frac{r}{2}u_{i+1,j}$$

simplifies to

$$-0.5\,u_{i-1,j+1} + 2u_{i,j+1} - 0.5u_{i+1,j+1} = 0.5u_{i-1,j} + 0.5u_{i+1,j}$$

To find the solution at the first time step, the equations are

$$\begin{aligned}
+\ 2u_{1,1} - 0.5u_{2,1} \qquad\qquad &= 0.5(u_{0,0} + u_{2,0} + u_{0,1}) = 0.0128, \\
-0.5u_{1,1} +\ 2u_{2,1} - 0.5u_{3,1} \qquad &= 0.5(u_{1,0} + u_{3,0}) \qquad = 0.0656, \\
-0.5u_{2,1} +\ 2u_{3,1} - 0.5u_{4,1} &= 0.5(u_{2,0} + u_{4,0}) \qquad = 0.2176, \\
-0.5u_{3,1} +\ 2u_{4,1} &= 0.5(u_{3,0} + u_{5,0} + u_{5,1}) = 1.0648.
\end{aligned}$$

The solution from the MATLAB function that follows is shown in Table 15.2 for the first five time steps, and in Fig. 15.11 for $0 < t < 1$. The true steady-state solution is $u(x) = x$.

Table 15.2 Temperature in a rod, solution by Crank–Nicolson method.

$t \backslash x$	0.0	0.2	0.4	0.6	0.8	1.0
0.00	0.00	0.0016	0.0256	0.1296	0.4096	1.00
0.04	0.00	0.034794	0.11358	0.28831	0.60448	1.00
0.08	0.00	0.078313	0.19968	0.39728	0.6714	1.00
0.12	0.00	0.11578	0.26343	0.46235	0.71491	1.00
0.16	0.00	0.14258	0.3069	0.50689	0.74231	1.00
0.20	0.00	0.16092	0.33678	0.53672	0.7609	1.00

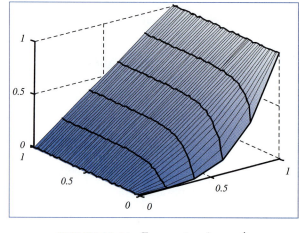

FIGURE 15.11 Temperature in a rod.

MATLAB Function for Solving the Heat Equation, Using Crank-Nicolson Method

```
function zz  = Heat_CN(f,  g1,  g2,  a,  T,  n,  m,  c)
%    to solve w_t = c w_xx              on  0 ≤ x ≤ a, 0 ≤ t ≤ T.
%     initial condition      w(x, 0) = f(x)       0 ≤ x ≤ a
%     boundary conditions    w(0, t) = g1(t);   w(L, t) = g2(t);
%     define mesh
%         n = number of subdivisions for x;
%         m = number of subdivisions for t;
%     define mesh spacing and parameters
    h = a/n;    k = T/m;    r = c*k/h^2;    rr = 0.5*r;
```

```
  x = h : h : h*(n-1);     t = k : k: k*m;
  w00 = feval(f, 0);    wx0 = feval(f, x);    wa0 = feval(f, a);
  w0t = feval(g1, t);   wat = feval(g2, t);
%   Define tridiagonal system
  d = (1+r)*ones(1 : n-1);
  aa = -rr*ones(1 : n-2);    aa(n-1) = 0;
  b = -rr*ones(1 : n-1) ;    bb(1) = 0;
  [dd, bb] = LU_tridiag(aa, d, b);
%  Solution for first time step
  cc(1) = rr*w0t(1)+ rr*w00+ (1-r)*wx0(1)+ rr*wx0(2);
  cc(2:n-2) = rr*wx0(1:n-3)+ (1-r)*wx0(2:n-2)+ rr*wx0(3:n-1);
  cc(n-1) = rr*wx0(n-2) + (1-r)*wx0(n-1) + rr*wa0 + rr*wat(1);
  x =  LU_tridiag_solve(aa, dd, bb, cc);
  w(1:n-1, 1) = x(1:n-1)';
%  for each time step, j = 2 ... m
  for j = 2 : m
    cc(1) = rr*w0t(j-1) + rr*w0t(j) + (1-r)*w(1,j-1) + rr*w(2,j-1);
    cc(2:n-2) = rr*w(1:n-3,j-1) + (1-r)*w(2:n-2,j-1) + rr*w(3:n-1, j-1);
    cc(n-1) = rr*wat(j-1) +rr*w(n-2,j-1) + (1-r)*w(n-1,j-1) + rr*wat(j);
    x =  LU_tridiag_solve(aa, dd, bb, cc);
    w(1 : n-1, j) = x(1 : n-1)';
  end
%  Display solution with initial and boundary conditions;
%  x from left to right
    zz = w';
    zz = [w0t    zz    wat];
    ww = [ w00    wx0    wa0];
    zz = [ ww,
           zz];
```

15.1.4 Heat Equation with Insulated Boundary

The form of the boundary conditions depends on the physical situation being described. Keeping an end of the rod insulated corresponds to specifying that the partial derivative u_x is zero at that end of the rod; i.e.,

$$u_x(0, t) = 0 \quad \text{or} \quad u_x(a, t) = 0.$$

We illustrate the modification to the explicit method for the case of the temperature of the rod given at $x = 0$, but the end of the rod at $x = a$ insulated, so that $u_x(a, t) = 0$.

The recommended approach to a boundary condition specified by a derivative is to add a fictitious point to the grid; for the situation described here, we extend the grid to include the point x_{n+1} at each time step. Using the central difference formula, we find that the boundary condition $u_x(a, t)$ becomes

$$\frac{1}{2k}\left[u_{n+1,j} - u_{n-1,j}\right] = 0,$$

or

$$u_{n+1,j} = u_{n-1,j}.$$

Applying the general update equation at $i = n$ gives

$$u_{n,j+1} = r\,u_{n-1,j} + (1 - 2r)u_{n,j} + r\,u_{n+1,j},$$

which includes the fictitious point. Substituting the information from the boundary condition, we get

$$u_{n,j+1} = r\,u_{n-1,j} + (1 - 2r)u_{n,j} + r\,u_{n-1,j} = 2r\,u_{n-1,j} + (1 - 2r)u_{n,j}.$$

The system of equations is

$$u_{1,j+1} = r\,u_{0,j} + (1 - 2r)u_{1,j} + r\,u_{2,j}, \qquad i = 1,$$

$$u_{i,j+1} = r\,u_{i-1,j} + (1 - 2r)u_{i,j} + r\,u_{i+1,j}, \qquad i = 2, \ldots, n-1,$$

$$u_{n,j+1} = 2r\,u_{n-1,j} + (1 - 2r)u_{n,j}, \qquad i = n.$$

For comparison, the equations for the explicit method (with u_0 and u_n given by boundary conditions) are

$$u_{1,j+1} = r\,u_{0,j} + (1 - 2r)u_{1,j} + r\,u_{2,j}, \qquad i = 1,$$

$$u_{i,j+1} = r\,u_{i-1,j} + (1 - 2r)\,u_{i,j} + r\,u_{i+1,j}, \qquad i = 2, \ldots, n-2,$$

$$u_{n-1,j+1} = r\,u_{n-2,j} + (1 - 2r)u_{n-1,j} + r\,u_{n,j}, \qquad i = n-1.$$

15.2   WAVE EQUATION: HYPERBOLIC PDE

The standard example of a hyperbolic equation is the one-dimensional wave equation

$$u_{tt} - c^2 u_{xx} = 0, \qquad \text{for } 0 \le x \le a \text{ and } 0 \le t.$$

Initial conditions are given for $u(x, 0)$ and $u_t(x, 0)$:

$$u(x, 0) = f_1(x), \qquad u_t(x, 0) = f_2(x), \qquad \text{for } 0 \le x \le a.$$

Boundary conditions are given at $x = 0$ and $x = a$:

$$u(0, t) = g_1(t), \qquad u(a, t) = g_2(t), \qquad \text{for } 0 < t.$$

Although the one-dimensional wave equation does not usually require a numerical solution, it serves as an introduction to higher dimensional wave equations, for which numerical methods are more likely to be worthwhile.

The mesh is given as before:

$$x_i = ih, \quad i = 0, 1, \ldots, n, \quad h = \Delta x = a/n,$$

$$t_j = jk, \quad j = 0, 1, \ldots, m, \quad k = \Delta t = T/m.$$

As with the heat equation, there are several choices for finite-difference approximations for u_{xx} and u_{tt}; each choice yields a method with certain characteristics—explicit or implicit technique, stability requirements, and truncation error. We consider an explicit method and an implicit method, each based on central difference formulas for the second derivatives.

15.2.1 Explicit Method for Solving Wave Equation

Replacing the space derivative in the wave equation by the difference formula at the jth time step, i.e.,

$$c^2 u_{xx} \Rightarrow \frac{c^2}{h^2} [u_{i-1,j} - 2u_{i,j} + u_{i+1,j}],$$

and replacing the time derivative by the difference formula at the ith space step, i. e.,

$$u_{tt} \Rightarrow \frac{1}{k^2} [u_{i,j-1} - 2u_{i,j} + u_{i,j+1}],$$

gives

$$\frac{1}{k^2} [u_{i,j-1} - 2u_{i,j} + u_{i,j+1}] = \frac{c^2}{h^2} [u_{i-1,j} - 2u_{i,j} + u_{i+1,j}].$$

In a similar manner to our approach for the heat equation, we define the parameter

$$p = \frac{ck}{h} = c \frac{\Delta t}{\Delta x},$$

solve for the unknown $u_{i,j+1}$, and rearrange the order of the terms on the right-hand side to obtain

$$u_{i,j+1} = p^2 u_{i-1,j} + 2(1 - p^2)u_{i,j} + p^2 u_{i+1,j} - u_{i,j-1}.$$

Since the solution is known for $t = 0$, we can solve for $u_{i,j+1}$, starting with $j = 0$. However, we do not know $u_{i,-1}$. To overcome this difficulty, we use the initial condition for $u_t(x,0) = f_2(x)$ and replace the time derivative by the centered difference formula to give

$$u_{i,1} - u_{i,-1} = 2k \, f_2(x_i).$$

The equation for u at the first time step now becomes

$$u_{i,1} = 0.5p^2 u_{i-1,0} + (1 - p^2)u_{i,0} + 0.5p^2 u_{i+1,0} + k f_2(x_i),$$

where the values of $u_{i-1,0}$, $u_{i,0}$, and $u_{i+1,0}$ are available from the initial condition $u(x,0) = f_1(x)$. The value of u at each subsequent time step can be found from the general equation

$$u_{i,j+1} = p^2 u_{i-1,j} + 2(1 - p^2)u_{i,j} + p^2 u_{i+1,j} - u_{i,j-1}.$$

There are two stability requirements, determined by the matrix of coefficients of u at the jth time step:

1. The sum of the coefficients of the $u(:, j)$ terms must be less than or equal to 2; this is satisfied for all choices of p, since $p^2 + 2(1 - p^2) + p^2 = 2$.
2. No coefficient of $u(:, j)$ is negative. (A negative coefficient on $u_{i,j-1}$ is fine.) This requires that $1 - p^2 \geq 0$, or $p \leq 1$ (i.e., $ck \leq h$). (For further discussion, see Ames, 1992, p. 266.)

Example 15.5 Vibrating String, Explicit Method, Stable Solution

Consider the motion of a vibrating string of unit length with both ends held fixed and an initial displacement described by the PDE

$$u_{tt} - u_{xx} = 0, \qquad \text{for } 0 < x < 1, \qquad 0 < t.$$

The initial conditions are

$$u(x, 0) = x(1 - x), \qquad u_t(x, 0) = 0, \qquad 0 < x < 1,$$

with boundary conditions of

$$u(0, t) = 0, \qquad u(1, t) = 0, \qquad 0 < t,$$

at $x = 0$ and $x = 1$, respectively. We first take a fairly coarse mesh, $h = \Delta x = 0.2$; the stability condition, $p = \dfrac{\Delta t}{\Delta x} \leq 1.0$, requires that $k = \Delta t \leq 0.2$. Using the maximum allowed value of Δt (so that $p = 1$) results in a simplification of the general equation for the first time step,

$$u_{i,1} = 0.5p^2 u_{i-1,0} + (1 - p^2)u_{i,0} + 0.5p^2 u_{i+1,0} + (\Delta t) \, g(x_i),$$

to the form $u_{i,1} = 0.5 \, u_{i-1,0} + 0.5u_{i+1,0} + 0.2g(x_i) = 0.5u_{i-1,0} + 0.5u_{i+1,0}$.

The initial and boundary conditions (bold), and the solution at the first time step (italics) are given in the following tabulation:

	$x =$	0.0	0.2	0.4	0.6	0.8	1.0
t	$j \backslash i$	0	1	2	3	4	5
0.0	0	**0.0**	**0.16**	**0.24**	**0.24**	**0.16**	**0.0**
0.2	1	**0.0**	*0.12*	*0.20*	*0.20*	*0.12*	**0.0**

The value of u at each subsequent time step can be found from the general equation $u_{i,j+1} = u_{i-1,j} + u_{i+1,j} - u_{i,j-1}$. The solution at the second time step (shown in italics) is shown in the following table:

$x =$		0.0	0.2	0.4	0.6	0.8	1.0
t	$j\backslash i$	0	1	2	3	4	5
0.0	0	**0.0**	**0.16**	**0.24**	**0.24**	**0.16**	**0.0**
0.2	1	**0.0**	0.12	0.20	0.20	0.12	**0.0**
0.4	2	**0.0**	*0.04*	*0.08*	*0.08*	*0.04*	**0.0**

The solution, using the MATLAB script that follows, is graphed in Fig. 15.12.

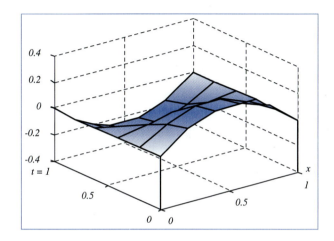

FIGURE 15.12 Vibrating string

MATLAB Script for Wave Equation

```
%  S_15_5
%  script for wave equation
%  The Hyperbolic PDE
%       w_tt - c^2 w_xx = 0        0 < x < a,  0 < t < T
%  Initial conditions
%       w(x, 0) = f1(x)        w_t(x, 0)= f2(x)       0 < x < a
%  Boundary conditions
%       w(0, t) = 0            w(a, t) = 0            0 < t < T
% define
a = 1                 % length of string
T = 1                 % length of time interval
n = 5                 % number of space steps
m = 5                 % number of time steps
```

```
h = a/n;                % space step size
k = T/m;                % time step size
c = 1;                  % coefficient of w_xx in PDE
f1 = 'x.*(1-x)';        % function to define initial displacement
f2 = ' 0*x';            % function to define initial velocity
x = h:h:(a-h);          % define space grid points
t = k:k:T;              % define time grid points
% initial displacement and velocity (as column vector)
wx0 = eval(f1)';        dwx0 = eval(f2)';
% initial displacement at x = 0 and x = a
w00 = 0;                wa0 = 0;
% define boundary condition at x = 0 and x = a
w0t = zeros(m,1);    wat = w0t;
% define computation parameters
p = (c*k/h)^2;       p2 = p/2;    pm2 = 2*(1-p);
%  Solution at first time step
w(1,1) = (1 - p)*wx0(1)+ p2*wx0(2) + k*dwx0(1);
w(2:n-2,1)=p2*wx0(1:n-3)+(1-p)*wx0(2:n-2)+p2*wx0(3:n-1)+k*dwx0(2:n-2);
w(n-1,1) = p2*wx0(n-2)+(1-p)*wx0(n-1) + k*dwx0(n-1);
%  Solution at second time step
w(1,2) = pm2*w(1,1) + p*w(2,1) - wx0(1);
w(2:n-2,2) = p*w(1:n-3,1)+pm2*w(2:n-2,1)+p*w(3:n-1,1)-wx0(2:n-2);
w(n-1,2) = p*w(n-2,1) + pm2*w(n-1,1) - wx0(n-1);
%  Solution at remaining time steps
for j = 3:m
  w(1,j) = pm2*w(1,j-1) + p*w(2,j-1) - w(1,j-2);
  w(2:n-2,j)= p*w(1:n-3,j-1)+pm2*w(2:n-2,j-1)+p*w(3:n-1,j-1)- w(2:n-2,j-2);
  w(n-1,j) = p*w(n-2,j-1) + pm2*w(n-1,j-1) - w(n-1,j-2);
end
%    Display solution with initial and B.C; x from left to right
zz = [ w0t    w'      wat ];
ww = [ w00    wx0'    wa0 ];
zz = [ ww,
       zz ]
x = 0:h:a;
t = 0:k:T;
mesh(x,t,zz)
```

15.2.2 Implicit Method for Solving Wave Equation

As is the case with parabolic equations, implicit finite-difference solutions have stability advantages for hyperbolic equations also. A simple implicit scheme (Ames, 1992, p. 284) results from replacing the time derivative by the difference formula at the ith space step:

$$u_{tt} \Rightarrow \frac{1}{k^2}[u_{i,j-1} - 2u_{i,j} + u_{i,j+1}],$$

and replacing the space derivative by an average of the differences at the $(j+1)$st and $(j-1)$st time steps

$$c^2 u_{xx} \Rightarrow \frac{c^2}{2h^2}[u_{i-1,j+1} - 2u_{i,j+1} + u_{i+1,j+1} + u_{i-1,j-1} - 2u_{i,j-1} + u_{i+1,j-1}].$$

The difference equation then becomes

$$u_{i,j-1} - 2u_{i,j} + u_{i,j+1} =$$

$$\frac{c^2 k^2}{2h^2}[u_{i-1,j+1} - 2u_{i,j+1} + u_{i+1,j+1} + u_{i-1,j-1} - 2u_{i,j-1} + u_{i+1,j+1}].$$

In a manner similar to that for the heat equation, we define $p = \dfrac{ck}{h}$, so that

$$-p^2 u_{i-1,j+1} + 2(1+p^2)u_{i,j+1} - p^2 u_{i+1,j+1} = 4u_{i,j} + p^2 u_{i-1,j-1} - 2(1+p^2)u_{i,j-1} + p^2 u_{i+1,j-1}.$$

Since the solution is known for $t = 0$, we can solve for $u_{i,j+1}$, starting with $j = 0$. However, we do not know $u_{i,-1}$. To overcome this difficulty, we use the initial condition for $u_t(x, 0) = f_2(x)$ and replace the time derivative by the centered difference formula to give

$$u_{i,-1} = u_{i,1} - 2kf_2(x_i).$$

The equations for $j = 0$ then have the form

$$4(1+p^2)u_{1,1} - 2p^2 u_{2,1} =$$
$$4u_{1,0} - 2p^2 kf_2(x_0) + 4(1+p^2)kf_2(x_1) - 2p^2 kf_2(x_2) + 2p^2 u_{0,1},$$

$$-2p^2 u_{1,1} + 4(1+p^2)u_{2,1} - 2p^2 u_{3,1} =$$
$$4u_{2,0} - 2p^2 kf_2(x_1) + 4(1+p^2)kf_2(x_2) - 2p^2 kf_2(x_3),$$
$$\vdots$$

$$-2p^2 u_{i-1,1} + 4(1+p^2)u_{i,1} - 2p^2 u_{i+1,1} =$$
$$4u_{i,0} - 2p^2 kf_2(x_{i-1}) + 4(1+p^2)kf_2(x_i) - 2p^2 kf_2(x_{i+1}),$$
$$\vdots$$

$$-2p^2 u_{n-1,1} + 4(1+p^2)u_{n,1} =$$
$$4u_{n,0} - 2p^2 kf_2(x_{n-1}) + 4(1+p^2)kf_2(x_n) - 2p^2 kf_2(x_{n+1}) + 2p^2 u_{n+1,1}.$$

The value of u at each subsequent time step can be found from

$$2(1+p^2)u_{1,j+1} - p^2u_{2,j+1} = 4u_{1,j} - 2(1+p^2)u_{1,j-1} + p^2u_{2,j-1} + p^2u_{0,j+1} + p^2u_{0,j-1},$$

$$-p^2u_{1,j+1} + 2(1+p^2)u_{2,j+1} - p^2u_{3,j+1} = 4u_{2,j} + p^2u_{1,j-1} - 2(1+p^2)u_{2,j-1} + p^2u_{3,j-1}$$

$$\vdots$$

$$-p^2u_{i-1,j+1} + 2(1+p^2)u_{i,j+1} - p^2u_{i+1,j+1} = 4u_{i,j} + p^2u_{i-1,j-1} - 2(1+p^2)u_{i,j-1} + p^2u_{i+1,j-1},$$

$$\vdots$$

$$-p^2u_{n-1,j+1} + 2(1+p^2)u_{n,j+1} =$$
$$4u_{n,j} + p^2u_{n-1,j-1} - 2(1+p^2)u_{n,j-1} + p^2u_{n+1,j-1} + p^2u_{n+1,j+1}.$$

This system of equations is tridiagonal and thus can be solved by the Thomas algorithm of Chapter 3. Iterative methods can also be used, since the linear system is diagonally dominant. (The diagonal elements are $2(1 + p^2)$, and the off-diagonal elements, two in each equation, are $-p$.)

This implicit method has unrestricted stability (Ames, 1992, p. 285; see Ames as well for a discussion of the general three-level implicit form. The preceding implicit method corresponds to $\lambda = 1/2$, the explicit method corresponds to $\lambda = 0$, and the general method has unrestricted stability for $\lambda \geq 1/4$.)

15.3 POISSON EQUATION: ELLIPTIC PDE

The standard example of an elliptic equation is the two-dimensional Laplacian or potential equation

$$u_{xx} + u_{yy} = 0, \qquad a \leq x \leq b, \qquad c \leq y \leq d,$$

or Poisson's equation,

$$u_{xx} + u_{yy} = f(x,y), \qquad a \leq x \leq b, \qquad c \leq y \leq d.$$

The simplest boundary conditions specify the value of the function along each of the four sides of the rectangular domain:

$$u(a,y) = g_1(y), \qquad u(b,y) = g_2(y), \qquad c < y < d,$$
$$u(x,c) = g_3(x), \qquad u(x,d) = g_4(x), \qquad a < x < b.$$

We define a mesh in the x–y plane:

$$x_i = a + ih, \qquad i = 0, 1, \ldots, n, \qquad h = \Delta x = (b-a)/n,$$
$$y_j = c + jk, \qquad j = 0, 1, \ldots, m, \qquad k = \Delta y = (d-c)/m.$$

We denote the (approximate) value of $u(x,y)$ at the point (x_i, y_j) as u_{ij} (see Fig. 15.13) and the value of the right-hand side, $f(x_i, y_j)$, as f_{ij}. Replacing the second derivatives by centered differences gives a system of algebraic equations for the function values at the mesh points:

$$\frac{1}{k^2}[u_{i,j+1} - 2u_{i,j} + u_{i,j-1}] + \frac{1}{h^2}[u_{i+1,j} - 2u_{i,j} + u_{i-1,j}] = f_{ij}.$$

However, unlike the situation with the wave equation, no information is given that allows us to solve these equations in a sequential manner. Due to the somewhat more extensive computations needed to obtain interesting results, we first present a MATLAB function for Poisson's equation and then illustrate the process with examples.

The first example is the potential equation problem solved earlier in Chapter 3. However, using the MATLAB function, one need not form the coefficient matrix explicitly. The second example is a Poisson equation with the same boundary conditions as those for the potential equation. Gauss-Seidel iteration is built directly into the MATLAB function Poisson. This means that changing the order of the updates would change the details of the intermediate results, but not the final answer.

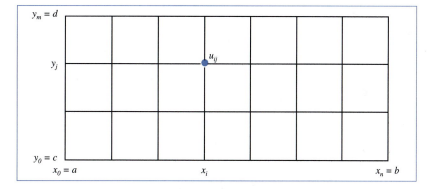

FIGURE 15.13 Mesh for Poisson and Laplace equations.

MATLAB Function for the Poisson Equation

```
function z = Poisson(f, g1, g2, g3, g4, a, b, c, d, n, m, max_it)
%   Solve the Elliptic PDE
%       u_tt + u_xx = f(x,y)                    a < x < b,  c < y < d
%   with boundary conditions
%       u(a,y) = g1(y)       u(b,y) = g2(y)                 c < y < d
%       u(x,c) = g3(x)       u(x,d) = g4(x)                 a < x < b
h = (b-a)/n;          k = (d-c)/m;     r = (h/k)^2;
c1 = 1/(2*r + 2);    c2 = r*c1;      c3 = c1*h^2;
x = 1:1:n-1;          x = a + h*x;    y = 1:1:m-1;     y = c + k*y;
%   evaluate boundary and initial conditions
wa(1:m-1) = feval(g1, y(1:m-1));   wb(1:m-1) = feval(g2, y(1:m-1));
wc(1:n-1) = feval(g3, x(1:n-1));   wd(1:n-1) = feval(g4, x(1:n-1));
```

```
for i = 1 : n-1
    fij(i, 1:m-1) = feval(f, x(i), y(1:m-1));
end
w = zeros(n-1, m-1);
for it = 1: max_it
%   solution at the 4 corners
    w(1,1) = c2*(w(1,2) + wc(1)) + c1*(w(2,1) + wa(1)) - c3*fij(1,1);
    w(1, m-1) = c2*(wd(1) +w(1, m-2)) +c1*(w(2, m-1) + wa(m-1)) - c3*fij(1,m-1);
    w(n-1,1) = c2*(w(n-1, 2) + wc(n-1)) + c1*(wb(1) + w(n-2,1)) - c3*fij(n-1,1);
    w(n-1,m-1) = c2*wd(n-1) + c2*w(n-1,m-2) + c1*wb(m-1)  ...
                              + c1*w(n-2,m-1)- c3*fij(n-1,m-1);
%   solution along the 4 sides
    w(2:n-2,1) = c2*w(2:n-2,2) + c2*wc(2:n-2) + c1*w(3:n-1,1) + ...
                        c1*w(1:n-3,1) - c3*fij(2:n-2,1);
    w(2:n-2, m-1) = c2*wd(2:n-2) + c2*w(2:n-2,m-2) + c1*w(3:n-1, m-1) ...
                        + c1*w(1:n-3, m-1) - c3*fij(2:n-2, m-1);
    w(1, 2:m-2) = c2*(w(1,3:m-1) + w(1,1:m-3)) + c1*(w(2,2:m-2) + ...
                                   wa(2:m-2)) - c3*fij(1,2:m-2);
    w(n-1, 2:m-2) = c2*(w(n-1,3:m-1) + w(n-1,1:m-3)) + ...
                        c1*(wb(j)+ w(n-2, 2:m-2))- c3*fij(n-1, 2:m-2);
%   solution at interior points
    for j = 2: m-2
        w(2:n-2, j) = c2*(w(2:n-2, j+1) + w(2:n-2, j-1)) + ....
                        c1*(w(3:n-1, j) + w(1:n-3,j))- c3*fij(2:n-2, j);
    end
end
% display solution with BC, x from left to right
wac = 0.5*(feval(g1,c) + feval(g3,a));
wbc = 0.5*(feval(g3,b) + feval(g2,c));
wad = 0.5*(feval(g1,d) + feval(g4,a));
wbd = 0.5*(feval(g4,b) + feval(g2,d));
z = w'; z = [ wa' z wb'];
wcc = [wac wc wbc]; wdd = [ wad wd wbd];
z = [ wcc, z, wdd];
```

Example 15.6 Potential Equation

Consider the equation

$$u_{xx} + u_{yy} = 0, \qquad 0 \le x \le 1, \qquad 0 \le y \le 1,$$

with boundary conditions

$$u(0, y) = y^2, \qquad u(1, y) = 1, \qquad 0 < y < 1,$$
$$u(x, 0) = x^2, \qquad u(x, 1) = 1, \qquad 0 < x < 1.$$

The solutions after 1, 5, 20, and 50 iterations are shown in Fig. 15.14.

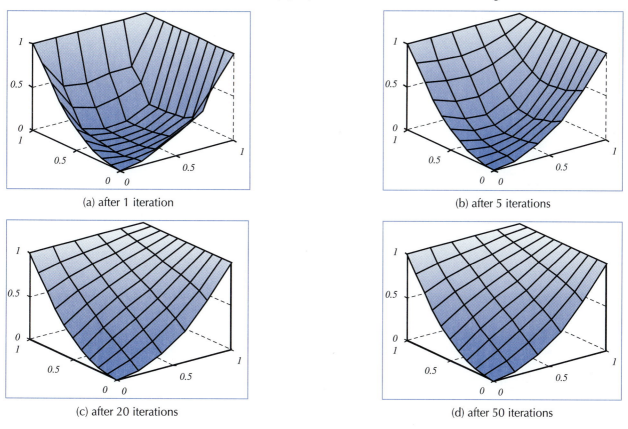

(a) after 1 iteration

(b) after 5 iterations

(c) after 20 iterations

(d) after 50 iterations

FIGURE 15.14   Solution of the potential equation.

MATLAB Script for Solving Poisson's PDE, Example 15.7

```
%   Script to solve Poisson's PDE
%       u_tt + u_xx = f(x,y)          a < x < b,  c < y < d
%   Subject to the boundary conditions
%   u(a,y) = g1(y)   u(b,y) = g2(y)    c < y < d
```

```
%     u(x,c) = g3(x)    u(x,d) = g4(x)      a < x < b
a = 0;   b = 1;   c = 0;   d = 1;    num_iter = 20;
n = 5;       m = 10;   h = (b-a)/n;    k = (d-c)/m;    r = (h/k)^2;
c1 = 1/(2*r + 2);   c2 = r*c1;   c3 = c1*h^2;
x = 1:1:n-1;   x = a + h*x;    y = 1:1:m-1;    y = c + k*y;
%       define and evaluate boundary conditions for Example 15.7
g1 = 'y.^2';    g3 = 'x.^2';
wac = 0;    wbc = 1;    wad = 1;    wbd = 1;
wa = eval(g1);   wb = ones(1,m-1);   wc = eval(g3);   wd = ones(1,n-1);
%    define and evaluate right-hand side of PDE
xx = x';
for j = 1:m-2
   xx = [xx    x' ];
end
yy = y;
for i = 1:n-2
   yy = [yy
         y];
end
ff = 'xx + yy';       f = eval(ff);      w = zeros(n-1, m-1);
for it = 1: num_iter
   %    solution at the 4 corners
   w(1,1) = c2*(w(1,2) +wc(1)) +c1*(w(2,1) +wa(1)) -c3*f(1,1);
   w(1,m-1) = c2*(wd(1) +w(1,m-2)) +c1*(w(2,m-1) +wa(m-1))- c3*f(1,m-1);
   w(n-1,1) = c2*(w(n-1,2) + wc(n-1)) + c1*(wb(1)+ w(n-2,1))- c3*f(n-1,1);
   w(n-1,m-1)= c2*wd(n-1)+c2*w(n-1,m-2)+c1*wb(m-1)+c1*w(n-2,m-1)- c3*f(n-1,m-1);
   %    solution along the 4 sides
   for i = 2:n-2
      w(i,1)= c2*w(i,2) +c2*wc(i) +c1*w(i+1,1) + c1*w(i-1,1) -c3*f(i,1);
      w(i,m-1) = c2*wd(i)+c2*w(i,m-2)+c1*w(i+1,m-1)+c1*w(i-1,m-1)- c3*f(i,m-1);
   end
   for j = 2:m-2
      w(1,j)   = c2*(w(1,j+1)+w(1,j-1)) +c1*(w(2,j) + wa(j))- c3*f(1,j);
      w(n-1,j) = c2*(w(n-1,j+1)+w(n-1,j-1)) +c1*(wb(j)+ w(n-2,j))- c3*f(n-1,j);
   end
   for j = 2:m-2 % solution at interior points
      for i = 2:n-2
         w(i,j) = c2*(w(i,j+1) + w(i,j-1)) + c1*(w(i+1,j) + w(i-1,j))- c3*f(i,j);
      end
   end
end
%     display solution with x going from left to right; also display BC
z = [ wa'  w'  wb'];   wcc = [wac  wc  wbc];   wdd = [ wad  wd  wbd];
z = [ wcc,
      z,
      wdd];
x = a:h:b;   y = c:k:d;  z, mesh(x,y,z)
```

Example 15.7 Poisson's Equation

Consider the equation

$$u_{xx} + u_{yy} = x + y, \qquad 0 \le x \le 1, \qquad 0 \le y \le 1,$$

with boundary conditions

$$u(0, y) = y^2, \qquad u(1, y) = 1, \qquad 0 < y < 1,$$
$$u(x, 0) = x^2, \qquad u(x, 1) = 1, \qquad 0 < x < 1.$$

The solutions after 1, 5, 20, and 50 iterations, based on the preceding MATLAB script, are shown in Fig. 15.15. The solution values change only slightly after the first 20 iterations.

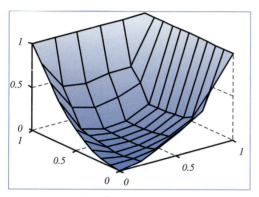

(a) after 1 iteration

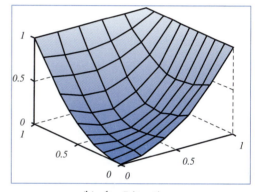

(b) after 5 iterations

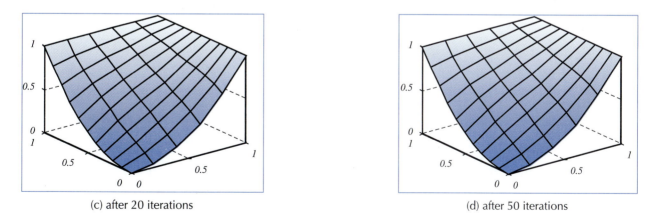

(c) after 20 iterations

(d) after 50 iterations

FIGURE 15.15   Solution of Poisson's equation.

Finite-difference methods for solving a two-dimensional Poisson equation

$$u_{xx} + u_{yy} = f(x, y)$$

on a rectangular region are based on dividing the domain of the problem into rectangular subdomains and approximating the solution at the mesh points. An alternative approach, known as the finite-element method, allows the domain to be divided into any convenient set of subregions (often triangular, but not necessarily of the same size). Rather than just finding the solution at the mesh or node points, an approximate solution of suitably simple form is found over the entire region. In the following discussion, we assume that the subregions are triangular.

The problem of solving the differential equation is converted into a corresponding problem of minimizing a functional that consists of an integral over the region (and, for certain types of boundary conditions, a line integral along the boundary).

To begin, consider a finite-element solution to an elliptic PDE of the form

$$u_{xx} + u_{yy} + r(x, y)u = f(x, y) \quad \text{on the region } R$$

and

$$u(x, y) = g(x, y) \quad \text{on the boundary of } R$$

The corresponding functional to be minimized is

$$I[u] = \iint\limits_{R} [u_x^2 + u_y^2 - r(x, y)u^2 + 2f(x, y)u] \, dxdy.$$

The region R is divided into p triangular subregions $T_1, T_2, \ldots, T_p$; the vertices of these regions are the nodes, $V_1, \ldots, V_n, V_{n+1}, \ldots, V_m$. Nodes $j = 1, \ldots, n$ are in the interior of R; the remaining nodes $j = n + 1, \ldots, m$ are on the boundary of R. Figure 15.16 shows a region divided into 14 triangular subregions.

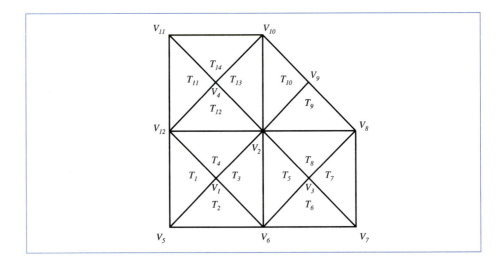

FIGURE 15.16   Region divided into 14 triangular subregions.

A finite-element solution of the PDE is a function

$$U = \sum_{j=1}^{m} c_j \Phi_j,$$

where the Φ_j are basis functions. There is a basis function corresponding to each node. The solution process consists of the following steps:

1. Define the subdivision of R by specifying the locations of the nodes.
2. Define each of the basis functions $\Phi_j, j = 1, \ldots, m$.
3. Determine coefficients c_j for the basis functions that correspond to boundary nodes $(j = n + 1, \ldots, m)$, so that the solution U satisfies the boundary conditions at those nodes.
4. Determine the coefficients c_j for the basis functions that correspond to interior nodes $(j = 1, \ldots, n)$, so that U minimizes the integral $I[u]$.

To find the coefficients corresponding to the interior nodes, we must minimize

$$\iint_R [U_x^2 + U_y^2 - r(x, y)U^2 + 2f(x, y)U] \, dxdy, \qquad \text{with } U = \sum_{j=1}^{m} c_j \Phi_j.$$

The minimum occurs where $\dfrac{\partial U}{\partial c_i} = 0$, for $1 \le i \le n$. This gives a linear system of equations $\mathbf{Ac} = \mathbf{d}$, where $\mathbf{A} = [a_{ij}], 1 \le i, j \le n$,

$$a_{ij} = \iint_R [\Phi_i]_x[\Phi_j]_x + [\Phi_i]_y[\Phi_j]_y - r(x, y)\Phi_i\Phi_j \, dxdy, \qquad (15.1)$$

and

$$d_i = -\iint_R f(x, y)\Phi_i \, dxdy - \sum_{j=n+1}^{m} c_j b_{ij}, \qquad (15.2)$$

in which

$$b_{ij} = \iint_R [\Phi_i]_x[\Phi_j]_x + [\Phi_i]y[\Phi_j]_y - r(x, y)\Phi_i\Phi_j \, dxdy,$$

$$1 \le i \le n, \qquad n + 1 \le j \le m. \qquad (15.3)$$

We now consider the basis functions Φ_j. We define Φ_j to be one at node j, zero at all other nodes, and linear on each triangular subdomain. For each triangle that has node j as a vertex, we find a plane that is one at node j and zero at the other two vertices; Φ_j is identically zero on any subdomain that does not have node j as a vertex.

Example 15.8 Finding Basis Functions

To illustrate the definition of the basis functions Φ_j, consider a region $0 \le x \le 3$, $0 \le y \le 3$, as shown in Fig. 15.17, that is decomposed into four triangular subregions, designated $T_1, \ldots, T_4$. The nodes are the vertices of the triangles, denoted $1, \ldots, 5$. Node 1, located at $(1, 1)$, is the only interior node in this diagram; nodes 2, 3, 4, and 5 are on the boundary.

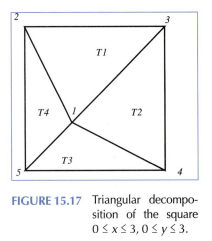

FIGURE 15.17 Triangular decomposition of the square $0 \le x \le 3, 0 \le y \le 3$.

We now find the five basis functions for this region. The basis functions corresponding to nodes $2, \dots, 5$ are each nonzero on only two of the triangular subregions. The second and third basis functions are illustrated in Fig. 15.18.

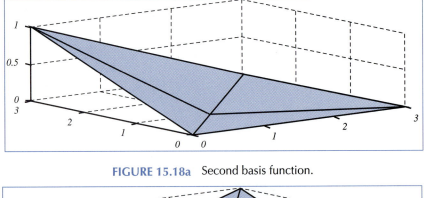

FIGURE 15.18a Second basis function.

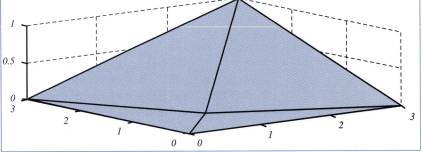

FIGURE 15.18b Third basis function.

The definition of the basis functions involves the determination of a plane that passes through three specified points. We want the jth basis function to be one at node j and zero at the other nodes. The equation of the plane that is equal to one at (x_1, y_1), zero at (x_2, y_2), and zero at (x_3, y_3) has the form

$$z = a + bx + cy,$$

where the constants $a, b,$ and c are found by solving the system

$$1 = a + bx_1 + cy_1,$$
$$0 = a + bx_2 + cy_2,$$
$$0 = a + bx_3 + cy_3.$$

The first basis function

Φ_1 is equal to one at node 1 and zero at nodes $2, 3, 4,$ and 5. Φ_1 is a plane on each of the four triangular subregions.

On $T_1, \Phi_1 = a + bx + cy,$ where $a, b,$ and c satisfy

$$1 = a + b + c,$$
$$0 = a + 0 + 3c,$$
$$0 = a + 3b + 3c \quad \Rightarrow \quad a = 3/2, \quad b = 0, \quad c = -1/2.$$

On $T_2, \Phi_1 = a + bx + cy,$ where $a, b,$ and c satisfy

$$1 = a + b + c,$$
$$0 = a + 3b + 3c,$$
$$0 = a + 3b + 0 \quad \Rightarrow \quad a = 3/2, \quad b = -1/2, \quad c = 0.$$

On $T_3, \Phi_1 = a + bx + cy,$ where $a, b,$ and c satisfy

$$1 = a + b + c,$$
$$0 = a + 3b + 0,$$
$$0 = a + 0 + 0 \quad \Rightarrow \quad a = 0, \quad b = 0, \quad c = 1.$$

On $T_4, \Phi_1 = a + bx + cy,$ where $a, b,$ and c satisfy

$$1 = a + b + c,$$
$$0 = a + 0 + 0,$$
$$0 = a + 0 + 3c \quad \Rightarrow \quad a = 0, \quad b = 1, \quad c = 0.$$

Thus,

$$\Phi_1 = \begin{cases} (3 - y)/2 & \text{on } T_1, \\ (3 - x)/2 & \text{on } T_2, \\ y & \text{on } T_3, \\ x & \text{on } T_4. \end{cases}$$

The second basis function

Φ_2 is equal to zero at node 1, one at node 2, and zero at nodes $3, 4,$ and 5. $\Phi_2 = 0$ on T_2 and T_3.

On T_1, $\Phi_2 = a + bx + cy$, where a, b, and c satisfy

$$1 = a + 0 + 3c,$$
$$0 = a + b + c,$$
$$0 = a + 3b + 3c \implies a = 0, \quad b = -1/3, \quad c = 1/3.$$

On T_4, $\Phi_2 = a + bx + cy$, where a, b, and c satisfy

$$1 = a + 0 + 3c,$$
$$0 = a + b + c,$$
$$0 = a + 0 + 0 \implies a = 0, b = -1/3, c = 1/3.$$

Hence,

$$\Phi_2 = \begin{cases} (-x + y)/3 & \text{on } T_1, \\ 0 & \text{on } T_2, \\ 0 & \text{on } T_3, \\ (-x + y)/3 & \text{on } T_4. \end{cases}$$

The third basis function

Φ_3 is equal to zero at nodes 1 and 2, one at node 3, and zero at nodes 4 and 5. $\Phi_3 = 0$ on T_3 and T_4.

As with Φ_1 and Φ_2, we form the linear systems to find the values of a, b, and c that define Φ_3 on T_1 and on T_2; we find that on T_1, $a = -1/2$, $b = 1/3$, and $c = 1/6$, and on T_2, $a = -1/2$, $b = 1/6$, and $c = 1/3$. So

$$\Phi_3 = \begin{cases} (-3 + 2x + y)/6 & \text{on } T_1, \\ (-3 + 2x + y)/6 & \text{on } T_2, \\ 0 & \text{on } T_3, \\ 0 & \text{on } T_4. \end{cases}$$

Note the symmetric form of Φ_3 on T_1 and T_2.

The fourth basis function

We can exploit the symmetry of the figure to find Φ_4 from Φ_2 by interchanging the roles of x and y and interchanging the triangular regions $T_1 \leftrightarrow T_2$ and $T_3 \leftrightarrow T_4$; doing this gives

$$\Phi_4 = \begin{cases} 0 & \text{on } T_1, \\ (x - y)/3 & \text{on } T_2, \\ (x - y)/3 & \text{on } T_3, \\ 0 & \text{on } T_4. \end{cases}$$

The fifth basis function

Φ_5 is equal to zero at nodes 1, 2, 3, and 4 and equal to one at node 5. $\Phi_5 = 0$ on T_1 and T_2. We find that

$$\Phi_5 = \begin{cases} 0 & \text{on } T_1, \\ 0 & \text{on } T_2, \\ (3 - x - 2y)/3 & \text{on } T_3, \\ (3 - 2x - y)/3 & \text{on } T_4. \end{cases}$$

Example 15.9 A Finite–Element Solution

Consider the problem

$$u_{xx} + u_{yy} = 0$$

with boundary conditions

$$u = x/3 \quad \text{for } y = 0, 0 \le x \le 3,$$
$$u = y/3 \quad \text{for } x = 0, 0 \le y \le 3,$$
$$u = 1 \quad \text{for } y = 1, 0 \le x \le 3,$$
$$u = 1 \quad \text{for } x = 0, 0 \le x \le 3.$$

The basis functions found in Example 15.8 are appropriate for problems defined on $0 \le x \le 3, 0 \le y \le 3$, with the triangular subdivision shown in Fig. 15.17.

To Find the Coefficients for the Nodes on the Boundary

For the given region, $U(\text{node } 2) = 1, U(\text{node } 3) = 1, U(\text{node } 4) = 1,$ and $U(\text{node } 5) = 0.$ Since we are looking for $U = c_1 \Phi_1 + c_2 \Phi_2 + c_3 \Phi_3 + c_4 \Phi_4 + c_5 \Phi_5$ to satisfy the boundary conditions, and because each Φ_j is zero except at node j, we must have $c_2 = c_3 = c_4 = 1$ and $c_5 = 0$.

To Find the Coefficients for the Interior Node

We have only one interior node, so we have only one coefficient to determine from the given equations. We must solve $Ac_1 = d$, where

$$A = \iint\limits_R [\Phi_1]_x [\Phi_1]_x + [\Phi_1]_y [\Phi_1]_y \, dx dy$$

and

$$d = -\sum_{j=2}^{5} c_j b_j,$$

in which

$$b_j = \iint\limits_R [\Phi_1]_x [\Phi_j]_x + [\Phi_1]_y [\Phi_j]_y \, dx dy, \qquad 2 \le j \le 5.$$

Because $c_5 = 0$, the calculation of b_5 is not required, but we do have a number of integrations to perform. We have used the fact that both $r(x, y)$ and $f(x, y)$ are zero in this example to simplify the expressions for A and d also. We note, for use in the following calculations, the areas of the triangular regions:

$$A_1 = \text{area}(T_1) = 3; \qquad A_2 = 3; \qquad A_3 = 3/2; \qquad A_4 = 3/2.$$

To Find A

$$\Phi_1 = \begin{cases} (3 - y)/2 \\ (3 - x)/2 \\ y \\ x \end{cases}, \quad [\Phi_1]_x = \begin{cases} 0 \\ -1/2 \\ 0 \\ 1 \end{cases}, \quad [\Phi_1]_y = \begin{cases} -1/2 & \text{on } T_1 \\ 0 & \text{on } T_2 \\ 1 & \text{on } T_3 \\ 0 & \text{on } T_4 \end{cases}.$$

$$A = \iint\limits_R [\Phi_1]_x[\Phi_1]_x + [\Phi_1]_y[\Phi_1]_y \, dxdy$$

$$= \iint\limits_{T_1} [0 + (1/4)] \, dxdy + \iint\limits_{T_2} (1/4 + 0) \, dxdy + \iint\limits_{T_3} (0 + 1) \, dxdy$$

$$+ \iint\limits_{T_4} (1 + 0) \, dxdy$$

$$= 1/4 \,(\text{area of } T_1 + \text{area of } T_2) + \text{area of } T_3 + \text{area of } T_4$$

$$= (1/4)(3 + 3) + 3/2 + 3/2 = 9/2.$$

To Find b_2

$$\Phi_2 = \begin{cases} (-x + y)/3 \\ 0 \\ 0 \\ (-x + y)/3 \end{cases}, \quad [\Phi_2]_x = \begin{cases} -1/3 \\ 0 \\ 0 \\ -1/3 \end{cases}, \quad [\Phi_2]_y = \begin{cases} 1/3 & \text{on } T_1 \\ 0 & \text{on } T_2 \\ 1 & \text{on } T_3 \\ 1/3 & \text{on } T_4 \end{cases}.$$

$$b_2 = \iint\limits_R [\Phi_1]_x[\Phi_2]_x + [\Phi_1]_y[\Phi_2]_y \, dxdy$$

$$= \iint\limits_{T_1} 0 + (-1/2)(1/3) \, dxdy + \iint\limits_{T_2} (0 + 0) \, dxdy + \iint\limits_{T_3} (0 + 0) \, dxdy$$

$$+ \iint\limits_{T_4} [(1)(-1/3) + 0] \, dxdy$$

$$= (-1/6)(\text{area of } T_1) + (-1/3)(\text{area of } T_4) = -1.$$

To Find b_3

$$\Phi_3 = \begin{cases} (-3 + 2x + y)/6 \\ (-3 + 2x + 2y)/6 \\ 0 \\ 0 \end{cases}, \quad [\Phi_3]_x = \begin{cases} 1/3 \\ 1/6 \\ 0 \\ 0 \end{cases}, \quad [\Phi_3]_y = \begin{cases} 1/6 & \text{on } T_1 \\ 1/3 & \text{on } T_2 \\ 0 & \text{on } T_3 \\ 0 & \text{on } T_4 \end{cases}.$$

$$b_3 = \iint_R [\Phi_1]_x[\Phi_3]_x + [\Phi_1]_y[\Phi_3]_y \, dxdy$$

$$= \iint_{T_1} [0 + (-1/2)(1/6) \, dxdy + \iint_{T_2}((-1/2)(1/3) + 0] \, dxdy$$

$$+ \iint_{T_3}(0 + 0) \, dxdy + \iint_{T_4}(0 + 0) \, dxdy$$

$$= (-1/12)(\text{area of } T_1) + (-1/6)(\text{area of } T_2) = -3/4.$$

To Find b_4

$$\Phi_4 = \begin{cases} 0 \\ (x-y)/3 \\ (x-y)/3 \\ 0 \end{cases}, \quad [\Phi_4]_x = \begin{cases} 0 \\ 1/3 \\ 1/3 \\ 0 \end{cases}, \quad [\Phi_4]_y = \begin{cases} 0 & \text{on } T_1 \\ -1/3 & \text{on } T_2 \\ -1/3 & \text{on } T_3 \\ 0 & \text{on } T_4 \end{cases}.$$

$$b_4 = \iint_R [\Phi_1]_x[\Phi_4]_x + [\Phi_1]_y[\Phi_4]_y \, dxdy$$

$$= \iint_{T_1} (0 + 0) \, dxdy + \iint_{T_2}[(-1/2)(1/3) + 0] \, dxdy$$

$$+ \iint_{T_3}[0 + (1)(-1/3)] \, dxdy + \iint_{T_4}(0 + 0) \, dxdy$$

$$= (-1/6)(\text{area of } T_2) + (-1/3)(\text{area of } T_3) = -1.$$

The Right Hand Side

$$d = -[c_2 b_2 + c_3 b_3 + c_4 b_4] = -[b_2 + b_3 + b_4] = -[(-1) + (-3/4) + (-1)] = 11/4.$$

The equation to be solved, $Ac_1 = d$, is $(9/2)c_1 = 11/4 \Rightarrow c_1 = 11/18$. The solution of the potential equation is $U = (11/8)\Phi_1 + \Phi_2 + \Phi_3 + \Phi_4$, which simplifies to

$$U = \begin{cases} 5/12 + (7/36)y & \text{on } T_1, \\ 5/12 + (7/36)x & \text{on } T_2, \\ (1/3)x + (5/18)y & \text{on } T_3, \\ (5/18)x + (1/3)y & \text{on } T_4. \end{cases}$$

Example 15.10 Using MATLAB to Find the basis Functions

We illustrate the use of a MATLAB script to generate the basis functions corresponding to each node in a finite-element grid with triangular elements. We describe the geometry in two arrays. The first, **V**, gives the coordinates of each of the nodes (interior nodes first). The second array, **T**, specifies the triangles by giving the indices of the three vertices that define each triangle. For the region illustrated in Fig. 15.16, there are 12 vertices and 14 triangles; the arrays are

$$
V = \begin{bmatrix} 1/2 & 1/2 \\ 1 & 1 \\ 3/2 & 1/2 \\ 1/2 & 3/2 \\ 0 & 0 \\ 1 & 0 \\ 2 & 0 \\ 2 & 1 \\ 3/2 & 3/2 \\ 1 & 2 \\ 0 & 2 \\ 0 & 1 \end{bmatrix}
\quad \text{and} \quad
T = \begin{bmatrix} 1 & 5 & 12 \\ 1 & 5 & 6 \\ 1 & 2 & 6 \\ 1 & 2 & 12 \\ 3 & 2 & 6 \\ 3 & 6 & 7 \\ 3 & 7 & 8 \\ 3 & 8 & 2 \\ 2 & 8 & 9 \\ 2 & 9 & 10 \\ 4 & 11 & 12 \\ 4 & 12 & 2 \\ 4 & 2 & 10 \\ 4 & 10 & 11 \end{bmatrix}
$$

We define the relevant parameters (or we could find them from the dimensions of **V** and **T**) as follows:

$$m = 12 \qquad \text{\% number of nodes}$$

$$n = 4 \qquad \text{\% number of interior nodes}$$

$$p = 14 \qquad \text{\% number of triangles}$$

For each node, we must find a basis function, which has the form $A + Bx + Cy$ on each triangle. We store the information in three arrays:

$$\mathbf{A}(m, p); \qquad \mathbf{B}(m, p); \qquad \mathbf{C}(m, p);$$

The row index gives the node number; the column index gives the triangular element. The computations to set up the three-by-three linear system for each triangular region and solve the system are given in the following MATLAB code:

```
%   Define basis function corresponding to each node, j = 1 . . . m
for j = 1: m
        for k = 1: p                          %      for each triangle
                for i = 1 : 3                  %      for each vertex
```

```
            AA(i, 1) = 1;                    %       form array
            AA(i, 2) = V(T(k,i), 1);
            AA(i, 3) = V(T(k,i), 2);
            if T(k,i) == j                   %       form right-hand side
                bb(i,1) = 1;
            else
                bb(i,1) = 0;
            end
        end
        x = AA\bb;                      %  solve system
        A( j, k ) = x(1);
        B( j, k ) = x(2);
        C( j, k ) = x(3);
    end
end
```

Although we do not need to display the definition of each basis function, it is informative to consider briefly what the information in arrays $\mathbf{A}$, $\mathbf{B}$, and $\mathbf{C}$ can tell us for this example. Each row of the matrix corresponds to a basis function, each column to a triangular element. The information about the basis function corresponding to node 1 is in the first row of matrices $\mathbf{A}$, $\mathbf{B}$, and $\mathbf{C}$. Node 1 is a vertex of triangles 1, 2, 3, and 4, so the only possible nonzero coefficients for the first basis function occur in the first four rows. Specifically, the first row of the three arrays are

```
A(1, : ) = [ 0  0   2   2  0 ......... 0],
B(1, : ) = [ 2  0  -2   0  0 ........ 0],
C(1, : ) = [ 0  2   0  -2  0 ........ 0];
```

This code tells us that the first basis function is

$$0 + 2x + 0y \quad \text{on } T_1,$$
$$0 + 0x + 2y \quad \text{on } T_2,$$
$$2 - 2x + 0y \quad \text{on } T_3,$$
$$2 + 0x - 2y \quad \text{on } T_4,$$
$$0 \qquad\qquad \text{on all other triangles.}$$

It is easy to verify that the function defined in this way has the required values at each of the vertices.

Example 15.11 Solving the Laplace Equation Using Finite Elements

We now solve the potential equation on $0 \le x \le 2, 0 \le y \le 2$, with the upper corner removed, as in Fig. 15.16. The boundary conditions are

$$u = 0 \quad \text{for} \quad 0 \le x \le 2, y = 0, \quad \text{and} \quad 0 \le y \le 2, x = 0,$$

$$u = x \quad \text{for} \quad 0 \le x \le 1, y = 2,$$

$$u = y \quad \text{for} \quad 0 \le y \le 1, x = 2,$$

$$u = 1 \quad \text{along the diagonal boundary.}$$

We continue the computations from Example 15.9; that is, we assume that the geometry has been defined and the basis functions have been computed. We also need the area of each of the triangular elements. In this example, each triangle is of area 1/4, so we set $H = 0.25 \times \text{ones}(1, 14)$. In general, for a triangle with corners at (x_1, y_1), (x_2, y_2) and (x_3, y_3), the area is $\text{Area}(T) = 0.5 \det (TT)$, where

$$TT = \begin{bmatrix} x_1 & y_1 & 1 \\ x_2 & y_2 & 1 \\ x_3 & y_3 & 1 \end{bmatrix}$$

To solve the problem, we must find the coefficients of the basis functions so that the linear combination $U = c_1 \Phi_1 + \ldots + c_m \Phi_m$ is the desired solution. We initialize the vector $\mathbf{c}$ so that the linear combination will satisfy the boundary conditions. For this problem, the BC are $U = 1$ at nodes 8, 9, and 10 and $U = 0$ at all other nodes; hence, we begin with

$$\mathbf{c} = [0 \quad 0 \quad 0 \quad 0 \quad 0 \quad 0 \quad 0 \quad 1 \quad 1 \quad 1 \quad 0 \quad 0].$$

We now set up the equations to determine the coefficients for the basis functions corresponding to the interior nodes. The following MATLAB code performs the computations analogous to eqs. (15.1)–(15.3).

```
for i = 1: n
    for j = 1 : n
        s(1:p) = B(i,1:p ).*B(j,1:p ) + C(i,1:p ).*C(j,1:p );
        AAA ( i, j ) = s*H';
    end
end
```

```
for i = 1 : n
    for j = n+1 : m
        k = j - n;
        s(1:p) = B(i,1:p ).*B(j,1:p ) + C(i,1:p ).*C(j,1:p );
        G( i, k ) = s*H';
    end
end
d( 1 : n ) = - G*c(n+1 : m)';
c(1:n) = AAA\d'
```

The final solution is linear on each triangular element and is of the form $A + Bx + Cy$, where A, B, and C are found by taking the linear combination of the basis elements. For this example, the coefficients for the linear combination are found to be

$$\mathbf{c} = [0.1154, 0.4615, 0.3654, 0.3654, 0, 0, 0, 1, 1, 1, 0, 0].$$

The code to find the final solution is

```
UA = A'*c';   UB = B'*c';   UC = C'*c';
U = [ UA    UB    UC ]
```

Thus, the final solution is

$$U = \begin{cases}
0 & + 0.2308\, x + 0 & y & \text{on } T_1 \\
0 & + 0\, x & + 0.2308\, y & \text{on } T_2 \\
-0.2308 & + 0.2308\, x + 0.4615\, y & & \text{on } T_3 \\
-0.2308 & + 0.4615\, x + 0.2308\, y & & \text{on } T_4 \\
-0.2692 & + 0.2692\, x + 0.4615\, y & & \text{on } T_5 \\
0 & + 0 & x + 0.7308\, y & \text{on } T_6 \\
-0.5385 & + 0.2692\, x + 1.0000\, y & & \text{on } T_7 \\
-0.8077 & + 0.5385\, x + 0.7308\, y & & \text{on } T_8 \\
-0.6154 & + 0.5385\, x + 0.5385\, y & & \text{on } T_9 \\
-0.6154 & + 0.5385\, x + 0.5385\, y & & \text{on } T_{10} \\
0 & + 0.7308\, x + 0 & y & \text{on } T_{11} \\
-0.2692 & + 0.4615\, x + 0.2692\, y & & \text{on } T_{12} \\
-0.8077 & + 0.7308\, x + 0.5385\, y & & \text{on } T_{13} \\
-0.5385 & + 1.0000\, x + 0.2692\, y & & \text{on } T_{14}
\end{cases}$$

The computed values at the nodes can be found from these formulas:

Node	x	y	U	Results from formula for
1	1/2	1/2	0.1154	$T_1, T_2, T_3,$ or T_4
2	1	1	0.4615	$T_3, T_4, T_5, T_8, T_9, T_{10}, T_{12},$ or T_{13}
3	3/2	1/2	0.3654	$T_5, T_6, T_7,$ or T_8
4	1/2	3/2	0.3654	$T_{11}, T_{12}, T_{13},$ or T_{14}
5	0	0	0	T_1 or T_2
6	1	0	0	$T_2, T_3, T_5,$ or T_6
7	2	0	0	T_6 or T_7
8	2	1	1	$T_7, T_8,$ or T_9
9	3/2	3/2	1	T_9 or T_{10}
10	1	2	1	$T_{10}, T_{13},$ or T_{14}
11	0	2	0	T_{11} or T_{14}
12	0	1	0	$T_1, T_4, T_{11},$ or T_{12}

Figure 15.19 shows a plot of the final solution.

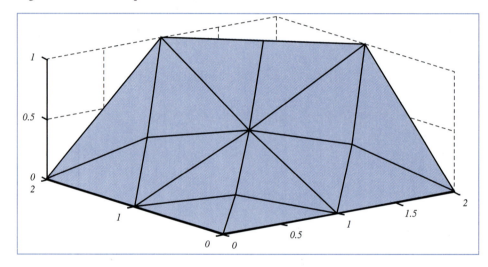

FIGURE 15.19   Solution to Poisson's equation using finite elements.

15.5   USING MATLAB's FUNCTIONS

MATLAB has several built-in functions that are helpful for visualizing the solutions generated by the finite-element method. The script that produces the plot in Fig. 15.19 illustrates the use of the MATLAB function `trimesh`. The basic function call requires specification of the node indices for each of the triangles (in array T) and the coordinates of the vertices of the triangular regions. The coordinates are given in three arrays, one for the x-coordinate, one for the y-coordinate, and one for the z-coordinate. An additional vector may be used to define edge color; if it is not user specified, edge color is proportional to the z coordinate.

The function `trisurf` is used in the same way as `trimesh`, but plots the surface defined by the triangular elements. The MATLAB code is as follows:

```
% S_plot_15_19
% plot for region in Figure 15.19
% define triangles by giving x, y, and z coord
x = [ 0.5      1        1.5      0.5      0  1  2  2  1.5  1  0  0 ];
y = [ 0.5      1        0.5      1.5      0  0  0  1  1.5  2  2  1 ];
z = [ 0.1154  0.4615   0.3654   0.3654   0  0  0  1  1    1  0  0 ];
              T = [ 1      5       12
                    1      5       6
                    1      2       6
                    1      2       12
                    3      2       6
                    3      6       7
                    3      7       8
                    3      8       2
                    2      8       9
                    2      9       10
                    4      11      12
                    4      12      2
                    4      2       10
                    4      10      11];
trimesh(T, x, y, z)
```

Finally, for more general polygonal regions, MATLAB has a function, `inpolygon`, to determine whether a given point is inside the polygon. The point or points to be checked are given in two vectors, **x** and **y**. The polygon is defined by two other vectors, **u** and **v**. The returned value is 1 if the point is strictly inside the polygon, 0.5 if the point is on the boundary, and 0 otherwise. The function call is `in = inpolygon (x,y,u,v)`. For example, to determine whether the points $(1, 1)$, $(2, 0)$, and $(3, 0.5)$ are inside the square $0 \leq x \leq 2, 0 \leq y \leq 2$, we define

$$x = [1 \ 2 \ 3]; \quad y = [1 \ 0 \ 0.5]; \quad u = [0 \ 2 \ 2 \ 0]; \quad v = [0 \ 0 \ 2 \ 2];$$

call the function as

$$\text{EDU>in = inpolygon(x, y, u, v)}$$

and obtain the result

$$\text{in} = 1 \quad 0.5 \quad 0$$

As expected, the results show that the first point is inside the square, the second is on the boundary, and the third is outside the square.

Heat Equation: Parabolic PDE: A finite-difference solution of the one-dimensional heat equation

$$u_t = c\,u_{xx} \qquad\qquad \text{for } 0 < x < a,\ \ 0 < t \le T,$$

with initial conditions: $\quad u(x, 0) = f(x), \quad 0 < x < a,$

and boundary conditions: $\quad u(0, t) = g_1(t), \quad u(a, t) = g_2(t), \quad 0 < t \le T,$

utilizes the mesh: $\qquad\qquad h = \Delta x = a/n, \quad k = \Delta t = T/m, \quad \text{with } r = \dfrac{ck}{h^2}.$

Explicit Method

$$u_{i,j+1} = r u_{i-1,j} + (1 - 2r)u_{i,j} + r u_{i+1,j}, \qquad \text{for } i = 1, \ldots, n - 1;$$
$$(0 < r \le 0.5 \text{ to ensure stability})$$

Implicit Method

$$u_{i,j} = (-r)u_{i-1,j+1} + (1 + 2r)u_{i,j+1} = (-r)u_{i+1,j+1}; \quad \text{(unconditionally stable)}.$$

Crank–Nicolson Method

$$-\frac{r}{2}u_{i-1,j+1} + (1 + r)u_{i,j+1} - \frac{r}{2}u_{i+1,j+1} = \frac{r}{2}u_{i-1,j} + (1 - r)u_{i,j} + \frac{r}{2}u_{i+1,j};$$

(unconditionally stable; better truncation error than the basic implicit method.)

Wave Equation: Hyperbolic PDE: A Finite-difference solution of the PDE

$$u_{tt} - c^2 u_{xx} = 0 \qquad\qquad \text{for } 0 \le x \le a, \quad \text{and } 0 \le t,$$

with initial conditions: $\quad u(x, 0) = f_1(x),\, u_t(x, 0) = f_2(x), \quad \text{for } 0 < x < a,$

and boundary conditions: $\quad u(0, t) = g_1(t),\, u(a, t) = g_2(t), \quad \text{for } 0 < t,$

utilizes the mesh: $\qquad\qquad h = \Delta x = a/n, \quad k = \Delta t, \quad \text{with } p = \dfrac{ck}{h^2} = c\,\dfrac{\Delta t}{\Delta x}.$

Explicit Method. The general form of the difference equation is

$$u_{i,j+1} = p^2 u_{i-1,j} + 2(1 - p^2)u_{i,j} + p^2 u_{i+1,j} - u_{i,j-1}.$$

The equation for u at the first time step

$$u_{i,1} = 0.5p^2 u_{i-1,0} + (1 - p^2)u_{i,0} + 0.5p^2 u_{i+1,0} + k f_2(x_i);$$
$$(\text{stability requires } p \le 1)$$

Implicit Method (Unrestricted Stability). The general form of the difference equation is

$$-p^2 u_{i-1,j+1} + 2(1 + p^2)u_{i,j+1} - p^2 u_{i+1,j+1} = 4u_{i,j} + p^2 u_{i-1,j-1} - 2(1 + p^2)u_{i,j-1} + p^2 u_{i+1,j-1}$$

The equations for $j = 0$ have the form:

$$4(1+p^2)u_{1,1} - 2p^2u_{2,1} = 4u_{1,0} - 2p^2kf_2(x_0) + 4(1+p^2)kf_2(x_1) - 2p^2kf_2(x_2) + 2p^2u_{0,1}$$

$$-2p^2u_{1,1} + 4(1+p^2)u_{2,1} - 2p^2u_{3,1} = 4u_{2,0} - 2p^2kf_2(x_1) + 4(1+p^2)kf_2(x_2) - 2p^2kf_2(x_3)$$

$$\ldots\ldots$$

$$-2p^2u_{i-1,1} + 4(1+p^2)u_{i,1} - 2p^2u_{i+1,1} =$$
$$4u_{i,0} - 2p^2kf_2(x_{i-1}) + 4(1+p^2)kf_2(x_i) - 2p^2kf_2(x_{i+1})$$

$$\ldots\ldots\ldots$$

$$-2p^2u_{n-1,1} + 4(1+p^2)u_{n,1} =$$
$$4u_{n,0} - 2p^2kf_2(x_{n-1}) + 4(1+p^2)kf_2(x_n) - 2p^2kf_2(x_{n+1}) + 2p^2u_{n+1,1}$$

The value of u at each subsequent time step can be found from:

$$2(1+p^2)u_{1,j+1} - p^2u_{2,j+1} = 4u_{1,j} - 2(1+p^2)u_{1,j-1} + p^2u_{2,j-1} + p^2u_{0,j+1} + p^2u_{0,j-1}$$

$$-p^2u_{1,j+1} + 2(1+p^2)u_{2,j+1} - p^2u_{3,j+1} = 4u_{2,j} + p^2u_{1,j-1} - 2(1+p^2)u_{2,j-1} + p^2u_{3,j-1}$$

$$\ldots$$

$$-p^2u_{i-1,j+1} + 2(1+p^2)u_{i,j+1} - p^2u_{i+1,j+1} = 4u_{i,j} + p^2u_{i-1,j-1} - 2(1+p^2)u_{i,j-1} + p^2u_{i+1,j-1}$$

$$\ldots$$

$$-p^2u_{n-1,j+1} + 2(1+p^2)u_{n,j+1} = 4u_{n,j} + p^2u_{n-1,j-1} - 2(1+p^2)u_{n,j-1} + p^2u_{n+1,j-1} + p^2u_{n+1,j+1}$$

Elliptic PDE

A Finite-difference Solution of Poisson's Equation

$$u_{xx} + u_{yy} = f(x, y) \qquad a \leq x \leq b; \qquad c \leq y \leq d.$$

with boundary conditions:

$$u(a, y) = \mathbf{g}_1(y) \qquad u(b, y) = \mathbf{g}_2(y) \qquad c < y < d$$
$$u(x, c) = \mathbf{g}_3(x) \qquad u(x, d) = \mathbf{g}_4(x) \qquad a < x < b$$

utilizes a mesh in the x-y plane:

$$x_i = a + ih, \qquad i = 0, 1, \ldots n \qquad h = \Delta x = (b - a)/n$$
$$y_j = c + jk, \qquad j = 0, 1, \ldots m \qquad k = \Delta y = (d - c)/m$$

the general form of the difference equation is

$$\frac{1}{k^2}[u_{i,j+1} - 2u_{i,j} + u_{i,j-1}] + \frac{1}{h^2}[u_{i+1,j} - 2u_{i,j} + u_{i-1,j}] = f_{ij}.$$

A Finite-Element Solution of an Elliptic PDE of the Form

$$u_{xx} + u_{yy} + r(x, y)\,u = f(x, y) \quad \text{on the region } R$$
$$u(x, y) = g(x, y) \quad \text{on boundary of } R$$

seeks to minimize the functional

$$I[u] = \iint\limits_{R} [u_x^2 + u_y^2 - r(x, y)u^2 + 2f(x, y)u] \, dxdy$$

where u is a linear combination of the basis functions. If R is divided into p triangular subregions, $T_1, T_2, \ldots T_p$, there is a piecewise-linear basis function corresponding to each node. The basis function corresponding to node j has the value one at node j and zero at all other nodes.

SUGGESTIONS FOR FURTHER READING

Our discussion of numerical methods for partial differential equations in this chapter provides only a brief introduction to an extensive area of research and application. The following are some of the many excellent sources for further study of these topics.

Ames, W. F., *Numerical Methods for Partial Differential Equations*, 3rd ed., Academic Press, Boston. 1992.

Boyce, W. E. and R. C. DiPrima, *Elementary Differential Equations and Boundary Value Problems*, 4th ed. John Wiley & Sons, New York, 1986.

Birkhoff, G. and R. E. Lynch, *Numerical Solution of Elliptic Problems*, SIAM, Philadelphia, 1984.

Celia, M. A. and W. G. Gray, *Numerical Methods for Differential Equations*, Prentice Hall, Englewood Cliffs, NJ. 1992.

Colton, D., *Partial Differential Equations*, Random House, New York, 1988. (This text includes a brief history of PDE, p. 49–53.)

Forsythe, G. E. and W. R. Wasow, *Finite-Difference Methods for Partial Differential Equations*, John Wiley & Sons, New York, 1960.

Garcia, A. L., *Numerical Methods for Physics*, Prentice Hall, Englewood Cliffs, NJ, 1994.

Golub, G. H. and J. M. Ortega, *Scientific Computing and Differential Equations: An Introduction to Numerical Methods*, Academic Press, Boston, 1992.

Haberman, R., *Elementary Applied Partial Differential Equations, with Fourier Series and Boundary Value Problems*, Prentice-Hall, Englewood Cliffs, NJ. 1983.

Hall, C. A. and T. A. Porsching, *Numerical Analysis of Partial Differential Equations*, Prentice Hall, Englewood Cliffs, NJ, 1990.

Meis, T. and U. Marcowitz, *Numerical Solution of Partial Differential Equations*, Springer-Verlag, New York, 1981.

Mitchell, A. R., *Computational Methods in Partial Differential Equations*, John Wiley & Sons, London, 1969.

Svobony, T., *Mathematical Modeling for Industry and Engineering*, Prentice Hall, Upper Saddle River, NJ, 1998.

Troutman, J. L. and M. Bautista, *Boundary Value Problems of Applied Mathematics*, PWS Publishing, 1994.

Zauderer, E., *Partial Differential Equations of Applied Mathematics*, 2d ed., John Wiley & Sons, New York, 1989.

The finite-element method is important in mathematics and engineering; the following references include discussion of the method from several different points of view.

Axelsson, O. and V. A. Barker, *Finite Element Solution of Boundary Value Problems*, Academic Press, New York, 1984.

Becker, E. B., Carey, G. F. and Oden, J. T., *Finite Elements: An Introduction*, vol. 1, Prentice-Hall, Englewood Cliffs, NJ, 1981.

Davies. A. J., *The Finite Element Method: A First Approach*, Clarendon Press, Oxford, U.K., 1980.

Mitchell, A. R., and R. Wait, *The Finite Element Method in Partial Differential Equations*, John Wiley & Sons, London, 1977.

Silvester, P. P. and R. L. Ferrari, Finite *Elements for Electrical Engineers*, 3d ed. Cambridge University Press, Cambridge, U.K., 1996.

Strang, G. and G. Fix, *An Analysis of the Finite Element Method*, Prentice-Hall, Englewood Cliffs, NJ, 1973.

Zienkiewicz, O. C. and Taylor, R. L. *The Finite Element Method*, 4th ed. vol 1, London: McGraw-Hill, 1989.

PRACTICE THE TECHNIQUES

For Problems P15.1–P15.10, solve the one-dimensional heat equation using the specified finite-difference method.

a. *Use the explicit finite-difference method with $\Delta x = 0.2$ and $\Delta t = 0.01$.*

b. *Use the explicit finite-difference method with $\Delta x = 0.2$ and $\Delta t = 0.02$.*

c. *Use the explicit finite-difference method with $\Delta x = 0.2$ and $\Delta t = 0.1$.*

d. *Use the implicit finite-difference method with $\Delta x = 0.2$ and $\Delta t = 0.1$.*

e. *Use the Crank-Nicolson method with $\Delta x = 0.2$ and $\Delta t = 0.1$.*

P15.1 Solve $u_t - u_{xx} = 0$, for $0 \le x \le 1, 0 < t < 0.5$, with initial condition $u(x, 0) = 0$, (for $0 \le x \le 1$), and boundary conditions $u(0, t) = 0, u(1, t) = t$ (for $0 < t < 0.5$).

P15.2 Solve $u_t - u_{xx} = 0$, for $0 \le x \le 1, 0 < t < 0.5$, with initial condition $u(x, 0) = x$, (for $0 \le x \le 1$), and boundary conditions $u(0, t) = 0, u(1, t) = 1$ (for $0 < t < 0.5$).

P15.3 Solve $u_t - u_{xx} = 0$, for $0 \le x \le 1, 0 < t < 0.5$, with initial condition $u(x, 0) = x(1 - x)$, (for $0 \le x \le 1$), and boundary conditions $u(0, t) = 0$, $u(1, t) = 0$ (for $0 < t < 0.5$).

P15.4 Solve $u_t - u_{xx} = 0$, for $0 \le x \le 1, 0 < t < 0.5$, with initial condition $u(x, 0) = 10$, (for $0 \le x \le 1$), and boundary conditions $u(0, t) = 0, u(1, t) = 0$ (for $0 < t < 0.5$).

P15.5 Solve $u_t - u_{xx} = 0$, for $0 \le x \le 1, 0 < t < 0.5$, with initial condition $u(x, 0) = \sin(4\pi x)$, (for $0 \le x \le 1$), and boundary conditions $u(0, t) = 0, u(1, t) = 0$ (for $0 < t < 0.5$).

P15.6 Solve $u_t - u_{xx} = 0$, for $0 \le x \le 1, 0 < t < 0.5$, with initial condition $u(x, 0) = \sin(\pi x) + \sin(2\pi x) + \sin(3\pi x)$, $(0 \le x \le 1)$, and boundary conditions $u(0, t) = 0$, $u(1, t) = 0$ $(0 < t < 0.5)$.

P15.7 Solve $u_t - u_{xx} = 0$, for $0 \le x \le 1, 0 < t < 0.5$, with initial condition $u(x, 0) = \sin(\pi x)$, (for $0 \le x \le 1$), and boundary conditions $u(0, t) = 0, u(1, t) = 1$.

P15.8 Solve $u_t - u_{xx} = 0$, for $0 \le x \le 1, 0 < t < 0.5$, with initial condition $u(x, 0) = x$, $(0 \le x \le 1)$, and boundary conditions $u_x(0, t) = 0, u_x(1, t) = 0$ $(0 < t < 0.5)$, i.e., ends insulated.

P15.9 Solve $u_t - u_{xx} = 0$, for $0 \le x \le 1, 0 < t < 0.5$, with initial condition

$$u(x, 0) = \begin{cases} 0, & \text{for } 0 \le x \le 0.2, \\ 20, & \text{for } 0.2 < x < 0.8, \\ 0, & \text{for } 0.8 \le x \le 1, \end{cases}$$

and boundary conditions $u(0, t) = 0$, and $u(1, t) = 0$ $(0 < t < 0.5)$.

P15.10 Solve $u_t - u_{xx} = 0$, for $0 \le x \le 1, 0 < t < 0.5$, with initial condition $u(x, 0) = x^2$, (for $0 \le x \le 1$), and boundary conditions $u(0, t) = 0$, $u(1, t) = 0$ (for $0 < t < 0.5$).

For Problems P15.11–P15.15, solve the wave equation using the following finite-difference schemes.

   a. *Use the explicit finite-difference method with $\Delta x = 0.1$ and $\Delta t = 0.1$.*
   b. *Use the explicit finite-difference method with $\Delta x = 0.1$ and $\Delta t = 0.2$.*
   c. *Use the implicit finite-difference method with $\Delta x = 0.1$ and $\Delta t = 0.2$.*

P15.11 Solve $u_{tt} - u_{xx} = 0$, for $0 \le x \le 1, 0 < t < 2$, with initial conditions (string plucked at midpoint, zero initial velocity)

$$u(x, 0) = \begin{cases} 0.2x, & \text{for } 0 \le x \le 0.5, \\ 0.2(1 - x), & \text{for } 0.5 < x < 1, \end{cases}$$

$$u_x(x, 0) = 0,$$

and boundary conditions $u(0, t) = 0$, and $u(1, t) = 0$ $(0 < t < 2)$.

P15.12 Solve $u_{tt} - u_{xx} = 0$, for $0 \le x \le 1, 0 < t < 2$, with initial conditions (string plucked at $x = 0.2$, zero initial velocity)

$$u(x, 0) = \begin{cases} 0.5\,x, & \text{for } 0 \le x \le 0.2, \\ 0.1 - (x - 0.2)/8, & \text{for } 0.2 < x < 1, \end{cases}$$

$u_x(x, 0) = 0$, and boundary conditions $u(0, t) = 0$, and $u(1, t) = 0$ $(0 < t < 2)$.

P15.13 Solve $u_{tt} - u_{xx} = 0$, for $0 \le x \le 1, 0 < t < 2$, with initial conditions $u(x, 0) = 0$ and $u_x(x, 0) = 0$, and boundary conditions $u(0, t) = 0$, $u(1, t) = 0.2\sin(t)$ (for $0 < t < 2$).

P15.14 Solve $u_{tt} - u_{xx} = 0$, for $0 \le x \le 1, 0 < t < 2$, with initial conditions $u(x, 0) = 0$ and $u_x(x, 0) = 0$, and boundary conditions $u(0, t) = 0$, $u(1, t) = 0.2\sin(\pi t)$ (for $0 < t < 2$).

P15.15 Solve $u_{tt} - u_{xx} = 0$, for $0 \le x \le 1, 0 < t < 2$, with initial conditions $u(x, 0) = 0$ and $u_x(x, 0) = \sin(\pi x)$, and boundary conditions $u(0, t) = 0$, $u(1, t) = 0$ (for $0 < t < 2$).

For Problems P15.16–P15.25, solve the potential equation using the finite-difference method with the specified mesh.

   a. *Use $\Delta x = 0.25$ and $\Delta y = 0.25$.*
   b. *Use $\Delta x = 0.2$ and $\Delta y = 0.2$.*
   c. *Use $\Delta x = 0.1$ and $\Delta y = 0.1$.*

P15.16 Solve $u_{xx} + u_{xx} = 0$, for $0 \le x \le 1, 0 \le y \le 1$, with boundary conditions $u(x, 0) = x$, $u(0, y) = y$, $u(x, 1) = 1$, and $u(1, y) = 1$.

P15.17 Solve $u_{xx} + u_{xx} = 0$, for $0 \le x \le 1, 0 \le y \le 1$, with boundary conditions $u(x, 0) = 0$, $u(0, y) = 0$, $u(x, 1) = x$, and $u(1, y) = y$.

P15.18 Solve $u_{xx} + u_{xx} = 0$, for $0 \le x \le 1, 0 \le y \le 1$, with boundary conditions $u(x, 0) = x$, $u(0, y) = 2y$, $u(x, 1) = 2$, and $u(1, y) = 1 + y$.

P15.19 Solve $u_{xx} + u_{xx} = 0$, for $0 \le x \le 1, 0 \le y \le 1$, with boundary conditions $u(x, 0) = x^2$, $u(0, y) = -y^2$, $u(x, 1) = x^2 + x - 1$, and $u(1, y) = 1 + y - y^2$.

P15.20 Solve $u_{xx} + u_{xx} = 0$, for $0 \le x \le 1, 0 \le y \le 1$, with boundary conditions $u(x, 0) = x^2 - 1$, $u(0, y) = -y^2 - 1$, $u(x, 1) = x^2 + x - 2$, and $u(1, y) = y - y^2$.

P15.21 Solve $u_{xx} + u_{xx} = 0$, for $0 \le x \le 1, 0 \le y \le 1$, with boundary conditions $u(x, 0) = x^2 + 1$, $u(0, y) = -y^2 + 1$, $u(x, 1) = x^2$, and $u(1, y) = 2 - y^2$.

P15.22 Solve $u_{xx} + u_{xx} = 0$, for $0 \le x \le 1, 0 \le y \le 1$, with boundary conditions $u(x, 0) = x^3$, $u(0, y) = y^3$, $u(x, 1) = x^3 - 3x^2 - 2x + 1$, and $u(1, y) = y^3 - 3y^2 - 2y + 1$.

P15.23 Solve $u_{xx} + u_{xx} = 0$, for $0 \le x \le 1, 0 \le y \le 1$, with boundary conditions $u(x, 0) = x^3$, $u(0, y) = y^3$, $u(x, 1) = x^3 - 3x^2 + x + 1$, and $u(1, y) = y^3 - 3y^2 + y + 1$.

P15.24 Solve $u_{xx} + u_{xx} = 0$ for $0 \le x \le 1, 0 \le y \le 1$, with boundary conditions $u(x, 0) = x^3$, $u(0, y) = y$, $u(x, 1) = x^3 - 3x + 1$, and $u(1, y) = y + 1 - 3y^2$.

P15.25 Solve $u_{xx} + u_{xx} = 0$ for $0 \le x \le 1, 0 \le y \le 1$, with boundary conditions $u(x, 0) = 0$, $u(0, y) = y^3 + y$, $u(x, 1) = 2 + x - 3x^2$, and $u(1, y) = y^3 - y$.

For Problems P15.26–P15.35, solve the potential equation (given in P15.16–P15.25, respectively) using the finite-element method with a mesh of 16 triangles. This mesh is similar to (an extension and rescaling of) that shown in Fig. 15.16; the triangles are defined in the matrices V and T, (compare to those given in Example 15.10.) Note that V_9 is now an interior node, the new node, V_{13} is a boundary node.

$$V = \begin{bmatrix} 1/4 & 1/4 \\ 1/2 & 1/2 \\ 3/4 & 1/4 \\ 1/4 & 3/4 \\ 0 & 0 \\ 1/2 & 0 \\ 1 & 0 \\ 1 & 1/2 \\ 3/4 & 3/4 \\ 1/2 & 1 \\ 0 & 1 \\ 0 & 1/2 \\ 1 & 1 \end{bmatrix}$$

and

$$T = \begin{bmatrix} 1 & 5 & 12 \\ 1 & 5 & 6 \\ 1 & 2 & 6 \\ 1 & 2 & 12 \\ 3 & 2 & 6 \\ 3 & 6 & 7 \\ 3 & 7 & 8 \\ 3 & 8 & 2 \\ 2 & 8 & 9 \\ 2 & 9 & 10 \\ 4 & 11 & 12 \\ 4 & 12 & 2 \\ 4 & 2 & 10 \\ 4 & 10 & 11 \\ 8 & 9 & 13 \\ 9 & 10 & 13 \end{bmatrix}$$

For Problems P15.36–P15.40, solve the Poisson equation.

   a. Use the finite-difference method with $\Delta x = 0.25$ and $\Delta y = 0.25$.

   b. Use the finite-difference method with $\Delta x = 0.2$ and $\Delta y = 0.2$.

   c. Use the finite-difference method with $\Delta x = 0.1$ and $\Delta y = 0.1$.

   d. Use the finite-element method with a mesh of 16 triangles, as described for P15.26–P15.35.

P15.36 Solve $u_{xx} + u_{xx} = 6x$ for $0 \le x \le 1, 0 \le y \le 1$, with boundary conditions $u(x, 0) = x^3$, $u(0, y) = y$, $u(x, 1) = x^3 - 3x + 1$, and $u(1, y) = -2y + 1$.

P15.37 Solve $u_{xx} + u_{xx} = 2x + 2 - 2y$ for $0 \le x \le 1$, $0 \le y \le 1$, with boundary conditions $u(x,0) = x^2, u(0,y) = y, u(x,1) = x2 + 1$, and $u(1,y) = 1 + y^2$.

P15.38 Solve $u_{xx} + u_{xx} = 2x + 2 - 2y$ for $0 \le x \le 1$, $0 \le y \le 1$, with boundary conditions $u(x,0) = x^2, u(0,y) = y, u(x,1) = x + 1$, and $u(1,y) = 1 + y^2$.

P15.39 Solve $u_{xx} + u_{xx} = 2(1+y)$ for $0 \le x \le 1$, $0 \le y \le 1$, with boundary conditions $u(x,0) = x^3, u(0,y) = y^2, u(x,1) = x^3 + x^2 + 1$, and $u(1,y) = -2y^2 + 4y + 1$.

P15.40 Solve $u_{xx} + u_{xx} = \sin(\pi x)$, for $0 \le x \le 1, 0 \le y \le 1$, with boundary conditions $u(x,0) = x, u(0,y) = y, u(x,1) = 1$, and $u(1,y) = 1$.

EXPLORE SOME APPLICATIONS

A15.1 The telegrapher's equation, $v_{tt} - c^2 v_{xx} + 2 a v_t = 0$, which governs propagation of signals on telegraph lines, is an example of a wave equation with damping. Investigate the numerical solution of this equation for a variety of initial and boundary conditions, and parameter values for a and c. (See Zauderer, 1989, or Svobodny, 1998, for discussion.)

A15.2 The standard inviscid Burger's equation,

$$\frac{\partial}{\partial t} \rho = -\frac{\partial}{\partial x}\left(\left(\frac{1}{2}\rho\right)\rho\right) = -\rho \frac{\partial}{\partial x}\rho$$

is a simple nonlinear PDE with wave solutions which describes the evolution of the density of an inviscid fluid. The generalized inviscid Burger's equation is

$$\frac{\partial}{\partial t} \rho = -\frac{\partial}{\partial x}\left(\left(a + \frac{1}{2}b\rho\right)\rho\right).$$

One application of this equation is in the modeling of traffic flow. The density of the traffic ρ depends on both density and velocity according to the equation

$$\frac{\partial}{\partial t}\rho = -\frac{\partial}{\partial x}F(\rho).$$

where $F(\rho) = \rho v(\rho) = \rho v_m(1 - \rho/\rho_m)$; that is, velocity is a linear function of density, with maximum velocity denoted v_m and maximum density denoted ρ_m. Investigate the solution of this PDE using different choices of finite-difference approximations for the partial derivatives. Take the initial density to be ρ_m for $-100 < x < 0$, and 0 for $0 < x < 500$; find the solution for $-100 < x < 500$. (See Garcia, 1994 for further discussion.)

A15.3 In the heat equation $u_t = cu_{xx}$, the parameter c is the thermal diffusivity of the material. Some typical values (cm^2/sec) are given in the following table, (adapted from Boyce and DiPrima, 1986, p. 515.)

Material	Diffusivity
silver	1.71
copper	1.14
aluminium	0.86
cast iron	0.12

Compare the termperature profile for rods of different materials, each with initial temperature of $100C$ and ends held at $0C$.

A15.4 Compare the termperature profile for rods of different materials (see A15.3), each with initial temperature of $100C$, with one end held at $0C$ and the other end insulated.

EXTEND YOUR UNDERSTANDING

U15.1 Compare the computational effort required to solve the one-dimensional heat equation using the explicit finite-difference method, the implicit finite-difference method, or the Crank-Nicolson method. The implicit methods (both basic and Crank-Nicolson) allow a larger time step than the explicit method; how much larger does it need to be to have the computational effort be the same as for the explicit method? Investigate these questions both analytically and experimentally for some of the problems P15.1–P15.10.

U15.2 Compare the computational effort required to solve the one-dimensional wave equation using the explicit finite-difference method and the implicit finite-difference method. The implicit method allows a larger time step than the explicit method; how much larger does it need to be to have the computational effort be the same as for the explicit method? Investigate these questions both analytically and experimentally for some of the problems P15.11–P15.15.

U15.3 Compare the computational effort required to solve the potential equation using the finite-difference method and the finite-element method. Investigate these questions both analytically and experimentally for some of the problems P15.16–P15.25.

U15.4 The finite-element method is well suited to domains that are more general than the simple rectangular regions illustrated in the text. Modify the domain for some of the problems given in the practice the techniques section (P15.16–P15.25) and solve the resulting problem using finite elements.

U15.5 The finite-element method is well suited to problems in which boundary conditions are more general than those illustrated in the text. Modify a portion of the boundary condition for some of the problems given in the practice the techniques section (P15.16–P15.25) to reflect a no-flux or insulated condition, i.e., take the outward normal to the boundary to be zero; then solve the resulting problem using finite elements.

U15.6 Consider the Poisson equation $u_{xx} + u_{yy} = f(x, y)$ $0 \le x \le 1; 0 \le y \le 1$, with boundary conditions

$$u(x, 0) = x \qquad u(x, 1) = 1 \qquad 0 < x < 1$$
$$u(0, y) = y \qquad u(1, y) = 1 \qquad 0 < y < 1$$

Take

$$f(x, y) = \begin{cases} 1 & \text{for } (x, y) = (1/3, 2/3) \\ 0 & \text{otherwise} \end{cases}$$

Choose an appropriate mesh, and solve using the finite-element method.

U15.7 Consider the Poisson equation $u_{xx} + u_{yy} = f(x, y)$ $0 \le x \le 1; 0 \le y \le 1$. with boundary conditions

$$u(x, 0) = x \qquad u(x, 1) = 1 \qquad 0 < x < 1$$
$$u(0, y) = y \qquad u(1, y) = 1 \qquad 0 < y < 1$$

Take

$$f(x, y) = \begin{cases} 1 & \text{for } (x, y) = (1/3, 2/3) \\ 0 & \text{otherwise} \end{cases}$$

Choose an appropriate mesh, and solve using the finite-difference method.

U15.8 Consider the Poisson equation $u_{xx} + u_{yy} = f(x, y)$ $0 \le x \le 1; 0 \le y \le 1$ with boundary conditions

$$u(x, 0) = x \qquad u(x, 1) = 1 \qquad 0 < x < 1$$
$$u(0, y) = y \qquad u(1, y) = 1 \qquad 0 < y < 1$$

Take

$$f(x, y) = \begin{cases} 1 & \text{for } (x, y) = (1/3, 2/3) \\ 1 & \text{for } (x, y) = (1/4, 1/2) \\ 0 & \text{otherwise} \end{cases}$$

Choose an appropriate mesh, and solve using the finite-element method or the finite-difference method.

Bibliography

Abramowitz, M., and I. A. Stegun (eds.), *Handbook of Mathematical Functions, with Formulas, Graphs, and Mathematical Tables,* Dover, New York, 1965.

Achieser, N. I., *Theory of Approximation,* Dover, New York, 1993.

Acton, F. S., *Numerical Methods That (usually) Work,* Harper and Row, New York, 1970.

Ames, W. F., *Numerical Methods for Partial Differential Equations,* 3d ed., Academic Press, Boston, 1992.

Ascher, U. M., R. M. M. Mattheij, R. D. Russell, *Numerical Solution of Boundary Value Problems for Ordinary Differential Equations,* SIAM, Philadelphia, 1995. (Originally published by Prentice Hall, Englewood Cliffs, NJ, 1988.)

Atkinson, K. E., *An Introduction to Numerical Analysis* , 2d ed., John Wiley, New York, 1989.

Axelsson, O., and V. A. Barker, *Finite Element Solution of Boundary Value Problems,* Academic Press, New York, 1984.

Ayyub, B. M. and R. H. McCuen, *Numerical Methods for Engineers,* Prentice Hall, Upper Saddle River, NJ, 1996

Barrett, R., J. Donato, J. Dongarra, V. Eijkhout, R. Pozo, C. Romine, and H. van der Vorst, *Templates for the Solution of Linear Systems: Building Blocks for Iterative Methods,* SIAM, Philadelphia, 1993.

Bartels, R. H., J. C. Beatty and B. A. Barsky, *An Introduction to Splines for use in Computer Graphics and Geometric Modeling,* Morgan Kaufmann, Los Altos, CA, 1987.

Becker, E. B., G. F. Carey, and J. T. Oden, *Finite Elements: An Introduction,* vol. 1, Prentice-Hall, Englewood Cliffs, NJ, 1981.

Boyce, W. E. and R. C. DiPrima, *Elementary Differential Equations and Boundary Value Problems,* 4th ed., John Wiley & Sons, New York, 1986.

Boyer, C. B., *The History of the Calculus and Its Conceptual Development,* Dover, New York, 1949.

Brent, R., *Algorithms for Minimization Without Derivatives,* Prentice-Hall, Englewood Cliffs, NJ, 1973.

Brezinski, C., *History of Continued Fractions and Padè Approximants,* Springer-Verlag, Berlin, 1991.

Briggs, W. L. and V. E. Henson, *The DFT: An Owner's Manual for the Discrete Fourier Transform,* SIAM, Philadelphia, 1995.

Burden, R. L, and J. D. Faires, Numerical Analysis, 6th ed., Prindle, Weber & Schmidt, Boston, 1996.

Celia, M. A., and W. G. Gray, *Numerical Methods for Differential Equations,* Prentice Hall, Englewood Cliffs, NJ, 1992.

Cheney, E. W., *Introduction to Approximation Theory,* McGraw-Hill, New York, 1966.

Coleman, T. F., and C. Van Loan, *Handbook for Matrix Computations,* SIAM, Philadelphia, 1988.

Colton, D., *Partial Differential Equations,* Random House, New York, 1988.

Conte, S. D., and C. de Boor, *Elementary Numerical Analysis,* 2d ed., McGraw-Hill, New York, 1972.

Dahlquist, G. "A Special Stability Problem for Linear Multistep Methods," *BIT,* vol. 3, 1963, pp. 27–43.

Dahlquist. G., and A. Bjorck, *Numerical Methods,* (Translated by Ned Anderson), Prentice-Hall, Englewood Cliffs, NJ, 1974.

Datta, B. N., *Numerical Linear Algebra and Applications,* Brooks Cole, Pacific Grove, CA, 1995.

Davis, P. J., *Interpolation and Approximation,* Dover, New York, 1975. (Originally published by Blaisdell Publishing in 1963.)

deBoor, C., *A Practical Guide to Splines,* Springer-Verlag, New York, 1978.

Dennis, J. E., Jr. and D. J. Woods, *New Computing Environments: Microcomputers in Large-Scale Computing,* edited by A. Wouk, SIAM, Philadelphia, 1987, pp. 116–122.

Dillon, W. R., and M. Goldstein, *Multivariate analysis : methods and applications,* John Wiley and Sons, New York, 1984.

Edwards, C. H., Jr. and D. E. Penney, *Calculus and Analytic Geometry*, 5th ed., Prentice Hall, Upper Saddle River, NJ, 1998.

Edwards, C. H., Jr. and D. E. Penney, *Differential Equations and Boundary Value Problems: Computing and Modeling,* Prentice Hall, Englewood Cliffs, NJ, 1996.

Edwards, C. H., Jr. and D. E. Penney, *Elementary Differential Equations with Boundary Value Problems* (3d ed.), Prentice Hall, Englewood Cliffs, NJ, 1993.

Eves, H., *Great Moments in Mathematics* (vol. 1, before 1650; vol. 2, after 1650), the Mathematical Association of America, Washington, DC, 1983.

Faires, J. D., and R. Burden, *Numerical Methods,* 2d ed., Brooks/Cole, Pacific Grove, CA, 1998.

Farin, G., *Curves and Surfaces for Computer Aided Geometric Design: A Practical Guide*, 2d ed., Academic Press, Boston, 1990.

Finizio, N., and G. Ladas, *An Introduction to Differential Equations, with Difference Equations, Fourier Series, and Partial Differential Equations,* Wadsworth Publishing, 1982.

Forsythe, G. E., and W. R. Wasow, *Finite-Difference Methods for Partial Differential Equations,* John Wiley & Sons, New York, 1960.

Forsythe, G. E., M. A. Malcolm, and C. B. Moler, *Computer Methods for Mathematical Computations,* Prentice-Hall, Englewood Cliffs, NJ, 1977.

Fox, L., *Numerical Solution of Two-Point Boundary Value Problems in Ordinary Differential Equations,* Dover, New York, 1990 (originally published by Clarendon Press, Oxford, 1957).

Fox, L., *An Introduction to Numerical Linear Algebra,* Oxford University Press, New York, 1965.

Fraleigh, J. B. and R. A. Beauregard, *Linear Algebra,* Addison-Wesley, Reading, MA, 1987.

Freund, R. W., G. H. Golub, and N. M. Nachtigal, "Iterative Solution of Linear Systems," *Acta Numerica I,* pp. 57–100, 1992.

Froberg, C. E., *Numerical Mathematics: Theory and Computer Applications,* Benjamin/Cummings, Menlo Park, CA, 1985.

Garcia, A. L., *Numerical Methods for Physics,* Prentice Hall, Englewood Cliffs, NJ, 1994.

Gear, C. W., *Numerical Initial Value Problems in Ordinary Differential Equations,* Prentice-Hall, Englewood Cliffs, NJ, 1971.

Golub, G. H., and J. M. Ortega, *Scientific Computing and Differential Equations: An Introduction to Numerical Methods,* Academic Press, Boston, 1992.

Golub, G. H., and C. F. Van Loan, *Matrix Computations,* 3d ed., Johns Hopkins University Press, Baltimore, 1996.

Greenbaum, A., *Iterative Methods for Solving Linear Systems,* SIAM, Philadelphia, 1997.

Greenberg, M. D., *Advanced Engineering Mathematics,* 2d ed., Prentice Hall, Upper Saddle River, NJ, 1998.

Greenberg, M. D., *Foundations of Applied Mathematics,* Prentice-Hall, Englewood Cliffs, NJ, 1978.

Greenspan, D., *Discrete Numerical Methods in Physics and Engineering,* Academic Press, New York, 1974.

Grossman, S. I., and W. R. Derrick, *Advanced Engineering Mathematics,* Harper & Row, New York, 1988.

Haberman, R., *Elementary Applied Partial Differential Equations, with Fourier Series and Boundary Value Problems,* Prentice-Hall, Englewood Cliffs, NJ, 1983.

Hager, W. W., *Applied Numerical Linear Algebra,* William W. Hager, Dept. of Mathematics, Univ. of Florida, Gainesville, FL. (originally published by Prentice Hall, Englewood Cliffs, NJ, 1988.)

Hair, J. F., R. E. Anderson, R. L. Tatham, and W. Black, *Multivariate Data Analysis,* 5th ed., Prentice Hall, Englewood Cliffs, NJ, 1998.

Hall, C. A., and T. A. Porsching, *Numerical Analysis of Partial Differential Equations,* Prentice Hall, Englewood Cliffs, NJ, 1990.

Hamming, R. W., *Numerical Methods for Scientists and Engineers,* 2d ed., McGraw-Hill, New York, 1973.

Hanna, O. T., and O. C. Sandall, *Computational Methods In Chemical Engineering,* Prentice Hall, Upper Saddle River, NJ, 1995.

Hibbeler, R. C., *Engineering Mechanics:Dynamics,* 7th ed., Prentice Hall, Englewood Cliffs, NJ, 1995.

Hibbeler, R. C., *Engineering Mechanics:Statics,* 7th ed., Prentice Hall, Englewood Cliffs, NJ, 1995.

Hildebrand, F. B., *Introduction to Numerical Analysis,* Dover, New York, 1987.

Hildebrand, F. B., *Advanced Calculus for Applications,* 2d ed., Prentice-Hall, Englewood Cliffs, NJ, 1976.

Himmelblau, D. M., *Basic Principles and Calculations in Engineering,* 3d ed., Prentice-Hall, Englewood Cliffs, NJ, 1974.

Hornbeck, R. W., *Numerical Methods,* Prentice-Hall, Englewood Cliffs, NJ, 1975.

Inman, D. J., *Engineering Vibration,* Prentice Hall, Englewood Cliffs, NJ, 1996.

Isaacson, E., and H. B. Keller, *Analysis of Numerical Methods,* Dover, New York, 1994. (Originally published by John Wiley & Sons, 1966).

Jaeger, J. C., *An Introduction to Applied Mathematics,* Clarenden Press, Oxford, 1951.

Jain, M. K., *Numerical Solution of Differential Equations,* John Wiley, New York, 1979.

Jensen, J. A., and J. H. Rowland, *Methods of Computation,* Scott, Foresman and Company, Glenview, IL, 1975.

Johnson, R. A. and D. W. Wichern, *Applied Multivariate Statistical Analysis,* 4th ed., Prentice Hall, Englewood Cliffs, NJ, 1998.

Kachigan, S. K., *Multivariate Statistical Analysis: A Conceptual Introduction,* 2d ed., Radius Press, New York, 1991.

Kahaner, D., C. Moler, and S. Nash, *Numerical Methods and Software,* Prentice-Hall, Englewood Cliffs, NJ, 1989.

Kammer, W. J., G. W. Reddien, and R. S. Varga, "Quadratic Splines," *Numerische Mathematik,* vol. 22, pp. 241–259, 1974.

Keller, H. B., *Numerical Methods for Two-point Boundary-value Problems,* Blaisdell, Waltham, MA, 1968.

Kollerstrom, N. "Thomas Simpson and 'Newton's Method of Approximation': An Enduring Myth," *British Journal for the History of Science,* vol. 25 (1992), pp. 347–354.

Kolman, B., *Introductory Linear Algebra with Applications,* 6th ed., Prentice Hall, Upper Saddle River, NJ, 1997.

Lancaster, P., and K. Salkauskas, *Curve and Surface Fitting: An Introduction,* Academic Press, Boston, 1986.

Leon, S. J., *Linear Algebra with Applications,* 5th ed., Prentice Hall, Upper Saddle River, NJ, 1998.

Leon, S. J., E. Herman, and R. Faulkenberry, *ATLAST: Computer Exercises for Linear Algebra,* Prentice Hall, Upper Saddle River, NJ, 1996.

Lorenz, E., "Deterministic Nonperiodic Flows," *Journal of Atmospheric Sciences,* vol. 20, pp. 130–141, 1963.

Mardia, K. V., *Multivariate Analysis,* Academic Press, London, 1980.

Maron, M. J., *Numerical Analysis: A Practical Approach,* Macmillan, New York, 1982.

Meis, T., and U. Marcowitz, *Numerical Solution of Partial Differential Equations,* Springer-Verlag, New York, 1981.

Morrison, D. F., *Multivariate Statistical Methods,* 3d ed., McGraw-Hill, New York, 1990.

Nelder, J. A. and Mead, R., *Computer Journal,* vol. 7, 1965, p. 308.

Nicolis, G. and I. Prigogine, *Self-Organization in Nonequilibrium Systems,* John Wiley & Sons, New York, 1977.

Ortega, J. M., *Numerical Analysis - A Second Course,* Academic Press, New York, 1972.

Ortega, J. M., and W. G. Poole, *An Introduction to Numerical Methods for Differential Equations,* Pitman Publishing, 1981.

Powers, D. L., *Boundary Value Problems,* 3d ed., Harcourt Brace Jovanovich, Orlando, FL, 1987.

Press, W. H., B. P. Flannery, S. A. Teukolsky, and W. T. Vetterling, *Numerical Recipes: The Art of Scientific Computing,* Cambridge: Cambridge University Press, Cambridge, U.K., 1986.

Rainville, E. D., *Elementary Differential Equations,* Macmillan, New York, 1958.

Ralston, A., and P. Rabinowitz, *A First Course in Numerical Analysis,* 2d ed., McGraw-Hill, New York, 1978.

Reinboldt, W. C., *Methods for Solving Systems of Nonlinear Equations,* SIAM, Philadelphia, 1974.

Reynolds, B. E., "The Algorists vs. the Abacists: An Ancient Controversy on the Use of Calculators," *The College Mathematics Journal,* vol. 24, no. 3, May 1993, pp. 218–223.

Rice, J. R., *Numerical Methods, Software, and Analysis,* 2d ed., Academic Press, New York, 1992.

Ritger, P. D., and N. J. Rose, *Differential Equations with Applications,* McGraw-Hill, New York, 1968.

Rivlin, T. J., *An Introduction to the Approximation of Functions,* Dover, New York, 1981. (Originally published by Blaisdell Publishing, 1969.)

Roberts, C. E., *Ordinary Differential Equations: A Computational Approach,* Prentice-Hall, Englewood Cliffs, NJ, 1979.

Shampine, L. F. and M. W. Reichelt, "The MATLAB ODE Suite", *SIAM Journal on Scientific Computing,* vol. 18, no. 1, 1997.

Sigmon, K. (ed.), *Matlab Primer,* Mathworks, Inc., 1998.

Silvester, P. P., and R. L. Ferrari, *Finite Elements for Electrical Engineers,* 3d ed., Cambridge University Press, Cambridge, U.K., 1996.

Simmons, G. F., *Calculus with Analytic Geometry,* McGraw-Hill, New York, 1985.

Simmons, G. F., *Differential Equations with Applications and Historical Notes,* McGraw-Hill, New York, 1972.

Simon, W., *Mathematical Techniques for Biology and Medicine,* Dover, New York, 1986. (Originally published by MIT Press, 1977.)

Smith, D. E., *A Source Book in Mathematics,* Dover, New York, 1959.

Spong and Vidyasagar, *Robot Dynamics and Control,* John Wiley & Sons, New York, 1989.

Stoer, J., and R. Bulirsch, *Introduction to Numerical Analysis,* Springer Verlag, New York, 1980.

Strang, G., *Linear Algebra and Its Applications,* 3d ed., Harcourt Brace Jovanovich, San Diego, CA, 1988.

Strang, G., and G. Fix, *An Analysis of the Finite Element Method,* Prentice-Hall, Englewood Cliffs, NJ, 1973.

Struik, D. J., *A Concise History of Mathematics,* 4th ed., Dover, New York, 1987.

Student Edition of MATLAB, The Language of Technical Computing, Version 5 User's Guide, Prentice Hall, Upper Saddle River, NJ, 1997.

Svobony, T., *Mathematical Modeling for Industry and Engineering,* Prentice Hall, Upper Saddle River, NJ, 1998.

Thomson, W. T., *Introduction to Space Dynamics,* Dover, New York, 1986. (Originally published by John Wiley & Sons, 1961.)

Thomson, W. T., *Theory of Vibrations with Applications,* Prentice Hall, Englewood Cliff, NJ, 1993.

Timan, A. F. , C. J. Hyman, N. I. Achieser, *Theory of Approximation,* Dover, New York, 1993.

Troutman, J. L., and M. Bautista, *Boundary Value Problems of Applied Mathematics,* Prindle, Weber & Schmidt Publishing, 1994.

Van der Pol, B. , "Forced Oscillations in a Circuit with Non-linear Resistance," *Phil. Mag.,* vol. 3, pp. 65–80, 1927.

Van Loan, C. F., *Introduction to Scientific Computing: A Matrix-Vector Approach Using Matlab,* Prentice Hall, Upper Saddle River, NJ, 1997.

Van Loan, C. F., *Computational Framework for the Fast Fourier Transform,* SIAM, Philadelphia, 1992.

Vargaftik, N. B., *Tables of the Thermophysical Properties of Liquids and Gases,* 2d ed., Hemishpere, Washington D.C., 1975.

Weinstock, R., "Isaac Newton: Credit Where Credit Won't Do," *The College Mathematics Journal,* vol. 25, no. 3, May 1994, pp. 179–192.

Young, D. M., and R. T. Gregory, *A Survey of Numerical Mathematics,* vol.1 and 2, Dover, New York, 1988.

Zauderer, E., *Partial Differential Equations of Applied Mathematics,* 2d ed., John Wiley & Sons, New York, 1989.

Zienkiewicz, O. C., and Taylor, R. L. *The Finite Element Method,* 4th ed., vol. 1, McGraw-Hill, London, 1989.

Zill, D. G. *Differential Equations with Boundary-Value Problems,* Prindle, Weber, & Schmidt, Boston, 1986.

Answers to Selected Exercises

Chapter 1

P1.1 $x = 1, y = 2$

P1.3 $x = 1, y = 1$

P1.5 $x = 1, y = 3$

P1.7   For $x_0 = 0.8$, $x_1 = 0.99957$, $x_2 = 0.90965$, $x_3 = 0.96928$; the conditions of the theorem are satisfied.

P1.9   For $x_0 = 0.5$, $x_1 = 0.75$, $x_2 = 0.4375$, $x_3 = 0.8085$; the conditions of the theorem are not satisfied.

P1.11 C_1: center $(1,0)$, radius $3/8$; C_2: center $(2,0)$, radius $1/2$; C_3: center $(3,0)$, radius 0; the disks are disjoint, so $5/8 \leq \mu_1 \leq 11/8$; $3/2 \leq \mu_2 \leq 5/2$; $\mu_3 = 3$.

P1.13 C_1: center $(1,0)$, radius $1/4$; C_2: center $(2,0)$, radius $1/2$; C_3: center $(3,0)$, radius $1/4$; the disks are disjoint, so $3/4 \leq \mu_1 \leq 5/4$; $3/2 \leq \mu_2 \leq 5/2$; $11/4 \leq \mu_3 \leq 13/4$.

P1.15 C_1: center $(1,0)$, radius $3/8$; C_2: center $(2,0)$, radius $1/2$; C_3: center $(3,0)$, radius $1/3$; μ_1 and μ_2 are within the union of the regions bounded by C_1 and C_2; $23/8 \leq \mu_3 \leq 25/8$.

P1.17   a. 10.9; b. 11.0; c. rel error for Part a is $-9 * 10^{-3}$, rel error for Part b is $9 * 10^{-5}$.

P1.19   a. $x_1 = 56.98, x_2 = 0.02$; b. $x_1 = 56.98, x_2 = 0.0176$; c. $x_1 = 56.9825, x_2 = 0.0175$.

P1.21   a. 1.2; b. 1.1; c. 1.0666 (Note, this is not better, the exact result is $\arctan(2) = 1.1071....$)

P1.23   a. 5; b. 4.5; c. 4.333... (The exact result is $(2^2 - 2^0)/\log(2) = 4.3281....$)

P1.25   a. 3.5343; b. 3.1474; c. 3.0184 (The exact result is 3.)

P1.27   (a. and b.) $0.92857 \leq y \leq 1.0714$; a. $1.9572 \leq x \leq 2.0429$; b. $1.9572 \leq x \leq 2.0429$

P1.29   (a. and b.) $1.9684 \leq y \leq 2.0316$; a. $2.9537 \leq x \leq 3.0463$; b. $2.9263 \leq x \leq 3.0737$

Chapter 2

P2.1 $x = 1.4142$

P2.3 $x = 2.6458$

P2.5 $x = 1.5874$

P2.7 $x = 0.49492$

P2.9 $x = 0.81904$

P2.11 $x = -2.8794, x = -0.6527, x = 0.53209$

P2.13 $x = -3.1055, x = 0.22346, x = 2.882$

P2.15 x = 2.8063

P2.17 x = -3.324, x = -1.6197, x = 5.9437

P2.19 x = 0, x = 1.3333, x = 2.5

P2.21 x = 0.21923

P2.23 x = 1

P2.25 x = 0.71137

P2.27 a. x alternates between 1 and -1; b. x = 0.2541; c. $x_0 = 0.5 - x = 0.44853$; $x_0 = 0 \to f'(x_0) = 0$ (Newton's method fails); d. x = 0.87055

P2.29 x = 2.029, x = 4.9132, x = 7.9787

P2.31 x = -0.70347

P2.33 a. x = 2.4781, x = 3; b. x = 2.7368, x = 2.7

P2.35 x = 0.12313

Chapter 3

P3.1 x = [1.1429, 1.0000, -0.7143]′= [8/7, 1, -5/7]′

P3.3 x = [1, 2, 3]′

P3.5 x = [1, 1, 1]′

P3.7 i) x = [1, 2, 6]′; ii) x = [-3, 5, -4]′

P3.9 x = [-1, 2, 0, 1]′

P3.11 x = [3, -4, -5]′

P3.13 x = [2, 1, -1]′

P3.15 x = [1, 1, 1, 1, 1, 1]′

P3.17 a. x = [0, 3]′; b. x = [-1, 3]′; without rounding x = [-1.001, 3.001]′

P3.19 a. x = [0, 5, 0]′; b. x = [1, 2, 3]′; without rounding x = [1.0005, 1.9995, 2.9995]′

P3.27 x = [1, 1, 1]′

P3.29 x = [1, -2, 5, 8]′

P3.31 x = [2, -5, -2, 1, -2, 2]′

P3.33 x = [-4, 3, -3, 4, 3, 3, 5, 5]′

P3.35 x = [-3, 1, -1, -2, 3, -4, -1, -1, 3, 0]′

P3.37 a. x = [4, -4, 4, 1, 2, 3, -4, 2]′

b. x = [-2, 1, 1, 0, 3, 0, -1, 5]′

c. x = [-3, -3, -2, 0, 4, -3, 3, 1]′

d. x = [5, 2, -4, -3, 2, -4, 0, -1]′

P3.39 a. x = [1, 0, 2, -1, 5, -1, -2, -5, -3, -2]′

b. x = [1, -1, -3, 4, -4, -4, -1, 2, 4, 0]′

c. x = [-2, 1, -5, 4, -1, 2, -4, 2, -2, 4]′

d. x = [1, 0, 1, -1, -1, 4, -4, -3, -3, -3]′

Chapter 4

(Results shown are exact, not values after 3 or 10 iterations.)

P4.1 x = [1, 2, 3]′

P4.3 x = [2, 1, -1]′

P4.5 x = [0.3, 1.8, 1.7]′

P4.7 x = [6, 3, 5, 2]′

P4.9 x = [0, 1, 0, -1]′

P4.11 x = [1, 2, 3, 4]′

P4.13 x = [1, -2, 3, 2, -1]′

P4.15 x = [-2, 4, -6, 2, -4, 7]′

P4.17 x = [-2, 1, 4, -6, 3, 2, -4, 7]′

Chapter 5

P5.1 x = 0.90644, y = 2.5704

P5.3 x = 1.38,   y = 1.6335

P5.5 x = 1.0784,   y = 1.9259

P5.7 x = 0.56451, y = 1.1579,   z = 1.5299

P5.9 x = 1.4901,   y = -0.68477,   z = 0.98001

P5.11 x = 0.29704, y = 0.67481,   z = 0.73066

P5.13 x = 0.33016, y = 0.47535,   z = 0.60284

P5.15 x = 0.57627, y = 0.36755,   z = 0.70639

Chapter 6

P6.1   a. L = [1   0   0
                2   1   0
                3   4   1]

   U = [1   2   3
          0   4   5
          0   0   6]

b. A⁻¹ = [1.5833   -0.1667   -0.0833
          -1.5417   1.0833   -0.2083
           0.8333   -0.6667   0.1667]

c. det(A) = 24

d. x = [1.3333   -0.6667   0.3333]′
   y = [2.1944   -2.8472   1.6111]′

P6.3   a. L = [1   0   0
                2   1   0
                1   2/3   1]

   U = [2   1   -2
          0   -3   6
          0   0   -1]

b. A_inv = [1/6   1/6   0
              0   1   -2
            -1/3   2/3   -1]

c. det(A) = 6

d. x = [1/3   -1   -2/3]′
   y = [-1/9   1/3   -1/9]′

P6.5   a. L = [1.0000   0   0
               0.5000   1.0000   0
               0.3333   1.0000   1.0000]

   U = [1.0000   0.5000   0.3333
          0   0.0833   0.0833
          0   -0.0000   0.0056]

b. [9   -36   30
     -36   192   -180
      30   -180   180]

c. 4.6296e-04

d. x = [3   -24   30]′
   y = [1791   -10116   9810]′

P6.7
a. L = [1   0   0   0
          2   1   0   0
          3   4   1   0
         -1   -3   0   1]

   U = [1   1   0   3
          0   -1   -1   -5
          0   0   3   13
          0   0   0   -13]

b. A_inv = [-0.2308   0.2051   0.3333   0.1795
              0.0769   0.4872   -0.3333   0.0513
              0.0000   -0.3333   0.3333   0.3333
              0.3846   -0.2308   -0.0000   -0.0769]

c. det(A) = 39

d. x = [0.4872   0.2821   0.3333   0.0769]′
   y = [0.0703   0.0677   0.0427   0.1164]′

P6.9   a. L = [1   0   0   0
                0   1   0   0
                0   0   1   0
               1/3   -1/9   1/9   1]

   U = [3   7   4   0
          0   3   13   3
          0   0   1   4
          0   0   0   -1/9]

b. A_inv = [-98   32   -24   295
              49   -16   12   -147
             -12   4   -3   36
               3   -1   1   -9]

c. det(A) = -1.0000

d. x = [205   -102   25   -6]′
   y = [-25724   12859   -3159   796]′

P6.11

a. L = [1   0   0   0   0   0
         2   1   0   0   0   0
         3   4   1   0   0   0
         1   0   0   1   0   0
         0   1   0 -1/3   1   0
         0   0   1   1   -2   1]

   U = [1   2   3   1   0   0
         0   2   4   0   1   0
         0   0   3   0   0   1
         0   0   0   3   6   12
         0   0   0   0   2   6
         0   0   0   0   0   1]

b.

A^{-1} =

   [11.0556 -14.5000   5.6667   1.9444 -9.1667 -5.3333
     -6.1944   7.7500 -2.8333 -0.8056   4.0833   2.1667
      1.8889   -2.0000   0.6667   0.1111 -0.6667 -0.3333
     -3.3333   5.0000 -2.0000 -0.6667   3.0000   2.0000
      2.8333   -6.5000   3.0000   1.1667 -5.5000 -3.0000
     -0.6667   2.0000 -1.0000 -0.3333   2.0000   1.0000]

c. det(A) = 36

d.

x =
   [-10.3333   4.1667   -0.3333   4.0000 -8.0000   3.0000]′
y =
   [-111.4352 67.8565 -23.2963 35.2778 -17.6944 1.2222]′

P6.13

a. L = [1   0   0   0   0   0
         2   1   0   0   0   0
         3   4   1   0   0   0
         1   0   0   1   0   0
         0   1   0   -1   1   0
         2   0   1   1   -2   1]

   U = [1   2   1   1   0   0
         0   2   2   0   1   0
         0   0   1   0   0   1
         0   0   0   1   6   12
         0   0   0   0   2   6
         0   0   0   0   0   1]

b.

A_inv =

   [52.50 -28.50   11.00   -7.50 -16.50 -10.00
    -16.25   9.75   -3.50   2.25   4.75   2.50
      9.00   -6.00   2.00   -1.00   -2.00   -1.00
    -28.00   15.00   -6.00   4.00   9.00   6.00
     12.50   -6.50   3.00   -2.50   -5.50   -3.00
     -4.00   2.00   -1.00   1.00   2.00   1.00]

c. det(A) = 4

d.
x = [1.00   -0.50   1.00   0.00   -2.00   1.00]′
y = [100.75 -31.625 17.00 -53.50   26.75   -9.00]′

P6.17   a. dd = [4   4   3]
                bb = [0   4   2]

             b. L = [1   0   0
                       4   1   0
                       0   2   1]

                 U = [4   2   0
                       0   4   1
                       0   0   3]

P6.19   a. dd = [5   3   2]
                bb = [0   3   3]

             b. L = [1   0   0
                       3   1   0
                       0   3   1]

                 U = [5   1   0
                       0   3   3
                       0   0   2]

P6.21   a. dd = [1   1   1   1]
                bb = [0   2   2   1]

             b. L = [1   0   0   0
                       2   1   0   0
                       0   2   1   0
                       0   0   1   1]

                 U = [1   3   0   0
                       0   1   2   0
                       0   0   1   5
                       0   0   0   1]

P6.23 a. dd = [1   2   4   4]
       bb = [0   1   3   3]

  b. L = [1   0   0   0
          1   1   0   0
          0   3   1   0
          0   0   3   1]

     U = [1   4   0   0
          0   2   2   0
          0   0   4   3
          0   0   0   4]

P6.25 a. dd = [5   1   1   4]
       bb = [0   2   3   1]

  b. L = [1   0   0   0
          2   1   0   0
          0   3   1   0
          0   0   1   1]

     U = [5   0   0   0
          0   1   2   0
          0   0   1   4
          0   0   0   4]

P6.27 a. dd = [1   2   3   4   5   6]
       bb = [0   2   3   4   5   6]

  b. L = [1   0   0   0   0   0
          2   1   0   0   0   0
          0   3   1   0   0   0
          0   0   4   1   0   0
          0   0   0   5   1   0
          0   0   0   0   6   1]

     U = [1   -5   0   0   0   0
          0   2   -4   0   0   0
          0   0   3   -3   0   0
          0   0   0   4   -2   0
          0   0   0   0   5   -1
          0   0   0   0   0   6]

P6.29 a. dd = [5   4   2   3   4   1]
       bb = [0   3   2   1   3   4]

  b. L = [1   0   0   0   0   0
          3   1   0   0   0   0
          0   2   1   0   0   0
          0   0   1   1   0   0
          0   0   0   3   1   0
          0   0   0   0   4   1]

U = [5   2   0   0   0   0
      0   4   0   0   0   0
      0   0   2   2   0   0
      0   0   0   3   4   0
      0   0   0   0   4   4
      0   0   0   0   0   1]

P6.31   L = [1.0000   0   0
             0.1667   1.00   0
             1.0000   0   1.00]

     U = [6.00   2.0000   2.0000
           0   1.6667   -1.3333
           0   0   -1.0000]

P6.33   L = [1   0   0   0
             0   1   0   0
            -1   0   1   0
             0   0   1   1]

     U = [-1   1   0   0
            0   1   -1   1
            0   0   1   0
            0   0   0   -1]

P6.35

L = [1.00   0   0   0   0   0
      0   1.00   0   0   0   0
      0   0   1.00   0   0   0
      0   0   0   1.0000   0   0
      0   0   0   0   1.0000   0
     -0.50   0.25   0   0.0833   0.0486   1]

U = [-2   6   4.0   0   0   0
      0   4   8.0   -0.50   0   0
      0   0   -0.5   3.25   1.50   0
      0   0   0   1.50   1.75   -3.0000
      0   0   0   0   -3.00   13.0000
      0   0   0   0   0   -0.3819]

P6.37 a. Doolittle form
       L = [1   0   0
            2   1   0
            4   3   1]

     U = [9   18   36
          0   4   12
          0   0   1]

b. Cholesky form

L = [3   0   0
       6   2   0
      12   6   1]

U = [3   6   12
       0   2   6
       0   0   1]

c. x_1 = [-1   2   1]'
    x_2 = [2   1   -1]'
    x_3 = [-2   -2   1]'

P6.39   Pivoting is required, Cholesky and Doolittle methods fail.

LU = PA = [2   -1   0   0   0   0
            -1   2   -1.0000   0   0   0
             0   0   -1.0000   2.0000   -1   0
             0   -1   0.6667   -1.0000   0   0
             0   0   0   -1.0000   2   -1
             0   0   0   0   -1   2]

L = [1.0   0   0   0   0   0
     -0.5   1   0   0   0   0
      0   0   1   0   0   0
      0   -0.6667 0   1   0   0
      0   0   0   1   1.0 0
      0   0   0   0   -0.5 1]

U = [2   -1.0   0   0   0   0
      0   1.5   -1   0   0   0
      0   0   -1   2   -1   0
      0   0   0   -1   0   0
      0   0   0   0   2   -1
      0   0   0   0   0   1]

c. solution using LU_pivot

xx_1 = [2   1   3 -1   -3 -2]
xx_2 = [1   2   3 -1   -3 -2]
xx_3 = [1 -1   2 -2   3 -3]

Chapter 7

Results after 10 iterations:

P7.1   a. m = 3.0001, v = [0.0000   0.5000   1.0000], error = 4.5601e-05, exact = 3
           b. m = 1.0000, v = [1.0000   0.0000   -1.0000], error = 5.8666e-05, exact = 1

P7.3   a. m = 3.0132, v = [1.0000   1.0000   0.0087], error = 0.0109, exact = 3
           b. m = 1.9768, v = [-0.9653   -0.9653   1.0000], error = 0.0290, exact = 2

P7.5   a. m = 3.0240, v = [-0.0106   0.2889   1.0000], error = 0.0162, exact = 3
b. m = 0.9990, v = [1.0000   0.9996   -0.0012], error = 0.0012, exact = 1

P7.7   a. m = 5.1521, v = [0.2367   1.0000   0.0529], error = 0.0355, exact = 5
b. m = 3.4033, v = [0.1618   1.0000   0.7092], error = 0.3437, exact = 3

P7.9   a. m = 2.0019, v = [0.2884   1.0000   0.5730], error = 0.0012, exact = 2
b. m = 0.9980, v = [0.2857   1.0000   0.5714], error = 5.4704e-06, exact = 1

P7.11   a. m = 4.0000, v = [1.0000   0.0010   -0.9980   0.0010], error = 0.0048, exact = 4
b. m = 1.9993, v = [0.0005   0.5002   1.0000   0.5002], error = 0.0011, exact = 2

P7.13   a. m = 4.9900, v = [0.9970   1.0000   0.0060   0.0030], error = 0.0172, exact = 5
b. m = 0.0000, v = [0.5000   1.0000   0.5000   0.0000], error = 5.6445e-15, exact = 0
(Hint: modify the inverse power method, or see hint for P7.19)

P7.15   a. m = 5.0000, v = [-0.7562   -0.1712   0.6250   1.0000], error = 2.6210, exact = 5;
after 50 iterations:
m = 5.0002, v = [-0.0000   1.0000   0.2500   0.4001], error = 1.0513e-04
b. m = 0, v = [0   0   0   1] (Hint: modify inverse power method, or see hint for P7.19)

P7.17   a. m = 4.0834, v = [-0.0005   -0.0592   0.4117   1.0000   0.5291], error = 0.1150, exact = 4
b. m = 1.9876, v = [0.5002   -0.4829   -0.9663   0.5166   1.0000], error = 0.0353, exact = 2

P7.19   a. m = 3.0132, v = [-0.0087   0.4869   1.0000   0.7566   0.5044], error = 0.0191, exact = 3;
after 30 iterations:
m = 3.0000, v = [-0.000   0.500   1.000   0.750   0.500], error = 5.6172e-06
b. m = -5.7135e-10, v = [1.0000   1.0000   -0.0000   -0.0000   -0.0000], error = 7.7881e-07, exact = 0;
converged after 12 iterations:
m = -7.0636e-12, error = 4.8669e-08
(Hint: Apply the inverse power method to B = A - 0.2I and then add 0.2 to the eigenvalue.)

P7.21   a. m = 8.7839, v = [-0.5198   1.0000   0.2923], error = 0.1514
b. m = 8.8657, v = [-0.5198   1.0000   0.2923], error = 0.1139;
from Matlab function eig: 8.8730

P7.23   a. m = 16.6077, v = [-0.5306   1.0000   0.2966], error = 0.2326
b. m = 16.7373, v = [-0.5306   1.0000   0.2966], error = 0.1713;
from Matlab function eig: 16.7460

P7.25   a. m = 45.0458, v = [-0.1743   1.0000   0.0506], error = 0.0013
b. m = 45.0454, v = [-0.1743   1.0000   0.0506], error = 0.0012;
from Matlab function eig: 45.0454

P7.27   a. m = -8.9669, v = [0.3685   -0.0528   1.0000], error = 0.6893
b. m = -8.7071, v = [0.3685   -0.0528   1.0000], error = 0.6384;
from Matlab function eig: -8.7460

P7.29 a. m = 57.2864, error =1.306
b. m = 58.0325, error = 0.8996
Eigenvector for parts a. and b. v = [1.0000   0.0220   0.1218 -0.6622]
Eigenvalue from Matlab function eig: 58.0982

P7.31 a. m = 48.2782 v = [-0.1454   1.0000 -0.1017 -0.0383], error = 0.0133
b. m = 48.2800, v = [-0.1454   1.0000 -0.1017 -0.0383], error = 0.0132;
from Matlab function eig: 48.2800

P7.33 a. m = 72.0000, v = [1.0000   0.3333 -0.6652   0.6681], error = 0.0746
b. m = 71.9997, v = [1.0000   0.3333 -0.6652   0.6681], error = 0.0746;
eigenvalue from Matlab function eig: 72.0000

P7.35 a. m = 33.3009, v = [-0.1043   0.4447 -0.5053   1.0000   0.2490], error = 0.0637
b. m = 33.3290, v = [-0.1043   0.4447 -0.5053   1.0000   0.2490], error = 0.0532;
eigenvalue from Matlab function eig: 33.3294

P7.37 a. m = 76.3303, error = 0.0742; b. m = 76.2918, error = 0.0502;
eigenvector for parts a. and b. v = [0.8155   0.1067   1.0000 -0.1053   0.4252   0.0853   0.3795];
eigenvalue from Matlab function eig: 76.2919.

P7.39 a. m = 194.6906, error = 0.7786; b. m = 194.7387, error = 0.7723;
eigenvector for parts a. and b. v = [-0.3087 1.0000 -0.6857 -0.0823 -0.5172 0.9594 0.3572 0.8342 0.0161];
eigenvalue from Matlab function eig: 194.7452

P7.41 a. The QR factorization of matrix A is
Q = [-0.2182 -0.6838 -0.6963
        -0.4364 -0.5698   0.6963
        -0.8729   0.4558 -0.1741]

R = [-4.5826   3.9279 -5.2372
        -0.0000 -1.2536   1.1396
        -0.0000 -0.0000   0.5222]
b. The QR eigenvalue method finds the upper triangular matrix
B = [3.0000   -0.6667 -7.4535
       -0.0000   1.0000   0.0000
        0.0000 -0.0000   1.0000]
with the same eigenvalues as A (on the diagonal): 3, 1, 1.

c. The upper Hessenberg matrix with the same eigenvalues as A is
AA = [1.0000   0   0
        -4.4721   3.0000 -6.0000
         0.0000 -0.0000   1.0000]

d. The upper Hessenberg matrix is converted to the upper triangular matrix
B = [3.0000   4.4721   6.0000
       -0.0000   1.0000 -0.0000
        0.0000 -0.0000   1.0000]
with the eigenvalues on the diagonal. (The computational effort for part d is approximately 1/2 that needed for part b.)

P7.43 a. The QR factorization of matrix A is

Q = [-0.8575   0.5145   0
       -0.5145 -0.8575   0
        0   0   1.0000]

R = [-5.8310   1.7150 -1.3720
        0   -1.0290 -0.3430
        0   0   2.0000]

b. The QR eigenvalue method finds the upper triangular matrix

B = [3.0147 -4.9970   1.4142
      0.0030   1.9853   0.0041
      0   0   2.0000]

with the same eigenvalues as A (on the diagonal): 3.0147, 1.9853, 2.0000.

c. The upper Hessenberg matrix with the same eigenvalues as A is A itself.

d. The results are the same as for part b, but with approximately 1/2 as many flops.

P7.47 a. Q = [0.2040 -0.4011   0.8930
                    0.9748 -0.0013 -0.2233
                    0.0907   0.9160   0.3907]

R = [-176.4540 48.2165 -22.3741
        -0.0000 -0.4061   2.9493
         0.0000   0.0000   0.8372]

b. B = [5.1175 21.0988 182.8169
         -0.0056   3.8943   7.3171
         -0.0001 -0.0014   2.9882]

e = [5.1175   3.8943   2.9882]

c. AA = [-36.0000   -9.4939   -5.9047
          172.7426   44.9453   26.0879
            0.0000   0.0879   3.0547]

d. B = [5.1175 -23.5183 182.5214
         0.0056   3.9911   -7.3038
        -0.0000   0.0147   2.8914]

e = [5.1175   3.9911   2.8914]

P7.51 a. Q = [-0.4339 -0.7071 -0.0638   0.5547
                    0.4339 -0.7071   0.0638 -0.5547
                    0.7593   0.0000 -0.3403   0.5547
                    0.2169   0.0000   0.9360   0.2774]

R = [-9.2195   9.2195 -4.4471   4.0132
      -0.0000 -5.6569   2.8284 -1.4142
      -0.0000   0   -1.1061   2.8504
       0.0000   0   0   1.6641]

b. After 10 iterations, the matrix is almost upper triangular

B = [3.9894 -0.0020 -0.3496 13.9731
      -0.0028   3.9995 -0.0908 -2.5377
      -0.0295 -0.0056   3.0302   3.6283
      -0.0001 -0.0000 -0.0048   1.9810]

e = [3.9894   3.9995   3.0302   1.9810]

c. Upper Hessenberg

AA = [4.0000   0   0   0
        8.3066   1.8406   0.8521 -12.0333
        0.0000 -0.2169   3.1594   0.2408
        0.0000   0.0000 -0.0000   4.0000]

d. B = [3.9894   0.2795 -8.1193 -11.3740
         0.0296   3.0462   2.0218   2.6984
         0.0000 -0.0173   1.9644   -2.8648
         0.0000 -0.0000 -0.0000   4.0000]

e = [3.9894   3.0462   1.9644   4.0000]

P7.55 a. Q = [0.1414 -0.9899   0   0
                    0.9899   0.1414   0   0
                    0   0   -0.5300 -0.8480
                    0   0   -0.8480   0.5300]

R = [-21.2132 10.1823 -20.9304   0
       -0.0000 -0.5657   5.0912   0
        0   0   -9.4340   -0.8480
        0   0   -0.0000   0.5300]

b. B = [4.0605 22.9972   9.5804 -19.1608
        -0.0028   2.9395 -1.0081   2.0161
         0   0   5.000   -8.0000
         0   0   0.0000   1.0000]

e = [4.0605   2.9395   5.0000   1.0000]

c. A is upper Hessenberg.

d. Householder function fails

P7.57

a. Q =

[-0.2626 -0.6607   0.4048 -0.4131   0.4000
  -0.3939 -0.5919 -0.4048   0.4131 -0.4000
  -0.2626   0.1376 -0.7625 -0.4131   0.4000
   0.6565 -0.3441 -0.2353 -0.4849 -0.4000
   0.5252 -0.2753 -0.1883   0.5029   0.6000]

R =

[-7.6158   6.3027 -7.6158   8.1410 -2.3635
   0.0000 -2.5052   1.5967 -2.6703   0.4405
  -0.0000 -0.0000 -2.3346 -1.8263   0.3012
   0.0000   0.0000 -0.0000 -2.6941   1.8679
  -0.0000 -0.0000   0.0000   0   0.8000]

b.

B =

$$\begin{bmatrix} 4.0552 & -0.0524 & 0.5977 & 1.0820 & 11.5716 \\ -0.0266 & 2.0007 & -0.0077 & 1.2381 & 3.5007 \\ -0.0591 & 0.0015 & 1.9828 & 2.7926 & 7.8998 \\ -0.0206 & 0.0005 & -0.0060 & 2.9631 & 2.7234 \\ 0.0002 & 0.0000 & -0.0001 & -0.0003 & 1.9982 \end{bmatrix}$$

e = [4.0552 2.0007 1.9828 2.9631 1.9982]

c.

AA =

$$\begin{bmatrix} 2.0000 & 0 & 0 & 0 & 0 \\ -7.3485 & 3.8889 & -0.0994 & -9.7992 & -8.4256 \\ -0.0000 & -0.9938 & 3.1111 & 0.0369 & 2.2768 \\ -0.0000 & -0.0000 & 0.0000 & 2.0000 & 0.0000 \\ -0.0000 & 0.0000 & -0.0000 & -0.0000 & 2.0000 \end{bmatrix}$$

d.

B =

$$\begin{bmatrix} 4.0552 & 0.8587 & 5.2410 & 7.0225 & 7.6099 \\ -0.0680 & 2.9786 & 5.1388 & 6.8344 & 4.2734 \\ -0.0000 & -0.0064 & 1.9662 & -0.0450 & -0.0288 \\ 0.0000 & -0.0000 & 0.0000 & 2.0000 & 0.0000 \\ -0.0000 & -0.0000 & -0.0000 & -0.0000 & 2.0000 \end{bmatrix}$$

e = [4.0552 2.9786 1.9662 2.0000 2.0000]

P7.59   a. QR_factor function fails.

b. QR_eigen fails (since QR factors are not available).

c.

AA =

$$\begin{bmatrix} -8.0000 & -5.7585 & -4.9735 & -7.0216 & -3.5777 \\ 13.8924 & 11.3316 & 7.5722 & 14.1866 & 9.1423 \\ 0.0000 & -1.5418 & 1.4703 & -3.9991 & -3.0447 \\ 0.0000 & -0.0000 & -0.1684 & 1.1980 & -1.7744 \\ -0.0000 & -0.0000 & 0.0000 & -0.0000 & 3.0000 \end{bmatrix}$$

d.

B =

$$\begin{bmatrix} 3.0127 & -0.7503 & -4.6326 & -3.7316 & -17.6593 \\ 0.0172 & 1.9878 & 0.8999 & 1.3603 & 22.4197 \\ 0.0000 & -0.0005 & 0.9995 & -1.7889 & 3.3341 \\ 0.0000 & 0.0000 & -0.0000 & 3.0000 & 0.7456 \\ 0.0000 & -0.0000 & -0.0000 & -0.0000 & -0.0000 \end{bmatrix}$$

e = [3.0127 1.9878 0.9995 3.0000 -0.0000]

P7.61   a. Q = $\begin{bmatrix} -0.9370 & -0.1735 & 0.3030 \\ 0.1562 & -0.9844 & -0.0808 \\ 0.3123 & -0.0284 & 0.9495 \end{bmatrix}$

R = $\begin{bmatrix} -6.4031 & 2.4988 & 2.6550 \\ -0.0000 & -7.7302 & -0.6941 \\ 0.0000 & -0.0000 & 1.2122 \end{bmatrix}$

b. B = $\begin{bmatrix} 8.8697 & -0.0970 & -0.0000 \\ -0.0970 & 6.0033 & -0.0000 \\ -0.0000 & -0.0000 & 1.1270 \end{bmatrix}$

e = [8.8697 6.0033 1.1270]

c. AA = $\begin{bmatrix} 6.0000 & 2.2361 & -0.0000 \\ 2.2361 & 4.0000 & 3.0000 \\ -0.0000 & 3.0000 & 6.0000 \end{bmatrix}$

B = $\begin{bmatrix} 8.8697 & 0.0970 & 0.0000 \\ 0.0970 & 6.0033 & 0.0000 \\ 0.0000 & 0.0000 & 1.1270 \end{bmatrix}$

e = [8.8697 6.0033 1.1270]

P7.65   a. Q = $\begin{bmatrix} -0.5946 & -0.2057 & 0.7772 \\ 0.4460 & -0.8887 & 0.1060 \\ 0.6690 & 0.4097 & 0.6202 \end{bmatrix}$

R = $\begin{bmatrix} -13.4536 & 23.1908 & 14.7172 \\ 0.0000 & -37.8707 & 7.5864 \\ -0.0000 & -0.0000 & 1.6879 \end{bmatrix}$

b. B = $\begin{bmatrix} 45.0454 & -0.0239 & -0.0000 \\ -0.0239 & 20.0000 & -0.0000 \\ -0.0000 & -0.0000 & 0.9546 \end{bmatrix}$

e = [45.0454 20.0000 0.9546]

c. AA = $\begin{bmatrix} 8.0000 & 10.8167 & -0.0000 \\ 10.8167 & 23.2308 & 13.8462 \\ -0.0000 & 13.8462 & 34.7692 \end{bmatrix}$

d. B = $\begin{bmatrix} 45.0454 & 0.0239 & -0.0000 \\ 0.0239 & 20.0000 & 0.0000 \\ -0.0000 & 0.0000 & 0.9546 \end{bmatrix}$

e = [45.0454 20.0000 0.9546]

P7.69   a. Q = $\begin{bmatrix} -0.9742 & -0.0262 & 0.2071 & 0.0853 \\ -0.0585 & -0.5679 & -0.0084 & -0.8210 \\ -0.0390 & -0.7166 & -0.4812 & 0.5034 \\ 0.2143 & -0.4041 & 0.8517 & 0.2555 \end{bmatrix}$

R = $\begin{bmatrix} -51.3225 & -2.7084 & -4.0918 & 19.5821 \\ -0.0000 & -13.8081 & -17.0130 & -16.6594 \\ 0.0000 & 0 & -11.7395 & 35.3765 \\ 0.0000 & 0 & 0 & 3.6758 \end{bmatrix}$

b. B = [58.0976 -0.1146   0.0060 -0.0000
        -0.1146 35.5004 -0.5341   0.0000
         0.0060 -0.5341 23.7782 -0.0000
        -0.0000   0.0000 -0.0000   0.6238]
    e = [58.0976 35.5004 23.7782 0.6238]

c. AA = [50.0000 -11.5758 -0.0000   -0.0000
          -11.5758 38.7463 11.6143   0.0000
           -0.0000 11.6143   8.0082   8.5860
           -0.0000   0.0000   8.5860   21.2456]

d. B = [58.0976 -0.1147 -0.0000   0.0000
        -0.1147 35.5242   0.0775   0.0000
        -0.0000   0.0775 23.7545   0.0000
         0.0000   0.0000   0.0000   0.6238]
    e = [58.0976 35.5242 23.7545 0.6238]

P7.73   a. Q = [-0.7894   0.1478 -0.2024 -0.5604
              -0.2046 -0.9784   0.0096   0.0267
               0.4093 -0.1021 -0.8578 -0.2936
              -0.4093   0.1021 -0.4723   0.7740]
          R = [-51.3079 -16.5764 33.1528 -33.1528
               0.0000 -17.4849   -2.0906   2.0906
              -0.0000   -0.0000 -27.0651 -20.8193
              -0.0000   -0.0000   0.0000   17.2938]
    b. B = [72.0000   0.0000 -0.0000   0.0000
             0.0000 18.0000   0.0000 -0.0044
            -0.0000   0.0000 36.0000   0.0000
             0.0000 -0.0044   0.0000   9.0000]
       e = [72.0000 18.0000 36.0000   9.0000]

    c. AA = [40.5000 -31.5000   0.0000   0.0000
             -31.5000   40.5000 -0.0000   -0.0000
               0.0000   -0.0000 18.8471   -3.8118
               0.0000   0.0000 -3.8118   35.1529]

    d. B = [72.0000 -0.0000 -0.0000 -0.0000
            -0.0000   9.0000 -0.0000   0.0000
             0.0000 -0.0000 35.9997 -0.0791
             0.0000   0.0000 -0.0791 18.0003]
       e = [72.0000   9.0000 35.9997 18.0003]

Chapter 8

P8.1   a. x = [1   2   3]
             y = [1   4   8]
             c = [0.5000 -4.0000   4.0000]

b. x = [1   2   3]
   y = [1   4   8]
   d = [3.0000   0.5000]
         4.0000   0]
   c = [1.0000   3.0000   0.5000]

P8.3   a. x = [4   9   16]
             y = [2   3   4]
             c = [0.0333 -0.0857   0.0476]
          b. x = [4   9   16]
             y = [2   3   4]
             d = [0.2000 -0.0048]
                  0.1429   0   ]
             c = [2.0000   0.2000 -0.0048]

P8.5   a. x = [0   1   2]
             y = [1   2   4]
             c = [0.5000 -2.0000   2.0000]

P8.7   a. x = [-1   0   1   2]
             y = [0.3333   1.0000   3.0000   9.0000]
             c = [-0.0556   0.5000 -1.5000   1.5000]

P8.9   a. x = [0   1   2   3]
             y = [0   1   0 -1]
             c = [0   0.5000   0 -0.1667]

P8.11   x = [0   0.6667   1.0000   2.0000]
            y = [2.0000 -2.0000 -1.0000 -0.5000]
            c = [-1.5000 -6.7500   3.0000 -0.1875]

P8.13   x = [0   0.6667   1.0000   2.0000]
            y = [4.0000 -4.0000 -3.5000 -0.5000]
            c = [-3.0000 -13.5000 10.5000 -0.1875]

P8.15   x = [0   0.5000   1.0000   1.5000]
            y = [1   2   1   0]
            c = [-1.3333   8.0000 -4.0000   0]

P8.17   x = [0   1   8   27]
            y = [0   1   2   3]
            c = [0   0.0055 -0.0019   0.0002]

P8.19

x = [-2   -1   0   1   2   3   4]
y = [-14.0000   0.5000   3.1000   0   -3.0000   0   16.0000]
c = [-0.0194 -0.0042   0.0646   0   -0.0625   0   0.0222]

Chapter 9

P9.1   a = 3.5000   b = -2.6667

x	y	(a*x+b)	(y - (a*x+b))
1.0000	1.0000	0.8333	0.1667
2.0000	4.0000	4.3333	-0.3333
3.0000	8.0000	7.8333	0.1667

err =   0.1667

P9.3   a = 0.1651   b = 1.4037

x	y	(a*x+b)	(y - (a*x+b))
4.0000	2.0000	2.0642	-0.0642
9.0000	3.0000	2.8899	0.1101
16.0000	4.0000	4.0459	-0.0459

err =   0.0183

P9.7   a = 2.8000   b = 1.9333

x	y	(a*x+b)	(y - (a*x+b))
-1.0000	0.3333	-0.8667	1.2000
0	1.0000	1.9333	-0.9333
1.0000	3.0000	4.7333	-1.7333
2.0000	9.0000	7.5333	1.4667

err =   7.4667

Chapter 10

P10.1   a. m = 1; a = 1/2, 1/2, b = 0, 1/2
          b. m = 2; a = 1/2, 1/2, 0, b = 0, 1/2, 0

P10.3   a. m = 1; a = 1/2, -1/2, b = 0, 1/2
          b. m = 2; a = 1/2, -1/2, 0, b = 0, 1/2, 0

P10.5   a. m = 1; a = 1/2, -1/3 , b = 0, -1/3
          b. m = 2; a = 1/2, -1/3, -1/6, b = 0, -1/3, 0

P10.7   a. m = 1; a = 1/2, -4/9 , b = 0, 0
          b. m = 2; a = 1/2, -4/9, 0, b = 0, 0, 0
          c. m = 4; a = 1/2, -4/9, 0, -1/18, b = 0, 0, 0, 0

P10.9   a. m = 1; a = 1/2, 1/4 , b = 0, 0.6036
          b. m = 2; a = 1/2, 1/4, 0, b = 0, 0.6036, 0
          c. m = 4; a = 1/2, 1/4, 0, 1/4, 0, b = 0, 0.6036, 0, 0.1036, 0

P10.11 a. m = 1; a = 1/2, -1/2 , b = 0, -1/2
          b. m = 2; a = 1/2, -1/2, 0, b = 0, -1/2, 0

P10.13 a. m = 1; a = 1/2, 1/2, b = 0, -1/2
          b. m = 2; a = 1/2, 1/2, 0, b = 0, -1/2, 0

P10.15 a. m = 1; a = 1/2, 1/3 , b = 0, 1/3
          b. m = 2; a = 1/2, 1/3, -1/6, b = 0, 1/3, 0

P10.17 a. m = 1; a = 1/2, 4/9 , b = 0, 0
          b. m = 2; a = 1/2, 4/9, 0, b = 0, 0, 0
          c. m = 4; a = 1/2, 4/9, 0, 1/18, b = 0, 0, 0, 0

P10.19 a. m = 1; a = 1/2, -1/4 , b = 0, -0.6036
          b. m = 2; a = 1/2, -1/4, 0, b = 0, -0.6036, 0
          c. m = 4; a = 1/2, -1/4, 0, -1/4, 0, b = 0, -0.6036, 0, -0.1036, 0

Chapter 11

P11.1   a. df = 0.0100
          b. db = 0.0100
          c. dc = 0.0100
          d. central difference with h = 2: dc2 = 0.0400
          dr = (4*dc _ dc2)/3 = 0

P11.3   a. df = 6
          b. db = 2
          c. dc = 4
          d. dc2 = 6.6667; dr = 3.1111

P11.5   a. df = 0.20
          b. db = 0.3333
          c. dc = 0.25
          d. dc2 = 0.25; dr = 0.25

P11.7   a. 25
          b. 21.7789
          c. 22
          d. 21.6411
          e. 21.4043

P11.9   a. 0.4083
          b. 0.4056
          c. 0.4056
          d. 0.4055
          e. 0.4054

P11.11 a. 1.5000
          b. 1.5675
          c. 1.6667
          d. 1.5708
          e. 1.5000

P11.13 a. 1.1667
b. 1.2075
c. 1.2222
d. 1.2092
e. 1.2000

P11.15 a. 1.3090
b. 1.4172
c. 1.3727
d. 1.4241
e. 1.4434

P11.17 a. 1.6089
b. 1.6520
c. 1.5507
d. 1.6528
e. 1.7365

P11.19 a. 5.4807
b. 5.2799
c. 5.2894
d. 5.2725
e. 5.2541

Chapter 12

P12.1
c. yy = [2.00   2.2100   2.4421   2.6985   2.9818...
3.2949   3.6409   4.0231   4.4456   4.9124   5.4282]

d. yy = [2.00   2.2103   2.4428   2.6997   2.9836...
3.2974   3.6442   4.0275   4.4511   4.9192   5.4366]

P12.3
c. yy = [1.00   0.9098   0.8343   0.7704   0.7155...
0.6679   0.6263   0.5895   0.5567   0.5274   0.5011]
d. yy = [1.00   0.9091   0.8333   0.7692   0.7143...
0.6667   0.6250   0.5882   0.5556   0.5263   0.5000]

P12.5
c. yy = [2.00   2.1905   2.3630   2.5194   2.6618...
2.7916   2.9104   3.0194   3.1197   3.2122   3.2979]

d. yy = [2.00   2.1903   2.3627   2.5191   2.6614...
2.7912   2.9100   3.0190   3.1192   3.2118   3.2974]

P12.7
c. yy = [2.00   1.9800   1.9212   1.8271   1.7030...
1.5559   1.3933   1.2230   1.0524   0.8878   0.7343]
d. yy = [2.00   1.9801   1.9216   1.8279   1.7043...
1.5576   1.3954   1.2253   1.0546   0.8897   0.7358]

P12.9
c. yy = [1.00   1.0008   1.0075   1.0265   1.0648...
1.1310   1.2375   1.4028   1.6569   2.0505   2.6732]

d. yy = [1.00   1.0010   1.0080   1.0274   1.0661...
1.1331   1.2411   1.4092   1.6686   2.0730   2.7182]

P12.11
d. yy = [1.00   0.7843   0.7040   0.7061   0.7564...
0.8187   0.8635   0.8697   0.8242   0.7227   0.5683]

P12.13
d. yy = [2.00   2.1237   2.2450   2.3643   2.4819...
2.5981   2.7129   2.8266   2.9394   3.0512   3.1623]

P12.15
d. yy = [5.00   4.2411   3.5621   2.9618   2.4416...
2.0013   1.6411   1.3608   1.1605   1.0403   1.00]

P12.17
d. yy = [3.00   2.9667   2.8724   2.7355   2.5755...
2.4158   2.2757   2.1670   2.0921   2.0464   2.0218]

P12.19
d. yy = [-1.00   -0.8884   -0.8298   -0.802   -0.7924...
-0.791   -0.7898   -0.7807   -0.7539   -0.6952   -0.5809]

(P 12.21-25, Results for ABM3, n = 10.)

P12.21
yy = [1.0000   1.1053   1.2236   1.3588   1.5144...
1.6948   1.9047   2.1492   2.4342   2.7658   3.1513]

P12.23
yy = [1.0000   1.1099   1.2409   1.3946   1.5727...
1.7770   2.0097   2.2736   2.5714   2.9063   3.2820]

P12.25
yy = [1.0000   1.0050   1.0203   1.0465   1.0851...
1.1385   1.2101   1.3049   1.4311   1.6015   1.8376]

Chapter 13

P13.1
a. uu = [2.0000   2.0000   2.0800   2.2480   2.5152...
2.8963   3.4100   4.0796   4.9336   6.0068   7.3413]

b. uu = [2.0000   2.0400   2.1688   2.3995   2.7491...
3.2394   3.8980   4.7587   5.8638   7.2649   9.0257]
exact, y= 1.5*exp(x) + 0.5*exp(-x) -x

P13.3

a. uu = [7.0000   6.2000   5.4400   4.7376   4.1050...
3.5503   3.0789   2.6940   2.3975   2.1903   2.0724]
b. uu = [7.0000   6.2200   5.4951   4.8350   4.2465...
3.7346   3.3028   2.9534   2.6878   2.5069   2.4112
exact, y = exp(-x) + x exp(-x) + x^2 - 4 x + 6

P13.5

a. uu = [-2.00   -1.20   -0.7200   -0.6624   -1.1296...
-2.2404   -4.1463   -7.0507   -11.2329   -17.0808   -25.1355]
b. uu = [-2.00   -1.360   -1.1616   -1.5471   -2.7004...
-4.8751   -8.4344   -13.9072   -22.0705   -34.0707   -51.6013]
exact, y = -exp(x) + exp(-x) - x.^2 +4*x -2

P13.7

a. uu = [2.0000   1.8000   1.6200   1.4580   1.3122...
1.1810   1.0629   0.9566   0.8609   0.7748   0.6974]
b. uu = [2.0000   1.8100   1.6381   1.4824   1.3416...
1.2142   1.0988   0.9944   0.9000   0.8145   0.7371]
exact, y = 2 exp(-x)

P13.9

a. uu = [1.0000   0.8000   0.6800   0.6200   0.6097...
0.6446   0.7241   0.8502   1.0272   1.2615   1.5613]
b. uu = [1.0000   0.8400   0.7402   0.6918   0.6912...
0.7384   0.8364   0.9907   1.2094   1.5028   1.8838]

P13.11

midpoint method:
uu = [1.0000   1.0000   1.0060   1.0242   1.0616...
1.1271   1.2332   1.3985   1.6508   2.0322   2.6053]

P13.13

Solution is similar to y = 2 cos(2x), fairly large n required for nice solution.

P13.15

midpoint method:
uu = [0   -0.6400   -1.2115   -1.7331   -2.2222   -2.6902...
-3.1443   -3.5889   -4.0269   -4.4601   -4.8899]

P13.17

midpoint method:
uu = [2.0000   2.0494   2.0976   2.1447   2.1908   2.2360...
2.2803   2.3237   2.3664   2.4083   2.4494]

P13.19

Euler's method:
uu = [5.00   6.3000   7.8200   9.5803   11.6016   13.9047...
16.5106   19.4407   22.7163   26.3591   30.3906]
exact, y = 2 x^2 + 3 x^3

P13.21

Euler's method:
uu = [3.00   3.3000   3.6600   4.0745   4.5399   5.0535...
5.6134   6.2183   6.8670   7.5587   8.2928]

midpoint method:
uu = [3.00   3.3300   3.7147   4.1507   4.6356   5.1677...
5.7456   6.3684   7.0351   7.7452   8.4982]
exact, y = 2 x^2 + 1/x

P13.23

midpoint method:
uu = [0   0.5400   0.9834   1.3495   1.6532   1.9060...
2.1169   2.2929   2.4397   2.5619   2.6631]

P13.25

midpoint method:
uu = [1.00   1.0000   0.9622   0.8807   0.7569   0.5975...
0.4130   0.2162   0.0208   -0.1595   -0.3125]

P13.27

midpoint method:
x = [0   0.1000   0.2000   0.3000   0.4000   0.5000   0.6000...
0.7000   0.8000   0.9000]

a = 1, uu = [1.0000   1.0950   1.1799   1.2541   1.3169...
1.3668   1.4015   1.4169   1.4055   1.3505

a = 2, uu = [1.0000   1.0800   1.1168   1.1071   1.0475...
0.9337   0.7605   0.5204   0.2016   -0.2192

a = 3, uu = [1.0000   1.0550   1.0126   0.8717   0.6364...
0.3176   -0.0655   -0.4803   -0.8718   -1.1323]

P13.29

midpoint method, on [1, 3]:

k = 1, uu = [1.000   0.980   0.8999   0.7172   0.3441...
-0.4089   -1.9740   -5.3898   -13.2966   -32.7878   -84.0125]

k = 2, uu = [1.000   0.960   0.8006   0.4442   -0.2615...
-1.6323   -4.3614   -10.0592   -22.6926   -52.6169   -128.4744]

k = 3, uu = [1.000   0.940   0.7021   0.1810   -0.8179...
-2.6792   -6.2099   -13.2143   -27.9828   -61.3645   -142.5102]

k = 4, uu = [1.00   0.920   0.6044   -0.0724   -1.3264...
-3.5583   -7.5656   -15.0492   -29.8918   -61.5631   -134.6992]

Note, using larger n shows that solutions actually decay more rapidly than results above indicate.

P13.31

t	x1	x2	x3	x4
a.				
0	1.0000	0	0	0
0.1000	1.2855	1.2707	1.6848	0.6997
0.2000	1.5438	2.7317	3.8321	1.6441
0.3000	1.7775	4.4741	6.6155	2.9190
0.4000	1.9890	6.6179	10.2687	4.6398
0.5000	2.1804	9.3235	15.1057	6.9627
0.6000	2.3536	12.8053	21.5499	10.0981
0.7000	2.5102	17.3510	30.1713	14.3305
0.8000	2.6520	23.3476	41.7391	20.0436
0.9000	2.7803	31.3158	57.2908	27.7552
1.0000	2.8964	41.9575	78.2258	38.1647
b.				
0	0	1.0000	0	0
0.1000	-0.2855	-0.2707	-1.6848	-0.6997
0.2000	-0.5438	-1.7317	-3.8321	-1.6441
0.3000	-0.7775	-3.4741	-6.6155	-2.9190
0.4000	-0.9890	-5.6179	-10.2687	-4.6398
0.5000	-1.1804	-8.3235	-15.1057	-6.9627
0.6000	-1.3536	-11.8053	-21.5499	-10.0981
0.7000	-1.5102	-16.3510	-30.1713	-14.3305
0.8000	-1.6520	-22.3476	-41.7391	-20.0436
0.9000	-1.7803	-30.3158	-57.2908	-27.7552
1.0000	-1.8964	-40.9575	-78.2258	-38.1647
c.				
0	0	0	1.0000	0
0.1000	0.1903	1.0803	2.5897	0.6997
0.2000	0.3625	2.3692	4.6508	1.6441
0.3000	0.5184	3.9557	7.3563	2.9190
0.4000	0.6594	5.9585	10.9390	4.6398
0.5000	0.7869	8.5365	15.7123	6.9627
0.6000	0.9024	11.9029	22.0987	10.0981
0.7000	1.0068	16.3442	30.6679	14.3305
0.8000	1.1013	22.2463	42.1885	20.0436
0.9000	1.1869	30.1290	57.6973	27.7552
1.0000	1.2642	40.6932	78.5937	38.1647
d.				
0	0	0	0	1.0000
0.1000	-0.0952	-0.5402	-0.7948	0.6502
0.2000	-0.1813	-1.1846	-1.8254	0.1779
0.3000	-0.2592	-1.9778	-3.1782	-0.4595
0.4000	-0.3297	-2.9793	-4.9695	-1.3199
0.5000	-0.3935	-4.2683	-7.3561	-2.4813
0.6000	-0.4512	-5.9515	-10.5493	-4.0491
0.7000	-0.5034	-8.1721	-14.8339	-6.1653
0.8000	-0.5507	-11.1231	-20.5942	-9.0218
0.9000	-0.5934	-15.0645	-28.3487	-12.8776
1.0000	-0.6321	-20.3466	-38.7969	-18.0824

P13.33

t	x1	x2	x3	x4
a.				
0	1.0000	0	0	0
0.1000	1.2855	1.0138	1.0659	0.2325
0.2000	1.5438	2.0713	2.2897	0.5408
0.3000	1.7775	3.1993	3.7161	0.9445
0.4000	1.9890	4.4291	5.3993	1.4674
0.5000	2.1804	5.7973	7.4047	2.1391
0.6000	2.3536	7.3473	9.8117	2.9959
0.7000	2.5102	9.1308	12.7170	4.0828
0.8000	2.6520	11.2099	16.2382	5.4548
0.9000	2.7803	13.6596	20.5188	7.1798
1.0000	2.8964	16.5705	25.7336	9.3412

P13.35

t	x1	x2	x3	x4
b.				
0	0	1.0000	0	0
0.1000	0.3321	1.0679	-1.0418	-0.9589
0.2000	0.7377	1.0345	-2.4739	-2.1003
0.3000	1.2332	0.8202	-4.5103	-3.5485
0.4000	1.8383	0.2996	-7.4663	-5.4783
0.5000	2.5774	-0.7224	-11.8090	-8.1414
0.6000	3.4801	-2.5466	-18.2323	-11.9044
0.7000	4.5827	-5.6338	-27.7692	-17.3060
0.8000	5.9294	-10.6863	-41.9590	-25.1414
0.9000	7.5743	-18.7694	-63.0963	-36.5873
1.0000	9.5833	-31.4941	-94.6029	-53.3901

P13.37

t	x1	x2	x3	x4
c.				
0	0	0	1.0000	0
0.1000	-0.2673	0.9647	2.7103	0.2569
0.2000	-0.3566	2.2283	4.7373	0.6605
0.3000	-0.3556	3.8099	7.2624	1.2748
0.4000	-0.3141	5.7966	10.5250	2.1888
0.5000	-0.2593	8.3361	14.8398	3.5262
0.6000	-0.2047	11.6412	20.6240	5.4580
0.7000	-0.1566	16.0026	28.4345	8.2203
0.8000	-0.1169	21.8114	39.0189	12.1377
0.9000	-0.0856	29.5929	53.3841	17.6562
1.0000	-0.0616	40.0525	72.8899	25.3870

P13.39

t	x1	x2	x3	x4
d.				
0	0	0	0	1.0000
0.1000	-0.9515	-1.2072	-0.1605	1.0952
0.2000	-2.1405	-2.9905	-0.6687	1.1813
0.3000	-3.3964	-5.1759	-1.5203	1.2592
0.4000	-4.4481	-7.4084	-2.6306	1.3297
0.5000	-4.9407	-9.1499	-3.8157	1.3935
0.6000	-4.4804	-9.7182	-4.7867	1.4512
0.7000	-2.7098	-8.3817	-5.1684	1.5034
0.8000	0.5868	-4.5112	-4.5472	1.5507
0.9000	5.3622	2.2172	-2.5515	1.5934
1.0000	11.1882	11.5937	1.0376	1.6321

Chapter 14

Linear shooting solutions use ode45

P14.1

a. xx = [0   0.0245   0.2158   0.4069   0.5984   0.7917   0.9881   1.1844   1.3808   1.5761   1.7686   1.9598...
2.1512   2.3443   2.5406   2.7370   2.9333   3.1290   3.1416]
   yy = [1.0000   1.1602   2.3767   3.5062   4.5098   5.3554   6.0100   6.4336   6.6100   6.5334   6.2148   5.6711...
4.9197   3.9798   2.8726   1.6550   0.3737   -0.9177   -1.0000]

b. x = [0   0.3142   0.6283   0.9425   1.2566   1.5708   1.8850   2.1991   2.5133   2.8274   3.1416]
    yy = [1.0000   0.9527   0.8113   0.5899   0.3103   -0.0000   -0.3103   -0.5899   -0.8113   -0.9527   -1.0000]

P14.3

a. xx = [0   0.0078   0.0703   0.1328   0.1953   0.2578   0.3203   0.3828   0.4453   0.5078   0.5703   0.6328...
0.6953   0.7578   0.8203   0.8828   0.9453   1.0000]
   yy = [10.0000   9.8856   9.0118   8.2076   7.4679   6.7877   6.1629   5.5892   5.0630   4.5807   4.1393   3.7357...
3.3673   3.0316   2.7263   2.4494   2.1989   2.0000]

b. x = [0   0.1   0.2   0.3   0.4   0.5   0.6   0.7   0.8   0.9   1.0]
    yy = [10.00   8.6195   7.4117   6.3564   5.4361   4.6352   3.9400   3.3386   2.8207   2.3772   2.00]

P14.5

a. xx = [0   0.0078   0.0703   0.1328   0.1953   0.2578   0.3203   0.3828   0.4453   0.5078   0.5703   0.6328...
0.6953   0.7578   0.8203   0.8828   0.9453   1.0000]
   yy = [2.0000   2.0626   2.5109   2.8698   3.1444   3.3406   3.4647   3.5235   3.5236   3.4720   3.3756   3.2410...
3.0747   2.8828   2.6711   2.4452   2.2099   2.0000]

b. x = [0   0.1   0.2   0.3   0.4   0.5   0.6   0.7   0.8   0.9   1.0]
    yy = [2.0   2.6998   3.1742   3.4469   3.5446   3.4958   3.3286   3.0709   2.7483   2.3844   2.0000]

P14.7

a. xx = [0   0.0245   0.2209   0.4172   0.6136   0.8099   1.0063   1.2026   1.3990   1.5953   1.7917   1.9880...
2.1844   2.3807   2.5771   2.7734   2.9698   3.1416]

  yy = [0   -0.2445   -2.0309   -3.5283   -4.7511   -5.7110   -6.4173   -6.8768   -7.0940   -7.0710   -6.8075   -6.3010...
-5.5466   -4.5370   -3.2625   -1.7108   0.1330   2.0000]

b. x = [0   0.3142   0.6283   0.9425   1.2566   1.5708   1.8850   2.1991   2.5133   2.8274   3.1416]
  yy = [0   -2.7723   -4.8234   -6.2039   -6.9479   -7.0738   -6.5847   -5.4685   -3.6976   -1.2284   2.0000]

P14.9

a. xx = [1.0000   1.0547   1.2377   1.4401   1.6452   1.8509   2.0579   2.2666   2.4770   2.6898   2.9058   3.1264...
3.3428   3.5558   3.7669   3.9774   4.1884   4.4013   4.6172   4.8378   5.0655   5.2910   5.5159   5.7406...
5.9637   6.1871   6.4128   6.6430   6.8803   7.1137   7.3424   7.5692   7.7962   8.0000]

  yy = [1.0000   0.9192   0.6588   0.3889   0.1364   -0.0923   -0.2945   -0.4664   -0.6049   -0.7074   -0.7720   -0.7975...
-0.7846   -0.7379   -0.6624   -0.5627   -0.4437   -0.3101   -0.1671   -0.0199   0.1260   0.2579   0.3713   0.4617...
0.5255   0.5615   0.5687   0.5465   0.4949   0.4191   0.3256   0.2191   0.1046   0]

b. x = [1.0000   1.7000   2.4000   3.1000   3.8000   4.5000   5.2000   5.9000   6.6000   7.3000   8.0000]
  yy = [1.0000   0.1872   -0.4242   -0.6985   -0.6096   -0.2622   0.1543   0.4474   0.5007   0.3157   0]

P14.11

xx = [1.0000   1.0703   1.2503   1.4541   1.7018   2.0047   2.3813   2.8604   3.3916   3.9541   4.5166   5.0791...
5.6416   6.2041   6.7666   7.3291   7.8916   8.4541   9.0166   9.5791   10.0000]
yy = [0   0.0456   0.1489   0.2458   0.3407   0.4306   0.5127   0.5833   0.6314   0.6592   0.6707   0.6711...
0.6635   0.6504   0.6333   0.6134   0.5914   0.5680   0.5437   0.5188   0.5000]

b. x = [1.0000   1.9000   2.8000   3.7000   4.6000   5.5000   6.4000   7.3000   8.2000   9.1000   10.0000]
  y = [0   0.3919   0.5626   0.6360   0.6599   0.6565   0.6374   0.6090   0.5752   0.5384   0.5000]

P14.13

a. x = [1.0000   1.0078   1.0703   1.1328   1.1953   1.2578   1.3203   1.3828   1.4453   1.5078   1.5703   1.6328...
1.6953   1.7578   1.8203   1.8828   1.9453   2.0000]

  y = [0.5000   0.5066   0.5634   0.6290   0.7049   0.7931   0.8958   1.0157   1.1557   1.3194   1.5106   1.7339...
1.9941   2.2971   2.6490   3.0568   3.5284   4.0000]

b. x = [1.0000   1.1000   1.2000   1.3000   1.4000   1.5000   1.6000   1.7000   1.8000   1.9000   2.0000]
  y = [0.5000   0.5937   0.7117   0.8615   1.0531   1.2987   1.6136   2.0164   2.5297   3.1804   4.0000]

P14.15

a. x = [0   0.0078   0.0703   0.1328   0.1953   0.2578   0.3203   0.3828   0.4453   0.5078   0.5703   0.6328...
0.695   0.7578   0.8203   0.8828   0.9453   1.0000]

  y = [1.0000   1.0048   1.0438   1.0846   1.1274   1.1724   1.2199   1.2702   1.3235   1.3803   1.4408   1.5055...
1.5750   1.6496   1.7300   1.8168   1.9110   2.0000]

P14.17

a. x = [1.0000   1.0078   1.0703   1.1328   1.1953   1.2578   1.3203   1.3828   1.4453   1.5078   1.5703   1.6328...
1.6953   1.7578   1.8203   1.8828   1.9453   2.0000]

  y = [0   -0.0213   -0.1848   -0.3376   -0.4819   -0.6193   -0.7508   -0.8776   -1.0005   -1.1201   -1.2370   -1.3516...
-1.4645   -1.5759   -1.6863   -1.7958   -1.9048   -2.0000]

P14.19
b. x = [0   0.0078   0.0703   0.1328   0.1953   0.2578   0.3203   0.3828   0.4453   0.5078   0.5703   0.6328...
0.6953   0.7578   0.8203   0.8828   0.9453   1.0000]
   y = [1.0000   0.9853   0.8736   0.7712   0.6773   0.5911   0.5119   0.4393   0.3727   0.3119   0.2563   0.2058...
0.1601   0.1190   0.0823   0.0499   0.0215   0.0000]

P14.21
b. x = [1.0000   1.0078   1.0703   1.1328   1.1953   1.2578   1.3203   1.3828   1.4453   1.5078   1.5703   1.6328...
1.6953   1.7578   1.8203   1.8828   1.9453   2.0000]
   y = [1.0000   0.9922   0.9343   0.8828   0.8366   0.7950   0.7574   0.7232   0.6919   0.6632   0.6368   0.6124...
0.5899   0.5689   0.5494   0.5311   0.5141   0.5000]

P14.23
b. x = [0   0.0078   0.0549   0.1019   0.1490   0.1963   0.2449   0.2974   0.3536   0.4133   0.4758   0.5383...
0.6008   0.6633   0.7258   0.7883   0.8508   0.9133   0.9758   1.0000]
   y = [1.0000   0.9983   0.9801   0.9488   0.9046   0.8477   0.7767   0.6863   0.5751   0.4416   0.2870   0.1191...
-0.0600   -0.2483   -0.4436   -0.6439   -0.8471   -1.0514   -1.2550   -1.3333]

P14.25
x = [0   0.0078   0.0703   0.1328   0.1953   0.2578   0.3203   0.3828   0.4453   0.5078   0.5703   0.6328   0.6953...
0.7578   0.8203   0.8828   0.9453   1.0000]
y = [0   0.0180   0.1611   0.3011   0.4356   0.5631   0.6829   0.7947   0.8988   0.9958   1.0861   1.1703   1.2491...
1.3229   1.3923   1.4577   1.5195   1.5708]

Chapter 15

P15.1
Solution at t = 0.5

a.	0	0.0683	0.1444	0.2364	0.3523	0.5000
b.	0	0.0682	0.1443	0.2363	0.3522	0.5000
c.	0	3.9062	-15.6250	29.6875	-25.6250	0.5000 (unstable)
d.	0	0.0693	0.1461	0.2381	0.3533	0.5000
e.	0	0.0682	0.1443	0.2365	0.3521	0.5000

P15.3
Solution at t = 0.5

a.	0	0.0010	0.0016	0.0016	0.0010	0
b.	0	0.0008	0.0012	0.0012	0.0008	0
c.	0	-44.2775	27.3650	27.3650	-44.2775	0 (unstable)
d.	0	0.0053	0.0086	0.0086	0.0053	0
e.	0	0.0005	0.0016	0.0016	0.0005	0

P15.5

Solution at t = 0.5

a.	0	0.0000	0.0000	0.0000	0.0000	0
b.	0	-0.0029	0.0048	-0.0048	0.0029	0
c.	0	-19809	32052	-32052	19809	0 (unstable)
d.	0	0.0000	-0.0000	0.0000	-0.0000	0
e.	0	-0.0621	0.1004	-0.1004	0.0621	0

P15.7

Solution at t = 0.5

a.	0	0.2012	0.4020	0.6020	0.8012	1.0000
b.	0	0.2009	0.4008	0.6015	0.8005	1.0000
c.	0	39.0625	-171.8750	334.3750	-299.3750	1.0000 (unstable)
d.	0	0.2081	0.4129	0.6127	0.8078	1.0000
e.	0	0.1985	0.3991	0.6022	0.7952	1.0000

P15.9

Solution at t = 0.5

a.	0	0.0825	0.1335	0.1335	0.0825	0
b.	0	0.0724	0.1000	0.1171	0.0618	0
c.	0	90250	-120000	87790	-38130	0 (unstable)
d.	0	0.4058	0.6610	0.6660	0.4141	0
e.	0	0.5248	-0.2946	0.3233	0.1623	0

P15.11

a. oscillations most easily shown graphically
b. unstable

P15.17

a.
$$
\begin{bmatrix}
0.0000 & 0.0000 & 0.0000 & 0.0000 & 0.0000 \\
0.0000 & 0.0547 & 0.1172 & 0.1797 & 0.2500 \\
0.0000 & 0.1172 & 0.2422 & 0.3672 & 0.5000 \\
0.0000 & 0.1797 & 0.3672 & 0.5547 & 0.7500 \\
0.0000 & 0.2500 & 0.5000 & 0.7500 & 1.0000
\end{bmatrix}
$$

P15.19

a.
$$
\begin{bmatrix}
0.0000 & 0.0625 & 0.2500 & 0.5625 & 1.0000 \\
-0.0625 & 0.0547 & 0.3047 & 0.6797 & 1.1875 \\
-0.2500 & -0.0703 & 0.2422 & 0.6797 & 1.2500 \\
-0.5625 & -0.3203 & 0.0547 & 0.5547 & 1.1875 \\
-1.0000 & -0.6875 & -0.2500 & 0.3125 & 1.0000
\end{bmatrix}
$$

P15.21

a.
$$
\begin{bmatrix}
1.0000 & 1.0625 & 1.2500 & 1.5625 & 2.0000 \\
0.9375 & 0.9688 & 1.1562 & 1.4687 & 1.9375 \\
0.7500 & 0.7813 & 0.9688 & 1.2812 & 1.7500 \\
0.4375 & 0.4688 & 0.6563 & 0.9688 & 1.4375 \\
0.0000 & 0.025 & 0.2500 & 0.5625 & 1.0000
\end{bmatrix}
$$

P15.23 a.
$$\begin{bmatrix} 0.0000 & 0.0156 & 0.1250 & 0.4219 & 1.0000 \\ 0.0156 & 0.1719 & 0.3438 & 0.6094 & 1.0781 \\ 0.1250 & 0.3438 & 0.4844 & 0.6250 & 0.8750 \\ 0.4219 & 0.6094 & 0.6250 & 0.5469 & 0.4844 \\ 1.0000 & 1.0781 & 0.8750 & 0.4844 & 0.0000 \end{bmatrix}$$

P15.25 a.
$$\begin{bmatrix} 0.0000 & 0.0000 & 0.0000 & 0.0000 & 0.0000 \\ 0.2656 & 0.2656 & 0.1875 & 0.0157 & -0.2344 \\ 0.6250 & 0.6406 & 0.4844 & 0.1406 & -0.3750 \\ 1.1719 & 1.2031 & 0.9687 & 0.4531 & -0.3281 \\ 2.0000 & 2.0625 & 1.7500 & 1.0625 & 0.0000 \end{bmatrix}$$

Subject Index

(Note that numbers in parentheses indicate that a reference is to an exercise.)

A

Abel, Niels Henrik 3
Absolute stability region 432
Acceleration 20, 21-22, 34, (38)
Adams-Bashforth method 424-426, 436, 459, 470-471
Adams-Moulton method 426-427, 436
Adams Bashforth-Moulton method 427-430, 434, 436-37, (438), 459-464, (472)
Airy's equation (472)
Al-Kashi, Jemshid 1
Approximate
  to n digits 13, 17, 18
  to n decimal places 13
Approximation, function 287-364
  (see also, least-squares approximation, Fourier methods, Pade approximation, Taylor) approximation
Arc length 367, 387, (400)
Areas 1
Archimedes 1, 42
A-stability 466
Assymptotic error constant 53, 56, 68
Augmented matrix 81

B

Babbage, Charles 2
Babylonian mathematics 1
Back substitution 80, 82, 84
Backslash division 100, 142
Backward difference formula 368-370
Banded matrix (132)
Bank balance (439)
Basis functions for finite-element method 535-546, (552-553)
Beam, deflection (75), 191, 200, 481, (476), 478, 483, 495-496, (502)
Bernoulli equation (440)
Bessel equation (472)
Bessel functions (285)
Big-Oh, (see Order)
Binary digit 16
Binary representation 15
Bisection 4, 41, 44-48, 49, 50, 52, 55, 56, 71, (72-73), (76), 135
Bit 15
Blasius equation (501)
Bouncing ball data (327)
Boundary condition
  Dirichlet 480, 481, 482
  insulated 521-522
  mixed 480, 484-486
  Neuman 480

Boundary value problem 477-500, (501-502)
    finite difference method 492-500, (501)
    shooting method 480-492, 499, (501)
Briggs, Henry 2
Burger's equation (553)
Building permits (286)
Bulirsch-Stoer method 254-257, (277-279)
Butcher's method 422
Byte 15

C

Cancellation error, 17
Census data (284)
Central difference formula 368-370, 397, (398), 492, 493, 497, 518, 523
Characteristic polynomial 432
Chebyshev equation (472)
Chemical processes (156) 228, 234, 250-251, 265, 297, (326), (439), 443, 447, 450, 458, (474-475), (501), (502)
Chinese mathematics 1
Cholesky form 159, 173-5, 182
Chopping arithmetic 16
Clamped boundary condition 288
Classic Runge-Kutta method 417-420, 435, (438), 454-458, (472)
Complex conjugate 29-30, 357
Composite integration methods 384-387
    Simpson 386-387
    trapezoid 20-21, 384-385
Computation, efficient 23-25
Computer arithmetic 15-16, (39)
Conjugate gradient methods 127
Convergence 3
    fixed point iteration 11-12, (36), 69
    geometric illustration of 10, 12, 112, 116, 118-119
    linear 48, 53
    MATLAB function
      fmins 153
      fzero 70
    order of 34, 52-53, 62
    quadratic 53, 62
    rate of 52, 56, 68, (225)
    tests for 13, (76)
      (*see also*, stopping conditions)
    use of eigenvalues for 10, 12, 127

Convergence, conditions for
    fixed-point iteration 11
    fixed-point iteration, for systems 148-149, (157)
    Gauss-Seidel 122
    Jacobi method 117
    Newton's method 62
    nonlinear finite difference method 500
    secant method 57
    SOR 126
Condition of a matrix 88 (*see also*, ill-conditioned matrix)
Crank-Nicolson method 518-522, 548, (551)
Crout form 159, 172, 182
Cubic equations 1-3
Cubic least squares approximation 301-303, (324-326)
Cubic spline interpolation 261-268, (276-278), (281-282)

D

Degree of precision 328, 381
Derivative, approximation of 365, 368-376, (398)
Derivative boundary conditions 521-522
Derivative initial conditions 523
Determinant of a matrix 178-179, (183)
Diagonally dominant matrix 87, 97, 116, (132)
Difference formulas
    for first derivative 368-371, 397, (398)
    for higher derivatives 372, 397, 509, 523, 527
    for partial derivatives 373, 503, 523, 527
Differentiation, numerical 368-373
    (*see also*, Richardson extrapolation)
Differential equations, partial 503-554
Differential equations, ordinary 403-500
    first-order 403-440
    higher-order 441-442, 444-445, 477-500, (501-502)
    systems 445-471, (472-476)
Direct methods 2
    (*see* also, Gaussian elimination)
Dirichlet boundary condition 480
Discrete least-squares 287-307, 321-322, (324-328), 329-341
Disease, spread (439)

Examples, *cont.*

    LU factorization 161, 162, 166-167, 167-168, 172-173, 174-175, 175-176, 178, 179, 179-180

    Mass-and-spring system 460

    Matrix inverse 179-180

    Midpoint method 412-413, 413-414, 449-450, 450-451, 454, 455-457

    Minimization 150, 152

    Motion of object with air resistance 404, 430-431, 461-463, 479, 488\

    Nonlinear finite difference method 497-498

    Nonlinear pendulum 442, 444, 446, 449

    Nonlinear shooting method 486-487, 488, 489-490

    Nonlinear system from geometry 136, 138-139, 142-143, 143-144

    ODE for Dawson's integral 413-414

    ODE-IVP 404, 442, 443 (*see also,* Examples: Adams-Bashforth, Adams predictor-corrector, Classic Runge-Kutta, Euler)

    ODE-BVP 478, 479 (*see also,* Examples: Linear finite difference method, Linear shooting method, Nonlinear finite difference method, Nonlinear shooting method)

    Oil reservoir modeling 288, 299, 304-305

    Pade approximation 318

    Parametric curves 229

    Piecewise polynomial interpolation 258, 260-261 (*see also,* Examples: Cubic spline interpolation)

    Planetary orbits (elliptical) 43, 51-52, 55, 367

    Poisson's equation 506, 533

    Polynomial interpolation 231, 233, 234, 235, 239, 239-240, 240, 246, 246-247, 247-249

    Population growth 289, 298

    Potential equation 531, 544-546

    Power method 193, 195, 196, 197

    QR factorization 208, 210-211, 214-215

    Rational-function interpolation 256-257

    Solving a small linear system
      direct methods 7, 80, 89, 89-90,
      iterative methods 112, 113, 118-119, 119-120, 123-124

    Systems of ODE-IVP 442, 443, 444, 446, 447, 449, 450, 451, 452, 453, 454, 455, 458

    Taylor's method 409-410

    Tridiagonal system 93, 96, 98, 166-167, 178

    Trigonometric interpolation and approximation 332-333, 334, 336, 340-341

    Two-link robot arm 137, 144-145, 467

    Wave equation 505, 524

    Waveforms for musical instruments 330, 356-357

    Weakly stable method 432-434

    Zeros of polynomials 7, 44-45, 49-50, 53-54, 54-55, 57-58, 58-59, 62-63, 64-65, 67, 69

Explicit methods for ODE 424-426, 435-436

Explicit methods for PDE 509-514, 523-526, 528-534

Extrapolation methods 388-391

F

Factorization of matrix (*see* LU factorization, QR factorization)

False position (*see* Regula falsi)

Fast Fourier transform (*see* FFT)

FFT 329, 342-360, (361-364)

Fibonacci, Leonardo 2

Finite-difference method for ODE-BVP 477
    linear (106), 492-496, 499, (501)
    nonlinear 497-498, 500, (501)

Finite-difference method for PDE 503, 507-533, (551-552)

Finite-element method for elliptic PDE 503, 507, 534-546, (552-553), (554)

Five-point formula 373

Fixed-point iteration 6-7, 34, (36-7), 69, (73)
    convergence theorem 11

Fixed-point iteration for systems 145-9, 154, (155-6)
    convergence theorem 148-9

Floating-point 15

Floating-point operations (*see* flops)

Floating sphere 42, 45-46, 59-60

Forces on a truss 79, 85, 91-92, (106), (132)

Flops 24, (107), (157), (187), (476), (554)
    basic Gaussian elimination 87, 92
    Fourier transforms 342
    Jacobi method 118
    Thomas method 97

Flow in a pipe (399)

Format, output 30-31

Forward difference formula 368-369, 370, 397, (398), (502), 508, 514

Forward elimination 80
Fourier methods 329-364
Fourth-order Runge-Kutta method 417-420, 435, (438), 454-458, (472)
Fresnel integrals (286), (400)
Function
    orthogonal 311
    rational 227, 254-257
Function approximation 3, 287-364
    (*see also*, Least squares approximation, Fourier methods)
Function approximation at a point 315-318
    (*see also*, Taylor approximation, Pade approximation)
Functional, minimization of 534
    (*see also*, Minimum of a function)

G

Gas law
    Beattie-Bridgeman (75)
    Peng-Robinson (74)
    van der Waals (74)
Gauss, Carl Friedrich 1
Gauss-Jordan method (107)
Gauss-Seidel method 109, 111, 118-122, 129, (130-131), 529-530, 531-532
    conditions for convergence 122
Gaussian elimination 4-5, 7-8, (36), 77-101, (102-107)
    basic 80-88, 100
    for tridiagonal systems 93-99, 101
        (*see also*, Thomas method)
    row pivoting 87-93, 101, (103)
    use by Chinese 1
Gaussian quadrature 392-395, 397, (399)
Generalized minimum residual method, *see* GMRES
Geometric figures 331, 340-341, 357-359, (362-363)
Gerschgorin Circle Theorem 12, 34, (37, 38), 513
Ginzburg-Landau equation (439)
Givens rotation 207, 213
Global truncation error, *see* error
GMRES 128
Gompertz growth curve 298
Gram-Schmidt process 311-312, (328)
Greek mathematics 1

H

Heat capacity (284)
Heat distribution, steady state in plane 503
    (*see also*, Laplace or Poisson equations)
Heat distribution, steady state in a rod (501)
Heat equation (temperature in a rod) 503, 504, 507-522, (551)
Hermite equation (472)
Hermite interpolation 227, 250-253, 274, (279-280), (288)
Hessenberg matrix 212-215
Heun's method 415, 417, 435
Higher-order differential equation 441-471, (472)
    conversion to system of first-order ODE 444-445
Hilbert matrix 88
Horner's method 2, 25, 34, (39)
Horner, W. G. 2
Householder
    matrix 203-205
    transformation (reflection) 202-206
Hyperbolic PDE 503, 505, 507, 522-528, 548-549, (552)
    (*see also*, Wave equation)

I

Ideal gas law (*see* gas law)
Identity matrix 28
Ill-conditioned matrix 88, 192
Ill-conditioned ODE 465
Implicit methods for ODE 424, 426-427, 435, 436
Implicit methods for PDE 514-522, 527-528
Inertial matrix 190
Initial-value problems 403-476
Integration, see numerical integration
Integrals
    cosine (399)
    Dawson 413
    elliptic (400)
    exponential (400)
    Fresnel (400)
    sine 366, (399)
Interpolation 227-275, (276-285)
    (*see also*, polynomial, Hermite, rational function, cubic spline)
Inverse matrix 179-181, (183-184)

Inverse power method 198-202, 217
Iterative methods 2 (*see* also: Jacobi, Gauss-Seidel, SOR, Bisection , Regula falsi, Secant, Newton, Muller, Fixed point Minimization, Power method, QR method for eigenvalues)
Iteration, termination conditions for 13
    (*see* also, stopping conditions)

J

Jacobi method 109, 111-118, 128, (130-131)
    conditions for convergence 117
Jacobian 135, 141, 143, 466

K

Khayyam, Omar 1
Kepler, Johannes 2, 43
Kutta, M. W. 2
Kutta's method for ODE 421

L

Lagrange, Joseph Louis 2
Lagrange interpolation polynomial 230-238, (276-277), 371, 381
Laguerre equation (472)
Laplace (or potential) equation 503, 506, 528-529, 531, (552-553) (*see also*, Elliptical PDE)
Lawson's method 422
Least squares approximation 287-315, 319-321, (324-328)
    continuous 307-315, 322
    cubic 301-303
    discrete 290-307, 321-322, (324-328)
    exponential 287, 289, 304, 322
    linear 287, 290-295, 321-322, (324-326)
    quadratic 296-300
    total 290
Leibnitz, Gottfried Wilhelm 2
Legendre equation (472)
Legendre polynomials (73), 312-315, (328), 395
Light intensity 306-307, (327)
Linear boundary-value problems 377, 480-485, 492-496, 499

Linear finite-difference method 492-496, 499, (501)
Linear interpolation,
    piecewise 258
    use by Babylonians 1
Linear least squares 292-297, 323-324, (326)
Linear shooting method 480-485, 499, (501)
Linear system, solving
        direct method (*see* Gaussian elimination)
        interative methods (*see* Jacobi, Gauss-Seidel, SOR)
Local trucation error (*see* Error, truncation)
Logarithms 2
Logistic population growth 289, 302, 303
Lorenz equation (156), (475)
Lotka-Volterra model (475)
Lower triangular matrix 159
        (*see* also, LU factorization)
LU factorization 159-182, (183-186)
        applications 175-181, (187), 515
        direct 171-175
            (*see* also Doolittle, Crout, Cholesky)
        for tridiagonal matrix 165-167
        using Gaussian elimination 161-164
        with pivoting 167-171

M

Mass-and-spring system (106), 460-461, (474)
MATLAB, introduction to 25-33
    clear 33
    command window 26-31
    comments 31
    editing 33
    formats 30-31
    functions and scripts 31-33
    Output 30
    Plotting 30
    programs 31-33
    save and execute 33
    special matrices 28
    variables 26
    Vector and matrix computation
MATLAB functions, built-in
    ch 1 (linspace, plot, hold, grid, log, disp, diary, input, eval, feval, clear) 27-33
    ch 2 (roots, poly, help, open, fzero) 69-70

Minimum of a function 149-152, 154, (155-156)

Motion of object with air resistance 404, 430-431, (439), 461, 479, 488, (474)

Muller's method 63-68, 71, (72-73)

Multi-step methods for ODE 423-431, 459-464 (*see* Adams-Bashforth, Adams-Moulton, Adams-Bashforth-Moulton predictor-corrector)

N

Napier, John 2

Natural cubic splines (*see* cubic splines)

Neuman boundary conditions 480

Newton's law of cooling (327)

Newton's method 2, 4
  function of 1 variable 58-63, 71, (72-73), 489-492
  systems of equations 135, 138-145, 154, (155-156)

Newton interpolation polynomial 238-245, (276-277)

Newton-Cotes formulas 365
  closed 376-381, 384-387, 397
  open 382-383, 397

Newton-Raphson method 2 (*see also*, Newton's method)

Nine chapters 1

Nodes for finite element method 535-547

Nonlinear BVP 486-492, 497-500, (501)

Nonlinear equations, finding roots of
  (*see* nonlinear functions, finding zeros of)

Nonlinear finite differences 497-499, (501)

Nonlinear function of one variable
  finding zeros of 3, 41-76
  (*see also*, bisection, secant, regula falsi, Newton's method, Muller's method)

Nonlinear functions of several variables
  finding zeros of 135-154
  (*see also*, Newton's method, fixed-point iteration, minimization)

Nonlinear pendulum 442, 444, 446, 449-450

Nonlinear shooting method 486-492, 499, (501)

Nonlinear system from geometry 136, 138-139, 142-143, 143-144

Normalized floating point system 15

Numerical differentiation 3, 364, 368-376
  First derivatives 368-371
  Higher derivatives 372
  Partial derivatives 373
  Richardson extrapolation 374-375

Numerical linear algebra 3, 77-134, 159-226

Numerical integration 3, 5-6, 20, 31, 32, 34, (38), 376-397, (399) (*see also* trapezoid, Simpson, Gaussian quadrature, midpoint, Romberg, Newton-Cotes)

Numerical round-off 3 (*see* also, Error, round-off)

Nystrom method for ODE 417

O

Oil reservoir modeling 288, 299, 304-305

Operation counts, *see* flops

Orbit 43, (474) (*see* also, planetary orbit)

Order (big-Oh) 14, 15, 20, 21-22, 34, 342, 370, 372-376, 409, 513, 518, 519 (*see* also, Convergence, order of)

Order of equations
  effect on accuracy 22-24, 87-88
  effect on convergence 116

Ordinary differential equations 3
  boundary value problems 477-502
    (*see also*, shooting, finite difference)
  initial-value problems 403-476 (*see* Taylor methods, Euler, Runge-Kutta methods, multistep methods, Adams-Bashforth, Adam-Bashforth-Moulton)
  stability 431-434

Orthogonal functions 311, (328). 338

Orthonormal functions 311, (328)

Orthogonal polynomials 308-313

Ostrowski Theorem 126

Overdetermined system 100

Overflow 15

Over-relaxation 123

P

Pade approximation 287, 316-318, 323, (328)

Parabolic PDE 503-504, 507-521 (*see* also Heat equation)

Parametric curves 229

Parasitic solution 465

Partial differential equations (PDE) 503-546 (*see* also, heat equation, wave equation, Poisson equation, finite element method)

Partial pivoting 87, 88-92

Spline interpolation (105), 257-268, 274-275, (277-279), (288)
Spring (73-74)
Spring-mass system (106), 464
Stability of finite difference methods for PDE 510, 512, 513, 524
Stability of ODE methods 431-434
Milne's method (440)
strongly stable method 432
weakly stable method 432-433
Steady-state heat distribution (*see* Heat equation)
Steepest descent method (*see* minimum of function)
Stiff differential equation 465-466
Stopping conditions 46, 55, 111, 113, 116, 122, 124, 143, 148, 150, 196
Straight-line approximations
(*see* Newton, regula falsi, secant, trapezoid)
Successive over relaxation, *see* SOR
Successive underrelaxation 123
Symmetric power method 196, 202
System of linear equations 77-134, 175-6, 292, 295, 310,
System of nonlinear equations 135-158, 497-498, 500
System of ordinary differential equations 441-476
(*see also*, Euler's method, Midpoint method, Runge-Kutta method, Multi-step methods)

T

Taylor approximation 316
Taylor, Brook 2
Taylor method for ODE-IVP 403, 405-411
first-order, *see* Euler's method
higher-order 409-411
Taylor polynomial 2, 14
one variable 14, 372
two variables 415
Telegrapher's equation (553)
Temperature conversion data (327)
Temperature in a rod (501) (*see also*, Heat equation)
Termination conditions
(*see* stopping conditions)
Thermal diffusivity (554)
Thirteen-point formula 373
Thomas method 95, 101, (103), (107), 528
Thomson, W. T. 190, 218
Three-point difference formulas 369-371

Torricelli's law (439)
Trace 201
Traffic density (554)
Trapezoid method for ODE 435
Trapezoid rule 8-9, 20, 34, 376-379
Tridiagonal matrix 93-9, 492-6, 513, 515, 518, 519, 528
Trigonometric approximation 334-341, 360, (361)
Trigonometric interpolation 332-3, 335-41, 360, (361)
Trigonometric polynomial 332, 360
Truncation error (*see* error)
Truss, forces on 79, 85, 91, (106), (132)
Two-point boundary value problem (*see,* Boundary value problem)
Two-link robot arm 137, 144-145, 467-469

U

Underdetermined system 100
Underflow 15
Upper Hessenberg matrix
Upper triangular matrix 159,
(*see also*, LU factorization)

V

Van der Pol equation (475)
Vapor pressure (285)
Viscosity (285)

W

Water draining (327), (439)
Wave equation 503, 505, 507, 522-528
(*see also*, Hyperbolic PDE)
Waveforms, musical instruments 330, 356, (362-3)
Wilkinson, 192
Word 15, (*see also*, bit, byte)

Z

Zero
finding zeros of a function
(*see* nonlinear function)
matrix 28

Author Index

A

Abramowitz, M. 283, 398, (400), 557
Achieser, N. I. 323, 557, 562
Acton, F. S. 154, 557
Ames, W. F. 373, 398, 519, 524, 527, 528, 550, 557
Anderson, R. E. 155, 559
Ascher, U. M. 500, 557
Atkinson, K. E. 35, 57, 62, 68, 71, 102, 117, 122, 210, 238, 378, 381, 395, 397, 423, 432, 557
Axelsson, O. 551, 557
Ayyub, B. M. (74-75), 282, 283, 398, (399), 471, (476), (502), 557

B

Barker, V. A. 551, 557
Barrett, R. 130, 557
Barsky, B. A. 229, 275, 557
Bartels, R. H. 229, 275, 557
Bautista, M. 500, 550, 562
Beatty, J. C. 229, 275, 557
Beauregard, R. A. 559
Becker, E. B. 551, 557
Birkhoff, G. 550
Bjorck, A. 35, 558
Black, W. 155, 559
Boyce, W. E. (75), 550, (554), 557
Boyer, C. B. 35, 557

C

Carey, G. F. 551, 557
Celia, M. A. 550, 558
Cheney, E. W. 323, 558
Coleman, T. F. 129, 558
Colton, D. 550, 558
Conte, S. D. 558

Brent, R. 72, 557
Brezinski, C. 323, 557
Briggs, W. L. 360, 557
Bulirsch, R. 255, 275, 561
Burden, R. 127, 558

D

Dahlquist. G. 35, 466, 558
Datta, B. N. 130, 558
Davies, A. J. 551, 558
Davis, P. J. 275, 558
deBoor, C. 275, 285, 558
Dennis, J. E. 155
Derrick, W. R. 471, 559
Dillon, W. R. 155, 558
DiPrima, R. C. (75), 550, (554), 557
Donato, J. 130, 557
Dongarra, J. 130, 557

Mead, R.   155, 560
Meis, T.   550, 560
Mitchell, A. R.   550, 551
Moler, C. B.   72, 129, 275, 558, 560
Morrison, D. F.   155, 560

N

Nachtigal, N. M.   128, 129, 559
Nash, S.   275, 560
Nelder, J. A.   155, 560

O

Oden, J. T.   551, 557
Ortega, J. M.   126, 128, 154, 437, 550, 560, 561

P

Pauling, L. C.   (74)
Penney, D. E.   72, (75), 404, 437, (439), (440), 558
Poole, W. G.   437, 561
Porsching, T. A.   550, 559
Pozo, R.   130, 557
Press, W. H.   71, 102, 154, 255, 275, 561

R

Rabinowitz, P.   35, 53, 72, 122, 192, 201, 360, 390, 395, 397, 561
Rainville, E. D.   561
Ralston, A.   35, 53, 72, 122, 192, 201, 360, 390, 395, 397, 561
Reddien, G. W.   275, 560
Reichelt, M. W.   437, 561
Reinboldt, W. C.   154, 561
Reynolds, B. E.   35, 561
Rice, J. R.   35, 72, 561
Ritger, P. D.   398, (400), 437, 561
Rivlin, T. J.   323, 561
Roberts, C. E.   437, 500, (502), 561
Romine, C.   130, 557
Rose, N. J.   398, (400), 437, 561
Rowland, J. H.   69, 102, 323, 398, 560
Russell, R. D.   500, 557

S

Salkauskas, K.   275, 560
Sandall, O. C.   (75), 437, (439), 471, (474), 500, (501-2), 559
Shampine, L. F.   437, 561
Sigmon, K.   561
Silvester, P. P.   551, 561
Simmons, G. F.   35, 561
Simon, W.   (74), 443, 471, (475), 561
Smith, D. E.   35, 561
Spong, M. W.   467, 471, 561
Stegun, I. A.   283, 398, (400), 557
Stoer, J.   255, 275, 561
Strang, G.   92, 102, 126, 129, 183, 218, 551, 561
Struik, D. J.   35, 561
Svobony, T.   550, (553), 561
Swenson, C.   72

T

Tatham, R. L.   155, 559
Teukolsky, S. A.   71, 102, 154, 255, 275, 561
Taylor, R. L.   551, 562
Thomson, W. T.   471, (474), 562
Timan, A. F.   323, 562
Troutman, J. L.   500, 550, 562

V

Van der Pol, B.   562
van der Vorst, H.   130, 557
Van Loan, C. F.   36, 87, 102, 127, 128, 129, 183, 201, 203, 218, 360, 558
Varga, R. S.   275, 560
Vetterling, W. T.   71, 102, 154, 255, 275, 561
Vargaftik, N. B.   282, 562
Vidyasagar, M.   467, 471, 562

W

Wait, R.   551
Wasow, W. R.   550, 558
Weinstock, R.   35, 562